SHAPING ENGLISH LITURGY:
STUDIES IN HONOR OF
ARCHBISHOP DENIS HURLEY

SHAPING ENGLISH LITURGY:
STUDIES IN HONOR OF
ARCHBISHOP DENIS HURLEY

EDITED BY
PETER C. FINN
JAMES M. SCHELLMAN

PREPARED BY
THE INTERNATIONAL COMMISSION
ON ENGLISH IN THE LITURGY
– A JOINT COMMISSION
OF CATHOLIC BISHOPS' CONFERENCES

THE PASTORAL PRESS
WASHINGTON, D.C. – 1990

UBI SPIRITUS, IBI LIBERTAS

IN COMMEMORATION OF THE
FORTIETH ANNIVERSARY
OF HIS EPISCOPAL ORDINATION
(19 MARCH 1947)
AND THE
FIFTIETH ANNIVERSARY
OF HIS PRIESTLY ORDINATION
(9 JULY 1939)
THE
INTERNATIONAL COMMISSION
ON ENGLISH IN THE LITURGY
DEDICATES
THIS COLLECTION OF ESSAYS
TO

DENIS EUGENE HURLEY, O.M.I.

ARCHBISHOP OF DURBAN
ADVOCATE FOR HUMAN RIGHTS
PROMOTER OF LITURGICAL RENEWAL
FAITHFUL SERVANT OF GOD'S PEOPLE

CONTENTS

THE MOST REVEREND
DENIS E. HURLEY, O.M.I.

Denis Eugene Hurley was born of Irish parents in Cape Town on 9 November 1915. After schooling in South Africa he entered the Oblates of Mary Immaculate in 1932 and was sent to Ireland for his novitiate. He began his studies for the priesthood in Rome in 1933, earning a licentiate in philosophy at the Angelicum in 1936 and a licentiate in theology at the Gregorian in 1940. Ordained a priest on 9 July 1939, Father Hurley continued his studies in Rome until the following year when the entrance of Italy into the Second World War forced his return to South Africa. On his return he was named a curate at the cathedral in Durban where he served until his appointment in 1944 as superior of the Oblates of Mary Immaculate Scholasticate in Pietermaritzburg. In December 1946, Denis Hurley was named vicar apostolic of Natal and was ordained bishop on 19 March 1947. At age thirty-one he was the youngest bishop in the Church. When the hierarchy was established in South Africa in January 1951, the vicariate apostolic of Natal became the archdiocese of Durban with Denis Hurley as its first archbishop.

A year later Archbishop Hurley was elected president of the Southern African Bishops' Conference and continued in that office until 1960. In 1960 he was named a member of the Central Preparatory Commission of the Second Vatican Council. He was present when the Council opened in October 1962 and attended all four sessions. At the first session he was elected to serve on the conciliar Commission on Priestly Formation and Christian Education. Archbishop Hurley made important spoken interventions at the Council on the draft documents dealing with the liturgy, the Church, religious freedom, the role of the laity, the formation of priests, and the Church in the modern world as well as written interventions on other aspects of the Council's deliberations. In 1965 Pope Paul VI named Archbishop Hurley a member of the Consilium for the Implementation of the Constitution on the Liturgy, and when the Consilium ceased to function in 1969, he was named a member of the newly-established Congregation for Divine Worship. He remained a member of that Congregation until 1974.

Archbishop Hurley was chosen by the bishops of South Africa as their representative at the Synod of Bishops in 1967, 1974, 1977, 1980, and was elected a member of the Consilium of the Synod by the Synod participants in 1974 and 1977. Elected by the bishops of Southern Africa to a further term as president of the conference in 1981, he continued in that office until 1987. As president of the Southern African Bishops' Conference Archbishop Hurley attended the Extraordinary Synod of Bishops in Rome in 1985.

Archbishop Hurley was named a Chevalier of the Legion of Honor by the French government in 1975. He has been the recipient of honorary doctorates from the University of Notre Dame (1970), the University of Natal (1978), the Catholic University of America (1982), Georgetown University (1987), and the University of Cape Town (1988).

Archbishop Hurley is recognized throughout the world as one of the leading Roman Catholic bishops of the Vatican II era. He is admired for his knowledge and positions on a wide range of issues facing the Church in the contemporary world. These include liturgical renewal, parish and community renewal, the formation of priests, marriage and family issues, and ecclesiological questions. Undoubtedly he is most regarded and admired for his deep commitment and courageous witness to the work of social justice, particularly in his native South Africa.

During the first session of the Council Archbishop Hurley participated in the discussions that led to the founding of ICEL a year later. He was present at the meeting at the English College in Rome on 17 October 1963 when ICEL was formally established, and his involvement with ICEL has continued since that time. Archbishop Hurley was elected chairman of ICEL's Episcopal Board in August 1975 and has been reelected to that office several times since by the bishops of the Board.

To commemorate his fortieth anniversary of episcopal ordination and to express gratitude for his vigorous and generous leadership of ICEL, the Episcopal Board and Advisory Committee during their meetings in Washington in January 1987 paid the following tribute to Archbishop Hurley:

> The joy and hope, the struggle and anguish of the people of this age and especially of the poor and those suffering in any way are the joy and hope, the struggle and anguish of Christ's disciples, and there is nothing genuinely human that does not find a response in their hearts. . . .

These words from the Pastoral Constitution *Gaudium et spes* of the Second Vatican Council are an apt commentary on the life and ministry of Denis Eugene Hurley, O.M.I., Archbishop of Durban.

On the occasion of the fortieth anniversary of his episcopal ordination and in recognition of his leadership of the International Commission on English in the Liturgy, the Episcopal Board and Advisory Committee dedicate the work of the revision of the Roman Missal to Archbishop Hurley with gratitude and affection. May his deeply felt commitment to the Church's liturgical renewal as evidenced at the Council, in his membership on the Consilium, and in his long years of service to ICEL inspire this great task and be an example to all who carry it on.

How blessed are those who live in your house, O Lord;
  they shall praise you all the day long.
Blessed are those who find their strength in you,
  whose hearts are set on the way to Zion.

✳ ✳ ✳

Archbishop Denis Hurley is a man of wide interests. His concern for liturgical renewal began well before the Second Vatican Council where he was an ardent proponent of the Constitution on the Liturgy. He had a major role after the Council in implementing the liturgical reform as a member of the Consilium for the Implementation of the Constitution on the Liturgy and as a founder and participant in the work of the International Commission on English in the Liturgy. The present volume, made up chiefly of essays on subjects liturgical, pays tribute to Archbishop Hurley's leadership and vision in the reform of the liturgy begun at the Second Vatican Council and continued in the twenty-five years since.

In the opening essay Bishop *Frederick Amoore* writes of Archbishop Hurley's commitment to social justice in the context of his native South Africa. The link between liturgy and social justice is indispensable, as Archbishop *Rembert Weakland* demonstrates, and indeed many of the liturgical pioneers of the first half of the twentieth century were deeply involved in the cause and work of social justice.

Archbishop Hurley foresaw that the historic work of the Council in the area of liturgical renewal was a beginning and a challenge. Much hard work would have to be done over a long period of time, and this would include the need for periodic reappraisals of what had been accomplished. In fact there could never be a time when one could say the renewal is completed, the end has been achieved. *Mark Searle, Thomas Krosnicki, Frederick McManus, Gilbert Ostdiek,* and *Mary Alice Piil* treat various historical and theological issues of the conciliar reform. Their studies, while acknowledging the signal achievement of the Vatican II reforms, suggest continuing topics and issues that have arisen out of an experience of those reforms over the generation just past.

The introduction of the vernacular on a wide scale through the Constitution on the Liturgy and post-conciliar enactments was a new experience for the Roman Catholic Church. Many difficult questions had to be faced with regard to vernacular texts that were worthy of the holy mysteries and suited to the literary cultures of twentieth century Catholics. The International Commission on English in the Liturgy has since 1963 had the task of preparing the vernacular texts for the conferences of bishops where English is spoken. *Patrick Byrne* points out a number of benefits that have resulted from Catholics worshiping in English. And various aspects of ICEL's work in preparing liturgical texts for the closing decades of the twentieth century are investigated by *Michael Hodgetts, Kathleen Hughes,* and *Frank Henderson.*

In articles 37-40 and 63, the Constitution on the Liturgy opened the way for what is sometimes called liturgical inculturation or acculturation. The elements of genuine inculturation have been a topic for study and discussion over the last two decades. Efforts have been made, particularly in Asia and Africa, to put the results of these discussions into practice. The continuing work of liturgical inculturation is clearly one of the major issues facing the Church as it looks toward the next century. *Andrew Borello* and *Paul Puthanangady* deal with some aspects of the relationship between liturgy and culture.

The 1969 *Ordo Lectionum Missae* has been hailed as one of the great accomplishments of the conciliar reform. The new Roman order of readings for the celebration of the eucharist has also had significant ecumenical repercussions. Some issues arising out of the use of the 1969 lectionary in the Christian Churches are dealt with by *Horace Allen* and *Eileen Schuller. Lawrence Boadt* focuses on the related subject of the psalms in his essay, which discusses a recent initiative to provide a translation of the psalms and biblical canticles for use in the Church's liturgical rites.

Through all of its twenty-five year history Archbishop Hurley has been closely involved in the work of ICEL. Since 1975 he has served as chairman of its Episcopal Board. *Frederick McManus* and *John Page* tell the story of ICEL's quarter century of service to the conferences of bishops where English is spoken. Their accounts are supplemented by excerpts from the memoirs of *G. B. Harrison*, one of the original members of ICEL's Advisory Committee, and by sections from the biography of *Percy Jones*, another of the original members of the Committee.

✳ ✳ ✳

EXCERPTS FROM ARCHBISHOP HURLEY'S SPEECHES DURING THE SECOND VATICAN COUNCIL

These excerpts from speeches given by Archbishop Hurley during the sessions of the Second Vatican Council give an impression of his contributions to the Council and serve to highlight the breadth of his interest and concerns. Though the speeches were delivered over a quarter century ago and addressed topics of concern to the Council Fathers, they remain in their overall intent and their broad lines of argument remarkably apt and up-to-date.

ON THE PASTORAL OBJECTIVE OF THE COUNCIL

(*Acta Synodalia*, vol. I, Period I, Pars III, Congregatio Generalis XXII, 19 November 1962, pp. 198-200)

I regard the present debate to be of the utmost value, because it concerns an absolutely fundamental issue, the purpose of the entire Council. On this purpose all are agreed, thanks be to God. We all say that the purpose of the Council is pastoral and this is what we all understand from the splendid words of the happily reigning Supreme Pontiff. There is no disagreement about this point. But— and it is a very big "but" —there is extreme disagreement about the interpretation of the word "pastoral."

Some declare that the Council can act pastorally simply by defining the truth, by safely storing the seed of the Gospel in the granary of dogmatic definitions. Others deny that defining truths suffices to attain the Council's pastoral objective, and they want the Council to speak in such a way that its very way of speaking will make it clear that truth is not merely to be safeguarded, but to be proclaimed; that the seed of the Gospel is not to be stored up in the granary of dogmatic definitions but to be scattered and sown throughout the world.

This then is the difference beween the two sides: whether it is possible for the Council to be pastoral simply through definitions that safeguard truth; or whether its pastoral character requires such a way of expression that whoever hears or reads its declarations will experience the power and sweetness of the truth.

If there is anyone who denies that it is possible for the Council to speak in such a way, then I suggest that the very beautiful schema prepared by the Secretariat for Christian Unity and entitled *De verbo Dei* be printed and distributed to the conciliar Fathers. That schema, as we have heard from a number of Fathers, breathes the sweet beauty of Sacred Scripture, and there is nothing that touches the hearts of believers and nonbelievers alike more than the fragrance of the Scriptures. . . .

The division about what belongs to the pastoral nature of the Council far exceeds the limits of the present debate. But I am absolutely sure that this division will enter into nearly all future debates. By the kindness of the Supreme Pontiff I was a member of the central preparatory commission and, as I remember it, the most frequent intervention on the various schemata—particularly those regarding faith and morals—pointed to their insufficiently pastoral character. Yet after so many such interventions I was amazed to discover that the schemata had been amended only slightly, and very slightly indeed, in a pastoral direction. After the debate of these last several days I now know the reason, namely, that those assigned the task of amending the schemata did not understand the word "pastoral" in the same sense as those who made interventions.

We are therefore at a crisis point in the Council and as far as I can see we will experience this same division in the debate on ninety percent of the schemata. What is to be done? I see now that when in the central commission we complained about the non-pastoral character of the schemata, we were voices crying in the wilderness. But there was no one there to hear our cry, no one who could and should have been concerned with this defect in the preparatory work. There was no central direction. There was no person or commission to give a clear interpretation of the pastoral objective of the Council, to direct and coordinate the labors of the individual commissions toward its declared purpose, to establish limits to the topics that would be presented to the Council. Therein lies the basic defect of the preparatory work; therein, so to speak, lies the original sin of this Council.

Esteemed Fathers, we cannot spend ten or twenty years debating schemata of a thousand pages and on every page face the same division about the meaning of the word "pastoral."

I do not question the usefulness of the debates of these past weeks, since they have brought to light the disagreement over the interpretation of the purpose of the Council. But now that this point has been made, we cannot argue endlessly about every individual manifestation of this disagreement. The issue must be resolved either by a general debate and vote in the Council *aula* or by the work of a special commission to be established by the Supreme Pontiff to deal with the issue between the first and second session of the Council. And if such a commission is established, it should receive a broad mandate to attend to the reviewing and shortening of schemata and to the improving of the order of their debate.

Only in this or a similar way can the Council be redeemed from the original sin of the preparatory work and reach a successful outcome.

※ ※ ※

(*Acta Synodalia*, vol. I, Period I, Pars IV, Congregatio Generalis XXXIII, 3 December 1962, pp. 197-199)

It is not pleasant to play the role of devil's advocate time and again in the conciliar debates, but in this stage of, so to speak, the Council's purgative way, there seems to be no escaping the task.

For the most part I am not greatly pleased with the Schema *De Ecclesia* because of a defect running throughout almost all the preparatory work for the Council: a lack of unity and coordination. A number of Fathers have complained about the inclusion in this schema of chapters on bishops, on the states of perfection, on the laity, and on ecumenism. I cannot understand how the work in preparation for a Council on unity could have been itself so lacking in unity.

For the solution of this problem it seems that there is nothing left but to propose again that between the first and second session the entire preparatory work be redone under the direction of a central and — excuse the word — centralizing commission, having the task of expressing clearly, in accord with the mind of the Supreme Pontiff, the purpose of the Council and of ensuring that the means necessary for achieving that purpose are applied, as His Eminence Cardinal

Léger [Cardinal Paul Léger, archbishop of Montreal] has already said this morning.

As to the purpose of the Council, there is practically no need for defining truths, since they are not in any danger that would call for conciliar consideration. Indeed I would venture to say that it is neither appropriate nor desirable to constrict certain teachings within the theological formularies of the past, since we are in the midst of a very fruitful stage of theological ferment arising from many causes, particularly from the renewed study of Sacred Scripture, of the documents of the Fathers and Church history, and from a growing concern for the needs of our contemporaries.

That concern is a pastoral concern, which must be the supreme concern of this Council, convened not to define truths, but to renew the pastoral activity of the Church. And with the help of God that activity will have as one of its foremost results an increased ecumenical effectiveness.

The nature and properties of "ecumenicity" have been clearly presented to us (especially by His Eminence Cardinal Bea and His Excellency Bishop de Smedt); other Fathers have spoken about the pastoral aspect. Permit me also to say a few things about the pastoral issue, in order that this effort, however small, may serve to make the idea clearer and sharper.

It belongs to the pastoral office to propose the truth to people in such a way that they are able to embrace it and so to live by it. The first requirement for this is a suitable way of presenting doctrine that consists not simply in adapting words and language, but in a manner of speaking that is not academic or rhetorical but plain and ordinary, yet precise; that is not juridical or desiccated, but that is imbued with a kind of unction and a love for God and neighbor.

In addition to this mode of expression, a further requisite is that doctrine be developed and explained so that of itself and as doctrine it has the power to give an answer to the questions with which people truly grapple about their final end, about God and his Christ. The truth should not of course be changed nor diminished, but it must be examined with deeper insight, brought back again to its source, developed more profoundly and extensively, and renewed in such a way as to be not only doctrine true in itself but doctrine *for the people* to whom we are sent. It must become teaching that has the effective and actual power to answer the just demands and questions of people. Our speech must not just say *something*, even something true, but must seek to say something to the people of these times. Let us remember the scholastic adage: "Whatever is received is received according to the mode of the recipient." And let us therefore speak in the Council in such a way as to give a new impulse to the preaching of the Gospel in today's world. Paul the Apostle dared to preach the Gospel to the Greeks in the language of the Greeks. The medieval doctors dared to express Christian truth in scholastic concepts and vocabulary. It therefore is the Church's tradition to accommodate its preaching to the needs of the people and of the times.

The Council of Trent called for, so to speak, a new type of bishop, and in Saint Charles Borromeo found the perfect model: a type of bishop who was no longer the feudal lord of the Middle Ages, no longer the humanist of the Renaissance, but a bishop who is a pastor in the face of the needs of post-Tridentine society. We have been sent to a very different kind of world. It is not like the post-Tridentine world, which at least in intention and in principle was favorable to religion; our world has little or no regard for religion, yet it struggles intensely with the problems of human existence on this earth and of the development of the world. Since we are the appointed pastors of this world and its people, we must search for some apt and, if need be, new way of speaking to them, or rather we must be present to them in the name of Christ and for the sake of Christ. Does not this new world need some new type of evangelical pastor, a pastor not less doctrinal than a Tridentine pastor, but one who is not content to present people with "doctrine *in se*," who is concerned with presenting doctrine of a kind or formulated in such a way that it responds to their questions? Was that not the meaning of the address of the Supreme Pontiff delivered in the Council *aula* on the eleventh of October? May God grant that from the Second Vatican Council a new generation of pastors may emerge, worthy to be compared to the great generation of Tridentine pastors, but who are pastors fully attuned to the world of this age and to its people!

On the Constitution on the Liturgy

(*Acta Synodalia*, vol. I, Period I, Pars I, Congregatio Generalis IV, 22 October 1962, pp. 327-328)

Since all that I wished to say has already been well said by others (although perhaps not by His Excellency [Archbishop Vagnozzi] the last speaker), moved by the charism of brevity, I yield my right to speak. [The following remarks were submitted in written form.]

It is undoubtedly a favorable sign that the schema proposed for the first debate is the schema on the liturgy. It is a most beautiful schema, filled, to use its own words, with a "warm and living love for Scripture" (SC art. 24). We must fervently hope that the other schemata will be enlivened by the same love. We should thank the preparatory commission from the bottom of our hearts for a schema so well composed.

What pleases me most is the schema's lucid exposition of the true and genuine nature of the liturgy and of its importance in the life of the Church. As the text makes so clear, the primary and supreme purpose of the Church is to give glory to God. The Church by its entire nature strives for the salvation of souls, or to put it in terms better suited to our times, for the salvation of the people of God. But the salvation of the people of God is the glory of God, according to the words of Psalm 105 (106): "Save us, O Lord our God, and gather us from among the nations, that we may give thanks to your holy name and glory in your praise" (verse 47).

The more therefore that anything in the Church glorifies God, the more directly does it contribute to the purpose of the Church. But the supreme means, although as the schema notes not the only means, of giving glory to God is the liturgy, and the primary manifestation of the Church is the full and active participation of the entire holy people of God in liturgical celebrations.

A further point relative to the liturgy deserving of the fullest consideration is that the Church cannot give glory to God without thereby receiving immediately and abundantly from the divine generosity the most precious gifts—the gifts of divine life, of faith, hope, love, and apostolic zeal. The liturgical movement must always have a twofold direction: the movement of the people's worship, prompted by the Holy Spirit, toward God the Father through Christ the Head; and the movement from God the Father toward his people through Christ the Head in the Holy Spirit. These gifts build up the Body of Christ, the people of God, and the Christian community.

The schema explains this idea very well by citing words from the Acts of the Apostles: "And they devoted themselves to the apostles' teaching, and fellowship, to the breaking of the bread and to the prayers . . . praising God and having favor with all the people" (Acts 2:42, 47). These words point out very well the three elements that make up the principal outward expressions of the Church's life and apostolic activity, namely, teaching, liturgy, and "favor with all the people," or the witness of a Christian life. By its nature the life of the Church is apostolic and missionary in character, and to form an apostolic spirit those three elements are necessary—teaching, liturgy, and the witness of Christian life. . . .

If we wish to renew the apostolic spirit in the Church (and this, I think, is an aim of this ecumenical Council), it will be necessary to reform the liturgical life, not apart from catechetical and moral renewal, but in close conjunction with them. And this reform can come about, it seems to me, only if the exposition in this schema of the importance of the liturgy is enthusiastically embraced and if the schema's intent concerning the participation of the faithful and the adaptation, structure, and language of the liturgy is faithfully pursued.

ON THE DECLARATION ON RELIGIOUS FREEDOM

(*Acta Synodalia*, vol. III, Period III, Pars II, Congregatio Generalis LXXXVIII, 22 September 1964, pp. 515-518; excerpt)

[. . .] There is one aspect of the question which I wish to consider, namely, the classical argument for the union of the Catholic Church with the State. It is necessary to deal with this argument, since to many of us it may seem to vindicate the so-called ideal condition, one, that is, which the Church of its nature desires to attain when it can with regard to its relations with civil society and its directive organism, called "the State." If the classical argument retains its force, our declaration cannot be said to be complete and accurate and must be emended at least in regard to the following proposition: "The civil powers possess no direct capacity and competence to determine or regulate the citizens' relations with their Creator and Savior."

The classical argument in its simpler and principal form runs as follows: Since each person is a social being by nature, each is obliged to worship God not only as an individual but also in a social manner. In order that this social obligation may be fulfilled, civil society as such is bound to acknowledge and worship God, and indeed in the manner in which God himself has indicated, namely, through the Catholic Church. Civil society is therefore bound to show special respect toward the Catholic Church and to provide it with assistance.

We all accept the principle, namely: Since each person is a social being by nature, each is obliged to worship God not only as an individual but also in a social manner. But the fallacy in the argument seems to consist in this, that from that accepted principle it makes a jump to the conclusion that therefore civil society must ensure the fulfillment of this obligation. I call this a fallacy because if God has established a special society in which people may fulfill their social obligation to worship, by that very fact civil society is exempt from such a duty. For it is a basic principle of Catholic sociology that civil society should do for its members only those things which they cannot do either for themselves or through some other society, for example, the family.

But in fact God has established a special society in which people can fulfill their obligation of social worship, namely, the Church. Under the New Testament, therefore, no obligation or competence is left to civil society in this regard. Therefore the following proposition of our schema is entirely acceptable: "The civil powers possess no direct capacity and competence to determine or regulate the citizens' relations with their Creator and Savior."

We must further consider that if, in virtue of the argument for union of Church and State, we hold that civil society of its nature has an obligation regarding divine worship, we implicitly assert the direct power of the Church over civil society. For the direct power of the Church extends to every area where the obligation regarding divine worship exists. And it should be noted that this is not a question of the power of the Church over civil society by reason of subject matter, that is, in regard to temporalities; to admit that civil society as such has an obligation in any way to have concern for social worship is to imply the power of the Church over civil society by reason of the very constitution of civil society.

Such a direct power of the Church over civil society must not be admitted. Therefore in our times and in keeping with today's understanding of these ideas the teaching on union between Church and State must be abandoned. There need be no fear that this would lead to harm for the Church; rather it should be expected to work for its advantage. Without that union the Church strives much more to exercise its influence on all members of society, and does not place its hope and trust in help expected from the State.

Finally, a further argument against religious freedom that is drawn from people's inadequacy regarding religious truth seems to me to be quite weak. We must recognize that people, both as individuals and as part of society, progress in the natural order from ignorance to the possession of truth, only slowly and through difficult paths, fraught with snares and pitfalls. This progress necessarily implies the danger of erring. And history in fact teaches us that people have never attained any important truth without first experiencing error. Those therefore who want human rights to depend on the possession of the truth implicitly deny to people the right of thinking, inquiring, discussing, and writing.

The conclusion is that freedom and rights belong to people not because they have already attained the truth, but in order that they might reach it. And if this conclusion applies to the natural order, it applies a fortiori to the supernatural order, for in elevating humankind God has not lessened human freedom but sanctified it.

ON THE CHURCH IN THE MODERN WORLD

(*Acta Synodalia*, vol. III, Period III, Pars V, Congregatio Generalis CVII, 22 October 1964, pp. 341-343; excerpt)

Although there are some good points in this schema, it seems to have a basic defect, which, as many have remarked, consists in the schema's having been composed before its purpose was clearly settled. On the contrary, the destination of a journey should be known before the journey begins.

His Excellency the relator has described the schema's purpose in paragraph 12 of his report: "The issue is to promote more and more a dialogue with all people, so that they may be heard concerning their ideas, conditions, and problems, and so that they in turn may know the mind of the Church regarding the more important conditions, trends, and problems of our times."

If this purpose had been settled on before the schema was composed and if it had been kept firmly in mind, we would not now be deploring its many defects. Among these I note the following.

1. In chapter 1 paragraph 5 [of the report on the schema] it is stated
that the schema must explain "the importance of earthly things for
the total vocation of man." But it seems to me that "to explain" exceeds the scope of the schema, since the schema takes as its objective
to promote dialogue, not to give a full explanation of the truth. To
promote dialogue is not to look for explanations from oneself alone
but from all the parties to the dialogue, **as was well pointed out yester-
day by His Excellency Archbishop Wojtyla, Archbishop of Cracow**
[emphasis in original]. And in fact there is no explanation in the
schema, and it would be amazing if there were one, since theology itself has not yet arrived at a true explanation of the issue in question.
This chapter of the schema seems not even to suspect the things that
are being discussed in recent times about the value of the natural order and its relationship to the supernatural end of humankind. . . .

Having said these things, I gladly declare that I accept the purpose of the schema as stated by His Excellency the relator in his
report: "The issue is to promote more and more a dialogue with
all people. . . ."

But with regard to the method of achieving this purpose, I humbly suggest that it should not be in the manner of a simple exposition of truth but in the manner of an exhortation to all orders and
members of the Church: to ourselves the bishops and other Fathers
of the Council, to priests and all religious, to laypersons in a special way—to parents, owners, workers, scientists, scholars—to all,
so that we all may show ourselves, according to our individual order, office, and capacity, to be concerned about the problems of the
world and about the need for working and cooperating with others
to find solutions. Such an exhortation, elaborated with pertinent
arguments, could serve as the *prooemium* of the schema.

After the *prooemium* there should be a discussion on the more
important problems of the times, including suitable considerations
and suggestions that may lead to finding a way of solution.

The first and greatest problem is clearly the theological problem of the true value of the natural order and its relationship to the
supernatural end of humankind. Mention should be made of the
ideas that have lately begun to be circulated and which have their
origin principally in the splendid vision, religious and scientific,
evolutionary and eschatological, of that illustrious son of the Church,
Pierre Teilhard de Chardin.

The issue is the idea of the presence of God in the world, a presence that is always creative, and of which St. Thomas has written

so beautifully. This is an idea also based on St. Paul's doctrine of cosmic Christology, on which Cardinal Meyer has spoken so well, an idea that sees an intimate connection between the presence of God in the world and, since the incarnation, the presence of Christ through his death and glorification. But there is a great problem that remains to be clarified, namely, whether the creative activity of the Word, with which people cooperate in fulfilling their own work in the world, is now the creative action of the Word incarnate and how this creative activity is related to the work of salvation. This, if I am not mistaken, is the greatest theological problem of this century.

There should also be a discussion of the particular problems that the schema already treats, but care must be taken to ensure that this treatment does not take on the appearance of being a simplistic and merely theoretical solution of problems that are extremely difficult and complex. As has already been said, the objective of the schema is not to present definitive solutions, but rather to urge the members of the Church of whatever order and condition to find solutions to the problems and to work with other people to apply these solutions. [. . .]

✳ ✳ ✳

(*Acta Synodalia*, vol. IV, Period IV, Pars III, Congregatio Generalis CXLII, 5 October 1965, pp. 395-397; excerpt from speech on Ch. IV of the Schema of the Pastoral Constitution on the Church in the Modern World, delivered in the name of seventy bishops)

[. . .] The paragraph on relations between the Church and the political society is well marked by the spirit of *aggiornamento*. Nor does it limit itself to juridical issues between the two so-called perfect societies. Our hope is that the term "perfect society" may disappear from our theological language, for it causes confusion in determining the relations between the Church and the political society. For the Church is called a society only in an analogical sense and its true nature is hidden in the mystery of God. It is also impossible to divide human activity sharply into the spiritual and the temporal, for all human acts in the temporal order belong also to the spiritual order because of their moral orientation.

For this reason there is need to qualify an expression used in paragraph 89, namely: "The Church, not wanting in any way by reason of its task and its competence to be confused with civil society. . . ." It is true that the Church does not wish to be confused with civil society. But it does wish to have an influence on civil society, because it seeks to consecrate all human activity, forming Christian consciences in such a way that people as citizens and as leaders of the earthly city can imprint a Christian direction upon social and political life.

For this reason I propose that the words in question be emended more or less as follows: "Because the Church is at once a sign and a witness of human transcendence, it does not wish to involve itself in any way in matters pertaining to the political society, except to form the consciences of people toward the right and faithful fulfillment of their civil responsibilities."

The new spirit is also evident in the statement of paragraph 89: "But (the Church) does not place its hope in privileges offered by civil authority. Indeed the Church will gladly renounce the exercise of certain legitimately acquired rights, when it is clear that such exercise would cast doubt upon the sincerity of its witness or that new conditions of life demand a different arrangement."

This is well put. We must acknowledge that in spite of the efforts of the authorities and members of the Church to avoid conflict with the civil powers, such conflicts will arise. They will arise because the true freedom of the Church is denied or because the Church is forced to defend human rights to life, peace, a just distribution of wealth, or a true social, cultural, and political freedom.

In the past we have perhaps insisted too much upon the rights of the Church and the antiphon "The Church claims the right" was too frequently repeated in theology and by the magisterium. Please God that in the future we will be concerned with at least as much zeal for human rights. And this, I hope, will be the result of the schema *De Ecclesia in mundo huius temporis*. In defending the freedom of the Church regarding human rights we will hardly be able to avoid conflict with civil authority. The difficulty will be to conduct ourselves in such conflicts as witnesses to the love of Christ.

Therefore I ask that to the text be added, for example, at the end of the chapter, words along the lines of the following: "The Church cannot agree in the essentials to the denial of this freedom (that is, freedom to proclaim the faith). Nor as Mother and Teacher of all can the Church tolerate injustices committed or permitted by the public authority against the people of any race or religion, and particularly injustices against the poor. The Church must raise its voice against such abuses of power, and it will at times come into conflict with the civil powers, but without ever ceasing to bear witness to Christ's love."

On the Dogmatic Constitution on the Church:
Bishops in the Church

(*Acta Synodalia*, vol. II, Period II, Pars II, Congregatio Generalis XLIV, 9 October 1963, pp. 364-366; excerpt)

Permit me to say a few things about this Chapter II, by touching on two themes: first on the ministries of bishop; second, on the role of priests.

[. . .] We may immediately notice a great disproportion in paragraph 19, which treats of the (bishop's) office of teaching and contains no less than fifty lines. At first glance this does not seem great, if we fail to notice that forty-one of these lines are on infallibility, which leaves only nine lines on the general office of preaching the word, the greatest ministry of the Church, given the time and labor expended on it. Not that the importance of things is to be measured merely by prolixity of words—but the great verbal disproportion here may lead to a like disproportion of ideas.

This consideration aside, the contents of the paragraphs cited are rightly and well put, if we consider only principles. For by the very nature of episcopal ministry it belongs to the bishop to teach, to sanctify, and to rule. But if we look at practice, at the reality itself, what do we see? The ministry of teaching and sanctifying in their daily actuality and in nearly all its aspects is fulfilled not by the bishop but by priests.

To ninety-nine out of a hundred of his flock the bishop appears as an unfamiliar and remote figure, a complete unknown at the personal and human level. It is up to him to establish general directives, to arrange and organize diocesan business, to coordinate the various projects and undertakings. But he most often has no direct hierarchic influence upon his flock; this is left to the priests, through whom the bishop does almost everything in the diocese. They are the bishop's hands and feet, his eyes and ears and voice. Just as no one can act except through bodily organs, so too all the things that the bishop wishes to accomplish, all that he may hope to be done, depend completely on his priests to be put into effect. We all know that in the reading of pastoral letters whether the bishop's words sound like the trumpet of the archangel or like a list from the telephone directory depends completely on the priests.

From this it is clear that the bishop exercises the offices of teaching, sanctifying, and ruling above all by leading his priests. Since in today's circumstances it is all but impossible for the bishop to draw near to his people directly, his greatest concern must be to provide his priests with pastoral leadership. Thus he can accomplish through them what he cannot do of himself. I think that this must be said explicitly in the schema; indeed a special paragraph should be drawn up on the bishop's pastoral leadership, namely, on how he should direct, organize, inspire, encourage, and assist his priests. But if it should be said that since this matter belongs to the practical order, it does not fit in with the character of a dogmatic constitution, I would answer by saying that even a dogmatic constitution must pay attention to *facts*. And the chief fact about the ministry of the bishop (particularly his office of teaching and sanctifying) is that in these times this ministry is being carried out by his priests, and therefore it is incumbent upon the bishop to provide the best leadership and support possible.

I confess that in all these things I speak as one less wise (2 Corinthians 11:23), since I am aware that I am incapable of showing in what this role of leadership consists. Still, I am sure that this is a most serious issue that should be dealt with in the schema. If in the last decades there seems to have been a slow response to the appeals of the Supreme Pontiffs concerning the social apostolate, missions, the apostolate of the laity, catechetical and liturgical renewal, the explanation, in my opinion, lies above all in the fact that we bishops have been unequal to the fulfillment of our leadership role. We have lacked the abilty to present the papal encyclicals to our priests as living teachings, so that they could then communicate them as living teachings to the people of God. Sad to say, the impulse toward Catholic renewal has not originated with us, but with special groups of priests and laity.

I am therefore completely convinced of this: when the schema treats of the episcopal office it must clearly state the principle that the fulfillment of this office consists above all in providing strong and gentle pastoral leadership to his priests, who, with the cooperation of religious and laity, must carry out the work that we ourselves cannot do.

From this serious consideration what naturally follows as a conclusion is the great importance of the order of the presbyterate for the carrying out of hierarchic ministries. . . . In order therefore that the priesthood may be dealt with as it deserves, I propose that Chapter II be divided into three articles, so that it treats clearly and distinctly each level of the hierarchy—episcopacy, priesthood, and diaconate.

✳ ✳ ✳

(*Acta Synodalia,* vol. II, Period II, Pars V, Remarks submitted in writing on the Dogmatic Constitution on the Church: the Conferences of Bishops; pp. 320-321)

During this debate I have now heard many times the admonition that the decisions of conferences of bishops do not possess juridic force. With great admiration I have listened to expositions on how great conferences have functioned successfully now for many years without their decisions having any juridic power. As a member of a hierarchy that has experienced the great generosity of the conference of bishops of Germany let me publicly in this Council *aula* offer my deepest thanks both to the entire conference and in particular to its beloved president Cardinal Joseph Frings.

In our conference of South Africa we have always successfully used the same principle (denying juridic force), as experience attests. In this matter we are indebted to His Excellency Martino Lucas, who when he was the Apostolic Delegate laid the main foundations of our conference; it is therefore pleasant to recall that we have learned the practice of collegiality first from the representative of Peter.

So much for the past, and I gladly grant that juridic power was not very necessary to the conferences in the past. What of the future? If matters are placed in the hands of the conferences to be decided juridically—liturgical matters, for example—they are undoubtedly decided by the conferences juridically. We cannot avoid the issue. This is the price of the "decentralization" that we all desire. If we wish to exclude all juridical power from the conferences of bishops, we reject "decentralization" and acknowledge ourselves to be incapable of assuming collegial responsibility. It would be a shame to admit such a thing in today's world, which more and more tends toward unity and in which we see nations prepared to lay aside their particular rights in order to foster and promote international collaboration.

Furthermore, if the conference of bishops lacks all juridical power, for individual cases special delegation from the Holy See will be required, and from this in the course of time the result may be that quinquennial faculties are granted not simply to the individual bishops but also to the conferences of bishops.

Esteemed Fathers, we are no longer deliberating in secret. Each and every item that we hear in the *aula* is shouted from the house tops; and in my opinion this is a good thing. Let us therefore ask ourselves: how do our words sound in the ears of the wide world? Do they sound like the words of people wanting only their own way, who on the one hand claim for themselves the right to share in ruling the universal Church, but on the other hand in the running of their own dioceses do not wish to impose any limitation or form of limitation on themselves, nor to resign because of advanced age, nor to accept the decisions of brothers in the episcopate?

It has been said that the faithful are disturbed by the constraint of monarchical episcopal power. My own experience at least contradicts this. But when laws and their application differ from one diocese to another, then the faithful cry out in complaint: "Is it ever going to be possible for you bishops to agree with one another?"

✷ ✷ ✷

DENIS HURLEY:
HIS WITNESS TO LOVE OF NEIGHBOR

Frederick Amoore

IN PRISON AND YOU CAME TO ME

On Good Friday in 1985 a procession of about three hundred people, following a two-meter wooden cross held by two clergymen, black and white, made its way round the streets of Durban, and eventually arrived outside Durban City prison. A service was held then as a gesture of solidarity with sixteen, who, accused of treason, were imprisoned there, and also with hundreds detained without trial in prisons all over the Republic of South Africa. Denis Hurley, Archbishop of Durban, led that service. He had visited the prison earlier in the week and he believed that those imprisoned had been uplifted, strengthened, and encouraged by that service. He himself might have been inside that prison, a risk for which he was prepared, and a story to be told later.[1]

FOR THE PEOPLE OF GOD

No tribute to the concern for the worship of God shown by Archbishop Hurley in his immense work for the liturgy would be complete unless accompanied by some account of his concern for the people of God in the midst of oppression, poverty, homelessness, and unemployment.

A South African, born in the Cape, but having lived most of his life, and all his episcopate, in Durban, he has been deeply involved in and concerned about the mass of evils that the world knows under the comprehensive title of apartheid. That hated word only came into the South African scene at about the time he was consecrated bishop, but much of the social evil associated with it, in the way of inequality between black and white, white privilege in the matter of housing, job opportunity, education, political power,

---

[1] See *Southern Cross*, 3 May 1985; *Diakonia News*, May 1985.

sporting and social activity, and a great deal else, had long marked the local scene. For the most part there was residential segregation, and even the churches in black areas were inferior to those in white areas. The area round Durban was one of growing industrialization, and there was a great mixture of people—Zulu, Indian, "colored," and white.

Like many other South Africans in the white community Archbishop Hurley grew up accepting the surrounding inequalities without much questioning of them. As happened with many others, when he went overseas, first to the novitiate of the Oblates of Mary Immaculate (O.M.I.) in Ireland in 1932, and then to Rome the following year, his perceptions were sharpened. The title of the thesis he presented for his licentiate was "Economic Domination by Credit Control," and this would indicate a growing concern with the needs and plight of ordinary people. After ordination he was appointed curate at Emmanuel Cathedral in Durban—a church set right in the midst of people and all the problems of life. On his seventieth birthday he told how his political conversion had followed his ordination and that while he had earlier resented the Mahatma Gandhi for disturbing the peace of the British Empire, he had later regarded him as a hero.[2]

After three years at the cathedral, he was appointed superior of the St. Joseph's Scholasticate in Pietermaritzburg, and after only three years there, he was nominated bishop, the youngest in the world. As bishop he became more aware of the needs of so many different kinds of people in what was fast becoming a great industrial area with a deprived rural hinterland.

The year after his episcopal ordination, in 1948, the white electorate of South Africa (there was a tiny minority of Cape "colored" men on the voters' roll still) brought in the National Party government (still in power today), whose policy was apartheid, a strict form of segregation and white group dominance, enforced not only by social custom but by legislation.

Very early in his episcopate, Archbishop Hurley had to confront these racial measures. A cartoon in the *Daily News* depicts him and Ambrose Reeves (then Anglican bishop of Johannesburg), coped and mitred, trying to pull back with their crosiers a Dr. Verwoerd ballooning up to the sky, laden with his Bantu Education Act. Within a year or two, he had been made chairman of the South African

---

[2] See *Southern Cross*, 24 Nov. 1985.

Catholic Bishops' Conference and was responsible for responding to the increasing mass of legislation enforcing apartheid which appeared year by year. Churches had invested heavily in education, and the Bantu Education Act was a very thorny question. Does the Church try to save something by attempting to cooperate with such legislation? Under his leadership the pronouncements of the Conference seemed to grow strong, from a mild reproof to a forthright statement of the demands of Christian social justice.

From this time on his public addresses, his writings, his actions bear witness to his profound appreciation of human dignity, his convictions that the Christian faith must bear strong witness in social, economic, and political life and that God is to be sought among the persons of the poor and the oppressed.

SOME MAJOR INFLUENCES

The work and teaching of Monsignor Cardijn, the founder of the "Young Christian Workers" with his principle of "Look, Judge, Act," had a profound effect on him; so too had the teaching of Teilhard de Chardin and the humanism of Maritain. In 1961 he was appointed to the Central Preparatory Commission of the Second Vatican Council, and the three years of the Council sessions were the foundation of much of his later teaching and witness. Vatican II strengthened for him the sense of identification with the poor and oppressed. In his public addresses he developed and publicized the teaching of *Gaudium et spes* on the dignity of the human person. For him, this and other documents were a revolution in Catholic thinking, taking it away from a renunciation of this world to the hope for its transformation.

In South Africa he became increasingly involved with the South African Institute of Race Relations, a body which, with its strong emphasis on the need for exhaustive research along with any pronouncements on socio-economic matters, went along with the principle of "Look, Judge, Act." In 1964 he was invited to give the Hoernle Memorial Lecture, to which he gave the title of "Apartheid, the Crisis of Christian Conscience." In 1965 he was elected president of the Institute, and his presidential address that year, "A Time for Faith," was followed in 1966 by another address, "Human Dignity and Race Relations."

DIAKONIA

The metropolitan area of Durban was becoming a microcosm of South Africa. Among the Zulu people there were factions and faction fights, difficult relationships between the Indian and other peoples, industrial problems, and the beginnings of strike action on a major scale. There were thousands of squatters and homeless people with increasing resentment and bitterness, especially among the youth, as the grip of apartheid legislation and administrative action grew tighter, and as people were moved away from their homes and lands to resettlement areas.

It seemed to the archbishop that this was an area in which Christian people could and ought to work together ecumenically. He made some preliminary suggestions to the Natal Council of Churches, and after some months, on 25 March 1976, seven Churches came together to set up Diakonia in Durban. He described it in this way:

> It is an effort to help the Church give practical expression to the Gospel in some aspects of the social scene in and around Durban. It is a time for rejoicing—and for trepidation, for new ventures are always uncertain. Trepidation is a very useful attitude. It drives us to prayer, to hope in God, to trust, not in our own efforts, but in the guiding hand and power of God.[3]

He was elected as the first president, and under his leadership Diakonia began to play an increasing part in Christian witness in Durban, addressing itself to such matters as the wages and service conditions of domestic workers, industrial conditions, youth problems, and much else.

Naturally such an organization attracted the hostile attentions of the government, and from time to time its affairs came under the investigations of the security police. Threats were made. In August 1985 the director, Paddy Kearney, was detained under section 29 of the Internal Security Act. Seven security policemen searched the Diakonia office, removing papers and files. Archbishop Hurley was there, and when he attempted to object, he was ordered off the premises. He later made a public protest at the high-handed behavior of the police as an attack on a Church body trying to do the work of Christ in the unjust and apartheid-ridden society of South Africa, and publicly expressed full confidence in Mr. Kearney.[4]

---

[3] *Diakonia News,* May 1976.
[4] See *Southern Cross,* 8 Sept. 1985; 23 March 1986.

In the following year, the archbishop was enabled by a judgment of the Natal Supreme Court to have Mr. Kearney released.

ACTS OF PUBLIC WITNESS

The conditions of detention by the security police meant that the family of the one detained often had no knowledge of the place of detention; there seemed to be no way of ensuring that the detainee was properly treated and cared for. There were many allegations of brutal treatment or of torture to secure the evidence sought by the security police. Solitary confinement, deprivation of food, electric shock treatment, and much else was alleged against the authorities, and there seemed to be no way of proving or disproving these charges. From time to time a detainee died in custody.

In April 1976, the archbishop addressed a meeting in the cathedral for Joseph Mduli, who had died in custody, and he called for a proper enquiry. The following year he held a memorial service in his cathedral for twenty-two people who had by this time died in detention. He spoke of the violence inherent in enforcing apartheid.[5]

During the middle of 1978 the various groups of squatters at Crossroads, outside Cape Town, were threatened by harrassment of all kinds with dire predictions of removal and relocation. Once more a service was held in Emmanuel Cathedral in solidarity with them. More than that, on 15 September the archbishop kept vigil for them by standing outside Durban Post Office and carrying a great notice-board drawing attention to the threats which were being made against the people of Crossroads. There were many squatters all round Durban, living a precarious existence in their makeshift huts of corrugated iron and cardboard, and the archbishop was well aware of their hardships. This incident shows the extent of his sympathy— people a thousand miles away in Cape Town mattered to him, just as did his own people close at hand.[6]

Very largely through Archbishop Hurley's influence the Catholic Church received observer status in the South African Council of Churches, and in 1976 he addressed the National Conference of the SACC on Mobilization for Peace. In this address he developed

---

[5] See *Diakonia News*, Nov. 1977.
[6] See *Diakonia News*, Nov. 1978.

a theme to which he returned from time to time, namely the difficulty of changing group attitudes, especially the attitudes of the white group. "The Church has given little attention to the ethics of group attitudes; in social morality we have scarcely come of age." Nevertheless he looked to the future in hope which was to be sustained by the power of prayer.[7]

In 1984 he took a prominent part in the launching of a campaign to attract a million signatures to a petition rejecting apartheid, seeking the creation of a non-racial, democratic South Africa, free of oppression, economic exploitation and racism, and opposing the Tricameral constitution. He asked Diakonia itself to collect ten thousand signatures of the total.[8]

SUMMONNED TO APPEAR IN COURT

Perhaps his most costly act of public witness arose out of a report issued by the Catholic Bishops' Conference and a subsequent press conference he held in February 1984 in connection with alleged police atrocities in Namibia. The report itself was drawn up in the light of a visit by members of the Catholic Bishops' Conference to Namibia and of the interviews and investigation carried out on that visit. Nevertheless the authorities did not like the report and the strong criticism of police and military actions contained in it.

From time to time during 1984 the police visited Archbishop Hurley, and eventually he was summoned to appear in court in October 1984. The charge was that he had contravened the Police Act by alleging police atrocities in Oshikulu and Kavango in South-West Africa, without having reasonable grounds for believing them to be true. When he arrived in court, the charge was postponed until February 1985.

During all this time, his diocese, the Catholic Church in Southern Africa, and very many other Christian Churches rallied strongly to his support. This was world news, for he was the first archbishop to appear in any court anywhere in the world for thirty-one years. Mass was offered for him in many places and prayer vigils were held.

Among those who attended the court on the day of the trial were bishops from England, Scotland, and Ireland, as well as many mem-

---

[7] See *Ecunews Bulletin*, 24 Aug. 1976.
[8] See *Diakonia News*, Mar. 1984.

bers of the local hierarchy. Then came the anticlimax; the prosecutor withdrew the charges on the ground that the telex sent by the journalist who had reported the matter was not sufficient evidence without further testimony.

Archbishop Hurley was described as the prophet who would not be silenced, one who was willing to risk going to jail so that the truth could be told. He himself regretted that the trial had never taken place; had it done so the truth about the atrocities in Namibia could have been established in a court of law. His final comment was:

> May God grant the grace of repentance to the offending party and the grace of forgiveness to the offended party so that reconciliation may result and peace and friendship come into its own.[9]

An incident of this kind did not deter him from further action. The next year he wrote to the Minister of Police strongly protesting against the killing of a child, Maggie Legwetu, as a result of police action with bird-shot at Kagiso in the Transvaal.[10] Shortly after this he went with others to interview the leadership of the African National Congress in Lusaka, because he felt that the ANC must be a part of any plans for a better future for South Africa. On his return he said that he felt that the Catholic Church in South Africa had been more concerned with opposing the injustices of apartheid than in actively promoting a democratic society.[11]

The continuing state of emergency has, among many other ill results, seriously affected the independence of the press, and has put a strong censorship on the reporting of civil strife, protests, and demonstrations of many kinds. A new periodical, *New Nation*, was launched by the Catholic Bishops' Conference in January 1986 and Archbishop Hurley as president of the conference declared its purpose in these terms:

> The lives of people in South Africa are strongly touched by political realities, so the "New Nation" will have much to say about them. It will endeavour to speak in truth and justice, love and freedom, and contribute to the unfolding of justice and peace.[12]

New Nation has rapidly proved its effectiveness as a thorn in the side of government policy; its first editor is suffering from detention without trial, and strong threats and warnings have been sent to the pa-

---

[9] *Southern Cross*, 27 Jan. 1985, 24 Feb. 1985, 3 Mar. 1985.
[10] See *Southern Cross*, 9 Feb. 1986.
[11] See *Southern Cross*, 4 May 1986.
[12] *Diakonia News*, Mar. 1986.

per, indicating that it could easily be closed down for the news and views it is publishing.

Archbishop Hurley is a man with a great heart, great enough to be concerned not only with the suffering in his own diocese, in South Africa and Namibia, but also that of the rest of the world. Halfway through his episcopate the University of Natal asked him to deliver a public lecture. His subject was "World Morality and World Community," and he spoke of his concern about the wealth of the West as contrasted with the tragedy of poverty and starvation in the Third World. On another occasion he spoke with deep feeling for a sobbing Vietnam, for Calcutta, and for the continuing warfare in the Middle East, in the Horn of Africa, and in Ireland.[13]

This concern for people throughout the years of his episcopate was the overflow of his love and service for Almighty God, for he knew that love of God and love of neighbor cannot be separated. His definition of neighbor was generous and wide. The teaching of the Church, particularly as expounded by Vatican II, was nothing unless it was shown to be just as relevant to daily life as it was to the worship of God for which he had so high a regard.

Any adequate account of his social teaching would need a whole book; the next few paragraphs can only point to some of the more important themes in his speaking and writing.

THE DIGNITY OF THE HUMAN PERSON

The Pastoral Constitution *Gaudium et spes* sets the heart of human dignity in the heart where the individual person is alone with God and possesses a law written by God; to obey this law is the very dignity of the human person.[14]

He shared in the promulgation of this and other documents of the Second Vatican Council declaring the dignity of the human person.[15] Then he looked around at his diocese and country and saw among the African people the breakdown of family life, the destruc-

---

[13] See Denis E. Hurley, "World Morality for a World Community," A Graduation Address to the University of Natal, *Theoria* 28 (May 1967), 10.

[14] See Vatican Council II, Pastoral Constitution on the Church in the Modern World *Gaudium et spes* [hereafter, GS], 7 Dec. 1965, no. 16.

[15] See Vatican Council II, Declaration on Christian Education *Gravissimum educationis*, 28 Oct. 1965, and Declaration on the Relationship of the Church to Non-Christian Religions *Nostra aetate*, 28 Oct. 1965.

tion of their traditional institutions and customs; the way in which grown men and women were addressed as "boy" and "girl." What could be more destructive of human dignity than the apartheid society in which he had to live.

So he chose as title for his second presidential address to the South African Institute of Race Relations (SAIRR), "Human Dignity and Race Relations."

> To recognise human dignity is a way of getting rid of racism and wrong nationalism, for being human is a value that transcends colour, race, and culture.[16]
>
> If you claim anything for yourself on the basis of human dignity, you can't refuse it to others or even consider them reprobate. Human dignity is beyond nationalism, class or caste distinction, and, in particular, it is indispensable to the peaceful development of South Africa.[17]
>
> Moral value is needed to create a South African cultural consensus, and that value must be respect for human dignity.[18]
>
> When a man realises, no matter how confusedly, that he has within himself the power of communication with the infinite, with the physical infinite of the universe and the spiritual universe of its Creator, he knows with a deep and unconquerable conviction that he is subservient to no other man, that only the infinite can demand the absolute dedication of his life, and the ultimate loyalty of his spirit.[19]
>
> This dignity was not clear from the beginning, but a truth of which man became aware in a flowering of rights and liberty, involving freedom against tyranny and slavery, liberty of speech, publication, assembly and religion, the status of women, and an attempt to deal with the wickedness of war.[20]

The archbishop declared his admiration for pacifists like Charles Yeats and attacked conscription for military service. He asked for conscientious objection to be allowed to moral and ethical objectors, and not only to pacifists on religious grounds. He himself does not seem to have taken up a pacifist position.[21]

---

[16] Denis E. Hurley, "Human Dignity and Race Relations," Presidential Address to South African Institute of Race Relations (Johannesburg: South African Institute of Race Relations, 1966), 12.

[17] Hurley, "Human Dignity," 6.

[18] Hurley, "Human Dignity," 3.

[19] Hurley, "Human Dignity," 3.

[20] Hurley, "Human Dignity," 2.

[21] See *Southern Cross*, 7 July 1985.

The Role of the Church in the World

Belief in God as Creator and Redeemer dominated the way in which Archbishop Hurley saw the Church in the world and the members of the Body of Christ as those who share in this creative and redeeming work. "When we work, we are most like God, God the worker, God the creator."[22] He felt that it was the burden of his career to guide the Church to a concern and responsibility in social and political matters. In an address to the Convocation of the University of Natal he said that a change was beginning to come over the Church from the days when it seemed to have assumed that it was not its job to react against great social evils. The Church was beginning to learn that the worst sins are social sins, vested interests, both those of financial and racial oligarchies and of parliamentary and peoples' democracies.[23]

He said on his seventieth birthday that Vatican II was one of the chief influences on him,

> deepening our understanding of the Church, the revelation of a completely new attitude of the church to the world, so that the church must love the world, must be involved in the world and exist for the world, here to enlighten, evangelise and sanctify the world—that vision is—I think—the inspiration of my life.[24]

On another occasion he said:

> So often in the past spirituality has consisted in resisting the blandishments of the world, with no thought as to how involvement in the material world is related to eternal life. Renunciation still has a place in Christian living, but today the church has had to reconsider its attitude and recognise a commitment to the world and to its transformation. Some patristic and mediaeval teaching almost looked forward to the destruction of the world. Now it seems to us less and less likely that the end of the world will bring a catastrophic conclusion to an environment into which so much dedicated endeavour has been poured.[25]

The archbishop pointed to the hope of St. Paul in the epistle to the Romans, "creation still retains the hope of being freed, like us, from

---

[22] *Diakonia News*, July 1984.

[23] See *Concept*, June 1974, 31-35.

[24] *Southern Cross*, 24 Nov. 1985.

[25] Denis E. Hurley, "The Cross and the World," in *PACSA* (1982), 5, Journal of the Pietermaritzburg Agency for Christian Social Awareness.

its slavery to decadence, to enjoy the same freedom and glory as the children of God."[26]

In 1982 Archbishop Hurley contributed a chapter, "Catholic Social Teaching and Ideology," to the book *Catholics in an Apartheid Society*. This gave him the opportunity of developing the teaching of *Gaudium et spes* and of the great sociological encyclical letters on the world, though with special reference to South Africa. "Christians must love the world in which they live, love human involvements, human achievements, perceive problems and come to grips with them, bringing the love of Christ to the situation."[27] There is a call to the laity who because of their baptism are the frontline troops of the Church, and indeed the bulk of its membership. His strong consciousness of the laity as the greater part of the Church appears in another symposium to which he contributed:

> The insistence on the role of the laity and the training of the laity has led to deeper theological thinking about the issues involved. Work, marriage, the family, and the basic significance of the temporal, take up more than ninety-nine percent of the average Christian's time. Work—was it the curse of Adam or was it something built into the human race, as an essential aspect of the image of God, making mankind a co-creator with God in the ongoing evolution of the world?[28]

He quoted from *Gaudium et spes* such passages as this: "For after we have obeyed the Lord, and in His Spirit nurtured on earth the values of human dignity, brotherhood and freedom, and indeed all the good fruits of our nature and enterprise, we will find them again, but freed of stain, burnished and transfigured."[29] He saw the world opened up before our eyes as an immense field for the practice of Christian love, with a million obstacles.[30]

A MILLION OBSTACLES

The million obstacles were all round him in the persons of those who supported and practiced apartheid, as well as the network of

[26] Romans 8:21.

[27] Denis E. Hurley, "Catholic Social Teaching and Ideology," in *Catholics in an Apartheid Society*, ed. A. Prior (Cape Town: D. Philip, 1982), 22-23, 34.

[28] Denis E. Hurley, "Beyers Naude: Calvinist and Catholic," Symposium paper in *Not Without Honour: Tribute to Beyers Naude*, ed. P. Randall (Johannesburg: Ravan Press, 1982), 77-78.

[29] GS, no. 39: Walter M. Abbott, S.J., ed., *The Document's of Vatican II* (New York: America Press, 1966; London: Geoffrey Chapman, 1966), 237.

[30] See Hurley, "Catholic Social Teaching and Ideology," in *Catholics in an Apartheid Society*, 43.

laws, custom, habits, and socio-economic practices which had grown
up over a period of more than three hundred years. So often in his
teaching, Archbishop Hurley returned to St. Paul's great hymn of
love[31] or to the great commandment to love God and neighbor. It
is the law of love that judges South African society. He reckoned
that ninty-five percent of the white population claims to share in
the Jewish or Christian tradition, and he asked how could this basic law of love be demonstrated in a situation where a minority of
the population occupy most of the land and enjoy superior opportunities in employment, education, leisure, and sport, as against
the majority of the population who are black and have no political
rights. When some defended apartheid as a way of preserving Christian civilization, he replied that Christians have a right to question
whether they wanted Christianity preserved in such a way.[32]

Among a number of doctorates, he received one from Georgetown University. The citation honored his "powerful witness to the
Christian ideals of justice and love for all, regardless of race. Many
have remained silent or blind in face of racial injustice. Archbishop
Hurley has not."[33]

Like many other clergymen he was accused of bringing politics
into the pulpit, or mixing politics with religion. He has had to be
critical of those white Catholics who have failed to follow the lead
of their bishops. Groups of Catholics have been formed to do just
this (and similar groups are to be found in other Churches as well).[34]
To them he replied that the call to keep politics out of religion is
really a call to keep the message of the Scriptures, the example, the
wisdom, the influence, the virtue, the holiness, and the freedom
of Jesus out of political life.[35]

It is all too easy to denounce the sin and to hate the sinner. That
was a trap into which he did not fall. He knew that it would not
be at all easy for white people to change their attitude or their priv-
ileged position. "No change for the better is unaccompanied by
suffering. A society enjoying power and privilege and a comfortable life will find change difficult, the suffering of conversion and
of living out the effect of sin."[36] He was fully alive to white fears of

---

[31] 1 Corinthians 13.
[32] See Denis E. Hurley, "Apartheid: The Crisis of Christian Conscience" (Johannesburg:
South African Institute of Race Relations, 1966), 1, 10.
[33] Southern Cross, 22 Feb. 1987.
[34] See J. deGruchy, The Church Struggle in South Africa (Cape Town: D. Philip, 1982), 99.
[35] See Diakonia News, Nov. 1984.
[36] Hurley, "The Cross and the World," in PACSA (1982), 10.

losing what seemed to be the guarantee of survival.

> It may be a case of too little, too late, but at least we are going hard
> in a specific direction, realising how difficult it is for large commu-
> nities to change their outlook when—as in the case of the whites—
> power and privilege have been characteristic of their social life.[37]

But he did not abandon his crusade. He realized the seeming
failure of Christian people to follow their Lord's teaching of Christian love. "Religion must often suffer the humiliation of seeing its
most relevant lessons applied by those who deny its belief."[38] It may
be a long struggle.

> Possibly by the nature of things, this apparent impotence of the
> church is inevitable. It is conceivable that we have just survived the
> first few hundred years of a new cultural period in the evolution
> of man, destined to supplant and to last as long as the ten thou-
> sand year period that began when men left the caves and embarked
> on the first agricultural revolution. As was said by the Abbé Brueil,
> we have only just cast off the last moorings which hold us to that
> neolithic age.[39]

But there must be no complacency; there is a great struggle.

> All the sinews of our being pull in the opposite direction, selfish-
> ness, pride, avarice, lust, the herd instinct, tribal loyalties and ani-
> mosities, the hunger for power and privilege that lock people into
> a blind dedication to their group concern—transformation involves
> much of the cross.[40]

He saw racism as a worldwide and not merely South African
problem, and he quoted Pope Paul VI's 1967 Encyclical *Populorum
progressio* to this effect:

> Racism is still an obstacle to collaboration among disadvantaged na-
> tions and a cause of division and hatred within countries when-
> ever individuals and families see the inviolable rights of the human
> person held in scorn, as they themselves are unjustly subjected to
> a regime of discrimination because of their race or their color.[41]

This teaching and warning continued throughout his episcopate:
in 1959 he said that the color bar must go within ten years to avoid

---

[37] "Pastoral Plan," *Southern Cross*, 2 Feb. 1987; see "Politicians Appeal to Conscience," *Sash*, 1 Jan. 1987.

[38] Hurley, "Human Dignity and Race Relations", 4.

[39] Hurley, "Catholic Social Teaching and Ideology," in *Catholics in an Apartheid Society*, 42.

[40] Hurley, "Beyers Naude: Calvinist and Catholic," in *Not Without Honour*, 80.

[41] Paul VI, Encyclical Letter *Populorum progressio*, 26 Mar. 1967, no. 63; cited by Hurley in "Catholic Social Teaching and Ideology," 41.

disintegration and total destruction in South Africa.[42] This was a warning long before Sharpeville, the Rhodesian war, Soweto and the Emergency of the eighties. The Churches must choose whether after liberation they will be remembered for the inspiration and encouragement received from them, or with a cold resentment for indifference to struggle and contest.[43]

Ecumenism

The foundation of Diakonia will have indicated Archbishop Hurley's commitment to ecumenism. He longed for the day when further steps to union might be achieved and the present barriers against receiving Holy Communion together would disappear. He showed great friendliness and was welcomed with great enthusiasm and affection at meetings, conferences, and synods of other Churches in South Africa. He was supportive of all Christians in their endeavors for peace and justice.

Beyers Naude had been a prominent minister of the Dutch Reformed Church, and a great supporter of the National Party government. His views underwent a dramatic change, and he had to give up his position in the Dutch Reformed Church. He founded the Christian Institute to promote a drastic change in the South African way of life. In a fierce and oppressive act, the Institute was banned, and Beyers Naude was subjected to grievous limitations on his life and liberty, being restricted in the times he could leave his house, and the places to which he might go. On his seventieth birthday Beyers Naude was presented with the book *Not Without Honour*, to which Archbishop Hurley contributed a chapter, "Beyers Naude: Calvinist and Catholic." He wrote of Naude as

> a sign of conversion to Christian love in its most demanding form, a sign of justice and transformation, of Christian collaboration against denominational barriers, a sign of what it means to be Calvinist and catholic, a sign of the cross of Christ and the hope of resurrection.[44]

---

[42] See A. M. Goguel et P. Buis, *Chrétiens d'Afrique du Sud Face à l'Apartheid* (Paris: l'Harmattan, 1978), 42.

[43] See Goguel et Buis, 61.

[44] Hurley, "Beyers Naude: Calvinist and Catholic," in *Not Without Honour*, 80-81. At one time Beyers Naude stood at the heart of power and influence in the Dutch Reformed Church and in the Afrikaner community. His views underwent a rapid change after the Cottesloe Conference between South African Church leaders and members of the World Council of Churches. His banning order, for five years, was very severe; he was confined to the magisterial district

Earlier he told of a moving encounter with a Methodist minister in which each acknowledged his failures and that of the Church to which he belonged in a great expression of humility. "We failed to seek the truth in love, and truth sought us in anger."[45]

At the opening of the Peace Library in Durban in 1982, Archbishop Hurley spoke of two other libraries which had been founded under the inspiration of the Mahatma Gandhi and he said:

> As Christians we apologize that our effort comes so late in the day, but we pray that it may be a sign to the one whom we call Lord and Saviour, and elicit the approval of the Mahatma who, I am sure, shares the joy of everlasting life with Christ.[46]

ALIVE TO MANY ISSUES

The area round Durban was one of rapid industrialization, and although authority tried from time to time to make strikes illegal, they went on. When questioned about a powerful strike for an improvement in wages and working conditions, the archbishop replied that these strikes were a sign that black fellow citizens of ours are capable of acting in a manner which is, by and large, peaceful and orderly.[47]

An important matter was education. There was strict segregation in government schools, and the private schools (that is, non-government, and for the most part under Church control) were accustomed to admit only white pupils. (There were a few schools which were non-racial.) During the sixties the segregationist policy of the private schools came under increasingly strong attack. In 1970 Archbishop Hurley said that all Catholic schools should be open to every pupil, no matter what his race, and six years later there was an instruction that all schools must be open to all races, whatever the law might say. He realized the double risk, that the government might close schools down and that white parents might withdraw their children from such private schools and send them to government schools. He said that this was a risk that had to be faced. In point of fact the government, in spite of angry speeches

---

of Johannesburg and apart from his family, was only allowed to meet with one person at any time. After five years, the order was renewed. He was deprived of his position as minister in the Dutch Reformed Church.

[45] Denis E. Hurley, "Facing Facts" (Johannesburg: SAIRR, 1966), 8.

[46] *Diakonia News*, May 1982.

[47] See Goguel et Buis, 61.

by some of its supporters, took no action at all, nor did parents notice-ably withdraw children. In fact many said that they were glad of the opportunity given to their children of mixing with boys and girls of other groups. Nor did the standard of education suffer, which was another fear.[48] From time to time he joined in pleas that all government education should be integrated, and that there should be one department of education for all, instead of the wasteful and divisive system of separate departments for each racial group.[49]

The teaching of Monsignor Cardijn, "Look, Judge, Act," had meant much to the archbishop and he encouraged the formation of a branch of Young Christian Workers (the society which Cardijn founded) in Durban. They sought basic rights for all workers, and their leadership suffered detention at the hands of the security police.[50]

One of the early actions of the Christian Institute, in which Beyers Naude had a major part, was the series of Sprocas Studies. These were a somewhat academic examination of various institutions, in-cluding the Church, in an apartheid society. By 1970 it was felt that a more action-related program was needed, and Archbishop Hurley presided at a meeting in 1971 at which the Black Consciousness Pro-gram was set up. This was to be in black hands—funds, though not control, were to come from the Christian Institute and the S.A. Coun-cil of Churches—and the program was to concern itself with black theology, work, youth projects, education. This was a movement which was soon to feel the killing effect of government action.[51]

From time to time the South African Defence Force would launch a military incursion into a neighboring state, claiming that they had received information that the African National Congress (ANC) was mustering forces there for a terrorist attack in some part of South Africa. Such an incursion was launched on Maseru, the capital of Lesotho, just before Christmas 1982. Forty-two citizens of Lesotho were killed in that attack, and many more injured; much damage was caused to houses and other property. Strong protests followed, both inside and outside South Africa, and Archbishop Hurley called upon all Catholics to offer prayers and church collections for the

---

[48] See M. Hope and J. Young, *The South African Church in a Revolutionary Situation* (New York: Orbis Books, 1981), 155-156.

[49] See *Southern Cross*, 1 Dec. 1985.

[50] See Hope and Young, 155.

[51] See Goguel et Buis, 61.

families of the victims of the raid, as a gesture of compassion, sympathy, and solidarity.[52]

One of the ways in which the government tried to meet demands for reform was the proposal in 1983 for a tri-cameral parliament. This added two other chambers, one for "colored" representatives and the other for Indian representatives, to the white House of Assembly. These representatives were chosen by the racial group so designated, and the new constitution was so arranged that the white house had ultimate control, even if all three houses had a joint sitting. To some this seemed a step forward, as being the first occasion on which the government had included people other than white in any kind of decision-making. Others condemned it bitterly, both because it was another act of discriminatory legislation, and even more because it completely ignored the largest section of the population, the great mass of African people. Archbishop Hurley commented as follows:

> We feel that everybody in South Africa has a right to share in the resources of South Africa, and a right to participate in the government of South Africa. Full participation may be difficult to reach immediately, but at least the principle should be enunciated and a method set up for gradual implementation. Instead, in this proposed constitution, we have the old principle of Apartheid re-emphasised to the exclusion of black people. In the light of the Christian principle of love, justice and brotherhood, we judge this draft constitution to be very lacking, and we cannot support it.[53]

In some quarters "reconciliation" has been regarded as a dirty word, as a cheap way of getting round the injustices perpetrated in the past. When Archbishop Hurley gave his support to the "Release Mandela" campaign he restored meaning to this word.

> Because the way of violence is so unpredictable, so destructive, so prolific of insoluble bitterness, religion has no other option but to promote reconciliation with all the strength and love at its command, a reconciliation which produces neither victors nor vanquished, because those vanquished by it are the authentic victors. The call to free Mandela, I see as a call for reconciliation. Reconciliation is a leap in the dark. But faith is a prior leap in the dark. And if we have made the first leap by believing in a gospel of reconciliation, why not make the second leap by endeavouring to practise it, even in politics—especially in politics![54]

---

[52] See *Rand Daily Mail*, 6 Jan. 1983.
[53] *Diakonia News*, Sept. 1983.
[54] *Diakonia News*, July 1980.

His Hopes

These actions are just a sample, taken from a period of many years, of the archbishop's wide sympathy and love for so many different people in their distress. He saw so much of evil, wickedness, and violence, but he was not without hope. So in a pastoral letter in 1986 he called for a day of fasting and penance once a month against the spiral of violence.[55]

In 1978 the University of Natal honored him with the award of a Doctor of Literature, and in his graduation address he spoke of the greatest summons of the Transcendental to draw on all the idealism, motivation, and inspiration to transcend the highest and toughest barriers that rise between us. Community instinct has a magnificent potential, but it is a liability if there is entrenchment behind group barriers. Reconciliation between antagonistic groups is a pioneering task. Only late in our century have we begun to understand something of the tough psychological sinews of group attitudes that seem to make conflict inevitable between human communities. Could South Africa be fired to do enough to ensure a peaceful resolution of agonizing problems and be the first great example in the world of such a breakthrough?[56]

He wrote on another occasion, "The love and sharing that should be the hallmark of Christian individuals and families must also become the norm for dealings between national and racial communities."[57] The major task lies in harnessing this tremendous power of love to meet the needs of the situation. "Christians must never yield to pessimism; the essential task of the Church remains, that of giving practical expression to Christian faith."[58]

The Man

A mark of the greatness of the man is that although so much of his teaching involved pointing out the wrongs of white-enforced laws, social and economic norms, and lifestyle in general, Archbishop Hurley did not become hard or bitter—not even when he

---

[55] See *Southern Cross*, 19 Jan. 1986.

[56] See Denis E. Hurley, Graduation Address 1978, in *Graduation Addresses* (Durban: University of Natal).

[57] Hurley, "Catholic Social Teaching and Ideology," in *Catholics in an Apartheid Society*, 41.

[58] Hope and Young, 157.

was criticized for words or actions. He did say that he felt that he was lacking in the human touch. That certainly did not come through; what was obvious was a warmth and friendliness, a humility and peace which make him a man greatly beloved.[59]

On his 70th birthday, Alan Paton paid him this tribute:

> Denis Hurley was not born in a lighthouse as some people imagine. His father was the keeper of the lighthouse at Cape Point, the guardian of the light that warns the sailors of dangers and guides them away from destruction.
>
> Now the son did not follow in his father's footsteps. But he became a lighthouse keeper too; the guardian of the light that warns of dangers and saves us from destruction. The lighthouse has become a symbol of light and hope and our Archbishop has been doing this work of warning and guiding for the greater part of his seventy years. And he has done it with great faithfulness for which to-day we give thanks.[60]

---

[59] See *Natal Daily News*, 17 Mar. 1987.
[60] Alan Paton, in *Hurley, 1947-1987*, booklet commemorating the fortieth anniversary of Denis E. Hurley as Archbishop of Durban (Durban: Archdiocese of Durban).

WORKS CITED

Abbott, S.J., Walter M. *The Documents of Vatican II*. New York: America Press, 1966. London: Geoffrey Chapman, 1966.

Archdiocese of Durban, *Hurley 1947-1987*, Booklet commemorating the fortieth anniversary of Denis E. Hurley as Archbishop of Durban. Durban: Archdiocese of Durban.

Concept, No. 5. Occasional Publication. Durban: University of Natal.

de Gruchy, J. *The Church Struggle in South Africa*. Cape Town: D. Philip, 1982.

Diakonia News. May 1976, Nov. 1977, Nov. 1978, July 1980, May 1982, Sept. 1983, Mar. 1984, July 1984, Nov. 1984, May 1985, Mar. 1986. Quarterly Publication. Durban: Diakonia.

Ecunews Bulletin. 24 Aug. 1976. Occasional Publication. Johannesburg: South African Council of Churches.

Goguel, A. M., and P. Buis. *Chrétiens d'Afrique du Sud Face à l'Apartheid*. Paris: l'Harmattan, 1978.

Hope, M., and J. Young. *The South African Church in a Revolutionary Situation*. New York: Orbis Books, 1981.

Hurley, Denis E. "Apartheid: The Crisis of Christian Conscience." Johannesburg: South African Institute of Race Relations, 1966.

———. "Beyers Naude: Calvinist and Catholic." Symposium paper in *Not Without Honour: Tribute to Beyers Naude*, ed. P. Randall. Johannesburg: Ravan Press, 1982.

———. "Catholic Social Teaching and Ideology." In *Catholics in an Apartheid Society*, ed. A. Prior. Cape Town: D. Philip, 1982.

———. "Facing Facts." Johannesburg: South African Institute of Race Relations, 1966.

———. Graduation Address 1978. In *Graduation Addresses*. Durban: University of Natal.

———. "Human Dignity and Race Relations." Johannesburg: South African Institute of Race Relations, 1966.

———. "The Cross and the World." In *PACSA* (1982). Pietermaritzburg: Pietermaritzburg Agency for Christian Social Awareness, 1982.

———. "World Morality for a World Community." In *Theoria* 28 (1967). Pietermaritzburg: University of Natal.

Natal Daily News (Durban). 17 Mar. 1987.

Rand Daily Mail (Johannesburg). 6 Jan. 1983. (Publication now ceased.)

Sash. 1 Jan. 1987. Johannesburg: Black Sash Movement.

Southern Cross. 27 Jan. 1985; 24 Feb. 1985; 3 Mar. 1985; 3 May 1985; 7 July 1985; 8 Sept. 1985; 24 Nov. 1985; 1 Dec. 1985; 19 Jan. 1986; 9 Feb. 1986; 23 Mar. 1986; 4 May 1986; 22 Feb. 1987. Catholic weekly newspaper published in Cape Town.

RITUAL REFORM

SEMPER REFORMANDA:
THE OPENING AND CLOSING RITES
OF THE MASS

Mark Searle

When the Second Vatican Council mandated a general restoration of the liturgy, it clearly acknowledged that liturgical celebrations involve processes of communication: "In the liturgy, by means of signs perceptible to the senses, human sanctification is signified and brought about in ways proper to each of these signs" (Constitution on the Liturgy *Sacrosanctum Concilium* [hereafter, SC], art. 7). Recognizing that, with the passage of time, the capacity of the Roman Mass for effective communication had been severely compromised, the Council ordered that "both texts and rites should be so drawn up that they express more clearly the holy things they signify" (SC, art. 21). One important step toward more efficient communication was to be a clearer articulation of the nature and purpose of the several parts of the Mass (see SC, art. 50), a step which was realized in the new Order of Mass of 1969 with the distinction between the liturgy of the word and the liturgy of the eucharist and the provision for opening and concluding rites which would constitute the gathered people as an assembly at the beginning and send them forth at the end.

The revision of the *Ordo Missae* was, as Pope Paul VI was profoundly aware, a matter of "serious and universal import,"[1] requiring the services of the best scholars in the Church, the consultation of the world's bishops, and the close interest of the pope himself. It was also a matter of the greatest sensitivity. Even before the 1967 Synod, but especially during and after that event, the pressures on the one side for radical reform and from other quarters for no reform

---

[1] Paul VI, Address to the members and *periti* of the Consilium, 13 Oct. 1966: *Documents on the Liturgy, 1963-1979: Conciliar, Papal, and Curial Texts* [hereafter, DOL] (Collegeville, Minn.: The Liturgical Press, 1982) 84, no. 630.

at all were quite extraordinary.[2] Ironically, the very importance which the Church attaches to the Mass created the kinds of conditions which resulted in what many believe now to have been among the least successful of the postconciliar reforms.[3]

This is not the place to attempt to recount the complex history of the reform of the Order of Mass,[4] or to pursue in any detail the reasons for which specific elements of the initial and concluding rites were adopted. Instead, by focusing on the opening and concluding rites, we will suggest that one of the major problems with the reform process was that it was essentially operating under conflicting guidelines. The Council had issued a number of directives intended to enhance the communicative qualities of the liturgy of the Mass, especially in SC, article 50;[5] but it had also insisted that "sound tradition be retained . . . [that] there must be no innovations unless the good of the Church genuinely and certainly requires them; care must be taken that any new forms adopted should in some way grow organically from forms already existing" (SC, art. 23). These two sets of principles, while not necessarily irreconcilable, posed the possibility of conflict and it is the thesis of this essay that, in the later stages of the reform, particularly, the urge to conserve overwhelmed the concern for effective communication.

Ritual is rather like speech in that it consists of a sequence of sign-units and communicates effectively when the sign-units are not only carefully chosen but carefully ordered in sequence. Good ritual, like good speech, requires careful attention not only to vocabulary, but also to syntax. While this analogy should not be pushed too far (for ritual is more like a full-length drama than a simple sentence), the distinction between the process of selection (the paradigmatic axis) and the process of combination (the syntagmatic axis) of the elements is one that is fundamental to any semiotic system, and can be applied fruitfully to the opening rites of the Mass.[6]

---

[2] See Annibale Bugnini, *La riforma liturgica (1948-1975)*, Bibliotheca "Ephemerides Liturgicae," "Subsidia" 30 (Rome: CLV-Edizioni Liturgiche, 1983), esp. 255-299.

[3] For a summary of the main criticisms, see Emil J. Lengeling, *Die neue Ordnung der Eucharistiefeier. Kommentar der Dokumente zum Römischen Messbuch* (Leipzig, 1970), 198-199. Also, R. Cabie, "Le nouvel *ordo missae*," *La Maison-Dieu* 100 (1969), 21-35. On the entry rites, Ralph Keifer, "Our Cluttered Vestibule: The Unreformed Entrance Rite," *Worship* 48 (1974), 270-277.

[4] This history has been recorded by the secretary of the Consilium, Annibale Bugnini, in his memoir *La riforma liturgica (1948-1975)*, esp. 332-388.

[5] See below, p. 65.

[6] On this see Karl Heinrich Bieritz, "Zeichen der Eröffnung," in Rainer Volp (Hrsg.), *Zeichen/Semiotik in Theologie und Gottesdienst* (Munich and Mainz: 1982), 195-221. My indebtedness to Bieritz's article will be obvious in what follows.

This will be the approach adopted here. Rather than commenting in detail on the individual items ("vocabulary") in the opening and concluding rites as they exist today, we shall compare the structure ("syntax") of both these rites in the present Mass with the form they had in the original draft prepared by the revisers in 1964. To provide a broader context for the comparison, we shall also examine the opening and concluding rites in their unrevised form (the Tridentine Mass) and in the eighth-century papal Mass which served in some sort as a model for the revisers. Finally, since liturgy is less a matter of texts than of performance, we shall look at how the revised Order of Mass is now being celebrated in some parishes of the United States.

The latter is marked by too many variations to admit of easy tabulation, but the main structure of the other rites can be seen synoptically in Table 1:

PRECONCILIAR MASS	ORDO ROMANUS I	SCHEMA 113	ORDO MISSAE 1970
Introit	Introit	Introit	Introit
Procession	Procession	Procession	Procession
Genuflects to altar	Bows to altar	Bows to altar	Bows to altar
Prayers at foot of altar	Prays (silent)	Sign of cross (silent)	
Ascends to altar	Sign of cross (silent)	Prays (silent)	
Kisses altar	Kiss of Peace	Kisses altar	Kisses altar
Blesses incense	Kneels before altar		
Incenses altar	Kisses Book of the Gospels	Incenses altar and people	Incenses altar
	Kisses altar		
	Goes to seat	Goes to seat	Goes to seat
			Sign of cross
	Greeting	Greeting	Greeting
		Introduction to *Kyrie*	Introduction to Mass
			Penitential Rite
Kyrie	*Kyrie*	*Kyrie*	*Kyrie*
Introit			
Kyrie			
[*Gloria*]	[*Gloria*]	[*Gloria*]	[*Gloria*]
[*Gloria*]			
Kisses altar			
Greeting	Greeting		
Collect	Collect	Collect	Collect
TABLE 1			

I. The Problem: The Rites on the Eve of the Council

Although it is common to speak of the "old Mass" as if it were a single rite, it had always existed in more than one form and continued to do so when the Second Vatican Council convened. Traditionally, there was the pontifical Mass, though most Catholics witnessed it but rarely; there was the Solemn High Mass, with deacon and subdeacon; there was the sung parish Mass, or High Mass, with priest, servers, and choir; and there was the Low Mass, with priest and server, but no singing, celebrated with or without a congregation.[7] Then, in 1958, the Congregation of Rites issued its Instruction on sacred music, which complicated matters by encouraging both the "dialogue Mass" and congregational participation in the *Missa in cantu*, or sung Mass, while permitting different levels of active participation in both. Though not common in the English-speaking world, permission had also been given in some countries, notably Germany, for the congregational singing of appropriate hymns at different points of the Mass, as well as for the reading of the Mass texts in the vernacular by a commentator or *Vorbeter*.

Nonetheless, despite this range of possible forms of the Mass and despite the fact that the basic pattern, both rubrically and in parish life, was that of the Low Mass, the sung parish Mass had emerged as the form favored by the Liturgical Movement as the basis of any attempt to develop active participation.[8] Behind this decision lay respect for the fact that this form of the Mass had served as the basic parish Mass from late antiquity until modern times. More important, the distinction between what was "public" and what belonged to the private devotion of the priest was much clearer here than in the Low Mass, as was also the proper distribution of ministerial roles. Since this was the form of the old Mass with which the study group charged with revising the Mass (*Coetus* X) was dealing, this is the form we shall examine here.

One of the gravest distortions of the Mass liturgy which had occurred over the centuries and which the reform was supposed to tackle was the duplication created when the priest began to recite for himself everything that had originally belonged to other min-

---

[7] On these forms of the Mass, see Aimé-Georges Martimort, ed., *L'Église en Prière* (Paris and Tournai: 1961), 306-313; and Josef A. Jungmann, *The Mass of the Roman Rite: Its Origins and Development*, one volume ed., tr. Francis A. Brunner, rev. Charles K. Riepe (London: Burns and Oates Ltd.; New York: Benziger Brothers, Inc., 1959), 147-168.

[8] Karel Amon, "Hochamtsregel und neuer Messordo," *Liturgisches Jarhbuch* 20 (1970), 209-215.

isters. The oddest manifestation of this was clearly the priest's reading the Scripture lections while they were being chanted by the deacon and subdeacon, but, as the following table makes clear, it was operative in the opening rites as well.

VERBAL CODE 1 [PUBLIC]	VERBAL CODE 2 [PRIVATE]	MUSICAL CODE	VISUAL AND KINETIC CODES	CONGREGATION'S ROLE
[Introit]	Prayers at foot of altar and orations	Plainchant or polyphony	Entry procession (usually very brief) Gestures at foot of altar; kiss of altar; incensation;	Watching Listening Movements and gestures (sign of cross, etc.)
	Blessing of incense Introit			
Kyrie Intoning of Gloria Gloria Greeting Collect	Kyrie Gloria	Settings from Kyriale or polyphony Chant	movements at altar Gestures of greeting and prayer Vestments Objects Spaces	Verbal: Response to Greeting; Amen after Collect (if not done by choir or ministers)
TABLE 2				

This table drawn up by Karl Heinrich Bieritz,[9] though a simplification, displays something at least of the complexity of any ritual event, drawing as it does on many "codes" or signifying systems simultaneously. What it also reveals clearly is the duplication mentioned earlier: the private performance by the priest of those parts of the liturgy entrusted to the choir. The visual and spatial codes (with the vested priest ministering, with his back to the people, in a separate part of the church building, at an altar somewhat removed from the people and the choir) confirm the message communicated by the way his texts are read: this private liturgy, performed by the ordained priest, is the official and indispensable liturgy. It may occasionally be interrupted by the choir, but the role and even the presence of choir and congregation are of quite secondary importance and not at all essential. At best, they hedge the priestly rite with sacredness. By the time the priest turns for the first time to greet the people and acknowledge their presence, the liturgy is well underway. Thus, despite whatever role the choral and congregational contributions may originally have had, this particular form of the opening rites of the Mass establishes from the outset a clear understanding of where the real liturgy lies and thus determines how the rest of the celebration will be interpreted.

---

[9] Bieritz, 197.

It is important to note that the messages being communicated here are not primarily verbal, but non-verbal. To focus on the texts alone is to miss most of what is going on and to overlook the fact that the congregation, for example, while often entirely deprived of any verbal interaction with the priest or the choir, is nonetheless a participant in the event as a whole in virtue of their watching, listening, and moving or gesturing more or less on cue. Similarly, it can be appreciated that the three texts sung in sequence—introit, *Kyrie* and *Gloria*—are less likely to communicate denotatively (i.e. in terms of their textual content) than connotatively, creating appropriate associations through their musicality. They served, it has been remarked, as an "overture" to the rest of the Mass.[10]

There was, therefore, a certain consistency in the messages being communicated by the opening rites of the Tridentine Mass—at least when the specific verbal contents were ignored—a consistency all the more remarkable given the haphazard and largely accidental way the elements had come together in the course of history. What secured this consistency was the triumph of the non-verbal: the Latin language effectively prevented close reading of the contents of the texts, while the architectural and decorative features of pre-Vatican II churches worked well with the musical and ritual codes to communicate this conception of a "double liturgy" of which one part was clearly official and indispensable and the other entirely subordinate and ancillary.

It was, however, the communication of an image of the Church and a conception of liturgy at odds both with the vision of Vatican II and with the early tradition which inspired it. In addressing the need to reform the Order of Mass, the Council had self-consciously adopted as its own the goal of Saint Pius V who, in the sixteenth century, had promulgated the reformed Roman Missal convinced that it had been restored *ad pristinam . . . sanctorum Patrum normam et ritum*.[11] Although that was neither true nor, in fact, possible in the sixteenth century, by the time of Vatican II the history of the Roman Mass had been exhaustively researched and fully documented. Josef Jungmann himself, in 1949, had argued that it would

---

[10] Bieritz, 199.

[11] Vatican Council II, Constitution on the Liturgy *Sacrosanctum Concilium*, 4 Dec. 1963, art. 50: DOL 1, no. 50. See Bull *Quo primum* of Pius V, 14 July 1570. In 1563, while the Council of Trent was discussing the reform of the Mass, a manuscript of a Gregorian sacramentary was sent up to Trent from the Vatican. Later the Commission appointed by Pius V also consulted ancient sources. Jungmann, 103-104.

now be easy enough to achieve the goal that had eluded Pius V and to "reconstruct" the Roman Mass as it was found in the earliest extant sources. By so doing, many of the problems of the present Mass—the multiplication of prayers, the multiplications of signs of the cross, the disarrangement of the sequence of prayers and rites, etc.—would be resolved. Yet Jungmann felt that such a solution would be too radical. What the reform of the Mass really needed was a master-builder who knew thoroughly both the historical tradition and the needs of the Church now and in the future.[12] Nonetheless, it is worth looking briefly at the papal Mass described in the *Ordo Romanus Primus (OR I)*, since this was the source of most later forms of the Roman Mass and because it offered the key to resolving the complexities of the opening and concluding parts of the Mass of Pius V.

II. THE MODEL: ORDO ROMANUS I

An *ordo*, in the history of the Roman liturgy, is a normative description of how a given rite is to unfold: rubrics in more or less narrative form. Since it was meant to serve as a guide to the performance of the rite and was not used during the rite itself, it contained no prayer- or chant-texts. The first of the *ordines Romani* in Monsignor Andrieu's critical edition[13] offers a full description of a papal Mass sometime after the year 700. It is Easter Day and the Mass is to be held in the basilica of Saint Mary Major. Theodore Klauser summarizes the events as follows:

> Early in the morning the Pope rode with a great following from his residence in the Lateran to the church, which at the previous day's mass had been announced as the place (or *statio*) where the papal mass was to be held. . . . The Pope was accompanied on the one hand by those who held high office in his administration, and on the other by the deacons, sub-deacons, and acolytes who were to act as ministers at the liturgy. They took with them from the Lateran treasury liturgical books, vessels, linen, and other equipment.

---

[12] Jungmann's proposals for a reform of the Mass are recorded by Johannes Wagner, "Zur Reform des 'Ordo Missae': Zwei Dokumente," in *Liturgia opera divina e umana. Studi sulla riforma liturgica offerti a S. E. Mons. Annibale Bugnini in occasione del suo 70 compleanno*, Pierre Jounel, Reiner Kacynski, and Gottardo Pasqualetti, eds., Bibliotheca "Epemerides Liturgicae," "Subsidia" 26 (Rome: CLV-Edizione Liturgiche, 1982), 264-267. Jungmann's reluctance to consider a wholesale restoration of the ancient Roman Liturgy is also apparent in his comments on the Tridentine reform in *The Mass of the Roman Rite*, 103.

[13] M. Andrieu, *Les ordines romani du haut moyen-age*, vol. 2, Spicilegium Sacrum Lovaniese 23 (Louvain: 1948), 74-108.

When they arrived at the stational church, the Pope, supported ritually on either side by two deacons (this was in fact the *sustentatio* of court ceremonial), went to the sacristy or *secretarium* which was situated at the front of the basilica. Here his followers, following the rules laid down in Byzantine court ceremonial, stood round and assisted him in the removal of his outer garments in order that they then might clothe him in his liturgical vestments. . . .

Meanwhile, all those taking part in the service, having processed from the church which had been announced as the place of assembly, had now for some considerable time been in their carefully allotted places in the basilica. The suburban bishops and the presbyters sat round the apse on their *subsellia* next to the throne; the choir (*schola cantorum*), consisting of men and boys, stood in a square partition on the nave side of the altar; and in the center of the nave itself was the congregation which was strictly divided with the men on one side, the women on the other, and the aristocracy in the front rows. The period during which they waited was interrupted by a solemn ceremony; an acolyte (with his hands covered) carried the Book of the Gospels into the basilica, and a subdeacon laid it reverently (*honorifice*) on the altar. In the sacristy, the Pope was informed as to which sub-deacon was to proclaim the *apostolus* (i.e. the epistle) and which member of the choir was to lead the singing; it was not permitted to make any alteration in this arrangement afterwards. Finally, the Pope gave a signal. Whereupon the candles of the seven candlesticks (*cerostatae*) were lit, the sub-deacon concerned put incense on the *thymiaterium*, and the choir, on the instructions of a messenger, began the Introit antiphon. (Lights, incense, and music at the Introit were, as we know, some of the privileges of secular origin to which the Pope also had a claim.) The Pope then, once more ritually supported, entered the church at the end of a solemn procession. At the head walked the sub-deacon with the thurible, then followed the seven torch-bearers, and last came the deacons and sub-deacons. . . .

When they arrived in front of the altar, four of the seven torch-bearers went to the right, and three to the left. The Pope reverenced the altar with a bow, made the sign of the cross on his forehead, and gave the kiss of peace to his assistant ministers down to and including the deacon. He then gave a signal, whereupon the *schola* brought the Introit psalm to an end with the "Gloria Patri", and the Pope waited for this to finish, kneeling on the apse side of the altar. At the "Sicut erat," he kissed the Book of the Gospels, then the altar, and went to his throne in the center of the apse, where, turning east, he followed the singing of the "litany" (i.e. the *Kyrie eleison*). When it seemed to him that a sufficient number of Kyries has been sung, he commanded the choir to cease. Turning now to the congregation (facing, therefore, west), he intoned the hymn "Gloria in excelsis Deo"; and while this was being sung, he again faced eastwards. When this was over, he turned round once more and greeted the people with the salutation *Pax vobis*. Immediately after this, facing east once more, he gave the bidding for the prayer *Oremus* and straight away said the Collect, leaving no time at all for private prayer. . . . After the Collect, the Pope sat down on his throne and all present sat down also.[14]

If we set this entrance rite out synoptically, as was done for the Tridentine Mass, its structure appears as follows:

VERBAL CODE	MUSICAL CODE	VISUAL AND KINETIC CODES	CONGREGATION'S ROLE
?	?	Meeting	Gathering at *statio*
	?	Walking together	Procession
		Congregation arranged by rank and gender	Entry into church
		[Pope arrives]	Waiting
		Entry of Gospel	Watching
Introit antiphon and psalm	Gregorian Chant	Pope and attendants enter church	Watching/listening
		Pope passes through schola, bows to altar, makes sign of cross, gives *pax* to senior ministers,	Watching
Doxology Introit antiphon		gives signal to schola	
		Pope kneels	
Kyrie – Litany	Plainchant	Pope, ministers, stand in silence	Listening/watching, facing east
		Pope signals to end *Kyrie*	
Gloria	Plainchant	Pope turns to intone *Gloria* Pope, ministers, listen facing east	Listening
Pax vobis Oremus	Chant	Pope turns to congregation, turns back	Responds?
Collect	Chant	to face east	Amen?

TABLE 3

---

[14] Theodore Klauser, *A Short History of the Western Liturgy*, tr. John Halliburton (London: Oxford University Press, 1969), 61-63. The basilica of Saint Mary Major, of course, faces west, but the *Ordo Romanus I* assumes the more common orientation of churches and represents the general practice of the papal Mass rather than the special particulars of Easter morning Mass in Saint Mary Major.

Setting out the structure of the rite like this reveals several important things about this liturgy.

In the first place, for all the variety of individuals and groups involved, it remains a single, integrated rite. The people gather, process to the church, and take their appointed places. The suburban bishops and other clergy also take their places in the apse, and the schola assumes its place between the altar and the people. They wait. The Book of the Gospels is carried in as a holy object and placed upon the altar. The liturgy proper gets under way with the entry of the pope, to the accompaniment of the introit and its psalm sung by the schola. On arrival at the altar, the pope signals and the introit cedes to the *Kyrie*, which is sung by the schola alone, but which is a ritual chant expressing the whole assembly's acknowledgement of the lordship of Christ. Similarly with the *Gloria*: it is sung by the choir alone, but the pope and ministers and people stand in their serried ranks facing east, looking beyond the assembly, beyond the space of the basilica, to the "Lord God, heavenly king, God the Father almighty." Finally, this solemn, imperial opening comes to a close when the pope, standing again at the head of his people, addresses God on their behalf in the name of Christ.

In effect, then, the opening rites of the *OR I* serve to establish various sets of hierarchically structured relationships. The rigidly stratified order of Roman society is manifest in the allocation of places to the different social classes; but the secular society and its ranks are in turn subordinated to the ecclesiastical orders, themselves hierarchically arranged with the pope at the summit. These two mirror orders of Church and society are themselves expressly subordinated in turn to the divine King and the heavenly court, as is clear from the unfolding of the rite. (It would be even clearer if the interior decoration of the basilica, with its depictions of the pantocrator, Mary, the queen mother, and the ranks of the apostles and martyrs, could be taken into account).

The rite unfolds in five stages. First, there is the entry procession of the faithful and clergy and their assumption of their appropriate positions in the basilica. Next, following the entrance of the Gospels, comes the entrance of the pope, an entrance which employs all the pomp and circumstance of the Byzantine court[15] and which bespeaks the exalted status of the bishop of Rome: lights,

---

[15] Klauser, 32-37.

incense, attendants, music. It is, as Johannes Wagner has remarked,[16] a *Staatsakt*, a ceremony of state, a formal civic event, reflecting the status and power of the Church in Rome and the empire. But then, third, this almost godlike figure, standing at the pinnacle of the ecclesiastical and civil orders, performs to Christ the very same gestures of obeissance with which honor has been accorded to him: he bows, crosses himself, kisses the altar and the Gospel book, and kneels before the altar. In this submission to the "God in the highest," he is joined, fourth, by the whole assembly. He shares the kiss of peace with the leading ranks of the clergy: the bishops, priests, and deacons; equally significantly, he stands facing east while the choir sings the *Kyrie*-acclamation and the hymn of the *Gloria*, standing at the head of his people, but with them over against the heavenly throne before which the earthly Church is gathered. Finally, with all these relationships established through proxemic, spatial, kinetic, and musical codes, they are articulated verbally in the pope's greeting of the people (*Pax vobis*) and then, facing east again with his back to the assembly, his chanting of the collect. The collect represents the conclusion, summation and climax of all that has gone before. K. H. Bieritz notes that the Roman collect is more a matter of form than of informational content, and characterizes it as a "public address to God," analogous with the loyal address with which rulers were greeted in antiquity.[17] It thus provides a conclusion which is all of a piece with the rest of the opening rites in this ancient papal Mass, a masterpiece of political theology!

These opening ceremonies rehearse and reveal the reality of the Church in its encounter with God in Christ, and do so in ways that show how the Church's self-understanding is necessarily shaped by the political and social realities of a given time and place. Because of this, there was never any question of simply returning to OR I in the reform of the *Ordo Missae*. The very time it took—the whole liturgy probably lasted about three hours—was problematic even in late antiquity.[18] Besides, modern forms of social organization are quite at odds with those presumed in this rite and consequently the relationship of the people to God is now conceived quite differently. In short, the conciliar mandate to restore "elements which

---

[16] Johannes Wagner, "Reflexionen über Funktion und Stellenwert von Introitus, Kyrie und Gloria in der Messfeier," *Liturgisches Jahrbuch* 17 (1967), 40.

[17] Bieritz, 206.

[18] Evidence for this is to be found in the omission of the sermon and the prayers of the faithful, and in the failure any longer to pause for silent prayer between the *Oremus* and the collect.

have suffered injury through accidents of history . . . to the earlier norm of the holy Fathers: could not be taken literally. Resurrecting the Roman liturgy of the seventh or eighth century, would have yielded nothing better than a "period piece," quite unsuited either to the convictions of the modern Church or to its pastoral situation, and thus contrary to the larger purposes of the Council.

Nonetheless, this rite had much besides its venerable antiquity to commend it. First, it was an integrated public ritual, unlike the opening of the Tridentine sung Mass, and it revealed how the different participants could each contribute to the liturgy as a whole by the exercise of their own proper functions. Second, it was a vivid illustration of how "the preeminent manifestation of the Church is present in the full, active participation of all God's holy people in these liturgical celebrations, especially in the same eucharist, in a single prayer, at one altar at which the bishop presides, surrounded by his college of priests and by his ministers" (SC, art. 41). Third, it demonstrated the importance of the entrance procession for inaugurating the liturgical celebration, especially when, as was already happening by this time, the political dimension of the various symbols was reinterpreted along more theological lines. Fourth, it provided a key to how the various elements of the opening rites, so jumbled in the Tridentine Mass, originally functioned. This, in turn, would suggest that a more coherent opening could be provided for the new Order of Mass and would even indicate some options. It is hardly surprising, then, that this liturgy, while not offering an exact blueprint, should have loomed so large in the minds of those charged with drawing up the new Mass.

III. THE FIRST DRAFT: SCHEMA 113

After the Second Vatican Council voted for liturgical reform, in its Constitution on the Liturgy *Sacrosanctum Concilium* (4 December 1963), steps were quickly taken to set the process in motion. The *Consilium ad exequendam Constitutionem de sacra Liturgia* (hereafter, the Consilium), a supervisory body of about forty bishops from all over the world, was established in January 1964, and the group of experts responsible for revising the Order of the Mass (*Coetus* X) was nominated in February.[19] The mandate given them read in part:

---

[19] Given the historical and pastoral questions involved, the *coetus* was supposed to be composed of specialists in both liturgical history and pastoral liturgy, but the former easily

To carry out art. 50 of the Constitution on the Liturgy: "The Order of Mass is to be revised in a way that will bring out more clearly the intrinsic nature and purpose of its several parts, as also the connection between them, and will more readily achieve the devout, active participation of the faithful.

For this purpose the rites are to be simplified, due care being taken to preserve their substance; elements that, with the passage of time, came to be duplicated or were added with but little advantage are now to be discarded; other elements that have suffered injury through accident of history are now, as may seem useful or necessary, to be restored to the vigor they had in the tradition of the Fathers."

Coetus X held a series of extended working sessions in April, May, and June, as well as a joint session with Coetus XV (structure of the Mass) in August. These meetings saw the establishment of working procedures, the identification of resources and guidelines to be followed in the revision process, and the enumeration of the various questions about the Mass which would require further research and discussion. Most important was the agreement reached by the coetus and confirmed by the Consilium on the need to establish a basic blueprint, or forma normativa, as it was called, on the basis of which different forms of the Mass (pontifical, concelebrated, private) could be elaborated, while preserving the substantial unity of the Roman rite. In the reform of the missal following the Council of Trent, that "normative form" of the Mass had been, as the rubrics of the Missal of Pius V made clear, the Low Mass, said by a priest accompanied by a server. In view of the developments in the Church's understanding of her liturgy in modern times, and especially in view of the mandate given by the Council, a different model would have to be adopted: that of the celebration of the gathered Church.

It was recognized that, ecclesiologically, the bishop's Mass, celebrated in the cathedral with a full complement of clergy and laity, was the ideal,[20] "but since this form of the Mass can only be used very rarely in ordinary parishes and communities, it does not seem

---

outnumbered the latter. The coordinator (relator) of Coetus X was Johannes Wagner and its secretary was Anton Hänggi, who was named a bishop in 1967 and succeeded by the Spanish Benedictine Adalberto Franquesa. Members included Mario Righetti, Theodor Schnitzler, Pierre Jounel, Cipriano Vaggagini, Pierre M. Gy, Josef A. Jungmann, Luigi Agostini, Joseph Gelineau, and Louis Bouyer. Msgr. Frederick R. McManus of the Catholic University, Washington, was a consultor to the group. See Bugnini, 332, footnote 1.

[20] See SC, art. 41: DOL 1, no. 41; Vatican Council II, Dogmatic Constitution on the Church Lumen gentium, no. 26: DOL 4, no. 146.

right to make the pontifical rite the norm for the celebration of the Mass."[21] The same was felt to hold true of the Solemn High Mass and the Mass with a Deacon. Consequently, the norm, or *Missa normativa* as it came to be called, was to be that of "the Mass celebrated with singing (*Missa in cantu*), with a reader and at least one server, with a schola or at least one cantor, and with the people singing."[22]

This decision, clearly faithful to articles 26-32 of the Constitution on the Liturgy, firmly fixed the foundations for the revision of the Order of Mass and would be important in determining the shape of the opening and concluding rites. Further guidelines would be found in article 50 (cited above, p. 65) and in article 34:

> The rites should be marked by a noble simplicity; they should be short, clear, and unencumbered by useless repetitions; they should be within the people's powers of comprehension, and as a rule not require much explanation.

In the light of such criteria, the opening rites of the Tridentine Mass were clearly problematic. As we have already noted, and as many in the Church had already complained before the Council, the beginning of the present Mass was a lengthy, cumbersome accumulation of elements from different historical periods lacking any clear logic or structure. The extensive "private" liturgy of the priest, the burden of three major chants—introit, *Kyrie* and *Gloria*—sung in sequence and without interruption, the practice of having two, often three, collects: these were identified as some of the practices calling for correction in light of the Council's directives.

By October 1964, a first sketch of a new *Ordo Missae* was drafted,[23] and it bore a remarkable likeness to the *OR I*: while choir and people sang the introit, the priest, together with the reader and servers processed to the altar; the priest bowed to the altar, approached to kiss it, and went to his chair. Meanwhile, the choir, winding up the introit, embarked upon the *Kyrie*. When the *Kyrie* was finished, the priest intoned the *Gloria*, if it was to be used that day. Otherwise, he immediately greeted the people and invited them to pray. After a short silence, the collect completed the rite.

While this work was in progress, the first Instruction (*Inter Oecumenici*) on the implementation of the Constitution on the Liturgy had appeared in September 1964, followed by the decree *Nuper edita*

---

[21] Schema 39, no. 11.

[22] Schema 39, no. 13.

[23] Schema 44: *Specimen provisorium exaratum ad primum schema praeparandum*, 22 Oct. 1964.

Instructione of 27 January 1965 publishing an interim Order of Mass and revised rubrics. As a result, major alterations were already introduced into the celebration of the Mass. In the opening rites, for example, the prayers at the foot of the altar were reduced by the omission of Psalm 42, while the vernacular was permitted for the chants (introit, *Kyrie, Gloria*) and the priest's greeting of the people. The "double liturgy" characteristic of the Tridentine Mass was eliminated with the ruling that the priest "is not to say privately those parts of the Proper sung or recited by the congregation," but "may sing or recite the parts of the Ordinary together with the congregation or choir."[24] Just as important, the introduction of the priest's chair and the lectern and the preference expressed for the free-standing altar[25] so as to permit movement all around it, altered the character of the opening rites from being the ceremonies with which the sacrificing priest entered upon his sacred functions to being the constitution of a worshiping assembly.

With the publication of these directives, the reform was already under way. As a result, *Coetus* X was able to consider its task simplified because a number of key decisions had already been made by the pope in permitting the promulgation of these documents.[26] Furthermore, the immediate implementation of partial changes both allowed the *coetus* to assess the value of the changes and prepared the Church at large for the definitive reform.[27]

In any case, the work of the *coetus* went on, blessed by the Consilium in September 1964 and April 1965,[28] but delayed by the illness of the *relator*, Johannes Wagner. It met in Paris, at the Saulchoir, for nearly three weeks in June 1965, and then at Nemi, near Rome, for a shorter session (15-19 September). The result was the first full draft of the *Missa normativa*, which was then circulated to the heads of all the other working groups for their evaluation. The draft was then lightly edited in response to these comments and finally submitted to the Consilium as Schema 113, dated 9 October 1965. With that, the *coetus* clearly felt that "the first stage of our work has come

---

[24] Congregation of Rites (Consilium), Instruction (first) *Inter Oecumenici*, 26 Sept. 1964, nos. 48, 57-58: DOL 23, nos. 340, 349-350.

[25] *Inter Oecumenici*, nos. 91-96: DOL 23, nos. 383-388.

[26] See Schema 90, 26 Apr. 1965.

[27] What was not immediately foreseen, but soon became apparent, was that the introduction of change and experimentation, once started, could not easily be kept under control. Unofficial "experimental liturgies," and the reactionary responses they and even the official reform provoked, soon came to cast a dark shadow over the work of the Consilium and especially of *Coetus* X. See Bugnini, 256-265.

[28] Schemata 39 and 90.

to a close. The matters which were to be thought through by us as
the experts in this first stage have been thought through enough.
Even the comments of the heads of the other working groups yielded
nothing of any importance which had not been fully discussed over
and over again in our own group."[29] The hope was that the Consilium, after reading the new order and attending two experimental celebrations, would approve it, with or without amendments,
and then take it home with them (for they were almost all diocesan
bishops) for six months' experimental use in selected places, before
making any final decision on whether to approve it or not. Unfortunately, this did not work out as planned, for the press got hold
of the story and stirred up a hornet's nest of suspicions, accusations,
and denunciations which not only delayed the final approval of the
Mass by several years, but led to an unhappy series of confronta-
tions, interventions and tugs-of-war[30] that, as much as or more than
Coetus X, were responsible for the final shape of the *Ordo Missae*.

The opening rites of Schema 113 (Table 4) provide strong evidence in support of the claim made by *Coetus* X for the whole of
this draft Order of Mass:

> We have taken the utmost care to ensure that the traditional form of
> the Mass be faithfully preserved. The *coetus* is persuaded that the
> changes it is proposing, far from destroying the venerable structure
> [of the Mass], clarify and in some ways enrich it, and are far removed
> from "archaeologism," rationalism, or sheer desire for novelty.
>
> Walking a middle path, we have attempted to restore the tradi-
> tional form of the Mass in such a way that the new *Ordo Missae* will
> serve contemporary pastoral needs and at the same time, perhaps,
> serve throughout the world, in all the churches originating from
> Rome, as an element of the substantial unity of the Roman Rite (SC,
> art. 38) and a stable foundation on which legitimate cultural varia-
> tions may be constructed (SC, art. 38).[31]

The traditional character of these rites is patent in that the basic
structure of the ancient Roman Mass has been restored: the proces-

---

[29] Schema 113a: *Relatio ad primum schema Ordinis Missae "normativae" patribus Consilii proponendum*, no. 3.

[30] See Bugnini, 340-388.

[31] Schema 113a, nos. 10-11. Schema 113 (*Schema primum Ordinis Missae normativae patribus
"Consilii" proponendum*) was accompanied by two other documents under the same number,
identified here as 113a (commentary) and 113b (questions submitted to the decision of the Consilium). All are dated 9 Oct. 1965. The Consilium met in late October and approved most of
what *Coetus* X had done. It also showed strong support for a penitential rite at the beginning
of the Mass, but was deadlocked on the proposal to omit the *Kyrie* when the *Gloria* was used.
The voting is reported in Schema 218, 19 Mar. 1967.

sion accompanied by an entry chant, the greeting of the altar and of the people, the acclamatory chant (*Kyrie, Gloria*) and the prayer of the day. There is even a mild tendency towards traditionalism, perhaps, in such touches as the silent sign of the cross made by priest and ministers on arriving at the altar (derived from *OR I*) or in the *coetus'* inability to bring itself to drop either the *Kyrie* or the *Gloria* or move them elsewhere in the Mass. On the other hand, in rationalizing and abbreviating the entry rites, in suggesting the use of the vernacular and having the people sing the chants, which in the *ordines Romani* are sung by the choir alone, they recognize the ecclesiological and pastoral realities of the twentieth century. And in the flexibility with which they approach such matters as the chants and the gestures of reverence, they display commendable openness to further development and refinement of the Order of Mass as it is assimilated by the different cultures of the Catholic world.

SCHEMA 113: ORIGINAL DRAFT OF THE *MISSA NORMATIVA*			
VERBAL CODE	MUSICAL CODE	VISUAL AND KINETIC CODES	CONGREGATION'S ROLE
Entrance Chant Latin or vernacular	Gregorian or polyphonic	Assembling Procession of priest and [deacon] servers [lectionary, lights, cross, incense] Arrive at altar Priest and ministers make sign of cross, pause awhile	Priest greets altar [Priest incenses altar and people] Assemble Sing
Greeting *Admonitio* *Kyrie* Greek or vernacular *or* *Gloria* Latin or vernacular *Oremus* Collect Amen	Chant [Chant] Gregorian or polyphonic Chanted or spoken	Priest faces people All remain standing	Respond Sing Respond
TABLE 4			

As Table 4 shows, the entrance rite has been simplified, but not impoverished. It constitutes a coherent syntagm, or sequence of sign-units, moving from the assembling of the faithful, through the formal entrance of the ministers and the greeting of the altar and people, to an acclamation of Christ present in the assembly and the first direct address to God in the name of all those congregated in Christ (collect). Some room is left for selection or substitution of elements (more or less solemn procession, *Kyrie* or *Gloria*, variable collects and introits), but the principles governing such selection according to liturgical seasons, feasts, and occasions, are clear enough. By making the *Kyrie* and *Gloria* interchangeable, the particular character of a given celebration is more clearly signaled and the sequence of units remains straightforward and logical, although the further step of allowing the omission of both the *Kyrie* and *Gloria* on occasions of least solemnity seems not to have been considered. Nonetheless, there were a number of "soft spots" where members of the *coetus* were not entirely of one mind or were unwilling to appear inflexible. It was these points which left the way open for further developments that, whatever their individual merits, served to obscure what had been clarified and to undermine what had been established in this draft. They can best be identified by considering the different codes involved.

Musical Code

The directives of the Constitution on the Liturgy, requiring on the one hand that the revised rites be adapted to the participation of the people while insisting that "the treasure of sacred music is to be preserved and fostered with great care" (art. 114), created a conflict which was not easily resolved. From the beginning, both *Coetus* X, responsible for the Order of Mass, and *Coetus* XIV and XXV, responsible for liturgical chants, had recognized that the accumulated musical treasures of Gregorian chant and polyphony were largely beyond the capacities of the average parish and that, if the entry chant was to be sung, some alternatives to the texts of the *Graduale Romanum* would have to be provided. Reciting the texts of the antiphons and psalms, or chanting them *recto tono* or to a psalm tone, would simply not serve the function of the entrance chant.[32] The solution adopted was twofold. Alongside the introit antiphons and psalms appointed in the Missal, and while intending that these should continue to be used *de more*, a new set of chants—*Communia*

---

[32] Schema 39, 30 Sept. 1964, nos. 23-30. "The primary function [of the entrance chant: antiphon and psalm] is to accompany the entrance of the celebrant and his assistants; the secondary function is to unify the participants as the assembly begins; third, it often gives expression, through word and melody, to the spirit of the day or the feast or the season" (no. 23). See also Schema 16, 17 June 1964, which contemplated allowing it to be replaced by another form of chant, such as a litany (no. 16), or else omitting the introit altogether and having the procession enter in silence on days of least solemnity (no. 17).

de Tempore[33] —would be drawn up for seasonal use. However, even this would not be enough, given the problem of translating the texts and providing them with settings suited to the different vernacular languages, as well as the demanding character of Gregorian chant. So it was agreed, and accepted by the Consilium,[34] that "other suitable chants (i.e. suited to the nature of the sacred action, to the occasion or the season) might also be allowed, in accordance with SC, article 38." In Schema 113a, a preference is declared for "appropriate psalms."

Similarly with the *Kyrie* and *Gloria*: the historic musical heritage was to be preserved, as the Council had required, but the requirements of the vernacular and questions about the function of the *Kyrie* made this goal difficult to attain here also. Nonetheless, with the priest's greeting and address to the people, as well as the collect, preferably being chanted (*cantans vel clara voce dicens*), and the entrance chant and *Kyrie* (or *Gloria*) sung, the intention of the *coetus* was unmistakable: a formal, sung liturgy was to be normative. In face of the pastoral difficulties such a standard posed, however, the *coetus* did not press the issue with as much vigor as would have been needed for the *sung* Mass to have emerged as the recognized norm.

Verbal Code

Where the texts of the Mass were concerned, *Coetus* X was firmly committed to the vernacular, but seems to have thought primarily in terms of vernacular translations of traditional Latin texts appointed for each celebration. This would have retained the character of the Roman Mass quite unmistakably, especially if the translations could be accommodated to the traditional chant modes. Where the entrance chant was concerned, however, this was clearly going to prove problematic, so that the possibility of allowing alternative chants had to be considered. The first step was to allow the use of a selection of simpler chants from the *Graduale Romanum*, but even this would not be enough. Hence the provision, noted above, for the composition of original chants. At the time, it was envisaged that these new texts, as well as their musical setting, would be carefully monitored by the conferences of bishops in terms of their suitability

---

[33] This was eventually published as the *Gradule simplex* in Sept. 1967. On the troubled history of this document and of the Instruction *Musicam sacram* of March of the same year, see Bugnini, 852-880.

[34] 5-6 Oct. 1964. See Schema 90, no. 2.

as entrance chants and of their appropriateness for the day or the season. In other words, it seems to have been thought that a new set of "propers" would emerge in each language, with a specific entrance chant assigned to each occasion. That, of course, was not what eventually happened.[35]

One way of reconciling the use of the vernacular with the need to ensure that new forms grew organically out of the old was to keep the verbal elements to a minimum. Since the sign of the cross was made by the ministers alone and in silence, the first spoken utterance in the Mass was the priest's greeting of the people. The provision of two other texts (based on greetings in the Pauline Epistles), besides the traditional *Dominus vobiscum*, enhanced not only the solemnity of the greeting, but its ability to establish contact between priest and people. However, it was the difficulty of moving without further ado into the *Kyrie* which initially opened a small hole through which a tide of verbosity was later to flow.

The problem was: whatever the original function of the *Kyrie*, what is its function in the Mass now? Though this was not at all clear, there was almost unanimous agreement among the liturgists that the *Kyrie* had become too familiar a part of the Roman Mass simply to be dropped altogether, and the suggestion that it be moved to provide a response to the newly-restored prayers of the faithful was not generally acceptable. So it was kept at the beginning. However, since it was thought improper to delay the presider's greeting once he had arrived at his place in the assembly, the *Kyrie* had to follow the first act of verbal communication between priest and people. But then it seemed rather abrupt—and perhaps to run the risk of mere formalism—if the chanting of the *Kyrie* were to begin without some sort of an introduction. Taking its cue from SC, article 35 ("short directives to be spoken by the priest or proper minister should

---

[35] The German musicologist, Helmut Hucke, who was a member of *Coetus* XIV (Chants of the Mass), has commented that the musical expectations held by the revisers of the Mass were very different from the values promoted by those who saw themselves as defenders of "sacred music." The liturgists (including liturgical musicians) responsible for the new rites thought in terms of Gregorian chant as being the norm, even if the texts were in the vernacular and even if they were sung by the whole congregation. The defenders of the Church's musical heritage, on the other hand, thought of this heritage primarily in terms of polyphonic music sung by highly-trained choirs. Different again were the expectations of those lands where there was a tradition of vernacular hymnody, especially the *Messlieder*. As Huck points out, where the traditions of "sacred music" were entrenched, the renewal of liturgical music made little headway; whereas in countries with little experience of either Gregorian or polyphonic music, the field was open for an explosion of new compositions and new forms of congregational singing. See Hucke in H. B. Meyer et al., *Gottesdienst der Kirche*, vol. 3, *Gestalt des Gottesdienstes* (Regensburg: Pustet, 1987), 164.

be provided within the rites themselves"), the *coetus* decided to suggest a brief *admonitio* to lead into the *Kyrie* and offered three selections in the commentary accompanying schema 113. In view of subsequent developments, these are worth looking at.

The first was simply borrowed from the Spanish (Visigothic) liturgy:

> Dearly beloved, with one mind let us call upon God, source of mercy and love, asking his forgiveness and an increase of grace.

The second was proposed by Italian members of *Coetus* X:

> Brothers and sisters, let us humbly confess our sins to God;
> let us pray with confidence for his mercy and pardon.
> Lord, regard not our sins.
> R. But wipe away our faults.
> Lord, have mercy.
> R. Lord, have mercy. . . . etc.

The third, based on the Trisagion, was of French origin:

> Holy God, holy and strong, holy and immortal One.
> Lord, have mercy. R. Lord, have mercy.
> You who suffered for us on the Cross.
> Christ, have mercy. R. Christ, have mercy.
> Remember us when you come into your Kingdom.
> Lord, have mercy. R. Lord, have mercy.

It is striking that, with the exception of the third form, and despite the absence of any formula of absolution following it, the *Kyrie* is now transformed from an acclamation of Christ (the function it served in *OR I*) into a plea for the forgiveness of sins. This was perhaps accidental, a result of the need to have the priest say something at this point, but, in the words of the commentary:

> The examples given show that it would be very easy to introduce *pro opportunitate*,[36] an act of confession of sins, of penance and contrition and of asking forgiveness, without burdening the beginning of the Mass or adversely affecting the Mass's structure. Indeed, many pastors and members of the faithful have strongly requested something of this kind before they proceed to the table of the Word and of the Lord's Body and such [holy] mysteries.[37]

By the time the definitive *Ordo Missae* came to be published, this *Kyrie* rite had developed into an autonomous penitential rite, usually

---

[36] "As may be opportune." Schema 258, 21 Nov. 1967, no. 4 defines the term *ad libitum* as referring to elements in the rite left to the choice of the priest, as opposed to *pro opportunitate* which refers to elements which properly belong in the rite but which can, under certain circumstances, be omitted.

[37] Schema 113a, no. 36.

in addition to the *Kyrie,* while the *admonitio* became, not an introduction to the *Kyrie* or *Gloria,* but an introduction to the Mass of the
day whose model brevity was in danger of being ignored in "opening remarks" capable of including a remarkable range of forms and
topics.

Movements and Gestures

Here perhaps the most remarkable innovation is the opening
rubric, "when the people have assembled." This was inspired by
the provision in SC, article 31, that "the revision of the liturgical
books must ensure that the rubrics make provision for the parts be-
longing to the people." It was also a self-conscious break with the
old rubrics which omitted any reference to the people's participation and began simply, *Sacerdos, omnibus paramentis indutus.* . . .

The actions themselves fall into three sections. First there is the
procession, consisting at least of priest and server but, *pro opportunitate,* consisting of deacon, bookbearer, acolytes with lighted candles, crossbearer, and thurifer. Next comes the actions associated
with the arrival at the altar, the taking of places and the greeting
of the people. Finally, the attention of priest and people is directed
to God and to Christ. It will be noted, however, that in contrast to
OR I where priest and people both face in the same direction (east)
in a posture of self-transcendence, in the new rite priest and people face each other in more populist mode, signifying the mystery
of Christ in the gathered assembly.

Unfortunately, this reconfiguration of the assembly is less effective than it might have been, because it receives no explicit support
from the verbal signs (texts). The musical code and signs, being left
largely undetermined, cannot be relied upon, either. And the same
is true of the spatial code: there is the minimal requirement of a
lectern, a presider's chair, and a free-standing altar, which should
have helped refocus the assembly as itself a sign of Christ's presence, but in actual fact they would usually have to be accommodated
in churches designed to express the separation of the people from
the presence of Christ represented by the person of the priest and
the eucharistic species.

Of all the codes, the verbal is the most easy to regulate, the visual and kinetic most difficult. Yet even in the minimal guidelines
provided by the rubrics, both strong and weak points are noticeable. The provision that the presider incense not only the altar but
the people seems a remarkably powerful symbol of the holiness of

the assembly and of its unity with Christ.[38] A less fortunate addition, perhaps, was the making of the sign of the cross by priest and ministers upon arriving before the altar. This gesture, like the brief pause which was to ensue before the priest approached the altar to reverence it, was clearly inspired by *OR I*, though appeal was made in the commentary to the identical practice at the beginning of each of the hours and other forms of prayer. Paul VI was to seize upon this and insist, despite repeated protests from *Coetus* X and the Consilium, that it be made by the whole congregation and accompanied by the Trinitarian formula, said aloud.

In sum, this is a simple and yet noble beginning to the Mass, in complete concordance with the Council's wishes, recognizably faithful to the Roman tradition yet clearly adapting it to a more contemporary ecclesiology. There is a single, coherent ritual process in which different groups of participants have their role and in which there is no reduplication of functions. It has a clean, lean logic, a structure simple enough for ordinary occasions but capable of considerable elaboration in more solemn circumstances: the community comes together, is constituted as an ordered assembly and turns to God first in acclamation (*Kyrie* or *Gloria*, depending on the feast or season) and then in the solemn opening prayer. But for all its strengths, it left open a number of doors for further interpolations of new material and seemed to expect a greater self-discipline from local Churches (for example, in the matter of music) than could be depended upon. The consequences are to be seen in the Missal of Paul VI and in what parishes have since made of it.

IV. THE DEFINITIVE TEXT: THE ORDO MISSAE OF 1969

The mood of the liturgists when they submitted the fruit of their labors to the Consilium in October 1965 seems to have been one of satisfaction and expectation; the discussions and vote of the Consilium, adopting the *Ordo Missae* for controlled experimentation, would have done little to dampen that mood. Yet a difficult road lay ahead and it would be another four years before the new Order of Mass would be published.

Developments relating to the *Ordo Missae* in this period were of a different order from the developments of the first stage in that

---

[38] Unfortunately, the incensation of the people survived in the successive drafts of the new Mass until Schema 281, 21 Mar. 1968, when it was dropped without comment.

they were no longer fully in the hands of the liturgists of *Coetus* X. The story has been told elsewhere,[39] but the results can be set out as in Table Five.

A quick comparison of tables 4 and 5 will show how much of Schema 113 remains in place and how much was altered between 1965 and 1969. Most striking is the influx of verbal elements following the presider's arrival at his seat, and the shift that has occurred in the balance of verbal and non-verbal elements and of singing to speech. The incensation of the people, for example, is no longer an option.[40] The sign of the cross, from being a silent gesture made by priest and ministers on arriving at the altar, is moved to a new and altogether more prominent role, involving the verbal participation of the whole congregation, while the *Gloria*, on the days it is appointed, will not replace the penitential rite and *Kyrie*, but will be added to them.

The effect of the alterations and additions is not merely a simple increase in the amount of words used. The grammar of the rite has been ignored and the concern for simplicity and clarity of the symbol-structure which were to ensure effective communication has yielded to a concern to salvage as many elements of the preconciliar rite as possible. The new role of the sign of the cross is a striking example of this. Coming before the greeting, it has a curiously divisive effect. As a conventional sign for the beginning of an act of prayer, it cuts off what preceded it from what follows. As a self-involving confessional formula, it sits uneasily with the greeting (itself trinitarian in two of the three formulae provided), and seems to represent the sort of duplication the reform was intended to undo.[41] The *admonitio* has also assumed a new function. In response to criticisms that the "lead-in" to the penitential rite was too exclusively focused on sin and penance and that something was needed to serve rather as an introduction to the Mass of the day, the rubric was changed.

The priest may introduce the faithful very briefly to the Mass of the day. The penitential act follows. The priest invites the faithful to repentance: "To prepare ourselves to celebrate the sacred mysteries, let us acknowledge our sins."

---

[39] Bugnini, 341-388.

[40] See footnote 39.

[41] *Coetus* X, with the overwhelming support of the Consilium, strongly resisted this change of function for the sign of the cross when various attempts to relate the sign of the cross to the greeting proved futile. The pope, however, remained adamant. See Schema 281, 21 Mar. 1968, and the two Addenda of 23 and 29 Apr. which document the struggle. In the final draft before publication (Schema 293, 24 May 1968), the Consilium still omits the public sign of the cross.

VERBAL CODE	MUSICAL CODE	VISUAL AND KINETIC CODES	CONGREGATION'S ROLE
Entrance Chant Antiphon/psalm or other in Latin or vernacular	Gregorian, polyphonic, other	Assembling	Assemble
		Procession of priest reader servers [cross] [thurible]	Sing
		Arrive at altar All bow Priest: ascends to altar kisses altar [incenses altar] goes to seat	
"In the name . . ."	Spoken/chanted	All make sign of cross	Sign of cross
Amen	"		Respond
Greeting	"		Respond
Intro to Mass	"	All remain standing	Listen
Penitential Rite	Spoken/chanted"		Confess
Absolution	"		Listen/Respond
Kyrie	Spoken/ch/sung		Recite/Sing
[Gloria]	["]		[Recite/Sing]
Oremus	Spoken/chanted		
Collect	"		Listen
Amen	"		Respond

TABLE 5

The result is a double introduction, one to the liturgy as a whole, the other to the penitential rite.

A similar duplication, the insistence that the *Kyrie* be used even on days when the *Gloria* was required, was also strenuously resisted because it perpetuated what was one of the most obvious problems of the old Mass: the burden of three consecutive chants of very different character—the entrance chant, the *Kyrie*, and the *Gloria*. From the beginning, the *coetus* had felt obliged to retain both the *Kyrie* and the *Gloria* at the beginning of the Mass because of their long history there. Nonetheless, there seemed no reason to think that the only way to preserve them both in the Roman Mass was to have them performed in the same liturgy. They could alternate, according to feasts and seasons, thereby enhancing the ethos of a given celebration by their musical and textual sign value. To have both together was usually described by the *coetus* as "unduly burdensome," but the real problem was that, syntagmatically, they do not belong together since they come from different realms of discourse, as it were. This issue and its outcome is merely another instance of the tension between renovation and conservation, a tension which, in the final stages of the reform process was resolved increasingly in favor of conservation. The net result was that the communicative efficacy of these opening rites was diminished through the heaping up, once again, of disparate elements. Concern to preserve elements of the past overrode considerations pertaining to the grammar and syntax of the rite.

Instead, communication seems to have been identified with the spoken word: the formula for the sign of the cross, the greeting, the introduction to the Mass of the day, the call to repentance, the penitential act, the *Kyrie*, [the *Gloria* on certain days], the call to prayer—itself open to elaboration—and finally the collect. But besides the accumulation of verbal elements, there was the mode of their execution. If there was no opening song, the introit antiphon was to be recited. Similarly with everything else that followed: if not sung, it was to be recited. In fact, the change of phrasing in the rubrics tended to encourage recitation, for whereas the earlier drafts presumed that the *Kyrie* and *Gloria* would usually be sung and used the phrase *cantans vel clara voce dicens* for the greeting, introduction and collect, the new Order of Mass and the General Instruction on the Roman Missal simplify the matter by using *dicens* every time, even for the "chants" of the Mass. Paragraph 18 of the General Instruction of the Roman Missal points out that *dicens* is "to be understood of both singing and saying,"[42] but there no longer seems to be quite the same concern to foster a sung liturgy, as opposed to a Low Mass with singing, perhaps out of concern for congregations with little musical talent.

The question of the role of singing in the entrance rites is a complex one. While there is no place here to go into the evolution of this question fully, it is generally true to say that the original draft of the Order of Mass envisaged that the singing of the introit, as well as the *Kyrie* or *Gloria*, would be normative, and that the greeting and collect, and even the *admonitio*, would be chanted, as in the *Missa cantata*. It was the twofold problem of the demanding nature of most of the Gregorian corpus and the difficulties created by the

---

[42] "In texts that are to be delivered in a clear, loud voice, whether by the priest or by the ministers or by all, the tone of voice should correspond to the genre of the text, that is, accordingly as it is a reading, a prayer, an instruction, an acclamation, or a song; the tone should also be suited to the form of celebration and to the solemnity of the gathering. Other criteria are the idiom of different languages and the genius of peoples.

In the rubrics and in the norms that follow, the words *say* (*dicere*) or *proclaim* (*proferre*) are to be understood of both singing and speaking, and in accordance with the principles just stated." Congregation for Divine Worship, General Instruction of the Roman Missal [hereafter, GIRM], 4th ed., 27 Mar. 1975, no. 18: DOL 208, no. 1408.

introduction of the vernacular for the maintenance of the church's musical heritage, which first began to qualify this presumption, as we have seen. Nonetheless, the General Instruction of 1970 underlines the importance of singing and suggests an ongoing role for the Latin chants in multilingual congregations (no. 19). At the same time it says:

> With due consideration for the culture and ability of each congregation, great importance should be attached to the use of singing at Mass; but it is not always necessary to sing all the texts that of themselves are meant to be sung.
>
> In choosing the parts actually to be sung, however, preference should be given to those that are more significant and especially to those sung by the priest and ministers with the congregation responding or by the priest and people together.

A footnote refers the reader to nos. 7 and 16 of the Instruction *Musicam sacram* of 5 March 1967, but it is nos. 27-36 of the same Instruction which actually spell out what should be sung and in what order of priority. Here we find that varying "degrees of solemnity" are provided for on a scale of 1 to 3. "These degrees must be so employed, however, that the first may always be used without the others, but the second and third never without the first."[43] Where the opening rites are concerned, these three degrees distinguish between the various elements as follows:

First degree: Priest's greeting and congregation's response; the opening prayer (collect).

Second degree: *Kyrie* and *Gloria*.

Third degree: Song for the entrance procession.

Furthermore, the *Ordo cantus Missae* (1972) provides music for the sign of the cross at the beginning of Mass, presumably because it is one of the parts of the Mass sung by the priest, to which the people respond. On the other hand, the provision in Schema 113 that the *admonitio* or introduction might be sung disappeared fairly early on and is not included in any of the official documents. The same is true of the penitential rite.[44]

---

[43] Congregation of Rites, Instruction *Musicam sacram*, 5 Mar. 1967, no. 28: DOL 508, no. 4149. The Instruction is following, without acknowledgment, the 1958 Congregation of Rites Instruction on music and liturgy, no. 25. In general, it appears that *Coetus* X (Order of Mass) and *Coetus* XIV (Chants of the Mass) were operating within the framework established by the 1958 Instruction.

[44] Schema 261, 27 Nov. 1967: *Coetus* XIV: De cantibus in Missa.

In principle, then, the "normative" form of the Mass remains close to that of the *Missa cantata* while allowing a large measure of adaptability. While the rules governing this adaptability are clear enough, they are included neither in the General Instruction itself, nor in the rubrics given in the Order of Mass, so that it is hardly likely that the preference for a rather formal, chanted liturgy will be realized (in either sense of the word) at parish level. The profusion of elements,—many being duplications: the sign of the cross and the greeting, the penitential rite and the *Kyrie*, the *Kyrie* and the *Gloria*—only further confuses the syntax of the rite and is surely one of the reasons for the unforeseen and sometimes strange variety of opening rites in evidence today.

V. The Result: The Opening Rites in U.S. Parishes

The success or failure of the revised rites is to be judged not so much by the reviews of liturgical experts as by the reception they have been accorded by local parishes in the nearly two decades since they appeared. It might therefore be instructive to take a brief look at the findings of the Notre Dame Study of Catholic Parish Life which, in the fall of 1983, observed and recorded two weekend Masses in each of thirty-six U.S. parishes.[45] Since these parishes were selected for study on the basis of factors other than their liturgical life, they represent merely a random sample of liturgical practice in the United States, but their geographic, demographic, and structural diversity makes them reasonably representative. It should also be noted that the observations were scheduled in such a way as to capture the practice of the parish on an average Sunday outside the major seasons of the Church year. Consequently the practices reported represent parish practice in Ordinary Time, and do not preclude greater solemnization of the rites on specific occasions.

The easiest way to see what U.S. Catholics have made of the revised Roman Mass is to look at parish celebration of the opening rites in terms of the codes previously identified.

---

[45] See Mark Searle and David Leege, *The Celebration of the Liturgy in the Parishes*, Report no. 5 of the Notre Dame Study of Catholic Parish Life, Aug. 1985. See also Report no. 6, *Of Piety and Planning: Liturgy, the Parishioners and the Professionals*, Dec. 1985; and Mark Searle, "The Notre Dame Study of Catholic Parish Life," *Worship* 60 (1986) 4, 312-333.

Musical Code

Of the seventy Masses observed, (two in each parish that had more than one Mass each weekend), only nine had no music or singing at all, while the rest exhibited a wide variety of repertoire and practice.[46]

The rules governing the choice of what will be sung at Mass seem not to be known in this country.[47] None of the first-level items (sign of the cross, greeting, collect) were chanted at any of the Masses observed. An entrance song was sung at nearly nine out of every ten main Sunday Masses, somewhat less frequently at Saturday evening or other Sunday Masses. In the absence of a sung entrance chant, the introit antiphon was commonly recited by the whole congregation as the priest entered, but sometimes silence was observed. At only four Masses was the *Kyrie* sung, usually as Form III of the penitential rite, while the *Gloria* was more than five times as likely to be recited than it was to be sung. It would seem as though the *coetus* need not have worried about the "burden" of singing three major chants one after the other: two of the three are usually just recited. Their concern to preserve the musical patrimony of the Church, in accordance with the directive of Vatican II, has also proved fruitless with the passage of time. In no instance was the entrance chant taken from the *Graduale* or the *Graduale simplex*. Only in one parish was any Gregorian chant used, and that was as a motet later in the Mass. The same was true of polyphonic music: only one parish attempted it, and then as an anthem at the preparation of the gifts or at communion.

The overwhelming body of music in use in the Church in the U.S., if this sample is somewhat accurate, consists of English-language hymnody and folk-style compositions, with a small sprinkling of ethnic music (Gospel songs, Polish or French hymns).[48] None of this is appointed for use or even officially approved by the conference of bishops, so that the criterion of appropriateness, to the degree that it is applied at all, is applied locally (usually by the music director or the organist, if not by the pastor), with little guidance

---

[46] At about one third of the Masses, the congregation was led in a rehearsal of one or more musical pieces before the Mass began, while occasionally the choir or the organist was still practicing as the people gathered.

[47] *Music in Catholic Worship* (Washington: United States Catholic Conference, 1972), promulgated by the U. S. Bishops' Committee on the Liturgy, makes no reference to paragraphs 27-36 of *Musicam sacram*.

[48] An important limitation of this study is that Hispanic parishes were not included among the parishes studied.

beyond that provided by the topical index at the back of some hymnals. The selection of appropriate music, consequently, is a major item of liturgical planning where it occurs.[49]

The effect of singing virtually only the entrance song and of using for that purpose self-contained hymns or songs whose relation to the larger liturgical complex depends entirely upon the sensibilities of local planners is to dismantle the traditional "overture" to the Mass and to set aside the "treasury" of sacred music for the Latin Mass which the Council was so anxious to preserve. On the other hand, parish practice has largely embraced the normative model insofar as it called for a *Missa . . . in cantu . . . [cum] ipso populo cantante*.[50] The primary goal of the reform, the active participation of the assembled faithful, has been met; but secondary goals, such as the preservation of the traditional repertoire of liturgical music and the "organic development" of new forms out of pre-existing ones, appear to have been abandoned. And because musical forms not merely decorate the rite, but are part of its structure, the result is a liturgical shape given to the opening rites which was not that intended by *Coetus* X.

reception of rite

Verbal Code

The shift in the musical structure of the rite has been accompanied by structural shifts resulting from changes in the use of the verbal code. Apart from the change wrought by the total disappearance of Latin in favor of the vernacular, a change which might have been anticipated,[51] the major difference between contemporary celebrations of the opening rites and that anticipated by the liturgists in Schema 113 is the great influx of spoken communication.

This development is partly cultural, no doubt, but it is also due to the changes made in the *Missa normativa* and noted in the last section. The problems noted there have been verified and even ex-

---

[49] Seventy-two percent of 1100 U.S. parishes covered in phase one of the Parish Study claimed to have some process of liturgy planning, but "liturgy planning," like "liturgy committee," turned out, on closer examination, to be an elusive concept. See *Of Piety and Planning*, 3.

[50] Schema 39, 30 Sept. 1964, 4.

[51] The Council's attitude was that "the use of the Latin language is to be preserved in the Latin rites," while opening the door to the use of the vernacular for the "readings and directives" and for "some of the prayers and chants" (SC, art. 36: DOL 1, no. 36). By the time the new Missal appeared, everything, including the eucharistic prayer, could be translated as long as the translations were approved by Rome. Nonetheless, the desire to preserve the Latin language in the liturgy was kept alive by groups such as the Latin Mass Scoiety and was endorsed from above. See Paul VI, Address to Latinists, 26 Apr. 1968: DOL 121, nos. 835-836.

aggerated in pastoral practice. In particular, the Notre Dame Study shows the following:

- the introit antiphon and psalm are never sung, although the antiphon is occasionally recited;

- the sign of the cross, juxtaposed to the greeting and the "introduction to the Mass of the day," is found awkward by many presiders;

- in at least half the Masses, presiders rearrange these elements and incorporate some or all of them in their own improvised greeting and introduction.

In two of the seventy Masses observed, the presider simply omitted the sign of the cross. In fifteen percent of instances, it was made *after* the greeting, and in another twenty-three percent of cases it was itself introduced by being included in the presider's opening remarks. In ten of the seventy Masses observed, the presider began by wishing the congregation "Good morning/evening." Only seventeen percent followed the model formula for the "introduction": a third of all presiders took the opportunity to welcome the congregation or specific groups in the congregation and about the same number made reference to the Mass of the day or to the readings appointed. Other topics included in the introduction to the Mass included reference to current events, announcement of the intention for which the Mass was being offered, and information about the page on which the Mass of the day was to be found.

The penitential rite, as already noted, was invariably spoken rather than sung. The third form (*Kyrie*-litany) was the most popular, being used forty percent of the time, with about one presider in five improvising the petitions. The *Confiteor* was the next most popular (twenty-eight percent), with the second form being used relatively seldom (nine Masses out of seventy). In exceptional cases, for example, the welcoming of a child for baptism) it was omitted altogether. With the *Kyrie* being sung at only four Masses, the spoken form of the verbal code is clearly dominant and that dominance is further accentuated by the recitation of the *Gloria* at five Masses out of every six where it was used. Then followed more spoken address in the form of the call to prayer and the collect. It is hardly necessary to point out that beginning the liturgy with a spate of words is not what *Coetus* X had in mind, and that its concern to do justice to the specific function of each part and to consider its contribution to the overall balance and structure of the Mass is not widely reflected in contemporary practice. In other words, the present practice is not only verbose, it also hiccups along; hence the efforts of so many celebrants to resolve the difficulties inherent in the official rite by adapting and improvising.

Kinetic and Visual Codes

The original draft of the Order of Mass (Schema 113) attempted to strike a balance between musical, verbal, and non-verbal codes. Speech was kept to a minimum, gestures were to speak for themselves. The procession was to include all those who exercised any special ministry. The arrival at the altar and the constituting of the assembly were marked by a series of signs of respect offered both to the altar and to the congregation. Contemporary American practice, on the other hand, is marked by a tilt away from the non-verbal and from the "ceremonies of respect." In part, this is symptomatic of a cultural attitude that does not stand on ceremony, preferring informality to formality.

Liturgically, this is expressed in the reluctance to ritualize the entry procession. In only about two-thirds of all Masses was there a procession through the assembly and then it invariably consisted of presider, servers, and the reader, without cross, book, or candles. Even at the main Sunday Mass, parishes rarely availed themselves of the options for solemnizing the rite: incense was not used in any of the Masses in the parishes surveyed; the cross was carried at ten of the seventy Masses; lights at two; the lectionary or Gospel book at fourteen. The option to reverence the people with incense, of course, no long exists, but the option to incense the altar was never used.

As far as the witness of diversified ministries is concerned, a cantor was present to lead the congregation at twenty-seven of the seventy Masses, while a choir or singing group was present at thirty-two. Lay readers were used at almost all Masses and usually entered in procession with the priest and servers if there was a formal entry procession.

U.S. liturgical practice has clearly departed in significant ways from the vision which guided the liturgists charged with drawing up the new Order of Mass. Changes introduced into the blueprint between 1964 and 1969 did not improve the design, and these design weaknesses have been dramatically shown up in parochial use. Or, to switch back to our original communications model, we might say that the elegance of the ritual complex drafted by *Coetus* X was compromised by a desire to retain elements from the Tridentine structure which complicated the new structure with mixed signals and inconsistent messages. Carried out in churches designed with a different conception of the Mass in mind by people necessarily conditioned by their previous experience of the Latin Low Mass— either in clinging to it or in repudiating it—the new entry rites hardly stood a chance.

VI. The Concluding Rites

While the concluding rites of the Mass did not present problems as many or as complex as the opening rites, a number of points of interest may be mentioned briefly.

One criticism constantly made of the structure of the traditional Roman Mass was the abruptness of its ending: it seemed to move too quickly from the communion to the dismissal.[52] The problem is illustrated in the model provided by the *Ordo Romanus Primus*:

> During the whole of the communion, the choir sang the antiphon and psalm proper to this part of the liturgy.
>
> It was the Pope who again decided when the communion anthem which the choir was singing should be ended. He went once more to the altar and, facing east, said the *oratio ad complendum* (which we call the Post Communion). Then a deacon called out to the congregation "Ite missa est," the congregation replied with the response "Deo gratias", and the Pope then proceeded in a solemn procession back to the sacristy, giving his blessing to each part of the congregation on the way.[53]

Thus, in the classic Roman liturgy, the Mass ended in fact with the communion. Once the distribution of the elements was complete, the pope recited a concluding prayer and the deacon dismissed the congregation. The pope's recession was rather less "solemn" than Klauser's account suggests, for after kissing the altar, the pope moved through the choir and out through the congregation, preceded by the thurifer and candlebearers but unaccompanied by any chant, pausing as he went to bless the various groups that intercepted him and asked his blessing. The liturgy was effectively over and the congregation began to break up, then, as soon as the dismissal was given immediately after the postcommunion prayer.

---

[52] Schema 16, 17 June 1964, no. 64, speaks of this issue as one *a multis agitata et etiam in Aula Concilii proposita*.

[53] Klauser, 68.

This abruptness had been somewhat softened over the centuries by the accumulation of various disparate elements deriving from the private Mass or from more recent public concerns of the Church. Thus, by the time of the Council, the ending of the Mass had been obscured by the medieval development of a public blessing of the whole congregation, by the public performance of the Last Gospel (originally the priest's private devotion), and by the addition of various public prayers, for example, for the conversion of Russia.

The abolition of these latter prayers (now redundant with the restoration of the prayers of the faithful at the end of the Liturgy of the Word) and of the Last Gospel was never in question and they disappeared with the publication of the Instruction (*Inter Oecumenici*) on the orderly carrying out of the Constitution on the Liturgy in September 1964.[54] With that, the swift conclusion of the Roman rite became once more apparent.

The proposal of *Coetus* X with regard to the concluding rites was really twofold. The first was to respond to popular demand and to fill out the structure of the Mass after the distribution of communion by introducing the option of "a hymn, a psalm, or other prayers of praise, *pro opportunitate*," to be used after the distribution of communion (and hence after the communion chant) and before the postcommunion prayer which completed the communion rite. The second proposal was to give more status to the final blessing by introducing two additional alternative forms which would both allow the blessing to be solemnized and to be adapted to the feast, season, or occasion. Indeed, the proposal that the last blessing be chanted was one of the earliest suggestions to receive approval from the Concilium, together with the proposal to switch the order of dismissal-blessing to blessing-dismissal.[55] Other changes found in Schema 113 included the transfer of the greeting, *Dominus vobiscum* from before the postcommunion (Tridentine Mass) to before the blessing, where it would serve as part of the valediction; and the offering of the opportunity to make community announcements before the blessing and dismissal. In this way, the devotional needs of the faithful to express gratitude and praise after communion would be met, while the bald dismissal of the ancient Roman rite would be developed into a clearly distinct valedictory and concluding part of the Mass.

---

[54] *Inter Oecumenici*, no. 48j: DOL 23, no. 340.

[55] Schema 16, 17 June 1964, 65-66. The Consilium approved these proposals in its meeting of October the same year. See Schema 90, 26 Apr. 1965.

ORDO ROMANUS I	TRIDENTINE MASS	SCHEMA 113	ORDO MISSAE 1969
Communion	[Communion]	Communion	Communion
Pope goes to altar	Priest goes to altar	Priest goes to chair	Priest goes to chair
	Reads Comm. Ant.	[praise/thanks]	Pause
	Kisses altar		[song or silence]
	Greeting		
PC prayer	PC prayer	PC prayer	PC prayer
	Kisses altar		
	Greeting	[announcements]	[announcements]
Dismissal	Dismissal	Greeting	Greeting
	Placeat	Blessing	Blessing
	Kisses altar	Dismissal	Dismissal
	Blessing		
	Greeting		Priest kisses altar
	Last Gospel		
All leave	Reverence to altar	Reverence to altar	Reverence to altar
Blessings	All leave	All leave	All leave

TABLE 6

The experience of concelebration, in particular, had shown that "the whole final part of the Mass would be clearer and more significant [if] the Mass ends, with the prayer and dismissal of the people, at the place where it began,"[56] namely the presider's chair. So, with the distribution of communion complete, the priest would return to his chair (after washing his hands), for the song or prayers of thanksgiving just mentioned. These would then be concluded with the postcommunion prayer, which marked the end of the Liturgy of the Eucharist. This reordering, qualified as *pro opportunitate* and thus allowing of exceptions, was approved by the Concilium in October 1965.

In the same session, the Concilium approved the basic shape of the concluding rites. Brief announcements could be made at this point, instead of between the gospel and the sermon as had been customary in many places. The final greeting of the people, no longer functioning as in the Tridentine Mass as a call to prayer, but as a valediction, would be "The Lord be with you" and would immediately precede the last blessing. The last blessing, in turn, would be switched with the dismissal, so as to precede it. In this way, the blessing, which originated as an informal blessing of the people as the pope or bishop made his way out of the church, was at last formally incorporated into the liturgy as part of a substantial closing ceremony, while the dismissal regained its operative function as the formal act of closure of the assembly. Again, the syntax of the rite was clear, while interchangeable elements allowed the specific

---

[56] Schema 113a, 9 Oct. 1965, no. 86.

character of a given occasion or season to be accommodated. From the beginning, it had been anticipated that the final blessing would be sung, as was usual in sung Masses, but more elaborate benedictions, modeled on medieval episcopal blessings, would be provided for different feasts and seasons. The *oratio super populum* would be restored for use in Lent. In keeping with the Roman tradition, the exit of the ministers occurs without ceremony and without accompanying chant: "the priest and ministers, after making appropriate reverence to the altar, leave; and all return to their good works, praising God."[57] It appears that this rather informal exit was never queried or discussed at any time in the process of revising the Mass, which is rather extraordinary when the human dynamics of the situation are considered, for parting is usually found awkward unless adequately ritualized. But perhaps this is a problem only for those in German- and English-speaking countries, who apparently feel an irresistable need for a "closing hymn" if a service is to be properly ended.[58]

In the definitive Order of Mass, the priest takes his leave of the altar with a kiss, just as he had greeted it with a kiss at the beginning of the Mass, but otherwise the shape of the closing rite remained unaltered. It is an appropriate ending to the whole liturgy, "short, clear, and unencumbered," according to the directive of SC, article 34. In practice, however, things are rarely that simple, as the study of the U.S. parishes revealed.

In U.S. parishes, the sequence of units in the concluding rite is often jumbled. The source of the difficulty seems to be that there is rarely a thanksgiving song after the distribution of holy communion: one Mass out of the seventy observed had a thanksgiving song sung by the people and another had a piece sung by the choir. The preference for a period of silence is understandable, given that a song after communion will often appear as a mere duplication of the song sung during communion. Instead, people tend to kneel in silence during the communion rite and then sit down when the presider moves back to his seat. Because they are sitting at this point, it apparently seems appropriate to many presiders to make the announcements here. The congregation then stands for the postcommunion prayer and for the blessing and dismissal. As a result, the

---

[57] Schema 113, no. 93.

[58] For German-speaking countries, see Heinrich Rennings, "Der Schlussteil der Messfeier," in Th. Maas-Ewerd and Klemens Richter, eds., *Gemeinde im Herrenmahl. Zur Praxis der Messfeier* (Einsiedeln: Benziger; Freiburg: Herder, 1976), 342-350.

postcommunion prayer, instead of being the conclusion of the communion rite, which is its traditional role, becomes part of the dismissal of the assembly; while the silence after communion, instead of giving birth to common prayer, is abruptly terminated by the notices. This, in turn, must surely redefine the nature of the silence: from being a deep well of prayer it becomes an empty silence of waiting for something to be said or done. Furthermore, the musical dimension of the concluding rites is substantially different from that envisaged as normative. Neither the blessing nor the dismissal were ever sung in the parishes visited; but every Mass celebrated with any music at all ended with a recessional hymn—an item unknown to the Roman liturgy!

This is not to suggest that one form or style of celebration is inherently better than another, but merely to point out that freedom of choice permitted by the Order of Mass, together with a further degree of freedom not permitted but nonetheless claimed, is resulting in patterns of celebration which are actually restructuring the Roman rite and profoundly altering its character. Here we have only examined the opening and concluding rites, but these so-called "secondary" parts of the Mass are crucial for defining the identity of the assembly and the nature of its common undertaking. Consequently, the inevitable effect of restructuring both these rites is to alter the character of the Mass as a whole. One might feel more confident that this was a legitimate and desirable process of acculturation if the ritual process involved in gathering and dispersing in the Roman rite were better understood in the parishes. But this at least can be said: for better or worse, the Mass as experienced by most English-speaking Catholics today is not the Mass envisaged by those—whether scholars or pastors—charged with revising the liturgy of the Roman Mass.

VII. Conclusions

While inculturation is usually discussed in terms of developing new texts or introducing new symbols—proposed by conferences of bishops and approved by Rome—the evidence seems to suggest that inculturation, far from being a deliberate step taken after commissions have studied the matter, has already begun as soon as a local Church attempts to make something of the texts and directives appointed for its use. It was always thus, of course, and the uniformity associated with the Latin Mass could only be secured up to a point. But the new *ordo*, with its flexibility, positively invites adaptation to local circumstances. At the same time, the compromise character of the document has meant that the principles underlying such adaptation—what we have referred to as the "grammar" of the rite—is not as evident as they might be.

Music is a particular case in point. In Rome, the issue was hopelessly compromised by the irreconcilable differences hinted at earlier and by the inability, consequently, to propose a coherent set of principles and procedures for assuring genuine continuity between the Latin sung Mass,[59] as it was known in its different musical styles before the Council, and the liturgies sung by the faithful in their own languages. In the English-speaking world, the close control over texts and music envisaged by the Consilium was never realized. It was an exceedingly complex pastoral task, with heavy emotional, economic, and political overtones. In the U.S., the bishops, wanting to encourage the creation of new liturgical music, removed virtually all constraints and effectively left the matter to the market to decide. As a result, instead of the sung liturgy envisaged by the architects of the new Mass, most English-speaking Catholics know only Low Mass with hymns or other religious songs, largely interchangeable one with another. What has not sufficiently been grasped is the way music—however it is used—affects the structure of the liturgy itself. The choice of musical *forms* determines the character of the whole rite, either working with the words and actions of the liturgy or compromising them. It was for this reason that the 1969 Instruction on the Translation of Liturgical Texts insisted that "the form of singing which is proper to every liturgical action and to each of its parts should be retained."[60] As Helmut Hucke points out,

> Music is not merely a setting for a text: it creates structures of it own. This is clear from the history of Church music and liturgy in the West. The history of our church music is not merely the history of our setting texts to music, nor the history of decking out the liturgy with musical ornamentation. It is rather the history of the gestures, signs, rites and structures of the liturgy, and thus an integral part of the history of the western liturgy itself. Until this is

---

[59] According to the 1958 Instruction on music and liturgy, the distinction between a *Missa in cantu* and a *Missa lecta* hinges upon what the priest does: if the priest sings his parts, it is a sung Mass; if he does not, it is a Low Mass with singing. It is precisely the practice of the priest singing the greetings and prayers which seems to be dying out in the U.S.

[60] Consilium for the Implementation of the Constitution on the Liturgy, Instruction on the Translation of Liturgical Texts *Comme le prévoit*, 25 Jan. 1969, no. 36a: DOL 123, no. 873.

grasped, the musical dimension of liturgical renewal will not be realized.[61]

At the 1967 Synod, a number of voices were raised in criticism of the amount of freedom allowed the priest in deciding what would be said and done in the rite. Although *Coetus* X and the Consilium insisted on preserving this freedom, postulating the need for local communities to be able to adapt the rite to circumstances of place and time as pastoral prudence might suggest, one wonders in retrospect whether less freedom might have proved more beneficial, both to priests themselves and to congregations. It is interesting to note how strict a rein was kept on the texts of the Mass, (other than those of the "Proper"), while the musical and ritual dimensions were left to find their own level. Yet the principle enunciated in the 1969 Instruction on the Translation of Liturgical Texts might usefully have been extended to the non-verbal codes of the liturgy:

> The creation of new texts will be necessary. But translation of texts transmitted through the tradition of the Church is the best school and discipline for the creation of new texts so "that any new forms adopted should in some way grow organically from forms already in existence" (SC, art. 23).[62]

Another way of putting this is to say that the Church at large needed (and perhaps still needs) the opportunity to learn the language of the rite, to be rehearsed in its grammar and syntax, formed by its spirit, before being allowed to create new dialects. The choice of the entrance song, for example, should rest on a firm grasp of the function of that chant and its relation to the season or the occasion; and it should be a choice made from a restricted number of alternatives, these alternatives being clearly differentiated in terms of their appropriateness to specific circumstances. The same would hold for the greeting. By providing three forms of greeting without suggesting any rules by which one might be selected over another in any given situation, choice is rendered entirely arbitrary. But arbitrariness is the death of meaning.

Given that these developments were not intended by those entrusted with drawing up the new Order of Mass, and given that they have occurred less by deliberate choice than by unreflected evolution, one wonders whether, two decades later, some public evaluation of the outcome is not called for. Perhaps the mandate of the

---

[61] Hucke, 164-165.
[62] Instruction *Comme le prévoit*, no. 143: DOL 123, no. 880.

International Commission on English in the Liturgy should now be extended beyond the text of the Mass to include the translation and inculturation of those other ritual codes touched on here. Their role in effective ritual communication may not have been as obvious as that of the spoken word, but their impact on the shape of celebration has proved surely no less significant.

GRACE AND PEACE:
GREETING THE ASSEMBLY
Thomas A. Krosnicki, S.V.D.

The introductory rites comprise the first of the six liturgical units of the revised Order of Mass in the Roman Rite.[1] As such, the unit includes seven structural elements: entrance song, sign of the cross, greeting, brief introduction to the liturgy of the day, penitential rite, *Gloria* and the opening prayer.[2] Authors have already expressed reservations about the functional quality of this liturgical unit in relation to the overall eucharistic structure.[3] Although the entire unit deserves a careful study, this article will focus on its most primitive element: the greeting.

FROM AUSTERITY TO SIMPLICITY

Anton Baumstark's law of liturgical evolution— "from austerity to richness" —is confirmed again as one traces the historical development √ of the eucharistic entrance rites. From the oldest sources to the Mass of Pius V, one is aware of a general movement from simplicity to complexity.[4] In a study of the elements within the entrance rites, one dis-

---

[1] The six structural units of the eucharist are: the introductory rites, the liturgy of the word, the preparation of the gifts and altar, the eucharistic prayer, the communion rite, the conclusion. See Congregation for Divine Worship, General Instruction of the Roman Missal [hereafter, GIRM], 4th ed., 27 Mar. 1975, nos. 24-57: *Documents on the Liturgy, 1963-1979: Conciliar, Papal, and Curial Texts* [hereafter, DOL] (Collegeville, Minn.: The Liturgical Press, 1982) 208, nos. 1414-1447.

[2] GIRM, no. 24: DOL 208, no. 1414, which outlines the parts of the introductory rites as the entrance song, greeting, penitential rite, *Kyrie, Gloria,* and opening prayer or collect. The brief introduction to the liturgy is placed under the heading "Penitential Rite" (see GIRM, no. 29). I consider as introductory elements the seven areas where there is verbal communication involving celebrant and assembly.

[3] Examples of informed criticism of the introductory rites can be found in such articles as: Charles W. Gusmer, "Reviewing the Order of Mass," *Worship* 57 (1983), 345-348; Ralph Kiefer, "Our Cluttered Vestibule: The Unreformed Entrance Rite," *Worship* 48 (1974), 270-277; Kenneth Smits, "A Congregational Order of Worship," *Worship* 54 (1980), 55-75; John F. Baldovin, "Kyrie Eleison and the Entrance Rite of the Roman Eucharist," *Worship* 60 (1986), 334-347.

[4] Anton Baumstark, *Comparative Liturgy* (Westminster, Maryland: The Newman Press, 1958), 19-23. In considering the antithesis between austerity and richness Baumstark affirms that the evolutionary process moves from the one to the other.

covers that the greeting, sometimes called salutation, is the most primitive of the seven. It is the nucleus of this structural unit of the Roman liturgy to which other elements were gradually affixed.[5]

Gregory Dix confirms the primitiveness of the greeting when he states that in the original outline of the Christian synaxis one finds the opening greeting by the officiant and reply of the assembly as the only element preceding the proclamation of the scriptural lessons.[6] A witness to this fact is Augustine. In fourth century Hippo, he says, he began the celebration of the eucharist with only a greeting to the people before the reading of the word.[7] Augustine's practice stands in stark contrast with that witnessed to in *Ordo Romanus I.* The elaborate introductory rites found in this solemn papal liturgy of the seventh century (with the practice dating back earlier), contain acts of reverence to the altar (bow), gospel book (kiss), and altar (kiss); the sign of the cross, kiss of peace to the ministers; introit, *Kyrie, Gloria,* greeting of the people, and collect prior to the proclamation of the Scripture.[8] An expanded introduction to the Roman eucharistic rite, as we more or less know it today, in fact, had been completed already by the end of the fifth century.[9]

In the 1965 schema for the *Missa normativa,* prepared by the Consilium for the Implementation of the Constitution on the Liturgy, the celebration was to begin with the song of the assembly. The ministers were to make the sign of the cross *in silence* during the music, before the celebrant greeted the assembly. Other introductory elements followed: penitential act, *Kyrie* (optional), *Gloria* (occasional), and collect.[10] Except for the penitential rite, which would remain

---

[5] Gregory Dix, *The Shape of the Liturgy,* 2nd ed. (London: Adams and Charles Black Ltd., Dacre Press, 1954), see chart between pp. 432-433. Dix notes that the greeting is the original nucleus of the Roman synaxis with the other introductory elements being of later origin, representing a second stratum of structural development: entrance chant c. A.D. 430; litany c. 495; *Gloria* c. 500.

[6] Dix, 38, 103.

[7] S. Agostino, *De civitate Dei,* 22, 8, 22; B. Dombart, A. Kalb, eds. *Corpus christianorum collectum a monachis O.S.B. abbatiae S. Petri in Steenbrugge, Series latina,* Prepols, Tunshout, vol. 48 (1955), 826: "*Procedimus ad populum, plena erat ecclesia, personabat uocibus gaudiorum: Deo gratias, Deo laudes! nemine tacente hinc atque inde clamantium. Salutaui populum, et rursum eadem feruentiore uoce clamabant. Facto tandem silentio scripturarum diuinarum sunt lecta sollemnia.*"

[8] Michel Andrieu, *Les Ordines romani du haut moyen âge* (Louvain: 1948), 221. See Cyrille Vogel, *Medieval Liturgy: An Introduction to the Sources,* trans. William Storey and Niels Rasmussen (Washington: The Pastoral Press, 1986), 159-160, for dates of composition and diffusion.

[9] Dix, 458.

[10] Annibale Bugnini, *La riforma liturgica (1948-1975),* Bibliotheca "Ephemerides Liturgicae," "Subsidia" 30 (Rome: CLV-Edizione Liturgiche, 1983), 338. Johannes Wagner, "Zur Reform des 'Ordo Missae': Zwei Dokumente," in *Liturgia opera divina e umana Studi Sulla reforma offertia S.E. Mons. Annibale Bugnini in occasione del suo 10 compleano,* Pierre Jounel, Reiner Kacynski, and Gottardo Pasqualetti, eds., Bibliotheca "Ephemerides Liturgicae," "Subsidia" 26, (Rome: CLV-Edizione Liturgiche, 1982), 275.

problematic to this day, the one area that Pope Paul VI commented on, when he reviewed the proposed *Missa normativa*, was the sign of the cross which he desired to be said aloud on all occasions. The secretary of the Consilium, Annibale Bugnini, suggested that it be done in that manner if there were no opening song. The Pope insisted with: "E' opportuno che la formula 'In nomine Patris' sia detta a voce alta dal sacerdote, con risposta del pololo."[11]

The post-Vatican II revision of the eucharist, in part at least, represents a reversal in the dynamic of Baumstark's law. If anything, it was a decided attempt to cut back, to simplify, and to clarify according to the directives of the Constitution on the Liturgy.[12] The *JJ* move toward ritual simplification is evident in the introductory rites of the Mass of Paul VI.   *Therein lies the experimental nature of it!*

THE 1969 ORDO MISSAE GREETING

Purpose and Function

As an element of the introductory rites, the greeting is intended to assist the faithful to "take on the form of a community and prepare themselves to listen to God's word and celebrate the eucharist properly."[13] More specifically, the General Instruction of the Roman Missal notes that the greeting has a twofold function: to declare that the Lord is present and to express the mystery of the fathered Church.[14]

Number, Source and Meaning

The *Ordo Missae cum Populo* provides four distinct greetings for use in the introductory rites:

1. *Gratia Domini nostri Iesu Christi, et caritas Dei, et communicatio Sancti Spiritus sit cum omnibus vobis.*

The source for this greeting is Paul's Second Letter to the Corinthians (13:13). It conveys the meaning of "wishing the faithful 'the grace of the Lord Jesus Christ,' but so as to direct the eye to God our Father as the source of all grace and to the Holy Spirit as the

---

[11] Bugnini, 372.

[12] Vatican Council II, Constitution on the Liturgy *Sacrosanctum Concilium*, 4 Dec. 1963, art. 50: DOL 1, no. 50.

[13] GIRM, no. 24: DOL 208, no. 1414.

[14] GIRM, no. 28: DOL 208, no. 1418.

active principle of its unfolding."[15] Like the greeting *Dominus vobis-cum*, this text is used as part in the opening dialogue of the anaphoras in some eastern liturgies.[16]

2. *Gratia vobis et pax a Deo Patre nostro et Domino Iesu Christo.*[17]

Several greetings in the Pauline letters provided the inspiration for this particular text. Repeatedly Paul wished the community grace and peace from God the Father and the Lord Jesus Christ. Frequently, the Father is explicitly referred to as "our Father," echoing the teaching of the Lord's Prayer.[18] The meaning is not all that clear. Exegetes such as Joseph Fitzmyer maintain that the *charis kai eirene* is more than a Pauline adaptation or combination of Greco-Roman *chariein* and the Jewish *shalom*.[19] He notes that the notions of covenant favor (*charis*) and peace (*eirene*) find their source in the Aaronic blessing (Numbers 6:24-26) but have a literary solemnity that is suggestive of liturgical formulae. "The two words are Paul's summation of the *bona messianica* of the Christian era."[20] Richard Kugelman, for example, believes that "grace" is the favor God shows and the gift he gives to those whom he saves in Christ while "peace" is the fruit of the salvation God gives in Christ.[21] It is the divine gift of peace which includes reconciliation and harmony that the president of the assembly wishes to those present for worship.

3. *Dominus vobiscum.*

The most ancient of liturgical greetings, found in most rites, the phrase *Dominus vobiscum* is of scriptural inspiration (see Ruth 2:4 and Judges 6:12). Since functionally it serves as a greeting, it is not to be interpreted as a statement of fact (e.g., "the Lord is (*est*) with you") but as a prayerful acclamation or salutation (*Dominus sit vobis-*

---

[15] Josef A. Jungmann, *The Mass: An Historical, Theological, and Pastoral Survey* (Collegeville, Minn.: The Liturgical Press, 1976), 166.

[16] For examples see F. E. Brightman, ed., *Liturgies Eastern and Western*, 2nd ed. (Oxford: The Clarendon Press, 1967), vol. 1: The Liturgy of the Syrian Jacobites, 85; The Byzantine Liturgy of the Ninth Century, 321; The Liturgy of St. John Chrysostom, 385, etc.

[17] In the Latin editions (*Missale Romanum* 1970, 1975) this greeting appears in the appendix with a musical setting. In most of the vernacular editions the greeting appears in place in the Order of Mass and the response of the people rather than the "Benedictus deus . . ." of the Latin is the same as for the other greetings, e.g., English: "And also with you"; German: "Und mit deinem Geiste"; Italian: "E con il tuo spirito."

[18] Matthew 6:9; Joachim Jeremias, *New Testament Theology: The Proclamation of Jesus*, 2nd ed. (London: SCM Press Ltd, 1972), 197.

[19] Joseph A. Fitzmyer, "New Testament Epistles" in Raymond E. Brown, Joseph A Fitzmyer, and Roland E. Murphy, eds., *The Jerome Biblical Commentary*, vol. 2 (Englewood Cliffs, New Jersey: Prentice-Hall, Inc., 1968), 224. Hereafter cited as JBC.

[20] JBC, 224.

[21] Richard Kugelman, "The First Letter to the Corinthians" in JBC, vol. 2, 255-256.

cum). Bernard Botte argues convincingly that, if it were a declarative statement or proclamation, the proper response on the part of the community would not be *Et cum spiritu tuo* but the *Amen* of assent.[22]

4. *Pax vobis.*

Reserved for the bishop, this alternative to the traditional *Dominus vobiscum* does not preclude the use of the other forms of greetings.[23] Repeating the salutation of the risen Lord to his apostles (John 20:20, 21, 27), the bishop, as a successor of the apostles, offers it as a greeting to the community. The exclusive use of this greeting by bishops (not priests or deacons) is attested to, for example, by John Chrysostom who notes that the bishop saluted the faithful as he entered the church with the *Pax vobiscum* and by the Council of Braga (563) which was unique insofar as it legislated that both bishops and priests should use the one same greeting *Dominus vobiscum*.[24]

A COMMON RESPONSE

Whereas the celebrant's greetings are variable and scriptural in source, the community's response *Et cum spiritu tuo* can be used invariably with all the greetings.

The traditional response has presented some difficulty for interpretation. It is generally accepted that it is not a Semitism but a "Christianism" based on the Pauline use of *pneuma* where the spirit is *"la partie spirituelle de l'homme la plus apparentée à Dieu, object immédiat des actions et des influences divines. . . ."*[25] It appears that more recent scholarship has moved away from Josef Jungmann's understanding of the response *Et cum spiritu tuo* as meaning "your person" or simply "you."[26] Henry Ashworth is quite explicit in his interpretation when he comments:

---

[22] Bernard Botte, "Dominus Vobiscum," *Bible et vie Chrétienne* 62 (1965), 34.

[23] *Caeremoniale Episcoporum* (Rome: Vatican Polyglot Press, 1984), 44. Paragraph 132, referring to the introductory rites of the Mass states: *"Postea Episcopus manus extendens, populum salutat, dicens: 'Pax vobis,' vel aliam e formulis in Missali propositis."* This, however, seems to be a restrictive directive as will be seen from comments on the possibility of creativity in the use of additional greeting texts. See note no. 32 below.

[24] Josef A. Jungmann, *The Mass of the Roman Rite: Its Origins and Development*, one volume ed., tr. Francis A. Brunner, rev. Charles K. Riepe (London: Burns and Oates Ltd.; New York: Benziger Brothers, Inc., 1959), 243.

[25] Botte, 37. In this regard Botte quotes C. Spicq, *Les épîtres pastorales* (Paris: 1947), 397.

[26] Josef A. Jungmann, *The Mass of the Roman Rite: Its Origins and Development*, tr. Francis A. Brunner, two volume ed., vol. 1 (New York: Benziger Brothers, Inc., 1951), 363, footnote 16:

The people's response *Et cum spiritu tuo* is also a prayer for God's
accredited minister. It is a prayer which asks that the creative activity and power of the Holy Spirit may fill his *pneuma* and enable
him to obey Christ's command "Do this in remembrance of me."[27]

One can understand then why traditionally the response *Et cum
spiritu tuo* has been used only when an ordained minister presides,
since the community's response refers to that "spirit" given through
the imposition of hands in the sacrament of ordination.[28] This nuance has been overlooked or intentionally set aside in some vernacular translations. The International Commission on English in
the Liturgy (ICEL), for example, uses this response with all ministers in its revised *Order of Christian Funerals* but has consistently translated *spiritu tuo* in the generic sense of Jungmann's "you." Could
it be that in such cases the meaning given to "you" (*spiritu tuo*) is
a reference to the spirit given to all in the sacraments of initiation?

Of course, ICEL has accepted the ecumenical translation of the
greeting prepared by the International Consultation on English Texts
(ICET). In 1970 ICET suggested that the appropriate translation of
the greeting and response would be: "The Spirit of the Lord be with
you. And also with you." The reason ICET did not translate *spiritu*
in the people's response was given: "If 'Spirit' is used in the greeting, it need not be used in the response." In light of the comments
that resulted from the use of the initial ICET translation of the greeting, in 1972 the English was changed to: "The Lord be with you."
It should be noted, however, that the people's response remained
unchanged (without the explicit reference to the spirit) although the
original argument for its omission by ICET was no longer valid. The
1975 ICET translation follows the 1972 text without additional comment or explanation.[29]

"This is a Semitism: *Spiritus tuus* = your person = you." Yet, in this same note, Jungmann
cites the patristic interpretation of "your spirit" as referring to the indwelling of the Holy Spirit
and to the fact that this counter-greeting "was even at an early age restricted to those endowed
with major orders, bishops, priests and deacons. . . ." One recalls that in the revised rites the
response *Et cum spiritu tuo* is still reserved for a reply to ordained ministers. The reason seems
to be linked with the deeper understanding of the response, referring to the spirit given in
ordination. See W. C. Van Unnik, "Dominus Vobiscum: the background of a liturgical formula,"
in A.J.B. Higgins, ed., *Studies in Memory of Th. W. Manson* (London: University Press, 1959),
270-305; Henry Ashworth, "Et cum spiritu tuo," *The Clergy Review* 51 (1966), 122-130; Emil J.
Lengeling, "Und mit deinem Geiste," *Gottesdienst* 8 (1974), 97-99.

   [27] Ashworth, 128.

   [28] Aimé Georges Martimort, ed., *La Chiesa in preghiera: Introduzione alla Liturgia*, 2nd ed.,
vol. 1 (Brescia: Queriniana, 1985), 71.

   [29] International Consultation on English Texts, *Prayers We Have in Common* (Philadelphia:
Fortress Press, 1970, 1972, 1975).

ADAPTATION OF THE GREETING

On the level of national conferences of bishops, initiative has been shown in officially expanding the number of greetings printed in the approved liturgical books. The 1983, second edition of the Italian *Messale Romano,* drawing from the Pauline corpus, includes four additional texts[30] and the German *Messbuch* of 1975 offers another five.[31]

The richest collection of salutations in the revised books of the Roman Rite, however, is found in the 1984 section of the Roman Ritual entitled *De Benedictionibus.*[32] Seventy-three initial greetings are provided covering a variety of specific occasions and only four of them are duplicates.[33] This is in clear contrast with the earlier sections of the revised ritual where, when a rite is celebrated within Mass, it is simply indicated that the salutation is to be taken from the *Ordo Missae* (for example, confirmation, ordination, and religious profession) or the suggestion is given that the celebrant offer a greeting in a friendly manner without any suggested fixed text. Such is the case, for example, in the celebration of baptism, reconciliation, marriage, and funerals.[34] *Pastoral Care of the Sick: Rites of Anointing*

---

[30] Conferenza Episcopale Italiana, *Messale Romano,* 2nd ed. (Rome: Libreria Editrice Vaticana, 1983).

[31] *Messbuch* (Einsiedeln und Köln, Germany: Benziger, 1975).

[32] *Rituale Romanum, De Benedictionibus,* (Rome: Vatican Polyglot Press, 1984). The office for the Pontifical Ceremonies selects texts from this corpus for eucharists celebrated by John Paul II. For example, at the Chrism Mass on Holy Thursday (1987), Pope John Paul used no. 532:

Deus, omnis sanctitatis fons et origo,
qui homines ad Christi sequelam semper
vocare dignatur, sit cum omnibus vobis.

On the Solemnity of Mary, Mother of God (1987) the Pope used a line from 2 Thessalonians 3:16:

Il Signore della pace
vi dia egli stesso la pace sempre e in ogni modo.
Il Signore sia con tutti voi.

[33] Numbers refer to the paragraphs in *De Benedictionibus* of the *editio typica* that are duplicates: no. 75 = no. 47, blessing of a family; no. 159 = no. 140, blessing of children; no. 160 = no. 141, blessing of children by laypersons; no. 863 = no. 846, blessing of a baptismal font. A number of the blessings are prepared for use by laypersons. It is interesting to note that whereas ordained ministers may use the texts offered in the *Book of Blessings* or some other text especially taken from Scripture (*alia apta verba e Sacris Scripturis praesertim deprompta*) no such provision is offered for the texts to be used by laypersons. None of the texts in the latter case have *Et cum spiritu tuo* as the people's response.

[34] In the case of baptism, marriage, reconciliation, and funerals, the character of the greeting is somewhat different from that of the eucharist. In these cases it seems to be more of a welcome and an opportunity to introduce the community into the meaning of the celebration. No mention is made that it should, if possible, be built on Scripture. The greeting does not take place from the presidential chair but, as the case may be, at the entrance of the church (e.g., funeral liturgy) or where the celebration begins (e.g., reconciliation room).

and Viaticum includes four rather uninspired greetings for possible use.[35]

In the area of the sacramental rites there seems to be some indication that additional greetings printed in place would be beneficial pastorally. Thus, the 1985 *Order of Christian Funerals*, adapted by ICEL, has introduced four new greetings for use in several stages of the funeral process. The vigil for the deceased includes the following three new texts for optional use:[36]

> May the God of hope give you the fullness of peace and may the Lord of life be always with you.

> The grace and peace of God our Father, who raised Jesus from the dead, be always with you.

> May the Father of mercies, the God of all consolation, be with you.

In the vigil for a deceased child, one additional new composition is offered:[37]

> May Christ Jesus, who welcomed children and laid his hands in blessing upon them, comfort you with his peace and be always with you.

In addition to the limited creativity emerging from the conferences of bishops and international language commissions such as ICEL, some initiative has been shown in the publication of private collections of greetings for use in the liturgy of the eucharist.[38] This raises

---

[35] See The Roman Ritual, *Pastoral Care of the Sick: Rites of Anointing and Viaticum* (Washington: ICEL, 1982), 55, 83, 149, 205. The texts include two from the *Ordo Missae*: "The grace of our Lord . . ." and "The grace and peace . . ." The two other texts are well known:
1. "Peace to this house and to all who live in it."
2. "The peace of the Lord be with you."

[36] *Order of Christian Funerals* (Washington: ICEL, 1985), 27, no. 69. This text prepared by ICEL is an adaptation of *Rituale Romanum, Ordo Exsequiarum* (Rome: Vatican Polyglot Press, 1969) and the 1970 provisional translation of the *editio typica, Rite of Funerals* (Washington: ICEL, 1970).

[37] *Order of Christian Funerals*, 139, no. 248.

[38] See note 32 for examples of papal creativity in this area; Bernard J. LeFrois, SVD, "*Ad Libitum* Greetings and Prayers for the Penitential Rite," *Boletin Eclesiastico de Filipinas* 57 (1976), 338-346; *Catequetica: Revista de Practica Pastoral* is published every two months by Editorial Sal Terrae, Guevara, 20, 39001 Santander, Spain. In this periodical the "Saludo" is actually what in English would be called the "introduction" to the celebration and not a greeting as such; *Dienst am Wort Gedanken zur Sonntagspredigt* is published every two months by Religiose Bildungsarbeit Stuttgart, Böheimstrasse 44, D-7000 Stuttgart 1, Germany; The "Liturgische Arbeitsgruppe in Bistum Aachen" which prepares *Sonntagsdienste* (Bergmoser + Höller, Karl-Friedrich-Strasse 76, Aachen, Germany) provides a new greeting for each Sunday, often in harmony with the gospel. On the 19th Sunday of the Year with the gospel reading from Matthew 14:22-33 (Jesus walks on the water), we find, for example:
> *Der herr, unser Gott, vergisst uns nicht.*
> *Er hört unser Rufen, lässt sich finden*
> *von denen, die ihn suchen.*
> *Er sei mit euch allen.*

the question concerning the freedom offered to the individual celebrant to be creative in the use of the opening greeting of the Mass.
Although the General Instruction of the Roman Missal makes no
explicit mention of the greeting as an area of presidential creativity,
the 1973 circular letter of the Congregation for Divine Worship
opened up the area by stating that "by their very nature these brief
admonitions do not require that everyone use them in the form in
which they appear in the Missal."[39] It would seem that by extension the principle of creativity could now encompass the greeting
element within the introductory rites as well. Furthermore, in view
of the developments within the *Ordines* (e.g., the indication in the
Book of Blessings that the celebrant may use *alia verba apta e Sacris
Scripturis praesertim deprompta* for the greetings) one can accept as
a principle that the introductory salutation within the eucharist lies
within the acceptable areas of creativity. Of course, due consideration must always be given to the use of the proper genre in light
of the function and meaning of this element within the introductory rites of the Mass. As a matter of pastoral practice, this is at present the generally accepted principle.[40]

PASTORAL SITUATION AND PRACTICE

When one studies the greeting in the context of the introductory rites, several problems emerge. The first concerns the verbosity
of the entire structural unit. The elements tend to produce a con-
gested, cluttered, and wordy ritual opening.

As noted earlier, the *Missa normativa* recognized this difficulty
and had proposed at least one suggestion in the right direction: the
sign of the cross made by the ministers in silence.[41] In this case, the

---

[39] Congregation for Divine Worship, Circular Letter *Eucharistiae participationem*, 27 Apr.
1973, no. 14: DOL, 248, no. 1988.

[40] See Gaston Fontaine, "Créativité dans la liturgie d'aujourd'hui," *Notitiae* 73 (1972), 151-156.
A summary is presented in the *Bishops' Committee on the Liturgy Newsletter*, vol. 1 (1965-1975),
339-340. In preparing new texts due attention should be given to the genre of the greeting.
I found the following text in a leaflet prepared for a wedding in Italy. Inadvertently the initial
greeting was turned into an epiclesis:

> *La grazia e la tenerezza di Dio, che è Padre*
> *l'amore di Cristo che ci rende figli*
> *la potenze dello Spirito che feconda e fa vivere*
> *che crea unità nella diversità*
> *che genera comune e famigila*
> *siano su Erminia e Carlo*
> *siano su tutti voi.*

[41] Bugnini, 338.

first words addressed by the one presiding over the eucharist would be the greeting of the assembly. This would follow the ancient practice where the first exchange between the presider and the assembly was the greeting. It should be noted that some conferences of bishops have moved in this direction by adapting the Roman Rite slightly. In Germany and French-speaking countries, the entire sign of the cross (including the *Amen*) is said by the priest celebrant alone.[42] Thus the first celebrant-assembly exchange is the primitive initial greeting.

The use of the sign of the cross and the greeting has been criticized as being repetitious. Often, in both texts the trinitarian statement can appear to be an unnecessary extended didacticism, as some authors have termed it. Rather than being a greeting, the initial salutation can become a lesson in trinitarian theology, a confession of trinitarian belief, or an anticipatory repetition of the creed.

The wordiness of the introductory rites is further compounded by the fact that the greeting may be followed by a few words of introduction to the liturgy of the day.[43] To alleviate this situation, there has been some (unfortunate) move in the direction of combining the greeting and introduction, at times ending the introduction with the greeting. The following German example for the Seventh Sunday of Easter illustrates this process:

> In these days between Ascension and Pentecost we are reminded that Christ our Lord and Redeemer is not visible among us. However, he is present in the power of his Spirit, when we are gathered together in his name. Prompted by this belief, we greet and bless one another when we say: The Lord be with you. And with your spirit.[44]

The above example brings to mind another danger that faces the use of the greeting and the introductory words. Together they can easily be developed into a mini-homily. Adolf Adam recognized this danger when he commented on the directives of the German *Messbuch*:

> Then they greet each other with one of the eight greetings which the Missal offers as a choice. It is, of course, possible for the priest to add personal greetings to the initial greeting. However, one

---

[42] Martimort, 227, footnote 14.
[43] GIRM, no. 29: DOL 208, no. 1419.
[44] Author's translation from *Dienst am Wort Gedanken zur Sonntagspredigt*, (1987), no. 3, 383. In this case the unit is referred to as "Eröffnung." Generally, as in the *Messbuch*, a distinction is made between "Begrüssung der Gemeinde" (Greeting) and "Einführung" (Introduction).

should be aware of the danger of superfluous subjectivism that in the long run would be hard for the entire congregation to bear.[45]

The additions one makes to the greeting or the replacement of the scripturally inspired text with so-called secular greetings has been commented on by several authors. Aidan Kavanagh, in his inimitable style, sttempted to find a reason for the use of the secular greeting. In *Elements of Rite* he speculates:

> The reason for which some presidents choose to greet the assembly with "Good morning, everybody" instead of "The Lord be with you" is difficult to fathom. It cannot be that the former is more appropriate to the assembly's purpose than the latter. Nor can it be that the first is theologically more sophisticated than the second. And since one would prefer not to entertain the possibility that the secular greeting is a mark of clerical condescension to the simple and untutored laity, the only alternative is to attribute the secular greeting's use to presidential thoughtlessness of a fairly low order.[46]

Lest one argue that Kavanagh would not be against the use of the secular greeting as long as the liturgical one is used along with it, a quote from another liturgist might clarify the matter from a liturgical point of view:

> Distortion of the formal greeting ("Good morning." "The Lord *is* with you") is inappropriate—a violation of the ritual bond already established by the song and procession. To say something like "Good morning" is to say loud and clear that the ritual is a barrier to communication. It is felt as a break from the pattern and is experienced as the celebrant's peeping over or around a wall of ritual at the people. . . . To say either "Good morning" or to change the greeting formula into a flat statement is to treat the congregation as if they were bored or ignorant.[47]

While aware of the contrary opinions,[48] I would agree with the Keifer-Kavanagh line of argumentation. My approach, however, is the consideration of the essential meaning and communicative function of the greeting within the structural unit. The specific function of the initial greeting is quite focused. "This greeting and the congrega-

---

[45] Author's translation from Adolf Adam, *Grundriss Liturgie* (Freiburg: Herder, 1985), 137.

[46] Aidan Kavanagh, *Elements of Rite: A Handbook of Liturgical Style* (New York: Pueblo Publishing Co., 1982), 77.

[47] Ralph Kiefer, *To Give Thanks and Praise* (Washington, D.C.: National Association of Pastoral Musicians, 1980), 109.

[48] Joseph M. Champlin, *The Proper Balance: A Practical Look at Liturgical Renewal* (Notre Dame: Ave Maria Press, 1981), 81-82.

tion's response express the mystery of the gathered Church."[49] The initial elements of the opening rites—the procession, opening song, sign of the cross—have established the setting or environment in which the assembly finds itself. There should be no doubt that this is a religious ambiance. The biblically inspired greeting which follows does not move the community back, out of that context, but moves it deeper into the mystery of its own being as a community of faith. The function of the greeting in this context is not one of welcome or casual recognition as "Good morning" is when said as one meets another on the street.[50] Rather, the specific function of the liturgical greeting is to mutually declare, affirm, and confess that the community has taken on a dimension bigger than itself. The eucharistic assembly is not simply a sociological grouping of individuals as at a purely nonreligious affair. The act of gathering to worship is not the result of purely human initiative; it is the result of grace calling individuals to become the ecclesial Body. Having been gathered to worship, it has become Church, engaged in a cultic act with the active presence of Christ in its midst.

CONCLUSION

In spite of some negative criticism of the present introductory rites, there is some indication that the area is not as problematic as others. In 1980 Kenneth Smits, commenting on the present order of worship, noted: "The opening song, sign of the cross, mutual greeting and call to worship flow nicely from more general activity to that which gives particular focus to the celebration."[51] In the United States a national study of the Order of Mass was undertaken by the Federation of Diocesan Liturgical Commissions and the Bishops'

---

[49] GIRM, no. 28: DOL 208, no. 1418. In this regard Robert Hovda comments that "no 'Good morning, sisters and brothers' is as worshipful an orientation after the opening song of the Sunday assembly as the sign of the cross and the scriptural greeting. The former spotlights the speaker; the latter, the purpose of the gathering." Robert Hovda, "The Amen Corner," *Worship* 61 (1987), 247.

[50] Fortunately communities are beginning to exchange personal greetings before the eucharist begins. Some contemporary church architecture fosters this type of exchange on the social level by the introduction of a gathering space at the entrance of the church. Some members of the community (celebrant, deacons, ministers of hospitality) make it a point to greet the people upon their arrival thus rendering the introduction of a casual greeting unnecessary and even reduplicative within the introductory rites.

[51] Smits, 60-61.

Committee on the Liturgy.[52] Commenting on the three year study, Charles Gusmer observes that "the results of the survey indicate a high comfort level and satisfaction with the revision of the Order of Mass."[53] He adds, however, that the introductory rites are too crowded and invariable and that in general—throughout the Order—the respondents desire more flexibility with the rites.[54]

As already noted, there has been some attempt to meet these criticisms of the introductory rites, and the opening greeting in particular. It would appear that in the future even more might be done.

Several specific conclusions might be drawn from a study of the initial greeting. First of all, the present form, the result of the Vatican II reform, is admittedly a significant improvement over the opening rites found in the Missal of Pius V. Secondly, those conferences of bishops and mixed or international commissions responsible for providing vernacular translations of the liturgical texts are to be commended not only for their translations but, at times, for the additions to and the adaptations of the rite of the Missal of Paul VI. Yet, the work has not been completed. Specifically, I would offer the following five areas of immediate concern:

1. Episcopal conferences, in adapting the rite to fit local cultural situations, might need to adjust the introductory rites in accordance with sound principles of inculturation.[55]

2. A distinction must be recognized and officially accepted between the Sunday and the weekday celebrations of the eucharist. On weekdays, given the nature of the assembly—its level of faith, degree of prayer experience, the frequency of its celebration—an adjustment of the introductory rites might prove beneficial. What is perhaps ritually useful on Sundays has already appeared as unnecessary and even overburdening on a daily basis. On weekdays there should be the option to omit elements in the introductory rites (as is already encouraged in Masses for children).[56] In

---

[52] Bishops' Committee on the Liturgy and Federation of Diocesan Liturgical Commissions, *The Mystery of Faith: A Study of the Structural Elements of the Order of Mass*, (Washington: Federation of Diocesan Liturgical Commissions, 1981) served as a useful tool for this national (USA) study of the *Ordo Missae*.

[53] Gusmer, 345.

[54] Gusmer, 345.

[55] Such adaptations in this direction can be seen in the Mass for use in Zaire and in the Order of Mass for India.

[56] Congregation for Divine Worship, Directory for Masses with Children *Pueros baptizatos*, 1 Nov. 1973, no. 40: DOL 276, no. 2173.

this case, the initial greeting might once again emerge as the nucleus of the introductory structural unit, at least on weekdays.

3. A greater use of imagination and creativity should be encouraged in the preparation of additional initial greetings for use especially on those occasions when sacramental rites are joined with the eucharist (for example, marriage, confirmation, etc.). These should be biblically inspired and precise while remaining specific enough to fit the special liturgical celebration.

4. Celebrants must be conscious of the liturgical meaning and communicative value of the initial greeting. Reading from a printed text is not the normal manner of extending a mutual salutation. The gesture, accompanying the greeting, must express the intent of the text rather than appear as a separate afterthought, made with such guarded hesitancy that it reflects an embarrassment to accept with confidence the role of one called to preside over the community at prayer.

5. The introductory rites, as the first complete structural unit of the liturgy of the eucharist, need to be reconsidered in view of the negative criticism raised. The ultimate question should be whether they achieve their intended goal. Do they truly assist those present to come to recognize and express their unique identity as the mystery of the Church gathered in common prayer with the Lord Jesus?

THE ROMAN ORDER OF MASS FROM 1964 TO 1969: THE PREPARATION OF THE GIFTS

Frederick R. McManus

In some sense this brief study is a partial reprise of a 1980 article, "The Genius of the Roman Rite Revisited."[1] With its perhaps overblown title, that article described the projected reform of the Order of Mass as it was tried out in Rome in late 1965 and contrasted it with the Roman Order of Mass promulgated in 1969. The thesis of the article was that the 1965 project had been greatly complicated (or enriched, depending on one's viewpoint) by 1969. The thesis had a particular validity if the 1965 project was judged as reflecting a basic, austere, and nuclear Roman eucharistic rite—and a potential starting point for cultural and other adaptation in different regions.

The present study has a more limited scope—the preparation of the gifts or "offertory rite"—but one pursued in greater detail: to describe the successive developments in that single area of the Roman Order of Mass over the course of the five-year period 1964-1969. This is done from a rereading of several schemata of the Consilium for the Implementation of the Constitution on the Liturgy [hereafter, Consilium] from this period.[2] Besides piecing together details in the five-year process, the paper will offer some judgments on the progress or regression reflected in the several drafts—and even propose some reworking that is still desirable, although such comments are of unlikely impact in the ecclesial climate of the late 1980s and early 1990s.

It is especially appropriate to include this study in a collection dedicated to Archbishop Denis E. Hurley of Durban. He was a mem-

---

[1] Frederick R. McManus, "The Genius of the Roman Rite Revisited," *Worship* 54 (1980), 360-378.

[2] A list of the schemata of the Consilium is given by Piero Marini, "Elenco degli 'Schemata' el 'Consilium' et della Congregazione per il Culto Divino (Marzo 1964–Luglio 1975)," *Notitiae* 18 (1982), 455-772. The present article deals only with the formal schemata and accompanying reports; all are from *coetus studiorum* no. 10, *de Ordine Missae*.

ber of the implementing Consilium from mid-1965; he was a founding member of the Episcopal Committee of the International Commission on English in the Liturgy in 1963;[3] and, still earlier, he was
one who both understood and supported the draft of the Constitution on the Liturgy when it was under review by the Central Preparatory Commission in 1962, some months prior to the Second Vatican
Council.[4]

The story of the Roman postconciliar commission has been told
best by its secretary, Annibale Bugnini, in a volume published
posthumously, La riforma liturgica (1948-1975).[5] This includes a documented account of the development of the revised Order of Mass,
which was done by a working group or coetus studiorum headed by
Johannes Wagner of Trier.[6] Bugnini's account goes beyond the substantive changes in the Order of Mass and the supporting reasons:
he describes the forces behind the developments, from the studies,
trial celebrations, and critiques to the 1967 meeting of the Synod
of Bishops and beyond, including the role of the Roman Curia and
especially that of Pope Paul VI. The latter was deeply involved at
several stages of the process before he made the final decision in
early 1969 to promulgate the revised Order.[7]

---

[3] See Frederick R. McManus, ICEL: The First Years (Washington: ICEL, 1981), 5-11. Archbishop Hurley drafted an organizational plan for ICEL in early 1963, prior to its formal establishment by the participating conferences of bishops in October of that year. He also drafted
ICEL's "mandate" (1964), which was approved by the founding conferences.

[4] Acta et Documenta Concilio Oecumenico Vaticano II apparando, Series I (Antepraeparatoria)
(Rome: Vatican Polyglot Press, 1960-1961); Series II (Praeparatoria) (Rome: Vatican Polyglot Press,
1964-1969). The Central Preparatory Commission discussed the draft (submitted by the Preparatory Commission on the Liturgy) at meetings from 26 Mar. to 2 Apr. 1962. For Archbishop
Hurley's intervention and votes, see Series II (Praeparatoria), II, 2: 77-78, 99, 314, 366, 491.
When voting favorably on the draft of the chapter on the eucharist, he stated that the reform
would "seem to promote the good of the Church, opening the way to evolution, lessening
the force of revolution" (evolutione viam aperiendo, revolutionis vim minuendo). In the commission Archbishop Hurley was next in seniority to Archbishop Marcel Lefebvre.

[5] Annibale Bugnini, La riforma liturgica (1948-1975), Bibliotheca "Ephemerides Liturgicae,"
"Subsidia" 30 (Rome: CLV-Edizione Liturgiche, 1983). Bugnini's account of the revision of the
Ordo Missae is given on pp. 332-388, with greater detail of background and narrative than the
schemata studied here reveal.

[6] This was the principal coetus dealing with the eucharistic celebration. Anton Hänggi
(later named Bishop of Basel) was secretary; in 1967 Adalberto Franquesa became pro-secretary.
For the composition of Coetus X, see Bugnini, 332. See also Robert Cabie, "Le nouvel Ordo
missae," La Maison-Dieu 100 (1969), 21-35; Johannes Wagner, "Zum Reform des 'Ordo Missae'
Zwei Dokumente," in Liturgia opera divina e umana: Studi sulla riforma liturgica offerti a S. E. Mons.
Annibale Bugnini in occasione del suo 70 compleanno, Pierre Jounel, Reiner Kaczynski, and Gottardo Pasqualetti, eds., Bibliotheca "Ephemerides Liturgicae," "Subsidia" 26 (Rome: CLV-Edizione
Liturgiche, 1982), 263-289. Bernard Botte's informal comments on the work of the Consilium
on the Mass are in the recently translated From Silence to Participation: An Insider's View of Liturgical Renewal, John Sullivan, ed. (Washington: Pastoral Press, 1988), 145-152.

[7] See Bugnini, 345-347, 354-360, 363-366. One major intervention of Paul VI is described
below, at footnote 48.

The Process of Revision: The Schemata

For convenience, the steps of the five-year process may be summarized in terms of the successive drafts of the *Ordo Missae*:

1. A provisional description of a revised Order of Mass and a report under the heading *specimen provisorium*, dated 22 October 1964.[8]

This tentative effort sums up preliminary considerations, without attempting to provide a draft *Ordo Missae* with rubrics and texts, as subsequent schemata do. It was the fruit of several meetings of the working *coetus*.

2. The first schema of the so-called *Missa normativa*, in versions dated 19 September and 9 October 1965, accompanied by an extensive report and a list of questions to be resolved by the members of the Consilium.[9]

It was this rite which, during the fourth period of the Second Vatican Council, was celebrated twice—once in French, once in Italian—with the participation of all the members and consultors of the Consilium. Largely because of press reports and reactions outside the Consilium, the work was almost interrupted at this point.

3. A second schema of the *Missa normativa* dated 24 May 1966, substantially the same as its predecessor.[10]

This draft relocated the sections of the lengthy supplementary report mentioned above under no. 2 as footnoted declarations or explanations. Subsequent schemata did not need a full report or introduction; instead they contained the Order of Mass itself, accompanied by explanations of new developments and variations.

After the revised Order of Mass was celebrated during the fall 1967 meeting of the Synod of Bishops, a period followed in which

---

[8] Schema no. 44 (no. 9 *de Missali*), 22 Oct. 1964: "Specimen Provisorium Exaratum ad Primum Schema Praeparandum" (7 pp.).

[9] Schema no. 106 (no. 12, *de Missali*), 19 Sept. 1965: "Schema Primum 'Ordinis Missae Normativae'," 9 Oct. 1965: "Schema Primum Ordinis Missae 'Normativae' Patribus 'Consilii' Proponendum" (24 pp.). This schema has two forms of the Roman *Canon Missae*, as well as a report of twenty-six pages and four pages of *quaesita* submitted to the members of the Consilium.

In general the pattern was that an individual *coetus* such as no. X would first submit its drafts and reports to a meeting of a central group of consultors, chiefly the *relatores* of the various *coetus*, just prior to a plenary meeting of the Consilium itself (the members of which were almost all bishops).

[10] Schema no. 170 (no. 23, *de Missali*), 24 May 1966: "Schema Primum Ordinis Missae Normativae" (37 pp.). To this were added five pages of *quaesita*, a general introduction to the question of new anaphoras (with texts), and further questions concerning *variationes*.

questions raised in the discussion and voting of the synodal Fathers had to be reviewed, together with the recommendations or decisions of Pope Paul VI—including those made in the light of three eucharistic celebrations in which the pope himself participated.[11]

4–7. A schema of 21 December 1967, reflecting in a preliminary way some of the issues raised by the Synod of Bishops,[12] followed by the schemata of 10 February 1968,[13] 21 March 1968,[14] and 24 May 1968.[15]

These four schemata, developed within a period of less than five months, together with reports of 21 November 1967 and 24 May 1968, represent the post-synodal stage of the Order of Mass. They differ considerably among themselves in detail but not in substance.[16]

8. In turn the schemata of this final stage of the process must be compared with the text of the *Ordo Missae* "restored by decree of the Second Ecumenical Vatican Council and promulgated by authority of Pope Paul VI." This was issued as of 6 April 1969, along with the Apostolic Constitution *Missale Romanum* (dated 3 April) and the first edition of the General Instruction of the Roman Missal.[17]

Overall the process can be seen in four stages: (a) preliminary project of 1964 (no. 1 above); (b) the first revised Order of Mass of 1965 and 1966 (nos. 2 and 3); (c) the emended schemata of 1967 and 1968 (nos. 4-7); (d) the promulgated Order of 1969.[18]

---

[11] See Bugnini, 341-366.

[12] Schema no. 266 (no. 44, *de Missali*), 21 Dec. 1967: "Schema Ordinis Missae cum Populo" (13 pp.).

[13] Schema no. 271 (no. 45, *de Missali*), 10 Feb. 1968: "Ordo Missae cum Populo" (20 pp.).

[14] Schema no. 281 (no. 47, *de Missali*), 21 Mar. 1968: "Ordo Missae cum Populo" (22 pp., including an *Ordo* for private celebration). The schema also has several addenda.

[15] Schema no. 293 (no. 51, *de Missali*), 24 May 1968: "Ordo Missae" (22 pp., including an appendix and an *Ordo* for private celebration).

[16] Bugnini (pp. 367-371) describes the concerns of officials of the Roman Curia and of consultants who were chosen by Paul VI during the period following the completion of schema no. 293, as well as the final issues raised and resolved by the pope (pp. 372-378).

[17] Paul VI, Apostolic Constitution *Missale Romanum*, 3 Apr. 1969: *Acta Apostolicae Sedis* [hereafter, AAS] 61 (1969), 217-222; ICEL, *Documents on the Liturgy, 1963-1979: Conciliar, Papal, and Curial Texts* [hereafter, DOL] (Collegeville, Minn.: The Liturgical Press, 1982) 202, nos. 1357-1366. Congregation of Rites [hereafter, SC Rites], Decree *Ordine Missae*, 6 Apr. 1969: *Notitiae* 5 (1969), 147; DOL 203, no. 1367.

The General Instruction of the Roman Missal *Institutio generalis Missalis Romani*, [hereafter, GIRM], issued by the Congregation for Divine Worship, deals with the rite of *praeparatio donorum* in nos. 49-53 (general description), 100-107 (presiding celebrant), 133 (deacon), 145 (acolyte), etc., but the development and content of this document are outside the scope of this paper: DOL 208, nos. 1439-1443, 1490-1497, 1523, 1535.

Coetus X held its first meeting 8-10 May 1964 in Trier at the Liturgisches Institut of which Johannes Wagner was director. The whole process thus took just short of five years.

[18] In his account Bugnini (pp. 332-388) gives a more complex pattern for the phases of the work; for clarity, the four stages listed here are simply based on the sequence of schemata.

This study illustrates the process in the case of the part of the Order of Mass which begins the eucharistic liturgy, the preparation of the gifts. The choice of this area or zone of the eucharistic rite of course implies nothing about the relative significance of the several parts of the Order of Mass. Nonetheless, from the beginning of the reform the existing offertory rite was seen as especially problematical: in texts, in structure or ritual, in underlying significance. Judgments concerning the rite ranged from the expansive concept of "taking" the bread and wine in Gregory Dix[19] to the cautionary stance of Bernard Capelle[20] to the massive gathering of complex historical data analyzed by Josef Jungmann.[21]

It is difficult to summarize these problems briefly; most of them will appear in the description of the schemata. Two extremes may be mentioned: on the one hand, any minimizing of the significant and necessary rite of bringing forward the elements for the eucharist, especially through merely token participation of the assembly; on the other hand and more seriously, any excess in the rite (a) that is proleptic in relation to the anaphora—the older and ongoing concern—and thus makes the presentation of gifts an offering and an end, even a sacrifice, in itself or (b) that even by a proper and reasonable emphasis somehow restricts the assembly to the offertory rite and thus almost excludes it from real participation in the "sacerdotal" anaphora that follows.

all 3 w/ foundation in ritual history

THE BASES FOR REVISION

First, the very nature of the project for a reformed Order of Mass as a whole must be summarily described. It is the rite of celebration for ordinary parochial circumstances, especially on the Lord's

---

[19] Gregory Dix, *The Shape of the Liturgy*, 2nd ed. (London: Adams & Charles Black Ltd., Dacre Press, 1945), 48-50, 110-123, 495-498.

[20] "Pour une meilleure intelligence de la messe. L'offertoire," *Questions liturgiques et paroissiales* 17 (1932), 58-67; "Quête et offertoire," *La Maison-Dieu* 24 (1950), 121-138; *Pour une meilleure intelligence de la messe*, 2nd ed. (Louvain: Abbaye du Mont César, 1955), 37-55, which begins "L'offertoire pose un problème." Abbot Bernard Capelle was a member of the Preparatory Commission on the Liturgy; he died in 1961.

[21] Josef A. Jungmann, S.J., *The Mass of the Roman Rite: Its Origins and Development (Missarum Sollemnia)*, two volume ed., vol. 2 (New York: Benziger Brothers, Inc., 1955), 1-100. Jungmann, who had been a member of the Preparatory Commission on the Liturgy and a *peritus* of the Conciliar Commission on the Liturgy, was a member of *Coetus* X of the Consilium. See also Kenneth Stevenson, *Eucharist and Offering* (New York: Pueblo Publishing Company, 1986), esp. pp. 105-116 on the preanaphoral prayers and Western medieval prayers.

Day. It is the exemplar—hence called the *Missa normativa* or later, when this term was misunderstood, the *forma typica*[22] —for all other grades and degrees of lesser and greater solemnity and for all other forms. These forms may range from the Mass without a congregation to the Mass in smaller and specialized assemblies such as home liturgies and celebrations with small children. They include both the principal and the secondary celebrations in parishes and similar communities on Sundays, feastdays, and weekdays; they extend to the stational Mass itself, presided over by the bishop of the local Church.[23]

It is the latter, formerly called the pontifical Mass, rather than the exemplary Sunday parochial celebration that fully actualizes the local Church and is the preeminent manifestation of the Church of Christ.[24] In one sense the eucharist presided over by the bishop is thus the norm and exemplar.[25] Nevertheless the reform of the Order of Mass, for obvious pastoral and practical reasons, was designed for the Sunday "sung celebration, with a reader and at least one minister, with a schola or at least one cantor, and with the people singing."[26]

Even at the end of the five-year period during which this development of the Order of Mass took place, one new element of

---

[22] In Chapter IV of GIRM (1969) the description of the different forms of celebration with a congregation begins with section A, *Forma typica* (nos. 82-126), which is translated in DOL as "Basic Form of Celebration." It is followed by distinct sections on the functions of deacons, acolytes, and readers, as already mentioned in footnote 17.

[23] For the concept of an extremely basic rite that is susceptible to the broadest accommodation and adaptation, see the article cited above in footnote 1, especially pp. 367-370.

[24] See Vatican Council II, Constitution on the Liturgy *Sacrosanctum Concilium* [hereafter, SC], 4 Dec. 1963, art. 41: DOL 1, no. 41. SC, art. 42, relates parochial and other liturgies presided over by presbyters to the celebrations of the whole local Church presided over by the bishops described in SC, art. 41.

[25] The revised *Caeremoniale Episcoporum*, published by decree of the Congregation for Divine Worship, 14 Sept. 1984, treats the stational Mass in Chapter I of Part II, nos. 119-170 (see Eng. ed., ICEL, *Ceremonial of Bishops* [Collegeville, Minn.: The Liturgical Press, 1989]). As a whole the 1984 ceremonial is better organized than its predecessor, originally published under the same title by authority of Clement VIII (Bull *Cum novissime*, 14 July 1600), but it is extremely diffuse and repetitive of directives found in the revised liturgical books of the postconciliar period. So far as the eucharist is concerned, the material of the episcopal ceremonial (nos. 119-186) would be better integrated into GIRM, along with the Directory for Masses with Children *Pueros baptizatos* (Congregation for Divine Worship, 1 Nov. 1973: AAS 66 [1974], 30-46; DOL 276).

[26] This is the language with which the *praenotanda* of the first draft of the *Missa normativa* (schema no. 106; see above, at footnote 9) begins. The theory or principle of this basic form of celebration, in full accord with SC, art. 49-50 (below, at note 28), had been developed at the very beginning of the process, for example, in a report of *Coetus* X dated 17 June 1964 (schema no. 16, no. 2 *de Missali*, p. 2); it is elaborated in another report dated 30 Sept. 1964 (schema no. 39, no. 5 *de Missali*, pp. 3-5). These schemata do not include an Order of Mass.

the Sunday parochial liturgy was still in beginning stages. In 1969 the conciliar restoration of an authentic diaconate was barely under way. For this reason the liturgical ministry of deacons is referred to in the various schemata and in the promulgated Order of Mass almost in passing.[27]

Two decades later, the specific diaconal liturgical ministry would in every sense pertain to the basic, exemplary, and thus "typical" eucharistic celebration. With some thousands of deacons now ministering in the United States, for example, it is not uncommon in ordinary parochial circumstances for the presiding priest to be assisted by a deacon at the chief Sunday eucharist.

The principles followed by the revisers are found in the Constitution on the Liturgy *Sacrosanctum Concilium*, both the general principles of Chapter I, which need not be recited here, and the direct conciliar mandate in Chapter II:

> 49. Thus, mindful of those Masses celebrated with the assistance of the faithful, especially on Sundays and holydays of obligation, the Council makes the following decrees in order that the sacrifice of the Mass, even in its ritual forms, may become pastorally effective to the utmost degree.

> 50. The Order of Mass is to be revised in a way that will bring out more clearly the intrinsic nature and purpose of the several parts, as also the connection between them, and will more readily achieve the devout, active participation of the faithful.

> For this purpose the rites are to be simplified, due care being taken to preserve their substance; elements that, with the passage of time, came to be duplicated or were added with but little advantage are now to be discarded; other elements that have suffered injury through accident of history are now, as may seem useful or necessary, to be restored to the vigor they had in the tradition of the Fathers.[28]

Simplification, elimination of elements duplicated or added "with but little advantage," restoration of "other elements that have suffered injury through accident of history"—these may now seem to be euphemistic references to the root-and-branch defects of the medieval and modern Roman liturgy. But the conciliar Fathers, fully aware of what was needed, overwhelmingly supported the reform of the

---

[27] The diaconal function is somewhat more carefully defined – but still as exceptional – in GIRM, nos. 127-141; no. 133 describes the deacon's function during the preparation of the gifts.
[28] SC, art. 49-50: DOL 1, nos. 49-50.

Order of Mass, no less than the principles: clarity and comprehensibility for the assembly, popular involvement and participation, and potential adaptability of a revised rite.[29]

The conciliar decision about the Order of Mass needs no more commentary than to point out the emphasis, first, on the communal celebration (and not on the low Mass or even private Mass which were given emphasis in the 1570 missal)[30] and, second, on the Sunday eucharist. In approving this mandate, the conciliar Fathers also had before them a general plan with slightly greater detail. This took the form of a *declaratio* or explanation, which reads, for the part of the rite being examined here:

> Among the individual parts of Mass, it seems that those at the beginning, at the offertory, at the communion, and at the end are in the greatest need of revision, especially because the Roman rite was taken over in Gaul and redacted according to a Gallic-Germanic genius in a new form which the Roman Church later adopted.
>
> Among other things, the following are proposed for some kind of revision. . . .
>
> d) The offertory rite should be so described and adapted that the participation of the people may be evident in a procession of offering, which might take place at least on more solemn days, either by the people themselves or by their representatives (as is still done in the Ambrosian liturgy).
>
> Likewise the prayers which accompany the offering should be so revised that it better corresponds with the meaning of an offering of gifts which are to be consecrated later. The significance of

---

[29] When put to a direct vote, the second paragraph of SC, art. 50 (not in the original draft of the constitution) was approved by 2249 of the conciliar Fathers; there were 31 negative votes. See *Acta Synodalia Sacrosancti Concilii Oecumenici Vaticani II*, 4 vols., indices (Rome: Vatican Polyglot Press, 1970-1980), II, 2: 335.

For the principles or policies of reform in general, see SC, art., 21-42, where they appear in Chapter I under four headings: (a) general norms; (b) norms drawn from the hierarchic and communal nature of the liturgy; (c) norms based on the teaching and pastoral character of the liturgy; (d) norms for adapting the liturgy to the cultures and traditions of peoples.

[30] *Missale Romanum ex Decreto Sacrosancti Concilii Tridentini Restitutum Pii V Pont. Max Jussu Editum*, promulgated by the Bull *Quo primum tempore*, 14 July 1570. In this missal—substantially unchanged in the edition of 1962, aside from additional proper Mass formularies (and the Holy Week revision of the 1950s)—the *Ordo Missae* simply ignores the sung elements of choir (or congregation) and is inconsistent in referring to the deacon "if it is a solemn Mass." The orientation is even more evident in the *Ritus servandus in celebratione Missae* (corresponding roughly to parts of the General Instruction of the Roman Missal); in this 1570 document the description of the Order of Mass is given in terms of the low or recited Mass, with interspersed paragraphs explaining the exceptional case of the sung liturgy, the *Missa sollemnis* or *Missa cantata*.

the prayer over the gifts should be restored by speaking it in a loud voice.[31]

Again, little comment is needed for these very preliminary plans. They had been worked up by the preconciliar Preparatory Commission and were submitted by the Conciliar Commission on the Liturgy to the bishops and other Fathers before they voted on the text of the Constitution on the Liturgy, article 50 quoted above, in order to illustrate the kind of reformed Order of Mass that was projected.

Preparation of the Gifts: The Point of Departure

The first and preparatory part of the liturgy of the eucharist in the Order of Mass is an area of the rite which had been complicated and confused by the extensive prayers said inaudibly by the presiding celebrant more than by major structural difficulties. These prayers, a medieval accretion "added but with little advantage," were well known—all out of proportion to their significance—to many educated Catholics prior to the revision, even though they were said inaudibly. They were found, for example, in the "Ordinary of the Mass" included in devotional books which were popular early in this century and in the hand missals which became moderately common in the decades before the Second Vatican Council.

The point of departure for reform was of course the Roman Order of Mass as celebrated in 1963.[32] This part of the Order of Mass needs to be described if only because in the late 1980s it has already been forgotten except by those who seek to perpetuate the so-called Tridentine Mass. The latter is certainly not the Mass of the Council of Trent in any real sense; it is the Mass of the 1570 Roman Missal of Pope Pius V. And, for the most part and certainly for the prepa-

---

[31] *Acta Synodalia* II, 2: 289; this was submitted to the conciliar Fathers on 8 Oct. 1963. The text had been in the schema of the Preparatory Commission on the Liturgy examined by the Central Preparatory Commission in March and April of 1962 (above, at footnote 4); see *Acta et Documenta*, Series II (Praeparatoria), II, 3: 103-104; III, 2: 29-30. As already mentioned, the need to relate any "offertory" of gifts to the eucharist itself, to be achieved in the anaphora, is a constant concern.

[32] The latest *editio typica* of the missal appeared in 1962, including the revised code of rubrics—prepared by the reform commission established by Pius XII in 1948 and approved by John XXIII in the motu proprio *Rubricarum instructum*, 25 July 1960. The exhaustive rubrical study by J. B. O'Connell, *The Celebration of Mass*, 3 vols. (Milwaukee: The Bruce Publishing Company, 1940-1941), was influenced by the progress of the liturgical movement and is clearly the best of its kind, but it reflects the almost absolute rigidity expected in modern times for the eucharistic celebration—either by the Apostolic See or by the teaching of rubricians.

ration of the gifts, that missal simply described the late medieval Roman Order of Mass. Indeed the offertory rite of 1570 is almost indistinguishable from the Order of Mass of Johannes Burchard published seven decades earlier—with the major exception that the post-Tridentine liturgical book omitted the presentation of gifts by the congregation.[33]

In the 1570 Order of Mass, as it still appeared in the Roman Missal of Pope John XXIII (of 1962), the offertory rite began with the presiding celebrant kissing the altar in greeting—after he had returned to the altar from the chair if he had been seated there for the sung profession of faith. He then faced the people to greet them, "Dominus vobiscum," while opening and rejoining his hands. The response was sung by a choir or said by a server. The priest faced the altar and again addressed the people, this time with the invitation to prayer, "Let us pray"—at a recited Mass extending and joining his hands as if in greeting but bowing his head to the altar cross.

Next the priest said the offertory antiphon appointed in the Mass formulary, quietly at a sung Mass, aloud at a recited Mass. If the liturgy was sung, the choir chanted the antiphon, sometimes augmented (or, in practice, even replaced) by a sung motet or the like. Otherwise there was silence during the rite.

The priest first took the paten or plate with the bread—either from the deacon or directly from the altar, having first removed the veil and pall from the vessels—and lifted it up in a gesture of offering. The bread for the communicants may or may not have been presented; more often than not the ministers, if they communicated, and the faithful in general would receive the eucharist from pre-consecrated elements—despite the sense and tradition and even the teaching of Benedict XIV, which was resurrected and reaffirmed by Pius XII.[34]

The priest raised his eyes to God, then lowered them, and offered the bread, saying inaudibly a prayer to God the Father. The prayer,

---

[33] Burchard's *Ordo Missae* (1502) is included in J. Wickham Legg, *Tracts on the Mass* (London, 1904), 119-174. Although the format and indeed language of the 1570 missal are very different, the substance of the rite is the same. One variant in Burchard's treatment is the *Missa sicca*, which does not appear in the 1570 missal, and the earlier *Ordo* is somewhat attentive to the role of the congregation, as the 1570 missal is not. For a recent summary see Burchard Neunheuser, "The Relation of Priest and Faithful in the Liturgies of Pius V and Paul VI" in *Roles in the Liturgical Assembly: the Twenty-Third Liturgical Conference Saint Serge*, tr. Matthew J. O'Connell (New York: Pueblo Publishing Company, 1981), 207-219, esp. 208-209.

[34] Pius XII, Encyclical Letter *Mediator Dei et hominum*, 20 Nov. 1947: *AAS* 38 (1947), 521-600; the pope bases no. 117 on no. 3 of the encyclical letter *Certiores effecti* of Benedict XIV (13 Nov. 1742).

expressive of an offering to God of the spotless, sacrificial host, illustrates the heart of the problem: an anticipation of the eucharistic prayer and the offering of the body and blood of Christ. It also illustrates the private and personal character of this series of silent prayers:

> Holy Father, almighty and ever-living God, accept this clean sacrificial offering [*hanc immaculation hostiam*] which I, your unworthy servant, make to you, my living and true God, for my numberless sins, transgressions and failings; I make it on behalf of those who are present here and of all faithful Christians, living and dead. May it bring salvation to them and to me, that we may attain everlasting life. Amen.[35]

After the prayer, the priest made the sign of the cross with the plate over the altar and placed the bread on the altar, that is, on the corporal (that had been spread by the deacon during the creed or by the priest himself at the beginning of a recited Mass).

The cup was prepared by the deacon and subdeacon, the later pouring the water after it had been blessed by the priest with the sign of the cross and a prayer said silently:

> You, O God, in a wonderful way created human nature in all its nobility, and you have still more marvellously renewed it. Grant then, that through the mystery of this water and wine we may have fellowship in the Godhead of Jesus Christ who humbled himself to share in our manhood and is your Son, our Lord, living and reigning with you in the unity of the Holy Spirit, one God, for ever and ever. Amen.

The prayer is a venerable Christmas collect somewhat artificially adapted to the context, to make the mixture of wine and water a symbol of the divine and human natures of Christ and of the *admirabile commercium*. In the absence of ordained ministers the priest himself prepared the cup in the same way but at the side of the altar.

In either case the priest took the cup and lifted it up in a gesture of offering, with his eyes raised throughout the saying of an-

---

[35] The English translations are taken from *Layman's Daily Missal, Prayer Book, and Ritual* (Baltimore: Helicon Press, 1962), one of the two or three better translations in use prior to the reform. A second was the elegant translation in *The Roman Missal*, edited by J. B. O'Connell and H.P.R. Finberg (London: Burns & Oates Ltd., 1949; New York: Sheed & Ward, 1950); another was *Daily Missal of the Mystical Body* (title on spine: *Maryknoll Missal*) (New York: P. J. Kenedy & Sons, 1957), the presidential prayers of which were later adopted for liturgical use in the dioceses of the United States until the ICEL translations became available.

On the development of these prayers and of parallel texts, see Paul Tirot, *Histoire des prières d'offertoire dans la liturgie romaine du VIIe au XVIe siècle*, Bibliotheca "Ephemerides Liturgicae," "Subsidia" 34 (Rome: CLV-Edizione Liturgiche, 1985).

other inaudible prayer—offering the cup of salvation. This time the
deacon assisted the priest in holding the cup and said the prayer
with him, while also raising his eyes:

> We offer you the cup of salvation, Lord [*Offerimus tibi, Domine, cali-
> cem salutaris*]; and we ask of your loving-kindness that it may come
> before your divine majesty with an acceptable fragrance for our sal-
> vation and that of the whole world. Amen.

Again, before placing the cup on the altar, the priest made the
sign of the cross with the vessel. (And the subdeacon removed the
plate and held it covered with a veil until after the eucharistic prayer.)

Next the priest joined his hands and placed them on the altar.
Bowing, he said inaudibly the verse *In spiritu humilitatis*,[36] which
is retained in the Order of Mass of 1969. Standing erect he then made
a gesture of extending and joining his hands preparatory to blessing, raising his eyes as well, and added a silent prayer of invocation, asking God the Sanctifier to come and bless "this sacrifice."
The words were accompanied by the sign of the cross made over
"the host and chalice" on the altar:

> Come, almighty and ever-living God, the Sanctifier: bless this sac-
> rifice set forth to the honor of your holy name.

There followed, in solemn or sung celebrations, the rite of incensation: the priest first blessing the incense with a prayer to God
through the intercession of Saint Michael; then incensing the offerings, cross, and altar, and returning the thurible to the deacon, each
action accompanied by a prayer; finally the deacon incensing the
priest and "others in order." The manner of each incensation was
minutely described; the details need not be recited. After the incensation (or after the blessing of the offerings), the priest washed
his hands at the side of the altar, reciting inaudibly seven psalm
verses with the doxology *Gloria Patri*.[37] A final silent prayer was added
by the priest, bowing at the center of the altar with his hands joined
and placed on it. Addressed to the Holy Trinity (unlike Roman
prayers), the text first declared that "we offer this offering" in memory
of the paschal mystery and in honor of the saints:

> Accept, Holy Trinity, this offering which we make to you [*hanc ob-
> lationem, quam tibi offerimus*] in memory of the passion, resurrection
> and ascension of Jesus Christ, our Lord: and in honor of blessed

---

[36] Adapted from the prayer of Azariah (Daniel 3:39-40). This is one of very many examples of the adaptation of biblical texts for liturgical use in the Roman rite.

[37] Psalm 26:6-12.

Mary, ever-virgin, of blessed John the Baptist, of the holy apostles Peter and Paul, of the saints whose relics are here [i.e., buried in the altar or under it], and of all the saints. May it bring honor to them and salvation to us; and may they whom we remember on earth plead for us in heaven. Through Christ our Lord. Amen.

Next the priest turned to face the people and made the ritual gesture of extending and joining his hands, while giving the invitation before the secret prayer; the invitation *Orate, fratres* was to be made in a slightly raised voice (so that those near the priest might hear and respond). The text of the invitation and the response made by the deacon and subdeacon, or by the server or those around the altar, is the one retained in the Order of Mass of 1969. In a low voice the priest added "Amen" to the response of the ministers.

The final element of the offertory rite was the variable secret prayer. On all but the greatest occasions it was augmented by additional prayers corresponding in number to the collects or opening prayers at the beginning of Mass. It was said without any additional invitation, with the priest extending his hands as during the collects, but inaudibly. Its final words were sung or said aloud, *Per omnia saecula saeculorum,* so that the response "Amen" might be given by the choir or the server. (This inevitably created the misapprehension by anyone paying attention that the concluding words of the secret prayer pertained to the preface of the canon which followed; the impression was reinforced by the printing of these few final words, in missals from 1570 to 1962, at the beginning of the several prefaces.)

As the Consilium undertook its reform of the Order of Mass, certain changes were made without much delay—as a part of the gradualism which characterized the reform during the decade 1964-1974. In the fall of 1964 three interim revisions were published which affected this part of Mass; they took effect 7 March 1965:

The celebrant is not to say privately those parts of the Proper sung or recited by the choir or the congregation [in this context, the offertory antiphon]. . . .

In solemn Mass the subdeacon does not hold the paten but leaves it on the altar.

In sung Masses the secret prayer or prayer over the gifts is sung and in other Masses recited aloud.[38]

---

[38] SC Rites, Instruction (first) *Inter Oecumenici,* 26 Sept. 1964, no. 48 a, d, e: AAS 56 (1964) 877-900; DOL 23, no. 340. The principle of the priest's not reciting texts sung by others was already well known, or should have been well known, from the revised rites of Holy Week (1951 and 1955).

Similarly in 1967, again as a part of the gradual reform, certain further changes were introduced into the offertory rite. The secret prayer or prayer over the gifts came under the rubric of a single presidential prayer to conclude the introductory rite (collect or opening prayer) and the communion rite (prayer after communion) – although the combination of two prayers with a single conclusion was still allowed. Ritually, the kissing of the altar at the beginning of the offertory was suppressed (among other repetitive kissings of the altar), and another minor simplification introduced:

> At the offertory, after offering the bread and wine, the celebrant places on the corporal the paten with host and the chalice, omitting the signs of the cross with paten and chalice.
>
> He leaves the paten, with the host on it, on the corporal both before and after the consecration.[39]

This second series of changes went into effect 29 June 1967. The two groups of modifications, slight as they seem, relieved the *coetus* of the Consilium which was revising the Order of Mass from resolving these matters separately. The norm that the presidential prayer over the gifts, which completes the rite of preparing the gifts and had long been called the secret prayer, should be sung or said aloud was of course a major clarification. Once for all it was made clear that, like the opening prayer and prayer after communion – and, to a certain extent, the concluding prayer after the general intercessions restored in 1964, this presidential prayer completes and even climaxes a structural area of the rite of Mass.

THE PREPARATION OF THE GIFTS IN THE SCHEMATA

1. *The Project of 1964: Specimen provisorium*

In the initial project of the Consilium,[40] the first element is the offertory song of the cantors and the people – the antiphon with psalm or some other chant. The allowance for an alternative of "some other chant" was in accord with the openness to diversity already found in the same 1964 project in the case of the entrance song.

During this song the priest goes from his chair to the altar, and the ministers bring the cup, wine, and water to the altar. The priest's

---

[39] SC Rites, Instruction *Tres abhinc annos*, 4 May 1967, nos. 4, 8, 9: AAS 59 (1967) 442-448; DOL 39, nos. 450, 454-455.

[40] For references to the successive schemata, see above, footnotes 8-10, 12-15.

reception of the gifts from the people is mentioned but is not described.

An overall rubric indicates that all the prayers said privately and silently by the priest may be omitted if he prefers to join in the singing of the people and the cantors.

A new text is given for the preparation of the cup by the priest, which takes place at once: "At the Lord's command, wine was made from water: may water mixed with wine become the wedding banquet."[41] The blessing of the water with the sign of the cross, from the old rite, is omitted.

Standing at the center of the altar, the priest first receives and then reverently holds the cup in his right hand and the vessel or plate with bread in his left (without any further or explicit gesture of offering). Before placing the vessels ceremonially upon the altar, he says a single formula: "As this bread was scattered over the mountains and was gathered into one and as wine from many vines flowed into one, so may your Church be gathered from the ends of the earth into your kingdom. Glory to you for ever."[42] A note adds that "the host of the celebrant" remains on the plate with the rest of the bread. A possible alternative is suggested for consideration: instead of holding the vessels in his hand while saying the prayer, the priest first places them on the altar ceremonially and then touches them reverently during the prayer.

Next the priest bows and says the prayer *In spiritu humilitatis* as in the 1570 rite. Then, if incense is used, he blesses it with a brief formula ("May this incense go up to you, Lord, and our prayer be directed like incense in your sight"). He incenses the gifts, making a single swing of the censer slowly and reverently around them; then he circles the entire altar and incenses it; finally he himself incenses the assembly.

The priest next washes his hands as customary (that is, at the side of the altar), but accompanies the act with a new and brief formula ("May we not go to prayer with a bad conscience. May the Lord pour clear water over us, and we shall be washed"). The prayer *Suscipe, sancta Trinitas* of the old rite is omitted.

---

[41] The symbolism of wine and water in reference to the human and divine natures of Christ and to the *admirabile commercium* is replaced in this text by the reference to the marriage at Cana—as a sign of the eschatological, messianic banquet, the supper of the Lamb. See SC Rites, Instruction *Eucharisticum mysterium*, 25 May 1967, no. 3 b: AAS 59 (1967), 541; DOL 179, no. 1232.

[42] Adapted and expanded from the Didachē, chapter 9.

Similarly, the invitation *Orate, fratres* and its response are omitted. Instead, the simpler invitation *Oremus* is indicated, along with the possibility of a "monition" by a commentator or the priest himself concerning the intention of the prayer over the gifts which is to follow—but without explicit mention of the pause for silent prayer (already specified for the opening prayer). Finally all stand and the priest completes the rite by singing or saying the prayer over the gifts; the people respond, "Amen." There is then a short pause before the beginning of the next part of the eucharistic liturgy, the solemn canon or anaphora.

This provisional outline of 1964 reflects agreement on several points. The traditional offertory song is the principal accompaniment (1) to the rites of bringing the gifts forward, preparing the altar and gifts, and solemnly placing them on the altar; (2) to the (possible) incensation of gifts, altar, and people by the priest; and (3) to the washing of his hands. A secondary accompaniment is the series of prayers said quietly or inaudibly by the priest; they are much abbreviated in the proposal and carefully avoid any "little canon" anticipating the eucharistic prayer and indeed any language of offering. Legitimate enough if properly understood, the dimension of offering must not be disproportionate. Just as significant is the fact that the saying of these prayers is left to the discretion of the priest, at least when there is singing in which he may join.

The only prayer said publicly is the prayer over the gifts, no longer said "secretly" of course. The place of this prayer in the structure, namely, as completing the rite, just as the collect completes the introductory rite, is enhanced by the brief pause before the dialogue with which the preface of the eucharistic prayer begins.

One would hardly say that this projected rite for the preparation of the gifts was perfect: several questions were left unresolved, and the private prayers of the priest, although remarkably improved over the medieval accretions, reflected a compromise of sorts. Nevertheless the rite described in 1964, called a *specimen provisorium*, respected the conciliar decree faithfully and offered important insights which will be taken up in the conclusions below.

2. *The First Missa normativa of 1965*

In the schema of the following year, the *Missa normativa* of fall 1965, the song to accompany the rites is first considered: either the customary antiphon with its psalm or some other chant again preferably from the psalms, that is suited to the character of the rite, the feast day, or the season. The ritual description begins with a relocation of the washing of the priest's hands: it takes place at the very beginning, while he is still seated at the chair, and no formula is appointed.

Only after the ministers have placed the book, corporal, and veiled cup on the altar does the priest go to the altar. The plate or plates or ciboria and the vessels with wine and water are brought forward by the people or the ministers. Other gifts not intended for the eucharist itself, if any, are received by the deacon (or the priest in the absence of a deacon) and taken by a minister to a suitable place near the altar.

The priest takes the plate with the bread from the deacon or minister, holds it in both hands raised a little above the altar, and says:

> As this bread was scattered and then gathered and made one,
> so may your Church be gathered into your kingdom.
> Glory to you, God, for ever.[43]

Then the priest places the plate on the altar. The deacon (or priest, in the absence of a deacon) next pours wine and a little water into the cup, without any formula. The priest receives the cup, holds it slightly raised above the altar with the help of the deacon, and says:

> Wisdom has built a house for herself,
> she has mixed her wine,
> she has set her table.
> Glory to you, God, for ever.[44]

He then places the cup on the altar.

The rest of the rite follows the 1964 project already described, including the prayer *In spiritu humilitatis* but with a few exceptions. The incense is not blessed, and only the gift (and not the altar and the people) are incensed. The reason is that the schema of 1965 has an incensation of altar and people by the priest at the beginning of the celebration and therefore avoids any duplication at this point. There is no mention of *Oremus* before the prayer over the gifts (sung or said in a clear voice), of the possible introductory "monition" by a commentator before the prayer over the gifts, or of the formal pause after that prayer before the anaphora is begun.

---

[43] Again, from chapter 9 of the Didachē, but different from the text in the 1964 document, in which the mention of the wine had been included.

[44] The text is adapted from Proverbs 9:1-2.

This is perhaps the simplest form of the rite in its several recensions from 1964 to 1969, with one notable exception, which is a change from the 1964 project: now the placing of the gifts of bread and wine on the altar is divided, and two distinct formulas, one for each element, are reintroduced.

Also notable is the placement of the washing of hands: it follows the ancient practice of a ceremonial washing of hands before prayer or before a sacred action, and thus comes at the very beginning of the liturgy of the eucharist—although it has appeared in various places in Western rites. Still another very appropriate possibility was considered, namely, just before the anaphora; the suggestion is attributed to an unnamed "most erudite expert" (Bernard Botte). The choice was influenced by the ancient practice still in use at pontifical Mass as described in the Ceremonial of Bishops of 1600[45] and, in principle, by the hope of showing the unity of the whole eucharistic rite.

In this 1965 schema the priest's role of taking the gifts and solemnly placing them on the altar, called a sacerdotal action, is kept carefully distinct (a) from the people's role, which is to bring forward the gifts for the eucharist along with other gifts, including money, and (b) from the ministerial role of the deacon: to receive the people's gifts, prepare the cup, and place the plate and cup in the priest's hands (i.e., not on the altar).

With regard to the texts, the intent was to remove anything referring to the offering of the body and blood of Christ, while changing the *elevatio* of the gifts into a solemn *depositio*. It was thought that the actions should not be without texts entirely, as in antiquity, but they are not to be proleptic, anticipating either the prayer over the gifts or, for that matter, the eucharistic canon.

3. *Schema of 1966 and the 1967 Synod of Bishops*

In the schema of May 1966, the Order of Mass of the preceding *Missa normativa* was reproduced, but in a different format, as already mentioned. Of much greater importance is what followed, namely, the many questions raised during the 1967 meeting of the Synod of Bishops. The reception of the whole Order of Mass by the synodal Fathers was mixed, but a considerable majority voted favorably: seventy-one absolutely *placet* and fifty-two *placet iuxta modum*

---

[45] *Caeremoniale Episcoporum*, Lib. I, cap. VII, no. 5.

—favorable but with a reservation or reservations; there were forty-three votes of *non placet* and four abstentions.[46]

An evaluation of the *modi* or reservations expressed bv the Fathers suggests some of the directions taken in the subsequent schemata—even though the individual *modi* came from a minority of participants in the Synod of Bishops.

In the part of the Order of Mass being considered, some favored the retention of three private formulas: for the bread and for the wine, as well as the prayer *In spiritu humilitatis*. The placement of the washing of the priest's hands at the beginning of the eucharistic rite was challenged as being disproportionately solemn. Despite the several complex problems associated with the invitation *Orate, fratres*—its restriction to the priest and ministers at sung Masses, the structural problem of a response which separates the invitation from the prayer over the gifts, the content of the texts, with concepts anticipatory of the anaphora—its retention was sought by some. Finally, a question had to be resolved concerning the mingling of water with the wine. The forced symbolism of the older text is evident: as already noted, it refers to the incarnation and the *admirabile commercium* rather than to a more pedestrian imitation of the Lord's Supper and thus, more profoundly, to the eucharistic meal, the messianic banquet.[47]

4. *Schema of December 1967*

In the next schema, several changes are introduced. To begin with, the washing of the priest's hands is relocated to its position after the incensation, with provision for an accompanying formula but without any text being specified. The same occurs for the preparation of the cup: space is left in the text for a formula to be added. An appendix to the schema proposes alternatives to the texts for the bread and wine given in the 1965-1966 schemata and Psalm 51:12

---

[46] Schema no. 258 (no. 42, *de Missali*), 21 Nov. 1967: "De Expensione Modorum Synodi" (13 pp.). This report contains questions from the *modi* of the synodal Fathers and also from Paul VI himself; it is not among the schemata with an *Ordo Missae*. Although the votes of individual synodal Fathers are not known, it may be presumed that the curial heads were among those who voted *non placet* or *placet iuxta modum*—thus making the proportion of the favorable votes of the elected Fathers from the other local Churches still larger and in a sense more representative of the Catholic episcopate. This representative role was intended as a function of the (ordinarily consultative) Synod of Bishops: see the expression *partes agens totius catholici Episcopatus* in Paul VI, Motu Proprio *Apostolica sollictudo*, 15 Sept. 1965: AAS 57 (1965), 776, and in Vatican Council II, Decree *Christus Dominus*, 28 Oct. 1965, no. 5, but not in canon 342 of the 1983 Code of Canon Law.

[47] See above, note 41.

for the washing of hands. In every case the private prayers are explicitly directed to be said inaudibly or silently, *secreto*, by the priest.

There are other changes as well. "Where the custom exists," the priest (the deacon is not mentioned) receives the gifts from the faithful at the entrance of the chancel. The deacon is not mentioned in the ceremonial holding of the cup, which is placed "on the corporal, at the right of the plate." The text *In spiritu humilitatis* is said inaudibly by the priest, bowed and with hands joined. Both the gifts and the altar, but not the people, are incensed. After the washing of his hands, the priest completes the rite by singing or saying—without any invitation, although *Oremus* is proposed in an appendix—the prayer over the gifts "at the center of the altar, with hands outstretched."

As should be evident, the modifications in the rite at this stage reflect some progress—or regression—toward the 1969 Order of Mass. The schema may be viewed as an interim step prior to the three schemata of the first five months of 1968.

5. *Schema of February 1968*

In the first schema of 1968, a strong affirmation was introduced concerning the bringing of the gifts to the altar:

> To foster and manifest the active participation of the faithful, it is desirable that, so far as possible, the faithful themselves—at least through some of their members—should make the presentation to the priest, by bringing forward what is necessary for the celebration of the eucharist and also bearing gifts to support the needs of the Church and the poor.

In later schemata this rubric is shortened but not changed in substance until it appears finally in the 1969 Order.

Three texts are given for the placing of the bread on the altar, two for the preparation of the cup, three for the placing of the cup on the altar, two for the washing of the priest's hands: Psalm 51:4 (the verse found in the 1969 Order of Mass) or Psalm 51:12. In each case the texts are alternatives and are to be said inaudibly, as is the verse *In spiritu humilitatis*, retained from the previous schemata.

At this stage of the process dissatisfaction with the private prayers of the priest remained strong. This is partly evident from the diversity of texts as compared with earlier efforts. Various possibilities had been envisioned from the first, in the hope of finding a poetic and symbolic manner of referring to the gifts without an explicit "offertory." Among the sources mentioned were the Ambrosian and Dominican rites, the prayers over the gifts in the old sacramentaries, or newly composed texts. It was clear, moreover, that the specialist, who might have preferred simply omitting all the prayer texts except the presidential prayer over the gifts, sought to have the "offertory prayers," whatever their text, made a matter of freedom, *pro opportunitate*. At one point, it was suggested that the private prayers be obligatory for Mass *sine populo*, optional for the *Missa normativa*; this proposed compromise ultimately failed, as will be seen below.

6. *Schema of March 1968*

In the next schema of 1968, the changes introduced reflect in part the intervention of Pope Paul VI referred to above. In particular, he expressed concern that the participation of the faithful should be expressed not only by bringing forward the gifts but by words as well—not in Latin, not silently, not reserved to the priest, but aloud. These words should also speak of the human work which is inserted into the holy eucharist through the elements of bread and wine.[48]

The two formulas for the bread and cup found in the March 1968 schema, which differ only slightly from those now familiar from the 1969 Order of Mass (below), were composed to include several elements: the bounty of God, from whom all good things come; the work of earth, which gives fruit in season; the industry and labor of humankind; the eucharist for the preparation of which the gifts are brought forward by the faithful. On the other hand, every misconception is to be avoided: it is not a sacrifice of bread and wine or an offering of the body and blood of Christ or a consecratory epiclesis. The two March 1968 texts lack the clause *quem [quod] tibi offerimus* which appears in the May 1968 schema below and in the definitive text of 1969—translated as "to offer" in English. This is the slight but meaningful difference that was introduced next.

Most significant from a structural point of view, a new direction is given concerning the two prayers: if there is no song to accompany the rite, they are regularly to be said aloud (despite the strong negative judgment of the revisers), and the people are to respond with an acclamation after each: "Blessed be God for ever."

---

[48] Schema no. 281 (no. 47, *de Missali*) addendum (I). 23 Apr. 1968: "Relatio ad Patres 'Consilii'" (6 pp.); (Addendum II, 29 Apr. 1968): "Relatio Subcommissionis Peculiaris De Ordine Missae" (7 pp.).

The schema also provides a brief text for the preparation of the cup, to be said inaudibly by the deacon (or by the priest in the absence of a deacon); it is the one found in the promulgated Order of Mass in 1969: "By the mystery of this water and wine may we come to share in the divinity of Christ, who humbled himself to share in our humanity."

As is apparent, the symbolism of the *admirabile commercium* is restored, but without the full prayer text of the 1570 rite. In this schema, too, Psalm 51:4 ("Lord, wash away my iniquity; cleanse me from my sin") is the only text given to accompany the washing of the priest's hands.

The chief ritual change in this schema is the direction that, after the priest incenses the gifts and the altar, the deacon or a minister incenses the people.

7. Schema of May 1968

The schema of May 1968 resolved some of the questions still open. As already mentioned, a definitive version of the prayers for the bread and the cup refers directly to offering—included but nuanced in the English translation:

> Blessed are you, Lord, God of all creation.
> Through your goodness we have this bread to offer,
> which earth has given and human hands have made.
> It will become for us the bread of life.
>   Blessed be God for ever.
>
> Blessed are you, Lord, God of all creation.
> Through your goodness we have this wine to offer,
> fruit of the vine and work of human hands.
> It will become our spiritual drink.
>   Blessed be God for ever.[49]

This time, however, there is a more restrictive direction: (1) The two formulas are to be said *inaudibly* (that is, ordinarily, whether there is song or not). (2) If there is no song, they *may* be said aloud

---

[49] The effect of the insertion of the verb *offerimus* in both texts, with its reintroduction of a perhaps excessive emphasis upon offering, was deliberately corrected in some translations by the use of words meaning "present" or "bring." This is commented upon by Robert Cabie, "The Eucharist," vol. II of *The Church at Prayer,* Aimé Georges Martimort, ed. (Collegeville, Minn.: The Liturgical Press, 1986), 204, footnote 37: "French: 'Nous te presentons'; Italian: 'ti presentiamo'; Spanish: 'te presentamos'; German: 'wir bringen vor dein Angesicht.' –The Order of Mass is not in full agreement with the thrust of the whole reform; thus it speaks of the 'offertory song' (for which there are no longer any set texts in the Mass formularies)."

(without response). (3) If they are said aloud, the acclamation of the people *may* be added.

It is of course this compromise that prevailed. In the above description, emphasis has been added to show the preferences indicated in the schema (and the 1969 *Ordo*) and also the optional nature of both the recitation aloud and, even then, of the congregation's response. This has been spelled out because of the very different way in which the directions of the promulgated rite have been carried out in common practice at Masses without song.

By way of summary of the 1967-1968 schemata (nos. 4-7, above), the ritual developments of the rite for the preparation of the gifts were principally in the location of the washing of hands; the participation of the people in bringing forward the elements for the eucharist and other gifts—which was refined but remain substantially intact; and the incensation, changed from an incensation of gifts and people by the priest to an incensation of gifts and altar, to which was finally added the incensation of the people by the deacon or, in the absence of a deacon, by a minister.

Textually, the two basic elements were unchanged, namely, the song—either the antiphon with psalm or some other chant—and the public prayer over the gifts. The private prayers were substantially changed and increased in number; the major innovation, in the absence of song during the rite, was the option of saying the formulas for the bread and the cup aloud, and the further option of a congregational acclamation in such a case.

8. *The Order of Mass of Pope Paul VI*

With the promulgation of the Order of Mass in 1969, the five-year process was completed. It remains only to note one change from the May 1968 schema, aside from a slight rephrasing of the rubrics. It is the restoration of the invitation *Orate, fratres* and full response before the prayer over the gifts from the 1570 Order of Mass. Throughout the development of the revised Order as reflected in the several schemata, either *Oremus* or no invitation at all had been the rule.

Conclusions to this review may take two forms. The first is a summary evaluation: whether the movement from the 1964 provisional project to the promulgated rite of 1969 was successful, unsuccessful, or relatively successful. The second is a series of idealistic reflections or recommendations: where the Roman Order of Mass—

no longer static after four centuries of nearly absolute rigidity—should now go, preferably as the continuing basic exemplar for culturally and regionally adaptable rites in the eucharistic celebration.

Conclusion I — An Evaluation

If the tests of The Constitution on the Liturgy, article 50, are applied—clarity, simplicity, discard of weaker elements, restoration of sounder elements—there was an overall falling off from 1964 to 1969, a dilution of an original project that was in closer harmony with the conciliar mandate. To put it differently, the initial plan while imperfect might have been a better point of departure for possible elaboration in actual celebrations and for cultural adaptation.

It is easy to enumerate the complexities which replaced simplicity and to suggest that the preparation of the gifts has assumed the very disproportionate emphasis that—aside from the participation of the people—was initially reduced. The weaknesses are several: retention of private prayers (improved as they are) said by the presiding celebrant and even said aloud, with a resultant increase of verbalization and the diminution of the prayer over the gifts; restoration not of older elements which might have provided sound precedents but rather of some part of the 1570 rite first discarded and then revived—like the *Orate, fratres* and response; restoration, along the same lines, of a complex rite of incensation that is duplicative, again instead of the clearer patterns initially planned; and a curious "little canon" even though the prayers for the bread and wine are not proleptic if they are precisely understood. It is hard to judge whether these evident weaknesses have made the rite less comprehensible to the assembly, but it is likely.

Nevertheless any comparison of the 1969 rite with that of 1570 (and 1963) suggests that the ultimate Order of Mass is relatively successful in the rite for the preparation of the gifts. An active if modest participation by the assembly in bringing forward the gift for the eucharist, along with other gifts of Christian charity; the enhancement of the prayer over the gifts—prescinding from the questions that can be raised about the numerous texts of this prayer; an elimination or reduction of minor and almost meaningless ceremonial gestures by the priest; the suppression of the formal offering gestures as if the bread and wine themselves were the Lord's body and blood—all these are sound changes in the direction of consistency and at least partial simplification.

A caveat must be added to this mildly negative evaluation, namely, that from 1964 to 1969 the simplicity of the rite gave way to needless complexity. There are schools of thought and in fact whole Christian rites which revel in enrichment and elaboration, duplication and amplification. The conciliar mandate of noble simplicity may seem incompatible with such religious and liturgical taste and sensibility. Yet the dichotomy is unreal: the ideal of a quasi-universal Roman rite makes sense only if it is extremely simple, even bare, but still completely open and susceptible to the very solemnity and enlargement that may be sought—preserving only the main lines of a comprehensible structure, a kind of framework of celebration.

CONCLUSION II – THE (UNLIKELY) FUTURE

It would be tempting to canonize the first proposal of 1964, if only because it was done in the immediate wake of the conciliar decree. Hindsight of two decades since the Order of Mass was promulgated permits a little greater sophistication. Some elements of the rite can be better analyzed in the light of what happened to the Order of Mass between 1964 and 1969 and indeed from 1969 to the present, as it has been celebrated in the living communities of the Church. Several possibilities may be discussed, unlikely as they appear in today's regressive and repressive climate.

1. Song

A psalm or hymn or other song is appropriate enough to accompany the preparation of the gifts, which involves the preparation of the altar (a small matter, although the spreading of the table cloth or corporal retains its sense), the presentation of the elements by the assembly, the preparation of the cup, and the actual taking of the gifts for the eucharist and placing them on the altar by the presiding priest. The insight that the president of the assembly should be free to join in this song should not be overlooked. Nor should the alternative of silence (i.e., without song) be entirely ruled out if it can support the several ritual acts leading up to the anaphora—provided that this silence is observed and shared by the priest also until the prayer over the gifts. Still another possibility is instrumental music to accompany the rite.

There is a pragmatic difficulty. If the private prayers are retained (below), it is almost inevitable that they will be said aloud by some priests and on some occasions. Already they have achieved an emphasis all out of proportion to their significance – and have complicated and weakened a fairly simple rite.

2. *Washing of Hands*

The proposal to locate the washing of the priest's hands at the chair and at the very beginning of the rite before the gifts of the assembly are brought forward was a tentative one. It is unfortunate that it was not carried over into general use, at least trial use. Again, the sign of peace as an additional or alternative ritual at the end of the liturgy of the word and at the beginning of the eucharistic liturgy has its own rationale[50] but is beyond the scope of this paper.

Possibly the symbolic washing before the eucharist begins – or even immediately before the preface of the anaphora – might have saved it from recent neglect and even disrepute. Inevitably it is now seen as a rite of small meaning, a needless cleansing after placing the gifts on the altar or incensing them. Instead the substantive tradition of the sign is as a symbol of ritual cleansing and preparation before the presiding minister enters upon the holy work of the eucharistic liturgy. At least the original recommendation of a washing of hands at the beginning is worthy of trial; if it is not successful in conveying some religious significance, there is not much reason to retain the washing at all.

3. *Procession of Gifts*

There seems now to be little danger of turning the representative carrying forward of the elements for the eucharist to be received by the ministers, along with gifts for the poor and other Church needs, into an autonomous sacrifice, a eucharist distinct from that of Christ, or a largely congregational rite that wrongly serves to exclude the lay faithful from the "clerical" eucharist that follows.

All these notions have served in the past to create a theological and liturgical wariness about expansive offertory processions. In general, this element of the restoration seems to have succeeded, provided always that (1) the bread and wine and water are indeed those to be used in the celebration and, after the eucharistic prayer, shared in communion of the body and blood of Christ[51] and (2) the other gifts of money and in kind are closely associated with, directed to,

---

[50] Including Matthew 5:23-24.
[51] GIRM, no. 283: DOL 208, no. 1673.

but distinct from, the eucharist of the Lord. None of this is achieved by a token display which does not manifest the sharing of the whole assembly in the eucharist.[52]

4. *Preparation of the Gifts*

Here the phrase is used more strictly of the actual preparation of the cup by the deacon (or by the priest in the absence of a deacon, although there is nothing to prevent an acolyte or other server from doing this). Whatever symbolism has been attached to the mingling of water with the wine, the retention of the rite is better understood as a traditional usage, whether in imitation of the Lord's Supper or not. The text now in use is as inappropriate an allegorism as was the prayer of the 1570 rite from which it is derived. To omit it completely was a better instinct.

Certainly there is no desire to elaborate further the preparation of the cup in the basic Roman rite which the Order of Mass is designed to describe. Whether done by the deacon or another minister or by the priest himself, it can best be relegated to the side table or credenza. As an alternative and simpler possibility, the preparation of the cup beforehand by the members of the assembly who bring the elements forward is also worth considering.

5. *Private Prayers of Priest (and Deacon)*

Perhaps the happiest resolution of this whole question would be to revert to one of the earlier norms: that the inaudible prayers be left optional, *pro opportunitate* – or simply suppressed entirely.

This is not idle iconoclasm. The fact is that the several prayers are a needless complication and prevent the priest, for example, from joining in the common singing of a psalm, hymn, or other song. Early in the process of reform, the implementing instruction of 1964 had established the principle that the priest might sing the ordinary parts of the Mass together with the people or choir, a principle equally valid for what were formerly called the proper parts, such as the song during the preparation of the gifts. Once for all, an option opened up for the priest to join in this singing might be an answer to the still unsatisfactory selection of prayers said inaudibly (or even aloud) by him.

---

[52] On this and other questions associated with the rite in concrete pastoral circumstances, see Michael H. Marchal, "A Consideration of the Offering in American Christian Liturgy," *Worship* 63 (1989), 42-47.

6. *Placing of the Gifts upon the Altar*

One great concern during the revision process, to distinguish the presentation and preparation of the gifts from their ceremonial *depositio* on the altar by the presiding priest, has been lost sight of. It is now common for a deacon or other minister to place the plate and cup or plates or ciboria and cups on the altar—from which, in a diluted and weakened ritual act, the priest lifts them (sometimes in a confusing offertory elevation), only to replace them on the altar.

This raises the other question of a single act of placing both bread and wine on the altar together instead of separate acts for each element, as the 1969 Order of Mass now directs.

Much can be said for and against placing both bread and wine on the altar table in a single act. It certainly weakens the distinction of the separate elements and the sign value evident both in the institutional narrative of the eucharistic prayer (and indeed in the several biblical accounts of the Supper) and in the giving of communion under both (separate) kinds. It might even enforce the aberration of referring to the eucharist under one kind (either species) as the body and blood of Christ, something the liturgical books carefully avoid. This is a kind of excess of the doctrine of concomitance, obscuring the very signs chosen in the Lord's institution.

On the other hand, and perhaps convincingly, simplification in itself may remain desirable. The single act of placing both bread and wine on the altar table together might help to keep this area of the eucharistic rite in proper, subordinate, and preliminary proportions. It would avoid, once for all, the anomalous placing of the gifts on the altar by deacon, minister, or priest himself before the ritual *depositio*. Whatever the meaning of that rite, it needs to be clear, certain, and simple.

7. *The Prayers for the Bread and for the Cup*

Although the simpler and neater solution would be to suppress the two prayers entirely and to unite the ritual acts as just considered, the two texts of the Order of Mass deserve their own evaluation.

In one way these two texts, each in the style of a berakah, are inspired. They are well composed (and well translated into English) and satisfy the exacting demands made for their content, as described above. Their thought and language enrich the Roman rite. The negative considerations, however, are serious and countervailing.

First, they introduce a new structure: they are spoken or recited rather than sung, a feature not noticeable when the prayer over the gifts is itelf spoken—but this only demonstrates how complex the structure has become with its different kinds of public prayer texts within a few moments of the liturgy. The thought of the variable prayer over the gifts is not always easy to explain, but at least it fits neatly into a clear and recognizable structure.

Next, the two prayers—they are blessings of God followed by petitions—interject a different style. This is not the place to consider the possibility of an overtly berakah style for the eucharistic prayer itself; it may be a legitimate alternative to what we have, and we surely need new anaphoras for the Sunday eucharist. But the intrusion of two brief examples of this style, with a Roman collect-style prayer to follow, is hardly a simple and comprehensible combination. And, while the content of the prayers may be unexceptionable, the dense ideas deserve expansion—possibly by way of incorporaton, in one celebration or another, into occasional variable prayers over the gifts.

8. *Incensation*

First, there is the question of the very inclusion of a rite of incensation. Its appropriateness, however, quite apart from traditional religious usage, should be evident even from the secular employment of burning incense, sweet smelling perfumes, flowers, even so mundane an example as room fresheners. Properly, it remains in the Order of Mass as an optional element of enhancement and solemnization—understandable in most cultures.

In this the schema of 1965 had an inspired proposal subsequently lost. Given that there should be an initial salutation of the altar as a symbol of Christ and as the table of sacrifice, it was proposed that the priest first greet the altar with a kiss or other conventional sign and then himself incense both the altar and the assembly. The latter remains as a valuable insight, corresponding, for example, to the Byzantine usage in which the presiding minister honors the Christian community with this ritual gesture.

In turn, this proposal of an initial incensation of altar and people by the priest himself suggested a reasonable limitation of the later incensation to the gifts themselves. This avoids repetition or duplication and provides a simpler sign, drawing attention to the gifts and honoring, even hallowing them. In the practical order it suppresses the lengthy and often awkward incensation of a whole series of individuals that is still sometimes seen—and sometimes comes into conflict with the prayer over the gifts or even the eucharistic prayer.

9. *Invitation to Prayer*

From a structural viewpoint, it is desirable that the prayer over the gifts, the concluding and desirably only expression of the rite in words, should follow the pattern of the other short presidential prayers, namely, with the invitation "Let us pray" followed by a brief but genuine period of silent prayer.

While there is nothing to prevent the free expansion of the invitation—in order better to focus, specify, and structure the period of silence—the continued use of the traditional *Orate, fratres* has its own problems of content and of the formal, lengthy response. The latter only serves, at present, to obscure the desirable relationship of the invitation to the prayer over the gifts.[53] In the five-year process seen in the several schemata, this invitation was an almost eleventh-hour addition or restoration.

At the same time the parallel with the opening prayer and the prayer after communion suggests strongly that there be a genuine pause in silence. It is clearly different (1) from the silence which may accompany the whole rite of preparation of gifts if there is no song and (2) from the silence which is a possible bridge between the prayer over the gifts and the eucharistic prayer (below).

10. *Prayer over the Gifts*

Various considerations dictate whether this is sung or only said solemnly. The structural parallels dictate that the assembly stand (at the invitation to prayer) so that the character of the presidential

---

[53] Partial solutions to the problem are found in the French and German missals, more adventurous than the English language sacramentaries.

Missel romain (Paris, 1977) has only a shortened version of the invitation: "Let us pray together at the moment of offering the sacrifice of the whole Church," but it retains a response, again in a shortened version: "For the glory of God and the salvation of the world."

Messbuch (Einsiedeln und Köln, Germany: Benziger, 1975) gives three possibilities, preferring either Form A or Form B of the invitation (or a variant of these), without response but with a short period of silence before the prayer over the gifts. Form A: "Let us pray to God, the all-powerful Father, that he may receive the gifts of the Church for his loving praise and the salvation of the whole world." Form B: "Let us pray." Form C, in third place, is a literal translation of the Latin invitation and response, as is found in English language sacramentaries.

The Italian sacramentary, *Messale romano* (Vatican City, 1983) provides four variants of the invitation, but includes the full response in every case.

prayer will be evident. This is not the place to consider either the content of the existing prayers over the gifts or the norms and opportunities for selection of these texts.

11. *Silence before the Eucharistic Prayer*

A small matter found in the 1964 project deserves to be revived, namely, a long enough pause between the prayer over the gifts and the opening dialogue of the preface of the eucharistic prayer to separate the first and second parts of the liturgy of the eucharist clearly and effectively. One alternative, that the priest bow to the assembly and that the assembly bows in response, may smack of archeologism—even though it would break up the two actions.[54]

If in the 1570 Order of Mass it appeared that the concluding words of the secret prayer were somehow the first words of the preface, ordinary practice of the 1969 Order seems not yet to have caught up with the distinction or transition. For example, while it may not be desirable for concelebrating priests to crowd around the altar, certainly their movement before or during the prayer over the gifts — or, worse, after the Sanctus—blurs the transition and weakens the unity of the eucharistic prayer.[55]

The General Instruction of the Roman Missal offers the possibility of a brief introduction to the eucharistic prayer by the priest at this point.[56] This is a legitimate occasion for a brief liturgical "monition," but it runs the danger of didacticism and excessive verbalization. A distinct moment of silence (after the priest has found the preface of the eucharistic prayer in *The Roman Missal* [*Sacramentary*]) might be a formal part of the rite, an opportunity for recollection, and and a separation of the rite of the preparation of the gifts from the more important anaphora that follows.

---

[54] Louis Bouyer, *Liturgical Piety*, Liturgical Studies I (Notre Dame, Ind. University of Notre Dame Press, 1955), p. 124, speaks of "that bow of acquiescence which is still prescribed in all Christian rites." The bow of the presiding celebrant at *Gratias agamus . . .* at the beginning of the eucharistic prayer and at *gratias agens* before the institution narrative have disappeared in the revised Order of Mass. On the contemporary question of bows and other gestures of priest and people, see Frederick R. McManus, *Liturgical Participation: An Ongoing Assessment* (Washington: The Pastoral Press, 1988), 14-18.

[55] GIRM, no. 167 [DOL 208, no. 1557] on this point could perhaps be more clearly stated, but if there is movement by the concelebrating presbyters it should follow the prayer over the gifts and should be completed before the presiding celebrant begins the dialogue of the eucharistic prayer.

[56] GIRM, no. 11: DOL 208, no. 1401.

Creative and cultural adaptation of the Order of Mass, left open and in fact invited by the missal of Paul VI, has seemed defunct since 1969, at least in the developed countries.[57] Perhaps two decades of celebration now suggest not only that kind of development but also a reworking of the basic (and then adaptable) Roman Order itself.

---

[57] GIRM, no. 6 [DOL 208, no. 1396]: "The purpose of this Instruction is to give general guidelines for planning the eucharistic celebration properly and to set forth rules for arranging the individual forms of celebration. In accord with the Constitution on the Liturgy (SC, art. 37-40), each conference of bishops has the power to lay down norms for its own territory that are suited to the traditions and character of peoples, regions, and various communities." On 5 Sept. 1970 the Congregation for Divine Worship issued an instruction, *Liturgicae instaurationes* [AAS 62 (1970), 692-704; DOL 52, no. 530], which in no. 12 practically negated the General Instruction's openness to adaptation and development.

CONCELEBRATION REVISITED
Gilbert Ostdiek, O.F.M.

INTRODUCTION

The Second Vatican Council, gathered in public session on 4 December 1963, gave its definitive approval to the Constitution on the Liturgy (*Sacrosanctum Concilium*). Paragraph 57 of that constitution, noting that "Concelebration, which aptly expresses the unity of the priesthood, has continued to this day as a practice in the Church of both East and West,"[1] extended the use of concelebration in the Roman Rite. The next paragraph directed that a new rite of concelebration be drawn up. Within a few months the new rite had been prepared and was ready for experimental use. The recollections of a member of one of the monastic communities entrusted with that experimentation pithily sum up this early experience of the concelebrated Mass.

> I remember that the first month or so there was euphoria. Everybody thought, "This solves all problems." By the second month there was a sort of subterranean murmur. By the third month the murmuring had broken out into the open and it became clear that this was not the solution. If the ordained concelebrants outnumbered the non-ordained monks, then it was worse than a Pontifical Mass![2]

In retrospect, the cameo experience thus described seems almost a prophetic anticipation of the twenty-five years of experience with concelebration that were to follow in the Church at large. Initial euphoria has given way to a murmuring that is now finding more frequent expression.[3] The questions being voiced cover a wide range

---

[1] Vatican Council II, Constitution on the Liturgy *Sacrosanctum Concilium* [hereafter, SC], 4 Dec. 1963, art. 57: ICEL, *Documents on the Liturgy, 1963-1979: Conciliar, Papal, and Curial Texts* [hereafter, DOL] (Collegeville, Minn.: The Liturgical Press, 1982) 1, no. 57.

[2] As described by Godfrey Diekmann, O.S.B., in an interview with H. Kathleen Hughes, R.S.C.J., in the spring of 1987.

[3] Traces of that reaction are recorded in: John F. Baldovin, "Concelebration: A Problem of Symbolic Roles in the Church," *Worship* 59 (1985), 32-47; Eligius Dekkers, "Concelebration — Limitations of Current Practice," *Doctrine and Life* 22 (1972), 190-202; Robert Taft, "Ex Oriente Lux? Some Reflections on Eucharistic Concelebration," *Worship* 54 (1980), 308-325.

of issues, from ritual aesthetics to theology to stipends. The question that seems most troubling concerns the central symbolism of the rite. Has the restored rite of concelebration so succeeded in symbolizing priestly unity, as the Council had hoped, that it also symbolizes, and even effects, a disunity in the community? Elisabeth Schüssler Fiorenza is not alone in alerting us to the problem of "festive 'con-celebrations' as the ritual manifestation of male bonding and male power."[4] The problem she names from a feminist perspective is also voiced by many lay people and by non-ordained members of religious communities. To highlight the source of their discomfort one only need rephrase her words to read "*clerical* bonding and *clerical* power."

This essay, then, will focus on two related issues: the shape of the rite and the unity it symbolizes. The first part of the essay will trace the history of the restoration of the rite of concelebration to put the issues within context. The second section will reflect on those issues in the light of the experience of the revised rite which we have accumulated over the past twenty-five years.[5]

RETRACING THE HISTORY

The history of the Vatican II renewal of the rite of concelebration can be told under four headings: the preconciliar background, the preparations for the Council, the debates and decisions during the Council, and the postconciliar implementation.

Preconciliar Background

The topic of concelebration, which occasioned one of the first great debates on the Council floor when Vatican II took up the schema on the liturgy, did not appear suddenly. It was in the 1920's and 1930's that the debate which was to reach the Council chambers got underway.[6] During those two decades several studies appeared

---

    [4] Elisabeth Schüssler-Fiorenza, "Tablesharing and the Celebration of the Eucharist," in David Power and Mary Collins, eds., *Can We Always Celebrate the Eucharist?*, Concilium 152 (New York: Seabury, 1982), 4.

    [5] In preparing this essay I have relied greatly on insights gained from my colleagues in the department of word and worship at Catholic Theological Union during a colloquium on concelebration held in Apr. 1987. Participants included: Kathleen Cannon, O.P., Edward Foley, O.F.M. Cap., John Huels, O.S.M., and H. Kathleen Hughes, R.S.C.J., who also graciously lent me a copy of her unpublished study on concelebration. Finally, comments offered by Frederick McManus have been of great help in clarifying the text of this article.

    [6] For a summary of these origins see Hendrik Manders, C.SS.R. "Concelebration," in Johannes Wagner, ed., *The Church and the Liturgy*, Concilium 2 (Glen Rock, N.J.: Paulist Press, 1965), 136-139.

which dealt with concelebration from the viewpoint of the liturgical movement and the history of Eastern liturgy.[7] These studies initiated a first round of discussion among scholars about the practice and meaning of concelebration.

A number of additional factors had come together to make concelebration a topic of widespread concern during the decades immediately before Vatican II. The first of these was a growing popular acceptance of the ideal, fostered by the liturgical movement, of a more communitarian liturgy. Though this communitarian impulse focused primarily on the participation of the congregation in the liturgy,[8] it was also being felt by the clergy. A second factor was the principle, strengthened under the pontificate of Pope Pius IX and affirmed by his own personal practice, that "every good priest celebrates the Eucharist every day, with the exception of those two or three days during Holy Week when . . . it is forbidden by the rubrics."[9] Thus, on the eve of the Council there was a firmly established expectation that every priest would celebrate daily even if there was no congregation in attendance. The third factor was the buildup of a far more numerous clergy who were less tied to the daily worship needs of a local congregation. Religious communities with large numbers of priests had to make daily provisions for multiple private celebrations. The same was true for the increasingly larger and more frequent gatherings of priests for retreats, study days, pilgrimages, etc. In those situations the expectation that all priests would individually celebrate their daily Mass created serious practical difficulties, not the least of which was a scandalous haste, and brought the principle of daily celebration into sharp conflict with the growing liturgical sensitivity to the communal character of the celebration.

Since the practice of concelebration was severely restricted under long-standing policies codified in canon 803 of the 1917 *Codex*

---

[7] Lambert Beauduin, "Concélébration eucharistique," *Questions liturgiques et paroissiales* 7 (1922), 275-285; P. De Meester, "De concelebratione in Ecclesia Orientali, praesertim secundum ritum byzantinum," *Ephemerides Liturgicae* 37 (1923), 101-110, 145-154, 196-201; J. M. Hanssens, "De concelebratione eucharistica," *Periodica* 16 (1927), 143-154, 181-210; 17 (1928), 93-127; 21 (1932), 193-219.

[8] See Pius XII, *Mediator Dei*, nos. 80-111: *Acta Apostolicae Sedis* [hereafter, AAS] 39 (1947), 552-562.

[9] Angelus Haussling, "Motives for Frequency of the Eucharist," in David Power and Mary Collins, eds., *Can We Always Celebrate the Eucharist?*, Concilium 152 (New York: Seabury, 1982), 26. In a footnote Haussling suggests that the theology underlying this practice reached a high point in the request/command of Pius XII to all priests to binate on Passion Sunday, 2 Apr. 1949, the day of his golden jubilee. See the Apostolic Exhortation *Conflictatio bonorum* 11 Feb. 1949: AAS 41 (1949), 58-61.

Iuris Canonici, there were attempts to find other ways to alleviate this situation. One solution was to synchronize the individual Masses of a number of priests.[10] Another solution was a communal Mass, the *messe communautaire*, in which one priest celebrated and the others assisted in alb and stole in the manner of the traditional Holy Thursday practice.

At the same time, the earlier, more contained discussion became a widespread debate about the history, theology, and liturgical practice of concelebration. For example, in 1953 an entire issue of *La Maison-Dieu* was devoted to the question of concelebration,[11] and concelebration was one of two major agenda items for the fourth international study meeting held at Louvain in September 1954,[12] one of a series of such meetings between 1951 and 1960 which brought together liturgical scholars and pastoral liturgists, with representatives from Rome often in attendance, to study and discuss issues in the reform of the liturgy.[13] In forums such as these discussion swirled around a number of questions.[14] What is the relative value of private celebration and communal celebration? Which is more beneficial to the spiritual life of the priest? Can a priest who assists silently at a *messe communautaire* be said to concelebrate? Or does valid concelebration require all priests to recite the eucharistic prayer together, especially the words of consecration? What light can liturgical history shed on the issue? Were instances of non-verbal participation found in liturgical history only "ceremonial" concelebration or were they truly "sacramental" concelebration, and can they serve as a precedent?

The details of that discussion need not be rehearsed here. For our purposes it suffices to highlight one significant shift that took place in regard to the meaning of concelebration. In the discussion several decades earlier, as Manders notes,[15] concelebration was seen to express at one and the same time the communal character of the liturgy, the hierarchical nature of the Church, and the unity of the

---

[10] A[imon-] M[arie] R[oguet], "Les messes synchronisées," *La Maison-Dieu* 35 (1953), 76-78.

[11] *La Maison-Dieu* 35 (1953), 3-78.

[12] For a summary report see Godfrey Diekmann, O.S.B., "Louvain and Versailles," *Worship* 28 (1953-1954), 540-543.

[13] See J. P. Jossua and Yves Congar, O.P., eds., *La Liturgie après Vatican II. Bilans, Études, Prospective,* Unam Sanctam 66 (Paris: du Cerf 1967), 113-114; Josef A. Jungmann, "Constitution on the Sacred Liturgy," in Hans Vorgrimler, ed., *Commentary on the Documents of Vatican II*, vol. I (New York: Herder and Herder, 1967), 2.

[14] For an overview of the discussion, see Manders, "Concelebration," 135-151; Katherine McGowan, *Concelebration: Sign of Unity of the Church* (New York: Herder and Herder, 1964), 72-109.

[15] Manders, "Concelebration," 138.

Church. In keeping with the ancient rule of "one community, one table, one Eucharist,"[16] the unity of the ordained ministry was never separated from the unity of the Church. Both were integral to the unity symbolized by the eucharist.

In the decades immediately before the Council, the new pastoral needs noted above lent great support and urgency to that earlier discussion. But under the impact of the new pastoral solutions, the discussion about the meaning of concelebration now took a subtle turn. Acting in consort in synchronized Masses or assisting together in the communal Mass, priests who had been accustomed to celebrating in isolation now experienced solidarity among themselves in a new and powerful way. The experience of the *messe communautaire*, Manders suggests, highlighted the unity of the priesthood itself at the expense of the more important understanding that the celebration unifies the whole community. By extension, the unity of the priesthood became the ideal for concelebration as well. And so, paradoxically, "in the middle of a period in which the liturgy was going to be de-clericalized, there arose a tendency toward clericalization of concelebration."[17]

In the midst of these discussions there were several papal and curial interventions which fixed boundaries that were to carry over into the conciliar period. In his encyclical *Mediator Dei*, issued in 1947 in support of the central agenda of the liturgical movement, especially its call for the presence and active participation of the faithful, Pope Pius XII rejected the position of those who argued against private celebration on the basis of the social character of the eucharist. Rather, he affirmed, even in that case the essentially public and social character of the eucharist is maintained by the fact that the priest offers it in the name of Christ and the faithful.[18] By these words he effectively insured the survival of private celebration for the immediate future. In an address given to cardinals and bishops several years later, he returned to the issue of communal versus private celebration, adding a refinement to the effect that priests assisting at Mass do not represent Christ and are therefore to be compared to lay persons attending Mass.[19] In his 1956 address to participants in the Assisi International Congress on Pastoral Liturgy, he adopted the current distinction between "ceremonial" and "sacramental" con-

[16] For references to patristic writings which state this rule, see Taft, "Ex Oriente," 322.
[17] Manders, "Concelebration," 143.
[18] *Mediator Dei*, nos. 95-97, also no. 83: AAS 39 (1947), 556, 553.
[19] Pius XII, Allocution, 2 Nov. 1954: AAS 46 (1954), 669-670.

celebration to affirm that only those priests who say the words "this is my body" and "this is my blood" truly concelebrate, since they alone act in the name of Christ.[20] To forestall any further controversy on the matter, the Holy Office reiterated in 1957 that "only he who pronounces the words of consecration celebrates validly."[21]

On the eve of the Council, then, a number of theological boundaries seemed effectively established: the value of private celebration, the requirement of verbal consecration for true concelebration, a minimalist theory of consecration as constituting the essence of the eucharistic sacrifice, the theological definition of the priesthood in terms of its unique power to act in the name of Christ, and a strong emphasis on the unity of the priesthood as the symbolic meaning of concelebration.

As to the pastoral solutions which had helped to rekindle and reshape the discussion, the practice of synchronized Masses, never one of great promise from the liturgical point of view, was forbidden by the Congregation of Rites in 1958.[22] That same decree, quoting earlier statements of Pius XII,[23] allowed communal celebration, the *messe communautaire*, for just and reasonable cause and with the authorization of the bishop.[24] It remained clear that although the communal Mass was allowed, the ideal of daily celebration of the eucharist by all priests remained intact and in favor. Thus, on the eve of the Council, the widespread hope for a solution to the problem of multiple private celebrations had begun to focus on extending the existing rite of concelebration itself.

Preparations for the Council

The announcement of Vatican II by Pope John XXIII on 25 January 1959, initiated a flurry of activity.[25] In May the Provisional Preparatory Commission, a central coordinating body composed of curial

---

[20] Pius XII, Allocution, 26 Sept. 1956: AAS 48 (1956), 718.

[21] Response to *Dubium de valida consecratione*, 23 May 1957: AAS 49 (1957), 370.

[22] *Instructio de Musica Sacra et Sacra Liturgia*, no. 39: AAS 50 (1958), 645.

[23] Pius XII, Allocution, 2 Nov. 1954: ASS 46 (1954), 670; Pius XII, Allocution, 22 Sept. 1956: AAS 48 (1956), 716.

[24] Congregation of Rites, Pius XII, Instructio, no. 38: AAS 50 (1958), 644.

[25] For a summary history of the preparatory work for the Council with particular reference to the liturgy, see Annibale Bugnini, *La riforma liturgica (1948-1975)*, Bibliotheca "Ephemerides Liturgicae," "Subsidia" 30 (Rome: CLV-Edizioni Liturgiche, 1983), 26-39. A detailed account of the preparatory work on concelebration can be found in Stanislaw Madeja, "Analisi del Concetto di Concelebrazione Eucaristica nel Concilio Vaticano II e nella Riforma Liturgica Postconciliare," *Ephemerides Liturgicae* 96 (1982), 6-15.

officials, was established to begin the initial preparations for the Council. On 18 June 1959, this Commission issued a letter inviting bishops, religious superiors, and Catholic faculties to submit agenda items. In June 1960, a permanent Central Preparatory Commission was named to oversee the preparatory work, and thirteen other preparatory commissions and secretariats were established and given particular areas of responsibility. Among these was the Preparatory Liturgical Commission.

Of the 2109 responses to the consultation letter, one fourth addressed the liturgy, including more than forty requests for a consideration of concelebration.[26] At its first general meeting in November 1960, the Preparatory Liturgical Commission divided its work among thirteen subcommissions. Responsibility for the question of concelebration was given to the third subcommission.[27] Its charge included: 1) a dogmatic and historical investigation of the origin, nature, and extension of ceremonial and sacramental concelebration; 2) whether concelebration can be allowed in the Latin Church, and if so, under what circumstances of place, time, and persons and with what rite; and 3) the ancient tradition of a single celebrant is to be kept for the Lord's Supper on Holy Thursday.[28] At its second general meeting in April 1961, the Preparatory Liturgical Commission discussed the first working draft of the schema on the liturgy, including five pages on concelebration prepared by the subcommission. In August a revised second working draft of the schema was sent to the members of the Commission for further observations. A third working draft came before the Commission at its third general meeting in January 1962, when it was discussed and revised further. The fourth and final working draft of the schema was presented to the Central Preparatory Commission on 2 February 1962.

---

[26] The consultation letter can be found in *Acta et Documenta Concilio Oecumenico Vaticano II Apparando* Series I (Antepreparatioria) [hereafter, ADCOVa] (Rome: Vatican Polyglot Press, 1960-1961), II-I, x-xi. The complete responses are given in ADCOVa, volumes II through IV.

[27] Bugnini, *La Riforma*, 27, lists the members as: Abbot Bernard Capelle (*relator*), Bernard Botte (secretary), and Archbishop Joseph Gogué, Anton Hänggi, and Aimé-Georges Martimort (consultors). Madeja, "Analisi," 9, footnote 23, includes Bishop Franz Zauner in the list of members.

[28] As cited in Madeja, "Analisi," 7: "A. Congrua instituatur investigatio tum dogmatica tum historica in originem, naturam et extensionem concelebrationis caeremonialis et sacramentalis. B. Utrum concelebratio admitti possit in Ecclesia latina. Et quatenus affirmative, quibus conditionibus quoad circumstantias loci, temporis et personarum; et quonam ritu. C. Feria V in Cena Domini servanda est antiquissima traditio Ecclesiae Romanae, ut unus tantum sacerdos celebrans Sacrum faciat."

At this stage, the schema included four articles (articles 44 to 47) on sacramental concelebration. The first article extended the use of concelebration; the second outlined rubrical revisions to be made in the rite; the third spoke of the oversight by the local Ordinary; and the fourth made allowance for each concelebrant to receive a stipend.[29] Though the text was to undergo another redaction before being sent to the Council Fathers as the official schema for conciliar debate, this pre-redaction version became available to them through unofficial channels and had an impact on their discussion.

Before tracing that further history, we might note the schema's stance on the dual issue of concern to us. The symbolic meaning of concelebration is not stated in the text itself, but rather in the accompanying apparatus. In addition to footnote citations, so-called *declarationes* were included in the text after each of the articles to provide the Council Fathers with background information and analysis. The *declaratio* for article 44 lists a number of reasons for extending the use of concelebration, namely: 1) to better manifest the unity of the Church in the unity of the priesthood; 2) to better foster the piety of priests and people; and 3) to alleviate the various practical difficulties and inconveniences.[30] Although ecclesial and priestly unity are held together in the first reason, the very phrasing suggests that the unity of the priesthood is seen as the more immediate and obvious symbolism. For it is through the priestly unity symbolized in concelebration that the unity of the Church itself is manifested. The other two reasons are practical and witness even more clearly to the stress on priestly unity which the pastoral difficulties created by separate celebrations had fostered.

As regards the shape of the rite, article 45 notes simply that "the rubrics of the Roman Pontifical are able to be retained"[31] and indicates the kinds of adaptation to be made. These words and the accompanying *declaratio* clearly accept a medieval form of the rite of concelebration as the working model for the revision.[32]

---

[29] See *Acta et Documenta Concilio Oecumenico Vaticano II Apparando* Series II (Preparatoria) [hereafter, ADCOVp] (Rome: Vatican Polyglot Press, 1964-1969), II-III, 107-110. The text of the articles is given in the appendix under the heading of preparatory schema.

[30] ADCOVp II-III, 108: "a) Unitas Ecclesiae in unitate sacerdotii melius demonstratur . . . b) Pietas magis fovetur, si plures sacerdotes simul litent, quam in diversis altaribus singillatim celebrant, sese invicem et populum molestia efficientes. c) Vitantur difficultates practicae et incommoda provenientia ex numero sacerdotum sive e penuria altarium et supellectilis, sive ex brevitate temporis."

[31] ADCOVp II-III, 108: "Quoad ritum, servari possunt rubricae Pontificalis romani."

[32] A proposal which in many ways anticipated the ritual revisions proposed in the schema can be found in Aimé-Georges Martimort, "Le Rituel de la Concélébration Eucharistique," *Ephemerides Liturgicae* 77 (1963), 147-168. Martimort had originally read this paper in August

The schema on the liturgy was the subject of lively discussion during the Central Preparatory Commission's fifth general session. When chapter two was taken up on 27 March 1962, more than half of the approximately eighty interventions commented on the articles on concelebration.[33] Though varying opinions and suggestions on concelebration surfaced and a vote was taken on chapter two as a whole, there was no protracted discussion of the issues and the Commission itself took no action to revise the articles on celebration,[34] nor did it consider the schema again in plenary session.

The schema was then turned over to an amendment subcommittee, one of three such subcommittees within the Central Preparatory Commission.[35] The subcommittee culled potential amendments from the observations made during the March meeting of the Central Preparatory Commission and sent them to the Preparatory Liturgical Commission for its response. These materials were brought to a full meeting of the subcommittee on 9 May, when a number of significant changes were made.[36] As regards concelebration, the extension authorized in article 44 was cut back drastically. The articles on the rite and its oversight remained unchanged, though their order was reversed. Article 47, concerning stipends, was eliminated completely. More importantly, the *declarationes* found throughout the text of the schema were deleted or reduced to informational footnotes. Thus, all the practical directives for liturgical reform proposed in the text of the schema were, in effect, divorced from the theological rationale which the *declarationes* had provided. And the implementation of all these directives was to be left to the Holy See, according to a note added at the beginning of the schema.[37] The proposed restoration seemed modest indeed.

---

of 1960, at the international meeting in liturgical studies held just prior to the eucharistic congress in Munich, and shortly thereafter he was named to the Preparatory Liturgical Commission's subcommission on concelebration.

[33] The minutes record 13 longer interventions and the 68 votes, almost all of which include observations and reservations of varying lengths (see ADCOVp II-III, 116-144).

[34] Compare this text with the text given in ADCOVp III-II, 33-37.

[35] On the subcommittee were: Cardinal Carlo Confalonieri (president), Father Vincenzo Fagiolo (secretary), Cardinal Clemente Micara, Cardinal Giacomo A. Copello, Cardinal Giuseppe Siri, and Cardinal Paul Emile Léger; with the later addition of Cardinal Joseph Frings and Cardinal Michael Browne. For this listing of the members and a chronicle of their work, see V. F [agiolo], ". . . e le Sottocommissioni . . . degli emendamenti," *L'Osservatore Romano della Domenica*, (6 Mar. 1966), 30-31. Cardinal Carlo Confalonieri also chronicled the amendment subcommittee's work for the Council Fathers (ASCOV I-II, 106-108).

[36] Bugnini, *La Riforma*, 38; Herman Schmidt, *La Costituzione sulla Sacra Liturgia. Testo, Genesis, Commento, Documentazione* (Rome: Herder, 1966), 120-122.

[37] ASCOV I-I, 263: "Huius Constitutionis mens est: tantum normas generales et altiora principia, generalem liturgicam instaurationem respicientia proponere, relinquendo Sanctae

On 23 June 1962 the amended schema was forwarded to the general secretariat of the Council, and on 13 July 1962, by authority of John XXIII, it was submitted to the Council Fathers as the official text for discussion.[38] However, someone familiar with the final draft of the Preparatory Liturgical Commission arranged that text and the amended text of the official schema in parallel columns, noting the variations. Like other such documents, this comparison of the two texts was distributed unofficially, apparently to give an account of the changes that had been made. The effect was to be the opposite of what had been intended.[39]

Conciliar Debates and Decisions

The schema on the liturgy was the first to be taken up during Vatican II. The schema came before the full Council assembly a total of five times, in keeping with the procedural steps established for the conciliar deliberations. The first four steps, discussion, amendment, modification, and vote, took place during the *congregationes generales* or general assemblies, the working sessions held four or five days a week while the Council was in session. The final step was formal approval, which occurred during a *sessio publica* or public session.

Sedi singula exsecutioni demandare." This note was excerpted from a much longer *declaratio* originally included in the *Proemium* (see ADCOVp II-III, 27). Isolated in this fashion, the note drew attention to itself and to a mindset that had led the Congregation of Rites to publish a flurry of ritual revisions during the years 1960-1962, seemingly in an attempt to keep the actual revision of the rites under curial control, leaving only the "larger principles" of liturgy to the conciliar discussion. The publication of the Apostolic Constitution *Veterum Sapientia* on 22 Feb. 1962 might be seen as a similar preemptive action anticipating the debate over whether Latin or the vernacular is to be used in liturgy (see Bugnini, *La Riforma*, 37; Schmidt, *La Costituzione*, 103-106, 116-117, 122).

[38] See *Acta Synodalia Sacrosancti Concilii Oecumenici Vaticani II* [hereafter, ASCOV] (Rome: Vatican Polyglot Press, 1970-1980), I-I, 262-303, for the complete schema; ibid., 280-282 for the articles and notes on concelebration. The articles on concelebration are given in the appendix under the heading of schema 1.

[39] Bugnini, *La Riforma*, 37; Schmidt, *La Costituzione*, 122-123. Bugnini's account hints at another fascinating bit of maneuvering. Apparently, a secretarial group was employed to do the actual work of redacting the text to incorporate the changes determined by the amendment subcommittee. It seems that the more conservative Cardinal Arcadio M. Larraona, who became president of the Central Preparatory Commission after the death of Cardinal Amleto G. Cicognani, established a parallel, shadow secretarial group with the intent of radically restructuring the schema of the liturgy. That intent finally came to nought when a key member of the group died in September 1962, long after the official amended schema had been distributed to the members of the Council.

Discussion on the liturgical schema began with its presentation during the fourth general assembly on 22 October 1962.[40] The chapter on the eucharist chapter II, which contained the articles on concelebration as well as two much-debated articles on vernacular in the Mass and on communion under both kinds, was discussed on the Council floor during five general assemblies, from 29 October through 11 November 1962. A total of 190 oral and written comments were addressed to chapter II.[41] Among these were thirty-nine oral and thrity-three written interventions on the question of concelebration.

The crucial concern early in the discussion was whether or not to extend the use of concelebration. Though there was significant opposition at first,[42] support for the proposed extension grew and eventually the interventions ran three to one in its favor. This shift was due in great measure to strong pleas concerning the pastoral needs of pilgrimage shrines[43] and religious communities,[44] to the kind of missionary urgency expressed by a spokesperson for 260 African bishops,[45] and to the ecumenical encouragement of the bishops of the Eastern Churches in which the ancient practice of "common celebration" had continued unbroken.[46]

Despite the weight given to pastoral needs, from the very beginning of the discussion it was also apparent that the Council Fathers were not content to base their decision on practical needs alone and many asked that "positive," that is, theological, reasons be given for the extension.[47] From explicit references to and citations of the reasons which had been given in the now-deleted *declaratio* of the fourth preparatory schema, there can be no doubt that the

---

[40] The text is given in ASCOV I-I, 262-303, followed by the *relationes* of the president and secretary of the conciliar liturgical commission, the successor to the preparatory liturgical commission which had drafted the document. The articles on concelebration (ibid., 280-282) are given in the appendix under the heading of schema 1.

[41] See ASCOV I-I, 331, 598-603; I-II, 9-158, 195-287; II-V, 870.

[42] See the adamant position taken by Cardinal Alfredo Ottaviani in his intervention (ASCOV I-II, 18-21). The applause that greeted his silencing by the chair when he had spoken well over the allotted time and his absence from several general sessions immediately thereafter clearly signaled that the assembly would remain free to express its own mind.

[43] See Bishop Pierre Mitheas Théas (ASCOV I-II, 139) and Archbishop Georges Hakim (ASCOV I-II, 234).

[44] See Abbot Gerard Sighard Kleiner, O.C.D. Cist. (ASCOV I-II, 48) and Abbot Primate Benno Gut, O.S.B. (ASCOV I-II, 127).

[45] See Bishop Jean van Cauwelaert (ASCOV I-II, 94-96).

[46] E.g., see Archbishop Joseph Khoury (ASCO VI-II, 83-85).

[47] E.g., see Cardinal Paul Emile Léger (ASCOV I-I, 602), Cardinal Augustin Bea (ASCOV I-II, 26), and Bishop Narciso Jubany Arnau (ASCOV I-II, 67).

"unofficial" distribution of that text in parallel columns with the official text was having an impact.[48]

Following the reasoning put forward in that earlier *declaratio*, speakers regularly cited the unity symbolized by the eucharist as the rationale for extending concelebration. There was, however, no consistent way of describing that unity.

Some were content to speak simply of the unity of the Church.[49] Some spoke only of the unity of the priesthood,[50] or of priests with their bishop.[51] Joseph Khoury, a Maronite archbishop, eloquently argued from a non-Western tradition that concelebration, which he called common celebration, is to be encouraged, first because the eucharist is the act of the community itself and then, following the thought of St. Ignatius of Antioch, because the eucharist is not simply the act of the presbyter, but of the presbyterate under the presidency or direction of the bishop. Thus, he concluded, the bishop's decision is needed only to withhold common celebration, not to grant it.[52] Still others, without specifying the relationship, spoke of the unity of the Church and of the priesthood,[53] or of the unity of priesthood and sacrifice,[54] or of the unity of people, priesthood, and sacrifice.[55] Finally, some saw the unity of the priesthood[56] or of the sacrifice[57] as the sign of the unity of the Church. It is apparent from this welter of expressions that the discussion had not yet succeeded in forging a consensus on how to express the unity symbolized by the eucharist. *the problem of conciliar debate?*

---

[48] The same can be said from another strand of the discussion not reported here, concerning how far to extend the use of concelebration. Those favoring a broader extension also called for a restitution of all or part of the less restrictive list of occasions for concelebration proposed in the fourth preparatory schema. See Abbot Kleiner (ASCOV I-II, 48) and Archbishop André Perraudin (ASCOV I-II, 123). Eventually almost all of these were restored.

[49] See Cardinal Léger (ASCOVI-I, 602).

[50] See Bishop Alberto Devoto (ASCOV I-II, 73).

[51] See Bishop Jubany Arnau (ASCOV I-II, 68), Bishop Eladio Vicuña Arauguiz (ASCOV I-II, 133), Bishop Franz Zak (ASCOV I-II, 151), Bishop Marino Bergonzini (ASCOV I-II, 206), Bishop John McEleney (ASCOV i-II, 250), Archbishop Paul Philippe (ASCOV I-II, 264).

[52] Ratio autem doctrinae, propter quam celebratio communis commendenda est . . . est quia celebratio eucharistica est proprius actus communitatis. . . . Et exemplum quam venerabile habemus Ignatii Antiocheni, secundum quem Eucharistia non est tam actua 'presbyteri' quam 'presbyterii', scilicet omnium sacerdotum, praesidente episcopo, si adest, secus, ex mandato episcopi. (Unde patet iudicium episcopi requiri non ad celebrationem communem concedendam, sed ut ab ea recedatur)" (ASCOV I-II, 83).

[53] See Bishop Charles H. Helmsing (ASCOV I-II, 46), Bishop Jubany Arnau (ASCOV I-II, 67), Bishop Arthur Elchinger (ASCOV I-II, 82).

[54] See Abbot Kleiner (ASCOV I-II, 48), Archbishop Neophytos Edelby (ASCOV I-II, 88).

[55] See Bishop Théas (ASCOV I-II, 139).

[56] See Abbot Kleiner (ASCOV I-II, 48), following the wording of the original *declaratio*.

[57] See Bishop Jacinto Argaya Goicoechea (ASCOV I-II, 201).

Regarding the shape of the rite, there were no more than a half dozen comments on article 45, and they were concerned with minutiae rather than with the basic direction being suggested for the restored rite.

At the end of the first period of the Council, the text of chapter II, along with the rest of the schema on the liturgy, was sent from the Council floor to the Conciliar Liturgical Commission to be amended in light of the oral and written interventions before the Council reassembled in the fall of 1963. The Commission, which had already taken up this task while the Council was still in session, divided the work of amendment among its thirteen subcommissions and met as a whole in the spring and in September of 1963, while the Council was in recess. Chapter II was assigned to a subcommittee on the eucharist.[58]

Seven amendments were proposed for a reorganized set of articles on concelebration.[59] The previous articles 44 and 45 were now combined into the new article 57. The beginning of this article was amended to read: "Concelebration, which aptly expresses the unity of the priesthood, has continued to this day as a practice in both the Eastern and the Western Church. For this reason, it has seemed good to the Council to extend permission for concelebration . . ." Significantly, the "positive reason" for concelebration requested in the debate had now been supplied. What is puzzling is that a wording was chosen which represented a minority approach among the welter of positions taken on the floor. In the *relatio*, Bishop Jesus Enciso Viana noted that the Commission had decided to substitute the phrase "the unity of the priesthood" for the formula "the unity of the Church" which some of the Council Fathers had recommended.[60] No further account is given as to why the Commission decided to make that change which was to draw so much comment after the extension was approved and implemented. The remaining amendments are devoted for the most part to restoring the cases for concelebration which had been deleted from the fourth draft of the preparatory schema.

---

[58] According to Madeja, "Analisi," 17, footnote 60, this subcommittee was composed of: Bishop Jesus Enciso Viana (president), Bishop Henri Jenny, Josef A. Jungmann, John B. O'Connell, and Damien Van den Eynde.

[59] See ASCOV II-II, 282.

[60] ASCOV II-II, 305: "Ubi de concelebratione agitur, proposuerunt quidam Patres ut ratio positiva adducatur, quae concelebrationem commendat, per formulam 'qua unitas Ecclesiae opportune manifestatur.' Commisio propositioni annuit, sed loco 'Ecclesiae' scripsit 'sacerdotii.'"

The Commission made one additional change, but did not propose it as an amendment to be voted on by the Council Fathers. Article 46, which had outlined the general shape of a revised rite of concelebration, was now reduced, in the new article 58, to the brief directive: "A new rite for concelebration is to be drawn up and inserted into the Roman Pontifical and Roman Missal."[61] Bishop Enciso Viana explained this change with the laconic note: "In this article we omitted all that touched on particulars and left only the principle of preparing a new rite."[62] Taken at face value, this decision simply eliminates details not worthy of full conciliar decision. However, the use of the phrase "new rite" does raise a question as to whether the Commission might have envisioned a more radical departure from the medieval rite than suggested in the previous version of the article.

The amended text of chapter II came back to the floor during the forty-third general assembly, on 8 October 1963.[63] By procedural rules, there was no floor discussion of the amendments. Voting on them took place during the forty-fifth general assembly, on 10 October 1963, with a yes or no vote. All seven amendments were approved by wide margins.[64]

The Council Fathers were asked to vote on the amended chapter II as a whole during their forty-seventh general assembly, on 14 October 1963. Their voting options were yes, no, and yes with modification (*placet iuxta modum*). Somewhat unexpectedly, the chapter received thirty-six no votes and 781 votes of yes with modification, thus failing to muster the two-thirds majority of unqualified yes votes needed to pass a text without modification.[65] The major stumbling block, represented by 558 of the *iuxta modum* votes, had to do with specifying in article 57 that the *local* Ordinary is the one who regulates concelebration.[66]

---

[61] SC, art. 58: DOL 1, no. 58.

[62] ASCOV II-II, 306: "Omisimus in hoc articulo omnia, quae particularia tangebant, et solum reliquimus principium de novo ritu conficiendo."

[63] For the amendments and the complete, amended text, see ASCOV II-II, 280-288, followed by the *relationes* of Cardinal Giacomo Lercaro and Bishop Enciso Viana which explained the proposed changes. The amended text of the articles on concelebration can be found in the appendix under the heading of schema 2.

[64] For the results of the votes, see ASCOV II-II, 435-436.

[65] Despite some initial uncertainty over the negative force of the *iuxta modum* votes, the view eventually prevailed that such votes were indeed positive, though with a proposal for amendment. See Jungmann, "Constitution on the Sacred Liturgy," 7, as well as footnote 70.

[66] See ASCOV II-V, 595-596.

At this point, then, the concern had shifted completely from questions of whether and how far to extend concelebration and for what reasons, to the question of control. This shift is surprising in that there was little apparent concern over the issue during the earlier floor discussions.[67] One can only speculate that two factors may have contributed to the fact that it became an issue now. The first is that Bishop Enciso Viana himself called attention to it in his *relatio* on the amendments.[68] The other is that the vote on this chapter was taken during the floor discussion of chapter II of the schema on the Church. In that discussion attention focused on such questions as collegiality and episcopal power, and religious exemption and the authority of non-local Ordinaries were often at issue, both below and above the surface.

In view of the 781 qualified votes, chapter II of the schema on liturgy was returned to the Conciliar Liturgical Commission for modification. After reviewing the results of the vote, the Commission prepared four *modi*, or modifications, to care for the major objections that had been raised.[69] The first of the *modi* added a sentence to article 57 specifying the local Ordinary's right to moderate concelebration in his diocese. The second, an editorial change in article 57, proposed an ecumenically more sensitive way of referring to the Church in the East and the West. The third concerned communion under both kinds. The fourth asked in effect that all the other modifications of chapter II requested in the qualified votes be set aside.

These four *modi* were brought back to the Council floor on 18 November 1963, during the sixty-ninth general assembly. They were explained in a lengthy *relatio* two days later, during the seventy-first general assembly.[70] There was no discussion of the modifications,

---

[67] Only three interventions had directly raised the question: Bishop Placido M. Cambiaghi (ASCOV II-II, 60), Bishop Pablo Barrachina Estevan (ASCOV II-II, 125), and Cardinal John D'Alton (ASCOV II-II, 195).

[68] ASCOV II-II, 294: "Requiritur iudicium Ordinarii. Disputatum est num deberemus dicere 'Episcopi' loco 'Ordinarii', ad vitandos conflictus ex maiori facilitate religiosorum oriundos. Praevaluit autem expressio 'Ordinarii.'" Again, no reason is given for the decision.

[69] These *modi* can be found in ASCOV II-V, 575-576.

[70] See the *relatio* by Bishop Enciso Viana, ASCOV II-V, 580-596, esp. 590-593 and 595-596 on concelebration. Though the total number of qualified votes had been high, Bishop Enciso Viana explained that the bulk of these votes concerned the regulation of concelebration by the local Ordinary and that on every other specific issue there was only a tiny minority of unfavorable or qualified votes. For that reason the fourth of the *modi*, really not a modification at all, was cast in the form of a *quaesitum*, asking if it pleased the voters to dismiss all the proposed modifications because none of them had mustered any significant support. The modified articles on concelebration are given in the appendix under the heading of conciliar constitution.

and a yes or no vote on them followed immediately. All the *modi* were passed[71] and a vote on the entire chapter II was also taken with overwhelmingly favorable results.[72]

During the seventy-third general assembly on 22 November 1963, the feast of St. Cecilia, the entire schema on the liturgy was voted on. It won approval with almost no dissenting voices.[73]

Finally, in a public session held on 4 December 1963 on the four-hundredth anniversary of the closing of the Council of Trent, the Constitution on the Liturgy was approved by formal vote.[74] The way had been opened for the rite of concelebration, seldom experienced in the post-medieval Church except on occasions such as ordination, to be used more widely. The dream, nurtured by the liturgical movement, of drawing priest celebrants away from their isolated celebrations and including them in a more communal celebration was ready to be fulfilled.

Postconciliar Implementation

Implementation of the conciliar decision to extend concelebration followed swiftly. On 25 January 1964 Pope Paul VI established the *Consilium ad Exsequendam Constitutionem de Sacra Liturgia* [hereafter, Consilium] to implement the Constitution on the Liturgy.[75] In March of that year the Consilium assigned the work of preparing the rites of concelebration and of communion under both kinds to a study group of experts under the direction of Father Cipriano Vagaggini, O.S.B.[76] The study group adopted as its working document a draft of a revised rite which an unnamed "specialist" had prepared the previous November, in anticipation. A round of con-

---

[71] For the results, see ASCOV II-V, 621.

[72] See ASCOV II-V, 631.

[73] See ASCOV II-V, 767.

[74] For the results, see ASCOV II-VI, 409.

[75] Paul VI, Motu Proprio *Sacram Liturgiam*, on putting into effect some prescription of the Constitution on the Liturgy, 25 Jan. 1964: AAS 56 (1964), 139-144; see DOL 20, no. 278.

[76] Bugnini, *La Riforma*, 131, footnote 2, lists the following members: Cipriano Vagaggini (*relator*), Adalberto Franquesa (secretary), Johannes Wagner, Aimé-Georges Martimort, Balthasar Fischer, Bernard Botte, Burkhard Neunheuser, Ansgario Dirks, and Rinaldo Falsini. Annibale Bugnini, who served as secretary of the Consilium, has recounted in several of his writings how the revised rite of concelebration was prepared. See his "Sei Mesi di Attività del 'Consilium ad exsequendam Constitutionem de Sacra Liturgia," *L'Osservatore Romano*, N. 220, 23 Sept. 1964, 5; "Acta Consilii," *Notitiae* 1 (1965), 94-104; "Il Rito della Concelebrazione," *L'Osservatore Romano*, N. 70, 26 Mar. 1965, 5; and especially *La Riforma*, 131-141. The information that follows can be found in these latter two works. See also Madeja, "Analisi," 29-31.

sultations and discussions between March and June produced two additional revised drafts. The last of these was forwarded to the Consilium on 6 June 1964, which prepared a fourth and final draft at its meeting of 18 to 20 June. In an audience with Cardinal Giacomo Lercaro, the president of the Consilium, Paul VI approved the revised rite *ad experimentum* on 26 June 1964.

Experimentation with the revised rite was entrusted first to six abbeys in various countries and then by indult to an increasing number of religious communities and gatherings of diocesan priests, with the permission and under supervision of the local bishop. Several Council Fathers were also invited to concelebrate with the Pope for the opening and closing of the third period of the Council, on 14 September and 21 November 1964. In all, there were over 1500 experimental uses of the revised rite from June through October of that year.[77]

On the basis of the comments and recommendations generated in the reports on these celebrations, and after further consultation and discussion, the Consilium revised the rite two more times, in December 1964 and January 1965. On 4 March 1965 Cardinal Arcadio M. Larraona, the prefect of the Congregation of Rites, presented the finalized *Ritus servandus in concelebratione Missae* to the Pope for approval. Paul VI promulgated the new rite on 7 March 1965. It was to take effect on Holy Thursday, 15 April 1965.[78]

The major outlines of the revised rite were as follows.[79] The principal celebrant carries out all the rites and prayers which a single celebrant normally does. Concelebrants, who are to be vested, take places at the altar with the principal celebrant from the preparation of the gifts through the communion rite. Using the appropriate gestures, they recite the institution account and the preceding and following portions of the eucharistic prayer together with the principal celebrant, whose voice should be more audible than theirs. Several other parts of the prayer may be assigned to individual concelebrants. Concelebrants communicate under both kinds.

At this point in retracing the development of the revised rite it may be helpful to pause and ask about the source of its inspiration. In their minds the drafters of the Constitution on the Liturgy and of the revised rite may have indeed envisioned a "new rite" differ-

---

[77] Bugnini, *La Riforma*, 134; "Il Rito," 5.

[78] Paul VI, Decree *Ecclesiae semper*: AAS 57 (1965), 410-412; DOL 222, no. 1788-1793.

[79] See Congregation of Rites (Consilium), *Ritus Concelebrationis* (hereafter, *Rite of Concelebration*), Introduction: (Rome: Vatican Polyglot Press, 7 March 1965), 13-18: DOL 223, nos. 1805-1809.

ing significantly from the medieval Roman rite. Early commentary on the revised rite reflects that assessment, noting that guiding principles were sought elsewhere.[80] These guiding principles were Pius XII's determination that saying the words of consecration together is required and suffices for valid sacramental concelebration, and the Council's reasoning that concelebration is to manifest the unity of the priesthood. These two principles inspired a simplified rite in which the priestly words and gestures of the concelebrants were radically reduced. Though some wished for an even greater reduction, this rite seemed daring enough and far removed from the medieval rite with its labored, simultaneous performance of all gestures and words by each of the concelebrants.

In retrospect, however, continuity with the medieval rite seems far more prominent than any discontinuity.[81] With medieval practice and theology the revised rite shares the underlying conviction that the unique role of the celebrant consists in the power to consecrate. That power is exercised only and adequately in pronouncing the words of consecration. When priests unite in consecrating, acting together *in persona Christi*, it is eminently clear that Christ is ultimately the one who offers the one sacrifice. Though ritual details may differ, the revised rite retains the basic shape of the medieval practice and its theology.

To resume our tracing of the history of the new rite, its general shape has remained intact since the revision, with only slight modifications. When additional eucharistic prayers were approved in 1968, the parts that can be said appropriately by individual concelebrants were specified.[82] These specifications and several other minor changes were incorporated into the rite of concelebration in the General Instruction of the Roman Missal, issued in 1969 and revised in 1975.[83]

The basic shape of the rite has thus remained consistent during the course of its preparation and implementation. There were, how-

---

[80] Pierre Jounel, *The Rite of Concelebration of Mass and of Communion under both Species* (New York: Desclee, 1967), 37.

[81] This was already intimated by another early commentator who notes that the new rite starts from the type of pontifical Mass. See Rinaldo Falsini, "Concelebration," in Teodoro Jiménez-Urresti and P. Huizing, eds., *The Sacraments in Theology and Canon Law*, Concilium 38 (New York: Paulist Press, 1968), 71.

[82] See the Congregation of Rites (Consilium), Norms, on the use of Eucharistic Prayers I-IV, 23 May 1968: *Notitiae* 4 (1968) 157-160; DOL 242, nos. 1931-1941.

[83] See Congregation for Divine Worship, General Instruction of the Roman Missal [hereafter, GIRM], 4th ed., 27 March 1975, nos. 153-208: DOL 208, nos. 1543-1598.

ever, several subtle ritual shifts worth noting. First, the earliest draft directed the concelebrants to use a "loud voice" when saying prayers along with the principal celebrant.[84] In the promulgated rite this directive has been modified so that the voice of the principal celebrant stands out over those of the concelebrants.[85] The General Instruction of the Roman Missal goes even further, specifically directing the concelebrants to recite the common parts of the eucharistic prayer *submissa voce* (in a softer voice), so that the congregation can hear the prayer without difficulty.[86]

Second, the earliest draft called for the concelebrants to accompany the principal celebrant to the altar for the preparation of the gifts. The second draft explicitly directed them to stand around the altar (*circa mensam altaris*). The fifth draft envisioned a similar placing of the concelebrants *circum altare*, but added the caveat that the assembly should be able to see the preparation rite. The promulgated rite substituted an alternate qualification, that the concelebrants not impede the preparation rite. Lastly, the General Instruction of the Roman Missal kept the *circa altare* directive, but with both of the previous qualifications, and instructs the concelebrants to take their place there only after the preparation rite.[87]

These two modifications indicate a measure of sensitivity concerning the affects of concelebration on the participation of the assembly. In the light of subsequent experience of the rite, a third modification seems less congenial to the assembly's role. Following the restrictions suggested in conciliar debate, the earliest draft of the revised rite had indicated that the number of concelebrants should be limited, and limitations were imposed during the experimental phase. The promulgated rite spoke only of an "appropriate" number. All such limitations were removed in the General Instruction of the Roman Missal,[88] open-

---

[84] See the text in Madeja, "Analisi," 36: "Has orationes omnes dicere debent alta voce una simul cum celebrante principali."

[85] "He [the principal concelebrant] is to take care to utter clearly and more audibly than the others the prayers that he is to sing or recite with the other concelebrants. . . . Similarly, they [concelebrants] say aloud those prayers that they speak alone or along with the principal celebrant. They should, as far as possible, . . . not be so loud that their voices are heard above that of the principal celebrant": DOL 223, nos. 1806-1807.

[86] GIRM, no. 170: DOL 208, no. 1560.

[87] See GIRM, no. 167: DOL 208, nos. 1556-1557. For the wording of these various stages of the text, see Madeja, "Analisi," 52.

[88] See GIRM, nos. 153-158: DOL 208, nos. 1543-1548. Initially some had envisioned no more than twelve concelebrants. Fear that concelebration would be limited to the elite soon led some to question such limitations. For additional comments on how the growing experience of the new rite gradually led to an expansion of the "appropriate" number, see Bugnini, *La Riforma*, 135. Note that at the same time the "official" attitude towards concelebration evolved from one of reluctantly allowing concelebration to one of promoting it.

ing the way for the large-group concelebrations that assemblies sometimes experience as overpowering.

One final topic remains to be traced, namely, the way the implementation documents understand the unity symbolized by the
eucharist. In the decades immediately before the Council and again
during the conciliar debates a broader and more integral way of im-
aging eucharistic unity had gradually given way to a sharper and
narrower stress on the unity of the priesthood. That focus became
exclusive when the Constitution named priestly unity as the sole
theological reason for extending concelebration.

Though the revised rite cites the conciliar formula of the "unity
of the priesthood"[89] and can be said to faithfully embody this more
restricted view, the documents accompanying the restoration seem
to reverse that narrowing down. In the 1965 decree promulgating
the revised rite, Paul VI consistently links unity of the priesthood
and unity of the sacrifice, speaking of concelebration with the bishop
presiding as "the preeminent manifestation of the Church in the
unity of sacrifice and priesthood and the single offering of thanks
around the one altar with the ministers and holy people."[90] Similarly, Cardinal Lercaro's letter to the conferences on liturgical renewal,
issued 30 June 1965, locates the doctrinal meaning of concelebration in the manifestation of the unity of sacrifice, priesthood, and
people.[91] The 1967 Instruction *Eucharisticum mysterium* from the Congregation of Rites affirms that concelebration expresses the unity
of the sacrifice and the priesthood, and of the people as well whenever they take an active part.[92] That document, like a 1968 instruction from the same Congregation dealing with the simplification of
pontifical rites, sees concelebration with bishop presiding and the
faithful taking active part as a special expression of that threefold
unity.[93] This ideal is also applied to religious communities in the
Declaration on concelebration of 7 August 1972 from the Congregation for Divine Worship.[94] Finally, the General Instruction on the

---

[89] See *Rite of Concelebration*, Introduction, no. 1: DOL 223, no. 1794. The only other implementation document to speak in these narrow terms is one from the Congregation for Divine Worship which concerns the renewal of priestly commitment at the chrism mass on Holy
Thursday. The formula is nuanced by the gathering of priests around their bishop: see DOL
315, no. 2556.

[90] Congregation of Rites (Consilium), Decree *Ecclesiae semper*: DOL 222, no. 1792 and passim.

[91] See DOL 31, no. 414.

[92] See DOL 179, no. 1276.

[93] See DOL 179, no. 1276 and DOL 550, no. 4458.

[94] *In celebratione Missae*, no. 1: DOL 226, no. 1814: "Concelebration is a sign and a strength-
ening of the fraternal bond of priests and of the whole community, because this manner of

Roman Missal also reflects the broader understanding of the unity symbolized by concelebration, that of priesthood, sacrifice, and people of God.[95]

The history we have retraced thus leaves us with a dichotomy. On the one hand, the revised rite is content, for the most part, to implement the Council's statement that concelebration expresses the unity of the priesthood.[96] On the other hand, the accompanying documents, with few exceptions, return to a larger theological vision of the oneness which such a celebration ought to symbolize. The experience of concelebration accumulated during the past twenty-five years witnesses to that same divergence of practice and theology and deserves further reflection.

REFLECTIONS

At the very outset of these reflections it should be acknowledged that concelebration hardly ranks among the most important of the revised rites experienced by the local assembly. It is also true that the experience of concelebration has varied widely, from serving as a badge of status in the parish celebration of a funeral or marriage to being a convenience for priests in a religious community. Despite these cautions, however, it remains true to say that our experience of the rite has also been shaped by more important paradigm shifts occurring in the liturgical renewal and can therefore serve as a barometer of the progress of that renewal. It is with an eye to that larger renewal and with a touch of devil's advocate that we now look at the name of the rite, its shape and meaning, other ritual models of "concelebration" in the revised liturgy, and some ideas for rethinking the rite and its meaning.

The Name of the Rite

A first shift concerns the very name of the rite. How we name a reality shapes how we perceive it and can, in the end, shape the

---

celebrating the sacrifice in which all share consciously, actively, and in the way proper to each is a clearer portrayal of the whole community acting together and is the preeminent manifestation of the Church in the unity of sacrifice and priesthood and in the single giving of thanks around the one altar." The shift to positive encouragement of concelebration, noted earlier, can be found in this document. See ibid., DOL 226, no. 1813.

[95] See GIRM, no. 153: DOL 208, no. 1543.

[96] One might argue that the rite implies a larger ecclesial unity when it is celebrated communally, in the midst of an assembly. This symbolism would be less true of a concelebration with only concelebrants present, as happens in large gatherings of priests. Curiously, GIRM places concelebration in a halfway position between celebrations with and without a congregation.

reality itself. When the Council convened, "concelebration" was an accepted term. In the early drafts of the schema on the liturgy the fuller title "sacramental concelebration" was used to name the rite, in contrast to "ceremonial concelebration."[97] In the conciliar discussions "concelebration" quickly became the common usage[98] and has remained the standard name for a eucharist celebrated by more than one priest.

There are, however, occasional glimpses of other usages as well. At times the term is used more broadly in other sacramental rites, such as confirmation, when those assisting the presiding bishop/priest are called "concelebrating priests."[99] The relation among the concelebrants who simultaneously anoint or absolve in communal celebrations of confirmation, anointing, and penance is not unlike that of celebrants in the preconciliar "synchronized masses." Another kind of usage which gives wider meaning to the term refers to the relation between presider and assembly, or between members of the assembly. The *Rite of Penance* notes that the penitent is with the priest celebrating the liturgy of the Church's continual self-renewal."[100] The General Instruction of the Roman Missal affirms that "the celebration of the eucharist is the action of the whole Church"[101] and evokes the image of a unified, shared action in describing the assembly's part in the eucharistic prayer.[102] Similarly, though language of concelebration is not used in the *Rite of Marriage*, such a usage would be consonant with the Western Catholic tradition that the couple administer the sacrament to each other.

The language of concelebration, like so much of our religious vocabulary, is in the process of being reshaped in the aftermath of

---

[97] See the titles of the first three texts in the appendix.

[98] Bishop Enciso Viana used this simple title to refer to the articles on concelebration in his *relatio* of the final conciliar text, though the title was eliminated from the official text (see ASCOV II-V, 590, 595). One speaker had objected to calling this *sacramental* concelebration, since that would hold true for all those who receive the Sacrament. See Archbishop Armando Fares (ASCOV I-II, 117): "Nam quotquot ad sacram mensam accedunt agunt concelebrationem sacramentalem seu frequentant Sacramentum."

[99] *The Roman Pontifical* [hereafter, *Pontifical*], chap. 3, Confirmation (Washington: ICEL, 1978), no. 9: DOL 305, no. 2518.

[100] The Roman Ritual, *Rite of Penance* (Washington: ICEL, 1974), Introduction, no. 11: DOL 368, no. 3076. The Latin reads: "Ita fidelis . . . una cum sacerdote liturgiam Ecclesiae continenter se renovantis celebrat": *Ordo Paenitentiae* (Rome: Vatican Polyglot Press, 1974), no. 11.

[101] GIRM, Introduction, no. 5: DOL 208, no. 1380.

[102] GIRM, no. 54: DOL 208, no. 1444: "The priest invites the people to lift up their hearts to the Lord in prayer and thanks; he unites them with himself in the prayer he addresses in their name to the Father through Jesus Christ. The meaning of the prayer is that the entire congregation joins itself to Christ in acknowledging the great things God has done and in offering the sacrifice."

Vatican II. The liturgical renewal has forced a major shift in our understanding of celebration, which provides the stem for "concelebration." The presence and the full, active participation of the assembly are hallmarks of the Vatican II liturgy.[103] In a fundamental sense, then, the entire assembly celebrates the eucharist. It is truly their action. A further dimension of the reform has been the recovery and distribution of a variety of ministries within the assembly.[104] The role of the ordained minister is to be situated within that context. The liturgical vision that emerges is one in which the members of a local Church gather to carry out the complex yet unified act of celebrating the Lord' Supper.

The shift on the liturgical level, from priest-centered liturgy to one which fully engages all present according to their order, embodies yet other paradigm shifts which were initially less apparent. The first is a shift in ecclesiology. The model of Church as institution has given way to that of the people of God. The people gather, not just to adore from afar and receive their individual grace, but to take part in the celebration that worships God and makes them a holy people. The second shift has to do with ministry and its sacramental root. If all participate in the celebration, all have been empowered to do so. Baptism replaces ordination as the primary sacrament of vocation and empowerment.

It is hardly surprising, then, that using the word "concelebration" to refer to only one ministerial role within the complex and varied act of celebrating the liturgy becomes problematic. The problem is not so much with the word itself as with a usage that restricts how we understand the reality of celebration. What the word usually names is the collective exercise of eucharistic presidency by ordained ministers in an assembly which could celebrate equally well with only one of them presiding. This assumption that the word refers only to what the priests do independently of the assembly has led, unfortunately, to many popular misconceptions about concelebration. The concern some felt about "a potential image of concelebration simply as a rite for the convenience of the ordained ministers at a meeting or gathering or as a practice largely intended for religious communities"[105] is too often realized. Or concelebration becomes a way of enhancing solemn occasions by having more priests present.

---

[103] SC, art. 14, 27: DOL 1, nos. 14, 27.

[104] SC, art. 28: DOL 1, no. 28.

[105] Frederick R. McManus, ed., *Thirty Years of Liturgical Renewal* (Washington: Office of Publishing and Promotion Services, United States Catholic Conference, 1987), 47.

The unspoken intimation behind these faulty impressions is that the word should name more than it in fact does. We need, then, to look at the rite and what it means.

The Shape and Meaning of the Rite

A second set of shifts concerns the shape and meaning of the rite. As noted earlier, the conciliar adoption of the "unity of the priesthood" as the theological rationale for extending concelebration stands out as a momentary narrowing down of the meaning of the rite in comparison to the larger vision expressed in the preceding discussion and the subsequent documentation. A reading of the acts of the first period of the Council also leaves one with the impression that the Council Fathers had not yet developed the art of truly debating issues on the floor, despite their numerous interventions on the "positive" reasons for extending concelebration. In that light, one might agree with the assessment that the Conciliar Liturgical Commission's substitution of "priesthood" for "church" in the statement of rationale was due primarily to a practical concern, that of renewing priestly piety.[106]

We have also noted that this restricted statement of meaning was one of the guiding principles in revising the rite, and that the revised rite, though initially seen as a radical departure from the model previously contained in the Roman Pontifical, remains in basic continuity with medieval theology and practice. In view of the theological constraints in possession before and during the Council, as well as the conciliar principle that any new liturgical forms "should in some way grow organically from forms already existing",[107] the boldness of that departure should not be underestimated. Nevertheless, according to another assessment, "the restoration of concelebration was done very hastily; there was a desire to get rid of the so-called 'private' Masses, but by transposing into the new rite all that could be saved from our way of celebrating them. Thus from the start the enterprise was off course and aimed at two different goals."[108]

Though these assessments of the shape and meaning of the revised rite may need to be tempered, they help us to understand why concelebration with its duplication of the presider's role and

---

[106] See Frederick R. McManus, "Foreword," in McGowan, *Concelebration*, xviii.
[107] SC, art. 23: DOL 1, no. 23.
[108] Dekkers, "Concelebration," 201.

its heightened priestly symbolism often seems to be at odds with the ritual style which is the trademark of the liturgical renewal. The renewal has aimed for sacramental signs and a ritual style which are "marked by noble simplicity" and which are "short, clear, and unencumbered by useless repetitions."[109]

This shift in ritual style embodies, in turn, a deeper shift in sacramental paradigm. Following the Council's stress on clear sacramental signs that speak to the believers and nourish their faith,[110] there has been a shift away from an earlier emphasis on sacramental causality and efficacy at the expense of sacramental significance, with a consequent minimalism and overriding concern for efficiency, to a greater sensitivity and care for the full symbolic dimension of the liturgy.[111] It is precisely as communicative signs that sacraments produce their effect, or as medieval theology put it, "significando causant." In a parallel shift, the meaning of a sacrament is sought not just in theological statements about the rite, but in the rite's very enactment of meaning. In more technical terms, there is a growing awareness that liturgy is first theology. There is also a growing awareness that the stated and enacted meanings may sometimes be at odds.

From a symbolic perspective, concelebration is open to several potential misunderstandings if not performed with great pastoral care. Though intended to express the unity of those exercising liturgical leadership in service to the assembly, the rite can become an act of simultaneous inclusion/exclusion within the assembly, effectively identifying the band of ordained ministers with each other and separating them from the assembly by vesture, spatial grouping, and coordinated speech and action. Even though the concelebrants join in the responses of the assembly, their presence requires no appreciably new ritual interaction with the assembly, and it does not respond to any ministerial need of the assembly that cannot be met by other kinds of ministers. And beyond a coordination of speech and action and the optional distribution of portions of the eucharistic prayer, concelebration makes no ritual demands for interdependence between the concelebrants in the exercise of their role; nor does it significantly alter the way in which the principal celebrant exercises the presider's role.

---

[109] See SC, art. 34: DOL 1, no. 34.

[110] See SC, art. 59: DOL 1, no. 59.

[111] See Bishops' Committee on the Liturgy [National Conference of Catholic Bishops], *Environment and Art in Catholic Worship* (Washington: Office of Publishing Services, United States Catholic Conference, 1978), no. 14.

In such situations, especially when done on a large scale, concelebration is easily subject to other symbolic interpretations. If concelebrants are not needed for the service of the assembly, concelebration can be seem to be a convenience for celebrants, a mark of honor for the assembly, a form of high solemnity, or an expression of priestly solidarity. Because the number of concelebrants can be expanded or contracted at will with no ritual effects other than logistics, concelebration can be misunderstood as "a kind of co-presidency of the concelebrating priests over the Eucharist, as if a committee were in charge of the liturgical proceedings,"[112] something the rite never intended. By the very fact that it is so eminently suited to symbolize the unity of the priesthood, concelebration can come into conflict with the more integral vision of eucharistic unity also adopted by the Council and summed up in the dictum, "one community, one table, one eucharist."[113]

Other Ritual Models

One other important shift set in motion by the Council might be noted. The liturgical reform decreed by the Council was to produce a wide-scale revision of the Roman rites incorporating a far more varied and complex exercise of liturgical ministry, including that of the assembly itself. The restored rite of concelebration was approved for experimental use only six months after the promulgation of the Constitution on the Liturgy. At that point the Church had no other examples or living experience of alternate ritual models to draw on. Such is not the case twenty-five years later.

If one brackets eucharistic concelebration with its special concerns about valid consecration, a wide range of ritual models of "concelebration" can now be found in the revised rites of Vatican II. A quick typology might include the following.

One other rite, that of the consecration of a bishop, shows an exact parallel to eucharistic concelebration. Co-consecrating bishops impose hands and recite the essential words of the sacrament along with the principal consecrator.[114] Note that this rite also places symbolic stress on the unity of those ordained to the episcopate.

Several sacraments provide for multiple priest-celebrants when the large number of people approaching the sacrament so requires.

---

112 McManus, *Thirty Years*, 47.

113 For a discussion of this "conflict of two theologies," see Taft, "Ex Oriente," 319-325.

114 *Pontifical*, chap. 12, Ordination of a Bishop, nos. 23-24, 26. See also Congregation of Rites (Consilium), Instruction (first) *Inter Oecumenici*, 26 Sept. 1964, no. 69: DOL 23, no. 361.

The language of concelebration is used occasionally, but the more normal usage is "assisting" or "being associated with" the celebrant. These sacraments typically call for each celebrant to perform the essential sacramental action and words for individual recipients, simultaneously but separately. Such sacraments include: infant baptism,[115] adult baptism,[116] confirmation,[117] communal penance with individual confession and absolution,[118] and anointing.[119] In these cases the exercise of ministry is clearly a function of need.

Another category might include the "concelebration" of other ritual gestures which are central but not essential elements of a sacrament. In these cases the assisting or associated priest-minister performs a gesture together with the celebrant, who alone says the accompanying words. Such gestures would include: the anointing with chrism at the baptism of infants[120] and adults;[121] the imposition of hands by assisting celebrants of confirmation,[122] by priests in the ordination of priests,[123] and by non-consecrating bishops in the ordination of a bishop;[124] and the act of standing beside the celebrant before performing a core ritual or sacramental gesture.[125] These communal gestures serve to associate the assisting ministers symbolically with the ministerial role of the celebrant whose sacramental action they will share.

The next two categories refer to how non-ordained members of the assembly take part in a celebration according to their particular order. In these cases the typical vocabulary is "participating in" and "joining with." The first such category would include participation in an essential sacramental action. In the Western Catholic tradition, as noted earlier, marriage presents a unique case of mutual, lay administration or "confecting" of the sacrament. The language used is that of "bestowing and accepting consent" or "declaring consent"[126] rather than "concelebration." In the case of reconcilia-

---

[115] The Roman Ritual, *Rite of Baptism for Children* (Washington: ICEL, 1969), no. 61.

[116] The Roman Ritual, *Rite of Christian Initiation of Adults* [hereafter, RCIA] (Washington: ICEL, 1985), no. 220.

[117] *Pontifical*, chap. 3, Confirmation, no. 28; RCIA, no. 228.

[118] *Rite of Penance*, no. 55.

[119] The Roman Ritual, *Pastoral Care of the Sick: Rites of Anointing and Viaticum* (Washington: ICEL, 1983), no. 110.

[120] *Rite of Baptism for Children*, no. 62.

[121] RCIA, no. 218.

[122] *Pontifical*, chap. 3, Confirmation, no. 25; RCIA, no. 228.

[123] *Pontifical*, chap. 10, Ordination of a Priest, no. 21.

[124] *Pontifical*, chap. 12, Ordination of a Bishop, no. 24.

[125] E.g., *Pontifical*, chap. 3, Confirmation, no. 25; RCIA, no. 228.

[126] The Roman Ritual, *Rite of Marriage* (Washington: ICEL, 1969), nos. 2, 25.

tion, medieval theology eventually determined that the penitent's acts are not part of the matter and form of the sacrament. Accordingly the penitent does not "concelebrate" reconciliation in the narrower contemporary use of that word. Yet, as noted above, the revised rite does employ a grammatically equivalent phrase, "celebrating with the priest," to describe the penitent's role.

A final category would include the whole range of ways in which members of the assembly participate, either together or in particular liturgical roles, in actions which are central though not "sacramental" in the technical sense of "confecting" a sacrament. Such participants would include: an assembly which shares in the act of offering the eucharist;[127] godparents and parents who join the priest in signing a child being baptized;[128] sponsors who lay hands on the shoulders of confirmation candidates during the anointing with chrism;[129] and godparents who place hands on the shoulders of the catechumens during the rite of election.[130] In keeping with the directives of Vatican II, these symbolic actions are performed in response to the assembly's need for participation and for a distribution of liturgical roles.

The array of ritual models found in the renewed liturgy is impressive indeed. What Vatican II did, in terms current in the preconciliar discussion on concelebration, was to restore to the liturgy a broad spectrum of sacramental and ceremonial concelebration such as the Church had not known since the early centuries.

Rethinking the Rite and Its Meaning

What the preceding reflections suggest is the need not only for pastoral sensitivity in the use of concelebration, but also for a more radical reassessment of the revised rite in light of twenty-five years of experience. It is helpful to reassess concelebration under three rubrics: how we name it, how its shape and meaning might be improved, and whether other ritual models in the revised liturgy provide us with potential paradigms for a more radical reshaping.

The name of the rite remains unexamined for the most part, though some have suggested alternate terms such as "co-celebration," "co-consecration," and "co-presidency." Each of these is not without its own difficulties. "Co-celebration," like "concelebration," still

---

[127] GIRM, no. 54: DOL 208, no. 1444.
[128] Rite of Baptism for Children, no. 79.
[129] Pontifical, chap. 3, Confirmation, no. 26; RCIA, no. 229.
[130] RCIA, no. 120.

risks isolating the role of the priests from that of the entire assembly. "Co-consecration" focuses too narrowly on co-recital of the words of consecration and lays the rite open to a minimalist theology of the eucharist. That minimalist tendency is too often verified in the liturgical practice of concelebrants who "say the words" without sharing the presidential role in any other way. "Co-presidency" is perhaps the most promising alternative. Though it can be misread as "presidency by committee," as suggested earlier, it does open the way to a needed re-imaging of the rite in terms of collegial presidency in service of the assembly. *Does it really need to be termed at all?*

What the name of the rite needs to recapture is the vision expressed elsewhere in the Constitution on the Liturgy:

> The preeminent manifestation of the Church is present in the full, active participation of all God's holy people in these liturgical celebrations, especially in the same eucharist, in a single prayer, at one altar at which the bishop presides, surrounded by his college of priests and by his ministers.[131]

Toward this end, a recovery of two concerns voiced in preconciliar and conciliar discussions can be of help. One is the collegial nature of eucharistic presidency, which must ultimately entail the symbolic leadership of the bishop in some manner. This concern was intimated in the conciliar debate on the regulation of concelebration by the local Ordinary and became explicit in another conciliar[132] document and in some of the early proposals for the restored rite.[133] The other concern is the integration of the role of the concelebrating priests with that of the celebrating assembly, as the conciliar vision requires.[134] On these two scores language of collegial presidency seems far more apt to describe the role of concelebrants.

Renaming the rite, however, is only a first step to recovering that conciliar vision. The rite needs to be reshaped to embody that larger meaning in two ways. First, attention must be given to integrating the role of co-presiders with that of the assembly, to recover the larger symbolism which locates the unity of priesthood within that of the

---

[131] SC, art. 41: DOL 1, no. 41. This same unified vision was expressed in many of the conciliar interventions in favor of extending concelebration, for example, by Archbishop Joseph Khoury (ASCOV I-II, 83). One notes with regret that such a vision of eucharistic unity was not chosen as the reason for concelebration.

[132] See Vatican Council II, Decree on the Ministry and Life of Priests, *Presbyterorum Ordinis*, 7 December 1965, nos. 7-8: DOL 18, nos. 262-263.

[133] See Martimort, "Le Rituel," 166.

[134] See also the conciliar intervention of Archbishop Armando Fares (ASCOV I-II, 117) quoted in footnote no. 98, above.

Church. This involves both preserving and proportionately enhancing the presence and active participation of the faithful in a communal celebration of this rite, as the Council recommended for all rites and especially the eucharist.[135] It also involves reducing whatever may be divisive in the rite. Pertinent reconsiderations would include the spatial positioning of concelebrants, the use of vesture, the manner of gesturing and speaking during the eucharistic prayer, and the way in which concelebrants receive communion.[136] The ideal is to identify the concelebrants in their role of service to the assembly without attracting undue attention to them. These reconsiderations will, of necessity, revive discussion of the theology of ministry, including the designation of the priest's role as one of acting uniquely "*in persona Christi.*"[137]

A second desideratum is a better integration of the concelebrants' actions to highlight their collegial character. Thus, for example, the co-recital of the institution narrative might give way to a recital by the presiding celebrant alone, in the presence of the others who thereby witness and affirm. This will require that both the earlier discussion of non-verbal, "ceremonial" concelebration and the 1957 decree of the Holy Office be reassessed in the light of our accumulated experience of the restored rite and of other ritual models. Another option might be a choral proclamation of the text which would replace co-recital with a more symbolic expression of interdependence among the co-presiders.

If working to improve the present rite while leaving its central design intact does not prove to be the final answer, two other solutions may be at hand. One is a less frequent use of concelebration. Such is increasingly the case, for example, in some communities of religious priests who have long experienced the rite on a daily basis. The vision of a more limited use which held sway for a time while the rite was being revised and discussed before and during the Council may be worth reconsidering. Replacing concelebration with attendance "*modo laicorum*" by priests, however, faces opposition from the official Church stance[138] and the pre-conciliar principle that every priest should celebrate Mass daily.

[135] SC, art. 27: DOL 1, no. 27.

[136] See Baldovin, "Concelebration," 45-47; Taft, "Receiving Communion—A Forgotten Symbol," *Worship* 57 (1983), 412-418.

[137] See Taft, "Ex Oriente," 319-325.

[138] See Congregation of Rites, Instruction *Eucharisticum mysterium*, 25 May 1967, no. 43: AAS 59 (1967), 564; DOL 179, no. 1272; Congregation for Divine Worship, Declaration *In celebratione Missae*, 7 Aug. 1972: AAS 64 (1972), 561; DOL 226, no. 1813.

The other solution is more radical. The form of the revised rite has remained firmly embedded in the tradition of the Roman Pontifical from which it evolved. Might it now be possible to envision a more radical departure from medieval origins than could have taken place when the rite was revised after the Council? It is at this point that other ritual models could be pressed into service as potential paradigms from which a new rite of concelebration could "grow organically," according to the conciliar principle. One such model would be the "traditional" Holy Thursday practice which the Council first intended to keep intact. The other ritual models, listed above, which are now part of the revised liturgy offer other possibilities. Thus, "assisting priests" might be associated symbolically with the word and action of the presider by imposing hands or standing with the presider during central moments. Again, the questions related to non-verbal concelebration and the 1957 decree of the Holy Office would have to be reopened, as well as that of stipends.[139]

In all such attempts to rename the rite, to improve it, or to give new shape to the visible presence and ritual participation of ordained priests in a eucharist celebrated under the presidency of another, the final resolution must remain true to the Council's vision of the symbolic unity of one community, one eucharist, one table, and one presidency.

CONCLUSION

The experience of the restored rite of concelebration which has accumulated over the past twenty-five years invites us to look again at the shape of the rite and the meaning it symbolically enacts. The initial euphoria we felt when the rite resolved our problems with multiple separate celebrations has given way to intimations that the rite as we know it may be at odds with major directions of the liturgical renewal.

Such questions surely deserve study and discussion. This essay has retraced the path by which the rite was restored in the hope of gaining new insight into the questions we now face about the rite's shape and meaning and of making some small contribution

---

[139] On the issue of stipends, see John M. Huels, "Stipends in the New Code of Canon Law," *Worship* 57 (1983), 215-224; M. Francis Manion, "Stipends and Eucharistic Praxis," *Worship* 57 (1983), 194-214.

to furthering the discussion. That discussion will be fruitful for the continued renewal of the liturgy only if it respects both the received tradition and the experience of those who receive and cherish it. The words addressed to the Council Fathers by one of the first to speak on the schema on the liturgy express well the spirit and perspective needed to carry on that work of discussion and renewal:

> praecipua manifestatio Ecclesiae habetur in plenaria et actuosa participatione totius plebis sanctae Dei in celebrationibus liturgicis. . . . Et haec restauratio fieri potest, mihi videtur, tantum si expositionem schematis de momento liturgiae ardentur amplectimur, eiusque vota de participatione fidelium, necnon de accommodatione structura et lingua liturgica fideliter prosequimur.[140]

---

[140] Archbishop Denis E. Hurley, O.M.I., as recorded in ASCOV I-I, 327-328: ". . . the preeminent manifestation of the Church is present in the full and active participation of all God's holy people in liturgical celebrations. . . . And, it seems to me, this renewal can take place only if we warmly embrace what the schema puts forth about the importance of the liturgy and if we faithfully carry out the schema's wishes regarding the participation of the faithful and the accomodation of liturgical structure and language" (author's translation).

SELECTED BIBLIOGRAPHY

Acta et Documenta Concilio Oecumenico Vaticano II Apparando Series I (Antepraeparatoria), Vol. I – IV. Rome: Vatican Polyglot Press, 1960-1961. [Separately bound *partes* of each volume are identified in notes with dash and Roman numeral after the volume number.]

Acta et Documenta Concilio Oecumenico Vaticano II Apparando Series II (Praeparatoria), Vol. I – III. Rome: Vatican Polyglot Press, 1964-1969. [Separately bound *partes* of each volume are identified in notes with dash and Roman numeral after the volume number.]

Acta Synodalia Sacrosancti Concilii Oecumenici Vaticani II, Vol. I – IV. Rome: Vatican Polyglot Press, 1970-1980. [Separately bound *partes* of each volume are identified in notes with dash and Roman numeral after the volume number.]

APPENDIX

PREPARATORY SCHEMA* (ADCOVp II-III, 107-109)	SCHEMA No. 1* (ASCOV I-I, 280-281)	SCHEMA No. 2* (ASCOV II-II, 286)	CONCILIAR CONSTITUTION* (ASCOV II-V, 578-579)
DE CONCELEBRATIONE SACRAMENTALI	DE CONCELEBRATIONE SACRAMENTALI	DE CONCELEBRATIONE SACRAMENTALI	
44. [*Usus amplificetur*]. Concelebratio tam in Ecclesia Orientali quam in Occidentali in usu hucusque remansit. In votis est ut ad plures casus extendatur quam in disciplina vigenti et praesertim: a) ad Missam chrismatis, feria V in Cena Domini; b) ad Missam conventualem et ad Missam principalem in ecclesiis, ubi plures sacerdotes adsunt quam utilitas fidelium requirit, salva semper cuiusque sacerdotis libertate individualiter celebrandi, non tamen eadem in ecclesia, eodem tempore; c) ad conventus sacerdotum, uti sunt exercitia spiritualia, cursus studiorum, peregrinationes, etc., praesertim ubi singulae Missae sine incommodo celebrari nequeunt; d) ad extraordinarias celebrationes festivas, exempli gratia occasione Synodi dioecesanae, visitationis pastoralis una cum clero illius paroeciae). [Declaratio] . . . **	44. [*Usus amplificetur*]. Concelebratio tam in Ecclesia Orientali quam in Occidentali in usu hucusque remansit. Concilio facultatem concelebrandi ad sequentes casus extendere placet: a) ad Missam chrismatis, feria V in Cena Domini; b) ad conventus sacerdotum, si ad singulares celebrationes aliter provideri non possit et de iudicio Ordinarii.	57. § 1. Concelebratio, qua unitas sacerdotii opportune manifestatur, in Ecclesia usque adhuc in usu Occidentali usque adhuc in usu remansit. Quare facultatem concelebrandi ad sequentes casus Concilio extendere placuit: 1° a) feria V in Cena Domini, tum ad Missam chrismatis tum ad Missam vespertinam; b) ad Missas in Conciliis, Conventibus Episcopalibus et Synodis; c) ad Missam in Benedictione Abbatis. 2° Praeterea, accedente licentia Ordinarii, cuius est de opportunitate concelebrationis iudicare eiusque disciplinam moderari: a) ad Missam conventualem et ad Missam principalem in ecclesiis, cum utilitas christifidelium singularem celebrationem omnium sacerdotum praesentium non postulet; b) ad Missas in conventibus cuiusvis generis sacerdotum tum saecularium tum religiosorum.	57. § 1. Concelebratio, qua unitas sacerdotii opportune manifestatur, in Ecclesia usque adhuc in usu remansit tam in Oriente quam in Occidente. Quare facultatem concelebrandi ad sequentes casus Concilio extendere placuit: 1° a) feria V in Cena Domini, tum ad Missam chrismatis tum ad Missam vespertinam; b) ad Missas in Conciliis, Conventibus Episcopalibus et Synodis; c) ad Missam in Benedictione Abbatis. 2° Praeterea, accedente licentia Ordinarii, cuius est de opportunitate concelebrationis iudicare: a) ad Missam conventualem et ad Missam principalem in ecclesiis, cum utilitas christifidelium singularem celebrationem omnium sacerdotum praesentium non postulet; b) ad Missas in conventibus cuiusvis generis sacerdotum tum saecularium tum religiosorum.
45. [*Ritus concelebrationis*]. Quoad ritum, servari possunt rubricae Pontificalis romani. Attamen optantur quaedam aptationes, scilicet: a) ut concelebrantes, oblatione peracta, stent circa altare vestibus sacerdotalibus, aut saltem alba et stola, induti; b) ut minuatur numerus precum a concelebrantibus simul dicendarum; c) ut communicare possint sub utraque specie; d) ut solus celebrans principalis gestus faciat et benedicat. [Declaratio] . . .	45. [*Opportunitas concelebrationis et numerus concelebrantium*]. De opportunitate concelebrationis et de numero concelebrantium, in singulis casibus, Ordinarii erit iudicare.	§ 2. Salva tamen semper sit cuique sacerdoti facultas Missam singularem celebrandi, non tamen eodem tempore in eadem ecclesia, nec Feria V in Cena Domini.	§ 2. 1° Ad Episcopum vero pertinet concelebrationis disciplinam in diocesi moderari: 2° Salva tamen semper sit cuique sacerdoti facultas Missam singularem celebrandi, nec vero eodem tempore in eadem ecclesia, nec feria V in Cena Domini.
46. [*Opportunitas concelebrationis et numerus concelebrantium*]. De opportunitate concelebrationis et de numero concelebrantium, in singulis casibus, Ordinarii loci erit iudicare. [Declaratio] . . .	46. [*Ritus concelebrationis*]. Quoad ritum, servari possunt rubricae Pontificalis romani. Attamen quaedam aptationes fiant, scilicet: a) ut concelebrantes, oblatione peracta, stent circa altare vestibus sacerdotalibus, aut saltem alba et stola, induti; b) ut minuatur numerus precum a concelebrantibus simul dicendarum; c) ut communicare possint sub utraque specie; d) ut solus celebrans principalis gestus faciat et benedicat.	58. Novus ritus concelebrationis conficiatur, Pontificali et Missali Romano inserendus.	58. Novus ritus concelebrationis conficiatur, Pontificali et Missali Romano inserendus.
47. [*Stipendium*]. Dispositio can. 824 Codicis Iuris Canonici, relate ad stipendium Missae, valet pro unoquoque concelebrante. [Declaratio] . . .			
* Drafted by Preparatory Liturgical Commission; presented to Central Preparatory Commission on 2 Feb. 1962. ** See footnote no. 30 for text.	* Redacted by Central Preparatory Commission; submitted to Council 13 July 1962; debated 11 Oct. 1962.	* Amended by Conciliar Liturgical Commission; resubmitted to Council 8 Oct. 1963; voted on 10 Oct. 1963.	* Modified by Conciliar Liturgical Commission; resubmitted to Council 18 Nov. 1963; voted on 20 Nov. 1963 and 22 Nov. 1963; promulgated 4 Dec. 1963.

THE LOCAL CHURCH AS THE SUBJECT OF THE ACTION OF THE EUCHARIST

Mary Alice Piil, C.S.J.

INTRODUCTION

In a consideration of the engagement of the assembly in the liturgical action, several images of actual Sunday assemblies come to mind. One is of an old woman participating in a parish Sunday liturgy where the renewal has been taken seriously by all. Another image is that of many bored individuals kneeling and staring into space as the presider says the eucharistic prayer. In contrast, another assembly enthusiastically sings the memorial acclamation in response to the invitation to proclaim the mystery of faith. Why does such diversity exist? Is it a question of further involving the assembly in a visible, tangible manner or is the question one of attitude? Whose eucharist is being celebrated? The old woman is obviously engaged in the act. Yet she sits quietly as the prayer is said. Active participation means more than having an activity to perform. It demands full engagement of the person which at times can be accomplished with little (or no) physical activity.

In the twenty-five years since the promulgation of the Constitution on the Liturgy (*Sacrosanctum Concilium*), the Order of Mass of the Missal of Pius V has undergone significant change. The gradual evolution of the Order of Mass resulted in the Missal of Paul VI. With the exception of local adaptations, this same Order of Mass is being celebrated in every parish using the Roman rite. Yet, great diversity is experienced. Why?

All change in the Church is gradual and that change which follows upon a significant council is particularly so. The reforms following upon the Second Vatican Council are themselves indications of the process of reception of the Council's teachings. In addition, the Church must now attempt to receive into its life the many reforms which flow from the teachings of the Council.

When the Church is in the process of liturgical renewal, the question of how the priest and faithful are engaged in the celebration of the Mass comes to the fore. This issue was raised in the sixteenth century when the Reformation theologians challenged the prevailing Western theology of the Mass which stressed the role of the celebrating priest.[1]

The major intent of the present reform appears to be to emphasize the full participation of the entire assembly in the eucharist. This shift in emphasis suggests the need for further development of a theology of priesthood in relation to the assembly's participation. Any conflict of theology of ministry, specifically the ministry of the presiding priest, present in the conciliar and postconciliar documents emerges as a result of the primary emphasis of the reform on the full, active participation of the faithful in the eucharistic act.

During this present reception period, the Church has been struggling with an articulation of a theology of the offering of the eucharist. At the same time, however, many postconciliar documents appear to receive the Council's teaching that the local Church is the immediate subject of the eucharist. Many documents do, however, restate a scholastic/Tridentine understanding of the role of the priest, developed when the assembled people were passive spectators rather than active participants in the celebration.

Questions regarding the active participation of the assembly and the offering of the eucharist have surfaced as a result of the revival of liturgical consciousness in the twentieth century. Before the Council, Pius XII addressed these issues in *Mystici Corporis* and in his masterpiece *Mediator Dei*. Pius XII's call for active participation reached its summit in *Sacrosanctum Concilium* of Vatican II. After the Council, the task of reception of this teaching was carried out by Paul VI and the Consilium for the Implementation of the Constitution on the Liturgy [hereafter, Consilium]. But the process of reception continues into the present with episcopal teaching, the reflections of John Paul II, and the legislation flowing from the Roman congregations. This article will trace the question of the subject of the eucharist through the official documents of these several periods, that is, preconciliar, conciliar, and postconciliar.

---

[1] See Reinold Thiesen, *Mass Liturgy and the Council of Trent* (Collegeville, Minn.: St. John's Press, 1965), 2-19.

Pius XII and Participation in the Eucharist

In order to grasp possible reasons for the diversity of interpretation which exists within the Church today, it is necessary to look beyond the Second Vatican Council to the very roots of reform which are found in the liturgical movement. Perhaps the most helpful of Roman documents in dialogue with this movement is *Mediator Dei*.[2]

Pius XII provided the necessary impetus to the twentieth century effort to bring about a revival of the liturgical life of the Roman Catholic Church with the publication of the encyclical letter *Mediator Dei*, 20 November 1947. Its teaching on the respective roles of priest and laity in the celebration of the eucharist served as a background for the subsequent teaching of official documents of the Roman Catholic Church on the subject of the active participation of all in the liturgical action. It also shaped the liturgical understanding of several generations of priests whose training in liturgy was greatly influenced by this work. However, while much of Pius XII's theology of the Mass was received without change in later Vatican documents, it was received within a new ecclesial perspective. Consequently, the decrees of the Second Vatican Council and various postconciliar documents reinterpret Pius XII's teaching in light of a renewed understanding of the nature of the Church.

In his encyclical letter *Mystici Corporis* (1943),[3] Pius XII distinguishes between the Church as a hierarchical, juridical-social organism and as a faithful people. The communion of the faithful people is viewed as existing on the spiritual level of the relations of love and grace between Christ and the believers and between the believers themselves. *Mediator Dei* adopts this perspective. Hence, when it deals with the Church as subject of the liturgical act, it distinguishes between the Church as a social organism and as a faithful people of God. The priest-representative of the Church, viewed as a social organism, acts in the person of both Christ and the Church. The faithful *offer* because they pray with and through the priest.

According to Pius XII, direct participation in the liturgical act is reserved to the priest. The priest alone is necessary for the completion of this act. Pius XII does indicate, however, that the faithful should be encouraged to participate actively in the Mass. The value

---

[2] Pius XII, *Mediator Dei, Acta Apostolicae Sedis* [hereafter, AAS] 39 (1947), 521-594: Eng. ed., *On the Sacred Liturgy* (Washington: National Catholic Welfare Conference, 1948).

[3] Pius XII, *Mystici Corporis*, AAS 35 (1943), 193-248: Eng. ed., *On the Mystical Body of Christ* (Washington: National Catholic Welfare Conference, 1943).

of this participation of the faithful lies in its pastoral effectiveness for the individual and is in no way necessary for the offering of the eucharist. However, Pius XII does leave the way open for further development of the role of the faithful in the liturgical act. The discussion continued at the Second Vatican Council.

THE CONSTITUTION ON THE LITURGY
AND THE CONCILIAR PERIOD

The Constitution on the Liturgy makes a special effort to stress the importance of the active participation of the laity in the eucharistic celebration. It views the eucharist of the local Church as the primary manifestation and realization of Church. Important to this celebration is the active participation of those present according to their roles. In general, the Constitution views the entire local assembly as active subject of the liturgical celebration. It does not view the priest alone as an active, direct subject. It is precisely from this perspective that the Council called for the reform of the rites. But questions remain. The Constitution on the Liturgy does not clarify the relationship of priest to faithful in the liturgical act nor does it attempt to articulate the relationship of the local assembly to the universal Church in the celebration of the eucharist. The first of these questions is addressed to some degree in other conciliar documents. But instead of clarifying the problem of the relationship, subsequent conciliar documents yield further ambiguity.

Vatican II's program for liturgical renewal was officially set in motion with the promulgation of the Constitution on the Liturgy on 4 December 1963. With his Motu Proprio *Sacram Liturgiam*[4] of 25 January 1964, Paul VI established an ad hoc committee known as the Consilium for the Implementation of the Constitution on the Liturgy.[5] Its purpose was to translate the conciliar principles into concrete ritual changes. The work of the Consilium, which was submitted to the (then) Congregation of Rites for approval and then to the pope for promulgation, progressed rapidly. Liturgical changes, particularly changes in the celebration of the Mass, were being made as

---

[4] Paul VI, Motu Proprio *Sacram Liturgiam*, on putting into effect some prescriptions of the Constitution on the Liturgy, 25 Jan. 1964: ICEL, *Documents on the Liturgy, 1963-1979: Conciliar, Papal, and Curial Texts* [hereafter, DOL] (Collegeville, Minn.: The Liturgical Press, 1982) 20.

[5] In 1969 the Consilium was made a special commission of the newly established Congregation for Divine Worship. See Paul VI, Apostolic Constitution *Sacra Rituum Congregatio*, 8 May 1969: DOL 94.

the Council Fathers continued their discussions. This enabled them to experience together the implementation of the changes which were a direct result of their deliberations, an experience that undoubtedly affected their future discussions and decisions. The effectiveness of the Constitution on the Liturgy, with its emphasis on the local Church and its recognition of the priesthood of all believers, was demonstrated by the influence it exerted on subsequent debates of other documents that emerged from the Council.[6] In the conciliar documents that followed the publication of the liturgy constitution, both a universalist/juridical and a local Church/communion ecclesiology are evident.

That the Fathers of the Second Vatican Council were aware of the need to relate the celebration of eucharist to their discussion of Church is apparent when one studies the several drafts of the Dogmatic Constitution on the Church (*Lumen gentium*). This is particularly evident in nos. 3, 7, and 11. In each case additions were made to earlier schemas of the document in order to highlight the relationship between eucharist and Church. While each of these articles points to the reception of holy communion as a sign and source of the unity of all believers, the Church set forth is the universal Church. There is, nonetheless, a shift in no. 26.

With an addition to no. 26, a shift has been made in which the local Church is viewed as truly Church when gathered around the bishop for the celebration of eucharist. The article affirms that the local community united with its bishop or his representative is truly Church. It is the duty of the bishop to regulate the liturgy so that it is truly a sign of the Church's unity. The bishop is referred to as "steward of the grace of the supreme priesthood." As such he is either to offer the eucharist or see that it is offered. This language is generally associated with a more traditional eucharistic theology. Viewed in the context of local Church ecclesiology, however, a shift has taken place. Emphasis is now put on the local assembly gathered around its bishop as immediate subject of the eucharist.

The Constitution on the Liturgy bases the active eucharistic participation of the faithful on baptism,[7] and the Constitution on the Church stresses this teaching: "The faithful on their part, in virtue

---

[6] The most significant documents in this regard are the Dogmatic Constitution on the Church *Lumen gentium* [hereafter, LG], the Decree on the Ministry and Life of Priests *Presbyterorum ordinis*, and the Decree on the Apostolate of the Laity *Apostolicam actuositatem*.

[7] See Vatican Council II, Constitution on the Liturgy *Sacrosanctum Concilium* [hereafter, SC], 4 Dec. 1963, art. 14: DOL 1, no. 14.

of their royal priesthood, join in the offering of the eucharist."[8] The nature of this mode of participation is briefly stated. The faithful are said to join in the offering of the eucharistic sacrifice which the priest both brings about and offers to God in their name.

The distinction between the common priesthood of the faithful and the ministerial priesthood follows the teaching of Pius XII in *Mediator Dei*.[9] Thus the two priesthoods are said to differ "in essence and not only in degree." The use of "in essence" is, perhaps, unfortunate. It could be interpreted to mean that the laity have an inferior degree of responsibility for the whole mission of the Church. But the discussion preceding the final formulation of this passage and the immediate context itself do not favor this interpretation. The phrase is simply meant to describe a new kind of ministry, mission, and authority of the ordained which is radically different from that of the laity because it is established by Christ and the Spirit.

The distinction indicates that a functional differentiation exists between ministerial and common priesthood. Beyond that the Dogmatic Constitution on the Church, in no. 10, affirms that the difference has a personal dimension grounded in ordination. Consequently certain kinds of ministry are reserved only to the ordained. This includes leadership of the eucharist.[10] However, it should be noted that the distinction between the role of the ministerial priesthood and that of the laity in the celebration of the eucharistic sacrifice was received in a new way by the Second Vatican Council. For, as we have seen, the Constitution on the Liturgy teaches that all present at the eucharist participate as direct subjects of the liturgical action.

However, the liturgy constitution does not provide a developed theological position on the question of the relationship between the participation of the faithful and that of the priest in the liturgical action. Only the two essential modes of participation of the priest-celebrant, in which the faithful have no part, are given close attention. The priest is said to be the only one who "makes present the eucharistic sacrifice and offers it to God in the name of all the people."[11]

---

[8] LG, no. 10: DOL 4, no. 140.

[9] See *Mediator Dei*, no. 67ff.

[10] Edward J. Kilmartin, "Lay Participation in the Apostolate of the Hierarchy," *The Jurist* 41 (1981), 346-347.

[11] LG, no. 10: DOL 4, no. 140.

Elsewhere in the Dogmatic Constitution on the Church as well as in the Decree on the Ministry and Life of Priests (*Presbyterorum ordinis*), reference is made to the differentiated roles of priest and laity in the offering of the eucharistic sacrifice. Number 11 of the Dogmatic Constitution on the Church, for example, states: "all take part in this liturgical service, not indeed all in the same way, but all in their proper way."[12] And no. 26 refers to the key role of the bishop in the eucharistic sacrifice. It points to the dominant role of the priest-celebrant and differentiates between the mode of offering of priest and laity.

The conciliar documents base the faithful's participation in the eucharist on baptism. A distinction is made between the participation of the common priesthood and the ministerial priesthood, but the theology of participation of each is not developed. Instead, reference is frequently made to former interpretations, particularly those of Pius XII. Ambiguity is thereby created within the conciliar documents concerning the participation of the faithful in the liturgical act.

POSTCONCILIAR LITURGICAL REFORMS (1964-1969)

The postconciliar documents produced during the years 1964 through 1969 demonstrate that their authors desired to remain faithful to the Council Fathers' directives regarding reform of the liturgy.

The first instruction for implementation of the principles set forth in the Constitution on the Liturgy *Inter Oecumenici* was published on 26 September 1964.[13] Of particular interest is the call for the vernacular in the chants and acclamations of the Mass, which may be sung or recited by the people. Thus the attention of the people may now be focused on the eucharistic prayer as they sing the acclamations in the vernacular.

Any discussion of the reforms of the Order of Mass must take into account the Decree *Ecclesiae semper*,[14] which promulgated the rites of concelebration and communion under both kinds. The decree, in its attempt to affirm the practice of concelebration with a clergy accustomed to celebrating individual, often private, Masses,

---

[12] LG, no. 11: DOL 4, no. 141.

[13] Congregation of Rites (Consilium), Instruction (first) *Inter Oecumenici*, on the orderly carrying out of the Constitution on the Liturgy, 26 Sept. 1964: DOL 23.

[14] Congregation of Rites (Consilium), Decree *Ecclesiae semper*, promulgating the *editio typica* of the rites of concelebration and of communion under both kinds, 7 March 1965: DOL 222.

stresses and highlights the role of the priest in the liturgical act and
fails to bring the role of the presider into relationship with that of
the assembly in this form of celebration.

The Introduction to the *Rite of Concelebration* does attempt to make
a clear distinction between the role of bishop (priest) presider and
concelebrants when in no. 13 it states that the principal celebrant
is to carry out all the rites and say all the prayers which he says
when no concelebrants are present. Thus, although some effort is
made to set up a clear relationship between presider and concelebrants in the celebration, questions remain as to the roles of priest
and assembly in the liturgical act.

In an address to the Consilium on 13 October 1966, Paul VI stated
several guidelines relating to the faithful's participation in the eucharist. The "task . . . is to make the liturgical rites plain and clear
to the majority of the faithful in their intelligibility, in their forms
of expression, in the way they are carried out."[15] Understanding is
essential for meaningful participation. Revision to ensure full,
meaningful participation is to be undertaken.

Paul VI stressed that all the particular Churches should be included in any discussion of the renewal of the rite. "The issue is
of such a serious and universal import that we cannot do otherwise
than consult with the bishops on any proposals before approving
them by our own authority."[16] This is a clear affirmation of the principle of local authority in the liturgy called for in the Constitution
on the Liturgy, article 22. Both the guidelines for the full participation of the faithful and the inclusion of particular Churches in the
discussion of reforms point toward a rite that allows for the full
participation of all in the liturgical act.

On 4 May 1967, the second instruction for the implementation
of the principles set forth in the Constitution on the Liturgy *Tres
abhinc annos* appeared. The instruction is particularly interesting from
two perspectives.

According to suggestions set forth in *Tres abhinc annos*, the Canon
is greatly simplified. Excessive genuflections and the multiplication
of "signs of the cross" are eliminated. The Canon may be recited
in the vernacular.[17] Thus, the Great Prayer of the Church is said

---

[15] Paul VI, Address to the members and *periti* of the Consilium, 13 Oct. 1966: DOL 84,
no. 633.

[16] Address: DOL 84, no. 636.

[17] See Congregation of Rites (Consilium), Instruction (second) *Tres abhinc annos*, on the
orderly carrying out of the Constitution on the Liturgy, 4 May 1967: DOL 39.

aloud in the language of the people so that active assent by the entire assembly in the Great Amen can take place. This ritual adjustment makes possible the participation of all the faithful in the fullness of the liturgical act.

The communion rite is also simplified according to norms in *Tres abhinc annos*. The priest and people together recite the "Lord, I am not worthy." As in the Canon, some "signs of the cross" are omitted. There is a fusion of the priest's and the faithful's communion pointing to the unity shared by all in the reception of holy communion. Since the reception of communion completes the liturgical act, and since the faithful are included in the same act of communion as the priest, it is possible to say that the rite itself indicates an underlying theological shift. The full, active participation of the laity in the liturgical act is now taken seriously.

Number 12 of the Instruction *Eucharisticum mysterium* contains the first specific postconciliar articulation of the distinction between the ministerial priesthood and the common priesthood of the faithful as exercised in the eucharist:

> The priest alone, insofar as he acts in the person of Christ, consecrates the bread and wine. Nevertheless the active part of the faithful in the eucharist consists in: giving thanks to God as they are mindful of the Lord's passion, death, and resurrection; offering the spotless victim not only through the hands of the priest but also together with him; and, through the reception of the body of the Lord, entering into the communion with God and with each other that participation is meant to lead to.[18]

In no. 11 of the same instruction the participation of the faithful is related to baptism, while in no. 42 the bishop's participation is related to ordination. In order to correctly interpret the relationship between the role of the bishop and the sacrament of ordination, it is necessary to look at the treatment of the role of bishop in context in this section of *Eucharisticum mysterium*.

The particular section which deals with the role of the bishop is derived from *Lumen gentium*, no. 26. Taken out of context, this section points to a traditional eucharistic theology. Seen, however, in the light of the broader discussion of eucharist and the role of the bishop, it is obvious that the entire, hierarchically organized, local assembly participates in the liturgical act. Here the influence

---

[18] Congregation of Rites, Instruction *Eucharisticum mysterium* [hereafter, EM], on worship of the eucharist, 25 May 1967, no. 12; DOL 179, no. 1241.

of article 41 of the Constitution on the Liturgy is evident, with its emphasis on the local community gathered around the bishop as primary manifestation of Church.[19]

The participation of priests in the Mass, according to their special sacramental sign, is discussed in no. 43 of *Eucharisticum mysterium*, which interprets article 28 of the Constitution on the Liturgy. Priests participate in the eucharist "by celebrating or concelebrating the Mass and not simply by receiving communion like the laity."[20] This view contrasts sharply with no. 12, in which the laity and priests are said to differ only in that the priest alone consecrates the eucharist.

With the promulgation of the Decree *Prece eucharistica* on 23 May 1968, the way was open for the creation of additional eucharistic prayers. Along with the adaptation and renaming of the Roman Canon, three new eucharistic prayers were provided. Since the whole body of believers takes part in the action, the prayers are designed with the faithful's participation in mind:

> Through the eucharistic prayer in the celebration of Mass the Church . . . has always continued to do what Christ did at the Last Supper and to offer thanks to the merciful Father for the wonderful works he has wrought in Christ to carry out the plan of salvation.[21]

In the course of the centuries, additions to the old Roman Canon were made which militated against its original clarity. Consequently, reform of the Roman Canon was a pastoral necessity in view of the concern for the active participation of the faithful. Along with the new eucharistic prayers, guidelines were provided to explain the structure and content of these prayers with the purpose of assisting the faithful to achieve their full, active participation, both internal and external, which the Council set as the goal of liturgical reform. The guidelines note the uniform and clear structure of the eucharistic prayers, which is designed to make the content of the prayers more easily intelligible and so enable fuller participation.

The faithful are directly involved in four key moments in the prayer: the introductory dialogue, the Sanctus, the memorial acclamation, and the Great Amen.[22] The purpose of this fourfold involve-

---

[19] EM, no. 42: DOL 179, no. 1271.

[20] EM, no. 43: DOL 179, no. 1272.

[21] Congregation of Rites (Consilium), Decree *Prece eucharistica*, promulgating three new eucharistic prayers and eight prefaces, 23 May 1968: DOL 241, no. 1930.

[22] See Pierre Jounel, "La composition des nouvelles prieres eucharistiques," *La Maison-Dieu* 94 (1968), 76.

ment, according to Frederick McManus, is "to keep everyone united to the inner purpose of the Eucharist, to celebrate the Lord's death and resurrection, and to make the Church's offering to the Father."[23] The need to include the faithful in the prayer is also explained by Jungmann:

> to say these prayers in the name of all and thus in the plural, was not considered sufficient. One also made sure of the express assent and joint action of the congregation. . . . The assent of the people was required in the Amen.[24]

The link between the remembrance of the Lord's death and the actual offering of the eucharist is contained in the anamnesis. John Barry Ryan demonstrates this point:

> The Anamnesis cannot be separated from the offering which follows it and the two elements are distinguished in order to unite them. "In the Anamnesis properly so-called" the idea of offering is included for it is the subject making the memorial of the mystery who offers. Two remarks are called for here. First of all, this memorial is not purely subjective for it is endowed also with a sacrificial sense expressed in the offering. Secondly, we say "Anamnesis properly so-called" for other parts of the EP include anamnesis or remembrance of the mighty deed of God or of His Christ. The difference is that in the berakah the Anamnesis was the motive for blessing God (as in the Preface) while in the "Anamnesis properly so-called" we have a liturgical cult act that actualizes and offers.[25]

Another change in the eucharistic prayer is the introduction of the explicit epiclesis. Traditionally, the epiclesis is found after the anamnesis. In the new prayers, the epiclesis is split. The prayers prior to the institution narrative point to a consecratory epiclesis. The effect of the twofold epiclesis is to call attention to the role of the Holy Spirit in the celebration. It is the Spirit who transforms the gifts of bread and wine presented by the people and offered in their name by the priest. At the same time, the Spirit ultimately sanctifies the recipients of the Body and Blood and unites them into one Body of Christ. The Spirit, who enables the Church to offer acceptable worship in union with Christ, is the living source of the life of faith. This aspect of the Spirit's activity in the celebration is

---

[23] Frederick R. McManus, "Liturgy Changes Oriented Towards the People," in National Catholic News Service (Washington: U.S. Catholic Conference, 18 Nov. 1968), 2.

[24] Josef A. Jungmann, *The Eucharistic Prayer: A Study of the Canon of the Mass*, trans. Robert L. Batley (Notre Dame: Fides, 1964), 31-32.

[25] John Barry Ryan, *The Eucharistic Prayer: A Study in Contemporary Liturgy* (New York: Paulist Press, 1974), 32-33.

not explicitly placed in the foreground of the eucharistic prayer. It
is implied, however, in the reference to the Holy Spirit as the ultimate gift communicated through the reception of holy communion. It is this Spirit who, according to Eucharistic Prayer IV, gathers
the communicants into the "one body of Christ" and so makes of
them "a living sacrifice of praise." Again, this pneumatological aspect of the eucharist affirms that the community gathered in the
Spirit is the immediate subject of the liturgical action.

The postconciliar documents produced during the years 1964
through 1969 demonstrated that their authors desired to remain faithful to the Council Fathers' directives regarding reform of the liturgy. During this same period, the *Ordo Missae* underwent constant
revision, progressively giving a more active role to the faithful. The
rite of the Mass was diversified, giving the celebrant, ministers, and
faithful respective roles in the celebration. A clear distinction was
made between the liturgy of the word and the liturgy of the eucharist.

The attempt to shift the focus from the celebrating priest to the
entire worshiping assembly was set in motion. The entire assembly performs the visible rite of the Church by actively participating
in the eucharistic prayer. The faithful unite their minds and hearts
with the prayers and intentions of the priest and they also actively
offer with him. The reforms of the Canon make it possible for the
faithful to participate in the offering. The entire eucharistic prayer
is said in the vernacular and the assembly responds to it with a series of acclamations. A distinction is made between the consecration, reserved to the priest alone, and the offering, in which all the
faithful participate. In the former, the priest who presides acts as
Christ's representative; in the latter, the faithful participate along
with the priest in the offering.

The reception of communion is the means of a more perfect participation in the offering; and so, the reception of communion during the celebration rightfully becomes the norm. In the revised
communion rite, the unity of priest and people is demonstrated in
the communion preparation and reception.

While it is clear that the faithful present participate in the liturgical act, difficulties remain. Attempts were made during this period to clarify the manner of participation of priest and faithful in
the offering. However, a full theological explanation of how priest
and faithful participate in the priesthood of Christ as it relates to
the offering of the eucharist was not developed.

Besides the changes introduced into the Mass during the period from 1964 through 1969, a proposed *Missa normativa* was introduced to the bishops at the 1967 Synod.[26] After experiencing the celebration of this modified rite, both the bishops and Paul VI provided reactions which helped to shape the 1969 *Ordo Missae*, which, together with the *Institutio Generalis Missalis Romani*, was promulgated in April 1969 in the Apostolic Constitution *Missale Romanum*.[27]

THE ORDER OF MASS OF PAUL VI (1970)

In the Apostolic Constitution *Missale Romanum*, Paul VI indicated the major changes in the new Missal. He referred to the General Instruction of the Roman Missal, which provides both regulations and explanations for the function of each individual participating in the celebration. In particular he mentioned that the eucharistic prayer with its collection of prefaces provided new possibilities for the active participation of the faithful, and he stated that the ritual had been simplified and the Word given a prominent place.[28] However, the new Order of Mass was greeted with some rather severe criticism in certain circles.[29] As a result, both the General Instruction and the Order of Mass were revised. The final redaction was published in the 1970 *Missale Romanum*. This text was promulgated together with a letter from the Congregation for Divine Worship on 26 March 1970.[30]

As a result of the negative criticisms of the 1969 edition of the General Instruction, an introduction was added in the 1970 edition and several significant changes were made in the original text. The introduction attempted to provide the historical context for the changes to calm the fears of traditionalists, who judged that the new Mass was calculated to undermine the traditional theology of the eucharist.

---

[26] See *Notitiae* 3 (1967), 353-380.

[27] See Paul VI, Apostolic Constitution *Missale Romanum*, approving the new Roman Missal, 3 Apr. 1969: DOL 202.

[28] See Paul VI, Apostolic Constitution *Missale Romanum*.

[29] One such reaction: A Group of Anonymous Roman Theologians, "A Critical Study of the Novus Ordo Missae," *Triumph* 4 (1969), 22-24.

[30] Congregation for Divine Worship, Presentation *Edita Instructione* of the changes introduced into the General Instruction of the Roman Missal, May 1970: DOL 205.

Congregation for Divine Worship, General Instruction of the Roman Missal [hereafter, GIRM], 4th ed., 27 Mar. 1975: DOL 208. This is a translation of the fourth edition of the General Instruction contained in the 1975 *editio typica altera* of the *Missale Romanum*. Variants of earlier editions of the General Instruction, including the second edition of 1970, are given in accompanying notes.

The Introduction highlights the key sections of the 1969 document which came under criticism. Together with the body of the text of the General Instruction, it provides evidence for the kind of presentation sought by the critics of the 1969 edition. Among the criticisms addressed, the subjects of anamnesis (with its stress on the memorial of the paschal mystery rather than an exclusive focus on the sacrifice of the cross) and ministerial priesthood are most relevant to the question of participation in the liturgical action.

The 1969 edition is prefaced by a decree of 6 April 1969 from the Congregation of Rites which states that the General Instruction is to replace the *Rubricae generales*, the *Ritus servandus in celebratione et concelebratione Missae*, and *De defectibus in celebratione Missae occurrentibus*.[31] It is noteworthy that the General Instruction provides a new outlook. It shifts from a prior concern for rubrical exactness to an emphasis on the nature of the Mass and its pastoral effectiveness. The 1970 edition, which is essentially the same, provides a theological statement for each component of the Mass for which it gives directives. These statements are generally summaries or quotations of Council documents which in some sense clarify the texts. Additions made in the 1970 edition emphasize the sacramental character of the ministerial priesthood, but do not devalue the role of the assembly in the offering of the sacrifice of Christ.

The General Instruction stresses that the role of the faithful is required because the eucharist is a celebration of the entire local assembly. Number 3 states reasons for the conscious, active, and full participation of the faithful in the Mass. First, "the Church desires this kind of participation"; second, "the nature of the celebration demands it"; and finally, "for the Christian people it is a right and duty they have by reason of their baptism."[32] The baptized are agents of the celebration, and active participation is encouraged so that all "may more fully receive its good effects."[33]

It is through active participation that the full effectiveness of the eucharist is realized for the gathered community. Therefore, the General Instruction provides for ritual changes which encourage participation. "There must be the utmost care therefore to choose and to make wise use of those forms and elements provided by the

---

[31] Congregation of Rites (Consilium), Decree *Ordine Missae*, promulgating the *editio typica* of the *Ordo Missae* and issuing the General Instruction of the Roman Missal, 6 Apr. 1969: DOL 203.

[32] GIRM, no. 3: DOL 208, no. 1393.

[33] GIRM, no. 2: DOL 208, no. 1392.

Church that . . . will best foster active and full participation and serve the spiritual well-being of the faithful."[34] In addition, common posture which "both expresses and fosters the spiritual attitude of those taking part"[35] is advocated. Since the acclamations are "the means of greater communion between priest and people"[36] they, along with other responses, are provided "in order to express clearly and to further the entire community's involvement."[37]

Every authentic celebration of the eucharist is directed by the bishop, either in person or through the presbyters, who are his helpers. Whenever he is present at a Mass with a congregation the bishop should preside over the assembly and associate the presbyters with himself in the celebration.[38] In addition to speaking of the role of the bishop or priest as that of presider, nos. 11, 12, and 13 indicate that the presider is also president of the congregation.

The priest engages the assembly in the four basic actions which constitute the eucharistic sacrificial meal, that is, taking, blessing, breaking, and giving. These actions, evident in the institution narrative in the New Testament and present in early liturgical texts, have always constituted the basic Christian eucharistic ritual. They have been given new expression in the *Ordo Missae* of Paul VI.

The General Instruction outlines the role which the presider holds in the eucharist: he is to greet the faithful; carry on a dialogue between himself and the assembly; invite the people to pray with him; and lead the people in the eucharistic prayer.[39] Numbers 7 and 10 relate the priest's action of presiding in the person of Christ to the particular ministry he is performing during the Mass. Traditional Catholic doctrine has repeatedly stated that the priest acts in the person of Christ. And although this is reinforced in the General Instruction, the emphasis on the priest as president/presider is a new one. These roles, together with the stress upon the participatory role of the faithful, caused concern among some that the role of the priest might be reduced to representation of the people rather than action in the person of Christ. The 1970 edition of the General Instruction remedied this by emphasizing the priest's role as representative of Christ.[40]

---

[34] GIRM, no. 5: DOL 208, no. 1395.
[35] GIRM, no. 20: DOL 208, no. 1410.
[36] GIRM, no. 14: DOL 208, no. 1404.
[37] GIRM, no. 15: DOL 208, no. 1405.
[38] GIRM, no. 59: DOL 208, no. 1449.
[39] See GIRM, nos. 28, 14, 32: DOL 208, nos. 1418, 1404, 1422.
[40] Compare no. 60 in the first edition of GIRM (1969) with the second edition (1970); see DOL 208, no. 1450, and accompanying footnote c.

Active participation in the eucharistic celebration is related to the experience of the full effects of the sacrifice. In no. 2, the fruits of the Mass are directly related to the individual's active participation in the rite. According to no. 56, the eucharistic celebration "is the paschal meal," and therefore "it is right that the faithful who are properly disposed receive the Lord's body and blood as spiritual food as he commanded. This is the purpose of the breaking of the bread and the other preparatory rites that lead directly to the communion of the people."[41] Thus this article stresses the importance of carrying through the symbolism of the meal as completely as possible in order that holy communion may be seen as being directly related to the sacrificial offering which just transpired.[42]

The Order of Mass of Paul VI provides a rite for the preparation of gifts whose rubrics explain that by bringing up the gifts the faithful express their participation. This procession with gifts represents a major shift from the parallel moment in the Tridentine Missal. The similar emphases of the Tridentine offertory and Canon were so close that the offertory was frequently referred to as the "little canon."

The revised rite for the preparation of the altar and the gifts calls for some of the faithful to be actively involved in the preparation rite. Many have said that the participation of the faithful in this rite is an essential element in the ritual.[43] What would seem to be essential is that some of the faithful bring the gifts to the priest, who receives them and places them on the altar in preparation for the eucharistic prayer. One might say that this ritual moment represents the "taking action" of the fourfold action which is the eucharist.

When this ritual action is either accompanied by the singing of a hymn, as suggested in the rite, or by the recitation of the two simple *berakoth* prayers by the priest, its utter simplicity is evident and therefore communicates clearly to the faithful that their role in this preparatory component is essential.

Several elements pertaining to the priest alone are carried over from the Tridentine Missal. The prayer *Deus qui* and the shortened version of Psalm 25 accompanying the *Lavabo* and the prayer *In spiritu humilitatis* are retained. All prayers are to be recited silently, however. They thus remain the private prayers of the priest and thereby

---

[41] GIRM, no. 56: DOL 208, no. 1446.

[42] See GIRM, nos. 5 and 56h: DOL 208, nos. 1395 and 1446.

[43] See Frederick R. McManus, "The New Order of the Mass, Part II," *American Ecclesiastical Review* 161 (1969), 405 and Karl Rahner and Angelus Haussling, *The Celebration of the Eucharist* (Montreal: Palm Publishing Co., 1968), 87, note 30.

enable the processional action of the faithful to be experienced in its fullness. When the prayers are said aloud, they can seem to anticipate the offering of the eucharist, which takes place during the eucharistic prayer.

Some would hold that the *berokoth* prayers themselves can become problematic. A spokesperson for this school is Ralph Keifer:

> The thanksgivings for the bread and the wine are prime examples of an approach which sought remedial compromise rather than real reform. They replaced an *apologia* for the personal unworthiness of the celebrant and an offering of the cup for the salvation of the world. Beautiful as the new prayers are, it can be asked what purpose is served by replacing old prayers which anticipated the anamnesis, or remembrance, of the eucharistic prayer with new ones which overshadow its praise and thanksgiving and are, in fact, authentic "blessings" (*berakoth*). Given this unsatisfactory revision, little more is needed than a poorly chosen hymn, or a misguided celebrant, for the rite to appear as a culminating moment of the eucharistic celebration.[44]

Of primary importance to the revision of the Missal of Paul VI, when considered in light of the theology of participation set forth in the Council documents, is the reform of the eucharistic prayer.

The eucharistic prayer is "the center and summit of the entire celebration."[45] It is recited by the priest who also engages the assembly in the opening dialogue and acclamations. The entire assembly is asked to "give thanks to the Lord our God."[46] The participation of the faithful in the eucharistic prayer is a dramatic change compared to their total lack of involvement in the Canon of the Tridentine Missal. The faithful's active participation in the rite is possible because of the vernacular. At several points during the prayer they are also encouraged to sing acclamations.

This ritual flow is designed to permit and foster the people's actual participation. In the opening dialogue and throughout the entire preface, the priest stands with hands extended and proclaims the reasons for giving thanks. The people, having been encouraged to give thanks, stand and pray together with the priest in reverent silence. The *Sanctus* is their hymn of praise and is a proper response to the many reasons for giving thanks.

---

44 Ralph Keifer, "Preparation of the Altar and the Gifts or Offertory?" *Worship* 48 (1974), 596.

45 GIRM, no. 54: DOL 208, no. 1444.

46 Opening Dialogue, Eucharistic Prayer, *Prayers We Have in Common*, 2nd rev. ed. (Philadelphia: Fortress Press, 1975), 14.

After the *Sanctus*, the prayer continues with the *Te igitur*, followed by the consecratory *epiclesis*. The gifts given by the faithful are now referred to as "our offering"; they are to "become for us the body and blood of Jesus Christ,"[47] through the power of the Spirit.

In the recitation of the institution narrative and through the accompanying gestures, the priest recalls the Last Supper. After raising the consecrated host and the chalice, he asks all to proclaim the mystery of faith. The assembled community, having shared in the Word and offered thanks, proclaims the great mystery:

> Dying you destroyed our death,
> rising you restored our life.
> Lord Jesus, come in glory.[48]

Both the *anamnesis* and the following prayer of offering are closely related. The priest prays:

> Father, we celebrate the memory of Christ, your Son.
> We, your people and your ministers,
> recall his passion, his resurrection from the dead,
> and his ascension into glory.[49]

The priest prays in the name of all: "We, your people and your ministers. . . ." The entire assembly makes the memorial and in so doing enters actively into the mystery with Christ.

The priest continues: "and from the many gifts you have given us we offer to you, God of glory and majesty, this holy and perfect sacrifice."[50] While the priest alone says the prayer, all present are involved in the sacrificial action.

Having offered the sacrifice in the name of all, the priest prays that the sacrifice will be acceptable to the Father and become a source of unity and strength: "Grant that we . . . may be filled with his Holy Spirit, and become one body, one spirit in Christ."[51]

The Church assembled prays for itself, for those not present, and for all the departed. These intercessions, made by the priest in the name of all, are found in each eucharistic prayer.

Since all Christian prayer to the Father is made through Jesus Christ, the eucharistic prayer concludes with the doxology, in which

---

47 Eucharistic Prayer I, *The Roman Missal* (*Sacramentary*) [hereafter, RM], 2nd Eng. ed., 1985.
48 RM, Memorial Acclamation.
49 RM, Eucharistic Prayer I.
50 RM, Eucharistic Prayer I.
51 RM, Eucharistic Prayer III.

the assembly proclaims that it is through, with, and in Christ that all glory and honor is given to the Father. The Great Amen is the faithful's final response and a sign of their acceptance of the entire eucharistic prayer.

In addition to the eucharistic prayer, the Missal of Paul VI made major revisions in the communion rite. This was done in order to permit greater participation by the faithful in the final two actions, the breaking and giving of the eucharist.

The Lord's Prayer and the breaking of the bread, which in the Tridentine Missal were linked by the fraction taking place during the doxology, are individual units in the new Missal. The breaking and giving actions are thus clearly distinct and visible. They are separated by the ritual action of the sign of peace, which was not present in the Tridentine rite. The *Agnus Dei*, recited previously as an independent prayer, is now sung or recited during the breaking of bread. A primary revision is the reception of communion. The separate or optional reception of communion by the faithful in the Tridentine rite is no longer the norm. Reception of the eucharist by priest and faithful form one unit. Finally, the elaborate ablutions after communion are simplified and may be done after the celebration or at the credence table.

The 1970 communion rite offers a variety of opportunities for the active participation of the entire assembly in the meal-action. The Lord's Prayer, said by the priest and assembly in unison, is followed by the sign of peace. The entire body is asked to exchange some ritual sign of peace and unity. As the priest-celebrant, assisted by other ministers, prepares the elements for distribution, the faithful participate in the action of the breaking of the bread through the singing of the Lamb of God. Then, together with the priest, all confess their unworthiness to receive the Lord prior to approaching the minister, who presents the Body and Blood to the individual in the giving action while saying: "Body of Christ," "Blood of Christ."

The General Instruction and Order of Mass of 1970 clearly stress that the entire local assembly gathered for eucharist is the subject of the official liturgical act. In earlier scholastic theology, the priest alone is immediate subject of the official ritual offering of the eucharistic sacrifice.

The ritual adjustments provide for full, conscious, and active participation of all members of the assembly in the liturgical action. Still, some articles of the General Instruction remain open to various interpretations. Thus the present period continues the process of reception of the teachings of the Constitution on the Liturgy and now includes a process of reception of the Order of Mass and the General Instruction of the Roman Missal.

ROMAN DOCUMENTS AFTER 1970

The period following the promulgation of the General Instruction and the Order of Mass yields legislation that interprets the reform and in some instances calls for further change.

Of particular interest is the General Catechetical Directory of 11 April 1971. The Directory provides guidelines for the formulation of national catechisms by the conferences of bishops. Its ecclesiological teachings follow the lead of *Lumen gentium*.[52] In other words, the Church is presented as a universal and local community. At the local level it is hierarchically organized and living in communion with the bishop of Rome through its local bishop.

The sacraments, in general, are described from a Christological viewpoint with the emphasis placed on the active presidency of Jesus Christ and the ministerial role of the priest, that is, his role to act as instrument of Christ in the celebration of the eucharist and in the administration of the sacraments. The role of the rest of the community in the sacramental celebration is not mentioned.[53]

The section which deals specifically with Holy Orders places stress on the role of the priest to represent "Christ's person" in the offering of the sacrifice of the Mass. No mention is made of the relationship of the priest who presides at the eucharist to the gathered community, particularly his function to represent that community.

The passage which takes up the subject of the eucharist also focuses exclusively on the mystery of Christ's activity in the sacrificial action and his real presence under the forms of bread and wine. Elsewhere one reference is made to the self-offering which the faithful make in the liturgy. Nowhere in the Directory, however, is the subject of the ritual participation of the laity in the eucharistic celebration discussed. This omission is difficult to explain, especially since the Directory explicitly intends to include those aspects of the theology of the eucharistic celebration which ought to be included

---

[52] Congregation for the Clergy, *Directorium catechisticum generale*, AAS 64 (1972), 97-176: Eng. ed., *General Catechetical Directory* (London: Catholic Truth Society, 1971).

[53] *Directorium*, 130; Directory, 48.

in every national catechism. But the neglect of this aspect of the liturgical celebration has the practical effect of relegating it to a secondary place.

The 1971 Synod of Bishops addressed the question of ministerial priesthood. The decree emanating from this gathering focuses primarily on the identity of the presbyter in light of conciliar reforms. Two statements are of particular interest concerning the question of participation in eucharist.

The first is related to the priest's role of "presiding over and effecting the sacrificial banquet wherein the People of God are associated with Christ's offering."[54] This section repeats the teaching of *Lumen gentium*, no. 28, but it yields no further clarification.

Of particular interest is the second statement. Within a discussion of the spiritual life of priests, the decree states:

> Even if the Eucharist should be celebrated without participation by the faithful, it nevertheless remains the center of the life of the entire Church and the heart of priestly existence.[55]

The Constitution on the Liturgy, no. 27, highlighted the communal nature of the eucharistic liturgy. As a matter of compromise, the phrase "even though every Mass has of itself a public and social character" was added to the very strong statement calling for communal celebrations. It is unfortunate that what was admitted to the Council document as a compromise becomes the primary focus in the discussion of eucharist in the Synod decree. There is no positive statement in the decree concerning the role of the assembly in the eucharistic action.

In the declaration *In celebratione Missae* from the Congregation for Divine Worship, 7 August 1972, attention is given to the distinction between the ministerial priest's role and that of the faithful in the liturgical action. Of particular interest to this discussion is the statement:

> Because of the distinct sacrament of orders, priests exercise a function peculiar to them in the celebration of the Mass when, either individually or together with other priests, by a sacramental rite they bring about the presence of Christ's sacrifice, offer it, and through communion share in it.[56]

---

[54] *De Sacerdotio ministeriali*, AAS 63 (1971), 898-922; *The Ministerial Priesthood and Justice in the World* (Washington: National Conference of Catholic Bishops, 1971), 14.

[55] *The Ministerial Priesthood*, 22.

[56] *In celebratione Missae*, AAS 64 (1972), 561-563; "Declaration on Concelebration," in *Study Text 5: Eucharistic Concelebration* (Washington: USCC, 1978), 2.

It has been demonstrated that the reform recognized a particular and differentiated role for the priest/presider in the liturgical action specifically because of his role as president of the assembly. *In celebratione Missae*, by indicating that all priests present participate in this differentiated role, confuses the development present in the General Instruction concerning the relationship of priest/presider to assembly.

In 1972, Paul VI in *Ministeria quaedam* established lay ministries.[57] Many questions are raised by this document, yet it has extended the possibility of a variety of liturgical ministries for the laity. It stresses the idea that the gathered community, a hierarchically ordered body, is active subject of the eucharistic celebration.

The question of the faithful's reception of communion from hosts consecrated at the Mass at which they are received has been an active one throughout this century. The practice was again put forth in the Constitution on the Liturgy, art. 55. Not only is the priest to receive from the host consecrated at the Mass, but so too are all the faithful. This serves to highlight the participation of all in the completion of the liturgical action in the reception of communion.

Pius XII stressed that the priest's communion alone was necessary to complete the sacrifice. In *Holy Communion and Worship of the Eucharist outside Mass*, 21 June 1973, all present are encouraged to receive "from the same sacrifice" and so experience a "more complete participation in the eucharistic celebration."[58] This is a clear example of the "reception" principle at work. While not explicitly negating Pius XII's teaching, the document strongly affirms the Constitution on the Liturgy. The act of receiving communion completes the meal-action. Both priest and faithful participate in the action in union.

CONCLUSION

The ritual reforms of the Mass emanating from the Council have consistently recognized the full participation of the faithful in the liturgical action. Yet, unless these reforms are understood they cannot be fully effective in bringing about a transformation of the faith community.

---

[57] Paul VI, Motu Proprio *Ministeria quaedam*, on first tonsure, minor orders, and the subdiaconate, 15 Aug. 1972: DOL 340.

[58] Congregation for Divine Worship, *Holy Communion and Worship of the Eucharist outside Mass*, Chapter 1, 21 June 1973: DOL 266, no. 13.

The documents treated in the last part of this paper are but a few examples of the diversity of thought present in Roman documents subsequent to the reform of 1970. Decrees continue to be ambiguous as to the specific manner in which priest/presider, priest/concelebrant, and other members of the assembly participate in the local Church's eucharist. This diversity of understanding permits a diversity of interpretation as to how priest and faithful participate. The diversity of interpretations in turn gives rise to a variety of liturgical experiences of the eucharist both for the priest who presides and for the other members of the assembly. Thus it is possible at this moment in our history to observe great diversity among our congregations as they gather to celebrate Mass on Sunday.

Two ecclesiologies, two eucharistic theologies, continue to exist side by side. When the congregation gathered for Sunday Mass truly understands that the eucharist is Christ's gift to the Church, that is, the local Church assembled under the leadership of the priest, presiding in the person of Christ, then the local Church will be seen to be the immediate subject of the action of the eucharist. In contrast, when the faithful attend Sunday Mass with the understanding that the priest acts for them, then no matter how many ritual changes there are, the laity will continue to see themselves as passive recipients of the eucharistic action.

SOURCES CONSULTED

Challancin, James. *A Liturgy for the Local Church*. Rome: Pontifical Institute for Liturgy, St. Anselm's University, 1980.

Crichton, James D. *Christian Celebration: The Mass*. London: Geoffrey Chapman, 1971.

Deekers, Eligius. "Concelebration-Limitations of Current Practice." *Doctrine and Life* 22 (1972), 190-202.

Jungmann, Josef A. *The Eucharistic Prayer: A Study of the Canon of the Mass*. Trans. by Robert L. Batley. Notre Dame, Ind.: Fides, 1964.

Keifer, Ralph. "Preparation of the Altar and the Gifts or Offertory?" *Worship* 48 (1974), 595-600.

Kelleher, Margaret Mary. "Liturgy: An Ecclesial Act of Meaning." *Worship* 59 (1985), 482-497.

Kilmartin, E.J. "Money and the Ministry of the Sacraments." *The Finances of the Church*. Edited by Bassett and Huizing. New York: Seabury Press, 1979, 104-111.

Kilmartin, E.J. *Church, Eucharist and Priesthood: A Theological Commentary*. New York: Paulist Press, 1981.

McManus, Frederick R. *Sacramental Liturgy*. New York: Herder and Herder, 1967.

Rahner, Karl and A. Haussling. *The Celebration of the Eucharist*. Trans. by W.J. O'Hara. New York: Herder and Herder, 1968.

Rahner, Karl. "Theses on Prayer in the Name of the Church." *Theological Investigations*, V. New York: Herder and Herder, 1966, 419-438.

Ryan, John Barry. *The Eucharistic Prayer: A Study in Contemporary Liturgy*. New York: Paulist Press, 1974.

LANGUAGE AND LITURGY

REVISING THE ORDER OF CHRISTIAN FUNERALS

Michael Hodgetts

I. CONSULTATION AND REVISION

Right from the beginning of the work of the International Commission on English in the Liturgy (ICEL) it had been understood that after some years of use the texts would need revising. The huge task of translating most of the liturgical books into English was not completed until 1978, but by then plans had already been made for the revision. For the pilot scheme the 1970 translation of *Rite of Funerals* was chosen, partly because it was one of the earliest ICEL texts, partly because it was in constant use (except in England and Wales, which had another version), and partly because it was reasonably short.

Early in 1981 two thousand workbooks were sent out all over the world, containing the Latin, the 1970 translation, and space for comments and amendments. The result was 700 pages of proposed amendments to a rite which, even including one-line antiphons, consists of only seventy texts. The secretariat in Washington rearranged all this material, so that all the comments on one prayer were together, and also analyzed them under the headings of "Structure/Language" and "Theological/Pastoral." To ensure fair play, the names of the respondents were deleted and replaced by a number and the country from which each of them came. Despite this, individual styles were clearly apparent, and the revisers became familiar with the approach of "Canada 5" or "England and Wales 17," while the vigorous comments of "U.S.A. 61" had a marked influence on the treatment of the Songs of Farewell. There can be no doubt that this consultation justified its considerable cost, and ICEL is grateful to all those who replied.

Under the heading of "Structure/Language" were requests for, among other things, a more complex structure, with subordinate clauses; greater attention to musicality and rhythm; a fuller use of expressions of praise and supplication; a greater willingness to use

Romance and polysyllabic words; and a more adventurous vocabulary. Comments under the heading "Theological/Pastoral" included
allegations of Pelagianism; requests for a more consistent theology
of the state between death and resurrection; requests for a warmer
tone which would offer consolation to the bereaved; and specific
points about the rendering of such words as *anima, famulus, lux ae-
terna* and so on.

In September 1982 ICEL's subcommittee on translations and revisions (TR for short) met in Washington to consider these comments.
Within a few minutes it became clear that we were of one mind on
the line to be taken. Although the detailed suggestions often contradicted one another, we agreed that considerable weight should
be given to the consultation, both because of the substantial response
and because the general sense of the answers was consistently in
favor of a fuller and richer style. We also judged that this, together
with many detailed amendments and modifications was perfectly
compatible with the ICEL principles of clarity, simplicity, and the
use of contemporary accidence and syntax. We therefore formulated
a number of principles which we thought should govern the revision, along with specimen texts conforming to these principles.

In November 1982 these principles were approved and further
refined by the Advisory Committee of ICEL, and TR was authorized
to go ahead. At a meeting of TR in Washington in May 1983, revised
versions were drafted of about a third of the seventy texts, and two
members (including the author of this article) were delegated to polish these and to produce drafts of the other two-thirds. This they
did in Auckland, New Zealand, in August 1983. The complete draft
was further amended and then approved by the full subcommittee
in Washington that December. In August 1984 the seventy prayers
were approved, with further minor changes, by the Advisory Committee in London and immediately afterwards considered by a joint
meeting of the Advisory Committee and the Episcopal Board. The
introduction and rubrics and the original prayers (which were dealt
with by two other subcommittees and were not in final form by August 1984) were approved at the next Advisory Committee meeting
in February 1985. The completed book entitled *Order of Christian
Funerals* was published by ICEL in October 1985.[1]

---

[1] *Order of Christian Funerals* (Washington: ICEL, 1985) [hereafter, *Order*]; *Ordo Exsequiarum* (Rome: Vatican Polyglot Press, 1969) [hereafter, Latin]; *Consultation on Revision: Rite of Funerals*
(Washington: ICEL, 1981) [hereafter, Workbook].

Three comments need to be made about this process of consultation and revision. The first is that the actual translators submit a text for consideration: they do not, as is sometimes suggested, impose it. A draft does not become an official ICEL text until the Episcopal Board has approved it by a two-thirds majority; and even then the decision to use it in a particular country rests with the bishops of that country. Since the hierarchy of England and Wales had in fact voted not to use the 1970 ICEL version of the funeral rites, it was clear to everyone that the episcopal scrutiny of the texts was no mere formality.

Second, it might be thought that the process was too complicated. It has now been somewhat simplified, as a result of experience gained in working on the *Order of Christian Funerals*, but since this was to be the model for the revision of all the liturgical books it was important that it should be done thoroughly and carefully. The shortcomings of some earlier ICEL texts were due largely to the haste with which they had to be produced; this time there was no deadline to meet and we could afford to have second and third thoughts.

Third, and more radically, it might be said that there is no need of committees at all: it would be enough to find a distinguished poet and commission him or her to translate the lot, subject only to examination by three or four theologians and liturgists. But, apart from the difficulty of finding a literary figure both able and willing to tackle such a huge assignment, there is another difficulty which arises from the oral nature of all liturgical texts. Most modern poetry is written for silent contemplation on the printed page, with a consequent emphasis on idiosyncratic imagery at the expense of clarity and rhythm. Liturgical language is intended to be spoken or sung and heard and must be judged by quite different criteria from those that apply to most twentieth-century literature. The exception, an important one, is modern poetic drama—a point to which I shall return.

In any case, although all of us had brilliant solutions that we could not persuade our colleagues to accept, the draft did improve steadily at each stage. A single example will illustrate the point. There is an antiphon to Psalm 51[2] which in the Latin runs, *Animam de corpore quam assumpsisti, Domine, fac gaudere cum sanctis tuis in gloria*. In the 1970 ICEL version this was rendered as:

> Lord, may our brother/sister, whom you have called to yourself, find happiness in the glory of your saints.

---

[2] Latin, no. 149; *Order*, p. 271, no. 347(4); Workbook, p. 73.

This is a cumbrous translation of a cumbrous original, and it is possible to wonder whether anyone has ever actually sung either. It
is too long and diffuse to be memorized as an antiphon; the optative "may" is weak; and alternatives like "brother/sister" are best
avoided in texts for singing, even when, as here, they are metrically
equivalent. Accordingly, with Philippians 1:23 in mind, a working
group draft of August 1983 ran:

> Dissolved and with Christ,
> rejoice with the saints in glory.

Here the imperative is stronger than an optative and avoids the need
for a change of gender, and *animam de corpore* is at least suggested
by the context of the Pauline quotation. Further, the antiphon falls
naturally into two phrases, one of two stresses and one of three,
so that musical setting is much easier.

The full subcommittee, however, meeting in Washington in December 1983, thought that "dissolved," especially as the first word
of the antiphon, would baffle the congregation, many of whom might
not be regular churchgoers or familiar with the epistles. So "dissolved" was altered to "transformed." But the Advisory Committee
in August 1984 thought that "transformed" was open to the same
objection as "dissolved." Then one of its members, remembering
1 Thessolonians 4:16 (which is one of the readings for a Funeral Mass)
and also 2 Corinthians 12:4, suggested "caught up." This was clearly
the neatest solution, evoking St. Paul's vivid words about "in the
body or out of the body" while not depending on them, and also
reinforcing the word "Christ" by alliteration. The final version therefore runs:

> Caught up with Christ,
> rejoice with the saints in glory.

It is doubtful if a single translator, however sensitive, would have
teased out all the considerations quite so pertinaciously.

II. SENSE AND FORM

This example also illustrates the difficulty of reconciling matter
and form – of rendering the Latin fully and of rendering it in a form
in which it can be used. Under the first heading are the problems
of verbal accuracy, avoidance of ambiguity, theological precision,
awareness of scriptural and patristic allusions, sensitivity to meta-

phors and so on. Under the second heading are the problems of syntax, English idiom, logical order, rhythm, sound and, for a sung text, suitability for musical setting. The trouble is that these two principles tend to pull in opposite directions. At one extreme, it would be possible to produce a rendering in which no nuance or allusion of the original was missing, but at the cost of making it cumbrous, difficult to follow, and probably very long. At the other extreme, it is possible to write a concise and penetrating prayer which retains only a phrase or two from the original. Both procedures can be defended, for different purposes, but if your brief is to produce a translation of the Latin for liturgical purposes you have to aim somewhere in the middle and risk getting kicked from both sides. More than that, it is not possible to adopt a single formula for every case, since the genre of the prayer influences how far you lean towards grammatical accuracy and how far towards effective performance. A phrase which causes no problems when spoken by a single celebrant may sound awkward when recited in unison, and still more so when sung by a congregation. It is true that with care and practice people can learn to negotiate even the most ungainly expressions (the first verse of "The Lord's my shepherd," for instance); but there is no reason why they should have to.

The actual procedure in the subcommittee was this. We started with our copies of the workbook, containing a summary of the consultors' points as well as the Latin and the 1970 ICEL translation. The Latin and the English were read aloud. Then the comments were considered, a line at a time where possible. Some of them were turned down as not weighty enough to justify a change. Some of them were simple corrections or improvements which could be incorporated without any trouble. More often, a change in one place involved other changes elsewhere. Sometimes it was necessary to redraft the entire prayer. Very often the consultors were agreed that a particular phrase was unsatisfactory but disagreed about what should replace it. Then we might seek inspiration in Roget's *Thesaurus* or, for words which made implicit allusions to the Vulgate, in various translations of the Bible. In one of the prayers (see Latin, no. 173), for instance, the phrase *praestolanda resurrectione* instead of the more usual *exspectanda resurrectione* is perhaps a reminiscence of Job 17:15 and 30:26. In this case (see *Order*, p. 84, no. 164D) we were unable to devise a formula which both suggested the allusion and also maintained the flow of the prayer. Such phrases would be easier to deal with if there was still a single familiar version of

the Bible, such as the Douay or King James versions, but we have
to accept that there is not.

When the revised draft was more or less satisfactory as a translation, it was read aloud again to be judged for euphony and rhythm.
More changes might be needed to eliminate jerky movement, unin-
tentional assonance or awkward collocations of consonants. Finally,
it was read a third time, to ensure that all members of the subcommittee were clear about all the decisions.

For an illustration of this procedure, we can take the *Subvenite*,
one of the Songs of Farewell at the final commendation.[3] For these
eight lines, there were twenty pages of proposed amendments. In
line 6, for *in sinum Abrahae*, the 1970 version had "to Abraham's side."
Some consultors wanted to keep that; some wanted other
paraphrases; some wanted "the bosom of Abraham"; one wanted
"of Abraham and Sarah." How were we to decide? If the phrase was
translated literally, would the mourners pick up the allusion to Luke
16:22? Would it matter if they were puzzled for a moment? How
far should we allow for the fact that some of them would not be
practicing Catholics? Is such a Hebraism acceptable in a sung text
but not in, say, a collect? Does poetry depend on obscurity and
challenges to the imagination? Would it be better to use some native English expression, such as "paradise"? On the other hand,
should one of our aims be to naturalize unfamiliar phrases by using them in the liturgy? "Paradise" itself was originally a Persian
word, introduced into Greek by Xenophon and then taken over by
the Septuagint for the "garden of delight" in Genesis 2:15. And if
we object to "the bosom of Abraham," should we also object to "Shalom" (which ICEL does not use), or to "Amen" and "Alleluia" (which
it does).

Lines 3 and 4 (the actual response) of the *Subvenite* pose another
tricky problem. In Latin they run, *Suscipientes animam eius, offerentes
eam in conspectu Altissimi*—participles which have no grammatical
connection with the *Requiem aeternam* which forms the third verse
of the responsory. In 1970, ICEL had "Receive his/her soul and present him/her to God the Most High." The transition from the soul
to the person is awkward, but referring to the soul as "it" would
be even more so. (The Latin *eam* is, of course, feminine grammatically, not personally.) There is no way of avoiding these problems
in English as long as you use the third person. But lines 5-6 are

---

[3] Latin, nos. 47 and 66; *Order*, p. 90, no. 174; *Workbook*, p. 32.

addressed directly to the dead person: "May Christ, who called you, take you to himself; may angels lead you to the bosom of Abraham (or whatever)." Many consultors commented on the confusion likely to be caused by this transition. So would it be simpler to put the whole thing into the second person: "May the saints of God come to your aid; may the angels come to meet you; receiving you and presenting you," and so on? That would avoid both the change of person and the alternative genders. But it would also make the opening less dramatic; and what happens, again, when we get to the "Eternal rest"–which most people thought should be left in the traditional form (as it was not in 1970), so that the congregation can join in without any stumbling?

Apart from all that, the 1970 text had already been set to music before the revisions began, so that to change it in any way at all would introduce yet another source of confusion. Against that it can be argued that this whole business of trying to sing prose responsories with lines of unequal length is a technique which works well enough with plainsong but is not native to English. When the Song of Farewell is sung, the minister is more likely to substitute a hymn, such as "Abide with Me."[4] So perhaps the solution would be to write original English hymns, incorporating thoughts and images from the Latin, like the one which I wrote for the Society of St. Gregory in 1976 and which has been used at the funerals of both my parents?[5] But in that case ICEL would be accused of not *translating* the Latin.

What we eventually did was, understandably, a series of compromises. In the *Subvenite* itself, only three changes were made from 1970: "Hasten to meet him" for the weaker "Come to meet him"; "the bosom of Abraham" for: "to Abraham's side"; and the traditional form of the "Eternal rest." But in the five alternative Songs of Farewell we were more radical. In each of them the verses were regularized, so that each verse had the same number of lines, and corresponding lines had the same number of stresses. This ensures that they can now be sung in any parish with a cantor capable of leading a Grail psalm. For "I know that my Redeemer lives," an alternative metrical version was provided as well, so that even a cantor is unnecessary. The effect of these changes in one of them, the *Libera me*[6], can be seen in a direct comparison between 1970 (the

---

[4] The *Order* includes English hymns on: p. 303, no. 375; p. 317, no. 387; pp. 327-330, no. 396.
[5] *Music & Liturgy* 2, no. 4 (Autumn, 1976), 115.
[6] Latin, no. 191; *Order*, p. 367, no. 403(7); Workbook, p. 37.

original ICEL version), 1971 (the version used in England and Wales), and 1985 (the ICEL revision).

1970   Lord, lead me out of the ways of darkness; you broke down the gates of death, and visited the prisoners of darkness; * you brought them light to let them see your face.

They cried out in welcome: "Redeemer, you have come at last!" * you brought them light. . . .

Give him/her eternal rest, O Lord, and may your light shine on him/her for ever; * you brought them light. . . .

1971   Deliver me, Lord,
from the path that leads to destruction.
You broke asunder the gates of Hell,
came among those who were in the regions of death,
and gave them the light to see yourself.
* Those who were imprisoned in darkness.

You have come, our Redeemer, they cried:
* Those who were imprisoned in darkness.

Lord, grant him/her everlasting rest:
and let perpetual light shine upon them.
* Those who were imprisoned in darkness.

1985   You shattered the gates of bronze
and preached to the spirits in prison.
* Deliver me, Lord, from the streets of darkness.

A light and a revelation
to those confined in darkness.
* Deliver me, Lord, from the streets of darkness.

"Redeemer, you have come!"
they cried, the prisoners of silence.
* Deliver me, Lord, from the streets of darkness.

Eternal rest, O Lord,
and your perpetual light.
* Deliver me, Lord, from the streets of darkness.

III. IMAGERY AND THEOLOGY

It will be noticed in this third version that no attempt has been made to tone down the imagery. Some consultors had expressed disquiet about phrases which seemed more reminiscent of Aeneid VI than of the Gospels. In the 1970 version a certain amount of adapting had been done, but the results were not satisfactory either as translations or as modern prayers. Since the 1985 *Order of Christian Funerals* was to include alternative original prayers, TR decided to translate the imagery of the Latin as it stood, as far as was consistent with intelligibility. So, in the example just quoted, "the gates of bronze" from Psalm 106:16 has replaced "the gates of death" for *portas aereas*, but "the gates of death" has in turn been kept, despite the misgivings of some consultors, in the prayer on page 335, no. 398(3), of the *Order*, where the Latin has *portas mortis*. If the minister judges that the imagery of a particular text may be alien or puzzling to the mourners, the minister can choose one of the alternatives. In this case, I think that the image of breaking down the gates is both vivid and poignant: in this quotation from *The Times* (London) of 9 May 1985 it was the natural phrase to use:

> For some, yesterday could only trigger memories of unbearable suffering. The Chief Rabbi, Sir Immanuel Jakobovits, addressed survivors of Hitler's attempted genocide beside the holocaust memorial in Hyde Park. "There is not a single Jew here who has not got next-of-kin who died in the camps," he said. Among those listening was an English Jew and former Intelligence Corps sergeant, Mr. Norman Turgel, who had helped to liberate Belsen camp. Beside him was his wife Gena; she had been in the camp for five years and was close to death when the Allies finally burst down its gates.

The same principle has been applied to the theology of the prayers (which is often difficult to distinguish from their imagery). Many of them were written before the theology of life after death assumed its present form.[7] Some expressions in them do not sit easily with sixteenth or twentieth century theology, and there were consultors who urged strongly that they should be "corrected." But since the Latin itself had already been revised in accordance with the Constitution on the Liturgy of Vatican II,[8] it was the subcommittee's view that it should be rendered accurately, even if inconsistently.

This does not mean that every Latin word must have a corresponding word in the English. ICEL has sometimes been accused of Pelagianism, because of its sparing use of phrases like *propitius*,

---

[7] See Richard Rutherford, *The Death of a Christian* (New York: Pueblo, 1980).

[8] Vatican Council II, Constitution on the Liturgy *Sacrosanctum Concilium*, 4 Dec. 1963, art. 81-82: ICEL, *Documents on the Liturgy, 1963-1979: Conciliar, Papal, and Curial Texts* (Collegeville, Minn.: The Liturgical Press, 1982) 1, nos. 81-82: *Ritus exsequiarum paschalem mortis christianae indolem manifestius exprimat, atque condictionibus et traditionibus singularum regionum, etiam quoad colorem liturgicum, melius respondeat. Recognoscatur ritus sepeliendi parvulos, ac propria Missa donetur.*

tua miseratione, and *famuli tui* and its avoidance of passive subjunctives and participles. In 1985 many of these deprecative expressions have been restored, but they may be balanced by greater concision elsewhere. Thus in the prayer on page 60, no. 117A, of the *Order* the phrase "in your wisdom" has been added to represent *vocare dignatus es* and to soften the suggestion, noted by several consultors, of an arbitrary act of God. But further down the same prayer the English text in 1970 read, "raise him/her up to live for ever with all your saints in the glory of the resurrection" but is now, much more pithily, "and be raised up in glory with all your saints." Often such expressions have been moved to the address as adjectives qualifying "God," where the Latin has only a brusque and unsupported *Deus*. If there is no such phrase in the body of the prayer, a suitable one may even be added, as in a prayer for a married couple (*Order*, p. 343, no. 398 [31]), which begins "Lord God, whose covenant is everlasting" instead of the plain "Lord" for *Domine* of a literal translation.

In translating the subjunctives, less use has been made of optative "mays" and more of imperatives (with or without deprecative expressions) and of final clauses and "grant thats." So in the prayer for the family of a baptized child, where the text of 1970 had "May we one day join him/her" for *Nos etiam cum illo aeterni gaudii tribuas esse consortes*, the 1985 text (*Order*, p. 146, no. 262A) has "so call us one day to be united . . . ." No one grammatical construction can express the whole theology of grace, but the revisers have taken care to avoid imputations of Pelagianism, even though they think that these imputations against their predecessors are unjustified.

A problem which caused considerable discussion was what to do about *anima*. The translators of 1970 were rightly chary of suggesting a Platonist and Cartesian psychology which can make the resurrection of the body seem an irrelevant postscript. It is the whole person, constituted by body and soul, who is redeemed and saved. Moreover, the distinction is not always well expressed in the Latin. The Latin text for the English prayer on page 336, no. 398(9), of the *Order* begins with a statement that to God *non pereunt moriendo corpora nostra sed mutantur in melius* (which to one consultor suggested "universal bodily assumption immediately after death") and continues with a petition that the *soul* of the deceased will be raised up on the last day (*ut suscipi iubeas animam famuli tui N. . . . resuscitandam in novissimo die*). In the *Subvenite* it is at least possible that the periphrasis *animam eius* was used to avoid the alternatives *eum*/*eam*, particularly awkward in a sung text; and, perhaps for the same reason, the common gender dative *ei* is twice used of the deceased in the *Qui Lazarum*, even though grammatically its only possible antecedent is Lazarus himself.[9] In English there is the further difficulty that any pronouns used with "soul" must be neuter, in contexts where "he" or "she" will have occurred a line or two before. It is noticeable that in the prayers at the graveside, where the distinction needs to be made more clearly than at any other point in the rite, the straight opposition of *corpus* and *anima* is only used twice in the Latin (see Latin, nos. 193, 195 and *Order*, pp. 370-371, nos. 405[2] and 405[4]). Elsewhere it is *corpora*/*famulus tuus*;[10] *fratrem nostrum*/*corpus eius*;[11] *famulo tuo . . . dormitio, et . . . resuscitatio*;[12] *caro*/*anima*;[13] *his qui Christo, commortui et consepulti, beatam spem resurrectionis exspectant*.[14]

In view of these problems, the 1970 translation avoided the use of "soul" where possible, though, as the *Subvenite* shows, not entirely. In the 1985 *Order of Christian Funerals* it has been used wherever the logic of the prayer demanded it and sparingly on other occasions where the problems could be overcome. In the prayer on pp. 336-337, no. 398(9), of the *Order* the phrase about the raising up of the soul has been retained, but with a number of words between, so that the shift of subject is less obtrusive. In the next prayer on p. 337, no. 398(10), of the *Order*, the corresponding Latin verbs have been rendered by a string of noun-phrases following "Grant to the soul of your servant N." as given below:

> Lord God, in whom all find refuge,
> we appeal to your boundless mercy:
> grant to the soul of your servant N.
> a kindly welcome,
> cleansing of sin,
> release from the chains of death,
> and entry into everlasting life.
>
> We ask this through Christ our Lord.
> R. Amen.

---

[9] Latin, no. 190; *Order*, p. 367, no. 403(6); Workbook, p. 36.

[10] Latin, nos. 53, 71; *Order*, p. 114, no. 218A (also p. 124, no. 226A and p. 370, no. 405[1]); Workbook, p. 42.

[11] Latin, nos. 55, 72; *Order*, p. 115, no. 219A (also p. 372, no. 406[1]); Workbook, p. 46.

[12] Latin, no. 194; *Order*, p. 371, no. 405(3); Workbook, p. 44.

[13] Latin, no. 195; *Order*, p. 371, no. 405(4); Workbook, p. 45.

[14] Latin, no. 199; *Order*, p. 114, no. 222B; Workbook, p. 50.

In this way, "soul" does not need a pronoun and the question of its gender is avoided.

In this and other prayers, for *animam/famuli tui* the 1970 version had "your son/daughter" or "our brother/sister." This rendering was much criticized, though it is worth noting that *frater* is sometimes used in the Latin.[15] "Servant" has been replaced in a number of prayers in the *Order of Christian Funerals*, not only because it is more literal but also because it avoids the awkwardness of constant alternatives divided by slashes for a deceased man or woman. The same applies to the use of relative clauses. "Servant" and "who" (or "whom" or "whose") are of common gender; "who," in fact, in all its cases is also both singular and plural. Alternatives cannot be eliminated altogether, but there is a case for avoiding them at least sometimes.

IV. STRUCTURE, TONE, AND RHYTHM

Mention of "who" brings up the vexed question of the vocative *qui* clause. This is one of the distinctive features of the Roman collect, and was used even in prayers to the pagan deities,[16] but has been avoided by ICEL because "God, who have . . ." is grammatically correct but sounds wrong, while "God, who has . . ." sounds better but is grammatically wrong. It can also result in excessively long sentences which are difficult for a hearer to take in. One of the Latin prayers (Latin, no. 194; see *Order*, p. 371, no. 405[3]) has no less than three *qui* clauses in succession, amounting to thirty-three words, between *Deus* and the beginning of the petition. Another Latin prayer (Latin, no. 195; see *Order*, p. 371, no. 405[4]) has four *qui* clauses, amounting to thirty-eight words. Even the most hardened addict of Latin structures might admit that in these cases there is something to be said for separate statements with semicolons or full stops between them. After considerable discussion and experimenting, the revisers have formulated a principle which they hope will be generally acceptable. This is that vocative "who" clauses can be used when (a) they are fairly short; and (b) *either* the subject of the clause is something other than God, as in "Lord, whose

---

[15] Latin, nos. 46 and 65; 48 and 67; 55 and 72 and 184; 56 and 75; 168; 180; 183; 185; 186; 224.

[16] E.g., Livy XXIX, 27, 1: *Divi divaeque qui maria terrasque colitis*; Virgil, Aeneid VI, 264: *Di quibus imperium est animarum*. The famous invocation at Georgics I, 5-42, has no less than seven clauses depending on vocatives and introduced by *qui, quem, cui, quae* or *quibus*.

mercy . . . ," *or* the verb-forms are the same in the second and third persons. In practice, this means that the tense of the *qui* clause must be aorist rather than present or perfect. So in the prayer on page 343, no. 398(29), of the *Order* the address runs, "Lord God, who commanded us to honor father and mother." Since "commanded" is both second and third person, there is no awkwardness. But there would be if the verb was "command/commands" or "have/has commanded." By mixing such "who" clauses with noun-phrases in apposition (like "Ruler of the living and the dead" for *qui vivorum dominaris simul et mortuorum*[17]) and with direct statements (like "You willingly gave yourself up to death" for *qui teipsum morti tradidisti*[18]) the revisers hope to have reached a workable compromise.

However accurate a prayer may be theologically and grammatically, it will sound unfeeling unless the tone is right. A warmer and less bald style can go some way toward consoling the bereaved, especially when the funeral is that of a child, or in some other way untimely. It is dangerously easy to preach at the mourners under the forms of praying for them and to suggest that there would be less pain in the world if people remembered what they have been told. As already mentioned, new prayers have been provided for various circumstances which are not provided for in the Latin texts; and in the translations we tried to be sensitive to the probable effect of words and phrases. In the Latin prayer (no. 169) a literal rendering of *pro amisso propinquo* would be "for their lost relative." The 1970 version had "for their dead brother/sister." But the 1985 *Order* (p. 349, no. 399[2]) has "receive N. into the arms of your mercy," making the phrase less formal and at the same time providing an equivalent to, though not a strict translation of, the Latin *clementissimam pietatem* and *suppliciter exorantes*. For the same reason, in the final commendation for an unbaptized child, "Let us support his/her parents in their sorrow" (Workbook, p. 31) is now "Let us pray with all our hearts for N. and N." (*Order*, p. 194, no. 330). In the preceding invitation to pray "There is sadness in the parting, but it should fill us with new hope" (Workbook, p. 28) has been rephrased to read: "There is sadness in parting, but we take comfort in the hope . . ." (*Order*, p. 366, no. 402[5]). And on page 371, no. 405(3), of the *Order* a literal rendering of *suorum membra* (Latin, no. 194) might be unfortunate in the case of a body mutilated in a car crash, and we there-

---

[17] Latin, no. 202; *Order*, p. 350, no. 399(3); Workbook, p. 58.
[18] Latin, no. 169; *Order*, p. 349, no. 399(2); Workbook, p. 19.

fore retained the 1970 paraphrase, "those who are his by faith." These may be little details, but the cumulative effect is considerable.

Even when the tone is right, as well as the meaning, the translators' job is not finished. There is an important difference between a detached collection of correct words and a coherent and usable prayer. There were many criticisms of the 1970 translation on this point, usually blaming the defect on the avoidance of single-sentence collects in the style of Cranmer. There is something in this diagnosis, but it is not complete. The Our Father shows that a prayer consisting of short paratactic clauses can still be rhythmical and coherent, and so does our Lord's prayer at the Last Supper in John 17. It is nearer the mark to say that too many monosyllables produce a jerky effect, as can be seen by comparing "Deliver us from evil" with "Set us free from all that is bad." But the real secret has to do with the number and disposition of the stresses. Roughly speaking, the stresses in English speech tend to fall into groups of two or three. When the units of meaning coincide with these groups, the sentence will sound rhythmical. Between the stresses there may be no weak syllables at all (as in "Our Father"), or one (as in "daily bread"), or two ("Give us this day"), or three ("Deliver us from evil"). It is possible to have four or even more weak syllables, as in "sacrament of the resurrection",[19] but if they are all monosyllables the sentence is liable to become slurred or fall apart.

This principle was the basis of the medieval alliterative verse, which had four main stresses, two on each side of a central pause. The stresses could be moved about freely within the half-line, so that the rhythm, while disciplined and of great strength, did not become monotonous. This tradition exercised a great influence on the Book of Common Prayer and the King James Bible and accounts for the rhythmical satisfaction which is often said to be lacking in more modern versions. But it is native to English of any period and does not depend on medieval or Tudor accidence and syntax. During this century it has come back into use, particularly for poetic drama.[20]

The members of the translations subcommittee were already thinking in these terms when Archbishop Hurley suggested that a possible model for a liturgical psalter could be found in T. S. Eliot's

[19] Latin, no. 172; *Order*, p. 336, no. 398(7); Workbook, p. 62.
[20] See E. Martin Browne, *Verse in the Modern English Theatre; The W. D. Thomas Memorial Lecture* (Cardiff: University of Wales Press, 1963).

Four Quartets.[21] The opening lines of "Little Gidding," which he quoted, are an excellent example of this form of verse and are worth repeating here:

> Midwinter spring is its own season
> Sempiternal though sodden towards sundown,
> Suspended in time, between pole and tropic.
> When the short day is brightest, with frost and fire,
> The brief sun flames the ice, on pond and ditches,
> In windless cold that is the heart's beat,
> Reflecting in a watery mirror
> A glare that is blindness in the early afternoon.

In the end, the psalter subcommittee opted for a stricter pattern, but Archbishop Hurley's suggestion has a wider validity. Contemporary verse drama by Eliot and others provides us with a series of works in modern idiom and syntax; many of them on religious and some on Scriptural themes; of lengths comparable to those of liturgical functions; in language heightened by rhythm, assonance, and alliteration; spoken aloud and in some passages sung; before people who, at least while the performance lasts, form a community; and including translations from ancient and modern classics.[22] Western drama has twice originated in religious celebrations and perhaps there is a debt to repay. While anything in the nature of regular verse would be obtrusive (sometimes we have altered a prayer to make the rhythm less regular, rather than more), modern poetic drama does provide a model for reproducing in English what St. Augustine called "a certain rhythmical quality at the endings, not flaunted but almost inevitable and, so to speak, squeezed out of the matter in hand."[23]

Direct imitations of the Latin cursus are usually unsuccessful because of the much higher proportion of monosyllables in English. But there is much to be learned from studying it and the classical

---

[21] TR working papers on prose rhythm were first drafted in February and August 1978. Archbishop Hurley's memorandum was contributed to the psalter subcommittee on 14 Nov. 1978.

[22] For discussions see Michael Hodgetts, "The English Tradition and Liturgical Reform," *Clergy Review* 62, no. 11 (Nov. 1977), 434-440; Kenneth Larsen, "Language as Aural," *Worship* 54 (1980), 18-34; Michael Hodgetts, "Sense and Sound in Liturgical Translation," *Worship* 57 (1983), 496-513.

[23] St. Augustine, *De Doctrina Christiana* IV, 26: ed. J.P. Migne in *Patrologiae cursus completus: Series Latina*, vol. 34, col. 117: *Nonnulla, non iactanticula sed quasi necessaria atque, ut ita dicam, ipsis rebus extorta, numerositas clausularum.* This is probably a reminiscence of Cicero, *Orator* 219: *Compositione potest intellegi cum ita structa verba sunt ut numerus non quaesitus sed ipse secutus esse videatur.*

writers on rhetoric who influenced it. Cicero's *Orator* and *De Oratore* are particularly useful here, because in them we have the reflections on technique of a widely-read scholar who was also an experienced advocate and politician, aware that too sing-song a rhythm in prose would only provoke derision.[24] Three of his points are worth bearing in mind by translators.

The first is what has been dubbed the Law of Increasing Members: that the last clause of a period should be at least as long as those which precede it.[25] This is not a rule to be applied mathematically, but it is true that a paragraph is often both clearer and weightier if the shorter members are got out of the way first. A good example is the antiphon already quoted:

> Caught up with Christ,
> rejoice with the saints in glory.

A longer and more elaborate example is the following section of the prayer on page 376, no. 408(2), of the *Order*:

> deliver his/her soul from death,
> number him/her among your saints,
> and clothe him/her with the robe of salvation
> to enjoy for ever the delights of your kingdom.

In one of the prayers over the place of committal (Latin, no. 194, *Order*, p. 371, no. 405[3]), already mentioned for the inordinate length of its *qui* clauses, a direct comparison with the 1970 version is instructive:

> and on the day of judgment
> raise him/her up to eternal life
> with all your saints.

Here the last member is too short and, as Cicero says, *infringitur ille verborum ambitus*, the period is broken off.[26] A slight rearrangement makes the ending of the 1985 version much stronger:

> and on the day of judgment raise him/her up
> to dwell with your saints in paradise.

The second Ciceronian point is that it is better to end with a long syllable: *verba melius in syllabas longiores cadunt*.[27] Clearly, this was

---

[24] Cicero, *Orator*, 197, 209.

[25] Cicero, *De Oratore* III, 186: *Aut paria esse debent posteriora superioribus aut, quod etiam est melius et iucundius, longiora*. For discussion see L. P. Wilkinson, *Golden Latin Artistry* (Cambridge: Cambridge University Press, 1963, 1970), 135-188.

[26] Cicero, *De Oratore* III, 186.

[27] Cicero, *Orator*, 194.

not always possible, but it did mean that a run of short syllables at the end of a period was to be avoided. Substituting stressed syllables in English for long ones in Latin, this is still a sound principle. Weak syllables which trail off after the last stress give an inconclusive effect and induce hesitancy in any congregational response which should follow. The most incisive ending is on a stressed syllable, and it is noticeable that the ICEL texts of the funeral rite produced in 1970 and in 1985 rarely allowed more than one weak syllable after the last stress of a sentence.

The third point is a corollary of the second and concerns the number of weak syllables between stresses in the body of the prayer. The more of them that there are, the more awkward the sentence is to speak. According to Blass's Law, Demosthenes rarely had more than two short syllables between long ones: "one can see how this would make for both ease and impressiveness in utterance."[28] Cicero remarks approvingly that "Demosthenes" thunderbolts would not have such force but for the rhythm with which they are hurled on their way."[29] Applied to English liturgical texts, this has meant that in congregational or sung prayers there are rarely more than two weak syllables between stresses and in other texts rarely more than three. Clearly, such words as "mystery," "sacrament," "covenant" and "Abraham" demand a certain flexibility, since they already have two weak syllables after the stress, apart from any prepositions or articles which may follow. But even here improvements can be made elsewhere in the line, as in one of the prayers (Latin, no. 174), where "to the company of Abraham" (1970) has now been altered to read: "to dwell with Abraham," (*Order*, p. 336, no. 398[9]). In the antiphon to Psalm 25 (*Order*, p. 268), 1970 had:

> Lord, see the depth of my misery and grief, and forgive me all my sins

with three weak syllables between the stresses in "misery and grief." The 1985 version in the *Order of Christian Funerals* avoids this with

> Look on my grief and my sorrow; forgive all my sins.

Similarly, the antiphon to Psalm 93 (*Order*, p. 272), which in the 1970 version read:

> Of earth you formed me, with flesh you covered me; Lord, my Redeemer, raise me up again at the last day.

---

[28] Wilkinson, *Golden Latin Artistry*, 143.
[29] Wilkinson, *Golden Latin Artistry*, 151; Cicero, *Orator*, 234.

is now stronger for its conciser form and slower rhythm in the 1985 version:

> From clay you shaped me;
> with flesh you clothed me;
> Redeemer, raise me on the last day.

Here "at" was changed to "on" to vary the vowel-sounds and to reduce the excessive number of dentals in "at the last day."[30]

Finally, two connected points of wider application than just the *Order of Christian Funerals*. The first is the view that the Latin structure is so much part of the meaning that it, as well as the content, should be reproduced in English. Both this and the opposite view have a long history.[31] Both are to be seen at work in the Aramaic Targums and the early Greek and Latin versions of the Bible. The translator's preface to the Book of Sirach (Ecclesiasticus), written about 130 B.C. by the Hebrew author's grandson, observed that Hebrew expressions do not have the same force (*ouk isodynamei*) when rendered into another language. Cicero thought that translated words should be weighed out, not counted out, for the reader, and that word-for-word versions were the mark of an unskilled interpreter.[32] Behind all this lie two different philosophies of language—both of which were held in succession by Ludwig Wittgenstein, arguably the greatest philosopher of this century. There is the logical atomist view that statements mirror, or should mirror, the structure of the world in their own structure, and therefore that to alter the structure of statements is to risk distorting the facts. And there is the language-game view that all uses of language are conventions with rules, like games, and therefore that forms of words only have meaning in accordance with the structures and conventions in which they are used.[33] Since both these views in one form or another can be traced back to Plato's *Cratylus*,[34] I do not propose to discuss the state of the question here—merely to note that the revisers are aware of it and that the test throughout has been *actuosa participatio*.

[*margin note:* 2 possib- ilit:es]

---

[30] Latin, no. 151; *Order*, p. 272, no. 347(5); Workbook, p. 74.

[31] It is sometimes said that the "thou" form was universal in English liturgical translation until the twentieth century. In fact, the very first full Latin-English missal, edited by William Crathorne in the 1720s, has "you" nearly everywhere—though he does forget and revert to "thou" from time to time. J. D. Crichton, "The Laity and the Liturgy from c. 1600 to 1900," *Worcestershire Recusant* 43 (June 1984), 1-14.

[32] Cicero, *De Optimo Genere Oratorum*, 14; *De Finibus* III, 15.

[33] Ludwig Wittgenstein, *Tractatus Logico-Philosophicus* (1922); *Philosophical Investigations* (1953).

[34] Though all three disputants assume that the unit of meaning is the single word rather than the sentence, Cratylus maintains that names are correct by nature, Hermogenes that they are so by convention.

The second general point is that this and other disputes about translation cut across national boundaries. There are admirers of Cranmer and admirers of twentieth-century English on both sides of the Atlantic (and the Pacific), and it would be a mistake to identify any style of English or theory of translation with any particular country. Discussions in committee rarely turned on national differences of usage—though both *Webster's Third New International Dictionary* and the *Oxford English Dictionary* were on the table as we worked. The process of translating and revising gives one a heightened awareness, not only of the richness and flexibility of the English language, but also of the universality of the Church. It has been a privilege to contribute to the revision of the *Order of Christian Funerals,* and from the experience gained on that it can be said with confidence that the prospects for the greater project of revising *The Roman Missal* are very good.

ORIGINAL TEXTS: BEGINNINGS, PRESENT PROJECTS, GUIDELINES

H. Kathleen Hughes, R.S.C.J.

INTRODUCTION

The English language *Sacramentary* of 1973 contained a collection of original compositions called "alternative opening prayers." In retrospect this may not seem particularly noteworthy since such prayers were obviously envisioned in the mandate of the International Commission on English in the Liturgy (ICEL), a mixed commission whose purpose was contained in the first point of its 1964 charter:

> . . . to work out a plan for the translation of liturgical texts and the **provision of original texts where required** in language which would be correct, dignified, intelligible, and suitable for public recitation and singing.[1] [Emphasis added.]

Nevertheless, the *Sacramentary* prepared under ICEL's supervision was the only vernacular translation of the *Missale Romanum* to incorporate original compositions in a first edition.

The following article will review the initial stages of ICEL's work in the area of original composition, examine the current original texts projects, and conclude with a commentary on ICEL's present Guidelines for the Composition of Original Texts.

BEGINNINGS

BACKGROUND

The work of ICEL in the area of original composition began in 1967. In that year, in a first attempt to determine the appropriate

---

[1] Charter of the International Commission on English in the Liturgy, cited in Frederick R. McManus, *ICEL: The First Years*, an ICEL Occasional Paper (Washington: International Commission on English in the Liturgy, 1981), 13. See also a fuller treatment of the charter in McManus, "ICEL: The First Years," a revised and expanded version of the occasional paper printed in this publication.

style of English translation of Latin prayer texts, ICEL published a variety of sample translations in various styles and invited comment and criticism. In addition, readers were encouraged to offer their own English versions of thirteen Latin texts.[2] ICEL hoped through this exchange to unearth potential translators. An examination of returns proved disappointing. Few respondents were equipped to produce acceptable translations of the collects; no one demonstrated a truly remarkable gift. A report prepared for ICEL on this stage of the process included the following summary:

> It may be that the limits imposed by the style and content of the Latin orations and their special rhetoric, their extreme brevity, their frequent lack of warmth and color—make any satisfactory translation impossible. This has occurred to more than one writer including the present one. Certainly, if they are to be done at all, we must find a translator with a touch of genius. And thus far no mute, inglorious Cranmers have appeared. Some of the respondents working together could produce a text decidedly superior to the present American Sacramentary. But its virtues would be chiefly negative. The prayers would not offend.[3]

The mandate of ICEL's Advisory Committee had clearly envisioned the composition of original liturgical texts. As lack of enthusiasm for the translators' efforts continued, interest in developing alternative prayers increased. In January 1969 the Consilium for the Implementation of the Constitution on the Liturgy, in the formal conclusion of the Instruction on the Translation of Liturgical Texts (*Comme le prévoit*), suggested the path to creative development:

> Texts translated from another language are clearly not sufficient for the celebration of a fully renewed liturgy. The creation of new texts will be necessary. But translation of texts transmitted through the tradition of the Church is the best school and discipline for the creation of new texts so "that any new forms adopted should in some way grow organically from forms already in existence" (Constitution on the Liturgy, art. 23).[4]

Immersion in the Latin euchological heritage had been, for those responsible for the preparation of the *Missale Romanum* of Paul VI, an important precondition for the composition of new Latin texts

---

[2] *English for the Mass: Part II* (Washington: ICEL, 1965).

[3] James Devereux, S.J., "On Translating the Prayers of the Mass: A Report to the International Committee on English in the Liturgy," 1967.

[4] Consilium for the Implementation of the Constitution on the Liturgy, Instruction on the Translation of Liturgical Texts *Comme le prévoit*, 25 Jan. 1969, no. 43: DOL 123, no. 880.

organically continuous with antecedent forms. Similarly, the Consilium recognized that the laborious work of translation would prepare for yet more radical liturgical reform, reform disciplined by familiarity with the Church's tradition of prayer and open to a future demanding vastly more creativity in the verbal expression of faith, celebration, and thanksgiving. After the publication of this Instruction, ICEL's Advisory Committee expanded its work on the collects to incorporate the composition of alternative prayers.

By 1970 twenty-five different authors and translators had participated in the collect project. In December of that year the secretariat circulated the work of seven translators and two authors to the Advisory Committee, together with a ballot to be marked "acceptable," "partial problems," "serious difficulty," "totally reject." Concerning the sample translations, the balloting and appended comments demonstrated that the Committee was far from a consensus: "on the whole the work is excellent . . . ," "some of the expressions can only be called grotesque . . . ," "though there are few really brilliant attempts, there are few that cannot be polished into some acceptable form." Of the individual translators, the very people found most inspired by some were totally rejected by others. On the other hand, of the two authors who had presented alternative prayer texts, one was clearly favored by the Advisory Committee, and the project to provide alternative prayers received the Advisory Committee's vote of confidence.

The next step for the Advisory Committee, according to its mandate, was to present some sample alternative texts, together with a careful program for their development, to the sponsoring conferences of bishops in order to obtain episcopal consent to the implementation of this project.[5] Thus was the "Yellow Book" produced, an inquiry addressed to all bishops (approximately 750) of the conferences of bishops participating in ICEL.

---

[5] The development of the alternative opening prayer program is an example of the way the Advisory Committee followed its four-step mandate, namely:

1. To work out a plan for the translation of liturgical texts and the provision of original texts where required in langugae which would be correct, dignified, intelligible, and suitable for public recitation and singing; to propose the engagement of experts in various fields as translators, composers, and critics and to provide for the exchange of information with the sponsoring Hierarchies and with other interested Hierarchies; and to give special attention, within the scope of this plan, to the question of a single English version of the Bible for liturgical use or at least of common translations of biblical texts used in the liturgy.
2. To submit this plan to the interested Hierarchies with a view to obtaining their consent.
3. To implement the approved plan.
4. To submit final recommendations to the interested Hierarchies for their approval.

PRELIMINARY CONSULTATION

The Yellow Book was a preliminary consultation on the style of the prayers of the Missal prior to the preparation of a complete draft version.[6] The book was divided into three sections. The first section contained a small sampling of prayer translations in a style considered conservative. To each translation were appended comments drawing attention to paraphrase, amplification, concretization, and change of metaphor. All the bishops of the eleven participating conferences were invited to reflect upon the style of translation and to accept or reject in principle the direction of this part of ICEL's program.[7]

A second section raised the question of brief, optional invitatories for the opening prayer, and included this rationale:

> The hope is that, at least on occasion, a brief introduction may reduce somewhat the abruptness of a succinct opening prayer and may be a constant reminder to priests of the need for a clearly defined, even if brief, period for the people to recollect themselves before the text of the opening prayer is said.[8]

---

[6] A certain argot has developed at ICEL for the various stages of a project. The Green Book is a preliminary draft sent out for comments and suggestions. The White Book is prepared, based upon the responses to the Green Book, and is the definitive phase of a project. The White Book is sent for adoption by conferences of bishops which, in turn, send it to Rome for confirmation. A Yellow Book was an unusual first inquiry in the project of collect preparation. As noted in an issue of the Newsletter of the U.S. Bishops' Committee on the Liturgy: "The actual translation of the whole body of prayers of the Roman Missal has been repeatedly postponed by ICEL . . . the broad questions of style have been discussed at six meetings of the Advisory Committee" [BCL Newsletter 7 (1971), 288]. The "Yellow Book" was published in the hope of resolving questions of translation and style.

[7] On the sample translations, the bishops were asked to respond to the following questions:
  1. Please rank the sample translations of prayers according to this scale:
     A–Excellent; B–Good; C–Fair; D–Poor.
  2. Is the style of translation of the prayers generally satisfactory?
  3. Should the translation of prayers be: a) simpler or more elaborate? b) freer or more precise? c) more "traditional" or more contemporary?
  4. Is the principle that the translation of prayers may include paraphrases of the Latin acceptable?
  5. Is the principle that the translation of prayers may include "moderate amplification" acceptable?
  6. Is the principle that the translation of prayers may "concretize" the original in the light of present-day circumstances acceptable?
  7. Is the principle that the translation of prayers may include new metaphors for those found in Latin acceptable?"
Questions cited in "Prayers of the Roman Missal: An Inquiry Addressed to the Bishops of the Episcopal Conferences Participating in the International Committee on English in the Liturgy" [Yellow Book] (Washington: ICEL, 1971), 14.

[8] "Prayers of the Roman Missal," 9.

Sample optional invitatories and a series of questions about their suitability followed.[9]

Finally, in a third section, several alternative prayers were included for the bishops' examination and evaluation. A note indicated that the alternative prayers remained within the norms of legitimate liturgical translation, reference being made to the Instruction on the Translation of Liturgical Texts, no. 34:

> The prayers . . . from the ancient Roman tradition are succinct and abstract. In translation they may need to be rendered somewhat more freely while conserving the original ideas. This can be done by moderately amplifying them or, if necessary, paraphrasing expressions in order to concretize them for the celebration and the needs of today.

This citation was included to legitimate an extension beyond what the Instruction had envisioned in that particular paragraph. As will be noted below, the alternative prayers employed the Latin text as a point of departure, but represented considerable original elaboration and development of the Latin.[10] At the end of the third section another series of questions was appended to test episcopal preferences.[11]

The following examples of prayers for the First Sunday of Advent are gathered from the various sections of the Yellow Book:

---

[9] The questions relating to the invitatories were:

8. Is the addition of optional invitatories to the simple "Let us pray" acceptable in the opening prayer?

9. Should the invitatories anticipate the motive or occasion (e.g., some aspect of God's goodness or mention of the feast) to be found in the body of the opening prayer?

10. Should the invitatories briefly refer to the petition to be found in the opening prayer?

11. If ICEL provides such invitatories, for optional use, would you recommend that they be included, by authority of your episcopal conference, in missals?

("Prayers of the Roman Missal," 14-15).

[10] Such was ICEL's intention in the preparation of alternative prayers as stated in the annual report of 1970 and reprinted in the *Bishops' Committee on the Liturgy Newsletter* [hereafter, *BCL Newsletter*] 7 (1971), 289.

[11] Questions concerning the alternative prayers:

12. Please rank the alternative prayers according to this scale (A.B.C.D. as above, note 7).

13. Are these alternative prayers generally satisfactory?

14. Should these alternative prayers be: a) simpler or more elaborate? b) more general or more concrete? c) more "traditional" or more contemporary?

15. Should ICEL provide alternative opening prayers for use at the discretion of the individual episcopal conference?

16. Should such alternative opening prayers be offered: a) together with simple translations? b) or in an appendix? c) or in a supplementary booklet?

("Prayers of the Roman Missal," 15).

Collecta

Da, quaesumus, omnipotens Deus,
hanc tuis fidelibus voluntatem,
ut, Christo tuo venienti iustis operibus occurrentes,
eius dexterae sociati,
regnum mereantur possidere caeleste.
Per Dominum.

Invitatory

Let us pray
(that during Advent
the Lord will help us show the world by joy and love
that we are preparing to celebrate the birth of Jesus).

Opening Prayer

Everliving God,
increase our strength of will for doing good,
so that Christ may find an eager welcome at his coming,
and call us to his side in the kingdom of heaven,
where he lives and reigns
with you and the Holy Spirit, one God, for ever and ever.

Alternative Opening Prayer

Father,
give us the strength of character
to live and work at peace with you and with each other
as Christ your Son has taught us.
When he comes again in glory
may we join him and all the family of man
in the eternal life of his kingdom,
where he lives and reigns
with you and the Holy Spirit, one God, for ever and ever.[12]

The following points should be noted. The invitatory was not composed for the First Sunday of Advent but for seasonal use during Advent. The bishops chose to include optional invitatories in the *Sacramentary* but strongly favored a close connection with the specific prayer which followed for example, by having the invitatory anticipate the motive, the occasion, or the petition in the body of the prayer.

---

[12] "Prayers of the Roman Missal," 3, 10, 3, 13.

The preceding opening prayer paraphrases the Latin in the third line and alters the metaphor in the fourth line. The bishops judged such modest adaptation to be in full accord with the Roman Instruction on the Translation of Liturgical Texts. In fact, with the deletion of "everliving" this translation survived intact through the Green Book and White Book phases of the *Sacramentary*.

The proposed alternative opening prayer was clearly inspired by the Latin text but represented a liberal expansion: a change of emphasis from "will" to "character," a lengthy interpretation of "doing good," an explication of Christ's coming as eschatological, an inclusive reference to all of humankind joined together in the everlasting life of the kingdom. More than seventy-five percent of the respondents rated this alternative prayer as excellent or good, but in general they requested alternatives that were simpler, more concrete, and more contemporary.[13]

Once the results of the consultation were studied, the Episcopal Board of ICEL gave its authorization to the preparation of alternative opening prayers. The decision of the Episcopal Board, based on the recommendation of the Advisory Committee, to include alternative prayers in the body of the missal rather than consign them to an appendix or a separate publication guaranteed their accessibility to celebrants and planners alike. In a word, they would be used.

---

[13] As might have been anticipated from such a survey, particularly a survey inviting critique, the overall response was mixed. A summary of the responses of the United States bishops to the Yellow Book inquiry included the following specific observations and conclusions:

There is a disturbing reaction of some to the simple translations, namely, comments that they are stilted, dry, cold, artificial, with preference for the alternatives. The specific mention of this problem, however, is from a minority—and the theological concerns over dilution of doctrine come from an even smaller minority.

Style. In spite of specific objections, a great majority judge the translations "generally satisfactory" (54-13). There is a preference for simpler translations (37-10) and more contemporary translations (32-16). A very small minority (3, 6, 12, 13) do not accept the four principles taken from the Roman Instruction [i.e. inclusion of paraphrase, moderate amplification, concretization, metaphor substitution].

Invitatories. Almost all respondents (64-5) favor the addition of invitatories and propose (61-4) that they be included in missals.

Alternative Prayers. With regard to the *style* of the alternative prayers, the response was generally favorable (54-9); a few individuals expressed strong preference for the alternatives over the simple translations. With regard to the *provision* of alternative prayers, the response was again favorable (53-8), with a large majority preferring their inclusion in the body of the missal (43; 14 favored a separate booklet).

Conclusion. The survey indicates that the translations are acceptable, although comments (and a tabulation of the judgments on individual prayers) reveal no great enthusiasm. Very large majorities asked for the inclusion of invitatories and alternative prayers.

[*BCL Newsletter* 7 (1971), 296. In addition to this general summary, a summary of the ranking of every prayer is available in the ICEL archives.]

As noted at the outset, only English-speaking conferences of bishops chose to provide alternative opening prayers for Sundays and major feasts in the *Sacramentary* issued under their authority. These texts were intended as a first step in the direction of no. 43 of the 1969 Instruction already quoted, the first significant attempt to produce a euchology more radically adapted to the culture of a people.[14] The challenge which faced ICEL was to create English-language, contemporary prayers for which no precise model yet existed.

SECOND PHASE OF WORK

The scope of the alternative prayer project was limited, the approach conservative. This was due in no small part to the demands of ICEL's major task: the translation of every new liturgical rite as it issued from Rome. Only a modest number of alternative prayers could be expected in the time available, and therefore a decision was taken to concentrate on alternative opening prayers for Sundays and solemnities. In terms of the proposed structure and style of these prayers, after some early discussion of the feasibility of free, poetic composition,[15] ICEL chose a more cautious approach:

> As much as possible, try to retain the substance and basic thrust of the Latin prayers (though not the style, particular metaphors or phrases, etc.). Your compositions should be sufficiently faithful to the Latin that it would be clear that the fresh composition is inspired by the old Latin prayer. The "Ordinary" Sunday prayers are just that—downright banal and telegraphic. These need some amplification; feel free to do so.[16]

These guidelines were sent to Robert Morhous, a Trappist monk of St. Joseph's Abbey, Spencer, Massachusetts. Morhous, who had done some translation work for ICEL, had first come to the attention of Ralph Keifer, the ICEL staff editor of *The Roman Missal*, at

---

[14] Subsequently, other mixed commissions began similar projects as their *Sacramentaries* were revised. Of particular note is the 1983 edition of the Italian *Sacramentary*, which includes numerous original prayers and alternative formularies.

[15] Robert Morhous, the author of many of the alternative prayers, indicated to me in conversation that originally there was some hope within ICEL of having three versions of the opening prayer: a literal version, an elaboration of the Latin prayer, and an extended original composition in poetic form. In fact, it was the decision of the Episcopal Board to propose only one alternative and thus the respective ICEL conferences gave approval to only one alternative text.

[16] From a letter (undated, but most likely written in the last quarter of 1971) written by Ralph Keifer to Robert Morhous inviting Morhous to try his hand at alternative prayers.

the University of Notre Dame where Morhous was working on a degree in liturgical studies and Keifer was on the summer faculty. During the summer of 1971 Morhous had written a research paper on "The Function of 'Oration' in a Contemporary English Liturgy." The summary section of that paper suggests what Morhous's orientation would be in preparing alternative prayers:

> I think it helpful to suggest that at least we not limit ourselves to just one style of ORATION in our services—namely that of the translated Roman ORATION. A wider use of the Hebrew BERAKAH type formulas might open up avenues to a more satisfying way of concluding our prayer services. Blank verse and the use of sprung rhythm appeal to a sense of dignity and lyricism at the same time. Imagery of a more biblical orientation with picture piled upon picture is something that has a satisfying effect on modern man who is so exposed to the random and the fleeting that logical neatness leaves him irritated. Poetry, with echoes of all that has gone before, appeals to me as having the most promise. But in this case there must be no attempt to simply "translate" a Latin prayer. The poetic expression must come right out of, and be elicited by, the theme of the service which has preceded.[17]

To these reflections Morhous appended "Twenty-Five Orations for Various Occasions in a Contemporary Style" together with references to Latin prayers which had served as point of departure. Though not without fault, there was something refreshingly new about the style and content of these prayers:

> Bread
> tasting of the earth
> but food for paradise
> has been set before us
>
> Not flesh but faith
> is nourished
> Not strength but hope
> is gained
> Not taste but love
> is satisfied
>
> Grant us Father
> that we may never cease
> to hunger for this bread
> never cease to long
> for this Word that makes you present

---

[17] Robert Morhous, unpublished paper, 15.

never cease to strain
for the truth that makes us bread[18]

       * * *

Eternal Father
by his birth as man
and his death on a tree
your Son Jesus Christ
came as a servant
and emptied himself
of divine prestige

Grant us the blessing
to follow him now
in love and humility
through the way
of his emptiness
to the sharing
of his glory[19]

       * * *

O God
who on this day
expose to our
gaze
the streaming light
of truth
and glory
unseal the secrets
hidden in the
silence
of your eternal
love
and draw your church
into the vision
you share
with your Only Son
Christ our Lord[20]

Morhous appeared to be well-suited to the alternative prayer project. His sample texts were judged appealing, his use of biblical imagery striking, his style one that would enhance and develop exceedingly dry and abstract Latin prayers.

---

[18] Morhous, 23. Inspiration: prayer after communion, First Sunday of Lent.
[19] Morhous, 24. Inspiration: opening prayer, Passion Sunday.
[20] Morhous, 20. Titled: Epiphany; no citation of source.

In the next two years Morhous provided the majority of the alternative prayers of the *Sacramentary*,[21] although the response to his first efforts for ICEL might well have daunted a lesser man.[22] The ICEL Advisory Committee and experts in various fields whom they consulted were unsparing in their critique. The consultors provided detailed comments on each of the fifteen prayers in the first collection of texts. These specific comments helped to clarify what the Advisory Committee and its experts, liturgists and linguists, poets and playwrites among them, were hoping to achieve. For example, the first prayer in the collection was that of the First Sunday of Advent. The Latin which was "to inspire" the alternative read:

Da, quaesumus, omnipotens Deus,
hanc tuis fidelibus voluntatem,
ut, Christo tuo venienti iustis operibus occurrentes,
eius dexterae sociati,
regnum mereantur possidere caeleste.
Per Dominum.

The opening prayer, in Green Book redaction, read:

Let us pray
    (that during Advent
    the Lord will give us the strength we need
    to work for his kingdom).

All-powerful God,
increase our strength of will for doing good
that Christ may find an eager welcome at his coming
and call us to his side in the kingdom of heaven,
where he lives and reigns. . . .

The first draft alternative prayer read:

Let us pray
    in Advent time
    calling with gentle longing
    waiting in silent prayer
    for the birth of Jesus in mystery. . . .

---

[21] Another author who provided a substantial number of alternative prayers was Peter Scagnelli of Rhode Island. The prayers of Morhous and Scagnelli were edited in the ICEL Secretariat after revisions were made by the individual writers in response to the directions of the Advisory Committee.

[22] Critics' comments included "too many phrases I find meaningless," "disastrous versions," "contrived and obscure," "awkward and sentimental," "in large quantities they are unbearable." One poet summarized her response: "When the language is burdened with an accumulation of unnecessary adjectives, when sentences are overly long and so tortured that their meaning is not immediately apparent, when the style is often dated, how can a modern Christian adopt such prayers?" These comments are from the correspondence between ICEL critics and Morhous, available in the ICEL archives.

Father in heaven, our hearts are expectant
straining for your beauty
and our minds are searching
reaching for light.

Increase our longing for the Savior who comes
and strengthen our waiting
through growth in love
that he may find us
at the dawn of his birth
rejoicing in his silent presence
and humbly
adoring
the light of his truth.

This we ask through Christ our Lord. Amen.

One critic commented on the departure of the alternative prayer from the *sense* of the Latin text, namely, its eschatological thrust. This person was not seeking slavish literalism but expansion based upon the fundamental thought of the original.

More critics, however, were preoccupied with questions of language and style. It was pointed out that the very richness of the imagery would boggle the mind of the hearer. The variety of images of expectation (expectation, straining, searching, waiting, longing) had been further complicated by a range of other images (love, rejoicing, adoring, truth), the total number of which could not be sustained in a prayer as brief as a collect.

The logic of the prayer was questioned: what could it mean to strengthen our waiting? why speak of silent prayer which is about to be proclaimed? how can one reach for light? Various words and combinations were found sentimental (gentle longing); awkward (for the birth of Jesus in mystery); just plain ugly (our hearts are expectant/straining for). The prayer was said to be too long, the style contrived, weighed down by unnecessary adjectives (humbly adoring—can we adore in any other way?). Several critics called attention to the impossible combination of sibilants and dentals: "Our hearts are expectant straining for your beauty and our minds are searching. . . ." As one respondent noted, "Prayers should not be written for the most slovenly of celebrants, but they also should not demand genius of oratorical skill."[23]

---

[23] Correspondence, ICEL archives.

These and other suggestions and comments were sent to the author with words of good cheer and a request for a second draft of the first set of prayers and a new series of prayers. The "revised Morhous" as it came to be called was once again circulated widely by the Advisory Committee for comment, and after this consultation, yet a third draft was prepared.

This cursory review of ICEL's development of alternative opening prayers is instructive from several points of view. It suggests the phases of an ICEL project: the development of a program by the Advisory Committee; the engagement of experts as translators, composers, and critics; the role of the Episcopal Board in approving projects at the very outset after an exchange of information with the Advisory Committee; the broad consultation that projects demand; and the day-to-day labors of the Secretariat in keeping all of ICEL's constituencies apprised of progress.

APPROVAL AND CONFIRMATION

The development of alternative opening prayers, and indeed, of several other "original texts"[24] in the *Sacramentary* was only one aspect of the whole *Sacramentary* project. Translation work continued apace. After the publication of the new *Missale Romanum* ICEL sponsored consultation throughout the English-speaking world in the attempt to check, correct, and refine its translations. In 1971 the Green Book *The Revised Roman Missal* was circulated to all the bishops of the member conferences. Prefixed to the prayers, prefaces, and blessings was an introduction summarizing the results of the Yellow Book inquiry, describing in detail the problems of translation, restating the principles of translation which had issued from Rome, and illustrating these principles and problems through lengthy commentary on nine different texts.[25]

---

[24] Other "original" composition in the *Sacramentary* would include the addition of an acclamation in the eucharistic prayer. This acclamation was included for several reasons: (1) for variety; (2) because of the problem of moving from the body of the prayer, which is addressed to the First Person of the Trinity, to an acclamation addressed to the Second Person; (3) because of a desire to introduce a third person acclamation (like *Benedictus qui venit* . . .) since the Roman rite did not have the tradition of other rites which might address Christ after the institution narrative; (4) to keep the paschal mystery free of the adoration-petition element of the third Latin text. The *Sacramentary* also included "original" variants on the *Ite, missa est*, because of dissatisfaction with the received "Go, the Mass is ended" or "Go, it is the dismissal."

[25] *The Revised Roman Missal* for study and comment by the bishops of the member countries of the International Committee on English in the Liturgy, Inc. (Washington: ICEL, 1971), i-ix.

The numerous responses elicited through the Green Book consultation included references to inconsistencies in the layout and format, attention to individual words and phrases, lists of "un-English" expressions, and a few general remarks, for example, deploring the translation of every generic term for goodness and virtue by the single word "love." The deluge of vitriolic rebuke which had greeted the appearance of the earliest booklets (*English for the Mass* I and II) was remarkably absent.[26] There were a good many positive reactions and evidence of a sense of humor about the perils and pitfalls of trying to please all of the people all of the time.[27] By and large the respondents, chiefly bishops and their experts, were happy with the progress of the translation work and the development of new texts.

In light of all the comments received, a small subcommittee[28] revised the prayers again. Only those prayers which were altered were then circulated for further comment, a slight departure from ICEL's usual White Book phase. The Advisory Committee debated the alternative prayer issue and the texts thoroughly once more. Although less than enthusiastic about both the translations and the alternative opening prayers, the Advisory Committee approved both sets of texts during its own meeting immediately prior to a joint meeting with the Episcopal Board in London. It was the recommendation of the Advisory Committee that the *Sacramentary* be adopted on a provisional basis for five years. The Episcopal Board approved the *Sacramentary* but rejected the recommendation of giving it a five-year provisional status. The Episcopal Board was more pleased than the Advisory Committee with the alternative texts, seemingly because their length and warmth contrasted well with the more spare translated texts.

---

[26] For example, "Most of the prayers are *personal*, between God and us, with little fol-de-rol about instruments. The effect is excellent"; "The use of the present tense in the PACs (prayers after communion) is most effective. By no means should it be abandoned. Only the present tense can convey the ever-present continuing action of God in our lives here and now." (*English for the Mass* was issued in 1966 as the first of the ICEL consultation books. It came out in two parts and contained translations of texts from the Order of Mass and renderings of selected psalm texts in various styles.)

[27] One critic wrote several lengthy disquisitions on words which he hoped would be laid to rest once and for all. The treatise on the word "banquet" concluded: "A huge agglomeration of people, consuming too many calories they don't need, sitting through boring speeches that put us to sleep—this is the common image of what we know today as banquet. Please, do we have to put up with *that* for all eternity?"

[28] This subcommittee of the Advisory Committee was composed of Harold Winstone (an Englishman and member of the Advisory Committee), Thomas Murphy (an Irishman and member of the Advisory Committee) and Ralph Keifer as general editor.

One by one, conferences of bishops approved the White Book *Sacramentary* and requested confirmation from Rome. In late 1973, the Congregation for Divine Worship, before taking its own action, sent the White Book to the Congregation for the Doctrine of the Faith. In a letter of 14 January 1974, Archbishop Bugnini forwarded to ICEL, as agent of the conferences in question, a short list of suggestions and amendments prepared by the Congregation for the Doctrine of the Faith, all of them concerning the alternative prayers.[29] The suggestions were treated as editorial matters for ICEL to resolve, after which the Congregation for Divine Worship was able to give the confirmation. What is remarkable, indeed, is that apart from questioning seven texts, all of them alternatives, the Congregation for the Doctrine of the Faith and the Congregation for Divine Worship raised no questions about the hundreds of other prayers, both translated and original, in the *Sacramentary*.

The texts had satisfied the Curia. Would they have any significance for the ordinary worshiper who, in many parts of the English-speaking world, would hear them for the first time on the First Sunday of Advent, 1974?

In the foreword which the conference of bishops of the United States attached to the General Instruction of the Roman Missal, the alternative opening prayers were introduced with these words:

> The prayers of the Roman Missal have been translated in a style which, for the most part, retains the succinct and abstract character of the original Latin. The translations do not ordinarily employ the development or expansion mentioned in the instruction on liturgical translations. In the case of the opening prayer on Sundays and

---

[29] Congregation for the Doctrine of the Faith, reference number 216/73. The comments of the Congregation are interesting, for example:

"Da emendare: *P. 238 Corpus Christi* . . . we worship you living among us in the sacrament of your body and blood. *Be for us in this eucharist strength to live the mystery of your presence. May we offer to our Father in heaven the broken bread of undivided love.* Queste espressioni sembrano a quanto strane ed anche equivoche: nella prima sottolineata, i fedeli potrebbero essere condotti a confondere la presenza di Cristo nell'eucharistia con quella in mezzo alla comunita. Nella seconda, non capiranno se si tratta dell'offerta del Pane eucharistico oppure se 'broken bread' e preso in senso metaforico per designare il loro proprio amore."

ICEL modified the text to read: "May we offer to our Father in heaven a solemn pledge of undivided love. May we offer to our brothers and sisters a life poured out in loving service of that kingdom where you live . . . ."

"Suggerimenti: *P. 32 Fourth Sunday of Advent*. Father, all-powerful God, *the mystery of your eternal Word took flesh* on our earth. . . . Espressione strana. Sarebbe meglio dire: Father, all-powerful God, *your eternal Word* took flesh on our earth. . . ."

(ICEL Archives; the total number of texts which the Congregation questioned was seven, all of them alternative prayers.)

some feasts, however, an alternative text is printed for use at the discretion of the priest.

The alternative opening prayers are not direct or faithful translations of the corresponding Latin text. They follow its theme or are inspired by it, but they are generally more concrete and expansive. The addition of such texts was prompted by the practice in other Roman liturgical books of offering alternatives and by the following statement in the 1969 instruction on translation: "Texts translated from another language are clearly not sufficient for the celebration of a fully renewed liturgy. The creation of new texts will be necessary. But translation of texts transmitted through the tradition of the Church is the best school and discipline for the creation of new texts so 'that any new forms adapted should in some way grow organically from forms already in existence'" (no. 43).

Thus, on those occasions when two opening prayers appear side by side, the one on the left is a faithful but not literal translation of the corresponding Latin prayer, the one on the right is an alternative prayer suggested by the Latin text and in harmony with its theme. Either text may be chosen by the priest.[30]

Some will judge that the alternative opening prayers are not original and creative enough. There is, indeed, a marked similarity of structure and theme between the translation and the alternative. However, *that* the alternative opening prayers exist at all is a major tribute to the International Commission on English in the Liturgy. These prayers represent a first, albeit timorous, step toward the celebration of a fully renewed liturgy.

Within the first ten years of ICEL's existence, the Commission prepared the translation of virtually every major liturgical rite as these revised texts issued from Rome. It would be easy to underestimate this achievement from our vantage point. Yet the scope of this work remains remarkable: despite the pressures being exerted throughout the English-speaking world for the revised rites in the vernacular, ICEL established a Secretariat, formed an Advisory Committee under the authority of its Episcopal Board, developed effective procedures and an extensive consultation method, and, in the process, elaborated working principles for its continuing agenda.

Once the major rites were completed, it was time to step back from the work and evaluate its effectiveness. Regarding the use of the alternative opening prayers, the first assessment of many was

---

[30] "Foreword to the Sacramentary," *Sacramentary* (Collegeville, Minn.: The Liturgical Press, 1974), 14.

positive: alternative prayers were now available; the alternatives were longer, thus allowing a community time to experience themselves at prayer before their *Amen* was invited; the alternatives seemed to have more substance, particularly during Ordinary Time when their counterparts (in Latin as well as in English) occasionally seemed to be vacuous; the alternatives were more concrete and, in a certain sense, more "this-worldly"; the alternative texts used more imaginative language and appeared to be more poetic. Such was the initial response.

Yet there was a second wave of response, one more reserved about the effectiveness of these texts, suggesting that the alternative opening prayers were occasionally too long and sometimes employed mixed metaphors or strained poetic constructions. There was also the question of their durability: would these alternative texts wear well over time? In short, original composition had been appreciated but it would be important to learn from the strengths and weaknesses of these alternative opening prayers as ICEL's work continued.

PRESENT PROJECTS

From the beginning of ICEL's history it was understood that all of its texts would be subject to a thorough examination and revision after a suitable period of time of actual liturgical use and evaluation. In 1981, ICEL launched this long-range revisions program with the understanding that the revisions process would take perhaps ten to fifteen years to complete. As noted in ICEL's *Newsletter*, "This time is to be one of careful and systematic study of these texts, followed by their revision based upon the results of an extended consultation for each rite."[31] Bishops and consultants throughout the eleven member and fifteen associate member conferences were asked to express their judgment on three distinct aspects of the revisions process: 1) the quality of the translation of particular texts; 2) the pastoral usefulness of the presentation and arrangement of ministerial books; and 3) instances where new or alternative texts in English might be helpful or necessary. The results of the third aspect of each consultation have provided the agenda for ICEL's subcommittee on

---

[31] *ICEL Newsletter* 9:1 (1982), no page.

original texts, a working group established in 1982.[32] An explanation of the projects of the original texts subcommittee now follows.

Scripture-Related Presidential Prayers

One of the first projects assigned to the subcommittee was to explore the feasibility of providing new presidential prayers that would be related to the three cycles of the Sunday readings. The need for new prayers seemed particularly acute during Ordinary Time when existing texts were less rich and inspired than during the major seasons. It had been reported to ICEL that the French mixed commission was developing such prayers for its revised *Sacramentary* and that other language groups were inclined to follow suit. Unlike the alternative opening prayers, which found their inspiration in their Latin counterparts, these new texts were to take their inspiration from the readings of the day, particularly the gospel.

The challenges and potential pitfalls of such a project may be immediately apparent to the reader. During Ordinary Time, the second reading is semicontinuous and thus unrelated to the first reading and the gospel. Furthermore, there is not always a single "theme" in a passage of Scripture but sometimes several themes. Would such prayers preempt the work of a presider in selecting the focus of his homily? In what way could we expect opening prayers to "echo" the Scriptures—a phrase which had been used to explain the project to authors—if the Scriptures had not yet been heard?

Another set of questions began to preoccupy the original texts subcommittee, namely, how to define an original text. Was the text "original" simply because it was not a translation? Would originality imply new content? new structure? new style? new uses of language or fresh vocabulary? In what would a genuine alternative to the structure and style of the translated prayers consist? By posing these questions and attempting to give some direction to those authors who were commissioned to begin the preparation of texts, the subcom-

---

[32] The two parallel tasks, translation and original composition, had once before been assigned to two separate subcommittees, but this proved to be an unhappy working arrangement at a time when committee oversight was less well developed and consequently subcommittees could actually proceed in different directions. Thus a single subcommittee, Translations, Revisions, and Original Texts (TROT), was responsible for all of ICEL's textual preparation. In 1982, when the work of translation and revision was again separated from that of original composition, it was with the understanding that both subcommittees would work in close collaboration with each other under the direction of the ICEL Advisory Committee and that each would elaborate guidelines for their respective translators, authors, and consultors.

mittee was compelled to draw up a set of guidelines. These were eventually drafted as Guidelines for the Composition of Original Texts. These guidelines were to continue to be refined in light of expert consultation and the experience of the subcommittee. The present redaction of these guidelines with a brief commentary will form the last section of this essay.

PRAYERS OVER THE GIFTS AND PRAYERS AFTER COMMUNION

The project to create alternative prayers over the gifts (POGs) and prayers after communion (PACs) antedates the reestablishment of the original texts subcommittee. The need for such prayers appeared, in the beginning, more critical than further alternative opening prayers because there seemed to be a "sameness" about these texts, a lack of originality of structure, content, and vocabulary.

The difficulties in this project are not unlike those difficulties reviewed above, but with an added nuance. The content of *each* of the presidential prayers is circumscribed by its location and function in the rite. Opening prayers (OPs) have a part in the function of the entire entrance rite, enabling the assembly to experience themselves as a community and to prepare to hear the Word and celebrate the Supper of the Lord. That is a very general function, and the content of the prayer may incorporate themes of feast, season, or occasion of celebration.

POGs and PACs are, by their nature, location, and function, much more restricted in their content and form than are OPs. POGs function to say: these are our gifts—the bread, the wine, our lives — we prepare them now for that great transformation. This is a most particular focus. There are only so many ways to say, in the language of prayer, that we place our gifts before the Lord. Too often, the temptation in a POG is to say proleptically that these gifts are consecrated to God's glory. That is to anticipate the eucharistic prayer and to confuse the nature of the rite of preparation, which is simply that—preparatory, with the consecratory nature of the eucharistic prayer. To suggest that these prayers be inspired by the Scriptures would not relieve this difficulty because the Scriptures could not generate a sufficient number of new images or constructions in light of this very modest function. That being said, it may be obvious that the subcommittee would abandon its initial agenda of preparing a large number of alternative POGs in favor of a small collection of texts which might serve as seasonal alternatives.

The content of PACs, too, is somewhat restricted by that prayer's nature, function, and location. The greatest challenge in drafting new PACs is to avoid making this prayer, essentially a prayer of petition as are all the presidential prayers, into a prayer of thanksgiving. Having just received the eucharist, it is natural for a community to experience the need to articulate praise and thanksgiving at this moment in the rite. But the function of a PAC is to say: now that we have received the bread of life and the cup of salvation, give us the grace to live what we have just enacted. So describing the PAC is to suggest implicitly that this prayer has a mission or sending function, one which might well become more concrete and explicit in original texts.

In the case of PACs a long discussion has ensued about the feasibility and the wisdom of preparing three sets of PACs for each Sunday, again according to the three-year Scripture cycle. Those in favor of such a project believe the content of these prayers might be enriched by taking their inspiration from the Scriptures of the day. Such is true, perhaps, for the petition section of the prayer, but just as there are only so many ways to say "these are our gifts," there are a limited number of expressions to say "we have just received communion." Again, this opening section of the prayer had quite a circumscribed range of vocabulary, and original composition has been made even more difficult by lack of uniform practice of reception from the cup. Those who do not favor preparing three Scripture-related PACs for each Sunday and solemnity point to the difficulty of preparing several hundred texts without resorting, in the petition, to language which might be too topical and contemporary and thus not appropriate to the diverse communities that would use them.

In preparation for the revision of the *Sacramentary*, the original texts subcommittee now intends to produce a modest number of alternative PACs whose petition section will be a concrete request for grace to remain faithful to the vision of the kingdom celebrated in the liturgy. The alternative PACs will be related to feast and season, just as the POGs, and both will be available in a single collection in the *Sacramentary*.

Eucharistic Prayers

The eucharistic prayer project was first discussed by the Advisory Committee in the mid-1970's. At that time six authors, all of them eminent sacramental theologians, accepted ICEL's invitation to compose eucharistic prayers. Of those texts, one prayer survived the winnowing and pruning process of extensive international consultation, critique, study, and reading aloud, an essential part of the preparation of texts which are to be heard and appropriated in the midst of an assembly. Now known as *Eucharistic Prayer A*,[33] that prayer, in preparation for the better part of a decade, was approved by the Episcopal Board of ICEL in 1986 and presented to the conferences of bishops, eight of which approved it and sent it to Rome for confirmation. The Congregation for Divine Worship did not confirm the actions of the conferences.

The challenges of preparing presidential prayers pale in comparison to composition of eucharistic prayers. The former task may have pitfalls; the latter has landmines! The structure of the eucharistic prayer is far more complex, the requisite elements are more numerous, the theological ambiguities arising from our complex euchological tradition are more open to debate and hence disagreement even among scholars, and the difficulty of sustaining a coherent poetic theme in a prayer of such length seems almost insuperable. From this enumeration of challenges, it is clear that a variety of gifts are needed for such composition: one must have a good grasp of theology, liturgy, and language, of traditional patterns and contemporary expressions of prayer.

A question arises with regard to this project: do we actually need more eucharistic prayers? Since the Roman Church seemed to survive quite nicely for hundreds of years with the Roman Canon, the addition of three new eucharistic prayers seemed a luxury and the addition of two prayers for reconciliation and three prayers for use with children an embarrassment of riches. Yet different countries have produced new prayers. The Swiss have prepared eucharistic prayers and the French-speaking Canadians produced a eucharistic prayer for the rite of marriage. It was the decision of the Advisory Committee not to issue English translations of these prayers, which are for special, occasional use, and to concentrate instead on the original composition of eucharistic prayers in English that might be useful to communities for their normative celebration: the Sunday assembly.

Bishops and others in the various conferences have requested new eucharistic prayers which will incorporate more acclamations

---

[33] ICEL, *Eucharistic Prayer A* (Washington: ICEL, 1986).

on the model of the children's texts, such acclamations giving the community a more participatory role in the great prayer of thanksgiving. Another request has been for a prayer for use with ritual Masses. Many conferences would like to have more prayers which might be used with the existing prefaces in the *Sacramentary*. This latter request may be more difficult to achieve because of the nature of a eucharistic prayer and the desire of most composers to create an original preface which will set the theme, tone, and style of the prayer. Composers may well regard preparation of prayers to be used with any preface to be preparation of a kind of generic prayer, ill-suited to an integral work of artistic composition such as a eucharistic prayer. An alternative, should an original composition beginning with the post-Sanctus be difficult to obtain, would be the development of festal and seasonal embolisms in continuity with the Roman euchological tradition.

Perhaps the greatest challenge faced in the eucharistic prayer project is the inevitably careful scrutiny each composition faces, both within the ICEL process and after it, for soundness of doctrine. Such examination is, of course, both necessary and helpful except in those instances where consultors hope to make of the eucharistic prayer a compendium of theology, complete in itself. No prayer can say everything there is to be said about God, Christ, the Blessed Virgin, the role of the Spirit, the nature of the offering Church, the history of salvation, the communion of saints, and so on. All of our prayers, both throughout the tradition and those recently composed, together, cannot contain or hope to express all there is to be said about the work of God in Christ which we celebrate. If our present euchology were scrutinized even half as thoroughly as newly composed prayers, we might find ourselves without adequate expression, perhaps even left mute, when gathered for worship. It is of the nature of ritual language that it suggests, hints, opens new levels of meaning, and invites us into a larger Christian story. The story unfolds in the telling, which is another way to say that our belief is gathered up in all of the language of our prayer, verbal and nonverbal, all of it inadequate and groping to speak of the mystery which is God and God-with-us.[34]

---

[34] For a full discussion of the narrative character of liturgical prayer, see H. Kathleen Hughes, *The Language of the Liturgy: Some Theoretical and Practical Implications*, an ICEL Occasional Paper (Washington: ICEL, 1982).

Texts for the Rites

The *Order of Christian Funerals* is the first fruit of the long-range revisions process of ICEL and illustrates well the process which every major rite will eventually undergo. The funeral rite was selected as the first rite to be revised for several reasons: it was one of the earliest rites to be translated; it was one of the least polished translations; and it was of manageable size. It was hoped that through work on this rite, ICEL and its subcommittees might be able to develop sound working procedures for the revision of larger rites. Work on the *Order of Christian Funerals* would also yield valuable insights about translations and original texts before work would commence on the revision of the *Sacramentary*.

The first stage of ICEL's revisions process, as noted above, includes consultation on the quality of the present texts, on the pastoral usefulness of the arrangement of the ministerial books, and on the question of the adequacy of existing texts to meet contemporary pastoral situations. It was this last category which, in the case of the consultation on the funeral rite, drew numerous suggestions, most of them sound, for the development of new texts. Requests were made for an adequate ritual for use in the instance of stillbirth, for situations where cremation is the choice of the family, or when death has occurred violently, suddenly, or by suicide. New texts were requested for a young person, for a spouse, for a non-Christian married to a Catholic, for one who died after a long and full life, a cirumstance in which grief may seem less appropriate. In addition, texts were desired which would supplement the prayers and other existing material in the Latin *editio typica*. In all, over forty new texts were composed for the *Order of Christian Funerals*.

Sacramentary Revision

In addition to the work on presidential prayers and eucharistic prayers, the original texts subcommittee is also exploring other possible additions for the revised *Sacramentary*. An extensive preliminary consultation among ICEL's constituency has highlighted some of the needs experienced by member conferences: for more weekday collects, alternative texts for the Chrism Mass, alternative texts for the Gloria, the blessing of water, the communion rite, for some orderly rearrangement of the existing *ad diversa* collection as well as additions to this collection. New prayers, prefaces, and solemn blessings have been requested for some solemnities and feasts. Additional interpolations and acclamations for existing eucharistic prayers are wanted. Examination of these requests was undertaken by the original texts subcommittee, which has made recommendations to the full Advisory Committee. Authorization of the original texts program, as for all of ICEL's programs, rests finally with the Episcopal Board. The *terminus ad quem* for the revised *Sacramentary* is 1992 or early 1993.

Through each of these individual projects, the original texts subcommittee has been able to articulate and refine the guidelines for the preparation of new texts. These guidelines could not have been prepared a priori, nor are they now considered definitive. They remain a "working paper" for the subcommittee and its collaborators since the subcommittee recognizes that it learns more about the structure and function of liturgical language with each consultation and with each new project.

While some of these guidelines may seem self-evident, it has become increasingly clear that they are not, even to some seasoned in the art of liturgical composition. The original texts subcommittee has, in fact, found it most fruitful to have new author-collaborators sit down with the subcommittee to discuss these guidelines and in order to achieve some consensus about their meaning and weight before launching new projects.

GUIDELINES FOR THE COMPOSITION
OF ORIGINAL TEXTS[35]

FUNCTION AND STRUCTURE

1. The author should keep in mind the function of the prayer, its place and purpose in the rite.

An author needs to bear in mind whether a text is essentially petition, thanksgiving, blessing, greeting, and so on. In addition, the purpose of the prayer needs to be respected, as for example, keeping the POG a modest statement of preparation, not a mini-consecratory prayer anticipating the eucharistic prayer. The location of a prayer will color its purpose. The PAC, for example, acts as a kind of fulcrum, concluding the communion rite and preparing the

---

[35] These guidelines have proven useful, *mutatis mutandis*, for those engaged in the work of translation for ICEL.

community for its dismissal. The very location of the PAC demands some attention to its "sending" or "missioning" purpose.

> 2. The prayers are intended for *proclamation* in the liturgical assembly.

Liturgical prayers are not primarily for private study or personal meditation, though such may, of course, take place. Authors must constantly remember that prayers will be proclaimed aloud. Thus, prayers need to be crafted in such a way that they may be heard and understood. The oral and aural effects of the language that is chosen for a prayer will be critical in its effective proclamation by the celebrant and its appropriation by the assembly.

> 3. While the traditional elements of a particular genre of prayer should be contained in the newly composed prayers, they need not in every instance follow exactly the structure of the prayers now in the *Sacramentary* or other ritual books.

This guideline suggests that the classic order of a collect (address, amplification of address, petition, result clause, conclusion) might occasionally be altered for a different rhetorical emphasis. The address of God need not be the first words of the text of a collect but might occasionally drop down further into the body of the prayer. The draft of an original text for Epiphany begins:

> We have seen the star of your glory
> rising in splendor,
> Lord God of the nations.
> The radiance of your Word-made-flesh
> pierces the darkness that covers the earth
> and signals the dawn of justice and peace.[36]

Similarly, all of the elements of a eucharistic prayer as developed in the General Instruction of the Roman Missal need to be present in any new composition yet there may be an original way to reorder certain elements for more effective proclamation. A case in point is the current question raised about the appropriate location of the anamnesis and its juxtaposition with the community's proclamation of faith.

> 4. The thoughts expressed in the prayers should have a logical coherence and unity and the prayers should have a coherent structure.

The internal unity and the logical ordering of a particular text will require close attention from a composer. Again, to take a col-

---

[36] *Opening Prayers for Experimental Use at Mass* (Washington: ICEL, 1986), 22.

lect as an example, the petition of such a prayer should flow from the address and amplification of address. In other words, the title chosen for God is not arbitrary but is closely related to the petition.

In longer compositions coherence is achieved by careful transitions. The most consistent criticism of the first draft of *Eucharistic Prayer A* was that there was need of a more explicit transition from the preface section extolling creation to the post-Sanctus section and its concentration on redemption. One critic remarked that reference to sin and redemption in the post-Sanctus seemed abruptly inserted into the narrative when there had been no trouble in paradise in the preface. In the final draft, four lines were inserted after the "Holy, holy," to establish a coherent transition:

> All holy God,
> how wonderful the work of your hands!
> You restored the beauty of your image
> when sin had scarred the world.[37]

5. The nature of the rite as well as the moment in the rite and its ritual context will influence the tone of the prayer.

This guideline was developed after the subcommittee's experience of working on the *Order of Christian Funerals*. The tone of a prayer appropriate for use in the home immediately after a death will be more intimate than that at a funeral Mass; the tone will attempt to respond to the immediate sense of loss and attend to the needs of the mourners. Similarly, the prayer at the closing of a coffin will recognize the heightened emotional response of the mourners at this moment. The circumstances of death, the age of the deceased, the length of illness or the suddenness of loss, all will affect tone. For these reasons, the variety of pastoral circumstances surrounding the death of a Christian dictated that a range of original texts of varying "tone" be available for choice by the sensitive minister.

CONTENT AND STYLE

6. The prayers must be doctrinally sound.

This guideline may appear to be self-evident. Liturgical texts must avoid any material of dubious doctrinal interpretation. At the same

---

[37] *Eucharistic Prayer A*, lines 18-21. The final draft of this text as well as a discussion of the results of the consultation process are found in *ICEL Newsletter* 12:3-4; 13:1-2 (1985-1986).

time, as noted earlier in this essay, only one or other facet of doctrine need be articulated in a given prayer. Not everything need be or can be said.

In addition, although the prayers must be doctrinally sound, they should not be a self-conscious collage of doctrine explicitly articulated. The reason the Nicene Creed is an infelicitous liturgical text is that it is a statement of doctrine about what we believe, a conciliar statement which subsequently crept into the liturgy as a test of orthodoxy. The distinction between *theologia prima* (the act of worship) and *theologia secunda* (systematic reflection on the event of worship) must be respected for the integrity of both.

> 7. Inspiration for the prayers will be found in the Scriptures, the seasons, and the theology underlying the various rites.

This guideline suggests that authors look to the Scriptures assigned to feasts, seasons, and ritual celebrations to inspire their composition. It also urges writers to steep themselves in the liturgical year and its underlying theological themes. References to baptism, for example, would be expected in some presidential prayers in Lent and the Easter season. Similarly, eschatological allusions would be appropriate in prayers used during Advent. Note the strong eschatological character of an original text draft for the First Sunday of Advent:

> Above the clamor of our violence
> your Word of truth resounds,
> O God of majesty and power.
> Over nations enshrouded in despair
> your justice dawns.
>
> Grant your household
> a discerning spirit and a watchful eye
> to perceive the hour in which we live.
> Hasten the advent of that Day
> when the weapons of war will be banished,
> our deeds of darkness cast off,
> and all your scattered children gathered into one.[38]

> 8. The prayers should have enough substance to draw the congregation into prayer and to afford inspiration for meditation.

The length of a text is less at issue here than its content, and particularly the possibility that a word or a phrase might touch the

---

[38] *Opening Prayers for Experimental Use at Mass*, 10.

listener and stay with that person after the prayer is finished. The kind of report received most happily by the original texts subcommittee after a limited experimental period with a text is that after a celebration listeners commented on one or other phrase which captured their imagination and drew them more deeply into prayer.

> 9. The themes of the prayers should be fairly universal so that they can be used in a variety of places and circumstances. In addition, these compositions are prepared for an international community and should avoid themes that might be suitable for a particular community or region but would be meaningless or confusing in other circumstances.

Universality suggests that texts be judged for their usefulness in a variety of Sunday assemblies of different circumstances, backgrounds, educational levels, classes, and so on. In addition, this guideline looks to the durability of texts: references to contemporary social evils might prove dated in a number of years. Immediate concerns will more appropriately find a home in the General Intercessions.

Not explicitly mentioned in this guideline is a matter of equal concern, namely, ensuring the suitability of the vocabulary of texts across cultures. Turns of expression can have differing meaning in various locales; words which are perfectly acceptable in one culture may have an unhappy, slang connotation in another.

> 10. As far as possible the author should avoid moving from the concrete to the abstract in prayer composition. A concrete prayer is one that is rooted in human experience and speaks of basic human concerns. Thus rooted in human experience, a prayer can be concrete and universal at the same time.

A comparison of the two opening prayers assigned at present to the Fourth Sunday of Lent may help to illustrate this guideline:

Opening Prayer

Father of peace,
we are joyful in your Word,
your Son Jesus Christ,
who reconciles us to you.

Alternative Opening Prayer

God our Father,
your Word, Jesus Christ, spoke
    peace to a sinful world
and brought (hu)mankind the gift
    of reconciliation
by the suffering and death
    he endured.

Let us hasten toward Easter
with the eagerness of faith
and love.

Teach us, the people who bear
his name,
to follow the example he gave us:
may our faith, hope and charity
turn hatred to love, conflict to
peace, death to eternal life.

We ask this . . .

We ask this . . .

The opening prayer is quite concrete in its address and amplification of address: the community rejoices in the saving work of Christ who is even now reconciling us to God. Two factors contribute to the abstraction of the petition in this prayer: the use of "Let us," while a conventional and polite way to avoid a more forceful manner of expression, has the effect of weakening the petition by its formalism; "hasten toward Easter" is a highly ambiguous phrase. A close analysis of this text might suggest that the community is really asking, in the midst of its Lenten journey, for the grace of faith and love in order to participate wholeheartedly in the conversion process which the Lenten journey demands. Yet the prayer suffers from abstraction and authors must recall that communities, in general, do not have prayer texts in front of them for careful textual analysis.

The alternative opening prayer for the same Sunday provides a striking contrast. In this prayer the community affirms that Jesus *has* reconciled all of humankind by his suffering and death. The community then asks the grace to be taught to follow his example. As Jesus reconciled the world to God by laying down his life, so those of us who bear his name ask to be able to do the same. The request is an imperative. It is elaborated further: the community seeks the grace to confront hatred, conflict, and death in order to bring love, peace, and eternal life to humankind. The community asks to participate in Christ's work of redemption. In this instance, as in the case of the translated collect, the community would not have the luxury of careful textual analysis on the spot. Nevertheless, the very explicit nature of the language of this text invites a community to commit itself to a concrete way of life through its "Amen."

11. The compositions should be clear, forceful, interesting, consistent, and imaginative.

When authors first read this guideline there is a tendency to say: "Lord, who can be saved?" Lord, who can possibly write an original prayer?

12. There should be a consistency of images, and care must be exercised not to use too many images in a single prayer, lest the hearers become confused.

Again, an example may prove helpful. The alternative opening prayer for the Seventh Sunday of Easter reads:

> Eternal Father,
> reaching from end to end of the universe,
> and ordering all things with your mighty arm:
> for you, time is the unfolding of truth that already is,
> the unveiling of beauty that is yet to be.
>
> Your Son saved us in history
> by rising from the dead,
> so that transcending time he might free us from death.
> May his presence among us
> lead to the vision of unlimited truth
> and unfold the beauty of your love.
>
> We ask this . . .

Regarding this prayer, one commentator wrote:

> Some prayers are definitely intended for the better-educated; indeed that for the Seventh Sunday of Easter would be more appropriate for a high-powered meditation. They require careful enunciation and would seem best suited to solemn celebrations, but then only after a realistic assessment as to whether they will communicate their message to a reasonable proportion of the particular congregation present—and enable them to pray. It is not sufficient that they should sound well: the criterion is whether or not they are effective as prayer.[39]

In this text there are too many ideas, too many images, for the prayer to be understandable. In addition this text illustrates well the problem posed by expressing nonempirical realities in the language of prayer and the larger question of whether liturgical prayer is able to accommodate philosophical concepts. A question each author must address is the question of intelligibility when a prayer is proclaimed aloud.

13. An effort should be made to open the prayers to a wide-ranging vocabulary. Color and poetic imagery, where possible, should be evident in the compositions. At the same time jargon or esoteric words should be avoided.

---

[39] John Ainslie, *Making the Most of the Missal* (London: Geoffrey Chapman, 1976), 36.

A wide-ranging vocabulary suggests to authors that they have the freedom, even the mandate, to employ words in prayer which may not have been found there in the past. Fresh vocabulary, however, becomes a matter of debate, the same word or phrase being lauded by some as striking, unusual, and very fine, or as jarring, totally distracting, and thus inappropriate by others. An example of divided opinion is the following draft of a prayer after communion:

> Living God,
>> your word has claimed us once again,
>> the meal of life renewed us.
>
> Send us from this assembly
>> into the kingdom of the world
>> with faith to resist it,
>> the courage to love it,
>> and the wit to transform it
>> into the Kingdom of your Son.
>
> This we ask in the name of Jesus the Lord.[40]

The word "wit" received an extraordinary number of comments, both positive and negative.

On the other hand, there have been instances when new modes of expression have been quite well received. One case in point is a text for the Christmas Vigil Mass which speaks of "this night's marriage of heaven and earth,"[41] an altogether lovely and satisfying image of the mystery of the incarnation.

> 14. The prayers should use inclusive language and avoid the use of language which may discriminate on sexist, racist, clericalist, or anti-Semitic grounds.

After receiving the deliberations of an ad hoc subcommittee on discriminatory language, ICEL developed an inclusive language policy with regard to the way we speak of one another in the community of faith, a type of language we have come to call the "horizontal" dimension of inclusive language. ICEL's policy grows out of its concern that each member of the assembly be engaged by the language which is proclaimed. In the words of the Instruction on the Translation of Liturgical Texts:

> The prayer of the Church is always the prayer of some actual community, assembled here and now. It is not sufficient that a

---

[40] *Presidential Prayers for Experimental Use at Mass* (Washington: ICEL, 1983), 23.
[41] *Opening Prayers*, 15.

formula handed down from some other time or region be translated verbatim, even if accurately, for liturgical use. The formula
translated **must become the genuine prayer of the congregation
and in it each of its members should be able to find and express himself or herself.**[42] [Emphasis added.]

ICEL's guidelines on inclusive language may be found in *Eucharistic Prayers*, a study booklet incorporating inclusive language into
the nine approved eucharistic prayers and including a statement of
ICEL's inclusive language rationale.[43]

> 15. Attention to the rhythm and cadence must be a primary con-
> sideration in the composition of new prayers.
>
> 16. Prayers should be composed in sense lines with a view to their
> being proclaimed well, heard, and easily understood.

These two guidelines develop more thoroughly a concern for
the proclamatory character of new compositions. Are there too many
weak syllables in a row? Does the prayer end on a strong syllable?
Is there a sameness about the number and type of speech stresses
in a sequence which makes the prayer become singsong in deliv-
ery? Rhythm and cadence also are examined for the musicality of
a text. All ICEL prayers are composed in sense lines so that they
can be proclaimed thoughtfully and intelligently without undue
reliance on the *Sacramentary*.

> 17. Authors should avoid stock-in-trade collect phrases.

"We beseech thee" and "vouchsafe" may have surfaced rather
often in older translations of the Latin collects. While we have moved
beyond these phrases, it is possible for a single author to develop
a repetitive pattern or construction quite unconsciously. This is an
eventuality to which the original texts subcommittee remains alert.

> 18. Original texts should in general be fuller than the correspond-
> ing ICEL translations.

One of the more controversial decisions of the original texts subcommittee has to do with the length of texts. The genius of the
prayers of the Roman rite was in their concision, an inimitable quality
in English. Consultations have underscored the benefit of texts which

---

[42] Instruction on the Translation of Liturgical Texts, no. 20: DOL 123, no. 857.

[43] *Eucharistic Prayers*, For Study and Comment by the Bishops of the Member and Associate Member Countries of the International Commission on English in the Liturgy (Washington: ICEL, 1980), 63-67.

are slightly longer, allowing the community time to get on board, so to speak, before the prayer has concluded. The additional length of a successful text will be achieved by the development of a single image or theme, however, rather than the juxtaposition of a variety of images or themes.

TRINITARIAN CONCERNS

19. Christian liturgical prayer is traditionally directed to the Father, through the mediation of the Son, in the power of the Spirit.

It was the Council of Hippo in 393 which stated: "In prayer, no one shall address the Son instead of the Father, or the Father instead of the Son, except at the altar, when prayer shall always be addressed to the Father."[44] With rare exception, the prayers of the Missal continue this tradition, naming the First Person of the Trinity in the address of the prayer, offering the prayer explicitly through the mediation of Jesus Christ, and, when the longer form of the conclusion is employed, stating the Spirit's role in sanctifying the community.

20. Care must be taken to respect the Trinitarian economy.

Titles traditionally ascribed to one person of the Trinity would not ordinarily be used for another. For example, the Father would not be addressed as the "Comforter" or the "Sanctifier," titles traditionally assigned to the Spirit.

21. Within the prayers, references to the different persons of the Trinity must be expressed clearly, especially when pronouns (for example, you, he) are being used.

In this as in so many of the guidelines, the proclamatory character of the prayer demands that pronominal references be clear, most often achieved by placing pronouns in close proximity to their antecedents.

22. Presidential prayers should be addressed to the First Person of the Trinity. This may be done in a variety of ways and authors are encouraged to incorporate a wide range of metaphors, especially those drawn from the Scriptures, in the forms of address of the prayers. The choice of address should be made bearing in mind the content of the balance of the prayer.

---

[44] C. J. Hefele, *A History of Councils of the Church* II, trans. H. N. Oxenham (Edinburgh: T. & T. Clark, 1896), 398.

As ICEL stated when it established its inclusive language policy, the question of God language is far more complex and one which does not admit of easy solutions: "Names and descriptions applied to God in biblical and liturgical texts have been almost exclusively male in character. ICEL recognizes that this raises serious questions on several different levels, and is pursuing a study of the matter."[45] As this issue continues to be probed by theologians and linguists, ICEL has drafted its guideline in an expansive way, hoping to break some new ground by developing a wider range of metaphors as titles for God, drawn most particularly from the Scriptures, but inspired as well by the rite in question and by the nature of the petition. A review of recent ICEL publications yields the following new titles, among others:

From the *Order of Christian Funerals* (1985)

God of endless ages
God of blessings
God of our ancestors in the faith
God of deliverance
God of those who hope

From *Eucharistic Prayer A* (1986)

Strong and faithful God
All holy God

From *Opening Prayers for Experimental Use at Mass* (1986)

God of majesty and power
God whose will is justice for the poor and peace for the afflicted
God of glory and splendor
Guardian of our homes and source of all blessings
Lord God of the nations
God of the covenant
God of light and life
God of all mystery, all wisdom, all truth

In each instance these titles have been employed because they enhance the content of the balance of the prayer: perhaps by underscoring a quality of God related to the petition; perhaps by setting the tone, as with the texts from the *Order of Christian Funerals*; perhaps by providing the transition, as in titles employed in the eucharistic prayer. The language chosen for the address of the prayer

---

[45] *Eucharistic Prayers,* 67.

is not arbitrary, but intimately related to the prayer composition as a whole.

With regard to the use of the traditional title "Father" in original texts, this title may still be found in those texts which refer explicitly to the Son, for example,

> Merciful Father,
> you sent your Son, the Lamb of God,
> to bear the sins of the world.[46]

or which are inspired by a Lectionary text within which "Father" is a strong reference, as in the Matthean passage (Matthew 5:13-16) which inspired the following prayer:

> Heavenly Father,
> you have called your Church
> to be the salt of the earth and the light of the world.[47]

> 23. While presidential prayers are traditionally addressed to the First Person of the Trinity, there are other genre (for example, litanies) which may be addressed to the Son or the Spirit. ✓

This guideline provides a clarification for the address section of prayers other than presidential texts (that is, opening prayers, prayers over the gifts, prayers after communion, and eucharistic prayers).

> 24. Attention must be given to the conclusions of the prayers in order that they express the mediation of Christ. The conclusion, whether standard or more inventive, should fit together with what has gone before in the body of the prayers. It may be interwoven within the prayer. If there is a doxology in the body of the prayer, it seems best to omit a full doxology in the conclusion. ✓

It is the Epistle to the Hebrews which most profoundly develops Christ's mediatorial role as our High Priest who stands before the throne of grace, living still to make intercession on our behalf. Such is the theological presupposition of Christian prayer. Thus, as we conclude a prayer we state our belief that Christ is our mediator. We "make our prayer through Christ, our Lord," or "We ask this through . . . ," or we say, "Grant this through. . . ."

Some original texts have concluded with a statement of Christ's mediation which is more interesting because it is woven into the body of the prayer, for example,

---

[46] *Opening Prayers*, 24.
[47] *Opening Prayers*, 28.

Heavenly Father,
you have called your Church
to be the salt of the earth and the light of the world.

Let not the flame of our love for each other grow dim
nor our taste for your truth be dulled,
but give us a vigorous faith and charity unfeigned,
that all may see our works
and give you the glory
through our Lord Jesus Christ, your Son,
who lives and reigns with you and the Holy Spirit,
one God, for ever and ever.[48]

or, while free-standing, it is composed to fit the particular feast or season as illustrated by this Advent conclusion:

We ask this through him whose coming is certain,
whose Day draws near:
your Son, our Lord Jesus Christ,
who lives and reigns with you and the Holy Spirit,
on God, for ever and ever.[49]

CONCLUSION

From the modest beginnings of preparing some alternative opening prayers, ICEL's work on original texts has mushroomed rapidly in the last several years. It should not be surprising that, as the revisions process has gotten underway, ICEL continues to receive numerous requests for original prayers and alternatives to existing texts in light of actual liturgical experience. Only with the passage of time and significant pastoral use of the rites has it been possible for English-speaking communities to recognize the strengths and weaknesses of the ritual language they employed as well as particular instances when existing texts were "not sufficient for the celebration of a fully renewed liturgy."[50]

Having cited, once again, the Instruction on the Translation of Liturgical Texts, we have come full circle and concluded a description of ICEL's work on original texts: beginnings, present projects,

---

[48] *Opening Prayers*, 28.

[49] *Opening Prayers*, 10. The original texts subcommittee has encouraged authors to consider composing one conclusion for use throughout a particular season. Repetition of the final lines of the opening prayer would be a subtle way of expressing the liturgical unity of the season. Consultants have commented favorably on this aspect of the consultation.

[50] Instruction on the Translation of Liturgical Texts, no. 43: DOL 123, no. 880.

and evolving guidelines. The work is slow. It is a discipline. It is also a solemn trust. The preceding pages have communicated something of the evolution of ICEL's work in this area, including the development of principles and working procedures. What these pages fail to communicate is the recognition by all involved in the work—authors, members of the original texts subcommittee, Advisory Committee, and Episcopal Board—of the awesome responsibility this work entails. With the leadership of persons like Archbishop Denis Hurley, O.M.I., the mystery of communication with God in liturgy is never lost sight of in the mechanics of the day-to-day. It is to Archbishop Hurley, in deep gratitude, that the original texts subcommittee has dedicated its work.

ICEL AND INCLUSIVE LANGUAGE

J. Frank Henderson

Inclusive language by definition is that which includes, comprehends, contains, or embraces. Negatively, it does not exclude or discriminate against. In a liturgical context, inclusive language recognizes, embraces, and facilitates the full participation of the whole worship- ✓ ing community. In addition, it does not discriminate against or show prejudice toward anyone, even if they are not members of the liturgical assembly.

The issue of inclusive language arose in North America in the late 1960s and early 1970s, and became widely known there in the early and mid 1970s. In subsequent years it became recognized in other parts of the world as well. As the principal agency for providing liturgical texts for English-speaking Roman Catholics around the world, ICEL had to deal with this increasing consciousness regarding inclusive language. This is the story of that process.*

THE CONTEMPORARY CONTEXT

The question of inclusive language represents the convergence of a number of social, linguistic, liturgical, and theological issues. A principal concern is the place of women in society and in the Church and contemporary challenges to a long history of subordination. This has sociological, psychological, economic, and legal, as well as liturgical and theological aspects. Similar questions arise regarding minority groups in general. In addition, the relationship of Christians to Jews and members of other faiths is also at stake.

---

* The principal sources used in this study were the minutes of meetings of the Advisory Committee, subcommittee on discriminatory language, and subcommittee on translations and revisions, together with other documentation related to these meetings. Minutes of Episcopal Board meetings were not examined. However minutes of joint Advisory Committee–Episcopal Board meetings were available, and in some cases reports of relevant actions of the Board were provided by the Executive Secretary. ICEL Annual Reports, Newsletters, and other publications were also consulted. Finally, this writer was a participant in the work of ICEL on inclusive language from 1977 to 1987.

At the level of language questions arise regarding the nature of linguistic change, and how social forces influence linguistic development. It is also now being recognized that language influences people in ways other than as purely cognitive communication. The nature of linguistic gender in English is changing, and how generic language is used is under scrutiny. Many are concerned that change not threaten beauty in language, but there are diverse views about what constitutes beautiful language.

Our age is probably the first to raise questions regarding the nature of liturgical language. The principles that guide the translation of Latin texts into contemporary vernacular languages are also much discussed. New principles, such as full participation and hospitality, now govern liturgical rites and their celebration. There are new liturgical texts, songs and readings, greater use of Scripture, a sharing of ministry, and an increased valuation of baptism. Experiments in liturgical inculturation are being conducted around the world, and cultural differences are acknowledged and respected. Male-female relationships are culturally influenced, however, and the subordinate place of women in many cultures is no longer readily accepted.

In theology the question of inclusive language is related to the broader question of how we speak of God today. It is influenced by shifts in perceptions of immanence and transcendence, by the rediscovery of feminine images of God in Scripture and Christian tradition, and by attempts to talk about the Trinity in contemporary ways. Today's increased appreciation of the humanity of Christ is also relevant, but Christ's humanness is perceived (at least by some) to be more significant theologically than his maleness. The Holy Spirit has been rediscovered in Western theology, and it is now appreciated that our tradition has applied both feminine gender and feminine images to the Spirit.

Also involved are questions in ecclesiology. What does Church membership mean, and are women fully members of the Church? The question of ministry comes up, and hence that of the place of women in ministry. Inclusive language is also an ecumenical issue, and one that both unites and divides Christians, often across rather than along denominational lines. It is also a global issue, though sometimes perceived and expressed differently in different countries and regions. Questions of relations of local Churches to the Church universal are raised. The ability of Church structures to discern and interpret the "signs of the times" as well as their ability to resist passing fads are at stake. Modern understandings of Scripture influence all of these points.

Inclusive language also raises interesting methodological questions. How does the Church—local and universal—learn, grow, and adapt? How does it accept life experience and social change as theological data? What is the most appropriate relationship between liturgists/theologians and bishops? What Church structures and processes promote or inhibit growth and development? How can a body like ICEL provide leadership and promote growth while respecting the ministry of the bishops? How can local Churches in different parts of the world respond to their own needs and value their own cultures, while also fostering unity within the Church as a whole and respecting the ministry of the bishop of Rome?

Most if not all of these issues and questions are still in a state of development and growth. Many are controversial and engender strong feelings. In such a context it is not surprising that the introduction of inclusive language into the worship of English-speaking Catholics has required education and changes in attitudes, could not be accomplished over night, and has led opponents of linguistic change to criticize ICEL for taking the issues of inclusive language so seriously.

THE ROLE OF ICEL

Arising out of the liturgical renewal fostered by the Second Vatican Council, ICEL has the task of providing English versions of the revised Roman liturgies. The first phase of this work consisted mainly of the translation of the Latin texts of the universal Church. More recently it has also involved arrangement and layout of materials, provision of pastoral-liturgical materials for the use of the minister, and the composition of original texts in English.

Limitations

Though ICEL has a particularly important role in the question of inclusive language in the liturgy, that role is limited in several respects. For example, ICEL does not determine either the Scripture texts that are assigned for liturgical use, or the biblical translations that are used. It likewise is not responsible for most of the musical texts used. Another limitation is simply that much of ICEL's work is that of translation of Latin originals. Though translation need not be slavishly literal, it must respect the original text.

ICEL does not impose the English liturgical texts it produces, but instead offers them to its eleven member and fifteen associate member bishops' conferences representing the countries or regions where English is used in the celebration of the liturgy. It is an agency of these conferences of bishops. The bishops may approve or reject this work, and each bishops' conference must obtain confirmation of its approval from the Congregation for Divine Worship before using ICEL texts. Any changes that ICEL might wish to suggest in presently published texts, for example, with respect to inclusive language, must receive the approval of those bishops' conferences that desire the changes, and that approval must be confirmed by the Holy See.

Opportunities

ICEL has consciously and intentionally implemented principles of inclusive language since 1975, though its understanding of this issue has evolved over the intervening period. What courses of action have been open to ICEL, and how has it worked?

First, liturgical books published in Latin since 1975 have been translated into English using inclusive language. The first such book was the *Rite of Commissioning Special Ministers of Holy Communion*, published at the beginning of 1978. Second, inclusive language has been introduced into final ("White Book") editions of liturgical books, even if draft ("Green Book") versions previously in circulation had not been entirely inclusive. For example, the 1982 edition of *Pastoral Care of the Sick: Rites of Anointing and Viaticum* is consistency inclusive with respect to persons, whereas the 1974 edition was not.

Third, principles of inclusive language are being applied in the revision of liturgical books that have been used in White Book versions for a number of years. The first completely revised rite is the *Order of Christian Funerals* (issued in 1985). *The Roman Missal (Sacramentary)* is being revised at the present time.

Fourth, ICEL has pointed out to the conferences of bishops remedies that are available within the existing versions of the liturgical books and that are within their competence to promote or implement.

Fifth, ICEL can provide emendations of particular liturgical texts even before the entire liturgical books which contain them are revised. These are offered to bishops' conferences and eventually require confirmation by Rome.

Sixth, ICEL can work with other Churches through the international and ecumenical English Language Liturgical Consultation to emend common texts with respect to inclusive language. A new, largely inclusive version of these texts will be published in 1990.

The story of ICEL's understanding and implementation of principles of inclusive language will now be recounted in more detail. It is important to note that all structures of ICEL have had a role to play: the Episcopal Board, the secretariat, the Advisory Committee (hereafter, AC), the AC's various subcommittees, especially that on discriminatory language, and individual members of these bodies.

Early ICEL Texts

Inclusive language was first named as a concern of ICEL in 1975, several years after its work had been completed on the liturgical books for the eucharist, liturgy of the hours, and rites of baptism, confirmation, marriage, penance, etc. Two points may be made regarding ICEL's use of language during the pre-1975 period. First, the language of these liturgies is not *totally* exclusive or discriminatory either with respect to people or with respect to God, though today it is accepted that there is a need for improvement in both areas.

In addition, ICEL took at least one positive step toward inclusive language even in its earliest work. Thus whenever *fratres* was used in Latin as an address to the assembly, the following footnote was added to the corresponding "brethren":

> At the discretion of the priest, other words which seem more suitable under the circumstances, such as *friends, dearly beloved, my brothers and sisters,* may be used.

LANGUAGE THAT DISCRIMINATES AGAINST WOMEN

The first phase of ICEL's conscious and intentional work on inclusive language was carried out from 1975 to mid-1977. It included commitment to the use of inclusive language, coming to grips with the scope, nature and extent, of the problem, establishing new structures to deal with this matter, and attempts to remedy problems in existing texts.

Commitment

This work began with a commitment to the use of inclusive language. At its August 1975 meeting:

> The Advisory Committee recognized the necessity in all future trans-
> lations and revisions to avoid words which ignore the place of
> women in the Christian community altogether or which seem to
> relegate women to a secondary role.

Neither the origins of this statement nor discussion surrounding
it are recorded. However, it has been the benchmark for all further
ICEL work on the liturgical texts, and has been reiterated on numerous occasions.

It is of interest that this commitment to the use of inclusive language preceded precise definition of the issue, extensive study of
principles, analysis of texts, or formulation of possible courses of
action.

Defining the Issue

ICEL soon proceded to define the scope of the problem of what
was then called "discriminatory language," though this definition
evolved in the course of time. At the beginning the issue was thought
of in terms of language that discriminates against women. The issue was finally defined in a "proposal concerning discriminatory
language" adopted in November 1977.

> The discriminatory language under consideration has to do with
> sex, race, color, culture, religion (e.g., anti-semitism), state in life
> (clericalism), and related matters, and the problem must be seen
> in the context of more general problems of social, legal, and eco-
> nomic discrimination against minority or underprivileged groups.
> Under this broad scope, the AC considers the issues of sexist, racial,
> and anti-semitic discrimination to be of particular urgency.

This broad perspective continued to guide ICEL throughout its
work on inclusive language. Language excluding women clearly was
the primary focus and priority, and is given most extensive discussion here. What ICEL has done regarding the other issues will be
considered more briefly.

Attempts to define the problem also led to an increasing awareness that language that excludes women has to do not only with
language referring to persons, but also language about God. This
part of the story will be told below.

A further aspect of the process of definition was in distinguishing between problems in scriptural texts and those of liturgical texts
per se. The first subcommittee on inclusive language felt strongly

that a new translation of the psalms was needed, as well as the elimination from the lectionary of passages "which reflect real or apparent discrimination." At the May 1977 Advisory Committee meeting
these points were acknowledged, but it was also recognized that
lectionary reform was not part of ICEL's mandate, and that a new
psalter (and possible new translation of the lectionary) was a long
way in the future.

Finally, lists began to be made as early as May 1976 of specific
examples of exclusive language in ICEL liturgical texts. A detailed
study of *The Roman Missal (Sacramentary)* in this regard was presented
at the second subcommittee meeting in 1978. Such lists have recently
been brought up to date in relation to the revision of the Order of
Mass of the Missal.

Structures

The next step was the establishment of structures and processes
to deal with the issue of inclusive language. Of course, the secretariat,
Advisory Committee, and Episcopal Board remained the major structures in this as in all other aspects of ICEL's work. However, the
need was soon felt for smaller, more focused and more specialized
groups to deal with this matter.

> In August–September 1976, the following action was taken: The Ad-
> visory Committee, with the approval of the Episcopal Board, has
> therefore set up a subcommittee to study the entire question—
> particularly doubtful words and phrases which are not open to a
> simple solution. This subcommittee will attempt to develop princi-
> ples from its study of specific language; it will be concerned not
> only with new translations and texts but with the long range revi-
> sion of texts.

Such a subcommittee was then established. Over the course of
several years its membership and responsibilities varied, and it was
always an ad hoc, rather than standing committee.

The first subcommittee met in March 1977. Its "primary goals . . .
were: to attempt to examine and understand the overall question,
to ascertain the extent of the problem in reference to ICEL texts, and
to suggest general policy and guidelines for future ICEL work." With
a number of new members, it met again in June 1978. At both times
the primary (though not sole) concern was sexist language. Subcommittee work then lapsed for several years, while developments
proceeded in the Advisory Committee and Episcopal Board.

At its May 1980 meeting, the Advisory Committee resolved "That a (new) small subcommittee be established to complete the discriminatory language project." This subcommittee met in May 1981 and April 1982. It then felt that its mandate had been completed, and the following resolution was adopted by the Advisory Committee:

> Be it resolved that, having completed its mandate, the Subcommittee on Discriminatory Language be dissolved. It is understood that the principles already adopted will be implemented in all future work of ICEL.

Courses of Action

The principles of inclusive language were applied to new translations from 1975 on, and later were applied to texts in the process of revision. These actions, however, did not affect liturgical texts already published and not due for revision for a number of years.

From the beginning, ICEL sought to introduce short-term remedies that could be applied to already published liturgical books. In August–September, 1976 the Advisory Committee adopted a report stating that "the Order of Mass, including the four eucharistic prayers . . . have been reviewed carefully to see what initial or minimal changes could be introduced without confusion and without weakening their thought or literary quality."

The recommendation was made that "in instances where a generic use of man, men, etc. has been introduced without necessity and redundantly, it may be omitted." Several instances of this usage were explicitly noted, including part of the eucharistic words of institution.

The Episcopal Board, however, decided in September 1976 that before proposing action it would be good to survey the conferences of bishops. In his letter of June 1977 the Chairman of the Board, Archbishop Denis Hurley, asked the opinion of the conferences on the following questions:

> a. whether objections against discriminatory language existed in their particular countries or regions;
>
> b. whether ICEL should provide some immediate interim solutions by introducing a slight rephrasing of liturgical texts, especially in the Order of Mass (specific examples were given);
>
> c. whether ICEL should postpone such rephrasing until the process of general revision had been developed and was under way.

By November of 1977 the responses of the bishops' conferences had been received. No criticism of liturgical texts on the grounds of discriminatory language was reported by Australia, England and Wales, India, Ireland, Pakistan, Philippines, and Scotland. It was perceived as a small problem in New Zealand and South Africa. The majority of Canadian bishops who responded felt that there were objections to discriminatory language in their dioceses. The U.S. bishops' conference also "recogniz(ed) that there are objections against discriminatory language in English liturgical texts."

However, most of the bishops' conferences opposed "some immediate, interim relief," and most also opposed taking discriminatory language into account even in future revision or else wished the revision process to be postponed for some time. Thus efforts to make short-term responses to the problem of discriminatory language were frustrated.

Formulation of Principles

The second phase of ICEL's work may be thought of as beginning with the November 1977 Advisory Committee meeting and concluding with the publication of the "Green Book" at the end of 1980. It was characterized by study of the issue and the formulation of principles and guidelines, particularly with respect to language that includes women. It concluded with further attempts to provide short-term solutions to the problem, and again these were not very successful. Inclusive language was regularly used in all new translations worked on during this period, however, and this process experienced no setback.

Plan of Action

At the November 1977 Advisory Committee meeting the Executive Secretary "began by recalling that the conferences of bishops had responded to Archbishop Hurley's letter . . . by rejecting any immediate solution and by endorsing a process of long-term study of this matter. (He) proposed that the next step must then be the commission of serious, scholarly studies on the question of discriminatory language from the theological, sociological, literary, etc., points of view."

Following extensive discussion, a "proposal concerning discriminatory language" was adopted by the Advisory Committee and approved by the Episcopal Board. After an introduction, it continued:

3. The secretariat is directed to engage the assistance of specialists in the field of sexist, racist, and anti-semitic discrimination, and collectively (a) to identify and collect pertinent existing literature in these fields, (b) to consult with other Churches and other appropriate bodies regarding this problem.

4. The materials, reports, and studies obtained as a result of this process should be collated by the secretariat and evaluated by a subcommittee which should consist of experts in the fields involved, and other concerned and knowledgeable individuals, and chaired by a member of the AC. The subcommittee should report to the AC and make both general and specific recommendations:

(a) regarding the removal of discriminatory language in existing texts and documents;

(b) regarding principles and procedures by which future mistakes can be avoided;

(c) regarding attitudes which have given rise to various forms of discrimination in the past;

(d) regarding the commissioning of such study papers as may seem necessary.

This was both an ideal and an idealistic program of action. Even as this resolution was being passed, the Executive Secretary and several Advisory Committee members seriously questioned whether it could be accomplished. In the end it was too much to ask of the structures and personnel of ICEL, and in addition, such a mammoth project proved not to be necessary. Around this time a large number of publications on this subject were appearing. This made it difficult to keep up with what was being written on inclusive language and the place of women in the Church. At the same time, this literature also provided many of the studies that had been envisioned by the Advisory Committee and thereby relieved the subcommittee of some its task. The difficulty of dealing with the study of matters such as this under the constraints of regular Advisory Committee meetings also became apparent.

Study Papers

This work began with the commissioning of three study papers, two of which were considered in detail at several meetings of the

Advisory Committee. To summarize a long and complex story, they were greeted with mixed feelings, being well received by some members while others were uncomfortable with their content and approach. In the end, suggestions were made for improvements and they were returned to their authors.

Though these papers did not find acceptance as "position papers" of ICEL regarding inclusive language, they did provide a valuable service in educating the Advisory Committee on this issue. They brought together much data on language that was found useful and acceptable. In addition, by challenging the Advisory Committee and going beyond what it as a body was able to agree with at the time, its members were helped to progress further in this area. The indirect influence of these papers on further developments is undeniable.

Work on these study papers also moved ICEL to define its competence and its approach to the question of inclusive language more precisely. By concentrating on liturgical/theological arguments, it was able to reach agreement among its own personnel and take positions which it felt competent to argue convincingly and which would gain acceptance within its constituency. The Advisory Committee became aware of how controversial the issue was, and how much criticism any action would provoke. It learned to avoid positions which it was unable to document or defend or convince others of, or which would generate too much controversy. While some felt that there was a certain amount of "giving in" and "retreating" involved in this, these limitations did not ultimately limit what ICEL was able to do with respect to inclusive language.

Draft Principles

All of this preparatory work led to the publication of a statement of principles regarding inclusive language and of guidelines for concrete action. What was finally published in 1980 under the title of "Statement: The Problem of Exclusive Language with Regard to Women" began as "Guidelines for Non-discriminatory Language in Liturgy." It was drafted during the June 1978 subcommittee meeting and contained a statement of principles concerning inclusive language plus concrete guidelines for the revision of texts in this regard. Both language referring to persons and language referring to God were dealt with. At the end a section recommended certain "optional, immediate solutions" that conferences of bishops could undertake immediately, prior to eventual production of new books. These were simply the deletion of "men" in the Nicene Creed and in the words of institution, and a reminder that ICEL already recommended the use of alternative greetings in place of "Pray, brethren."

This document was discussed at length and received quite divided reactions when presented to the November 1978 Advisory Committee meeting. It became clear that extensive revision was required in order to make it generally acceptable, and it was revised several times during the meeting in order to be able to present it to the Episcopal Board a few days later.

Most of the objections were to the section on language referring to God. This was the first time that the Advisory Committee had considered this issue, and members were not ready to make recommendations regarding this subject without further study and documentation; most of this section was deleted but further work on the issue was promised.

The revised document was accepted by the Advisory Committee to be circulated as a tentative or interim document accompanied by an introduction and questions. The Episcopal Board accepted it on these grounds, but in light of the response of the conferences of bishops to Archbishop Hurley's 1977 letter, voted to remove the section on "optional, immediate solutions." However, these were communicated to the presidents of the conferences of bishops by letter.

Eucharistic Prayers

At this point, another facet of the story has to be introduced. The Advisory Committee had in general accepted the "dis-ease" of the Episcopal Board and the bishops' conferences with attempts to make immediate, optional emendations to liturgical books already in use, and was taking a long-term approach to the improvement of liturgical texts with respect to inclusive language. For some time, however, the possibility of making additions to and changes in the eucharistic prayers had arisen in other contexts. For example, interpolations (as in the German Missal) and additional acclamations (as used in the eucharistic prayers for children) were being considered for the sake of greater congregational participation. In addition, concern about possible theological misunderstanding of a few texts had led to a desire to emend some of the eucharistic prayers, even prior to their eventual revision.

To these concerns was now added that of inclusive language. Of special concern was Eucharistic Prayer IV, whose very exclusive post-sanctus section was said to lead some communities not to use this text. In addition, the "for us men" of the institution narrative of all the eucharistic prayers was of concern.

Between late 1978 and mid 1980 the subcommittee on translations and revisions and the Advisory Committee prepared inclusive language versions of the nine approved eucharistic prayers. In addition, it proposed that these be published together with the Principles referred to above, plus a bibliography on the question of inclusive language. These documents were considered by the Episcopal Board in September 1980, and their publication by the Advisory Committee was authorized. The "Green Book," officially titled *Eucharistic Prayers*, finally went to press in late 1980, with an introductory letter by Archbishop Hurley.

The 1980 Green Book

This document contains an introduction, the full texts of the eucharistic prayers in their emended versions, an explanation of the emendations that were proposed, the statement of principles, and a bibliography.

Two emendations that were made in Eucharistic Prayer IV are given by way of example. First, "and lead all men to the joyful vision of your light" was changed to "and lead them (referring to "creatures") to the joyful vision of your light."

A longer passage was emended to read:

> You formed the human race in your own likeness:
> male and female you created them
> and set them over the whole world
> to serve you, their creator,
> and to rule over all creatures.
> Even when they disobeyed you and lost your friendship
> you did not abandon them to the power of death,
> but helped all people to seek and find you.
> Again and again you offered them a covenant
> and through the prophets
> taught them to hope for salvation.

What principles were enunciated in the Green Book, and what guidelines for action were proposed?

The "General Principle" stated in the 1980 Green Book is the following:

> Both sound theology and pastoral sensitivity require that the language used in all liturgical texts, as well as in all other aspects of liturgy, for example, preaching, should not only permit but indeed facilitate the full participation of women in the worship of the Church.

This statement follows a Preface (by Archbishop Denis Hurley) and an Introduction (by the Advisory Committee). The preface alludes to societal and linguistic changes:

> The fuller participation of women in the social life of a growing number of countries is raising serious questions for languages like English which, for historical and cultural reasons, have reflected male predominance in their vocabulary, grammar, and syntax. Emerging sensitivities are no longer at ease with conventions that appear to exclude women from designations that should have a universal human extension.

A liturgical basis is added: "liturgy must reflect a deep concern for the whole people of God and an awareness of the sensitivities of every part of it."

The Advisory Committee's introduction begins with a statement regarding language:

> As a powerful tool of communication, language must be used in worship with the greatest care and precision. Modern studies have established the fact that language performs a highly important role in how one comes to perceive one's self and others. Furthermore, the range of symbols and images used determines the scope of the religious understanding and practice of the people of God, and if this range of symbols is limited, so also will be their understanding and practice. The way one is named within the worshiping community—and whether one is named at all—could affect the way one lives the Christian life.

An ecclesiological conclusion is then drawn:

> The failure of much of liturgical and theological language adequately to recognize the presence of women seems effectively to exclude them from full and integral participation in the life of the Church, and this exclusion can prevent the whole Church from experiencing the fullness of Christian community.

The question of "invisibility" is then dealt with further:

> Women . . . hear themselves mentioned only infrequently and often are not addressed at all. Their personal crisis with respect to

Church life is precipitated by appreciation of the truth of the principle _lex orandi, lex credendi,_ that is the Church believes as it prays. The experience of many women leads some to conclude that the Church considers them unimportant participants in its life and worship. Because of this problem of exclusive language and the obstacles to heartfelt participation which it creates in worship, some people have felt constrained to abandon corporate worship altogether.

The Introduction goes on to consider several basic liturgical and theological principles:

Today it is recognized that each and every Christian is called to, and indeed has a right to, full participation in worship. One basis for this appreciation is a deeper understanding of the meaning and power of the sacraments of Christian initiation. . . . Stemming from the baptismal anointing in the Spirit, we now have a greater recognition of the dignity and responsibility of each Christian to participate fully in the life of the Church. Christian worship arises out of and depends upon an integral and active assembly of the baptized, and it is hindered and made less perfect and less acceptable to the extent that some members of the community feel excluded from full participation in it.

It is then noted that the use of vernacular languages in worship has played a part in raising awareness: "When Catholics began to pray in their own tongues, attention was drawn to the fact that much traditional language in worship did not in fact permit full participation by those members of the community who were women."

Finally, the problem of biblical texts is raised:

Biblical language . . . must be carefully examined with respect to its influence on women's participation in worship, especially as it grew out of and in some ways reflects a time and culture considerably removed from our own.

Because several biblical translations were being revised at the time, "a full discussion of these matters will not be undertaken here."

Three specific areas of concern are identified: language addressing and referring to the worshiping community; language referring to God; and language referring to women. (The question of language referring to God is discussed separately below.)

Language _addressing and referring to the worshiping community_ is considered under three headings:

a. Terms such as men, sons, brothers, brethren, fraternity, and brotherhood now are understood to refer exclusively to males, al-

although from the perspective of the history of language these words once had a broader meaning. It is no longer acceptable to use this type of language in liturgical texts (unless the text does refer specifically to males) or to address such texts to any liturgical assembly in which women participate.

b. Texts such as man, mankind, forefathers, family of man, and certain uses of he, his, and him once were generic terms which could be used to include both men and women. Because these terms are in fact often used to refer only to males, their use has become ambiguous and increasingly is perceived to exclude women. Wherever possible, therefore, these terms should not be used. . . .

c. [. . .] "Brothers and sisters" or other inclusive phrases should be used [where the Latin has *Orate, fratres* or the like], if women form part of the worshiping assembly.

The question of language referring to women is dealt with as follows:

Some liturgical texts imply the inferiority of women and their natural subjection to men. These texts generally are biblical or biblically inspired and reflect the culture in which they were composed or culturally conditioned theological argumentation. An example would be the subjection of wives to husbands indicated in Ephesians 5 and Colossians 3. The problems that arise from such texts may in some cases be relieved by more careful translation; in other cases particular verses or entire pericopes may have to be deleted from liturgical use, and there is ample precedent for such selectivity. Another possible solution is careful explanation of the texts. Each passage requires individual study and judgment regarding the approach that is to be taken.

The emended eucharistic prayers published in the Green Book were approved immediately by the bishops' conferences of the United States and of Canada. Eventually they have come to be accepted by most of the other ICEL member bishops' conferences as well. Approval of these emended liturgical texts implies acceptance also of the principles upon which the emendations were carried out and which were printed immediately following the liturgical texts themselves. To what extent explicit approval was given these principles by the various bishops' conferences is not known.

As is standard procedure in the case of new or revised liturgical texts, the bishops' conferences individually have asked Rome to "confirm" these texts. Approval was soon given to change "for all men" in the institution narrative to "for all" and for the few other small changes that did not involve questions of inclusive language. Other changes were not approved. The present (March 1988) position of the Congregation for Divine Worship is that the inclusive language emendations proposed in the 1980 Green Book will be considered in the context of the larger project of the revision of the Missal.

Finally, ICEL, through its psalter subcommittee, later published a second statement of principles regarding inclusive language. It is to be found in the introduction to the *Consultation on a Liturgical Psalter* (1984). 𝄢

LANGUAGE REFERRING TO GOD

A third phase of this story may be thought of in terms of the work of ICEL on language referring to God during 1981 and 1982. The subcommittee held two meetings on this subject and made its final report to the Advisory Committee in November 1982. This report admitted:

> The situation with respect to (this issue) is both in a state of flux, and in need of further study; the perceptions of these issues also vary widely among and within the English-speaking countries. It therefore does not seem appropriate for ICEL to take definite positions on these issues at the present time. However, they are matters to be wrestled with, and certainly should not be forgotten or neglected in current and future work with liturgical language.

The subcommittee's recommendations were never adopted explicitly, but only implicitly through acceptance of the final subcommittee report. However, they have been extensively implemented in practice.

As was recognized in the 1980 Green Book, "names and descriptions applied to God in biblical and liturgical texts have been almost exclusively male in character, and ICEL recognizes that this raises serious questions on several different levels. . . ." Many questions and concerns have been raised regarding the origins, meaning, and consequences of this practice. However, the subcommittee decided to consider only a single issue, which at the same time was most basic, profoundly theological, and least controversial. This was the relationship of human language to the nature of God. The basic concern was that male or masculine language about God leads some to think that God is a male being.

Divine Names

One specific question concerns the divine name "Father." It has two types of usage in liturgical texts. One is in trinitarian formulas such as the sign of the cross, baptismal formula, blessings, some apostolic greetings, creeds, and doxologies. The other is in addresses of collects, prefaces, and eucharistic prayers.

An historical study carried out by one subcommittee member showed that *Pater* has only rarely been used in the addresses of Latin collects. In the present *Missale Romanum* only twenty-one out of approximately 1400 collects are so addressed. A detailed study of the ICEL English language version, however, showed that some 560 collects contain "*Father*" in the address. Similarly, "Father" is found more often in the English texts of the eucharistic prayers than in the Latin originals.

Senior members of the Advisory Committee explained that "Father" was used so frequently in order to make clear to the hearer that Roman presidential prayers are addressed to the First Person, a point which in some cases might otherwise not be evident until the conclusion. In addition, euphony was a consideration; "Father" sounds better than "God" at the very beginning of a prayer. (Beginning prayers with the single monosyllable "God" is still avoided by ICEL on the grounds of euphony.) Finally, the use of "Father" may also show greater appreciation that God is personal, and immanent as well as transcendent.

ICEL texts also showed an increase in the use of "Lord" compared to the Latin. In large part this was in formulas such as "Lord God" or "Lord our God," which were used to avoid the euphony problem mentioned above. The Executive Secretary had explained at the second subcommittee meeting that "Lord" had sometimes also been added for the sake of rhythm.

Images and Pronouns

Analysis of contemporary and historical liturgical texts also showed that the range of images, attributes, and metaphors used for God in liturgical language is relatively small. "Almighty," "eternal," and "merciful" predominate.

Finally, third-person pronouns for God are not used in collects, eucharistic prayers, etc.; only second-person pronouns are appropriate. However masculine third-person pronouns are used for God in some blessings, prefaces, and other types of prayers.

Principles

The general principle that was proposed to guide ICEL with respect to language referring to God is the following:

> Although no human language is adequate to express the nature of God, every effort should be made to use language that least distorts, narrows, or hampers our appreciation, understanding, experience, and relationship with God.

This has been applied in several ways. The subcommittee recommended that "no attempt should be made to completely eliminate 'Father' from liturgical texts," and suggested that the Lord's Prayer, the Creeds, baptismal formula, doxologies, and similar texts be excluded from consideration in this regard. However, the subcommittee recommended that the:

> use of (Father) should be rationalized, especially in view of its quite infrequent use in certain of the Latin prayers. . . . euphony alone should no longer be the major basis for its use in place of *Deus* and *Dominus*; problems of euphony can be dealt with in other ways. It is suggested that there be an explicit reason for the use of "Father" in each case in which it is not in the Latin.

The consistent practice of ICEL in recent years has been to use "Father" in translated texts when *Pater* is in the Latin, but not otherwise. The *Order of Christian Funerals* (1985) is the first liturgical book in which this principle has been expressed.

The subcommittee "suggested that a wider range of images and attributes for God be used in future prayer texts, including fuller use of the biblical tradition in this regard." This recommendation has been incorporated into ICEL's Principles of Revision and Guidelines for the Composition of Original Texts now in force.

The question of masculine pronouns for God was dealt with first by ICEL's psalter subcommittee. In their first psalm translations no masculine pronouns were used at all for God. The subcommittee on discriminatory language endorsed this work and added, "Though good English usage and construction probably will not allow the complete elimination of masculine pronouns for God from all liturgical texts, this usage probably can and should be reduced."

ICEL did not actually deal with liturgical texts that contained third-person masculine pronouns for God until it began to revise the general intercessions for Good Friday. Such pronouns were present in draft revisions submitted to the Advisory Committee in September 1987. After discussion of this matter, there seemed to be consensus among the Advisory Committee that as a general rule, masculine pronouns for God should not be used in liturgical texts. However, this point was not submitted to a vote, and more recently the issue has been reopened.

OTHER CONCERNS

The last phase of ICEL's work concerns the questions of anti-semitic and racist language, and that which includes the laity. Some of these were part of ICEL's early agenda, but work on them was not concluded until 1982.

The Jewish People

The question of anti-semitic language—language that discriminates against the Jewish people—became part of ICEL's agenda as early as 1977, and a final report and recommendations were made at the November 1982 Advisory Committee meeting.

The general principle recommended was simply that "prayers should not be formulated in such a way that they seem to cast Judaism in a negative or derogatory light. This is the case, for example, when Judaism is treated merely as the preparation for the fullness of redemption in Christ."

The Reproaches, which are optional texts, were considered to be fundamentally not anti-semitic. The recommendation was made that ICEL continue to print the Reproaches, that it not compose or include alternative texts, but that efforts by individual bishops' conferences to compose or officially sanction alternative texts be encouraged.

This issue did not arise again until 1985-1987, when the general intercessions of the Good Friday liturgy and the prayers after the readings of the Easter Vigil were being revised. Great sensitivity to the implications of these texts for the Jewish people was expressed by the subcommittee on translations and revisions and by the Advisory Committee, and some of these prayers have been redrafted several times because of such concerns; this process has not yet reached completion.

Race and Color

The question of language that might discriminate on the basis of race or color was first raised in 1977. Advisory Committee members "pointed out that discriminatory language also embraced the linking of white with pure, light, etc. in the liturgical texts and the linking of black with darkness, sin, evil, etc." Specific complaints regarding this type of liturgical text have never been received by ICEL, nor voiced by Advisory Committee or Episcopal Board members from Africa or Asia.

The Secretariat wrote to several members of the Black and Hispanic Catholic communities in the United States, asking "if you or others . . . have experienced any words or phrases in the liturgical texts as racist." Those who responded stated that there really was no problem in this respect in the present liturgical texts. The images of light and darkness were not found offensive as now used, though care needs to be exercised in this regard.

Laypeople

Finally, questions of language that includes the laity has also been considered. At its November 1977 meeting the Advisory Committee stated that "the discriminatory language under consideration has to do with . . . state in life (clericalism)." A resolution was proposed in November 1978 that "a statement be prepared regarding liturgical language that may be considered to discriminate against the lay members of the Church." However, this was not adopted, in part because it was considered a matter of lower priority, and in part because it was thought that the matter was already covered by previous resolutions.

CONCLUSIONS

The course of ICEL's work on inclusive language clearly was not simple or direct but instead convoluted and at times even melodramatic; it could not have been predicted in advance. One consistent thread was the commitment to the use of inclusive language initially expressed in 1975. Progress was also slow; it takes a good deal of time for a liturgical book to go through the entire process and reach the parish priests and people in the pews. It proved impossible for ICEL to make major interim changes in liturgical books already published, and at least eighteen years will have passed between the initial commitment to inclusive language in 1975 and the hoped for publication of the revised Roman Missal in 1993.

Among the various structures and institutions that are responsible for providing liturgical books for the English-speaking Roman Catholics of the world, ICEL has consistently provided leadership with respect to inclusive language. For many years it worked alone and without support, and received considerable criticism. Its work in this area is still viewed with suspicion in some quarters.

Some reservations regarding the use of inclusive language have been based on fears that good English grammar and construction would suffer and that inclusive language could not be beautiful. ICEL has not wavered in its commitment to good language and has found that with care, expertise, and steady effort, inclusive language can be achieved and good English style maintained.

It is interesting to note that many who are opposed to the use of inclusive language in general have not noticed when it is used in specific liturgical texts. Archbishop Denis E. Hurley has worked for the inclusion of all people in Church and society during his long ministry as bishop in troubled South Africa. This has been an inspiration to other members of ICEL in their efforts to include all persons in the worship of the Church through the use of inclusive language. It is an honor to dedicate this paper to him.

PASTORAL BENEFITS OF ENGLISH IN OUR LITURGY

Patrick Byrne

INTRODUCTION

After twenty-five years, we take the use of English in our liturgy for granted. A generation has grown up in the vernacular liturgy and is now raising its children. Catholics who are middle-aged or older have grown accustomed to worship in their own language and rarely give a thought to the old days of liturgy in Latin. This paper invites us to reflect on all that it means to have made such a major change in our public worship, and to appreciate anew the benefits that have flowed into our lives from this renewed liturgy.

In the earliest centuries of the Church's life and worship, Christian liturgies were celebrated in the language of the people. As these original languages became less current, the liturgy followed the people and moved to their new language. In this way, for example, the liturgy at Rome changed from Greek to Latin around the time of Pope Damasus I (366-384). After the barbarian invasions and during the early middle ages, this principle—already evident in 1 Corinthians 14:13-19—came to be forgotten in the Western Church. When the modern European languages began to develop before the year 1000, the liturgy remained in Latin. As a result, the people of northern Europe and, later, the peoples of Africa, Asia, Oceania, and the Americas were converted to a Church whose liturgy was in Latin rather than the language of the people.

Almost 450 years after the Protestant Reformation began, the Second Vatican Council officially approved a limited use of the vernacular, the language of the people, in the liturgy. Spurred on by the enthusiasm of pastors and people, conferences of bishops soon moved almost the entire body of liturgical texts, old or new, into the current language of the community. Believers were much more ready to sing their *Amen* once they could understand what their presiding priest or bishop was saying to them and to God in their name.

THE EXPERIENCE OF LITURGY IN OUR OWN LANGUAGE

From the blessing given to a mother or parents before birth, to baptism, confirmation, the weekly celebration of eucharist, the regular celebration of reconciliation, to marriage or religious profession or ordination, to anointing, the reception of viaticum, and to funeral and burial: from birth to death the Church community accompanies us with the liturgy. In its rites and blessings we dedicate our day and our life to God, giving thanks and praise for God's generous goodness, and praying for ourselves, our family, the Church, and the world. Since Vatican II, the liturgy has been touching our lives *in English*, in words we easily understand and use and respond to, in terms we understand without intellectual strain, without the use of bilingual participation aids. We hear God speaking directly to us in the words and the actions of the liturgy.[1] The following texts and prayers from our new rites illustrate what we are experiencing in our liturgies today.

> Father,
> through your holy prophets
> you proclaimed to all who draw near you,
> "Wash and be cleansed,"
> and through Christ you have granted us rebirth in the Spirit.
>
> Bless these your servants
> as they earnestly prepare for baptism.
>
> Fulfill your promise:
> sanctify them in preparation for your gifts,
> that they may come to be reborn as your children
> and enter the community of your Church.
>
> We ask this through Christ our Lord. Amen.
>
> (*Rite of Christian Initiation of Adults*, no. 196)

Parents and godparents, this light is entrusted to you to be kept burning brightly. These children of yours have been enlightened by Christ. They are to walk always as children of the light. May they

---

[1] See Congregation for Divine Worship, General Instruction of the Roman Missal, 4th ed., 27 Mar. 1975 [hereafter, GIRM], Introduction, nos. 12-13: ICEL, *Documents on the Liturgy, 1963-1979: Conciliar, Papal, and Curial Texts* [hereafter, DOL] (Collegeville, Minn.: The Liturgical Press, 1982) 208, nos. 1387-1388, which mentions that great enthusiasm has been shown for the use of the vernacular in the liturgy. *Notitiae*, the journal of the Congregation for Divine Worship, reported that 343 languages had been approved for liturgical use to the end of 1978 (see *Notitiae* 3 [1979], 385-520, for many detailed lists and charts). In the past decade, more languages have been added to these.

keep the flame of faith alive in their hearts. When the Lord comes, may they go out to meet him with all the saints in the heavenly kingdom.

(*Rite of Baptism for Children*, no. 64)

God our Father,
complete the work you have begun
and keep the gifts of your Holy Spirit
active in the hearts of your people.
Make them ready to live the Gospel
and eager to do his will.
May they never be ashamed
to proclaim to all the world Christ crucified
living and reigning for ever and ever. Amen.

(*Rite of Confirmation*, no. 33)

The body of Christ. Amen.

The blood of Christ. Amen.

(*The Roman Missal*)

I, N., take you, N. to be my wife. I promise to be true to you in good times and in bad, in sickness and in health. I will love you and honor you all the days of my life.

I, N., take you, N. to be my husband. I promise to be true to you in good times and in bad, in sickness and in health. I will love you and honor you all the days of my life.

(*Rite of Marriage*, no. 25)

Almighty Father,
grant to these servants of yours
the dignity of the priesthood.
Renew within them the Spirit of holiness.
As co-workers with the order of bishops
may they be faithful to the ministry
that they receive from you, Lord God,
and be to others a model of right conduct.

(Excerpts from the Prayer of Consecration in chap. 10,
The Roman Pontifical, Ordination of Priests)

The Lord has freed you from sin.
May he bring you safely to his kingdom in heaven.
Glory to him for ever. Amen.

(*Rite of Penance*, no. 47)

God of compassion,
our human weakness lays claim to your strength.

We pray that through the skills of surgeons and nurses
your healing gifts may be granted to N.

May your servant respond to your healing will
and be reunited with us at your altar of praise.

Grant this through Christ our Lord. Amen.

> (*Pastoral Care of the Sick: Rites of Anointing and Viaticum*, no. 125)

May the angels lead you into paradise;
may the martyrs come to welcome you
and take you to the holy city,
the new and eternal Jerusalem.

> (*Order of Christian Funerals*, no. 176)

Brothers and sisters in Christ, this is a day of rejoicing: we have come together to dedicate this church by offering within it the sacrifice of Christ.

May we open our hearts and minds to receive his word with faith; may our fellowship born in the one font of baptism and sustained at the one table of the Lord, become the one temple of his Spirit, as we gather round his altar in love.

> (*Dedication of a Church and an Altar*, chap. II, no. 30)

May the Lord Jesus,
who lived with his holy family in Nazareth,
dwell also with your family,
keep it from all evil,
and make all of you one in heart and mind.

> (*Book of Blessings*, chap. 1,
> I. Order for the Blessing of a Family, no. 60)

BENEFITS OF ENGLISH IN THE LITURGY

The use of our own language in worship during the past two and a half decades has helped us to experience the liturgy more fully as the "primary and indispensable source from which . . . to derive the true Christian spirit" (Constitution on the Liturgy [SC], art. 14: DOL 1, no. 14). A comparison of today's liturgy in the vernacular with the Latin liturgies of thirty years ago indicates a number of benefits in the life of the praying community.

1. *Pastoral Effectiveness and Understanding*

"The proof of the pudding is in the eating" is a familiar maxim. The pastoral effectiveness of the use of the English language in the liturgy is to be seen clearly in the benefits to the People of God who are touched by the liturgy in their parishes and in other gatherings of the faithful. They understand what is being said. In the readings they hear God speaking directly to them, in their own language. When the Scriptures are proclaimed in faith to the people of faith, God is using these words to touch hearts and change lives. We hear the prayers being addressed to God in our name, and are able to pray aloud with the community in our own language. The invitations and introductions are spoken directly to us. "The use of the vernacular in the liturgy may certainly be considered an important means for presenting more clearly the catechesis on the mystery that is part of the celebration itself."[2]

The good effects of liturgy in the language of the people extend to the presiders, the ministers, and all the people. Even children are able to grasp many of the effects of the liturgy through good use of language and the accompanying use of strong symbols in the liturgical action.

2. *A Clearer Message*

When we are taking part in liturgy, the texts are read or proclaimed or prayed in our own language, and we can let them speak to us directly. There is no barrier of another language, no obstacle to prevent the worshiper's clear understanding of what is happening, no need any longer to have to say, "When we say *et cum spiritu tuo* we mean 'and with your spirit.'" The texts of the liturgy have greater effect when they speak clearly to us. English texts that are expressed in concrete Anglo-Saxon terms tend to be less abstract than those using terms derived from the Romance languages. Good liturgy needs to have a balance of both, but always with clarity of proclamation and understanding as an important criterion.

3. *Use of Modern English*

When the *Book of Common Prayer* was issued by Edward VI in 1549, it was naturally produced in the language of the day, the English of its time. In those early days of modern English, long flowing

---

[2] GIRM, Introduction, no. 13: DOL 208, no. 1388.

sentences, subordinate clauses, inflections, and subjunctives—carried over from Latin and from medieval English—were still a part of the language, although they would gradually drop out over the succeeding centuries. The language of the Prayer Book and of the King James and the Douai-Rheims Bibles remained the standard language for prayer and worship in English until the second half of the twentieth century. By that time, this "Church language" had become archaic and remote from daily life, and seemed unreal, irrelevant, something one put on only when going to church.

After the International Commission on English in the Liturgy (ICEL) was formed in 1963, one of its major contributions to the prayer language of the English-speaking world was to choose to use good modern English rather than sixteenth century language in the liturgy. Although today's English at first seemed to be a little flat, especially when used in long sentences with subordinate clauses, soon the vigor of modern English asserted itself. Sentences varied in length, and shorter ones were used more often. A variety of literary forms came into our texts, and soon the natural strength of our language made itself felt: modern English put itself at the service of modern worship in the Roman Catholic Church in the English-speaking world. By the use of modern language, worship became relevant and closer to life in today's world.

4. Deeper Participation

Vatican II called for the people's active participation in the liturgy because of their share by baptism in the priesthood of Christ: we are God's priestly people. This participation in the worship and the work of Jesus is both our privilege and our responsibility. As a result of the development of modern Catholic liturgies in the vernacular, we have been able to experience participation by song, word, listening, gestures, postures, and silence (see SC, art. 30: DOL 1, no. 30). We have become more comfortable with taking part in the liturgy, and have let this experience lead us closer to Christ and each other. The community is no longer content to be silent spectators at a drama: now they have become sharers in the liturgical action. It is their liturgy, one in which they take an active part.

Now that we have become familiar with the words and rites of the liturgy and the flow of the Church's year of prayer, we are able to deepen our reflection on the meaning of the words, actions, gestures, and symbols used in the liturgy. In turn, these elements of worship are entering more fully into the life of the community.

The greeting or kiss of peace is now fully accepted by most, and many are able to articulate its meaning in practice, its message for daily living.

5. *Sharing in Ministry*

This deeper participation has made many more aware of their baptismal call to ministry. Sharing in the ministries of the liturgy has encouraged them to go further and take a more active role in other ministries within the Church and to the wider community. By basing their ministry in the liturgy, they are nourishing it with the eucharist as the source and center of all Christian living, and are being helped to extend God's kingdom each day. To the Sunday liturgy they bring their efforts at living their Christian faith all week. Their life is leading them to liturgy, and the liturgy is leading them back into life.

Liturgical ministers, especially those who use the liturgical texts—including musicians, singers, ministers of communion, readers, presiders, preachers, deacons, presbyters, and bishops—are beginning to see that liturgy goes far beyond words. They are becoming aware of the need for better proclamation; for good gestures and postures; for a sense of presence; for appropriate vesture, and for a suitable architectural setting. Many now recognize the need for the sensitive use of liturgical symbols and clear signs that speak to the worship assembly fully. Some examples include the generous use of oil, real bread, communion under both forms, good music, well-trained ministers, and dignified books.

6. *A Growing Sense of Ownership*

Today, most of our communities are becoming more comfortable with the liturgy in their own language, and are taking advantage of the freedom offered for adaptation. Many invitations and introductions may be stated in "these or similar words,"[3] and presiders and ministers are using these opportunities. Intercessions at morning and evening prayer and in the general intercessions of the eucharist are usually developed by local communities, based

---

[3] Examples in the rubrics of the Order of Mass include the rite of blessing and sprinkling holy water and the penitential rite. In the third form of the penitential rite, "the following or other invocations" may be used. This freedom was made more explicit by the Congregation for Divine Worship in the Circular Letter *Eucharistiae participationem* to the presidents of the conferences of bishops, on the eucharistic prayers, 27 Apr. 1973, nos. 14, 16: DOL 248, nos. 1988, 1990.

on the models given in the liturgical books. Where alternatives are offered (as in the penitential rites and other opening rites), some communities are taking advantage of this, and provide a suitable variety in their celebration. And some families, schools, and other communities are beginning to compose prayers and blessings for various events outside the liturgy. These follow the spirit of the liturgy and help people to be more in tune with the Church's spirit of worship.

This growing sense of ownership has led communities to see the importance of good liturgy. Now they are willing to work for better celebrations through parish liturgy committees, musicians, and other ministers. They are ready to spend more of the community's resources on helps for musicians and ministers, on music and hymn books and instruments, and on vestments and furnishings. The changes in the liturgy have led to a full revision of the liturgical books, and each community has had to provide these for its celebrations. As well, educational material and training opportunities for presiders, other ministers, and all members of the assembly have been made available in many parishes to enable all to participate more fully in celebrating and living the liturgy.

7. Growth in Music for the Liturgy

Strong developments in the field of music for liturgy have resulted from the use of the vernacular in Catholic worship. The importance of music in worship was discussed by the Second Vatican Council (see SC, art. 112-121, also art. 24: DOL 1, nos. 112-121, 24). As congregational singing became more common, there was a rapid development of new texts and music for hymns in English, and then beyond hymns to Mass settings and psalm tones. Folk music became quite popular in North America and elsewhere. New hymnals were edited by national or regional liturgical commissions and by commercial enterprises. As renewed books for the sacraments and other rites were issued by the Congregation for Divine Worship, new ritual music was commissioned at various levels.

Appropriate music for the liturgical seasons was developed and became familiar through regular use. More attention was paid to the ministries of music in the community—including choir, instrumentalists, cantors, and leaders of song—and training, resources, and good instruments became of greater concern. During the 1970s and 1980s, music was developed for the liturgy of the hours in monastic communities and in parishes. As congregational singing became the norm in most places, it was soon recognized that the Gregorian repertoire of the past was no longer appropriate for general use in parishes. While at first anything available was used in worship, gradually communities and musicians began to use more discernment, and discarded what was not appropriate for use in Christian worship. A variety of styles came into use, and still remain.

In the 1980s the quality of music was considered to be important. Communities began to recognize the importance of musical unity within the elements of the eucharistic prayer, and acclamations were through-composed. Today new hymns, Mass settings, and music for the rites, the hours, and the seasons continue to come onto the market, and specialized hymnals for ethnic or cultural groups have been prepared. In most communities people are comfortable with singing during the liturgy. Churches of different Christian denominations are sharing more of their music and are aware both of their own tradition and of what is taking place within the larger Christian community. Good composers and musicians are continuing to assist the People of God to sing their praise and to participate more fully in the liturgical action.

8. *Development of Liturgical Commissions and Offices*

The Second Vatican Council called for national and diocesan commissions for liturgy, music, and art (see SC, art. 44-46: DOL 1, nos. 44-46). Since 1963, many regional, national, and international commissions, offices, conferences, associations, and other organizations have been established for the development and encouragement of good liturgical formation and celebration. Most of them started working on and with liturgical texts in the vernacular, but soon moved into liturgical formation. In many parishes, schools, religious communities, hospitals, and some prisons, people have gladly responded to the invitation to work together for better worship and prayer in the community.

Strong leadership is being given in liturgy at many levels. Liturgical education at university and postgraduate level has increased and has become ecumenical and international. Publishers have flourished and have provided educational guidance and many good texts, along with some imperfect material.

Dioceses have set up liturgical commissions and offices: most provide training sessions for the people in parish ministries, and some have published helpful material. Many parishes have a liturgy or worship committee that helps in developing local celebrations, in forming ministers, and in working for a stronger prayer life in the community. Many national and international organizations have become ecumenical in their membership or work with similar organizations from other major Christian Churches. They share texts, ideas, publications, developments, formation, and experience, both formally and informally. All these developments have given a strong boost to the Church's liturgy, and enable more people to deepen their life of prayer and worship.

9. An Expression of Theological Growth

The discussions and documents of the Second Vatican Council often reflected the influence of different theologies. The result was that the Council moved the Church's theological understanding forward in a number of important areas. And this renewed theological understanding formed the basis of much that went into the renewal of the liturgy. Because we now worship in our own language, English-speaking Catholics throughout the world better grasp and are being formed by this theological renewal expressed in the words and actions of the liturgy. The following are elements of this renewal.

— Recognition of Christ's place: Christ's place in God's loving plan for our salvation is newly recognized. Jesus is the center of all human history. The paschal mystery is the saving death-resurrection of Jesus, seen as one great act of God's love for us. This mystery is celebrated in the liturgy and shared by us in the eucharist, the sacraments, and other rites and in our prayer, crosses, and daily living.

— Church as the People of God: The Church is seen as the People of God, the Body of Christ, the community, the assembly (*ekklesia, qahal*), which includes all baptized Christians. Today we realize that the Church is always in need of renewal and reform (Decree on Ecumenism, no. 6: DOL 6, no. 6).

— Recognition of many forms of ministry in the Church: We understand that all are called in baptism to share in Christ's priesthood, and are challenged to work (in ministry) and worship (in liturgy and prayer) with Christ to glorify God and save the world. We see that the members of the hierarchy share in the baptismal priesthood with all the faithful, and also have a ministerial priesthood of service to all. Bishops, priests, and deacons are brothers as well as leaders of the community. Ministry is seen as flowing from our baptism (in sharp contrast with the preconciliar view of "Catholic action" as the sharing of the laity in the apostolate of the hierarchy). Participation in the liturgy is always seen in this fuller context of life and prayer flowing from our baptismal sharing in Christ's priestly service.

— Acceptance of ecumenism: The Catholic Church recognizes and accepts and honors the baptism of other Christians, their membership in and relationship with the Church, and the duty of all who believe in Christ to work and pray together for unity, based on the unity of the Trinity. Ecumenism is seen as the work of all Catholics, to be lived in a spirit of dialogue, cooperation, and love for all our sisters and brothers in Christ. We are to work actively with the Spirit of Jesus to move closer to Christ and to one another, being open to the developments and movements of the Spirit that are beginning to bring Christians closer together.

— Openness to the work of God in non-Christian religions: The Holy Spirit calls all Christians and people of good will to work together to better human life in society. We work with others to make this a better world for all. We seek to avoid all forms of prejudice, racism, and rejection of people because of their language, creed, nationality, type of work, physical or mental ability, or gender (the expression "the weaker sex" no longer appears in our liturgical texts, but barriers are still raised to prevent full participation of women in ministries not requiring ordination; the question of inclusive language is discussed below).

— Missions: We see the work of missionaries as living the Christian life to the fullest. They are called to recognize the good already planted by God in other cultures, and to give witness to these cultures by challenging them with the full message of the Gospel, the Good News that God loves us all in Christ and calls us all to share in the life of the kingdom. Missionaries also invite the cultures they live with to teach the Church by their God-given gifts and insights.

— Acceptance of a positive view and theology of creation ("and God saw that all he had made . . . was very good," Genesis 1: 31): Liturgical texts reflect a positive theology of creation by moving away from exorcisms of evil in creation to recognition of the goodness of God's work (contrast the preconciliar exorcism over water and the present blessing of water on Sundays). We accept the goodness of this creation as a means toward God rather than an obstacle (we no longer "despise the things of this earth and long for the things of heaven," but rather use the things of this life as a means to salvation for all). God's saving and loving presence is recognized and welcomed in creation, in other people, and in natural events.

— A more positive approach to life: The Pastoral Constitution on the Church in the Modern World recalls the People of God to a more sensitive and positive approach to their life and witness. It sees the Church as faithful to Christ in the midst of a world in need of Christ's healing love. The Church is called to be light, witness, sign, loving concern, a daily living proof that God can and does work among us to save all.

The change from Latin to the language of the people in our worship both reflected and — to a certain extent — caused these developments in our thinking. As we pray and worship, if we listen to the positive attitudes expressed in our renewed liturgical texts we are being affected by them. As these theological changes are discerned and recognized, they affect our action, our liturgy, our reflections in theology and slowly become a normal part of our thought patterns and our way of life.

10. Ecumenical Impact

The effects of the use of the vernacular in the Latin Catholic Church's liturgy have extended to other Christian Churches. When ICEL chose to use modern English in its texts, other Churches took notice of this leadership and used the occasion of updating their worship books to move gradually into modern English as well. Since the early 1970s, through the International Consultation on English Texts (ICET),[4] ICEL and various national and international Church bodies have developed a set of common texts which are now being

---

[4] ICET was formed in the late 1960s by representatives of a number of Churches throughout the English-speaking world for the purpose of preparing agreed translations of common liturgical texts. After ICET issued its second revised edition of *Prayers We Have in Common* (Philadelphia: Fortress Press, 1975), it seems to have ceased its activity. Following an exploratory meeting in 1983, the Consultation on Common Texts (CCT), an ecumenical liturgical association of more than a dozen Churches in Canada and the United States, and ICEL sponsored the development of the English Language Liturgical Consultation (ELLC) to carry on the work begun by ICET. ELLC met in 1985 and 1987 and conducted a worldwide consultation on the need for updating the thirteen ICET texts. A revised set of texts, along with principles and detailed notes, will be published shortly by Abingdon Press (Nashville, Tenn.).

used in worship by all major Christian Churches around the English-speaking world.

11. *Renewed Appreciation of Universality and Richness*

In the days of the Latin liturgy, it was said that Catholics could go to Mass anywhere in the world and be at home. This was true because of the shape of the rite and the familiar sounds (and silences) of an unknown language. Today, English-speaking people can fit in perfectly in the liturgy in any country where English is spoken; in other areas, the shape of the rite is the same, but the language is that of the local believing community. Though we may not understand this language, we know the general thrust of the service, and we are able to pray with the assembly and offer ourselves with them in the eucharistic prayer and participate by communion. The experience of participating in another language may help us to appreciate the value of using our own language in our worship. The experience of worship in another culture may offer us some new insights into the meaning of what we do in liturgy and in life.

One unexpected benefit has resulted from the use of modern languages in the liturgy. When we compare texts as they are rendered in different languages, we can see how each language has chosen to bring out certain nuances of the original Latin, to emphasize elements which are particularly close to the spirit of the season or feast, or to express the text in a way that touches the particular culture. A comparison of the different linguistic versions shows once more how rich are the original texts of the Roman liturgy.

Toward the Future

There have been many rich developments in the liturgy in the past twenty-five years. Now we realize that the twenty-first century is only a decade away. Pope John Paul II is calling it the beginning of the third millennium of Christianity, and is strongly encouraging us to work for unity among Christians, to grow in the spirit of Vatican II, to be the Church living and working and worshipping in the modern world. How can the renewed liturgy contribute to our entry into the next century?

During the years before Vatican II, many liturgists felt that the arrival of the vernacular would solve many, if not most, of our problems. It would enable people to participate in the primary and indispensable source of the true Christian spirit, and so lead us closer to Christ in our daily living. As the vernacular came to be used, the development of suitable translations and the provision of renewed liturgical books took up much energy. Then we were led into deeper participation, and we became aware of the need and values of ministry. As we grew in ministry, we became aware of the need for ecumenical cooperation and inclusive language. As we grow in these, we are sensing the need of cultural adaptation of the liturgy so that it both grows from our own culture and proclaims the Good News to it. The Spirit continues to challenge us!

1. *Cultural Adaptation*

The Second Vatican Council recognized the importance of culture in several of its documents.[5] Culture is the way our humanity expresses itself in a particular place and time, and through which we hear the Gospel and give praise to God. All human cultures have shared in the unseen guidance of the Spirit, but are still in need of further challenge by the Good News that God loves us and has sent Jesus Christ to be our Lord and brother and savior.

The Constitution on the Liturgy offered some notes to help local Churches adapt the liturgy to the culture and traditions of their people (see SC, art. 37-40: DOL 1, nos. 37-40). Further scope for adaptation is described in the General Instruction of the Roman Missal, including postures, gestures, the arts, architecture, furnishings, altars, vessels, vestments, and local calendars. In many cases, these have not yet been fully explored by liturgical commissions and bishops' conferences.

In the liturgical movement, the beginnings of cultural adaptation were recognized in the areas of translation of rites into modern languages. The Consilium for the Implementation of the Constitution on the Liturgy provided an excellent document of guidelines on the translation of liturgical texts, and pointed out the need for proper freedom in translation. The translation of texts from Latin was seen as the first step, the school of cultural adaptation.[6] These guidelines have been followed in the 1970s and the 1980s,

---

[5] See Vatican Council II, the Pastoral Constitution on the Church in the Modern World *Gaudium et spes*, 7 Dec. 1965; Constitution on the Liturgy *Sacrosanctum Concilium*, 4 Dec. 1969; Decree on the Church's Missionary Activity *Ad gentes*, 17 Dec. 1965; and Declaration on Non-Christian Religions *Nostra aetate*, 28 Oct. 1965.

[6] See the Instruction on the Translation of Liturgical Texts *Comme le prévoit* issued by the Consilium for the Implementation of the Constitution on the Liturgy on 25 Jan. 1969. This document was issued in six major languages: the French text is given in *Notitiae* 5 (1969), 3-12;

and have led gradually to the alternative opening prayers in the Sunday Masses in the Sacramentary (*The Roman Missal*, 1973) and to the new or original texts in *Pastoral Care of the Sick: Rites of Anointing and Viaticum* (1982) and the *Order of Christian Funerals* (1985). At present, some conferences of bishops are looking at different ways of adapting the *Rite of Christian Initiation of Adults* (1985) and the *Book of Blessings* (1987).

Further steps will depend on the needs as seen by conferences of bishops, and the openness of the Congregation for Divine Worship and the other agencies of the Roman Curia. In the late 1960s, for example, the Catholic Bishops' Conference of India developed a form of liturgy adapted to Indian culture. These adaptations were approved by the Congregation for Divine Worship in 1969.[7] Since then, however, there seems to be a reluctance on Rome's part to allow other conferences of bishops to make changes of a similar nature. At the time of writing, little progress seems possible, but a more positive outlook may develop before long as many cultures explore their roots and see the need and desirability of cultural adaptation in the liturgy.

2. *The Challenge of a Fast-changing Language*

English is spoken by people in many different nations. It is the basic language in many countries that once formed part of the British Empire. It is the *lingua franca*, the language of communication, in countries which are divided by a variety of tribal tongues. English is influenced by many patterns and causes: by its ability and openness to absorb new words from other languages, by the fact that it is spoken as a second language by many, and by its acceptance as the worldwide language of commerce, aviation, science, and other important and influential fields of human activity.

Given these and other influences, English is most adaptable. Thousands of new words come into the language each year, and old words take on new or additional meanings.[8] Some of these new

---

the English text is contained in DOL 123. The final paragraph states that "translation of texts transmitted through the tradition of the Church is the best school and discipline for the creation of new texts so 'that any new forms adopted should in some way grow organically from forms already in existence' (SC, art. 23)."

[7] See *Notitiae* 6 (1969), 365-374. The indult was granted on 25 Apr. 1969. The twelve specific changes include postures, gestures, ceremonial objects, vestments, and the order of service.

[8] In 1987, the second unabridged edition of *The Random House Dictionary of the English Language* (New York: Random House, 1987) replaced the first edition of 1966. In twenty-one years, there were 50,000 new entries, including new words and new meanings for old words. This averages out to 2381 new entries a year!

uses may affect the language of liturgical prayer and the scriptural readings, at least in some countries or cultures.

One area in which English is becoming more socially sensitive is that of inclusive language. No longer is it considered desirable to say "man" when both men and women are meant: "people do not live on bread alone" (Matthew 4:4) is acceptable, "man" is not. This understanding involves both a change in prayer texts and a fresh approach to scriptural translation.[9] It has come upon the scene only since the early 1970s.

This is not a passing fad. Concern for inclusive language is a further step toward social justice and Christian sensitivity, an opening to all God's people. This is the work of God's Spirit, stirring us up through many seemingly secular events, groups, and movements. In English-speaking countries civil groups, governments, other Churches, Scripture translators, educators, social activists, and some conferences of bishops have heard this breathing of the Spirit, and are beginning to move ahead: can those who claim to worship *in spirit and in truth* (see John 4:23) be far behind? (In other languages, where all nouns are assigned a gender, the problem is not seen as yet. It is only beginning to be recognized by a few people at this time, but this awareness will grow.)

By its nature as a living, international language, English will continue to change and develop and to bring new challenges—as yet unsuspected—to pastors, ministers, and translators. We must be prepared to recognize these openings and discern them, and work to help our liturgical language meet these pastoral challenges, so that we may continue to praise God in song and word and life to the best of our ability.

Does this imply that bishops' conferences and organizations like ICEL will need to monitor language changes constantly? Does it suggest the need for more frequent revisions of texts, perhaps every twenty years? In the light of two decades of experience, perhaps there is need of a less cumbersome system for approval of liturgical texts than that established by Vatican II in 1963 (see SC, art. 22 and 36: DOL 1, nos. 22 and 36).

---

[9] In the general editor's foreword, dated Nov. 1984, The New Jerusalem Bible (Garden City, N.Y.: Doubleday, 1985) states: "Considerable efforts have also been made, though not at all costs, to soften or avoid the inbuilt preference of the English language, a preference now found so offensive by some people, for the masculine; the word of the Lord concerns women and men equally" (page v).

3. *The Importance of Proclamation, Movement, Silence*

An area of continuing concern is the manner in which liturgical texts are proclaimed in the worshiping assembly. The use of sense lines in many ICEL texts provides a certain guidance to the minister who reads them aloud, but a growing sensitivity for words and sentence structure and for the flow and rhythm of English needs to be developed at the local level. Each minister who reads texts aloud in the community's worship needs to develop a feel for English poetry and prose, to grasp the strength and ruggedness of English speech patterns, and to appreciate the melding of solid Anglo-Saxon and Teutonic words and rhythms with the flow and nuances of the Romance languages. Those who read prayers and Scripture texts in the assembly need to grow in their sense of timing, to know which words to hold a little longer, which words to stress, how long to pause at a punctuation mark or whenever meaning demands this.

This is a field which is unexplored in most communities of faith, and one where we can learn much from good speakers on radio and television. Good actors and others involved in the movement arts can help ministers—from servers and ushers to readers and presiders—to move with grace and economy, always aware that they are there to serve the community and make its worship more beautiful by their every movement or stillness.

Similarly, the whole community needs to come to appreciate the value of silence in our worship. It is a time for active reception of God's word, for allowing the Spirit of Jesus to speak in our hearts (see Romans 8:26-28), for accepting the call to prayer and reflection. Silence in prayer is an invitation to open our hearts to the Lord and the people of God in love and service. It is a call to praise and thank, to ask and receive, to forgive and be forgiven. Silence in our personal prayer and in our liturgy is an active presence of our loving God, a presence that enriches and deepens our worship. Silence is a form of active participation (see SC, art. 30: DOL 1, no. 30).

4. *Encouragement of Responsible Creativity*

There were some years in the late 1960s and early 1970s when many individuals attempted to write new texts, especially eucharistic prayers, for the liturgy. These seem to have evaporated after the sacramentaries were issued in 1974 and 1975 with nine approved eucharistic prayers. Though some people are still tempted to "embroider" prayer texts, they usually end up with wordiness in place of the "soberness and sense" of the Roman liturgy.[10]

Today, however, many communities are providing good texts for the parts they are encouraged to compose: introductions, invitations, acclamations for the third form of the penitential rite, and the general intercessions. This responsible approach to liturgical creativity has been positive. As well, more people are comfortable with creating prayers for a variety of occasions outside the Church's liturgy: meetings, classes, picnics, family gatherings, and mealtimes. School children are encouraged in their classes to compose or write prayer texts and to develop services of the word. Given this groundswell of positive and responsible creativity, some are now beginning to ask if there are not still further areas for adaptation and development of prayers and prayer forms in the liturgy, within the framework of the Roman tradition.[11]

Other areas for future development are Bible celebrations and devotions. Word services are encouraged by Vatican II for feasts and their vigils, during Lent and Advent, and in communities where a Sunday eucharist cannot be celebrated (see SC, art. 35,4: DOL 1, no. 35, 4). While some work has been done here and there, in general most parishes and communities have not taken this up in a strong way, except for a pastoral or simplified form of morning and evening prayer in some places. Devotional practices have been encouraged (see SC, art. 13: DOL 1, no. 13),[12] but again, many com-

---

[10] "The genius of the native Roman rite is marked by simplicity, practicality, a great sobriety and self-control, gravity and dignity. . . . In two or three words, . . . essentially soberness and sense." Edmund Bishop, *Liturgica Historica* (London and Toronto: Oxford University Press, 1918, 1962), 12 and 19.

[11] Today one hears teenagers and others exclaiming how "bored" they are at Mass: "It's the same thing Sunday after Sunday!" Perhaps there is room for a creative development of some of the prayers of the communion rite; for more eucharistic prayers; for a variety of forms (such as the *berakah* or blessing prayer in place of one of the three collects), more dialogue or sung acclamations in the eucharistic prayers (as in those for children), fuller preparation, better preaching, and a full use of creativity where it is already permitted and encouraged (see the Circular Letter *Eucharistiae participationem*, 27 Apr. 1973, referred to in footnote 3 of this essay, nos. 1-19: DOL 248, nos. 1975-1993). Presiders—bishops, priests, deacons, and laity—need to remember that good liturgy requires much more "than the mere observance of the laws governing valid and lawful celebration; it is also their duty to ensure that the faithful take part fully aware of what they are doing, actively engaged in the rite, and enriched by its effects" (SC, art. 11; DOL 1, no. 11).

[12] On 2 February 1974, Pope Paul VI issued his Apostolic Exhortation *Marialis cultus*, on Marian devotion (DOL 467). He offered scriptural, liturgical, theological, and anthropological bases for sober devotion to Mary, the mother of Jesus. The principles given in this document apply to other forms of Catholic devotions as well, and amplify the brief statement of the Constitution on the Liturgy, art. 13 (DOL 1, no. 13).

munities have done little about these. The next decade or two could see strong growth in these areas.

This is a new stage in our growth, and one that needs to be discerned both as a movement of the Spirit of God and as a contribution to liturgical adaptation in each culture which is ready for this. If such developments are to be pursued, a balance will need to be maintained between the depth of our liturgical tradition and the breadth of the richness of modern life in its many aspects.

CONCLUSION

The introduction of English into the Roman Catholic liturgy in the past quarter century has allowed the innate strength of the Church's worship to come forward and become a part of the people's life. The use of our own language with its vigor has added to the vitality of community prayer and worship, and it invites us to enter even more fully into the true spirit of Jesus Christ.

When we look back to what Vatican II began, we can be truly grateful to the Lord for the pastoral benefits that have come to us from the use of English in the liturgy.

CULTURE AND LITURGY

THE CONTEXTUALIZATION OF LITURGY AND ESPECIALLY LITURGICAL TEXTS:
THE TENSION BETWEEN THE UNIVERSALITY OF THE LITURGY AND THE SPECIFIC SITUATION OF THE LOCAL CELEBRATING COMMUNITY

Andrew Borello

In the renewal of the liturgical life of the Church that has flowed from the Second Vatican Council, a major factor has been the possibility of the liturgy of the Roman rite being celebrated in the language of the people.[1] This has allowed the people a more active participation in the liturgy, which in turn means that there is likely to be a deeper sense of the liturgy in their lives. The implications of this renewal are vast, but the applications have only started to bear fruit and the process is already fraught with controversy. Rather than concentrating on what such renewal actually demands, too many people are concerned with the letter of the law in the application of renewal. It is certainly not sufficient to have arrived at the point of translating the Roman rite into the vernacular[2] —this can only be the first stage in a much wider process of adaptation—and anyone who argues for a halt or reversal of the process has missed the point of the Second Vatican Council.

Placing the liturgy within the language of the people has allowed them to move toward realizing what liturgy is all about. But it is only an opening and will have to be seen through if it is to have any real effect on their lives. The liturgy has to enter into their lives and their manner of living,[3] and as long as it remains a reality divorced from their lives and all that they experience in living, it

---

[1] See Vatican Council II, Constitution on the Liturgy *Sacrosanctum Concilium* [hereafter, SC], 4 Dec. 1963, art. 21 and 36: ICEL, *Documents on the Liturgy, 1963-1979, Conciliar, Papal, and Curial Texts* [hereafter, DOL] (Collegeville, Minn.: The Liturgical Press, 1982) 1, nos. 21 and 36.

[2] See National Liturgical Office, Canadian Conference of Catholic Bishops, *National Bulletin on Liturgy* 17 (Sept.–Oct. 1984), 204-205.

[3] See SC, art. 10-11: DOL 1, nos. 10-11.

will not become the center of their lives. In turn, this means that it will fail to attain the purpose for which it has been so thoroughly reformed and in which it needs to continue to be reformed. The situation is an urgent one which must find a solution if the Church and its liturgy are not to become increasingly irrelevant. So while the letter of the law is contemplated and applied, the serious opportunities given to the Church to bring its liturgy into the actual realm of people's lives are missed.

Where does the problem lie? The problem seems to be twofold. First, that liturgy is not understood and that its implications are not lived out by those who celebrate it.[4] The second is fear—fear of letting go and allowing various peoples to express themselves, their culture, and their situation in the individual and unique way that belongs to them and their desire to enter into relationship with God through their liturgy, particular and authentic to them. In the whole process of moving the liturgy into the vernacular, a tension has been created between the universality of the liturgy and the need for it to enter into the more specific life experience of the local celebrating community. Such a tension, if acknowledged, becomes the very encouragement to growth in the Church and its liturgy. Yet the tension cannot be resolved by recourse to either the need for universality, uniformly enforced, or to a localization of the liturgy that denies universality. The very nature of the liturgy demands that it be both universal and real to a given community. The liturgy is a universal reality, celebrated by local communities, in which the universality is manifested in a pluriformity of liturgical expressions. If this were recognized and allowed, then it would be possible to realize the full potential of the reformed liturgy. As long as fear and ignorance dominate, this will not be possible because someone other than the community will determine what is allowed and what may not be done. This does not mean a free-for-all in the liturgy. Certain elements are clearly determined, but there are sufficient areas where there could be creative movement toward an authentic liturgy celebrated by the local community in their awareness of where God is leading them and of the very real situation they are living

---

[4] It is all too easy to celebrate liturgy divorced from the reality of life, as if the liturgy mysteriously achieves its purpose apart from the actual involvement of those who celebrate it. This is an alarming attitude that has been fostered by the Church and which continues to be propagated by many members of the Church, simply because it demands far less from the community and the individual members of the community. Some indication of what is required of the community is indicated in SC, art. 14: DOL 1, no. 14.

in. What must happen is that within the areas determined by the Church (and that means determined by the liturgy itself) the celebrating community must be able to give expression to the riches of its own culture and the situation which is its daily life.[5]

The appeal is, therefore, for a liturgy inculturated and contextualized. Perhaps one of the most significant areas is that of liturgical language and it is within this area that the problem seen is most clearly experienced. The vernacular is not a sufficient consideration because much more is at stake. There is, unfortunately, no clearcut blueprint which can be applied. Rather, according to certain principles, each community is going to have to be given the freedom to move and to work toward a plurality of expressions within the broad framework of the Roman rite. This article will attempt to look at those principles with the hope that others will take this whole process further for the benefit of all local Churches.

THE PROBLEM OF TALKING ABOUT ADAPTATION

While the Constitution on the Liturgy (*Sacrosanctum Concilium*) makes clear provision for cultural adaptation and even recommends that this be carried out as an essential expression of the liturgy,[6] the whole issue is a lot less simple to carry out in practical terms, for the reasons already indicated. What is the state of the whole situation of adaptation? To talk of such a process implies that there is an easily identifiable culture which is clearly categorized so that it may be purified of those elements that would be in conflict with the theology of the Church or the nature of the liturgy. Unfortunately this is seldom the case. More and more people have become deculturized or have entered into a movement of rapid cross-culturization which leaves them unaware or confused about their cultural iden-

---

[5] "True to the spirit of Vatican II the Church continues to renew and shape her liturgy, 'in order that the Christian people may more securely derive an abundance of graces from the sacred liturgy' (SC, art. 21). However, there is an aspect of liturgical renewal which needs an urgent and more careful attention. It is not enough to reshape every now and then the texts and rituals of the Roman liturgy according to the pastoral needs here and now and the dictates of liturgical scholarship. Renewal implies also the realization of those 'links between the message of salvation and human culture,' especially when the Church gives that message a better expression in liturgical celebrations (GS, no. 58)." Anscar Chupungco, *Cultural Adaptation of the Liturgy* (Ramsey, N.J.: Paulist Press, 1982), 1.

[6] See SC, art. 37-40: DOL 1, nos. 37-40.

tity.[7] Contrary to what many would say about this question of cultural identity, it is a vital issue in the consideration of the religious experience and the worship response. For too long, theologians have considered the religious experience as a universal reality that cuts across cultural awareness. Yes, all peoples will experience God, but they do so in a way that is determined by their culture (and the situation in which they find themselves living). Their idea of God, the way in which they perceive themselves and their relationship to God, their social orientation and structures, their life involvements will all determine the way in which they form and live out involvement with God.

This lack of or loss of cultural awareness is a great problem. Without it, it becomes impossible to talk of religious experience and the response of a life to God. If a people are unaware of who or what they are, of God in their midst or of their social responsibilities, then it makes no sense to talk of the commandment of love being present within that people. How can they experience and identify God if they are not aware of themselves or of God as present to them? The blame for this loss of a sense of God has been placed upon secularization of the contemporary world, but it seems that this process of secularization follows on a deeper problem and that is the issue of deculturization. A people that loses its cultural identity loses its means of recognizing God and the whole sense of God. Because the experience of God is incarnational, the process of deculturization leaves a people isolated from that within which God is made incarnate for them. In losing a sense of their culture, they are left without a sense of identity as a people, so that God (present among them as a people and incarnate in their culture) is no longer seen and experienced as being among them. This process of deculturization is alienation at its deepest level.

The Church battles on with this problem and it does so with great faith that somewhere the reality of God will break through this phenomenon and God will still be experienced. Yet the answer seems to lie in the Church discovering again a sense of a given peo-

---

[7] "In many parts of the world, liturgical reform and renewal must be viewed in the context of popular efforts to regain a cultural identity. There are at the present time strong movements to rediscover and foster traditional values and customs that have shaped the life of various peoples for many generations. Furthermore, in those parts of the world where Western theology and the Roman liturgy have been imposed on people whose thought patterns and symbol systems are more Eastern than Western, the Church and her rituals have regularly maintained an immigrant status." R. Kevin Seasoltz, O.S.B., *New Liturgy, New Laws* (Collegeville, Minn.: The Liturgical Press, 1980), 182.

ple's identity and becoming aware of the culture that they are living within. It may be a radically altered culture and heritage, but it is that which still determines them, even if they are totally unaware of it. They need to touch again that experience of themselves as a cultural entity and to allow it to have a more conscious place in the way in which they live and worship. Here the liturgy needs to become more sensitive to the full situation of a people (not just the cultural elements) and to lead them into an awareness that is brought into the encounter with God.

Related to the issue of non-awareness of cultural identity is the widespread problem of urbanization.[8] There are those peoples who are very aware of themselves as a cultural entity because they have been kept in isolation from other cultural groups or from the effects of urbanization and the resultant pressures that it places upon them. If there is to be a process of adaptation in this situation, then there are few added complications and some definite result can be expected. This will not be the case where a cultural group has been subjected to the process of urbanization and the coming together of different cultural groups. In this situation, to talk of adaptation becomes more difficult because it is so hard to determine what culture one is moving toward. In a multicultural group, which culture should be singled out?[9] Where a process of evolution (or degeneration) is taking place, which stage of the process should be singled out as the base on which to adapt or inculturate? Where such a problem exists, it seems almost impossible to speak of the entry of culture into theology or liturgy, at least for a whole people living in such a complexity of cultures and experiencing the evolution of themselves as a people. Rather one might well have to look to the individual community entering into this process of adaptation—being able to identify where they are. Obviously they could not carry this out alone, but within a set of guidelines, they might well be able to move toward a liturgy of their own. The question is then whether the Church can possibly conceive of such freedom being given to such communities.

Part of the problem that will be raised in such a solution will be that of the communitarian experience and identity of a given

---

[8] "No traditional cultural form vanishes completely from the consciousness or the subconscious of the society which it nurtured over generations and on which it imprinted a particular character. That is why museum pieces are not utterly alien to the daily life of a nation. A question has been raised on the phase of culture which is best suited for adaptation. Should traditional forms be discarded in favour of modern ones?" Chupungco, 76-77.

[9] For various definitions of culture, see Seasoltz, 190, and Chupungco, 77.

group. Inherent in urbanization and a loss of cultural identity is the loss of a communitarian sense. One of the concerns of the renewed liturgy is the creation of a sense of community, since it is a community that celebrates the liturgy. The liturgy of itself will not be able to create that sense and an effort is required to move it in that direction. Once a community identity is found, it will be possible for that community to work toward a more authentic liturgy which reflects its identity and concerns and makes it possible for all its members to enter into an ongoing religious experience and growth. And it will be precisely here that a contextualized liturgy will arise, going beyond the concerns of culture into the overall reality of that community. In turn, the community will grow in the realization of all that the liturgy asks in terms of personal and communitarian relationships with God.

While much is said about this quality of relationship with God, both on the individual and communitarian level, little is done to realize it, almost as if people were too afraid to move in this direction. There is a crippling presence of apathy and indifference among peoples who move toward urbanization and the more materialistic way of life that accompanies it. Much of this can be ascribed to a loss of a sense of being a person—a process of dehumanizing alienation. Just as there must be a recovery of a sense of community, so the individual has to gain a sense of personhood to counter the movement toward dehumanization. The relationship with God that the liturgy fosters must of its very nature draw the person away from this alienation from self and others. Becoming aware of self and valuing one's identity as person, the individual will be able to build community. In the same way the concern with community must be a concern with the individual person within that community and must encourage the person to an even greater awareness and acceptance of self. This interaction of the individual and community as they achieve a sense of identity will allow them to move along the path of self-actualization. Since this interaction is not just realized on the horizontal or human level but, in terms of liturgy, includes the vertical, God draws the individual and community into the realization of salvation by restoring to them the wholeness that signifies God's creational intention. All of this takes place within liturgy for it is here that the person encounters God and, through God, the community of believers and is drawn into the person-to-person I-thou relationship. The liturgy must, therefore, touch the actual situation of that person within the community. Again we move toward the reality of a contextualized liturgy and see at the same time a further problem that faces the Church in the area of liturgical renewal. All too often the person fails to be seen or to be acknowledged by the liturgy, which is almost as if the liturgy were saying that God is divorced from the life of that person and uninterested. This would seriously deny the whole meaning of the incarnation.

Finally, there is a problem that seems to be one which belongs more to those areas of mission where priests are too few in number to see to all the liturgical needs of a given community. The community itself will have to see to its own liturgy with the occasional help of a priest. Often the liturgy of the people will be more appealing to them than the formal official liturgy of the Church. The danger is that the priestly sacramental liturgy of the Church becomes increasingly insignificant and with that there is a serious loss of the sense of sacrament. How does this come about? The people who must celebrate non-sacramental liturgies within their communities do so in a way that allows them to express the culture and situation of that community. These alternate liturgies express more closely the natural religious response of a given community and are thus seen as more worthwhile. For such communities there is a great deal of confusion since the sacraments are said to be more important than para-liturgies, yet in their experience the very opposite is true. This makes it increasingly important to move toward liturgies that express themselves within a given cultural context and so touch the lives of those who celebrate those liturgies.

A DEFINITION OF LITURGY

This may seem a rather unlikely question to ask, considering that this is a collection of liturgical essays, but it seems vital to answer it in view of the fact that one of the major obstacles to liturgical renewal is a forgetfulness about what liturgy is (even on the part of those who write with authority on the subject).

Liturgy aims at creating an encounter between the mystery of salvation and the lives of those who celebrate it.[10] This involves the celebrating community being drawn into this mystery that is Christ himself, and the mystery becoming a reality in their lives. Certainly the liturgy makes Christ present in the various modes of that pres-

---

[10] See SC, art. 10: DOL 1, no. 10.

ence, but equally important is the availability of the community to that presence, since the whole point of Christ's being in their midst is to encounter them. Such an availability and openness to encounter cannot be determined by the liturgy objectively, but depends rather on the subjective situation of those who celebrate it. While the mystery is certain and is known, it remains hidden to those who do not move forward to experience it, whether they move or are moved toward that encounter. The liturgy, therefore, needs to assist them in this movement toward encounter rather than create an obstacle to it.[11]

This means that the life reality and self-awareness of the community are vital to the liturgy, which cannot be celebrated in ignorance of the community situation and context. There can only be such an encounter if there is an awareness of self and a desire to become aware of God—each member of the community needs to move closer to self-knowledge, to the other members of that community and the situation in which they find themselves through the encounter with Christ. And this encounter reveals what self and other are and ought to be. Such a growth in awareness means that the community comes to a deeper encounter and a deeper realization of the mystery itself, until it is Christ who lives in that community and is revealed in that life situation.

There is a further implication to this in that liturgy not only makes the mystery present, it also allows the individual and the community to discover this mystery within—the reality of Christ within the person and the actual cultural context.[12] While this is an accepted missiological principle, does it not apply equally to those cultural situations that are considered to be Christian? It seems that the same process works here too, especially if some sense of that culture can be grasped once again. This means that the person of Jesus is rendered present by the liturgy in order to be encountered and to be identified as already present in the person and the situation.

In view of this, it becomes increasingly necessary to consider this aspect of the liturgy—that the liturgy takes into account the people who celebrate it and seeks to draw them into relationship with

---

[11] "Worship cannot be legislated, for it is the free and loving response of the whole person to a loving God. It is not magic, nor is it mere ceremony, but it is the conscious acknowledgment of the sanctifying power of God that finds expression through the ritual celebrations of the Church. Worship is based upon the fundamental principle of our total dependence on God." Seasoltz, 205.

[12] Vatican Council II, Decree on the Church's Missionary Activity *Ad gentes*, 7 Dec. 1985, nos. 8-14, 21.

Christ. It is too easy to consider liturgy as a set and determined procedure to be acted out irrespective of the participants because it is only involved in objective realities. Already this would be an achievement for those who look at liturgy solely as an offering of praise to God for the divine activity. There can be no praise unless the action of God is experienced and is known so that a community knows what it is paying honor to God for. The concept of the glorification of God depends upon the fact that we glorify God by fulfilling what God has given us to do. We will only achieve this if we are in fact touched by God and if we reach the point of offering praise out of the lives that we live, as divinely determined. Liturgy has, therefore, to become life and has to be fed by those lives being offered in and through that liturgy.

The life situation of each community is going to differ, not only because of cultural differences, but also because of varying socio-economic and political factors.[13] It is this that has to be of concern to the liturgy and into this situation that the liturgy has to reach, so that the mystery of salvation might become reality incarnate for those peoples and determine their lives and the response that they make before God.

It is not enough to sit back and feel that Christ has done it all. The whole mystery of our salvation, achieved by Christ, has here and now to become reality for those who are moved by Christ to share in it. As long as it remains as an external reality, it makes no difference to that community and, being celebrated by them, is of little consequence to them. Instead, when they are moved to see this as the very center of their lives, it begins to be what Christ intended and what the Church is there to achieve for all generations, until the kingdom is achieved.

The Second Vatican Council, when referring to the liturgy, stresses the whole issue of the participation of the people.[14] What is spoken of is more than just making appropriate responses and

---

[13] Social justice is becoming increasingly important to the Church. This is as it should be, but there is a very real danger of imposing this need on the liturgy rather than allowing it to flow into the liturgy—the danger that social justice is more important than God. Chupungco has the following to say: "The liturgy is not a forum for the propagation of social and political ideologies, however Christian these may be in orientation. Indeed, it is only after the community has been imbued with them that the liturgy can admit them as elements of prayer. A 'liberation liturgy' can only mean that the people's aspiration for liberation has been assumed by the Church into the realm of worship. Although such a liturgy will be influenced by the ideology and language of the movement, it will have to be rooted in the Word of God and centred on the Christian mystery." Chupungco, 65-66.

[14] See SC, art.14: DOL 1, no. 14. See also Chupungco, 68.

executing certain gestures. Participation means a life involvement in what is celebrated and not just a presence or active involvement at the time of the liturgy. Eventually liturgy and the lives of those who celebrate it have to become one. The difficulty here is that most people do not believe that liturgy and life are connected in this way or that their participation could ever be expected to be so demanding. And so a community is likely to settle for far less than they might achieve, unless they are led to have a greater vision of what liturgy is. As long as we spend time worrying about rubrics without a sense of the deeper demands, liturgy will have little or no effect on our lives and on those around us.

If such an interaction between the mystery of salvation and the life of the community is to be achieved, then a far greater openness is going to be required on the part of those who structure liturgy and would seek to centrally control what is acceptable and what is not.[15] It is so easy to prevent participation in the liturgy by simply ignoring or deliberately cutting out the life situation of a given people. Liturgy can only be celebrated in context, in the given situation of a people/community. The community has to be aware and true to itself in order to bring all that into the encounter possibility. Everything is of value to the liturgy when it allows participation toward this total life involvement. There has to be a movement away from the idea of certain aspects of life being sacred and others not (being perhaps too secular?)[16] —those that are sacred would be acceptable and those that are not are not acceptable. All of life is sacred if it comes from God and accords with the divine purpose and plan. And even sin is the point of return to God, who uses even this to achieve his purpose.

Through the liturgy Christ seeks to enter into the reality of our lives and into our human experience so that he might be experienced there and come to be known. In this way Christ is able to touch our lives and be one with us in all that happens to us. Certainly it may be very difficult to attain this in liturgy, but it is very much a goal to be sought after. If Christ does not turn away from our

---

[15] SC, art. 22, clearly states that it is the Church which determines what liturgy is without dealing with the need of this authority to explore areas of the liturgy that need to be extended/altered/developed within the sphere of the actual community that celebrates liturgy. There is need for the issue of freedom to be looked at.

[16] Because the liturgy is considered as sacred activity, it is placed within the corpus of Church concerns that may not be touched for fear of it being desecrated. Liturgy has to be open to growth and development on an ongoing basis. Now suddenly to consider it beyond such a process is to relegate it to certain ossification.

humanity, why are we so determined to inflict this turning away on ourselves? Could there again be fear of what such a living liturgy might do to our lives; a fear that we would again lose control and Christ would take over? Surely we have to be open to this, and if Christ accepts our humanity then we must be able to do that as well. This will demand of us that we stop being judgmental about what would be acceptable/appropriate to him and what not. Rather there are two points of judgment—the reality of Christ and the salvation which he offers to that community (determined in Scripture and tradition) and the actuality of the community. Added to this is the guiding presence of the Spirit, who makes the liturgy of that community possible and who guides them, if allowed, to fulfill themselves in Christ.

If there is a danger of losing sight of the actual situation of the community, there is as grave a danger of losing sight of Christ present in that community. They have to come to know and respond to Christ with the gift of their lives. All too easily we ignore this dimension in trying to be relevant. What liturgy must be concerned with is the person of Christ and what he holds out to that community of the work of salvation being achieved in them through the Spirit. The community needs to grow in awareness of the presence of Christ, not by divorcing him from what they are living through, but by seeing Christ there, involved in all that happens to them.

THE DEMANDS OF THE INCARNATION

In considering these aspects of the liturgy, an underlying issue at stake is that of the incarnation. All that is said presumes again and again an acceptance and appreciation of this reality.[17] And it is here that a problem lies, for while we accept in theory the idea of the incarnation, we do not put this theory into practice in our lives. It remains a nice theory, but not a driving force that gives us the courage to let go of our fears. Christ has become one like us in all things but sin, and this demands of us that we learn to see him as totally involved with all that happens to us. Christ is with us in the midst of all that happens to us in order to lead us to know him and to live again because of his relationship with us. As long

---

[17] The comments made by Chupungco on the incarnation are particularly pertinent to this whole consideration. See Chupungco, 58-60.

as we look at Jesus as the historical person and fail to see him as the Christ, eternally actual and present in the here and now because of the liturgy, we will fail to understand and live out the incarnation within the whole paschal mystery.[18] Jesus is the presence of God in our world, sharing our humanity so that we might see and hear and touch God. This incarnation is directed toward our full experience of God in order that we might come to make a response of our lives to God on the basis of that experience. Because of his being not only incarnate, but also risen, Christ continues to be available to us so that we might experience him in the here and now and not simply by looking back to him and his life as a model of how we should live our lives. Christ's presence is available to us in the sacramentality of the Church and its liturgy, by which he is made present to us (in sacrament).

Jesus was incarnate within a specific historical period and given people. The fact that he was born a Jew is not an arbitrary choice — this was the people chosen by God so that a covenant relationship with them could prepare the way for the Son to come into the world, as one of them. Jesus is the incarnation of God as a Jew with a given cultural and religious heritage. The New Testament is at pains to indicate that Jesus is the fulfillment of all that is foreshadowed in the history of salvation among the Jewish people. He did not distance himself from that world, but was part of it and spoke to it. He identified himself as a Jew and was profoundly aware of the cultural and religious heritage that was his and the period of history in which he lived. At the same time, he spoke in such a way that he transcended that given situation so that his message might in future speak to all peoples and situations; might be concretized and might be found to be relevant because it becomes identified with that situation.

Just as Jesus is one with his Jewish situation and is the fulfillment of that situation, so he is to be found already present in each cultural situation and he comes in the fullness of his revelation to fulfill what is already there of himself and his Gospel. All revelation takes place in and through the living Word. This happens imperfectly until that Word comes as the person, Jesus Christ, and it continues to happen until the experience can be identified in the actual making known of Jesus. Jesus is the one who fulfills all im-

---

[18] See E. Schillebeeckx, O.P., *Christ the Sacrament of the Encounter with God*, (New York: Sheed and Ward, 1963), 64 and 72.

perfect forms of revelation, including that revelation which is experienced in a people and its cultural identity. This demands then that Jesus encounter each and every culture to allow them to recognize the Christ within and so move toward the realization and fulfillment of their relationship with him. Within the whole task of mission, it becomes essential to respect the forms of revelation and to seek to bring about an encounter between the "hidden" Jesus and the Jesus who is the fulfillment of all revelation. If the Church fails in this process of identification of the Christ within, it runs the risk of imposing the revealed Jesus (in whatever form he is presented by those who act as missionaries) instead of allowing Jesus to emerge within the very depths of the life of that people. The imposition leaves a people untouched by Christ, and Christianity is more than likely to remain external and superficial to that people. The alternate approach will allow a depth of faith experience within their culture and tradition and a sense of the Church being theirs, and they a part of the Church. Very clearly the early Church did not keep its message and life to that Jewish situation, but moved with all that it was to touch all nations in order to make this message and life a reality among those various peoples.[19] This period of the Church's history is very much one of transculturation which is adaptation, and it is this that made missionary expansion a possibility and is still as relevant to the fulfillment of the Church's mission today. Very clearly this stemmed from an immediate sense and experience of the incarnation, something that seems to have gotten lost along the way.

The very concept of the incarnation demands the inculturation of the mystery of Christ in each age and situation in which the Gospel is to be proclaimed and to be lived. The whole point of the incarnation lies in the fact of Jesus' entering into a given situation to share in the humanity of those people. This must include Christ's awareness of and response to their social, political, and economic situation. Without this total involvement, it becomes impossible for us to conceive of our sharing life with him, but of being forced into a position of nominal adherence by which he becomes a model of life for us.

---

[19] "Essential aspects of that tradition are the phenomena of liturgical adaptation and the reinterpretation of historical data. For example, Jesus himself gave a new orientation to the Jewish rites to which he and his disciples were heirs; he situated them in the context of his own life and mission. . . . But Christianity not only adapted Jewish religious practices to its own purpose; it also adapted itself to the culture of prospective converts beyond Judaism." See Seasoltz, 183.

Jesus Christ has a universal significance as the Lord and Savior of all peoples, the one who offers to all the same possibility of salvation. It is Christ who is the point of unity, as he approaches each and every people/community in the diversity of their nature. This means that what Christ has done he is still doing, and the incarnation which gives rise to the life that he offers the world is a continuous reality for all to be touched by. The incarnation is so easily relegated to the actual moment in history in which it occurs—a past event to be looked upon with wonder, but not in such a way that it would make any present difference. Yet the resurrection seals the life of Jesus (incarnation, public ministry, passion and death) as an eternal and actual reality, so that all that Jesus has done and fulfilled in his life may in the risen Christ be experienced by all peoples of all times. Since the incarnation is the foundation of this whole life and reality of Jesus, it needs to be experienced as such in the life of every Christian community. Because of the eternal and actual nature of the event, Christ's incarnation can and must be realized in each situation and community. The incarnation is the same reality, but experienced in different ways by differing peoples. In fact it needs to be experienced by each people/community according to their diversity in order for it to be a universal reality which touches all peoples. The unity of the event lies in the fact of the incarnation itself and its universality in the fact that it is experienced by all peoples in a way that is unique to them. The wider the inculturation of the Gospel, the greater the expression of the universality of that Gospel and of the Body, that is, the Church.

THE PROCESS OF CULTURAL ADAPTATION

The Constitution on the Liturgy moves into the whole area of cultural adaptation to make it possible for people of different cultures to have a deeper sense of participation in the liturgy. Such adaptation is governed by articles 37-40, which allow for three types of adaptation—accommodation, acculturation, and inculturation. In order to be able to deal with this question of adaptation, it will be necessary to clarify what is meant by these different terms, with particular reference to the Roman rite.[20]

---

[20] The book by Chupungco on cultural adaptation deals wonderfully with the subject. Extensive use is made in this section of pages 81 to 86 in which he defines what is meant by the three forms of adaptation.

Accommodation deals with the celebrative elements as they are performed already by the celebrating community. This may or may not involve cultural adaptation. In the revision of the liturgical books, provision is made for such elements. This is not the alteration of the rite, but rather the inclusion of elements already in use in celebration in the given community.

Acculturation may be described as the process whereby cultural elements which are compatible with the Roman liturgy are incorporated into it, either as substitutes or as illustrations of euchological and ritual elements of that Roman rite. Acculturation involves the change of the Roman rite by a cultural element, where the change is one of substitution or illustration. This involves a thorough knowledge of the formal (euchology and the structural ordering) and the theological elements of the Roman rite, so that the element to be illustrated or substituted is known and can be responded to as adequately as possible. At the same time there has to be a profound knowledge of the cultural elements so as to substitute adequately or illustrate one in the Roman rite.

Culture is to be understood as the sum total of a people's thought and language patterns, values and beliefs, rituals and traditions, literature and art. Underlying it is the people's genius or their inner spontaneous mode of reacting to reality which is expressed in language and translated into rituals and traditions.[21] In identifying the elements of a culture that are to be acculturated, it will be necessary to purify these elements of anything that is in conflict with the mystery of salvation, anything bound up with superstition or error, and then to reinterpret them in the light of that same mystery so that they express adequately what that mystery is all about.

Inculturation may be described as the process whereby a pre-Christian rite is endowed with Christian meaning. The original structure of the rite together with its ritual and celebrative elements is not subjected to radical change, but its meaning is altered by the Church to express the Christian mystery. Instead of drawing a cultural element into the Roman rite, there is a process of christianiz-

---

[21] This definition of culture is taken from Seasoltz, 190, and the *National Bulletin on Liturgy* 19 (Sept.–Oct. 1986). "It is the context in which we live. It is the lens through which we view reality, the filter through which the world comes to us, through which we interpret the world. . . . Our culture is a framework, a cataloguing system, a set of shelves on which we have a place for everything. Our culture is the way we contact the reality of the world, touch it, understand it and become part of it." *National Bulletin on Liturgy* 19 (Sept.–Oct. 1986), 213. Such a view goes beyond what is normally accepted and places us within the whole scope of this essay. It is a most useful statement to keep before us.

ing an element of the culture by the alteration of the meaning of that cultural rite. Ideally the whole of life should be inculturated by the mystery of salvation—all of life being given a new meaning according to the Christian message.

This last form of adaptation comes close to being what liturgy is all about.[22] The process of the mystery of Christ is brought into encounter with the reality of the lives of those who celebrate and vice versa, so as to transform that life situation according to that mystery. This indicates just how vital our definition of liturgy is for us and just how far it is seeking to go—the making present of Christ in the world so that the world might be transformed by him.

THE CONTEXTUALIZATION OF LITURGY

Up until this point, we have been concerned with cultural adaptation. Our consideration now needs to be widened to go beyond the issue of cultural adaptation into contextualization. A culture cannot exist in isolation, but is very much caught up with the situation in which it is lived out, so that the consideration of the culture of people needs also to include the issue of the present, actual situation or context in which a given people finds itself. Frequently a change of situation alters the way in which the culture is perceived and lived out so that neither the cultural nor contextual issue can be considered in a static manner. A particular culture is a product of a certain situation, is influenced by both the historical development of a people and their present situation, and in turn has its influence on that situation and its future development. Too little consideration is given to the study of the situation and the reflection of it in the liturgy, almost as if the situation is not worthy of consideration. Yet the process within the movement of the liturgy into

---

[22] "There can be no doubt that the liturgy does indeed make use of forms and symbols it finds in culture. . . . Yet neither Gospel nor Church nor liturgy becomes adaptively identified with any of the cultural elements. The assembly absorbed them as it renovated them to bespeak not their original pagan messages, but the message of Jesus Christ. In this sense the liturgy filtered, changed, preserved, and adapted cultural elements to itself. . . . The moral of this seems to be that the liturgical assembly is normally always in the business of absorbing cultural elements into itself in a rich diversity of ways and over long periods of time. . . . It is more a lump of clay dug from the earth, shaped by people's hands, bearing their fingerprints, and sparked by divine genius in Christ if the people remain faithful to him. The liturgy thus survives cultures even as it adapts them to itself. The process can perhaps be monitored and remarked upon, but it probably cannot be forced or retarded for very long." Aidan Kavanagh, O.S.B., *Elements of Rite* (New York: Pueblo Publishing Company, 1982), 56-57.

a given culture will demand not only the acknowledgment of the culture (translation), but the entry of that culture into the formation of liturgy (adaptation) and finally the realization that liturgy needs to reflect and relate to the context so as to allow the mystery of salvation to penetrate that context and to transform it. The incarnation of the Gospel is a placing of the Gospel within a situation and a discovery of that Gospel as present there in all that is happening. Such a contextualization of the Gospel needs to be reflected in a contextualization of the liturgy. While cultural adaptation is vital, is this contextualization of the liturgy not a more immediate possibility?

In a celebrating community in which there would be several major language/culture groups, which might be tribal grouping as well, the difficulty will lie in determining which cultural group to choose in order to carry out the process. Yet all those people are involved in an actual situation. If it were possible to create in them an ongoing awareness of what is happening to them as a community, it would then become possible to move them toward an awareness of their cultural identity and of the problems that exist among them as a multi-cultural community. This awareness will never develop if their situation is simply ignored. Most communities face problems within community and also the pressures of wider social, economic, and political issues. To be a truly Christian community in the situation of the modern world is nearly impossible and yet that is exactly what has to be achieved. In order to be Christian, many communities avoid the confrontation of their problems and in this they are aided by the approach that is taken to the liturgy and to liturgical spirituality. As we have seen, this is, in fact, a denial of the very nature of the liturgy.

This process of contextualization of the liturgy would have to work on two levels, that is, a non-adaptation and an adaptation process. Such an activity would depend very much on the involvement of the community and their readiness to open themselves to what would be involved in both of these processes.

The *non-adaptation process* would not involve any alteration of the liturgy itself, but would rather involve a better utilization of the liturgy as it already stands. Since the view of liturgy sees it as solely God-directed, the liturgy is frequently presented as such with little or no effort to relate it to the reality of the lives of those gathered to celebrate it. If such an effort is made, there is a great deal of benefit to be gained. This would be a process of maximizing the benefits

gained from a more effective celebration of the liturgy. It would require various stages of implementation:

1. *Liturgical Formation*—If the problem lies in ignorance, then the
pastor and community must be trained to know what liturgy is and
to be able to celebrate it more and more effectively. The liturgy is
the very heart of the life of a community, the point toward which
all its activity is directed and the point from which all its power flows.
Such formation must go beyond technique to touch the full vision
of liturgy and all that this involves.

2. *The Development of an Awareness of the Actual Life Situation of
the Community*—Because for so long people have been told not to
look at their lives, this is likely to be a difficult task for many of them.
The analysis needs to touch the situation and then to move toward
discovering what God would want of the community in order to
deal with that situation and make it increasingly Gospel-oriented.

3. *Exploration of the Mystery of Salvation as Revealed through the
Old Testament and Fulfilled in the Life of Jesus*—Often that mystery is
experienced but is not recognized because Jesus is not known. This
can be done very effectively in the liturgy, since it is possible to touch
this mystery both intellectually and experientially in this situation.
Since the mystery is not experienced apart from the given situation, it needs to be related to the situation to open up further the
whole growing in awareness of the community. As the process moves
forward, these two points of mystery and situation will become one.
This will demand shared preparation of the liturgy (introductions
to the liturgy, the readings, and the various aspects of the actual
celebration; homily; intercessions; music; audio-visuals, and all other
dimensions of the celebration that might need to be handled). Only
in this way can the full significance of the readings and the euchology be drawn out so as really to touch the lives of the community
rather than simply to be a text for a particular moment of the celebration.

Regarding the *process of adaptation* toward contextualization, the
same aspects as found in cultural adaptation are applied here:

1. *Accommodation*—This would involve the inclusion of elements
of celebration. The Roman rite could be considered to be the bare
bones of a liturgy which could develop greater complexity by the
addition of further elements. This would not be the alteration of
the Roman rite but its expansion.

2. *"Accontextualization"*–This would be the inclusion of contextual elements into the liturgy as substitution or illustration of elements in the Roman rite. This would touch the euchological elements probably more than the ritual ones.

3. *"Incontextualization"*–This would be the giving of a Christian meaning to elements and aspects of the life of the people so that they could be part of the celebration of the mystery of salvation. It is the penetration of the mystery into the actuality of people's lives by showing them the meaning of the events, people, situations, etc. in terms of the mystery so that they become celebrative.

Ideally there should be a twofold process carried out on an on-going basis—adaptation and contextualization—and this should be carried out in the three areas specified for each of the activities. However, it might well be easier to see the process developing through contextualization into adaptation and then the two proceeding together. While consideration has been given to cultural adaptation, little consideration has been given to this process of contextualization, possibly because it is considered to be automatic. Yet the poverty of development in this area certainly would indicate very little thought or regard for this whole issue. Much will have to be done to look at this area and to see the question of contextualization in a more creative light. Suggestions will be made in regard to the euchology of the liturgy, since this seems to be a vital area of consideration and one which can be fairly easily looked at. This does not mean that these suggestions will necessarily be met with loud approval.

LITURGICAL LANGUAGE

Language is probably one of the most powerful tools of adaptation and contextualization. Perhaps because of the enormous power of language, it is also an area very much feared and of enormous controversy. Because of this, many of the implications of language in the liturgy have been avoided or side-stepped. Although the vernacular has been recognized as having a place in celebration, not everything has been done to get vernacular to be used effectively as a means of allowing the expression of a people's culture and context. Rather the unity of the Roman rite has been of greater concern. The vernacular may be used, provided it accords with the Latin base texts. This ensures that there is a clearly established uniformity of what is prayed by the Western Catholic Church. But this does not allow a people to express themselves in liturgy. Their growth as a celebrating community is sacrificed to a uniformity of rite with the result that the whole sense of the universality of the Church is lost.

The Latin texts can act as a base upon which to build. In a first stage of translation, a fairly accurate presentation needs to be made in order to feel the way in which the euchology is presented and to gain something of the theological insight into the prayer forms. From this it would be possible to begin to move with greater freedom to acculturation, that is, allowing a contextualized culture to express itself linguistically.[23] There is unlikely to be a neat process forward which would make the publication of approved liturgical books easy, but this would allow a people to enter into the prayers. While we invite them to pray, the liturgical prayers often do not express their situation or the spirit of their praying.

The difficulty with liturgical language lies in finding a form which is adequate to the task of expressing the reality of the mystery of salvation and the life situation of the people asked to express themselves through these prayers.[24] The translation of the Scriptures in the vernacular has aroused much comment and disapproval, so the same must be expected in the case of the liturgical prayers. The expression of the mystery in language is always going to present us with problems—it is an attempt to express the infinite in finite terms. Religious language does exist in varying degrees in different people and it has been developed with the same variance. Some languages have a very developed religious dimension which expresses the mystery adequately, but others are less fortunate and much work has to be done. This will be particularly true where revelation has not been explicitly experienced. The implicit expressions of revelation will have to be developed to be able to express the explicit revelation experienced in Christ.

---

[23] "The insufficiency of translation is now accepted as a matter of fact, especially in non-Western countries. The use of the vernacular has made the liturgy intelligible but not closer to the heart of the people. Beneath every translation is a message originally communicated to another people. A translation, even in paraphrase form, cannot adequately transmit this message to the people of this age and culture without breaking away from its original mode of expression. Adaptation necessarily implies the composition of new liturgical texts." Chupungco, 73.

[24] "Each liturgical tradition has its own vocabulary and grammar. And while all the traditions share some central words and grammatical constructions in general, they remain specifically distinct." Kavanagh, 96. The problem lies in determining what that "liturgical tradition" is in order to find a vocabulary and grammar.

The situation is further complicated where a particular people have undergone a process of secularization and have rapidly lost a sense of God and of religious language. For such a people to express adequately the mystery in their language is complex.[25] These people may have the words, but not the sense and experience of those words, which simply renders them meaningless. This means that we need to ask ourselves whether there is everywhere a religious language which people use and can identify with. Criticism of the translators in many situations has been that they have not used a sufficiently liturgical or religious language and have relied too heavily on the ordinary language of the people. That may be a valid criticism where a people have a definite way of speaking to and about God which is clearly distinguished from their ordinary way of speaking.[26] Where there is not a specific way of speaking to God, no specifically liturgical dimension of the language, then there is more of a problem. To create such a religious language or to return to an early form of expression to be used in liturgy runs the risk of being meaningless and of not allowing the people to enter into the liturgy. At the same time there has to be something that indicates that liturgy is involved—does it have to be solely the function of language? Surely there is the rite that accompanies the words, and attention may be needed here and not just in the area of language.

The two requirements must be the mystery and the people called to live in and through that mystery. The language must be intelligible to the people and must allow them to participate. As well, it must be adequate to expressing the realities that are being celebrated and to lead the participants into the depths of that experience of the very truth, Jesus Christ. The principle of orthodoxy seems to be essential to safeguarding both the mystery and the life situation of the people—the language has to be true to mystery and to the people (true of who and what they are and of the situation that determines their lives). Such a concern in translation and in the creation of new texts must never be lost sight of. To produce a text which sounds wonderful but which denies the whole truth of God is point-

---

[25] "But the depth of liturgical adaptation is measured . . . by the use of language . . . and the real test is the kind of language that the liturgy employs. As long as the Church prays and speaks in a foreign language whose patterns of thought and mode of expression is alien to the people, all efforts at adaptation remain superficial. This means that the Church has not penetrated the realm of the spirit nor fully appreciated the native genius of the people." Chupungco, 72.

[26] See Chupungco, 74.

less. Those who hear it must be able to be part of it and it must lead them into the total gift of themselves to God, to live out all that is God's will. While it is less usual to look for heresies today, they still exist and they will be found in the translations and new prayers produced as alternatives. Care must be taken to see them as relating to the truths about God and about people and the situations that they live in. A concern for orthodoxy will, therefore, make it possible to translate and create beyond translation in a way that is true to what the Church is all about and what it seeks to achieve in and through the liturgy.

Once we begin to move beyond the mere accuracy of translation, there will be a far greater possibility of allowing a culture and the life situation of a people to be expressed adequately. Such a process needs to be ongoing as the awareness of a community grows. The appeal could be for the creation of a spontaneous approach to liturgical prayer, as was the case in the early Church. But this would only be possible where a community and especially the presider in that community had learned the art of liturgical prayer (many think they have and produce some horrendous results). Until such an ideal exists, there will be need for prayers to be produced which in their accuracy, style, form, literary quality, and liturgical format embody the full reality of liturgical prayer. A question mark needs to be placed, then, in front of the present translations and even the original Latin texts—are they all that they should be? This needs to be done before too many people waste their energy criticizing the way translations deviate from the original texts.

The need to develop new prayers will be determined by the extent to which the changing situation of a given community touches their consciousness and needs to be reflected in their liturgy. Certainly the situation does change, and if the community is moving with those changes so their prayers and their whole liturgical celebration will have to change in order to reflect that in celebration. Again it becomes a question of keeping a finger on the pulse of the community and of allowing them to enter into the whole process of developing liturgy. Such a sensitivity to the life situation of the community is revealed in the Masses found at the time of the barbarian invasion of Rome as produced by Pope Vigilius.[27] It is this approach that needs to be adopted in approaching the creation of

---

[27] See L. C. Mohlberg, L. Eizenhöfer, P. Siffrin, eds., *Sacramentarium Veronense*, 3rd ed., Rerum Ecclesiasticarum Documenta I (Rome: Herder Editrice e Libreria, 1978).

texts which will involve the people in praying and worshiping out of their situation—their hopes and fears, their successes and failures, their frustrations, struggles, moments of crisis, and above all in their faith in God, whom they trust, will rescue them and save them from their enemies.

To make the texts more contextual is to make them more concrete. If this is achieved, then it cannot be done for a whole spectrum of peoples. It has to be done at the level of the local Church or even within a given community. Certainly the sense of liturgical prayer must be gained from the first process of translation or from the improvement on this first process. From then on the process of developing liturgical texts is to have the greater freedom to move in new directions and to achieve a closer identification with the prayers themselves. With such an identification, it will be possible to use the prayers and liturgical texts as a source of preaching—of exploring the mystery in relation to where a given community is going under the guidance of God.

AN UNRESOLVED CONFLICT

What has been said to this point is open to debate on many levels, but perhaps nowhere more seriously than in the conflict over the identity of the local Church in relation to the universal Church. While we acknowledge that there has to be control, there has also to be the freedom to move within the given context, and no centralized authority really has the ability to assess the situation as the local Church has. The local Church must be aware of the universality of the Church, but it is not central control that determines the universality of the Church, nor is it uniformity. The universality of the Church lies in the person of Jesus and a common faith expressed in the Church's teachings. This universal truth can and must express itself in many spiritualities and in many varying liturgical forms. Rather than seeing the tension that exists between the universal and the local Church as wrong and a denial of universality, we should instead see it as the very vitality of the Church. A healthy situation exists where the community can be aware of its own identity and give liturgical expression to this and at the same time remain in touch with the reality of the wider Church to which that community belongs (both the local Church gathered around the bishop and the overall Church). The destructive position that could be adopted by a community is twofold—that it becomes so engrossed in itself that it loses touch with the wider realities or that it sees only beyond itself and has no sense of its own identity. Apart from this tension there is no real hope of life, and a community must be able to live through this continuing tension.

But there is a more serious problem and that is the artificial tension that is created in the name of fostering a sense of universality in the Church through uniformity. A major principle of the Second Vatican Council is that the Church expresses its universality in pluriformity and not uniformity. Yet this is denied in the liturgy where the movement is away from pluriformity toward uniformity.[28] Liturgy cannot ever be uniform since it varies by the very communities that celebrate it and it becomes a question of the uniqueness of each and every community gathered together as a celebrating assembly. If this principle is not acknowledged, then there is an increasing failure to develop and foster communites that are celebrating assemblies.

It is in the very fact of cultural adaptation and contextualization that the Church expresses its universality. The Church has to be contextualized in order to realize the incarnation of the Gospel and its universal teaching and so to be universal in life rather than just in teaching or name. This will respect the uniqueness of a people and of a community and their right to worship with the whole Church as a people or community. It is precisely this that liturgy is given to establish and not a uniform way of doing things. Obviously uniformity has many advantages, for it simplifies the whole question of translating, adapting, and contextualizing liturgy by removing the need for this to be done. There is also less risk in setting a uniform liturgy that everyone will carry out uniformly. But then the incarnation was a risk and would make no sense if it were not. God's presence in the liturgy is a form of divine vulnerability and therefore a risk for God. The fact that these issues need to be considered at all is indication of the degree of that divine risk. And God certainly seems to have very little problem with this.

Since there is a policy expressing a desire for uniformity in the liturgy, it is necessary to know that there is nothing in the nature of the liturgy that justifies such a policy. The Roman rite can ex-

---

[28] "This pluralistic view of the Church will not destroy the universality of the Church; rather it will promote it, since there can be no universal Church unless there are in fact local churches. But these local churches will be truly local only if they have their own distinctive culture and traditions." Seasoltz, 188.

press itself in a pluriformity of cultural and contextual expressions without denying its unity. And even if new rites within the Roman family were to be developed, they would not be destructive of the unity of the liturgy, but would rather express the universality. The desire for a uniform policy is an imposition of other needs and issues upon the liturgy. This seriously damages the whole sense of liturgy since it makes the liturgy a vehicle of other needs and concerns (uniformity, discipline and control, restatement of centralized authority, fear of handing over authority to the local Church, ignorance, a deliberate attempt to reverse the vision of Vatican II). How can this negative trend be reversed? This policy seems to be in full swing and to have support which makes it difficult to deal with. Yet if it is not, there are many problematic situations that arise out of it. The Church and its liturgy will become increasingly irrelevant and will miss the point of what they are and what they are there for. People will move toward a liturgy that is not imposed, but that arises from their own lives (culture and context). Since this will not fall within the region of sacraments or of liturgy as determined by the Church (which it must be), the whole unity and sense of the Church will be denied.

TOWARD THE FUTURE

If an adequate answer is to be found to this question as it relates to the liturgy, the Church will have to find again the vision and spirit of the Second Vatican Council and to open it so that it flowers and bears the fruit that lies potentially within the seed that the Council sowed. The fear of letting go from centralized authority will have to be overcome. As the Church specifies what liturgy is and creates that liturgy, it has little to fear. This cannot be changed. But the Church can and must learn to let that liturgy develop and move in new and varying directions according to the nature of differing peoples. The very fact that the liturgy was reformed according to the Roman rite of the fifth century, was done to allow such development to take place. This liturgy represents a high point of creativity, but also simplicity and sobriety which makes it ideal for adaptation and contextualization.

Unless the Vatican gives a lead in this process, little will happen. And if the Vatican actively works against it, then the consequences will be serious for the future growth and flowering of liturgy.[29] A very real choice faces the Church and the tragedy lies in the fact that it does not see it or will not see it. To allow the liturgy to become pluriform within the Roman rite and to move into an authenticity that comes from being the liturgy of a given people is to make it possible for the liturgy to be the life-force of that people and to become the center of their lives. To fail to do this is to force people away from the liturgy and into the development of alternative liturgies, a development which would seriously threaten the unity and existence of the Church.

Much has been said in many quarters about cultural adaptation. This will be vital, and not only for mission countries. The appeal made here is for a similar process to be allowed in terms of contextualization, particularly with regard to the ways in which language is used in the liturgy and the life situation of a people is brought into vital encounter with the mystery of salvation. The community must be able to celebrate liturgy in language that they identify with, language which is able to express their concerns and make it possible for them to experience the reality of God, who comes to bring them life. The liturgy has to be experienced as real to them and their lives in such a way that it will alter them and bring them to live in union with God and according to the Gospel that God's Son, Jesus, has revealed in action. This has to be the primary concern. The liturgy should not be used for some ulterior motive, and our concern should not be to preserve it as a monumental museum piece, intact and unrelated to those who are drawn into realizing it by celebrating it in their lives.

If the Church can go beyond its human need to remain in control and can allow the Spirit to move, then there is the potential in the liturgy for the Church to be renewed and to experience once again a position on center stage in our modern world.

---

[29] "It is imperative, however, that we always keep in mind the further stage of development involving the adaptation to local and regional conditions and the more radical accommodations of the liturgy to the diverse cultures of the world." Seasoltz, 201.

"Within the tradition set forth in the liturgical books themselves, the liturgical worship must be its own business." Kavanagh, 25.

CULTURAL ELEMENTS IN LITURGICAL PRAYERS

Paul Puthanangady, S.D.B.

The introduction of the vernacular has had more far-reaching consequences than those probably envisaged by the Fathers of Vatican II. The Council declared that Latin is the liturgical language of the Roman rite but permitted the use of the vernacular, subject to special regulations.[1] From the documents of the official Church that gave guidelines for the translation of the liturgical texts during the postconciliar period, it is clear that what was intended was not a literal rendering of the Latin text issued by the Roman Congregation. The Consilium's 1969 Instruction on the Translation of Liturgical Texts (*Comme le prévoit*) says: "<u>Translations, therefore, must be faithful to the art of communication in all its various aspects, but especially in regard to the message itself, in regard to the audience for which it is intended, and in regard to the manner of expression</u>."[2] The purpose of changing the liturgical language is the pastoral nature of the liturgy itself, that is, to make liturgy become a pastoral action which consists in helping the people respond to the revealing God in and through their life-situations. For this reason, it is very clear, a mere translation of the liturgical texts would not be sufficient.

> The prayer of the Church is always the prayer of some actual community, assembled here and now. It is not sufficient that a formula handed down from some other time or region be translated verbatim, even if accurately, for liturgical use. The formula translated must become the genuine prayer of the congregation and in it each of its members should be able to find and express himself or herself. . . . translation of the liturgy therefore often requires cautious adaptation.[3]

---

[1] See Vatican Council II, Constitution on the Liturgy *Sacrosanctum Concilium*, 4 Dec. 1963, art. 36: *Documents on the Liturgy, 1963-1979: Conciliar, Papal, and Curial Texts* [hereafter, DOL] (Collegeville, Minn.: The Liturgical Press, 1982) 1, no. 36.

[2] Consilium for the Implementation of the Constitution on the Liturgy, Instruction on the Translation of Liturgical Texts *Comme le prévoit* [hereafter, Instruction], 25 Jan. 1969, no. 7: DOL 123, no. 844.

[3] Instruction, nos. 20 and 21: DOL 123, nos. 857 and 858.

A close study of the Roman liturgical texts shows that they were formulated with a pastoral preoccupation and hence they reflected the cultural and historical situation of the people who took part in the liturgy. The many formularies of the Mass texts for Christmas found in the Verona Sacramentary[4] are witnesses to the pastoral concern of the president of the liturgical assembly to make the texts reflect the life-situation of the community. Hence the pastoral objective of vernacularizing liturgy today will be achieved only if texts that reflect the life of the community are used in the celebration. The inadequacy of the translated texts for a pastorally fruitful celebration is becoming more and more evident every day, especially in the third world countries of Africa and Asia. Even though in India the present texts are used in English or other local vernaculars, they convey very little of the rich content that these texts are supposed to contain. Original composition of liturgical prayer is becoming a real need if the liturgical celebrations are to be pastorally relevant. In order to achieve this the composers of original texts need to be equipped with certain criteria and guidelines because the transition from an established text to a freely composed text is not easy, especially for those who have been accustomed to a particular style of texts for many years.

SOME CHARACTERISTICS OF LITURGICAL PRAYER TEXTS

In this section of my article I do not intend to give an exhaustive analysis of the subject, but to highlight a few elements that seem to be essential in liturgical prayer.

1. *Liturgical Prayer Is Proclamation*

It should express the mystery of Christ to the people of today in such a way that they are able to respond to it with their life and not merely by assent to an intellectual statement. Through the liturgical proclamation the mystery becomes present. The cultic reality, therefore, should be translated into cultural expressions. The richness of the mystery that is proclaimed is such that it defies any translation. It is only through cultural expressions that the nuances will become evident and the mystery itself will be unfolded under a new

---

[4] See L. C. Mohlberg, L. Eizenhöfer, P. Siffrin, eds., *Sacramentarium Veronense*, 3rd ed., Rerum Ecclesiasticarum Documenta I (Rome: Herder Editrice e Libreria, 1978).

aspect which hitherto was unknown. Then it becomes a real proclamation. The following are some conditions that need to be met if
this proclamatory character of liturgical prayer is to be brought out
more clearly:

a. It should speak the language of today.

b. It should use a language that is used by the people in order
to enter into communication.

c. It should be in a language that can be used in a community.

d. It should bring the riches of revelation easily within the reach
of the people.

Vague, if unarguable

2. Liturgical Prayer Is an Act of Transmitting Tradition

"Tradition" as it is used here means not so much the doctrinal
formulation of the early Church as the experience of the Mystery
of Christ in a given community. Even if we consider the doctrinal
formulation, it is only with a view to capture the experience. In the
formulation of the liturgical prayer, this original experience is given
a new expression in such a way that the people will not only know
the content of the original experience, but will be able to have their
own experience of it. In this way they will keep alive the living tradition rather than receive a mere formula. In order to achieve this,
the liturgical prayers that are composed should have some of the
following characteristics:

a. They should have a sacred character, that is, they should be
capable of communicating the experience of God.

b. They should possess biblical vigor. The biblical element in
the prayers must be such that they communicate not only the
words of the Bible but create in the people an emotional response.
For this it may be necessary to change images and phrases.

c. They should have a proper rhythmic order, appropriate arrangement of phrases, and a determined manner of proclamation (or singing—in India we need one text for singing and
another for reciting).

THE TEXTS OF THE ROMAN MISSAL

In the liturgical tradition of Rome we must distinguish the so-
called "genius of the Roman rite" from its Christian content. The

composers of the liturgical prayers tried to express the Christian content through formulations that reflected the cultural peculiarities of Rome. This can be illustrated by analyzing a few texts of the *Missale Romanum*. We find pagan religious terms, legal terms, military terms, and medical terms used in the prayers of the *Missale Romanum* of the pre-Vatican II period. Some of these are retained in the *Missale* published by the Congregation for Divine Worship after Vatican II.

1. *Pagan Roman Religious Terms*

The liturgical texts of the Roman rite were influenced by many linguistic and cultural factors other than the Roman culture over the course of centuries. The liturgical Latin of the Missal reflects also the images and thought patterns of the Middle Ages. However, here we are taking only a few examples to illustrate the influence of the Roman culture on the liturgical texts of the past.

> *Quaesumus*: This is one of the oldest elements of Roman prayer forms. It occurs in the pleonastic construction *precor quaesoque* in the ancient formula of prayer recorded by Cato: *Mars pater, te precor quaesoque, ut sies volens propitius mihi* and in those set down by Livy.[5]

> *Supplicatio*: In Roman religious language this was the technical term for the public celebration of thanksgiving or petition during which the temples were opened and the images of the gods brought outside on couches while the pontifex performed the sacra.[6]

> *Sacrare, Consecrare*: This means to dedicate to God in a ritual action. *Sacrare* was one of the verbs used in pagan Latin for "to dedicate to the deity." But the employment of the verb *sacrare* in its gerundive form is frequent in the Roman prayer formulae. It is very interesting to note that the gerundive of cultic verbs appears frequently also in the ancient pagan Roman prayer formulae. It would seem that this has a stylistic reason since it adds a certain broadness and loftiness to the prayers.

> *Propitius*: This is one of the oldest Latin words used to express humanity's basic sentiments toward the higher Power.

---

[5] Mary Pierre Ellebracht, C.P.P.S., *Remarks on the Vocabulary of the Ancient Orations in the Missale Romanum* (Utrecht: Dekker & Van De Vegt N.V. Nijmegen, 1963), 120.

[6] Ellebracht, 149.

It is also an expression of the most natural attitude of the ancients toward the deity as the protector of humanity. This was frequently used in early Roman prayers.[7]

2. *Legal Terms*

The concern for precision in the use of words is a characteristic of the ancient Romans. It stemmed from their legalistic attitude and affected the formulation of their prayers. The very careful effort to use the most apt word to express things that concern God is clearly reflected in the formulation of the prayers of the Roman Missal. This resulted in prayer formulas that are rich in theology but lacking in emotional content. Emotional content is very important in the celebration of worship. Liturgical prayers are not speeches about God but manifestations of the outpouring of the hearts of the devotee and of the people gathered together for celebration. We can find many examples of this juridical character in the Roman liturgical prayers.

> *Indulgentia*: From its primary meaning of "leniency" or "tenderness," this word became, especially under the empire, a technical term for exemption from punishment granted by the emperor to one convicted of a crime. In the Christian sense it took on the sense of "forgiveness of sins" or more especially of the official pronouncement of that forgiveness in the rite of reconciliation. The same can be said, for example, of the words *absolutio* and *remissio*. These words truly fail to communicate the loving kindness of God, which is an essential characteristic of the New Testament dispensation of salvation.
>
> *Intercedere*: It was used by Latin authors to mean "to become a surety for." The Church adopted it to express the mediatory power of Jesus Christ and of the Church itself. This led to a legalistic understanding of the liturgical and sacramental action which deprived them of that personal character which is the specific quality of the new relationship between God and humanity established by Jesus Christ. When we look at the term *intercessio*, the legal character becomes evident. This noun was used in Roman political life to mean the interposition of a veto by a magistrate, the entrance of a third party between the two others in order to protect the one against the other.[8]

---

[7] Ellebracht, 142.
[8] Ellebracht, 159.

Suffragium: In the time of the republic it referred generally to an individual's vote for a magistrate. Under the empire, it came to be used for the intercession of an influential person before the emperor or other rulers, especially to help someone secure an office.[9] This term is used in the liturgical prayers to indicate the mediation of saints with God.

3. Military Terms

We find that the early Church considered martyrs as those who fought for Christ. Christian life itself, lived in the midst of persecutions and opposition, was seen as a battle. The Roman prayers use military terms to express the reality of Christian life and witness.

Munimen: This meant "rampart" and is used in the Roman orations to indicate the power of God against sin. We read in the prayer *super populum* of Thursday after the Fourth Sunday of Lent in the old Missal, *Populi tui, Deus, institutor et rector, peccata, quibus impugnatur expelle: ut semper tibi placitus, et tuo munimine sit securus.* Over against the *peccata* by which the people of God are attacked, a *munimen* by God is set up.

Praesidium: This is a term used to indicate an auxiliary force or support. The military significance of the term is evident in the following prayer of Ash Wednesday in the old Missal: *Concede nobis, Domine, praesidia militiae christianae sanctis inchoare jejuniis: ut contra spiritales nequitias pugnaturi, continentiae muniamur auxiliis.* Here the garrison for the warfare itself is indicated. The fasting is considered as military force against the evil of sin.

Vexillum: The Cross is called the calvary banner: *Jesu Christi Domini nostri corpore et sanguine saginandi, per quem Crucis est sanctificatum vexillum . . .* (Secret, 14 September in the old Missal). The Cross was compared in early Christian literature to the military standard because of the cross-form of these standards.[10]

4. Medical Terms

The saving God's action in the ancient world, especially in the Roman Empire, was compared to a healing action. This was in a

---

[9] Ellebracht, 72.
[10] See the hymn *Vexilla Regis*, composed by Venantius Fortunatus.

special way attributed to the god Aesculapius. The philosophers, too, were fond of using medical terms in an applied sense to designate moral deficiencies. The stoics in particular had developed a complex system of moral as well as physical philosophy in medical terms.[11]

> *Infirmitas*: In classical Latin this meant "weakness" or general indisposition. In the colloquial speech it came to be used for physical illness as well. In the Roman prayers it is used to express humanity's inability in the face of its duties to God: *qui in tot adversis ex nostra infirmitate deficimus . . .* (Collect, Monday of Holy Week in the old Missal).
>
> *Medicina*: This word was used in the science of medicine and sometimes referred to the healing remedy as such. In the Christian usage it became a term for "grace": *Caelestem nobis, praebeant haec mysteria, quaesumus, Domine, medicinam . . .* (Secret, 20th Sunday after Pentecost in the old Missal).
>
> *Purgare*: This was a technical medical name for cure by the administration of a laxative. It is used in the Missal to indicate the purifying effect of the sacraments. The vices are supposed to be the germs that prevent Christians from living in good health. The sacraments free them from these germs: *Haec nos communio, Domine, purget a crimine . . .* (Postcommunion, Monday after the Second Sunday of Lent in the old Missal).

The few examples that we have studied show that the cultural element played a very important role in the formulation of liturgical prayers. When we translate the Roman prayers into our vernaculars, a mere rendering of the words in their linguistic equivalent will not only fail to convey the full meaning of the prayers, but it can at times distort that meaning. A reformulation of the content is therefore necessary. This ultimately would mean the freedom for every Church to compose its own euchological formulas.

AN EFFORT TOWARD THE INCULTURATION OF LITURGICAL PRAYERS

In the overall policy of inculturation in liturgy adopted by the Catholic Church in India, there is a project for creating euchological

---

[11] See Ellebracht, 179.

texts that reflect the cultural genius of the nation. Some attempts were made to implement it by composing a few prefaces for the proper of the Masses for India, but the most important effort was the composition of the Indian Eucharistic Prayer.[12] We shall now examine some parts of this prayer.

1. *The Introduction to the Preface*

Instead of the traditional dialogue of the Roman liturgy we used "mangalacaranam" in a dialogue form. Mangalacaranam is a prayer for God's blessing on a religious rite. God is called upon to help so that our action may be rightly performed. This seems to be the most appropriate way of transposing to the Indian context the introductory dialogue.

> *Cel:* May your Holy Spirit, O God, enlighten our minds, and open our lips that we may sing the wonders of your love.[13]
>
> *Cong:* Help us Spirit Divine to proclaim God's mercy.
>
> *Cel:* Let us praise and thank the Lord, our God, whose majesty pervades the universe.[14]
>
> *Cong:* Great is his name and worthy of praise.
>
> *Cel:* Let us celebrate the glory of the Lord whose splendour shines in the depths of our hearts.[15]
>
> *Cong:* Glory to Him in whom we have our being.

There is definitely a new style here. In the Roman preface the introductory dialogue is addressed to the congregation, while here it is in the form of an invocation to God. This puts in evidence a special characteristic of liturgical prayers composed according to the Indian genius. Such prayer maintains the community character of the prayer while it stresses a vertical orientation. The whole community begins the prayer of thanksgiving by an act of invocation to God; in the Roman pattern, by contrast, the style of a statement is kept in the introduction to the prayer of thanksgiving.

---

[12] This was not approved by the Conference of Bishops, although they permitted it for experimentation. This permission was withdrawn at the request of the Congregation for Divine Worship in 1975.

[13] Rigveda 3, 62, 10.

[14] Iso Upanishad 1.

[15] Bhagavadgita 15, 15.

2. *Trinitarian Life*

"In this wondrous way, O God, you called them to share in your own being, your own knowledge, your own bliss." This is an effort to translate into Indian categories the idea of trinitarian life. The expression "Being, Knowledge, and Bliss" translates the Sanskrit expression of "Saccidananda," which means reality, awareness, and bliss ("Sat" = reality = Father; "Cit" = awareness = Son; and "Ananda" = Bliss = Spirit). In the Indian context this interpretation of the divine life makes much more sense than the highly intellectual and abstract term "trinity." The use of this interpretation in the liturgy gives to the prayers a much more relevant and experiential content than that which is conveyed by the use of the traditional trinitarian formula. This becomes all the more evident in the concluding doxology of the Eucharistic Prayer:

> *Cel:* In the Oneness of the Supreme Spirit through Christ who unites all things in his fullness, we and the whole creation give to you, God of all, Father of all, honour and glory, thanks and praise, worship and adoration, now and in every age, for ever and ever.
>
> *Cong:* Amen. You are the fullness of Reality, One without a second. Being, Knowledge, Bliss. Om, Tat, Sat.

The celebrant's conclusion uses to a great extent the Roman terminology; however, the formulation uses a more descriptive, all-inclusive language. The response of the congregation is a real act of acknowledgment of God whose fullness of life flows into the congregation. The final phase, "Om, Tat, Sat," is a profession of faith by which the community recognizes God as the only reality that exists and matters.

3. *Praise of God the Creator*

> The whole of creation praises your great glory who in the beginning started the work of creation through primaeval sacrifice, and decorating the universe by the power of splendour of your Word, change darkness into light, and nothingness into being.

According to the Christian understanding, God created everything out of love. In the Indian understanding creation takes place through a sacrificial act of God. This sacrificial act is understood as an act of interior burning. It is as it were an explosion of the inner energy of God. In that sense it can be the equivalent of love and thus we have here the Indian understanding of the Christian concept of creation. When we use these expressions in our prayer texts they touch the worshipers in their inner being and awaken genuine religious experience.

4. *The Redemptive Act of God*

> Because we disobeyed you who are goodness itself we lost eternal life: dharma declined; ignorance immersed us in spiritual darkness. Nevertheless, in the indescribable tenderness of your love, you remembered us and promised us salvation. Through the prophets and establishers of dharma, you revealed to us the message of salvation in various ways.

Here we have the use of two words: "dharma" and "ignorance." These are two typical words in Indian religious terminology. The former indicates social order while the latter indicates the sinful state of humanity. Sin is called lack of awareness (ignorance) of the divine reality. The redemptive work of Christ which is commemorated in the eucharistic celebration frees the world from all types of injustice and sinfulness. The use of these two words in the Eucharistic Prayer truly contextualizes the eucharistic proclamation, making it something that happens here and now in the Indian life-situation. The use of these two words gives to the participants of the eucharist an experiential awareness of the redemptive work of Christ as it is being celebrated through the medium of expressions that vividly depict the state of disorder and sinfulness. The work of the prophets and that of Jesus Christ is to re-establish "dharma," that is, to bring about order in the lives of people and thus create a just world which bespeaks the kingdom of God.

From these few examples it becomes clear that the use of expressions taken from the religious language of India can make the liturgical proclamation actual and thus a genuine celebration of the original mystery. Naturally, such borrowing of terms can also, at times, lead to misunderstanding since these words have some connection with a particular understanding of the Divine and its relationship with the world. To illustrate this I would like to give two examples: the word "avatara" from Indian religious terminology is at times interpreted as "incarnation." Now the term "avatara" means an appearance of the divinity from above, while incarnation signifies an involvement in history. It is a manifestation from below. Another example would be to translate "trinity" into "trimurti." "Trimurti" refers to the three forms in which God is manifested, while "trinity" is not a mere triple manifestation of God in the world. Hence a proper interpretation of the terms in the light of the mystery of Christ is necessary in order to unfold the hidden riches of God's plan and lead to new and richer responses from the people. Only when we can bring our liturgical proclamation to this level can we make our liturgy become an authentic channel that communicates Christian God-experience to people.

SOME SPECIFIC CHARACTERISTICS OF THE INCULTURATED LITURGICAL LANGUAGE IN INDIA

A people's vision of reality determines to a great extent their linguistic style. In India the reality is apprehended in its totality and expressed by describing the whole. As a consequence we have many words to indicate the same thing, each one highlighting a special characteristic. In an intellectual presentation there is an attempt to define the reality through a process of establishing its identity by abstraction; the stress here is more on differentiation than description. As a consequence the words contain meanings which are not fully expressed. There may be greater precision with regard to identity, but the richness of the object is lost in its formulation.

1. *Poetic Character*

In the formulation of the liturgical texts, it is very important that the descriptive and poetic style be followed because these texts appeal primarily to emotions. The Roman prayers with their linguistic precision often fail to communicate the experience to our Indian people. This is clearly seen in the fact that many of our communities have two marriage and funeral rites: one conducted at home with formulas and signs taken from the Indian culture and another conducted in the church with the official Roman texts. This shows the need to reformulate the liturgical prayers according to the cultural genius of India if liturgy is to be authentically communicative and participatory.

2. *Elaborate in Expression*

Emotional language abounds in adjectives and adverbs. This happens because experience is often ineffable and hence no expression is adequate enough to convey its full content. In liturgy we should use emotional language; but in the Roman liturgy this is not the case. As a consequence the Roman prayer formulas communicate very little of experience to the participants in India, who are accustomed to speak of God and speak to God using many adjectives and qualifying words:

> Lord, you are my father and mother, my friend, my guru and my master. Worshipful Lord, you work my weal and read the secrets of my heart. Sincere and best of my masters, in whom all loving-kindness dwells, protector of your suppliants, omniscient and all-wise, all-powerful friend of virtue and destroyer of vice and sin, Master, there is no holy master like yourself, no enemy of his master like myself.[16]

Going through the preceding text one gets a very typical example of the elaborate formulation of prayer which is found in the religious texts. This also clearly shows that the words in the prayers are not so much intellectual expression, but the pouring out of the heart by a devotee, who is not bothered about logic and sequence and does not worry about the repetition of the same idea. The devotee is intent on expressing experience, and all the words used have to be understood in the light of experience. By speaking in this vein, the devotee is not merely communicating ideas, but sharing his or her experience. Hence the one who listens must listen with the heart. It is formulations such as these that will make liturgy meaningful and relevant to our people.

3. Use of Images in Prayer Formulas

In India all communications about God are made through images and not through concepts. The very concept of God differs in the East from that in the West in this respect. While in the West the openness of God is expressed through the affirmation of one in opposition to many, in India the idea of oneness is the result of the harmony of many, who differ among themselves and even at times apparently contradict one another. An example can illustrate this:

> Not understanding, and yet desirous to do so I ask the wise who know, myself not knowing; who may he be, the One in the form of the unborn, who props in their place the six universal regions? They call him Indra, Mitra, Varuna, Agni or the heavenly sunbird

---

[16] *Ramacharita Manesa, Ayodhya Kanda*, taken from "In Diverse Ways" (Poona, 1970), 125.

Garutmat. The seers call in many ways that which is One; they speak of Agni, Yama, Matarisvan.[17]

The one who has discovered the supreme atman dwelling in the heart, without parts, without a second; the universal witness, neither being nor non-being attains the pure form of the supreme atman.[18]

Here we have a variety of experiences put together in images, each of which has its originality and uniqueness. God-experience is not conceptualized, but expressed in images. If we translate the attributes of God as given in the Roman prayers, they would never be able to communicate the richness of the content because of the poverty of the images that they evoke; at times they evoke no images at all, leaving the listener to be lost in intellectual dryness. In India the prayers have to use descriptive, image-filled expressions. As a consequence they will be longer than the concise formulations of the Roman Missal. The texts of the Roman Missal do not lend themselves to the proclamatory character of liturgical prayer; before they succeed in awakening the participants to an experience, they are concluded.

CONCLUSION

These reflections show that it is not possible to have meaningful liturgical prayers and formulas through translations. Even at the stage of translation, a mere word-for-word rendering of the text will only result in very poor collections of liturgical texts. We need to have more elaborate, image-evoking formulas taken from the culture of the people even as we try to make meaningful translations. But the best way of formulating liturgical texts can be none other than the development of original compositions. This would require a profound experience of the mystery of Christ as well as a delicate sensitivity to and deep-rootedness in one's cultural heritage. This would also call for greater autonomy of the local Church in liturgical matters. The role of Rome should not be to create texts and rites for the local Churches, but to make sure that the local efforts to express the mystery of Christ remain within the orthodoxy of faith, leaving ample room for creativity in formulations.

---

[17] Rigveda 1, 164, 6.
[18] Kaivalya Upanishad 23.

At this juncture, I would like to note another problem that we will have to face in this matter, that is, the lack of preparedness of the local Church to take up this initiative. The training and formation in liturgy in the past has systematically eliminated all possibility of the creation of a meaningful liturgy. Since pastors have had to discover meaningfulness in a given text or to make meaningful an action that was not really so for the people, their main concern has been to explain the signs rather than to evoke experience by using signs that were natural to them. This has had a negative influence on their ability to be creative. It is necessary, therefore, to train them to it, and this will be possible only if they are allowed to make some experiments in composition. Undoubtedly such experiments will also at times result in mistakes and deviations. Will Rome permit this? From what we can see in the present legislation, I do not think that the Roman congregations are prepared to do it. In that case, where is the possibility for creating original compositions? This is a question that the prophets of liturgical renewal will have to answer. I leave it to them.

JUSTICE AND LITURGY

LITURGY AND SOCIAL JUSTICE

Rembert G. Weakland, O.S.B.

The earliest scholars of the liturgical movement were, for the most part, monks; yet they seemed intuitively to have understood the intrinsic relationship between the liturgical reform and a renewed thrust toward social concerns. These pioneers knew that the basic values in any liturgical reform would lead to a similar revitalization of social involvement. Their instincts were correct, even though we are only now beginning to realize their dreams.[1]

Liturgy and Social Concerns: The State of the Question

It would be helpful to ask why the relationship between liturgy and social justice was so self-evident to such scholars and pastoral ministers as Lambert Beauduin (1873-1960) and Virgil Michel (1890-1938) but then seemed to become less emphasized, almost lost, in the period directly before Vatican Council II, values that we are trying with difficulty to recapture today. Bryan Hehir summed up the experience of all of us in the pre-Vatican II era when he wrote:

> The historical relationship of the liturgical movement and social ministry in the United States during the first half of this century illustrates the potential of one dimension of the Church's life to en-

---

[1] A useful introduction to Virgil Michel's thinking can be found in: Virgil Michel, O.S.B., *The Social Question: Essays on Capitalism and Christianity*, selected and edited by Robert L. Spaeth (Collegeville, Minn.: St. John's University, 1987). He has also been the subject of many recent monographs that are helpful for obtaining a vision of the relationship he saw between liturgy and social concerns. See, for example, R.N. Franklin, "Virgil Michel: An Introduction," *Worship* 62 (1988), 194-200, and Kenneth R. Himes "Eucharist and Justice: Assessing the Legacy of Virgil Michel," *Worship* 62 (1988), 201-224. Beauduin's positions were less articulate and led to less activism but they were no less clear. For the general theme of the relationship between liturgy and social justice the best, and as yet unsurpassed, work is *Liturgy and Social Justice*, Mark Searle, ed. (Collegeville, Minn.: The Liturgical Press, 1980). A more recent summation of this relationship can be found in "Liturgy and Social Justice," by Edward Foley, O.F.M. Cap., in *Economic Justice: CTU's Pastoral Commentary on the Bishops' Letter on the Economy*, John Pawlikowski, O.S.M., and Donald Senior, C.P., eds. (Washington, D.C.: The Pastoral Press, 1988).

rich the other. One of my first approaches to the systematic study of Catholic social teaching came through reading the *Proceedings* of the Liturgical Conference. In those volumes the names of Godfrey Diekmann, O.S.B., Reynold Hillenbrand, Shawn Sheehan, H. A. Reinhold and Bill Lenoard, S.J. complemented those of John A. Ryan, Bishop Has, George Higgins and Jack Egan. The theme of the Church as the Body of Christ was elaborated in terms of the Church at worship and the Church in witness. The resources were solid in quality but sparse in quantity. The key texts were *Mystici corporis, Mediator Dei,* and the social teaching of Leo XIII, Pius XI, and Pius XII. From these texts was fashioned a theological basis for a style of worship with a strong social consciousness and a style of ministry rooted in the sacraments.[2]

New feasts that had been introduced into the Church's calendar before Vatican II also showed this aspect of the double reform. So, for example, the feast of Christ the King has a definite liturgical and social dimension. Christ was portrayed as King of the universe and that kingship affected all of creation. The feast of the Sacred Heart, too, had a social dimension. Although the practice outlined was highly devotional, it was not without its concern for the needs of others. The heart of Jesus was open to all needs and meditating on that open heart would bring the faithful to a similar opening up to the needs of others. These sentiments were summed up by Pope Leo XIII in his encyclical, *Mirae Caritatis* (1902), on the eucharist. Here Leo clearly states the intrinsic connection between the eucharist and the bonds of charity that unite all Christians.[3] The articulation of the relationship between works of charity and the liturgy by Pope Leo led to *Mystici corporis* (1943) by Pope Pius XII. In paragraph 8 of that document, Pope Pius XII, in looking at what was happening in the Church, could talk in the same breath about the revived interest in the sacred liturgy and the works of Catholic social action.[4] Later he was to join the eucharist and its celebration with a sense of being a member of the social body of Christ. ("His social body" is an interesting and expressive phrase, but it was not taken up by others.) In *Mediator Dei* (1947) Pius XII makes this connection even more clear. In paragraph 34, when he is speaking of the effects of the unity of the sacramental life on the Church, he states:

---

[2] Foreword to *Liturgy and Social Justice,* Mark Searle, ed. (Collegeville, Minn.: The Liturgical Press, 1980), 9.

[3] Claudia Carlen, I.H.M., ed., *The Papal Encyclicals, 1878-1903* (Raleigh, N.C.: 1981), 499-507.

[4] Claudia Carlen, I.H.M., ed., *The Papal Encyclicals, 1939-1958* (Raleigh, N.C.: 1981), 38.

Not only through her ministers but with the help of the faithful individually, who have imbibed in this fashion the spirit of Christ,
the Church endeavors to permeate with this same spirit the life and
labors of men—their private and family life, their social, even economic and political life—that all who are called God's children may
reach more readily the end He has proposed for them.[5]

In the post-World War II period, most especially in Europe and
among European liturgists, this connection seems to have been de-
emphasized and came close to being lost. In the U.S.A. the liturgical movement of the late 1940's and 1950's continued to emphasize
a social dimension and a sharp ecumenical one, as well. But its influence on the pastoral life of the Church in the U.S.A. was not yet
strong and everywhere pervasive. The meetings of the Liturgical
Weeks seemed to become less and less in touch with the masses,
in spite of the urgency and depth of the themes treated. The major
theme in 1955, for example, was precisely "Liturgy and the Social
Order." Most often these weeks afforded to the participants a chance
for personal renewal, but they did not affect the universal Church
nor the agenda of the coming Vatican Council II.

For these reasons, one does not find in the documents of Vatican Council II a clear and inspiring paragraph on the relationship
between liturgy and social action. One would have expected in the
Constitution on the Liturgy (*Sacrosanctum Concilium*) a whole section on this vital connection.

In article 9 of that document the following uninspiring text occurs: "To believers, also, the Church must ever preach faith and penance, prepare them for the sacraments, teach them to observe all
that Christ has commanded, and invite them to all the works of charity, piety, and the apostolate. . . ." Article 10 comes closest to articulating this vision. Here the liturgy, especially the eucharist, is
seen as the fountain of grace for the sanctification of all the baptized and the place where the glorification of God is achieved. It
is described as the end to which all other activities of the Church
are directed. Rightly, the liturgy is not seen as the only activity of
the Church and its members, but it is seen as giving life to all other
activity, as well as providing the place where that activity is renewed
and given meaning beyond its human or secular value.[6]

---

[5] Carlen, *The Papal Encyclicals, 1939-1958*, 126.

[6] Vatican Council II, Constitution on the Liturgy *Sacrosanctum Concilium*, 4 Dec. 1963: ICEL,
Documents on the Liturgy, 1963-1979: Conciliar, Papal, and Curial Texts [hereafter, DOL] (Collegeville,
Minn.: The Liturgical Press, 1982) 1, no. 10.

Such a *lacuna* was bound to affect the liturgical renewal and reinforce the attitude among some that the liturgical reform of Vatican Council II was purely external and cosmetic, as serious for some as rearranging the deck chairs on the Titanic. Perhaps that lack was noted early on after the issuing of the Constitution on the Liturgy because the theme is explicitly treated, although in a convoluted way, in the first implementation document *Inter Oecumenici* (1964). In paragraph 5 the implementation document states explicitly that the aim of the Constitution on the Liturgy was not simply to bring about changes in texts and rites, but, rather, to give new inspiration and encouragement to the instruction of the faithful and to pastoral activity "that will have their summit and source in the liturgy (see Constitution on the Liturgy, art. 10)."[7]

Inter Oecumenici ties true worship and genuine social activity together by seeing them as ways of carrying out in the concrete the paschal mystery of Christ. Thus, it states:

> Pastoral activity guided toward the liturgy has its power in being a living experience of the paschal mystery, in which the Son of God, incarnate and made obedient even to the death of the cross, has in his resurrection and ascension been raised up in such a way that he communicates his divine life to the world. Through this life those who are dead to sin and conformed to Christ "may live no longer for themselves but for him who for their sake died and was raised" (2 Corinthians 5:15).[8]

But one still has a right to be somewhat disappointed by the lack of a strong and clear statement on the relationship between the liturgy and building up the kingdom of God here and now.

The Synod of Bishops held in 1971 issued a document called Justice in the World; here one would have expected a clear teaching on the relationship between liturgy and social justice. One paragraph on the topic can be found. It is short and cursory. The primary optic it assumes is that the liturgy is didactic and serves a necessary educational tool for justice. The liturgy also, it is admitted, cements the bonds of solidarity. In general, however, the treatment is shallow and perfunctory.[9]

---

[7] Congregation of Rites (Consilium), Instruction (first) *Inter Oecumenici*, 26 Sept. 1964: AAS 56 (1964), 878; DOL 23, no. 297.

[8] *Inter Oecumenici*, no. 6: AAS 56 (1964), 878; DOL 23, no. 298.

[9] The edition published by Joseph Gremillion in *The Gospel of Peace and Justice* (Maryknoll, N.Y.: 1975), pp. 513-529, is useful because it is numbered by paragraphs, thus facilitating citations. The original is not so numbered.

Pope Paul VI mentions liturgy several times in his apostolic exhortation *Evangelii nuntiandi* (Evangelization in the Modern World, 8 December 1975).[10] He stresses the role of the homily at liturgy and how it can change the lives of the listeners. Later he makes it clear that one cannot separate evangelization from "sacramentalization," as if the second could take place without interior participation. He, thus, identifies a true reception of the sacraments with interior conversion. Nevertheless, this treatment is not a full nor a complete and satisfying articulation of the role of liturgy in changing society and people.

One of the more satisfying papal documents in the postconciliar Church that treats of the relationship between liturgy and social concerns is the letter *Dominicae cenae* of Pope John Paul II sent in 1980 to all the bishops of the Church. In paragraphs 5 and 6 the Holy Father points out the relationship between eucharist and charity, eucharist and neighbor. Eucharist as source and sign of charity helps the faithful to see the dignity and value of each person in the eyes of God. "If our eucharistic worship is authentic," he wrote, "it must make us grow in awareness of the dignity of each person."[11] It goes on to say that "we must also become particularly sensitive to all human suffering and misery, to all injustice and wrong, and seek the way to redress them effectively."[12]

It should also be noted that the Introduction to the Lectionary (Second Edition, 1981) is a vast improvement on previous documents in this regard. In paragraph 6 it sums up the relationship between the two elements thus: "the faithful's participation in the liturgy increases to the degree that as they listen to the word of God spoken in the liturgy they strive harder to commit themselves to the Word of God made flesh in Christ. They endeavor to conform their way of life to what they celebrate in the liturgy, and then in turn to bring to the celebration of the liturgy all that they do in life."[13]

But in examining all of these postconciliar documents of papal or Roman origin one is hard pressed to find a single, clear presentation of the important link between liturgy and social concerns. Perhaps the final document cited, that of Pope John Paul II, is the

---

[10] Vincent P. Mainelli, ed., *Official Catholic Teaching in Social Justice*, A Consortium Book (Willmington, N.C.: McGrath Publishing Company, 1978), 294-446.

[11] John Paul II, *Dominicae Cenae*, no. 6, (Boston: Daughters of St. Paul, St. Paul Editions, 1980), 11.

[12] *Dominicae Cenae*, 11.

[13] The Roman Missal, *Lectionary for Mass*, 2nd Eng. ed., 1981, Introduction, no. 6.

clearest and most explicit. In any case, one would have to admit that the liturgical reform in its official sources did not have the same social thrust as the pre-Vatican II papal documents and the writings of the first liturgical scholars.

LITURGY AND SOCIAL CONCERNS

There are three value perceptions that must be present to relate liturgy to social concerns. One could say that these three perspectives are present in both liturgy and the Church's social mission and tie them together. They were alluded to in *Mediator Dei* by Pope Pius XII.

First of all, there can be no liturgy and there can be no true Christian social involvement without a sense of community or solidarity. There have been volumes written by liturgists about the meaning of the assembly in worship, but the argument basically resolves itself into the statement that liturgy is not a private devotion but an act of the people of God, called together by Christ himself and united with him through the action of the designated minister.[14] In order to have liturgy there must be a sense of union with Christ and through and with him to others. The assembly is, thus, not just any group that happens to be together; it is a group that is called, that lives by faith, and that expresses that faith through the liturgical act, especially the paschal mystery of the death and resurrection of Jesus Christ. In the eucharist, in particular, this awareness of union with others is present, but it must be verified in all the sacraments. Eucharist implies also the willingness to serve others, as John's Gospel, which is read in the liturgy of Holy Thursday with the washing of the feet, makes most clear.

If piety is permitted to remain only on the level of personal devotion, then no liturgy is possible and no concern for social justice evolves. Perhaps the reason why the generation following the Second World War did not see this connection was precisely because they did not see the communal dimension of the liturgy, its relationship to the whole community. Many still interiorly resist the liturgical renewal since it disturbs (thank God!) their private devotion.

---

[14] The most scholarly and thorough examination of this topic can be found in *Roles in the Liturgical Assembly: The Twenty-Third Liturgical Conference Saint Serge*, trans. Matthew J. O'Connell, (New York: Pueblo Publishing Company, 1981). See also Johannes Wagner and Helmut Hucke, eds., *The Church Worships*, Concilium 12 (New York: Paulist Press, 1966), and *Liturgy*, vol. 1, 1981.

Second, there is a special connection between the spiritual growth
of a believer and the liturgy. I place this aspect second since that growth ②
comes about in and through the presence and mediation of others
and not just in the private relationship between the individual and
God. Sometimes, in our concern lest the communal dimension of liturgy be lost, we are hesitant to talk about the personal growth that
takes place in the liturgy and in action. The whole process described
in the *Rite of Christian Initiation of Adults* is based on the presupposition that growth in holiness must take place, not just in the candidates, but in the entire community. Again this aspect of growth was
neglected because of the fear of falling into a privatized pietism. Now
we have reached the point where the integration of growth and liturgy can be discussed and analyzed. In this way liturgy will become
integral to the entire spirituality of the person.

Liturgy without personal spiritual growth could easily be turned
into mere ritual without conviction. Jean Sullivan describes this danger in this way:

> If love is not to be reduced to a new formalism or community to
> ritual while pretending to overcome divisions of money, class and
> race, they have to avoid ideology and sentimentalism, which means
> that they must begin to be fulfilled. Otherwise, in spite of all good
> intentions, love and ritual become only more examples of inertia,
> made worse by fakery. To believe that love can be intellectualized
> and made as obligatory as ritual, that people can be taught about
> a community of sharing in abstract terms, is to open the way to all
> sorts of illusions.[15]

But a parallel case can be made for social concerns: they must
not remain something one does, but become a way of life and an
integral part of one's spirituality. In this sense we can say they must
become an essential part of the lifestyle of any disciple of Christ.
One brings to the liturgy and then takes back into the world, but
in a renewed and hopeful way, the love and concern one has for
others and for building a world of justice and righteousness.

For the believer both the liturgical dimension and the social
counterpart must be a way of living out the paschal mystery. Both
are the paschal mystery realized in our day in each one of us. The
act of dying and rising takes place with Christ in the liturgy in its
sacramental form; but it is again lived out in life over and over after

---

[15] Jean Sullivan, *Morning Light: The Spiritual Journal of Jean Sullivan*, trans. Joseph Cun-
neen and Patrick Gormally (New York: 1988), 24.

we leave the assembly. In this respect the two aspects, liturgy and life, are held together as different ways of growing in the mystery of the death and resurrection of the Lord. To make that bond clear to the believer the liturgy demands that all offer the sacrifice, according to their distinctive ministerial function, with Christ. One should, thus, not neglect the importance of the offering of self with Christ at the eucharist. The offering makes sense only when the liturgy, that is, the paschal mystery being celebrated, is lived out in sacrifice for others, just as Jesus suffered, died, and rose for others. The internal disposition needed for participation at liturgy is the same as that needed for true social involvement in building the kingdom of God: offering of self for others just as Jesus did. True discipleship becomes a part of liturgy and life through such offering.

Third, there must be the conviction that the mission of the Church is to continue that of Christ himself, namely, that of sanctifying the world and recapitulating all things to the Father. The mission of sanctifying this world is another way of saying that the Church has a clear and definite mission to this world here and now. That mission was given to it by Christ and, thus, it is integral to the whole concept of being Church. Faith becomes a broader concept than just the salvation of the individual soul, since that salvation depends on how each one takes up the cross daily and follows Christ. That cross includes his mission of proclaiming the Good News of the kingdom, of bringing hope to those in need. Liturgy is always a calling to keep in mind that the true mission of the Church will never end until the final coming of the Lord. On the other hand, it also makes it clear that the here and now is where the kingdom is being built. Pope Paul VI expressed this conviction in these terms: "Those who sincerely accept the Good News, through the power of this acceptance and of shared faith, therefore gather together in Jesus' name in order to seek together the Kingdom, build it up and live it."[16]

Obstacles to Renewal

The first obstacle to renewal of both liturgy and social ministry is the concept of liturgy as private devotion. Many have already out-

---

[16] Paul VI, Apostolic Exhortation *Evangelii nuntiandi*, 8 Dec. 1975, no. 13: Mainelli, ed., *Official Catholic Teaching in Social Justice*, 399.

lined the difficulties within our culture for an authentic liturgical
and social renewal because of the hyper-individualism and personal-
ism that affects our culture.[17] That tendency militates against a sense
of solidarity and community and makes true liturgy and social consciousness impossible. Instead of leading to authentic liturgy, such
tendency in our culture fosters a highly personalized religious
manifestation where the accent is on the personal relationship between the individual and God and where the criterion seems to be
what the individual gets out of the relationship. M. Francis Man-
nion, in an excellent analysis of these trends, has called this
manifestation the "subjectification of reality." It has been studied
at length by recent sociologists, the classic work in the field being
Habits of the Heart by Robert N. Bellah and his associates.[18] The need
for a sense of community and solidarity has been strongly emphasized in the Economic Pastoral Letter of the Bishops of the United
States as essential for a social consciousness.[19] Without denying the
need for personal virtue and discipline, one could assert that both
liturgy and social ministry become problematic if a sense of community and solidarity does not evolve.

Connected with this tendency is the expectation that liturgy will
be entertainment. In our culture, when we participate in any large
gathering we do so to be entertained. It is difficult, especially for
the young, to see liturgy as participation in another sense. The importance of how ritual communicates and relates to both the past
and present moments has not been explained to them and, for that
matter, it has not been clarified to all Christians to a sufficient degree. In the same way, personal virtue is important for spiritual
growth; but that growth depends, too, on being with others. Often
the Gospel points out that true growth in discipleship comes about
by denying oneself, not by seeking self. Virtue, from a Christian
point of view, does not exist in a vacuum.

Since this obstacle, regardless of the fact that it is the most important, has been thoroughly analyzed by others, I would like to
treat at greater length of another obstacle found in our religious culture, one that comes from our false notion of how the events of this

---

[17] For an outstanding essay on this theme see M. Francis Manion, "Liturgy and the Present Crisis of Culture," *Worship* 62 (1988), 98-123.

[18] Robert N. Bellah, Richard Madsen, William M. Sullivan, Ann Swidler, and Steven M.
Tipton, *Habits of the Heart: Individualism and Commitment in American Life* (Berkeley: 1985).

[19] "Economic Justice For All: Catholic Social Teaching and the U.S. Economy" in *Origins*
16, 1986. Paragraphs 329-331 deal specifically with liturgy and social awareness.

world relate to the kingdom and especially to its ultimate manifestation. The correct relationship between liturgy and social concerns is disfigured by a kind of schizophrenic spirituality that has evolved around us in recent decades and that comes from the way many perceive the relationship between religion and world, or religion and politics, or religion and society. This second obstacle is connected to the first one of privatization but has its own theoretical and theological reinforcement. One could say that the relationship between liturgy and social concerns is colored by how one sees the relationship between the Church and its mission to the world.

Within the liturgical renewal there was a secondary strain that was very important: one could call it neo-Platonic. It too militated against any relationship between liturgy and social justice. It relied mostly on texts from the Johannine literature and saw the Church and world in an irreconcilable antagonism. American audiences were introduced into this strain through Louis Bouyer's book *Liturgical Piety* (1954).[20] In Chapter 19 of that work Bouyer dealt with "the Mystery and the World." Although he admits the need for a Christian to do good, he presents the Johannine antagonism between world and Church as the vision in which the liturgy here and now takes place. Since this antagonism will be resolved only at the end of time, he explains, the role of liturgy is to keep the eschatological hope alive and must not compromise with this world. One could also call this the "oasis" theory. In such a view there would be no need for a chapter on how liturgy relates to social ministry since the latter is not viewed as integral to the eschatological picture.

In this vision of liturgy one does not look for signs of God's activity outside the Church in the world, signs that might relate to the presence of the same God in the sacraments. Liturgy becomes the place where the divine mysteries are celebrated over against the world. One can see in this vision the struggle to come to terms with how—as H. Richard Niebuhr put it—Christ relates to culture. In that classic study the view articulated by Bouyer would be called "Christ against culture."[21] The advantage of this approach is that it gives a sense of identity or elitism to those who are members of the Church; that liturgy reinforces this sense of election. It is not important that liturgy be understood by the participants, as it can

[20] Louis Bouyer, *Liturgical Piety*, Liturgical Studies 1 (Notre Dame, Ind.: University of Notre Dame Press, 1954).

[21] H. Richard Niebuhr, *Christ and Culture* (New York: 1951). The second part of this book is entitled, "Christ against Culture," 45-82.

achieve its aim of unification of the elect as they wait for the eschaton through the very mystery itself. Other possible manifestations of the eschaton outside of liturgy are ignored as unimportant. How other aspects of the kingdom, those in the beatitudes or in the last judgment parable of Matthew, relate to liturgy is a question that does not have to be asked.

One cannot accuse this vision of being hyper-personalistic since a sense of Church and community is present; but it tends toward a spiritualization of Church so that there is no need to ask the question of how the Church relates to the world and how the liturgy is a part of that relationship.

This view could well be contrasted with that of other authors. I cite but two, both having been written before Vatican Council II. The first example is given in Charles Davis's book *Liturgy and Doctrine* (1960) and in particular the seventh chapter which is entitled, "Eschatology."[22] In that chapter Davis writes: "The reason for such a period (this present and first intermediate eschatological period in which we exist now) is to give to men the opportunity of associating themselves freely with the new creation and of cooperating with its gradual penetration into the world."[23] The second state in which Christ comes again "will show the meaning of human history and how God has been present in it, directing it to his purpose."[24] The relationship between our present life and final resurrection Charles Davis formulates in this way: "Further, the greater sense of the corporate character of the Christian life makes us more aware of the corporate elements in eschatology, namely, the Second Coming, the Resurrection, the last judgement and the restoration of the material universe."[25] In H. Richard Niebuhr's terms this description would fit the classification of "Christ the Transformer of Culture."[26]

My second example of contrast with the view of Louis Bouyer and a neo-Platonic thrust will be an article by Bishop Joseph J. Blomjous of the diocese of Mwanza in then Tanganyika.[27] I cite this example in particular because it shows how the missions were wrestling with these problems in a very real and vital way before the Vatican Council II. Blomjous wrote in 1960: "In the present sit-

---

[22] Charles Davis, *Liturgy and Doctrine* (New York: 1960).
[23] Davis, 114.
[24] Davis, 115.
[25] Davis, 119.
[26] Niebuhr, 190-229.
[27] Bishop Joseph J. Blomjous, "Mission and Liturgy," in Johnannes Hofinger, S.J., ed., *Liturgy and the Missions* (Collegeville, Minn.: The Liturgical Press, 1960).

uation of the Church in the missions there are probably no more necessary or more urgent matters than these two: social action and liturgical action, and the integration of the two into a mature Christian life."[28] The only way this could come about according to Blomjous was through the building of community, but community based on the unity of faith, on the Christianization of morals, and on liturgical participation. "Only when a parish lives its Christianity as a community in Christ and with Christ, and receives strength from that experience for the charitable and apostolic activity toward its fellow men, only then can we speak of a mature Christian society."[29] Blomjous calls for truly active participation of all Christians in the liturgical life of the parish, a living out of the *kerygma*, the message of the Gospel, and the evangelizing of the native cultures, so open as they are to a spiritual vision of the material world. Blomjous asked in this article the major questions that would arise in the subsequent Council about to begin.

This vision of both Davis and Blomjous was present in the Pastoral Constitution on the Church in the Modern World (*Gaudium et Spes*) of Vatican Council II, but it is not so evident in the Constitution on the Liturgy. One cannot say, on the other hand, that the vision of Bouyer triumphed either. Nevertheless, the neo-Platonic strain, with its emphasis on mystery, on antagonism, on the "otherworldly" quality of liturgy, still remains among us to be dealt with.

In all honesty one would have to admit that this neo-Platonic strain has provided a needed corrective or balance to another obstacle to liturgical and social renewal: one could call it a neo-Pelagianism, a sentiment, namely, that holds even implicitly that human persons are capable of solving all problems by themselves. This also affects how they worship; liturgy for them becomes fixed on the human community and not on the mystery of Christ. This strain fixes almost exclusively on the human contribution and its manifestation. One saw it in liturgies in the seventies that relied heavily on creating a strong human experience for its own sake. Here liturgy was often used to support a pre-agreed theme or message. Liturgy was, thus, manipulated to fit the ideology of the planners and not left free to challenge and energize.

Liturgy at its best is an oasis only in that it gives a sense of hope because God is at work in our midst. It is at its best when it uses

---

[28] Blomjous, 41.
[29] Blomjous, 43.

every human means and creativity, not for their own attractiveness, but to center on and interpret the biblical and sacramental meaning. The human is very much present but never as the ultimate achiever of salvation and redemption. Liturgy is at its best when the participants are sent out to transform the world, but are not naive about the potential inherent in it for evil. The Catholic tradition is not that of the Amish; the world must be transformed and the risk of contamination must be taken. Victory comes, so the liturgy constantly reminds us, from God; we are but his instruments.

Liturgy, like social concerns, takes seriously the Isaian texts about the kingdom and seeks to build such a kingdom of peace and justice. These signs of the eschatological kingdom are also here and now signs of hope. All events of the world are brought into the realm of the liturgy. The prayers of the faithful should reflect these cosmic concerns, the unity of the kingdom in the here and now with what went before and with what will come. The partial realization in mystery of the eschaton here and now through the work of the Holy Spirit is celebrated at each liturgy and worked out in each striving for social justice.

One could speak also about a fear that creates a new obstacle to liturgical and social renewal: it is the fear, namely, that soon the liturgy will become dispensable and the entire accent will be on action, or the social gospel, as it is called. There is no doubt that this temptation could be fatal in the U.S.A. because of our pragmatic and action-oriented culture. There is a tendency on our part to see our work as our prayer, to want to accomplish visible acts and to neglect prayer. We are told that before long this can lead to disaster, but we have all seen many examples of it. It can also lead into the semi-Pelagianism cited above.

The need for worship should be evident to a Christian. It provides the objective unifying force within the community, among the individuals, and between them and the community. It provides, as well, the motivation needed for action, and, although it keeps that motivation in the realm of the spiritual and religious, it does so in such a way that it does not remain in the realm of the abstract nor does it fall into the temptation of thinking that one can accomplish the work at hand without God's graces. More than anything else it objectifies the unity of the whole body of Christ in such a profound way that no human sentiment can accomplish. That unity has its origin in Christ. Liturgy is, thus, absolutely necessary so that the work of each individual relates to the work of the whole.

Liturgy and Social Awareness

I recall celebrating Mass many years ago in a relatively small town in Pennsylvania where there was but one large major industry. At that Sunday Mass the owner of the industry sat side by side with those who worked there. It was a visible sign that in the liturgy there is no class nor rank. The Gospel was to be preached to all without distinction. No one was above it nor outside its challenges. At communion one could see all ranks of managers and workers mingle to receive the eucharist. It was a kind of reminder that in the next life the order might be indeed reversed.

I contrast that with a Mass I celebrated many years later in Europe in the castle of one of the wealthiest families in the world. There the owner was at a special prie-dieu in the center, the rest of the family was behind him on the ground floor, all the servants were in the balcony looking down. God must have been smiling because we all knew that it was the same Gospel that was being preached to all alike (by chance the reading of the day emphasized the dangers of riches!) and we knew it was the same Christ who was received in communion by all. The distinctions built by human hands crumbled before the mysteries of faith. Liturgy of itself makes a social statement.

No community that worships together can hear the parable of the Good Samaritan or the story of Lazarus and the rich master without being changed. The proclamation of the Gospel is a constant challenge to the community to purify itself of prejudice and to move toward a true respect for all its members. Jesus' treatment of the poor and his mission to them changes their role in secular history as well as in the history of the kingdom. The proclamation of the Gospel affects how people relate to one another, how they view one another, and how they act toward one another. Works of justice are inspired by the liturgy, demanded by the liturgy.

Liturgy also leads to personal sacrifice for the kingdom. There is no way of assisting at the liturgy, for example, on Holy Thursday at the washing of the feet, and then of being indifferent to the needs of others. Liturgy leads to service. As head of the Benedictine Confederation I had the privilege of assisting many times at meetings of our Benedictine monks in the Far East. They taught us much about recapturing our tradition of mystical prayer, but we had much to teach them about the relationship between liturgy and social awareness. Liturgy does not permit one to withdraw into oneself, even to the heights of mystical union, without calling us again to the fact that union with Christ also implies suffering with him for others. The closer one comes to Christ in mystical prayer, as in liturgical, the closer one comes to others and especially to the needy and the poor. If liturgy is an oasis, it is so only insofar as it unites us more closely with Christ and, thus, with the world and with all those loved by Christ. One with him is one with all his children.

Liturgy never minimizes the here and now; but it also never forgets that the final phase of the kingdom is yet to come. It keeps that perfect balance for us in life between realism and hope, between human weakness and divine providence, between prayer and action. Because of that role it looks backward and forward to all other activity, whatever its nature might be. Liturgy then becomes the yeast needed for fullness of life in the kingdom.

These concepts constituted the vision of the early liturgical reformers and bound their concern for liturgical renewal with that of social justice. They saw it as one unified piece. A renewal of our ecclesial life in terms of such a vision has only been partially accomplished in this post-Vatican II Church. There is still much to be done.

LECTIONARY AND SCRIPTURE

THE ECUMENICAL IMPORT OF LECTIONARY REFORM

Horace T. Allen, Jr.

Among the evidences of personal greatness and prophetic insight are the corporate and conciliar structures which certain persons encourage and direct. Archbishop Denis Hurley's commitment to the work of the International Commission on English in the Liturgy (ICEL) is such evidence. The purpose of this article, in tribute to His Excellency, is to trace the enormous influence ICEL has had in matters ecumenical ever since its inception in the deliverances of √√ the Second Vatican Council of the Roman Catholic Church. This tribute is written from a profoundly Protestant point of view, which may or may not lend it much credence, but which will surely indicate that it can hardly pretend to speak of the expressed intent or agenda of ICEL through these two decades, but only of its widespread effects. This then is an interpretation from "outside the gates" of the labors of a trusted and effective partner in ecumenical, liturgical research and creativity.

With its first decree the Constitution on the Liturgy (*Sacrosanctum Concilium*),[1] the Second Vatican Council surprised everyone except those who for several decades before had "eyes to see and ears to hear" in matters liturgical. This first, and perhaps most shattering, deliverance of the Council Fathers is still reverberating up and down the various Churches and ecclesial communities of Christendom. There is good reason for this: it speaks directly to that most obvious and central activity of Christians, however simple or humble, their weekly and daily prayer and praise of the God of their salvation. Nothing could be more important, and therefore more inviolate. All liturgists know this but many have great difficulty in believing it. Thus this decree, especially in the context of all the Council had yet to do, set off a chain reaction whose explosions con-

---

[1] Vatican Council II, Constitution on the Liturgy *Sacrosanctum Concilium* [hereafter, SC], 4 Dec. 1963.

tinue to punctuate weekly Mass and daily prayer. And Churches whose "experts" were but "observers" at Rome are still struggling to become "expert" in the significance for their own liturgical life of the Constitution on the Liturgy. Of that story, more later.

What was even more surprising in the wake of the 1963 decree was the swiftness with which a resultant ecumenical, liturgical agenda made its way to center stage in official conciliar bodies such as the World Council of Churches (WCC), especially in the English-speaking world. This latter observation suggests that the logic of the catholicity of the Roman Church continues to express itself in a world in which the new universal language is not Latin but English. Thus Paul Theroux in his latest fascinating chronicle of railway travel: "English is the unofficial language of the new China."[2] The further fact is that the most widely-distributed document the World Council of Churches has ever published, Faith and Order Paper No. 111, is entitled *Baptism, Eucharist, and Ministry* (BEM).[3] The most casual historian of the two decades between the Council's decree and the World Council's paper would have to concede some kind of linear relation. In a brief and action-filled twenty years Rome and Geneva together have tackled the "tough nuts" of denominational identity and ecumenical stumbling. Nor were their conclusions all that disparate. Essential to such a developing consensus over such a period of years has been a large network of consultations, committees, and commissions, bilateral and multilateral. ICEL has been a principal partner in that development, because of its role of carrying forward the vernacular liturgical renewal among English-speaking Roman Catholics worldwide and thus of speaking for that renewal to a whole array of national Protestant bodies some of which exist only in more or less formal international configurations. ICEL, therefore, was central to the formation in 1964 of the North American Consultation on Common Texts (CCT), in 1969 of the International Consultation on English Texts (ICET) which produced *Prayers We Have in Common* (1970, 1971, and 1975)[4] and more recently, the English Language Liturgical Consultation (ELLC) which will shortly publish its reworking of those texts as *Praying Together*.

---

[2] Paul Theroux, *Riding the Iron Rooster—By Train Through China* (New York: G.P. Putnam's Sons, 1988), 115.

[3] Faith and Order Paper No. 11, *Baptism, Eucharist, and Ministry* (Geneva: World Council of Churches, 1982).

[4] International Consultation on English Texts, *Prayers We Have in Common* (Philadelphia: Fortress Press, 1970, 1971, 1975).

Thus, it has been that ICEL has served both the immediate and the more distant preoccupations of the Roman Council in expediting the "vernacularization" of our sacred liturgical texts in as wide an ecclesial context as could be put together. This may well not have been ICEL's primary agenda, but it was a vital side-effect of its efforts. The way from the Constitution on the Liturgy to *Baptism, Eucharist, and Ministry* has been almost breath-taking; ICEL has greatly encouraged those of us who have been chasing along.

All of this leads to the more specific business as intimated by the title of this article, namely, the way in which the publication in 1969 of *Ordo lectionum Missae* (OLM)[5] by the Holy See radically transformed the ecumenical liturgical relationships between that See and so many of its "separated sisters." It does not stretch the historical record to suggest that the liturgical use of the Bible was the crucial point of contention in the sixteenth century. It underlay the stress on the use of the vernacular, the development of congregational psalmody and hymnody, the advocacy of preaching and much of the critical theology of the Reformers, to say nothing of their revision of the liturgy for the Sacrament of the Lord's Supper. In their estimation, the magisterial tradition of the Church, including its liturgical actions and texts, had totally and dangerously supplanted the authority of the Word of God. This consciousness has never departed the Protestant mind.

It must be confessed, sadly, that this, as all triumphalism, never noticed its own shaky presuppositions, especially as historical-critical biblical studies began raising all manner of awkward questions, and non-liturgical worship increasingly became preoccupied with conversion, pietism, or humanistic and sociological agendas. The theological surprise which Karl Barth and Dietrich Bonhoeffer represented in Protestantism, with their biblical preoccupations, is directly traceable to these tendencies. In North American Protestantism, the Liberal/Fundamentalist standoff had become "the only game in town," and as a result Neo-orthodoxy has yet to be fully appreciated, since Tillich and Niebuhr and now Liberation theologians became the dominant players. Thus, as in the previously mentioned development of liturgical texts, Rome has helpfully intervened at the critical point of the liturgical use of the Bible. Who would have thought that the 1970's would witness the enthusiastic appropriation by

---

[5] Congregation for Divine Worship, *Ordo lectionum Missae* (Rome: Vatican Polyglot Press, 25 May 1969).

Protestant Churches and Communions throughout the world, especially English-speaking, of a Roman Lectionary table! Thus the sixteenth century Reformation was stood on its head and the ecumenical movement given a dimension no one had expected. Because of its textual preoccupations, and its mandate from the bishops' conferences to include the ecumenical dimension and interests in its program, ICEL was drawn into this development as well even though it was not technically part of its primary agenda. ICEL, necessarily, became the place where lectionary negotiations found their Roman focus and response because of the international context of this discussion, however important it would be that national episcopal conferences also be involved. And it must be remembered that for national Protestant Churches, without strong or reliable international connections, the worldwide ("ecumenical") dimension is quite important especially as the World Council has been so slow to enter into this particular discussion.

The rapidity with which English-speaking Protestantism took up the Roman *Ordo* of 1969 may be taken as evidence of the excellence of that document, but also of Protestantism's often ambiguous approach to the Bible which in fact was often more like an avoidance pattern. This appropriation of OLM '69 will be detailed in the section of this article which is immediately to follow. The contextual point to be noted here is the essential role of ICEL and its archepiscopal leadership, in making possible a dialogue in depth concerning what most Protestants would have regarded as the "wildest" of all ecumenical cards, a Roman proposal concerning the reading and preaching of the Bible at the public worship of the Lord's Day. Perhaps, one might reflect, inter-communion is not the prior question; a Protestant might think that the Bible is, and how surprising that Rome might have many of the answers, liturgically speaking!

So much for prologue. This article intends to address *Ordo lectionum Missae* in two ways. The first is to see it as a significant theological event which in its ramifications may open up quite a number of thorny questions which confront all Christians and in that way provide them with a much broader base for Chrisitan unity than has previously been defined. The issue is, of course, the centrality for all Christians of the Bible as the *locus classicus* of the definition of "faith," as in the apostolic definition of "one Lord, one faith, one baptism." First then, OLM as Ecumenical Event.

OLM as Ecumenical Event

In a report to the Episcopal Board of ICEL in 1982 Msgr. Frederick McManus spoke of the ecumenical use of OLM in the English-speaking world in these superlative terms: "by far the most successful and practical ecumenical progress in Christian Worship since the Second Vatican Council. . . ."[6] This reflection surely validates the careful way in which the Roman framers of OLM reviewed many lectionary systems including current projects and proposals and included in their discussions Protestant observers. The proliferation of the use by non-Roman Churches of this new table of readings for the Lord's Day has nevertheless come as something of a surprise to those who prepared and promulgated it. As hinted above, it was after all not at this point that Protestants were looking to Rome for help! But, of course, those Churches of the Episcopal and Lutheran families were working with much the same system which OLM reformed, and were equally aware of its weaknesses, especially as it excluded the Hebrew scriptures. And Churches which had abandoned any such system, such as this author's, were beginning to search out alternatives to what had become a largely unreliable and quixotic pattern of individual pastors relying on their own rather subjective canons.

The first Church in North America to take the Roman table into its liturgy was in fact the United Presbyterian Church, U.S.A., along with its Southern and Cumberland counterparts. They were engaged in producing a service book and hymnal (*The Worshipbook*, 1970 and 1972)[7] to implement its new *Directory for Worship* (1961)[8] which had put it back in touch with its Genevan roots in the liturgical reforms of Calvin himself. The author of this constitutional document was the Rev. Dr. Robert McAfee Brown who became one of the Protestant observers at Second Vatican Council. Adoption of this Directory had liberated North American Presbyterians from their dependence on the largely Puritan *Westminster Directory for Worship*

---

[6] Frederick R. McManus, "Report on the Consultation on Common Texts to the Episcopal Board of the International Commission on English in the Liturgy," Washington, 6 Mar. 1982.

[7] The Joint Committee on Worship for Cumberland Presbyterian Church, Presbyterian Church in the United States, and The United Presbyterian Church in the United States of America, *The Worshipbook: Services and Hymns* (Philadelphia: The Westminster Press, 1972).

[8] United Presbyterian Church in the U.S.A., *Book of Order*, Constitution of the United Presbyterian Church in the United States of America, Part II, 1977-78 ed. (New York: General Assembly of the United Presbyterian Church in the U.S.A., 1978).

(1645, 1788)[9] with its recommendation (universally ignored) of strict chapter-by-chapter "course reading." On the basis of Brown's document this new book for worship was prepared. Its initial intention was to include a two-year lectionary cycle based on a proposal of Alan McArthur known as the "Peterhead Lectionary."[10] It recast the calendar according to a year-long trinitarian pattern, and provided two years of readings, three per Sunday. A provisional edition of this was included in a trial paperback volume published in 1966.[11] The Committee preparing this revision of the 1946 *Book of Common Worship*[12] was stopped in its tracks, however, by the 1969 appearance of OLM. A perceptive member of the committee who was both a liturgist and a linguist, the Rev. Dr. Lewis A. Briner, then Dean of the Chapel at McCormick Theological Seminary in Chicago, saw the significance of what was happening ecumenically and convinced his colleagues to jettison the two-year sequence in favor of an adaptation which he prepared of the Roman pattern. (Ironically this same decision was faced in Great Britain as the Joint Liturgical Group [JLG] of the United Kingdom published its own version of the two-year thematic scheme in 1967, but unhappily the decision went the other way, setting up the difficult situation at the present time wherein of the three dominant systems now in use or under study, two are closely linked, i.e. the Roman, and *Common Lectionary* [CL],[13] whereas the third is quite different, i.e. that of the Joint Liturgical Group.[14])

In North America, however, the use and adaptation of the Roman system continued apace, as shortly after 1969 the Episcopal and Lutheran Churches published their own versions of OLM in paperback format for testing purposes and subsequently in hardbound official books: the *Book of Common Prayer* (1979)[15] and the

---

[9] United Presbyterian Church in the U.S.A., *The Constitution of The Presbyterian Church in the United States of America Being Its Standards Subordinate to the Word of God* (Philadelphia: The Office of the General Assembly, 1956).

[10] A. Allan McArthur, *The Christian Year and Lectionary Reform* (London: SCM Press, 1958).

[11] United Presbyterian Church in the U.S.A., *The Book of Common Worship: Provisional Services and Lectionary for the Christian Year* (Philadelphia: Westminster Press, 1966).

[12] United Presbyterian Church in the U.S.A., *The Book of Common Worship* (Philadelphia: The Board of Christian Education of the Presbyterian Church in the U.S.A., 1946).

[13] Consultation on Common Texts, *Common Lectionary: The Lectionary Proposed by the Consultation on Common Texts* (New York: The Church Hymnal Corporation, 1983).

[14] The Joint Liturgical Group of the United Kingdom, *The Calendar and Lectionary*, Ronald C. D. Jasper, ed. (London: Oxford University Press, 1967).

[15] Charles Mortimer Guilbert, Custodian of the Standard Book of Common Prayer of the Episcopal Church in the United States, *The Book of Common Prayer and Administration of the Sacraments and Other Rites and Ceremonies of the Church* (New York: The Church Hymnal Corporation and the Seabury Press, 1979).

Lutheran Book of Worship (1978).[16] In the meantime the United Methodist Church made an edition available in 1976,[17] while the Disciples of Christ and the United Church of Christ in the U.S.A. adopted for voluntary use the Presbyterian version. These developments were materially assisted by the publication of a consensus edition in pamphlet form by the ecumenical Consultation on Church Union (COCU),[18] representing (at that time) nine Protestant denominations seeking fuller unity. This pamphlet, incidentally, became the most widely-sought publication in the Consultation's history.

In Canada the United Church (formerly Methodist, Presbyterian and Congregational) undertook experimental use of the Roman system in a number of parishes, and the Anglican Church produced a pamphlet (1980)[19] making it available. Subsequently, that Church published the ecumenical adaptation of the Roman lectionary, *Common Lectionary*, in its *Book of Alternative Services* (1985).[20] This presumably reflected the intent of a notable resolution of the 1978 Lambeth Conference of Bishops of the Anglican Churches throughout the world which declared:

> The Conference recommends a common lectionary for the Eucharist and the Offices as a unifying factor within our Communion and ecumenically; and draws attention to the experience of those Provinces which have adopted the three year Eucharistic lectionary of the Roman Catholic Church.[21]

Thus, the Roman OLM was joined in the ecumenical scene by a series of denominational variants, perhaps as necessary as unexpected. It fell to the (North American) Consultation on Common Texts in 1978 to convene a meeting in Washington, D.C., to begin the process of harmonizing these variants with their Roman parent. Representatives of thirteen Churches in the United States and Canada attended. Special participants included the Rev. Fr. Gaston Fontaine, C.R.I.C., who had served as Secretary of *Coetus* XI, the

---

[16] Inter-Lutheran Commission on Worship, *Lutheran Book of Worship* (Minneapolis: Augsburg Publishing House and Philadelphia: Board of Publications, Lutheran Church in America, 1978).

[17] Section on Worship of the Board of Discipleship of the United Methodist Church, *Word and Table: A Basic Pattern of Sunday Worship for United Methodists* (Nashville: Abingdon Press, 1976).

[18] Commission on Worship of the Consultation on Church Union, *A Lectionary* (Princeton: Commission on Worship of the Consultation on Church Union, 1974).

[19] Anglican Church of Canada, *The Lectionary* (Toronto: The Anglican Book Centre, 1980).

[20] Anglican Church of Canada, *The Book of Alternative Services of the Anglican Church of Canada* (Toronto: Anglican Book Centre, 1985).

[21] *The Report of the Lambeth Conference 1978* (London: CIO Publishing, 1978), Resolution no. 24.

Rev. Fr. Reginald Fuller of the Episcopal Church in the U.S.A. and the Rev. Dr. James F. White, then President of the North American Academy of Liturgy.

There was general affirmation at the conference of the importance of a common table of Scripture lections based on the Roman OLM. There was also agreement on matters of calendar, psalmody, and terminology. It was recommended that the CCT convene a small working body to effect these concerns and in particular to:

> provide readings that are more completely representative of the Hebrew Bible and not simply prophetic or typological; this includes the possibility of aligning the Old Testament passage with the New Testament selection rather than with the Gospel.[22]

It is this decision, embodied in the result of this body's work (the North American Committee on Calendar and Lectionary [NACCL], chaired by Lewis Briner) which has provided much of the content of the theological discussion which has ensued and which will be described in the next section of this essay.

The working principles of NACCL were set forth by this writer in a report to the international fellowship of liturgical scholars, *Societas Liturgica*, at its meeting in Paris, France in 1981 as follows:

> 1. The basic calendar and structure of three readings presupposed by the Roman Lectionary are assumed.
>
> 2. The Gospel pericopes are assumed with only minor textual rearrangement to accomodate churches which use a Bible for liturgical use rather than a Lectionary.
>
> 3. The New Testament pericopes are largely accepted with some lengthening of pericopes and minor textual rearrangement to include contextual material such as apostolic and personal greetings and local ecclesial issues.
>
> 4. The typological choice of Old Testament pericopes has been addressed in that this has been the area of most serious criticism of the lectionary from Catholic and Protestant scholars and pastors. In response, the Committee has proposed a revision of the Roman table for a number of Sundays of the Year in each of the three cycles. The lessons are still typologically controlled by the Gospel, but in a broader way than Sunday by Sunday, in order to make possible semi-continuous reading of some significant Old Testament narratives.[23]

---

[22] "Minutes of the Consultation on Common Texts," Washington, 28-31.

[23] Horace T. Allen, Jr., "Address to *Societas Liturgica*," mimeographed, Paris: 25 Aug. 1981.

The finished product of this working group was published in 1983 as *Common Lectionary*.[24] It amounts to a limited revision and ecumenical harmonization of the several variants of OLM. It is now in widespread use in North America by Presbyterian, Disciples', Congregational, United Methodist, and United Churches. Episcopal and Lutheran Churches have authorized trial use. As noted above, the Anglican Church of Canada has published it in its *Book of Alternative Services*. As reported in the English Language Liturgical Consultation, of which ICEL is one of the constituent bodies, it is in trial use by Protestant and Anglican Churches in New Zealand, Australia, and South Africa. Indeed, it may be observed that the only place in the English-speaking world where ecumenical use of the Roman Lectionary, or its daughter, *Common Lectionary*, is not taking place is Great Britain. The reason for that has already been noted and is a matter of continuing discussion and negotiation between ELLC and CCT.

To recount this history of inter-Church conversation and adaptation, a process which in its own way as a phenomenon of the English-speaking world is a notable example of the "indigenization and adaptation of rites," is however only to touch the surface of this extraordinary ecumenical event.   *ecumenism ≈ communication*

Beneath and behind the growing consensus represented by the development and use of CL as an ecumenical adaptation of OLM, there has been the formation of extensive networks of scholarly and bureaucratic persons and offices. The CCT, for instance, now numbers in its active membership representatives from thirteen Anglican and Protestant Churches, the Polish National Catholic Church and the Roman Catholic Church through ICEL and the respective Bishops' Conferences of the U.S.A. and Canada. This must be attributed in large part to its commitment to this lectionary project. In addition, such a project has required fiscal support in addition to the "clerical" and secretarial support which ICEL has always provided. This fiscal help has been reflected in the budgets of a number of national church budgets. And, as CL has become more widely used than simply in North America, international connections have been made or reactivated as in the instance of the convocation of the English Language Liturgical Consultation in Boston, Massachusetts (1985), in Brixen, Italy (1987), and again in York, England (1989), to take up the lectionary question and to carry forward the

---

[24] Consultation on Common Texts, *Common Lectionary*.

textual agenda of the former International Consultation on English Texts which met last in London, England in 1974. The latest such development is the decision of the JLG of Great Britain to participate in CCT's continuing evaluation of CL in order to begin the process of British participation in lectionary reform.

Such networks and inter-relationships, especially in fields as highly charged as liturgy and Scripture studies, once made, are not easily dissolved or forgotten. Nor should they be. They become integral to the larger patterns of ecumenical reality which, as already noted, is already officially focussing on liturgical issues by virtue of the extensive discussion (not limited to the Western churches) of the WCC's BEM document. One might even be permitted a speculative and hopeful word to the effect that putting these networks of liturgical and lectionary consultations in place may well serve a new stage of inter-Church conversation as Orthodox Churches in North America adopt the use of English in liturgical celebration.

Looking locally rather than nationally it is also possible to discern enriching patterns of ecumenism as a result of lectionary reform. It has been the delightful experience of this writer and academician, because of national responsibilities (1970-75) in the course of introducing the Presbyterian Churches' *Worshipbook*, to travel widely and regularly for the purpose of continuing education of pastors. Throughout the continental United States, because of the congruence of OLM, its denominational variants, and more lately CL, there have mushroomed weekly clerical study groups whose purpose is corporate Scripture study for homiletical preparation. Here is a form of ecumenism which can only be described as a "pearl of great price." Here the local clergy, intimately involved with their pastoral tasks and realities, experience a unity which is vocational and biblical. Here they discover that the deepest unity of Christian people is that which is found in their common dependence on the life-giving Word of God. Here is "lavish" opening of the "richer fare" of "the table of God's word" which even the Vatican Council Fathers never anticipated, to say nothing of a seriousness about the sermon by means of which "the mysteries of the faith and the guiding principles of the Christian life are expounded from the sacred text during the course of the liturgical year."[25]

In addition, one can describe an intra-parish phenomenon of the same sort, whether in Protestant, Anglican, or Catholic contexts.

---

[25] *SC*, art. 52: ICEL, *Documents on the Liturgy, 1963-1979: Conciliar, Papal, and Curial Texts* (Collegeville, Minn.: The Liturgical Press, 1982) 1, no. 52.

That is the process whereby, also on a weekly basis, clergy, readers, musicians, and liturgy planners gather to give shape to the Lord's Day celebration(s) on the basis of the scriptural center. If anything, this is for Protestants a more novel experience, not having been propelled so totally as by Vatican II into the reform of rites. This too, in its own way, is a kind of ecumenism whereby the local people of God enter into the heart and center of the universal acclamation of the Church on the Lord's Day at ambo and altar-table.

This sort of local activity has given rise, as inevitably it must, to a vast enterprise of creating, composing and publishing of new songs, prayers, homiletical commentaries, and even rituals. Indeed, the CCT's own process of preparation of CL was more than once interrogated by interested (and occasionally nervous) publishing houses eager to know how to anticipate what would most certainly materialize in what for them is "the market."

At the same time, though more recently, a *corpus* of catechetical literature has begun to make its appearance in Protestant circles. This is probably a more unprecendented experience there than in the more Catholic and liturgical traditions. The reason for this is simply that the educational effort of Protestant congregations has historically been almost antithetical to its formal worship, being lay-led, fairly informal and often occuring at precisely the same time as public worship. Now to be able to integrate that program with what is happening in worship provides for an important new set of options whereby the liturgical life of the young *and* the older may be brought into some measure of congruence. In this regard, Protestantism, with its usually moralistic children's sermons and alternate assemblies, shares the dilemmas Catholics know well in relation to so-called "children's Masses."

Finally, the ecumenical reform of the lectionary has opened vast new vistas for the exercise of music and other arts in the liturgy. For far too long the Churches of the West have lived their musical lives in terms of fixed and largely Northern European or Roman musical repertoire. The combination of vernacular use (in place both of Latin and of Elizabethan English) and lectionary renewal, however, exploded that security and set off a wave of musical experimentation and creativity which well may be unparalleled in the history of Christian worship. It is not only that new texts are now needed to function in liturgies which are themselves new literary creations, but also that whole new systems for joining texts to tunes are needed. This has raised enormous questions of the appropriateness of various musical idioms, the relationship of so-called "sacred" to "secular" music, the singability and participatory quality of church music and most recently, the relationship of performed music of classic dimensions to the action and space of worship.

Not to be ignored, however, is the pressure lectionary reform has created explicitly for hymnic and responsory texts (and tunes). The three-year cycle of lections has uncovered the woefully inadequate biblical base of even the most extensive collections of hymnody among Protestants. When one recalls that the very origins of the hymn as such, with Isaac Watts and the Wesleys in the seventeenth and eighteenth centuries, was in order to provide richer biblical experience for singing (beyond the confines of the Psalter) one realizes how inevitable it is that to expand the lectionary's scope is also to demand a hymnological revolution, or at least, renewal.

This too is the point at which psalmody itself must enter into a new phase. Texts and tunes are now "up for grabs" as well as the development of whole systems whereby in metrical, responsory, antiphonal and through-composed ways, those 150 canonical hymns may once again make their musical way into the hearts, minds and memories of the faithful. The Church has not often had to undertake such a task. It is safe to say that no Christian Communion for whom the Psalter and song are understood to be coordinates is not hard at work in such a project of ritual creation. Thus does ICEL, to great ecumenical appreciation, steadfastly pursue its Psalter project, the first commercial published fruits of which have now appeared.

Yet another aspect of the artistic side of lectionary reform is the way in which not only musicians but also other artists (graphic, dance, environment) are enabled by the use of a renewed and enriched lection table to coordinate and integrate their efforts and creativity. In Protestant worship the choral anthem has become a predictable fact of life as the production for the whole community of a small body of largely amateur singers. Depending on the resources of the congregation this operation is more or less elaborate. The dawning use by over fifty percent of the pastors of many Protestant bodies of a lectionary table has suddenly provdied the possibility of integrating these anthem texts into the center of Sunday's proclamation, as well as the hymns to be sung by all. For many Protestant church musicians, in churches both large and small, this has revolutionized their work and opened important new lines of mutual ministry with preachers and pastors, as well as within liturgy planning groups. In turn, this possibility has provided agenda for the growing voluntary association in many denominations of musicians and other artists, for national and regional conferences and workshops and increasingly sophisticated publications. For several years, for instance, this writer provided a regular column in the Presbyterian Association of Musicians' journal *Reformed Liturgy and Music*[26] which simply suggested a number of hymns from the books currently in use which would complement the lections for the day.

One could continue piling up this sort of evidence from local, regional, and national sources. The ecumenical impact of OLM is more than impressive and certainly more than expected. Preaching, catechetics, hymnody, psalmody, other artistic forms, have all been stimulated as rarely before. Even that bastion of Protestant free-church preaching, the venerable Lyman Beecher Lectureship at Yale University, sought out this liturgist to speak in 1987 on the relationship of preaching to worship and in particular, the meaning of the use of the Roman Lectionary and its offspring in CL. As was said on that occasion, "a re-formation of the Liturgy of the Word whose basis is a Roman document must be, even for the Beecher Lectureship, news." Underneath this "news" however there lie some very "old" issues of disputed theology. Let us turn to them therefore if only to take a measure of the deep significance of lectionary reform as an ecumenical event. The same point could be put in another traditional formula: let us turn now to how it is that lectionary reform has itself alerted the Churches to the continuing dialogue between *lex orandi* and *lex credendi*.

OLM AS THEOLOGICAL EVENT

The publication in 1969 of *Ordo lectionum Missae* has brought to the surface a number of important theological questions which were at issue in the sixteenth century controversies though not as though they had never been discussed before. The importance of the present situation is that the positions are not so sharply drawn and that a generally irenic climate seems to prevail. Because these issues touch on Scripture and liturgy they penetrate deeply into ecclesiology. There is space in this essay only to speak in outline form of five:

---

[26] *Reformed Liturgy and Music*, Peter C. Bower, ed. (Louisville, Ky.: Ministry Unit on Theology & Worship of the Presbyterian Church, U.S.A.).

1. Word, Sacrament, and the Church;
2. Canon and Calendar;
3. Typology and the Hebrew Scriptures;
4. Patriarchy in Canon and Church;
5. Scripture and Tradition.

1. *Word, Sacrament, and the Church*

Catholic ecclesiology is fond of affirming the eucharistic center of the being of the Church in the world; Protestant ecclesiology is just as fond of locating the Church's *esse* in the Word of God. The liturgical practice of these communities has generally been thoroughly expressive of these convictions. Thus the Catholic churches have invariably celebrated holy communion each Lord's Day, if not daily, though not necessarily in conjunction with the preaching of the Word, and the Protestant churches have invariably gathered on the Lord's Day for preaching though on most such days neglected to celebrate the Sacrament. To be sure, neither side would consent to an unequivocal theological legitimization of this dialectic, or even, for that matter, to an absolute liturgical standoff. Catholics would contend that the reading ("proclamation") of the lessons for the day was a sufficient ministry of the Word, and Protestants would point to their monthly or quarterly eucharistic observances as evidence of their commitment to sacramental worship. But the contrasting liturgical practice surely spoke volumes to the ordinary people of God in terms of the relative importance of Word and Sacrament.

This state of affairs is all the more astonishing in the light of centuries of theological and liturgical pronouncements of the necessary complementarity of Word and Sacrament and the normative character of the ritual pairing of these events. It is noteworthy that the major figures of the sixteenth century, except for Zwingli who rejected the very concept of sacrament, agreed with the Roman Missal (if not practice) that the Lord's Day service at its fullest would always include both the reading and preaching of God's Word and the celebration of the Lord's Supper. Nevertheless, the cloudy primitive history of the uniting of these two rites at least suggests that the unity of the two has never been thoroughly understood, and perhaps just as rarely experienced. But, the liturgical norm has persisted along with its theological rationale.

A look at the rationale will be helpful in order to judge the significance of the effect on this question of OLM. The first point which is usually adduced for the regular pairing of Word and Sacrament is that they mutually inform one another in such a way as to witness to the centrality and truth of the incarnation. In Word-and-Sacrament the Word is, in the midst of the Christian assembly, "made flesh." The creative and revelatory word of Scripture and tradition is proclaimed by reading and preaching in such a way as to identify the reality and even personality of God in physical form under the species of bread and wine. Conversely, the concreteness of the sacramental elements grounds the intellectual and spiritual nature of Word in human experience. So to proclaim the Gospel both in word and concrete act, in idea and event is to witness directly, liturgically, and convincingly to the "Word made flesh" of the Fourth Gospel.

This way of thinking about the role of sacraments in incarnational theology also provides us with some very critical insights into both "Word" and "Sacrament," the two sides of this one classic rite. On the one hand, the conjunction of Word and Supper assures us that the Word of God is not coterminus with human words either the written ones in Scripture or the spoken/sung ones in proclamation. The sermon therefore is neither the "be-all" nor the "end-all" of worship. Not only does the service not end with the sermon; it is comprehensive of the sermon; indeed, the scripture-sermon event alone is truly both incomplete and also mis-leading as to the nature of the dominical presence among us. "Faith" may come by hearing (Romans 10:17), but the love of God seems to be found in communal events, such as eating and drinking together, becoming "one loaf" and sharing "one cup."

On the other hand, the conjunction of Word with Supper assures us that the Supper is not dependent on its signs alone, whatever they are, bread, wine, wafer, juice, body, blood. It is not the formula which is essential but the loving Word of promise, spoken in the only way the Church knows: a rhythm of Scripture, sermon and prayer attesting the living and revealed Word, Jesus Christ, who makes us his body and life in the communal meal: "We for our part have crossed over from death to life . . . because we love our brothers [and sisters]" (1 John 3:14).

A second point of theological rationale for the pairing of Word and Sacrament has to do with a *tertium quid* which is the timing or day for this dialectical event: the Lord's Day. As Word and Sacrament fell apart in their weekly co-incidence the reason for their Lord's Day occurrence became obscured. The interplay of creative Word and redemptive Sacrament was muted since Catholics experienced sacramental celebration on any day of the week and Protestants became used to celebrating the Lord's Day most frequently without the sacrament. For Protestants the day of the Word came to be understood in terms of a sabbath mentality and for Catholics the Mass on Sunday came to be understood in terms of an obligatory enactment of the death rather than the resurrection of Christ. To recover the connection of Word and Sacrament therefore, might mean a recovery of the resurrection, experienced weekly, in the family seder of Christians, celebrated as is only right, not only on that day which is the first day of the week but on the day which is also therefore the eighth day, the *Yom Yahweh*, the "Day of the Lord."

OLM has in a number of important ways given shape to this theological rationale for a proper and normative wedding of Word and Sacrament. Obviously its provision of such a rich selection of biblical material is bound to strengthen the biblical content of eucharistic celebrations and their homilies. More particularly, its "in course" methodology in Ordinary Time, its commitment to reading the Synoptic Gospels year by year, its use of the Fourth Gospel in the festival seasons, its use of Acts, Revelation, and the Johannine Epistles in the Easter Season, all testify to a liturgical use of the Scriptures which is also respectful of their literary form and theological assumptions. Also, the Ordinary Time respect for the Lord's Day as a festival in its own right and the setting of those days in a sequence which arises out of the Christmas-Paschal feasts and leads toward the Christ the King-Advent eschatological climax encourages that recovery of the Lord's Day as the kairotic suspension between the Lord's resurrection and return. As Karl Barth has put it:

> It is no longer the time of Easter, and it is not yet the time, i.e., the moment of His return. The community moves from the one point to the other like a ship—a constantly recurring picture—sailing over an ocean a thousand fathoms deep. The Lord Himself is in the midst, but He is also at the one point and the other, as the One who has come and the One who comes, concealed as the author and finisher of its faith (Hebrews 12:2) both in its beginning, in the event of which the Easter message speaks, and also in its end, to which this event and its own beginning refers it.[27]

In short, OLM has become for both Protestants and Catholics, perhaps for different reasons and by different dynamics, the occa-

---

[27] Karl Barth, *Church Dogmatics*, IV/1 *The Doctrine of Reconciliation*, tr. G. W. Bromiley (New York: Charles Scribners' Sons, 1956), 728.

sion for a reuniting of the liturgies of Word and Sacrament and in that way for a rediscovery of the nature of the Church as the resurrection community for whom, because of the fulfillment of the incarnation, the Word of God becomes not only flesh but life.

2. *Canon and Calendar*

We have here another dialectical pair which, as in the case of Word and Sacrament, needs a re-affirmation of their true unity. Although there are those who seriously question the integrity of any lectionary system which forces the biblical Canon into the shape of the Christian calendar. So says noted biblical scholar James A. Sanders: "the calendar tyrannizes the canon in the lectionary format as traditionally conceived . . . the canon is cut up into bits and pieces to serve the calendar."[28] There are at least two issues here. The more general question is the use of brief *pericopes* which may seem to be denuded of their context, and the more particular question (which we will take up in the next section of this essay) as to how well these pericopes are "mated" on any given Lord's Day, especially when it comes to the splicing together of "Old" and "New" Testament passages.

Here we need address only the first concern, that of the integrity of selected pericopes. One would like to think that the canon-criticism school of biblical scholarship would notice in the Roman Lectionary an impressive sensitivity to this worry. After all, it is precisely the primary assumption of this school that the biblical books must be read first of all as the products of the communities which created and received them. That is, they wish, if one understands them aright, to read the canonical documents in the context of their use . . . and that must mean, liturgical use! That is the primary intent of OLM: to make possible the responsible liturgical use of these books by "cutting" them into manageable sections, and in the case of the Epistles and Synoptic Gospels to read them in as sequential a way as possible, given the constraints of the calendar, Lent-Easter being the chief "interruption." It is a lively enough hypothesis to remember in this regard that the Synoptic Gospels and the Pauline Epistles, as well as Acts, might have been edited for just such a purpose, though the pericopes may well have been rather longer than our liturgies can permit. In this sense one could contend that the

---

[28] James A. Sanders, "Canon and Calendar: An Alternative Lectionary Proposal," in *Social Themes of the Christian Year*, Dieter T. Hesel, ed. (Philadelphia: Geneva Press, 1983), 258.

genius, not the failure, of the calendrical assumptions of both the Roman and Common Lectionaries is to begin with Christmas-Epiphany and proceed directly into the sequential lections of Ordinary Time right through to Advent (now understood as the conclusion of the "Year") with the Paschal season embedded in its midst as the center of the whole "wheel." (The Old Testament question will be discussed in the next section.)

The other observation which is essential to a consideration of Canon-Calendar is in fact similar to the matter of Word and Sacrament. It has to do with the incarnation of the Word. To read the Word – the Canon – in a temporal sequence is in another way to respect the "enfleshing" of the Word. For Protestants who have not observed the calendar, or who *have* observed the calendar but not as a lectionary system, this is a vital recovery. That is: in many "Free Churches" the Bible was read with no reference whatever to a calendar, and more recently, the introduction of a seasonal Christian calendar was not accompanied by any lectionary system. This latter situation resulted in what for Protestants was something of an unevangelical anomaly: seasonal ceremonies and symbols with no reference to biblical content. This is part of the explanation of how Advent came to be understood exclusively in terms of "getting ready for Christmas" rather than as an eschatological time.

We may say therefore that the Roman/Common Lectionary, both in its festival Sundays and its Ordinary Sundays, at least in terms of the New Testament, does justice to the demands of both Canon and Calendar. It is instructive at this point to contrast this judgement with an analysis of that other system in use in Great Britain, the two-year thematic lectionary produced by the Joint Liturgical Group. As already described, this system radically reworks the calendar so as to provide a Trinitarian division: nine Sundays before Christmas wherein the "controlling lesson" is the Old Testament pericope; Christmas to Pentecost wherein the Gospel is the controlling lesson; and Pentecost (21 to 23 Sundays) wherein the Epistle is the controlling lesson. There are two annual cycles and each Sunday is given a theological theme. This scheme replaces christological time with theological reflection both in terms of the annual trinitarian arrangement and the incarnational point of the more traditional calendar-and-lectionary, and does even greater violence to the canon by imposing on each "set" of three readings a theological "idea." This discussion is now underway as between the CCT and JLG and in the deliberations of the English Language Liturgical Consultation. Such a discussion would have been moot had not the years 1967-1969 seen the publication of both OLM and the work of JLG, and impossible had not ICEL taken so active a part in the creation and support of CCT and ELLC.

3. Typology and the Hebrew Scriptures

Here we come upon the most serious theological question yet. It was identified by the 1978 Washington, D.C. Consultation on the Roman Lectionary as the one area in which it needed careful revision. The Consultation agreed with Prof. Sanders that "the Old Testament especially is subordinated in Christian lectionaries to at best a supporting role to the New Testament passages chosen. Its main function in most lectionaries is to serve the Christian view of promise and fulfillment in which "the Old Testament is seen as promise and the New as fulfillment."[29] Fr. Fontaine in his exposition of the basic principles of the Roman Lectionary says much the same sort of thing, though not quite as explicitly: "Generally the Old Testament reading and the Gospel are harmonized. . . . In any case the Old Testament and Gospel passages shed light on one another, and such a choice makes it possible to appreciate more fully the overall unity of salvation-history."[30] A perceptive Lutheran commentator, Arland Hultgren, has observed that "The Old Testament is read generally in light of its fulfillment in Jesus Christ, so that salvation history is portrayed, but it is set forth in a punctiliar way—with the Gospel letting parts of the Old Testament shine through selectively, rather than in a semicontinuous fashion in analogy to the semicontinuous reading of the Gospels and the Epistles."[31] He continues, "Old Testament readings are frequently presented as background for the Gospel readings.[32]

This issue cuts deeply into that bedrock business of how it is that the Christian community receives the Hebrew Scriptures as the Word of God, and by implication, that red-hot business of how the Christian community continues to relate to the people of those Scriptures, the Jews.

Common Lectionary attempts to correct an overly typological or Christological use of the Hebrew Scriptures, in the context of that

---

[29] Sanders, 258.

[30] Gaston Fontaine, C.R.I.C., "Commentarium ad Ordinem Lectionum Missae," Notitiae 47 (1969), 256-282: unpublished tr., International Commission on English in the Liturgy, 7.

[31] Arland J. Hultgren, "Hermeneutical Tendencies in the Three-Year Lectionary," in Studies in Lutheran Hermeneutics, John Reumann, ed. (Philadelphia: Fortress Press, 1979), 148-149.

[32] Hultgren, 149.

Christological calendar, by opting for exactly the suggestion of the Lutheran writer, Professor Hultgren, namely, the semicontinuous reading of the Old Testament during Ordinary Time. And even in this revision a certain broad-based typology is respected in that in the year of Matthew's Gospel (Year A) the Patiarchal and Mosaic narratives are read, and in the year of Mark's Gospel (Year B) the Davidic narrative is read, and finally in the year of Luke (Year C) the Elijah-Elisha narrative is read along with selections from the twelve Minor Prophets.

It must be admitted that this whole matter is made more urgent than it has traditionally been due to the fact that in most of our Churches the setting wherein the Old Testament would have been read thoroughly and "in course," the Daily Office, has ceased to exist as a feature of the prayer life of ordinary Christians and their families. This has put unnatural pressure on the Sunday lectionary to fill in these biblical gaps, thus aggravating the question of how to do so without violating the inner integrity of the Old Testament especially.

Another historic lectionary usage helps to grasp this ongoing discussion. Those Churches which have kept alive the Daily Office in any form, such as the Episcopal, Lutheran, and Roman Catholic, have also lived more contentedly with a Sunday biblical tradition which, at least at eucharist, never included an Old Testament lection. As a result perhaps, the contemporary inclusion of such can only be countenanced as an adjunct to the Epistle-Gospel "pair." Whereas in Churches which have not followed the classic lectionary of the West there is a familiarity with the Old Testament which is quite different, even if that pericope would be the only lesson of the day! This may be said to be particularly true of Churches in the black community.

If it can be said that the Roman Lectionary, with its "typological" assumptions has opened up this question, it cannot be said with any such assurance that Common Lectionary has settled it. Common Lectionary has made one proposal, as outlined just above, which is quite debatable, but the prior question(s) cannot be avoided. Interestingly, the usefulness and acceptability of CL to the more catholic and sacramentally-oriented Churches in the English-speaking world may well turn on this theological matter. It is therefore also a matter of prime ecumenical concern. How interesting, however, that we have come to a point *again* in the discipline and liturgy of the Church in which the critical issue is that of the use of the Hebrew

Scriptures. Nor is the issue confined to hermeneutics or liturgics; one might make bold to say that as this question works itself out so also will certain other questions having to do with the Church's "mission" to the Jews, its attitude toward that Jewish institution known as "Israel," and to those other Semites who also regard themselves as children of Abraham, the Muslims. When dealing with the Bible it would seem, politics is never far away.

4. *Patriarchy in Canon and Church*

Following rapidly upon the previous political problem comes yet another: patriarchy as it dominates both Scripture and "synod." Here the virtue of OLM rapidly becomes its own Achilles' heel. Precisely insofar as lectionary reform has opened the Scriptures more lavishly for the people of God, many of those people now notice that the Scriptures, like the Church they know so well, exhibit an ambiguous if not downright negative attitude toward women in comparison with men. Further, this seems more obvious in the Old Testament than in the New and thus CL finds itself in greater trouble at this point than OLM. Thus, in a penetrating essay in Concilium, Marjorie Proctor-Smith concludes, concerning CL:

> It is evident that the lectionary's hermeneutical principles fail to take women seriously as active, significant agents in salvation history. They are regarded as adjuncts to male actors, they are important in relation to marriage; otherwise they are expendable. . . . One also notes the lectionary's tendency, when a reading seems too long, to omit the material about women, even if that material lies in the middle of the passage. . . . It could be argued, of course, that women are not terribly visible or active in the Bible itself, and perhaps the lectionary simply accurately reflects that regrettable fact. But it is the function of a lectionary precisely to be selective rather than representative.[33]

In this most pointed way Proctor-Smith raises the prior question as to the possibility that a lectionary system may either aggravate or mitigate this scriptural "problem." Her colleague, Elisabeth Schüssler-Fiorenza, has carried this argument further by asserting in *Bread Not Stone*:

> In conclusion, a feminist hermeneutic of proclamation must on the one hand insist that all texts identified as sexist or patriarchal should

---

[33] Marjorie Procter-Smith, "Images of Women in the Lectionary," in *Women—Invisible in Church and Theology*, Elisabeth Schüssler-Fiorenza and Mary Collins, eds. (Edinburgh: T. & T. Clark, 1985), 59.

not be retained in the lectionary and be proclaimed in Christian worship or catechesis. On the other hand, those texts that are identified
as transcending their patriarchal contexts and as articulating a liber-
ating vision of human freedom and wholeness should receive their
proper place in the liturgy and teaching of the churches.[34]

Once again, the Book-Church dialectic is cracked open: which
governs which? Does the Church interpret the book or does the book
judge the Church? This is the great and foundational issue of the
sixteenth century disputes. It is the issue of Scripture and Tradition. It too looms up as we consider the liturgical use of Scripture.

5. *Scripture and Tradition*

In one of its more thoroughly debated deliverances the Second
Vatican Council declared as part of the Dogmatic Constitution on
Divine Revelation (*Dei verbum*):

> Sacred Tradition and sacred Scripture, then, are bound closely to-
> gether, and communicate one with the other. For both of them, flow-
> ing out from the same divine well-spring, come together in some
> fashion to form one thing, and move towards the same goal. . . .
> Hence, both Scripture and Tradition must be accepted and honored
> with equal feelings of devotion and reverence. Sacred Tradition and
> sacred Scripture make up a single sacred deposit of the Word of
> God, which is entrusted to the Church.

To these twin realities of revelation is then added the Magisterium
as the "servant" of the Word of God. But all is enclosed in a "single
deposit of faith."[35]

So there can be no setting of Scripture and Tradition, much less
the Church's teaching office, in antipathy or antagonism to one another. One may not contradict the other; they stand together as served
by the teaching ministry of the Church. That is exactly the truth of
which the revised liturgy for Mass, with its lectionary system, is the
liturgical icon. In Word and Sacrament sacred Scripture is paired with
the sacred Tradition of eucharistic worship. In the liturgy of the Word
the Scripture is spoken both in its own words and in those of the
preacher, who serves as the local manifestation of the Magisterium.
The function of the lectionary system is to insure of the Scriptures
that they may speak with their fullest and richest integrity in order

---

[34] Elisabeth Schüssler-Fiorenza, *Bread Not Stone* (Boston: Beacon Press, 1984), 18-19.

[35] Vatican Council II, Dogmatic Constitution on Divine Revelation *Dei verbum*, 18 Nov.
1965, nos. 9-10: Austin Flannery, ed., *Vatican Council II: The Conciliar and Post Conciliar Documents*, 1981 ed. (Northport, New York: Costello Publishing Company, 1981), 755-756.

that the teaching be similarly rich and full and also in order that the eucharist, in its calendrical rhythm, will be expounded also by the proclamation of the Scriptures and the proclamation of the living Church.

Such an event certainly does not lay to rest the manifold and intricate theological questions which *Dei verbum* addresses, as did the sixteenth century, but it does set out a concrete and repeated liturgical framework as paradigm and icon for a prayerful approach thereto. To ask the liturgy to do more is to wreck it; to ask it to do less is to demean it.

CONCLUSION

If this essay has in any way successfully argued its point it may then be agreed that the publication by the Holy See in 1969 of *Ordo lectionum Missae*, as the mandate of the Second Vatican Council in the Constitution on the Liturgy, article 51, was an event of both ecumenical and theological importance for the entire Christian community. In that event, the service of the International Commission on English in the Liturgy in support of the development of *Common Lectionary* and, indeed, of the ecumenical bodies, CCT, ICET, and ELLC, has been worthy of praise and thanksgiving by all Christians. Indeed, we of the Protestant persuasion might well follow in the *Ad Limina* footsteps of our father in God, Karl Barth of Basel, in the year 1966. Reflecting on his interrogatory visit to Rome and an audience with the Holy Father he has mused for many of us:

> How would things look if Rome (without ceasing to be Rome) were one day simply to overtake us and place us in the shadows, so far as the renewing of the church through the Word and Spirit of the gospel is concerned? What if we should discover that the last are first and the first last, that the voice of the Good Shepherd should find clearer echo over there than among us?
>
> It could very well be possible that we others might find more to learn from the Roman Church than Rome for its part would have to learn from us, as we still assume with undue self-satisfaction. Is not the problem posed for the Word Council of Churches by the Roman Council (Vatican II) one of repentance and so of renewal of *our* churches, of all the non-Roman churches assembled in the World Council.[36]

So may, and must, we all pray, *Veni, Creator Spiritus*.

---

[36] Karl Barth, *Ad Limina Apostolorum: An Appraisal of Vatican II*, Keith R. Crim, tr. (Richmond, Va.: John Knox Press, 1968), 75-76, 79.

SELECTED BIBLIOGRAPHY

Horace T. Allen, Jr., Preaching in a Christian Context," being the Lyman Beecher Lectures on Preaching, Yale Divinity School, 1987. Available on cassette tapes from the School, 409 Prospect Street, New Haven, Conn. 06510.

Peter C. Bower, ed., *Handbook for the Common Lectionary*. Philadelphia: The Geneva Press, 1987.

Consultation on Common Texts, *Common Lectionary*. New York: The Church Hymnal Corporation, 1983; with an Introduction by Horace T. Allen, Jr.

Fred Craddock, et al., *Preaching the New Common Lectionary: Year B*. Nashville: Abingdon Press, 1984.

Fred Craddock, et al., *Preaching the New Common Lectionary: Year C*. Nashville: Abingdon Press, 1985.

Reginald H. Fuller, *Preaching the New Lectionary: The Word of God for the Church Today*. Collegeville, Minn.: The Liturgical Press, 1976.

Dieter T. Hessel, ed., *Social Themes of the Christian Year*. Philadelphia: The Geneva Press, 1983.

Joint Liturgical Group of the United Kingdom, Donald Gray, ed., *The Word in Season*. Norwich: The Canterbury Press, 1988.

John Reumann, ed., *Studies in Lutheran Hermeneutics*. Philadelphia:Fortress Press, 1979.

James A. Sanders, *Canon and Community: A Guide to Canonical Criticism*. Philadelphia: Fortress Press, 1984.

SOME CRITERIA FOR THE CHOICE OF SCRIPTURE TEXTS IN THE ROMAN LECTIONARY

Eileen Schuller, O.S.U.

Of all the liturgical reforms mandated by the Second Vatican Council, few were more comprehensive or influential than the call for a revision of the Lectionary. After three hundred years of reading the same Scripture passages over a one-year cycle as prescribed by the *Roman Missal* of 1570, there was now to be a major change in the biblical readings heard by all Catholics throughout the world week-by-week as they gather for Sunday liturgy. In the Constitution on the Liturgy (*Sacrosanctum Concilium*) the Council Fathers expressed their vision poetically, "The treasures of the Bible are to be opened up more lavishly, so that richer share in God's word may be provided for the faithful."[1] and pragmatically, "In sacred celebrations there is to be more reading from holy Scripture and it is to be more varied and apposite."[2]

With surprising alacrity, given the potential scope of the task, these general principles were enfleshed in a Lectionary, that is, a set Order of Readings for Sundays, weekdays, feasts of the Saints, Ritual and Votive Masses, and Masses for Various Occasions. Promulgated on 25 May 1969, the *Lectionary for Mass* was available and mandated for use by local parishes on the First Sunday of Advent 1971. A revised edition, released in January 1981 by the Congregation for the Sacraments and Divine Worship, involved only slight changes and additions.[3]

---

[1] Vatican Council II, Constitution on the Liturgy *Sacrosanctum Concilium* [hereafter, SC], 4 Dec. 1963, art. 51: ICEL, *Documents on the Liturgy, 1963-1979: Conciliar, Papal, and Curial Texts* [hereafter, DOL] (Collegeville, Minn.: The Liturgical Press, 1982) 1, no. 51.

[2] SC, art. 35: DOL 1, no. 35.

[3] The Decree of 21 January 1981 lists the major changes in this second edition: a significantly expanded introduction; the Neo-Vulgate edition as the source for the biblical references; optional readings added so that there is a three-year set of texts for the celebrations of the Holy Family, the Baptism of the Lord, Ascension, and Pentecost; lectionary references incorporated for the rites of sacraments and sacramentals and Masses which are new since 1969. In addition, there are a few minor modifications in the selection of verses for individual passages.

Today the Roman Lectionary stands as one of the permanent achievements of the vision of the Second Vatican Council. Furthermore, in a move largely unforseen in the 1960's, numerous Protestant Churches throughout the world have adopted its basic format and readings, with more or less extensive modifications.[4] In the oft-quoted words of the Methodist liturgical scholar James White, the Lectionary has become "Catholicism's greatest gift to Protestant preaching, just as Protestant biblical scholarship has given so much impetus to Catholic preaching."[5]

A relatively small number of key principles govern the formation of the Lectionary and determine its basic shape: a wide-ranging choice of biblical texts, assignment of the more important biblical passages to Sundays and solemnities, semicontinuous reading of the apostolic and gospel writers during the Sundays of Ordinary Time, selection of the Old Testament text to correlate with the gospel text during Ordinary Time, and "harmony of another kind"[6] during the seasons of Advent, Lent, and Easter. Undergirding all these more specific details are two fundamental premises: the Lectionary is composed "above all for a pastoral purpose,"[7] and finds its thematic unity in the paschal mystery—it is Christocentric.[8]

These foundational principles were succinctly articulated in the Introduction to the *Lectionary for Mass* in 1969, and further expanded and developed in the 1981 Introduction.[9] The past twenty years have seen the development of a substantial body of secondary literature

---

[4] The most significant of these revisions is that proposed by the Consultation on Common Texts (CCT) under the title *Common Lectionary* (New York: The Church Hymnal Corporation, 1983). A history of the project and its rationale is given in the Introduction (pp. 7-27). See also, James M. Schellman, "*Common Lectionary:* The Lectionary Proposal by the Consultation on Common Texts," *Ecumenical Trends* no. 11 (December 1985), 164-168.

[5] James White, *Christian Worship in Transition* (Nashville: Abingdon, 1976), 139.

[6] See The Roman Missal, *Lectionary for Mass*, 2nd Eng. ed., 1981 [hereafter, LM], Introduction, no. 67.

[7] LM, Introduction, no. 58.

[8] For an intitial statement of this principle, see Godfrey Diekmann, O.S.B., "Labores Coetuum a Studiis: De Lectionibus in Missa," *Notitiae* 11 (Nov. 1965), 334, section no. 4. This principle is not as directly stated in the Introduction to the *Lectionary for Mass* and is often overlooked or misinterpreted; see the fine discussion of William Skudlarek, *The Word in Worship: Preaching in a Liturgical Context* (Nashville: Abingdon Press, 1981), 39-40.

[9] A few other statements of principle are articulated in the Introduction but not developed at any length nor consistently applied. One example is the statement of intent in no. 64 "the parts have been selected and arranged in such a way as to take into account . . . the hermeneutical principles discovered and formulated through contemporary biblical research." Certainly the decision to assign a specific Synoptic Gospel to each year and to read it as a whole can be seen as an application of *Redaktionsgeschichte*. In other cases, however, little attention seems to have been paid to the work of biblical criticism; for example, the division of Genesis 1:1–2:2 at the Easter Vigil, rather than the complete unit to 2:4a (though the latter is the division on Tuesday, Fifth Week in Ordinary Time, Year I).

on the Lectionary, both pastoral and scholarly. Some studies are expository and explanatory, demonstrating how these principles are implemented in the Sundays of the three-year cycle;[10] other studies are more analytical and critical.[11] Probably the aspect of the Lectionary which has engendered the most sustained controversy and criticism is the way in which the Old Testament texts are chosen; a number of commentators (particularly but not exclusively biblical scholars) have pointed out the limitations and even the dangers which stem from selecting (for a major part of the Church year) only those Old Testament texts which harmonize with or somehow are related to the gospel of the day.[12]

A. SPECIFIC CRITERIA FOR CHOOSING THE READINGS

In the Introduction to the *Lectionary for Mass* (1981), following upon the statement of guiding principles of selection and organization, there is a sub-section entitled "Main Criteria Applied in Choosing and Arranging the Readings" (nos. 73-77). Here four additional criteria are listed and briefly elaborated: "(1) Reservation of some books on the basis of the liturgical seasons, (2) Length of texts, (3) Difficult texts, (4) Omission of texts."

These specific criteria have received surprisingly little attention or commentary in the literature of the last two decades. The purpose of this paper is to examine these criteria, to give some examples of how they seem to have been implemented in the Lectionary, and to suggest how they might provide a framework for enabling us to treat some sensitive pastoral questions that are currently be-

---

[10] For example: John H. Fitzsimmons, *Guide to the Lectionary* (Great Wakering, Essex: Mayhew-McCrimmon, 1981); *Proclaim the Word: The Lectionary for Mass*, Liturgy Study Text Series 8 (Washington: United States Catholic Conference, Publications Office, 1982); Ralph A. Keifer, *To Hear and To Proclaim: Introduction, Lectionary for Mass: Commentary for Musicians and Priests* (Washington: National Association of Pastoral Musicians, 1983).

[11] A series of scholarly articles on the Roman and other lectionaries make up a special issue of *Interpretation* 31 (Apr. 1977); see particularly the articles by Gerard S. Sloyan, "The Lectionary as a Context for Interpretation," 131-138, and Lloyd R. Bailey, "The Lectionary in Critical Perspective," 139-153. Arland J. Hultgren, "Hermeneutical Tendencies in the Three-Year Lectionary," in *Studies in Lutheran Hermeneutics* (Philadelphia: Fortress Press, 1975) refers specifically to the Lutheran lectionary, but his analysis is more far-reaching. For a critical questioning of some of the basic premises, particularly in the selection of Old Testament passages, see John J. Pawlikowski and James A. Wilde, *When Catholics Speak About Jews* (Chicago: Liturgy Training Publications, 1987).

[12] All of the studies mentioned above raise this issue. For a somewhat different perspective, see Joseph Jensen, "Prediction-Fulfillment in Bible and Liturgy," *Catholic Biblical Quarterly* 50 (1988), 646-662.

ing raised about the use or abuse of specific biblical readings, particularly those dealing with women and with Jews.

1. Reservation of Some Books on the Basis of the Liturgical Season

The first criterion (no. 74), the continuation of the Church's long-standing tradition of reading certain texts at fixed times in the liturgical year, is relatively straightforward and needs little comment. The Acts of the Apostles is read during the Easter season, the Gospel of John in the latter weeks of Lent and in the Easter season, and the prophet Isaiah during the Advent and Christmas seasons.

2. Length of Texts

The second criterion (no. 75), the issue of the appropriate length for a text, is much more crucial than it might seem at first glance. As we will discover shortly, it is only when we have some sense of the "normal" length of a lectionary passage that we can then suggest that a particular passage has been lengthened or shortened by a conscious decision.

In contrast to the early Christian community which read "the memoirs of the apostles or the writings of the prophets as long as there is time,"[13] the Lectionary claims to follow a *via media* in terms of length of passages. A distinction is made between narrative texts which can be longer in order to tell a complete story, especially since they "hold the people's attention," and those texts which must be shorter because of "the profundity of their teaching" (no. 75).

In terms of the Sunday lectionary, what does this *via media* look like in practice? Narratives from the Old Testament often have about ten verses, although a few are slightly longer (for example, the story of Sodom and Gomorrah, Genesis 18:20-32). When the natural story unit is longer, verses are deleted; from Genesis 15:1-18, the story of the making of the covenant with Abraham, only verses 5-12 and 17-18 are read; from the story of the call of Samuel in 1 Samuel 3:1-20 only nine verses are used; the anointing of David in 1 Samuel 16:1-13 is reduced to seven verses. An exception is made for the readings at the Easter Vigil which are all, both narrative and prophetic, longer than the norm. Thus, when the story of the sacrifice of Isaac (Genesis 22:1-18) comes on the Second Sunday of Lent B, it is edited for

---

[13] Justin Martyr, *Apologia* 67.

the sake of brevity to verses 1-2, 9-13, 15-18, while the complete passage is read at the Vigil. Non-narrative passages are usually four to eight verses, although there are a few longer texts such as Isaiah 11:1-10 and Baruch 5:1-9.

In the Synoptic Gospels, many pericopes by their very nature fall into relatively short units. Narrative passages are often ten to fifteen verses, although a few stories are longer (such as the Prodigal Son or the Emmaus story). The epistle readings are most often six or seven verses, very occasionally up to ten verses.

In about forty instances (the majority from the gospels), both a long version and an alternative shorter version are given "to suit different situations" (no. 75). Oddly enough, at times the original selection is actually rather short (for example, Matthew 4:12-23 which is only twelve verses allows the option of verses 12-17 only; 1 Thessalonians 4:13-18 allows a shorter version of verses 13-14). Although the Introduction notes specifically that "the editing of the shorter version has been carried out with great caution" (no. 75), questions can be raised about some underlying hermeneutical suppositions. For instance, apparently passages about women are deemed optional and are frequently omitted in the shorter version. If the short version is consistently read, a congregation would not hear the story of the cure of the woman with the hemmorrhage (Mark 5:25-34), the story of the woman who anoints Jesus before his Passion (Mark 14:3-9), or the list of the women who traveled with Jesus and "provided for them out of their own resources" (Luke 8:1-3).

3 & 4. *Difficult Texts and Omission of Texts*

More complicated than the issue of length are the criteria entitled "Difficult Texts" and "Omission of Texts" (nos. 76-77). The Introduction admits quite bluntly, "texts that present real difficulties are avoided for pastoral reasons" (no. 76). It goes on to explain that a difficulty may be objective (complex literary, critical, or exegetical problems) or subjective (related to the faithful's ability to understand the text). But lack of religious education and formation either on the part of the people or the pastor is not adequate reason for excluding a text. The final statement "often a difficult reading is clarified by its correlation with another in the same Mass" suggests that some difficult passages have in fact been included.

In addition to omitting a passage completely, one way to cope with difficulties is to omit only specific verses. The Roman tradition has always been willing to do this,[14] as opposed to other traditions which insist that a passage of Scripture be read in its entirety.[15] There is, however, a clear recognition of the danger "of distorting the meaning of the text or the intent and style of Scripture" (no. 77) by a cut-and-paste approach. Verses may be omitted for two reasons: (1) the text would have otherwise been unduly long; (2) the presence of a verse that "is unsuitable pastorally or that involves truly difficult problems" in a passage which is otherwise important to read.

B. Omission of Difficult Texts

Since we do not have a clear statement of how criteria three and four were implemented when it actually came to selecting specific passages, we must examine the Lectionary itself to see what "difficult" or "unsuitable" passages or verses have in fact been omitted and so arrive secondarily at some understanding of what these criteria meant to the editors. An immediate caveat is in order; the task is more difficult and less objective than it might seem at first glance. Sometimes, it is obvious or at least relatively clear why certain passages or verses are not used; these are the instances which best serve our purpose of illustrating general principles. However, in many cases a complex set of factors appear to be involved and a certain degree of subjectivity is inevitable.

1. *Omission of Difficult Texts in the Old Testament*

It is particularly in scrutinizing the choice of Old Testament texts that it is virtually impossible to determine whether a specific passage has been omitted because it is judged to be "difficult" on critical, pastoral, or theological grounds. On the one hand, it is obvious that most of the lengthy sections of legal material, ritual and sacrifical ordinances, and priestly prescriptions about purity and impurity are not judged suitable or necessary for reading in the Christian assembly; not surprisingly, only five percent of Leviticus (less than forty verses) is included in the entire Lectionary.

---

[14] Gaston Fontaine, C.R.I.C., "Commentarium ad Ordinem Lectionum Missae," *Notitiae* 47 (1969), 273, no. 42, for a list of such omissions from the *Roman Missal* of 1570. It can be noted that none of these are from the Sunday lections.

[15] The custom in many Protestant Churches of reading from the chancel bible or of having the congregation follow along in their own bibles militates against the omission of verses.

With a book like Genesis, however, it is hard to determine what specific passages have been omitted because of perceived difficulty since only approximately thirty percent of the total number of verses of Genesis are ever used in the Lectionary.[16] One can pick out certain stories that never appear, and suggest that they were omitted as obviously difficult (for example, the mating of the sons of God with the daughters of men, Genesis 6:1-4; Noah's drunkenness, Genesis 9:20-27; the thrice-told tale of a patriarch's lie about his wife, Genesis 12:10-20, Genesis 20:1-18, Genesis 26:1-14). Yet the question remains: were these stories really judged difficult, or were they omitted simply because of the constraints of space; after all, less than a third of the total book is read? Furthermore, the stories which are mentioned above do not seem particularly difficult when set beside stories which were chosen: for example, the cruel expulsion of Hagar and Ishmael into the wilderness (Genesis 21:8-21), or Esau's deceit in obtaining Jacob's blessing (Genesis 27:1-29).

If it is difficult to understand the dynamics involved in the choice of some passages and the omission of others in Genesis, recall that this is one of the Old Testament books used most extensively in the Lectionary. Only a few other biblical books (such as Isaiah) include thirty percent of their text in the Lectionary; for many books, even those which are read semicontinuously in the weekday lectionary, the figure is much less (for example, about eight percent of the total verses of Judges and Joshua, ten percent of Job, thirteen percent of Jeremiah).

The situation is further complicated since in places where the editors had extensive amounts of material at their disposal, they seem to have chosen precisely the more problematic texts in the book. Two examples can illustrate this: only five passages are selected from the entire book of Judges, but one is the harsh tale of the killing of the daughter of Jephthah in accord with her father's ill-advised vow (Judges 11:29-39);[17] many of the beautiful oracles and easily-understood stories

---

[16] Readings from Genesis are more frequent than this number might suggest, but many pericopes are read more than once (the Creation-Fall story of Genesis 1–3, the rainbow as sign of the covenant of Genesis 9, the Call of Abraham of Genesis 12, the making of a covenant with Abraham of Genesis 15, the visit at Mamre and the bargaining for Sodom and Gomorrah of Genesis 18, the sacrifice of Isaac of Genesis 22 – all these passages appear twice or three times). It is not only narrative material which is repeated; note the triple use of Isaiah 35:1-10 (or sections thereof).

[17] This is not to say the passage should not be read. For a strong argument for its inclusion in public reading and memory see Phyllis Trible, *Texts of Terror* (Philadelphia: Fortress Press, 1984), 93-116. My point is simply that it is not easy to determine how the editors of the *Lectionary* applied their criterion of "difficult" with a text such as this.

from the book of Jeremiah never appear, but we do read the rather odd prophetic sign of the soiled loincloth (Jeremiah 13:1-11).

Furthermore, as we have already noted, the Introduction does make provision for the inclusion of difficult texts when these are correlated with another text in the same Mass (no. 76). The combination of this principle with the typological reading of the prophets has lead to the inclusion of some passages which, in and of themselves, would be considered by Old Testament scholars ambiguous or abstruse; the Lectionary, of course, understands that they are to be read christologically and thus clarified by the gospel. Three examples would be: Isaiah 22:19-23, the dismissal of Shebna and the investiture of Eliakim with "the key of the House of David" (read in light of Matthew 16:13-20 "I will give to you the keys of the kingdom"); Zechariah 12:10-11, the description of mourning in the plain of Megiddo for "the one whom they have pierced" (read in combination with the prediction of the Passion in Luke 9:18-24); and (with a somewhat different relationship between the two readings) the arcane laws of Leviticus regarding leprosy, Leviticus 13:1-2, 45-46 read in conjunction with Jesus's cure of the leper, Mark 1:40-45.

2. Difficult Texts in the Gospels

The situation is, of course, very different when we turn to the Gospels. The three-year lectionary cycle was chosen precisely because it allowed the Gospels to be read in their entirety.[18] Of course, only a portion of each Gospel is covered in the Sunday cycle, approximately sixty-three percent of Mark, sixty percent of Luke, fifty-seven percent of Matthew.[19] But when we examine the Lectionary as a whole, almost all the verses of Mark appear at some point (with the exception of a few transitional phrases such as Mark 12:28a). Conspicuous by its absence from the Lectionary is Mark 13:1-23, "the Little Apocalypse"; however, it is not that this apocalyptic language and theology is judged too difficult for modern congregations, for the parallel sections from Luke are read (Luke 21:5-24; only Mark 13:21-23 does not appear at all). Since Matthew and Luke are longer Gospels, there are over one

---

[18] Although a four-year lectionary was considered which would have allowed for a much fuller reading of the Old Testament material, this was explicitly rejected by the planning committee; one primary reason was that the gospel and epistle material could be adequately covered in a three-year cycle. See Fontaine, 263; also Claude Wiener, "L'Élaboration du Lectionnaire Dominical et la Consultation de 1967," La Maison-Dieu 166 (1986), 41.

[19] These figures are taken from Jean Perron, "Les Évangiles du Dimanche," La Maison-Dieu 166 (1986), 109. The figures will vary slightly depending upon what is included in the Sunday cycle.

hundred verses of each which are not included in the Lectionary; however, in every case, the parallel text is read from one or both of the other Synoptics.

There is some evidence that difficult gospel texts are not read in the Sunday assembly, but are reserved for use on weekdays. This can only be speculation; the stated principle of presenting "the more important biblical passages" (no. 65) on Sundays and the solemnities of the Lord also comes into play. Examples of pericopes which one suspects appear only on weekdays because of their difficulty include: the story of the Gerasene Demoniac (Matthew 8:28-34 and Mark 5:1-20; the Lukan version is not read at all); the passage about the demon which leaves the house and returns with "seven other spirits more evil than himself" (Luke 11:24-26; the Matthean version is not used); the woes on the Cities of Galilee with their harsh language and the specificity of a difficult list of place names (Matthew 11:21-24, Luke 10:13-15); the complicated midrashic exegesis of Psalm 110 "the Lord said to my Lord, you are my son" (Mark 12:35-37; the two Synoptic parallels are not read at all); the statement that none of those present will see death until the return of the Son of Man (Mark 9:1, Matthew 16:28; on the Twenty-Second Sunday in Ordinary Time, Year A, the text ends at verse 27).

Finally, the Gospel of John is read in its entirety, except for some fifty verses. There is no apparent difficulty in some of the unused sections (for example, John 7:3-9, 11-24, 31-36; 12:34-43) and concern for the appropriate length of passages probably dictated their omission. It is harder to judge whether occasionally some passages may have been omitted because the editors perceived a pastoral difficulty with the harsh language about the Jews (for example the omission of John 8:43-50 "the devil is your father" and 6:70-71 "one of you is a devil"). On the other hand, some of the passages which show Jewish support for Jesus do not appear either: "there were many who did believe in him, even among the leading men" (12:42-43); "look, the whole world is running after him" (12:17-19).

3. *Omissions in the Acts of the Apostles*

The selection of readings from the Acts of the Apostles is governed by the decision to divide the book among the days (both Sundays and weekdays) of the Easter season.[20] In maintaining an

---

[20] A fair number of additional passages are found in the sanctoral cycle and Masses for Various Needs and Occasions: Acts 7:44-50, 11:27-30, 12:1-11, 13:32-39, 22:3-16, 26:19-23, 28:7-16.

appropriate length for each reading, less than one half of the book is covered; readings from the first fifteen chapters are almost continuous, whereas in the last chapters only isolated short sections appear.

Again, it is a matter of considerable guesswork to determine where and how the criterion of "difficulty" is operative. Two types of texts stand out. In contrast to "regular" miracle stories which are included (such as Peter's healing of the lame man, Acts 3:1-10), passages which deal with magicians, prophets and the use of supernatural powers are conspicuous by their absence: the lie of Ananias and Sapphira and their sudden deaths (5:1-11); the story of Simon the Magician, (8:9-13, 18-25); the prophet Agabus (11:27-30);[21] the magician Elymas (13:6-12); the sooth-sayer slave girl (16:16-21, the reading now starts at verse 22 with very little context); and the Jewish exorcists (19:11-20). The absence of one or two of these stories might be simply considered a function of the length of the book, but the consistency suggests that these texts were judged as difficult and omitted. Secondly, having noted that the Synoptic texts which treat of the midrashic interpretation of Psalm 110 appear only on weekdays, it is not surprising to find that the similar exegesis of Psalm 110 in Acts 2:34-35 is judged too difficult to include; in a somewhat similar vein, the complex intervening of psalmic texts in 13:34-41 is not part of the weekday readings.

4. *Omission of Epistle Texts*

With regard to the Epistles (and the book of Revelation could be included here also), the situation is similar to the Old Testament. The amount of material is much more extensive than what can be included in the allotted number of days (Sundays and weekdays) in the established two and three year cycle, especially since the very concise style of the Epistles and "the profundity of their teaching" (Introduction, no. 75) necessitates shorter rather than longer pericopes. Thus, a certain caution is called for in presuming that in every passage not read there is "a real difficulty" in the text itself or in contemporary pastoral understanding.[22]

The First Epistle to the Corinthians illustrates the problem. About sixty percent of the total verses are included in the Lectionary. It is

---

[21] Although this passage is not in the semicontinuous reading for weekdays, it is used as an alternate in the Mass for Those Suffering from Famine or Hunger.

[22] For an exploration of some of the factors possibly involved in the selection of epistle texts for the Sundays, see Michel Trimaille, "Les Livres du Nouveau Testament—Deuxièmes Lectures," *La Maison-Dieu* 166 (1986), 83-105.

tempting to suggest that certain passages have been omitted because they do not readily apply to modern life and sensibilities: texts about the desirability of widows not marrying (7:8-9); the situation of the unbelieving marriage partner (7:12-16); issues of circumcision and slavery (7:17-24); the demand for a woman to have her head covered in church (11:2-6); yet, other texts equally difficult in terms of their relevance for today are included: Paul's call for celibacy because "the world as we know it is passing away" (7:29-31), and detailed discussion of "food sacrificed to idols" (8:1-13 and 10:14-22). The complete omission of chapter 14 on the spiritual gifts is to be noted and is surely to be explained in terms of a perceived difficulty (particularly in light of what we have just seen of the omission of the more charismatic stories in Acts). Some texts which seem abstruse, even unintelligible to the modern reader because of the elaborate midrashic style of exegesis and allegory surprisingly are included, such as the Exodus allegory "and they all drank from the spiritual rock which followed them, and the rock was Christ" (10:1-6), and the complicated new Adam/old Adam typology (15:45-49). Other texts which would seem easily susceptible to theological misinterpretation are still selected, as 2 Corinthians 5:17-21, "God made the sinless one into sin."

C. OMISSION OF VERSES

When we turn to the fourth criterion "the omission of verses within a text" (no. 77), it is easier to draw up a concrete list of passages where this is operative. Clearly, in many cases, the constraints of length are the reason for the omission of verses. That is, a text is chosen for its fundamental importance and then verses deemed non-essential are omitted to bring the text to an accepted length, thus allowing the inclusion of many passages where the unedited biblical text would simply be too long for public proclamation. The stated principles of the Lectionary also allow for verses to be omitted because of the "pastoral unsuitability" of a particular verse/s in a passage which otherwise should be included (no. 77). However, when faced with an actual lectionary pericope with verses omitted, it is often a subjective judgment as to whether the omission is a factor of length or whether something has been judged "unsuitable." In examining a broad range of texts with verses omitted, certain general patterns emerge—although in almost every case contradictory examples can also be cited:

1. *Stage Directions*

Verses which provide "stage directions" are frequently omitted. Often these come at the beginning and end of the pericope and provide information about the setting, movement of characters to or from the scene or some other purely transitional phrases, all basically non-essential to the text. Two typical examples from the Sunday readings would be the omission of 1 Samuel 16:13b "as for Samuel, he rose and went to Ramah" and Mark 10:1 "leaving there, he came to the district of Judaea and the far side of the Jordan." However, in a number of instances in the Gospel pericopes, geographical indicators are included, even when they bear no intrinsic relationship to the story; for example, the inclusion of Mark 7:31 "Returning from the district of Tyre he went by way of Sidon toward the sea of Galilee, right through the Decapolis region"; or the odd beginning to the story of the woman taken in adultery from John 8:1 "Jesus went to the Mount of Olives. At daybreak, he appeared in the Temple again. . . ."

2. *Names of People and Places*

Omitted are lists of names of people and places which, although part of the biblical text, have little relevance when Scripture is read in a liturgical context (not to mention the very real potential for garbled pronunciation!). Typical examples would be the omission of the description of the four rivers of Paradise in Genesis 2:10-14; the formulaic lists of the peoples in the land "the Kenites, the Kenizzites, the Kadmorites, the Hittites and the Perizzites . . ." in such passages as Genesis 15:19-21; the names of the Levites present with Ezra and Nehemiah at the reading of the law (Nehemiah 8:7); the list of the names of the seven churches in Revelation 1:11b. However, other lists of names are included, perhaps because they are judged more integral to the text: Acts 2:9-11 with the list of visitors from throughout the world to Jerusalem on the first Pentecost; Luke's careful concern to specify the year of John the Baptist's preaching, when "Pontius Pilate was governor . . . Herod tetrarch of Galilee, his brother Philip . . . (Luke 3:1-2). The theological justification for some retentions is less obvious (for example, Isaiah 66:19b "to Tarshish, Put, Lud, Moschech . . .").

3. *Non-essential Information*

In addition to stage directions and lists of names and places, certain other information is judged non-essential and routinely omitted.

This includes verses or partial verses which are etymologies (Genesis 16:13-14 "this is why this well is called the well of Lahai Roi . . ."); "modernizing" or explanatory comments within a narrative (Judges 6:24b "this altar still stands at Ophrah of Abiezer" or Judges 11:39b "from this comes the custom in Israel . . ."; and unfamiliar mythological references (Job 9:13 "Rahab's minion's still lie at his feet"). At times it is less clear that the detail is simply superfluous; Micah 6:5 is omitted, presumably because of the vague references to Balaam, Shittim, and Gilgal, but a form critical approach to the passage would argue that this retelling of the events of salvation history is an essential component of the covenant lawsuit.

4. Harsh Verses

Many of the verses which are omitted are in some way harsh; they deal with the wrath of God, the slaughter of people, and condemnation of sinners. A few examples can illustrate: in the account of the covenant renewal ceremony at Shechem, Joshua 24 retells God's saving deeds, climaxing in verse 18a, "what is more, the Lord drove all these people out before us, as well as the Amorites who used to live in this country," but the Lectionary skips to verse 18b and leaves out this harsh memory of the expulsion of the original inhabitants of the land. The lengthy story of Elijah and the prophets of Baal is read continuously (1 Kings 18:20-39, 41-46) except for verse 40, "they seized them (the prophets of Baal) and Elijah took them down to the wadi Kishon and he slaughtered them there." From the New Testament, we have the chopped reading of Revelation 22:12-14, 16-17 omitting the condemnation in verse 15: "These others must stay outside: dogs, fortunetellers, and fornicators, and murderers, and idolaters, and everyone of false speech and false life." Finally, there seems to be a tendency, particularly in the Sunday lections, not to end a reading with a negative phrase. Isaiah 66:10-14, for example, remains an entirely positive text "to his servants the Lord will reveal his hand" since the final phrase is omitted "but to his enemies his fury" (Isaiah 66:14c); note that the Matthean Beatitutdes conclude at 5:12a, rather than finishing the verse with "this is how they persecuted the prophets before you."[23]

It is instructive to look closely at how the Lectionary handles a specific cluster of Old Testament texts which talk of the wrath of

---

[23] The Matthean text of the Beatitudes also ends at 5:12a all fifteen times this passage is used in Masses for Various Needs and Occasions, Proper of Saints, and Ritual Masses; in the weekday lectionary all of verse 12 is included.

God and punishment of sinners to the third and fourth generation. In the relatively short reading for Trinity Sunday from Exodus 34:4b-6, 8-9, verse 7 is omitted completely: "for thousands he maintains his kindness, forgives faults, transgression, sin; yet he lets nothing go unchecked, punishing the father's fault in the sons and in the grandsons to the third and fourth generation." In comparison, for the feast of the Sacred Heart, the complete text of Deuteronomy 7:9-10 (which scholars see as dependent on Exodus 34) is maintained: "he punishes in his own person those that hate him. He is not slow to destroy the man who hates him; he makes him work out his punishment in person," suggesting perhaps that the theological problem is not divine punishment of the sinner per se, but visiting the sins of fathers upon their sons to the third and fourth generation. Yet, in the long version of Exodus 20, verse 5 is kept: "and I punish the father's fault in the sons, the grandsons and the great-grandsons of those who hate me . . . ," suggesting that the Lectionary is not totally consistent in omissions. Finally, it should be noted that in the weekday cycle Exodus 34:5b-9 is read in toto; the editors seem more ready to include problematic verses in the weekday lectionary, even when these same verses are not read in the context of the Sunday assembly. (Just as problematic gospel passages were reserved for the weekday lectionary.)

In certain of the above passages, concern for length could be a factor, but something more is clearly involved. It is certainly far too simplistic to claim that all the harsh sayings of the Bible have been systematically excised, leaving us with a watered-down, weak, and sentimental version;[24] the many condemnatory texts in the Lectionary simply belie that charge. Yet there is some sensitivity at work on occasion, which results in the omission of certain harsh verses, particularly on Sundays or at the very end of a passage.

5. *Omission of the Unseemly*

A particular group of omissions are verses which have to do with something "unseemly," either in terms of bodily functions or sexu-

---

[24] In some circles (particularly letters to the editor), this has been a favorite critique of the Lectionary by people ready to extrapolate from an omission in a single passage to a general principle. For a few examples of many which could be compiled, see Question and Answer Section, "Who Chose the Readings for the new Missal?" *Homiletic and Pastoral Review* (Oct. 1986), 70, and R. H. Richens, "The Close of the Gregorian Era," *The Ampleforth Journal* LXXVI (1971), 59 who berates the revisers of both the Lectionary and the Missal for "a highly significant policy . . . the elimination of 'negative' themes or their transfer to Lent."

ality. Here the Lectionary exhibits what has been described as "a delicacy bordering on squeamishness."[25] Such concern seems to lie behind the careful editing of 1 Corinthians 6:13c-15a, 17-20 so as to leave out any mention of joining "to the body of a prostitute" (15b, 16); the reading of Job 7:1-4, 6-7 but not the rather gruesome description of Job's physical condition in verse 5; and the omission of references to menstruation in Ezekiel 36:17b and in the story of David and Bathsheba (2 Samuel 11:4b). On at least two occasions, eunuchs and prostitutes are simply removed from the text: in the first case, the result is a rather odd retelling of Jeremiah's deliverance from the well (Jeremiah 38:4-6, 8-10) in which his rescuer appears out of nowhere, since verse 7 which introduced "Ebed-melech, the Cushite, a eunuch attached to the palace" has been omitted. In the second case, the Lectionary reads a rather lengthy passage from the Epistle of James (2:14-24, 26) describing the place of good works, but chooses to omit totally verse 25 where the author gives a concrete example of a person "justified by her deeds," since the exemplar is "Rahab the prostitute."

On the other hand, one is occasionally surprised by the very explicit passages which are included in their entirety (for example, the reading from Isaiah 66:10-14c with its lengthy description of being suckled at Jerusalem's breasts, savoring "with delight her glorious breasts"). At times, it is difficult to be sure of the editor's intent; is the omission of Isaiah 6:2b (when the text is read on Sunday) "two to cover his face, two to cover his feet and two to fly" in the description of the seraphim an attempt to shorten the passage by removing unnecessary detail, or was the editor concerned about the euphemistic usage of "feet" in Hebrew (a subtlety largely lost anyway on a modern congregation)?

6. Omission to Highlight the Link with the Gospel

Sometimes only those verses are selected which highlight the correlation between the first reading and the gospel; this can mean that the original focus and intent of the Old Testament passage is virtually obliterated. For example, in reading only verses 7-10 of Isaiah 58, chosen so as to correlate with Matthew 5:13-16 ("your light will rise in the darkness"/"you are the light of the world") the passage becomes a general exhortation to "share bread with the hungry"

---

[25] Gerard Sloyan, 138.

and the whole contrast of a true/false fast is lost. Similarly, by reading only a few verses (4-5 and 17-19) from Jeremiah 1, verses which relate specifically to the gospel concern of "a prophet to the nations," the whole dynamic of a call narrative disappears. At times the christological typology leads to the omission of verses which are not easily applied to Jesus as, for example, in the Third Servant Song (Isaiah 49:3, 5-6) where verse 4 is omitted, "I have toiled in vain, I have exhausted myself for nothing."

D. Conclusion: Pastoral Implications

Our examination of the implementation of criteria three and four "Difficult Texts" and "Omission of Texts" has served to highlight the sometimes forgotten fact that the Roman Lectionary has never had as its goal the reading of the complete Bible. The use of Scripture in the liturgy is not solely, or even primarily, catechetical; "getting through it all" is not an end in itself. By definition, a lectionary is always "selective rather than representative—it chooses to include some texts and to exclude others."[26] Implicit in any lectionary is the acknowledgment that not every passage of Scripture either needs to be or should be read publicly in the Christian assembly.

Certainly there is reason for a healthy caution here. The decision to choose some biblical texts and omit others in the Church's official liturgical life is not without its perils. No one wants to end up with a "Reader's Digest" version of the Bible, carefully edited to offend no one. As Lloyd Bailey pointed out some years ago, there is a real danger that "those very sections which we would relegate to the state of 'obsolete' or incongruous are the ones which we need most to hear!"[27] The Roman Lectionary tradition has always sought to provide "the faithful with a knowledge of **the whole of God's word**, in a pattern suited to the purpose" (LM, Introduction no. 60, emphasis added). But, in the end, this concern for "the whole of God's word" must be balanced with the realities of the "pastoral purpose" which the Lectionary seeks to serve (no. 58), for only in this way can the Order of Readings truly correspond to "the requirements and interests of the Christian people" (no. 60).

---

[26] Marjorie Procter-Smith, "Images of Women in the Lectionary" in *Women— Invisible in Theology and Church*, Elisabeth Schüssler-Fiorenza and Mary Collins, eds., Concilium 182 (Edinburgh: T & T Clark, 1985), 52.
[27] Bailey, 149.

Although this close examination of some formative principles may seem at first glance a somewhat abstract and theoretical exercise, it does provide a useful framework for considering some of the more difficult questions which are being raised in the Church today about certain aspects of the Lectionary. Two issues immediately come to mind.

At a time of heightened concern for the presence and role of women both in society as a whole and in the Church, serious questions are being asked about why certain biblical texts about women are included in the Lectionary and others are omitted.[28] What should be our attitude toward the reading, particularly in the context of the Sunday assembly, of passages like Ephesians 5:21, "Wives should regard their husbands as they regard the Lord" or Colossians 3:18, "Wives, give way to your husbands, as you should in the Lord"? What about texts which emphasize the father over the mother (Sirach 3:2-6, 12-14), or omit all references to mothers as we "praise illustrious men" in "a list of generous men whose good works have not been forgotten" (Sirach 44:1-10, 13-14—read on the Feast of Joachim and Anne!)? Are there grounds for omitting such texts as these which are either misogynist in and of themselves or liable to be interpreted as such?[29]

Our discussion throughout this paper has demonstrated that the question cannot be belittled, nor automatically resolved by piously recalling that "all Scripture is inspired by God and can profitably be used for teaching . . ." (2 Timothy 3:16). The same principles which we have seen operative elsewhere in the Lectionary apply in this situation. There is no more necessity, or even possibility, to read aloud in the Christian assembly every text about women than there is to read every biblical text on a host of other topics. Many of the texts most negative to women are already omitted (for example, 1 Timothy 2:13, "A woman ought not to speak because Adam was formed first

---

[28] The most comprehensive examination of the issue is the article of Marjorie Procter-Smith, footnote 26. Procter-Smith based her study on the *Common Lectionary*; my forthcoming article in the *National Bulletin on Liturgy* (Ottawa: Canadian Conference of Catholic Bishops, National Liturgical Office, 1989) will examine the texts about women (both those included and those omitted) in the Sunday Roman Lectionary. Many contemporary feminist theologians and biblical scholars take as a given that "all texts identified as sexist or patriarichal should not be retained in the lectionary and be proclaimed in Christian worship or catechesis" (Elisabeth Schüssler-Fiorenza, *Bread Not Stone: The Challenge of Feminist Biblical Interpretation* (Boston: Beacon Press, 1984), 18-19.

[29] Many contemporary unofficial translations of the Lectionary have suggested substituting other passages for these texts that are offensive to many women. For example, although the standard passages are translated in the *Lectionary for the Christian People*, Gordon Lathrop and Gail Ramshaw, eds. (New York: Pueblo Publishing Company, 1986, 1987, 1988), the editors express the hope that "future lectionary revisions will choose other readings more appropriate for today's church" (A, xiv). In *An Inclusive-Language Lectionary* (published for the Co-operative Publishing Association in Atlanta: John Knox Press; New York: The Pilgrim Press; Philadelphia: The Westminster Press, 1983, 1984, 1985), alternate readings are given in the Appendix.

and Eve afterward"; Sirach 25:24, "Sin began with a woman and thanks to her we all must die") or used only on a weekday, not on Sunday (Genesis 3:16, "Your yearning shall be for your husband . . . yet he will lord it over you"). The Lectionary's own stated principle of taking into account "the hermeneutical principles discovered and formulated through contemporary biblical research" (LM Introduction, no. 64) can prove helpful. Two of the most controversial texts which are presently included in the Lectionary (Ephesians 5:21-32 and Colossians 3:12-21) belong to the specific genre of "Household Codes," which express standard Greco-Roman relationships between recognized groups: slaves/masters, wives/husbands, children/parents. At times, the Lectionary already implicitly recognizes the cultural and time-bound nature of much of this type of material; it omits entirely sections which refer to slaves and masters (for example, Colossians 3:22),[30] or leaves out the specific reference to slaves, thereby reshaping such passages into general admonitions to all Christians (1 Peter 2:20b-25). Many are asking if today the passages about women in the Household Code should not to be treated in a similar nuanced manner.

Equally serious questions have been raised in recent years about how certain texts in the Lectionary speak about the Jews. The 1974 Vatican Guidelines for Christian-Jewish Relations recognized the very real problem of biblical texts "which seem to show the Jewish people in an unfavorable light." The Guidelines bluntly name two specific areas of concern: the harsh and derogatory passages about the Pharisees (for example, the "Woes" of Matthew 23, most of which is included in either the Sunday or weekday lectionary), and the particular issue of the Passion Narratives, above all the Gospel of John (read every Good Friday) with its distinctive presentation of "the Jews" as the virtual embodiment of evil and darkness.[31] In addition, many other texts currently used in the Lectionary (including

---

[30] The slaves/masters section is read from Ephesians 6:1-9, but only in the weekday lectionary where, possibly, the semicontinuous reading alerts the reader to the specific genre of this material.

[31] In addition to these questions that the Vatican Guidelines themselves raise about particular passages, some scholars would question the whole prophecy-fulfillment approach which underlies the choice of the Old Testament reading in Ordinary Time. This is a much broader question and extends far beyond the particular concerns of this article. In addition to the critiques mentioned earlier (footnote 11, and in particular that of Pawlikowski and Wilde), see also Darrell J. Fasching, ed., *The Jewish People in Christian Preaching* (Lewiston: Edwin Mellen Press, 1984) and Eugene J. Fisher "The Roman Liturgy and Catholic Jewish Relations Since the Second Vatican Council," in *Twenty Years of Jewish-Catholic Relations*, Eugene J. Fisher, A. James Rudin, and Marc H. Tanenbaum, eds. (New York: Paulist Press, 1986), 135-155.

the speeches in Acts, "You [Jews] put to death the Author of Life," Acts 3:15, and much of Paul's discussion of the Law, "those who rely on the keeping of the Law are under a curse," Galatians 3:10) are equally open to misinterpretation. The problem is more prevasive than might seem at first glance and is exacerbated since many of the texts which provide a counterbalancing positive view of the Jews are read only on weekdays but never heard by the Sunday assembly (for instance, the rescue of the apostles before the Sanhedrin by the intervention of Gamaliel "a Pharisee . . . who was a doctor of the law and respected by the whole people" Acts 5:34-40).

Obviously our specific area of concern—the choice of Scripture readings about Jews in the Lectionary—cannot be isolated from and, in fact, must be resolved in light of the whole rethinking which is going on in Catholic theology today in terms of the relationship of the Church and the Jewish people. With regard to the use of the Scriptures in the liturgy, the issue must be approached on at least three different levels: no one change will be sufficient. Thus, scholars are exploring whether certain difficult terms can be translated in a way which better expresses their true meaning; it may be possible to continue to use certain passages if a term like *Ioudaioi* in John's Gospel can be translated other than as "the Jews."[32] Second, a highly developed level of homiletic and catechetical sensitivity is demanded from anyone preaching and teaching, especially in Holy Week, so that "homilies based on the liturgical readings will not distort their meaning, particularly when it is a question of passages which seem to show the Jewish people as such in an unfavorable light."[33] But better translations and homilies are not the whole answer; we still come down to the question: are there some texts or

---

[32] See, for instance, Malcolm Lowe, "Who were the Ioudaioi?" *Novum Testamentum* 18 (1976), 101-130. For a different translation, see Gerard Sloyan, "Israel as Warp and Woof in John's Gospel," *Face to Face: An Interreligious Bulletin* 9 (1982), 17-21. Recently the Canadian Conference of Catholic Bishops in *Passion Narratives for Holy Week* (Ottawa: CCCB, 1987) approved the decision to translate *Ioudaioi* as "Jewish leaders" or "Jewish authorities" in John 18:14, 31, 36, 38, 19:7, 12, 14, 31, 38. They point out that the words "the Jews" are used when speaking of the religious authorities or leaders of the Jews rather than the whole people: "Lest the actions of the leaders of that time be taken as an excuse for condemning all Jewish people then or now, these references have been amended to specify the one involved" (79).

[33] 1974 Vatican Guidelines, note 4. A case can be made that every biblical text can and should be read without omission and then preached upon, directly and forcefully, in such a way that the issue of anti-semitism in the New Testament is clearly faced; this line of approach is espoused by Raymond Brown, "The Passion According to John" *Worship* 49 (1975), 126-134. While perhaps an ideal solution, many are less sanguine than Brown about the reality of such a level of preaching in many of our parishes and as this article has attempted to show, such education and training is not demanded for dealing with other difficult biblical passages.

verses which must simply be omitted as "pastorally unsuitable"? Recognizing precisely the freedom which the Lectionary has always exercised in omitting particular verses, one can apply the same principles to texts about the Jews. Thus, in a recent edition of the Passion Narratives for proclamation in Holy Week, the verse of Matthew 27:25, "Let his blood be on us and on our children," is left out because "in our history, some Christians have used this line as an excuse for persecuting Jewish people or for accusing them of Christ's death."[34] Much joint discussion by Scripture scholars, liturgical experts, and participants in Jewish-Christian dialogue is still necessary to explore all the ramifications of such a decision.

Our examination of numbers 74-77 of the Introduction to the Lectionary has raised many questions. The statements in the Introduction are general and do not always yield clear and definitive answers on how to handle individual cases. But the fundamental principles are clear; flexibility and pastoral concern are essential in choosing which texts of Scripture are to be used when the Christian assembly gathers for public worship. As we ponder the future of the Lectionary, these same principles can lead us to new decisions about what biblical texts need to be included and omitted if the Church is to continue to be "nourished spiritually at the table of God's word" (LM, Introduction, no. 10).

---

[34] *Passion Narratives for Holy Week*, 79.

PROBLEMS IN THE TRANSLATION OF SCRIPTURE AS ILLUSTRATED BY ICEL'S PROJECT ON THE LITURGICAL PSALTER

Lawrence Boadt, C.S.P.

TRANSLATION: FORM AND MEANING

Language is made up of words, grouping of words in a coherent system, and expressiveness, i.e. intonation, stress, and verbal or gesturing signals. These words and their organization are symbols that communicate ideas and it requires both the speaker (or writer) and the hearer (or reader) to know the code that lies behind them. Both parties must have a mutual understanding of the basic meaning of the symbols in order to communicate. But this means that the symbol system of words that is language has no absolute meaning value, but only the relative value that comes from the shared context in which both sides accept a mutually learned meaning for the words. Even this shared context is not absolute, however, since one party may have a much deeper or broader knowledge of the range of meaning possible for a given word or word-grouping. Mutual understanding is also affected by the expansion of the lexical stock or range of meaning for given words since languages regularly coin new words or reapply common words in a new way. Teenage slang as well as scientific technical vocabulary constantly add to modern languages. Language is at root a part of a living culture whose perceptions and values, whose conceptual frameworks and usages, constantly change. Even so-called dead languages from ancient cultures have been structured and written in their age as living communication and require the decipherer to recapture the senses of the words as they were originally understood.

A language is made up of two essential components: form and meaning. They cannot be entirely divorced from each other, but are certainly distinct.[1] In most languages, the same meaning can be ex-

---

[1] See John Beekman and John Callow, *Translating the Word of God* (Grand Rapids: Zondervan, 1974), 19-25.

pressed in different ways, for example, by different grammatical constructions, or by different lexical choices (alternate vocabulary, syno-
nyms), or by a different style such as the choice of figurative metaphor
in place of a narrative description. Translation from one language to
another involves the communication of a message from one grammatical, phonological, and lexical system to another which may or may
not have the same forms available or in common use as the original
language. The receptor language, that is, the language into which the
translation is being made, must use the forms available in its own language system to express the meaning of the original language. The
translator is faced with having to know the context of the original language and its grammar, as well as the contexts of the receptor language which will best reproduce the equivalent meaning.

In light of these considerations, two of the important factors that
a translator must be especially sensitive to are (1) the *Wortfeld* of a word,
its semantic range, which may not correspond one to one with a word
in the other language; and (2) the use of idioms, expressions that are
peculiar to a language and often outside the normal grammatical form
or used in an unusual fashion. In Hebrew, for instance, the word *hesed*
is an important term for religious piety. It can mean in some contexts
what English would call "covenant obligation or duty" (Deuteronomy
7:12; 1 Samuel 20:8), in other contexts "pity" or "mercy" (Isaiah 54:8;
63:7), and in some later biblical passages, it comes to mean specifically "doing good deeds" (2 Chronicles 6:42, 35:26).[2]

No single English equivalent is available for this entire range of
meaning. In Hebrew, too, the idiomatic usage for having sexual inter-
course is to "know" a person, *yādaᶜ*, (see Genesis 4:1; Judges 19:25).[3]
It would hardly communicate the message of the original text to translate the Hebrew word into English in these contexts as "to make your
acquaintance." Idioms are particular to a language and can rarely be
transferred directly into another.[4] But idiomatic usage and differing
ranges of meaning for corresponding words are but two examples of
the problems that face translators. Some languages regularly use a
reflexive form as in English, but others normally prefer to express this
by the passive voice, as does Italian. English generally expresses the
verb "to be" in sentences while Hebrew, among others, does not. The

---

[2] See Katherine Doob Sakenfeld, *The Meaning of Hesed in the Hebrew Bible: A New Inquiry*,
vol. 17 of *Harvard Semitic Monographs*, gen. ed. F.M. Cross (Missoula, Mont.: Scholars Press, 1978).
[3] See the article, "*yadaᶜ*" in *The Theological Dictionary of the Old Testament*, eds. G. J. Bot-
terweck and H. Ringgren (Grand Rapids: Eerdmans, 1986), 5:464.
[4] See Beekman and Callow, *Translating the Word of God*, 29.

work of translation requires a knowledge of two diverse symbol systems, each with its own rules and means of expression, in order for the translator to bring across a single meaning from an original language to a target, or receptor, language.

THE TRANSLATION OF THE PSALMS AS SCRIPTURE

Because the psalms claim a sacred character as the Word of God to humans, the Church has always placed great stress on the message. The translation of biblical books requires that the translator take great care to avoid any distortion in meaning of the original Hebrew or Greek.[5] Modern critical scholarship has identified many ancient literary genres in which the psalmists expressed their thought, and these are often very important clues to understanding the intention of the ancient authors. Many centuries have passed since the psalms were composed, and it is naturally more difficult for us to understand completely their nuances of idiom or *Wortfeld* since we are far removed from the living context of the Hebrew of ancient Palestine. The identification of the literary genre of a psalm, however, assists the translator in pinpointing the purpose of a psalm and its possible function or setting in the liturgical life of Israel.[6] The same can be said of efforts to isolate rhetorical devices and stylistic techniques used by the psalmists.[7] Modern biblical scholars give considerable attention to these questions because they are essential in bridging the gap between a long-dead culture and our own twentieth century ways of thinking, no matter which modern language we speak. It has been a constant concern of the Roman Catholic Church in this century to master knowledge of the ancient world in order to understand the meaning of the sacred text through the forms in which it was expressed.[8]

---

[5] See Vatican Council II, Dogmatic Constitution on Divine Revelation *Dei verbum*, 18 Nov. 1965, no. 9: *Vatican Council II: The Conciliar and Post Conciliar Documents*, ed. Austin Flannery, O.P. (New York: Costello Publishing, 1981), 755.

[6] See Klaus Koch, *The Growth of the Biblical Tradition* (New York: Charles Scribner's Sons, 1969); and E. T. Ryder, "Form Criticism of the Old Testament," *Peake's Commentary on Holy Scripture*, gen. ed. Matthew Black (Nashville, Tenn.: Nelson, 1962), 91-95.

[7] See James Muilenburg, "Form Criticism and Beyond," *Journal of Biblical Literature* 88 (1969), 1-18; Aloysius Fitzgerald, "Hebrew Poetry," *Jerome Biblical Commentary*, ed. R. E. Brown, J. A. Fitzmyer, R. E. Murphy (Englewood Cliffs, N.J.: Prentice Hall, 1968), 238-244.

[8] Already in 1893, Pope Leo XIII called for mastery of ancient Oriental languages and ways of speech for the biblical commentator in his Encyclical *Providentissimus Deus*, 18 Nov. 1893, par. D, 2, a. Pope Pius XII, in his 1943 Encyclical *Divino Afflante Spiritu*, 30 Sept. 1943, par. 35-40, affirmed the need to study form criticism as well.

But once the message of the original is understood, it is not acceptable merely to discard the ancient Hebrew literary forms in which it is cast. The Consilium for the Implementation of the Constitution on the Liturgy, for example, issued guidelines in 1969 in its Instruction on the Translation of Liturgical Texts that address this explicitly:

> The divine word has been transmitted to us under different historical forms or literary genres and the revelation communicated by the documents cannot be entirely divorced from these forms or genres. In the case of biblical translations intended for liturgical readings, the characteristics of speech or writing are proper to different modes of communication in the sacred books and should be preserved with special accuracy.[9]

An example would be the lament psalm form. The psalm of individual lament is the most frequent type in the Psalter. It has a distinctive shape made up of at least four elements: address to God, a description of the lamentable state of the psalmist, prayerful petition for help, and a promise of praise or sacrifice.[10] A translator needs to respect this striking character of the lament psalm in order to convey fully its message which is not merely the meaning of the words, but the sense of prayer that wells up from helplessness toward the only source of strength and aid, God.

This necessary respect for the literary form of the individual psalms, however, is only the first step. But it naturally leads into the second essential consideration of a translation of the Psalter, namely, that it is poetry. This is the broadest literary category that can be identified for this body of literature and the most important. The psalms are not didactic works, or legal codes, or prophetic instruction and catechesis. Poetry has a different function from that of educational genres. It uplifts and stimulates the creative and imaginative side, it focuses on the emotional expression of faith, and it creates beauty by which we see ordinary reality in a new and more inward way. Perhaps that is why the Church has almost instinctively not chosen any psalms to be lectionary readings at the eucharist, but employed them instead as the responses to what is read. Any

---

[9] Consilium for the Implementation of the Constitution on the Liturgy, Instruction on the Translation of Liturgical Texts *Comme le prévoit* [hereafter, Instruction], 25 Jan. 1969, no. 30: ICEL, *Documents on the Liturgy, 1963-1979: Conciliar, Papal, and Curial Texts* [hereafter, DOL] (Collegeville, Minn.: The Liturgical Press, 1982) 123, no. 867.

[10] See Claus Westermann, *Praise and Lament in the Psalms* (Atlanta: John Knox, 1965, 1981), 173-194.

translation of the Psalter faces this added hurdle. It must be not only faithful to the meaning, it must try to capture that dimension of poetic beauty and artistry of language that transforms the meaning into an esthetic experience for the reader (worshiper) in the target language as well.

Still a third consideration for a translation of the psalms stems from their origins in a liturgical setting. The language of liturgy has often been thought to be so sacred that it really did not matter whether people understood all the words as long as they entered into the spirit of the prayer.[11] The reforms of the Second Vatican Council moved in a healthier direction by insisting on both intelligibility and the involvement of the community in liturgical formulations. The Constitution on the Liturgy (*Sacrosanctum Concilium*) states clearly:

> In this reform both texts and rites should be so drawn up that they express more clearly the holy things they signify and that the Christian people, as far as possible, are able to understand them with ease and to take part in the rites fully, actively, and as befits a community.[12]

The last phrase is echoed in more detail by the Consilium's Instruction on the Translation of Liturgical Texts:

> The prayer of the Church is always the prayer of some actual community, assembled here and now. It is not sufficient that a formula handed down from some other time or region be translated verbatim, even if accurately, for liturgical use. The formula translated must become the genuine prayer of the congregation and in it each of its members should be able to find and express himself or herself.[13]

This has decided implications for any psalm translation that is intended primarily for liturgical use. The translation should not focus primarily on a slavish rendition of words but on the living power of the imagery and meaning as it is expressed poetically by the original language. The translation should then focus on how this can best be conveyed in the target language in order to engage the readers or hearers with that same immediacy and contemporary expressiveness.

---

[11] See Josef A. Jungmann, S.J., *Liturgical Worship* (New York: Frederick Pustet, 1944), 140-141.
[12] Vatican Council II, Constitution on the Liturgy *Sacrosanctum Concilium*, 4 Dec. 1963, art. 21: DOL 1, no. 21.
[13] Instruction, no. 20: DOL 123, no. 857.

FORMAL EQUIVALENCE AND DYNAMIC EQUIVALENCE

All translation seeks to communicate the meaning of the original. But there has been a great deal of controversy over whether the best means to do this is by using a form that closely parallels the form in the original language, or by choosing the more ordinary or natural form of the receptor language that would express the same meaning. These two theories of translation are sometimes called "literal" and "idiomatic";[14] and sometimes "formal equivalence" and "dynamic equivalence."[15] Both sets of terms have problems. In the first pair, both words have other meanings, and there is always the danger that the idea of a literal transfer of a *form* from one language to another could be confused with the theory of literal interpretation of Scripture, where every word must be given its customary or usual meaning. The use of "equivalence" in the second pair sounds very much like exact duplication, and even the developer of the phrase has moved to "formal correspondence" as a more adequate term.[16] In the formally equivalent translation, the form of the words corresponds more closely to that of the original language than of the receptor language, while in a dynamically equivalent translation the form more closely resembles that of the receptor language.

Both types of translation seek to render accurately the meaning of the original text and at the same time make complete sense in the receptor language. Both try to capture some of the spirit of the original language and its particular literary genres. The implication of such basic goals is that the form must bend more than the content. It would not be acceptable, for example, to maintain or reproduce the Hebrew style of parallel lines by twisting the meaning of a passage. However, it may be acceptable to move away from exact parallelism in order to preserve the meaning more closely.

Formal equivalence translations generally try to preserve as far as possible the grammatical constructions of the original language, its tense and number markers, its word order, and often even consistency in word use by always reproducing a given word in the original language by the same chosen word in the receptor language, no matter how fuzzy the matching *Wortfeld*. The most slavish of formally equivalent translations would be an interlinear version, in which even the proper grammar rules and order of the receptor language are put aside

---

[14] See Beekman and Callow, 20.
[15] See Eugene Nida, *Toward a Science of Translating* (Leiden: E. J. Brill, 1964), 159.
[16] See E. Nida and C. Taber, *The Theory and Practice of Translating* (Leiden: E. J. Brill, 1969), 202.

to write a one-to-one correspondence with the grammar and word order of the original language. Sometimes, this can render idiomatic or figurative expressions so literally that the real meaning is lost. Thus most formally equivalent translations are modified types in which the translators make allowances whenever necessary to ensure that the meaning of a passage is not distorted. Puns, alliterations, similes, and metaphors require adjustments. And few modern, formally equivalent translations of the Bible attempt any word-for-word concordance of a term from the original language in all of its occurrences. Nevertheless, many critics adamantly insist that such formal equivalence rarely does justice to the full meaning of the original language, but falls back on an awkward grammar and style that create ambiguity and confusion as to the precise meaning of a passage because they are so foreign or unnatural to the way the receptor language expresses itself.[17]

A dynamic equivalence translation concentrates on making the meaning of a passage clear according to the best current linguistic forms in the receptor language. Naturalness is an important ingredient in seeking to render the spirit of the original passage. Good modern dynamic equivalent translations, such as the Good News Bible or the New English Bible, bring a freshness to their style which does not sacrifice accuracy even if some of our favorite passages sound much different from what we were used to. Martin Luther is reported to have said, "If the angel had spoken to Mary in German, he would have used the appropriate form of address; this, and no other word, is the best translation of whatever the phrase in the original may be."[18] That is, Luther himself was acutely conscious that the salutation of the angel Gabriel should be rendered according to standard German greeting formulas and not the original Greek forms if the sense of intimacy and naturalness was to be communicated. By following this approach, we avoid the risk inherent in formal equivalence of tailoring our own contemporary religious language to ancient Hebrew patterns. The influence of the King James Version over three centuries has had this effect in English. Besides filling our language with Hebraisms, it has become the source of many fundamentalist points of interpretation based on a naive word-for-word correspondence with the Hebrew original.[19]

---

[17] See Beekman and Callow, 22-24.

[18] Beekmann and Callow, 24.

[19] See Luther Weigle, "English Versions Since 1611," *Cambridge History of the Bible* (Cambridge: Cambridge University Press, 1963), 361-382, esp. 370-373.

An idiomatic approach also helps in the difficulties of matching the *Wortfeld* or lexical range of a word in one language with the roughly corresponding word in the other. A tension must always exist in this regard in the ability of a translation to go beyond what *must* be conveyed to what *may* be there also in the overtones of a word. For example, Hebrew has no strict past, present, or future verb tenses the way English does, so the rendering of verbal phrases is frequently open to a number of levels of static, transitive, or even progressive senses which the translator must decide upon for such verbal forms as the *qal* ("perfect" tense, usually with a past or present sense) and the *yiqtol* ("imperfect" tense, most often with a future or progressive sense).

DYNAMIC EQUIVALENCE AND THE PSALMS

In planning for the translation of a liturgical Psalter, it seems most natural to look for the strengths of the dynamic equivalence or idiomatic approach over the restrictiveness of the formally equivalent method. Because liturgical use demands intelligible, expressive, and poetic language, as well as the self-involvement of the worshiper with the language of the psalm, the stress in translations must fall on the linguistic forms of the receptor language to achieve them. This does not mean that everything in an idiomatic translation can be said differently from the Hebrew original form. Proper names and the major institutions of the Bible, such as temple, altar of sacrifice, etc., must be rendered literally if we are to preserve any historical connection to the life-setting of the original communicators of the biblical message. An unduly free translation such as the Cotton Patch version of Paul's Epistles,[20] which places the audience and situation of Paul's epistles in the southern United States, changes the setting so drastically that it becomes more of an analogy or accommodated version of Paul's message. It is not simply a paraphrase that highlights certain points, but a new meaning, and thus loses its right to be considered a translation at all.

On the other hand, a dynamically equivalent method can overcome many acute problem areas faced by literal renderings: archaic understandings of terms, misleading gender customs (such as the use of "sons of Israel" or "brothers" to render passages where all

---

[20] See Clarence Jordan, *The Cotton Patch Version of Paul's Epistles* (New York: Association Press, 1968).

Israelites or Christians are meant). This can be achieved by the use of poetic meter in English where a literal rendering from the Hebrew poem would sound wooden and by employing stately prose for the original epic poetry of parts of Genesis and the prophetic books which does not come across in English as poetry at all. In each of these cases, there is often no adequate way to convey the original language by a strict correspondence in modern English.

It should also be stressed that a faithful dynamic equivalent translation will respect the literary form of the original psalm so that poetry remains poetry, and laments or hymns of victory retain their characteristic genres. However, it does not mean that Hebrew rhythm or metrical accentuation can be carried over into the target language. This would result in loss of the poetic nature of the psalm in English, since the rhythm and verse accents are unique to each language.[21]

Poetry relies strongly on figurative language. The use of images of comparison or substitution is common: metonymy, synecdoche, hyperbole, metaphor, and simile. These require some care in translating so that the power and effectiveness of the image is not lost. Related to these are such devices as euphemism, symbolic action verbs ("nail the case down"), and idioms built around metaphorical actions (for example, "her eyes popped out"). In many such cases, some part is implicit or abbreviated. Thus, in a metaphor the point of comparison is often not stated. When Jesus tells the envoys of Herod to "go, tell that *fox* . . . ," he leaves the hearer to figure out that Herod is playing a cunning game with Jesus.

The Hebrew Scriptures often employ metaphorical imagery in this manner, especially in involved parables and allegorical passages, such as Ezekiel 16, 17, 19, 31, 32 and Isaiah 14. It was expected by the original writer that the audience would make the connections to contemporary events and people. In translation, these sometimes require clarification to make sense. In Ezekiel 26:2, the Hebrew says of the city of Tyre: "she is broken, the gates of nations." The King James Version added an explanatory phrase but turned the whole line into prose: "she is broken *that was* the gates of the people." This is both the challenge and the danger in the dynamically equivalent approach. In the poetic language of the Bible, much can be lost by transferring a figure or metaphor into a plainer statement even if

---

[21] Instruction, no. 37: DOL 123, no. 874, reads: "Liturgical hymns lose their proper function unless they are rendered in an appropriate verse rhythm, suitable for singing by the people. A literal translation of such texts is therefore generally out of the question."

the meaning remains faithful to the original. Thus, in Proverbs 10:17 the Hebrew poet uses the metaphor of the road in the proverb, "A path of life belongs to anyone who accepts correction; but whoever spurns a warning will go astray." But the Good News Bible loses the power of the road imagery in its prosaic rendition that eliminates the metaphor: "People who listen when they are corrected will live; but those who will not admit they are wrong are in danger."[22] These are only two illustrations of the sensitivity required in dealing with figurative language.

The ICEL Liturgical Psalter Project

Part of the original mandate of the International Commission on English in the Liturgy (ICEL) was to produce a Liturgical Psalter that would provide a faithful translation of the psalms suitable for singing or recital by cantors, choirs, and congregations.[23] Thus this Psalter's primary focus, unlike that of other available translations, would be its ability to be set easily to music. By providing such a translation oriented to the possibilities of liturgical use, this project would make it possible for complete psalms to be given full settings and would make use of through-composed music. Because familiarity with the psalms in Catholic tradition was largely confined to priests and religious who recited the daily Office, it seemed highly desirable to expose the ordinary Catholic, who only knew the psalms through the truncated form of responsorial psalms and antiphons, to a wider appreciation of the psalms in their wholeness. These ICEL psalms would be made available as an alternative where desired. They would not replace the present approved psalm translations already used in the liturgy, but supplement them.

Very specifically, therefore, behind the decision to consider a new translation rather than accept or revise an existing translation was ICEL's concern to broaden the musical possibilities, particularly in the Mass. At present, because of the requirement to use only existing translations of Scripture approved by individual conferences of bishops, mus-

---

[22] It is worth the distinction drawn between dead metaphors, that is, well-known frozen or stereotyped expressions, and live metaphors, those closely associated with real life activities that must be thought of before understanding how a speaker is using the metaphor. Thus there is a stronger moral for daily life in the live metaphor that mixes real experience with symbolic expression, as when Jesus tells his largely farming audience the parables about sowing seed or gathering in the harvest. See Beekman and Callow, 132-136.

[23] For further details about the Liturgical Psalter project, see Frederick R. McManus, "ICEL: 1963-1965," printed in the present volume. This article considers the aims of the original mandate.

cians and liturgists have been largely confined to chant modes or variations that can handle widely uneven line lengths and erratic stanza divisions. Hopefully, a new translation concerned for more regular line and stanza division could open up the psalms to modern melodic styles and allow more varied musical compositions for congregational use.

Already, the Instruction on the Translation of Liturgical Texts had encouraged the special treatment of biblical texts that were intended to be sung. It proposed that special attention be given to dividing the psalms into stanzas for easier use.[24] And for biblical verses used in antiphons, responsories, and versicles, it was suggested that they be given a different verbal form which would be more suitable for singing. The Instruction also noted that the custom of adapting biblical passages for liturgical use is found in ancient antiphonaries.[25] One of the major goals of the Liturgical Psalter project, then, was to extend this directive to the entire range of psalms used in the liturgy. For the psalms could be treated very much like hymns, with the special proviso that their full and accurate meaning be preserved by a faithful translation. At the same time, they would fulfill the mandate that "hymns very often need a new rendering made according to the musical and choral laws of the popular poetry in each language."[26]

A Sketch of the Translation Process

The project was formally inaugurated in 1978. It was approved as a pilot effort by both ICEL's Advisory Committee and Episcopal Board. An ICEL Liturgical Psalter Subcommittee of ten members was formed to oversee the work and to prepare an initial "Brief" or statement of purpose and procedures which would guide the project. It was intended from the beginning that this Brief would explain the procedures of the subcommittee and be revised regularly to keep it fully expressive of the project's goals and principles. A group of six Hebrew scholars were invited to submit translations of three or four psalms from the Easter cycle of the Mass liturgy based upon the statements in the Brief. These pilot translations were evaluated by the subcommittee and, as a result, two of the translators were asked to be a regular part of the new project.

---

[24] See Instruction, no. 36b: DOL 123, no. 873.
[25] See Instruction, no. 36: DOL 123, no. 873.
[26] See Instruction, no. 37: DOL 123, no. 874.

A working group was then formed composed of these two translators, two musicians, two liturgists, and a poet. Initially it was chaired by a staff member of the ICEL Secretariat, Mr. James Schellman.[27] This group met in May 1979 and decided upon two immediate steps: (1) a revision of the Brief incorporating insights derived from the pilot attempt at translations the previous year, and (2) the commissioning of a base translation of ten psalms from the Easter cycle by one of the translators, this effort to be critiqued by the second translator. This work was submitted to a part of the working group later that year to be reviewed for literary considerations and in order to attempt some ad hoc musical settings. A month later, the translators met again to refine the translation further, and in December the primary translator met with the poet to attempt a highly poetic and literary improvement of the base translation. The finished work was sent on to the musicians and liturgists for their comments.

At this stage, the ten psalms were presented to the full Episcopal Board of ICEL for discussion and a decision whether the project should be continued. Approval to proceed was given. The full subcommittee then met in the second half of 1980. All of these psalms were gone over and refined still further, and five were considered to be at a finished stage (Psalms 22, 23, 26, 95 and 98). These were sent to five composers who were asked to set them to music as best they could within a three-month period. The subcommittee met again in March, 1981 to review the musical settings that had been submitted and to send out the remaining five psalms (Psalms 66, 91, 100, 118 and 145) for musical composition. Shortly after this the ICEL Advisory Committee again reviewed the progress of the project and made suggestions. Finally, in late 1981, the working group put the finishing touches on a consultation booklet that included the translation of the psalms, their musical settings, liturgical comments on their use, and explanatory textual notes on the translations choices. This was sent to a wide variety of liturgical communities and professionals in the field for comment and evaluation after trial use during the Easter season of 1982.

Further work was done on these ten psalms and another thirteen in preparation for a second consultation during 1984. And the same basic procedures have been followed in work on still another

---

[27] The committee was subsequently chaired by Father Daniel Coughlin of the Advisory Committee, and currently by Sister Mary Collins, O.S.B., also a member of the Advisory Committee. Mr. Peter Finn serves as the coordinator of the project on the ICEL staff.

fifty psalms and canticles from other biblical books in the years since.[28] The method being used is thorough, involves many specialists working together, and requires that all participants follow the common set of principles enunciated in the Brief.

THE NATURE OF ICEL'S BRIEF ON THE LITURGICAL PSALTER

The Brief is divided into seven sections that cover all major aspects of the project:[29]

1. definition of the project;
2. the received tradition of liturgical use of the psalms;
3. the implications of recent psalm study;
4. textual considerations in the preparation of a liturgical psalter;
5. the scope of the present project;
6. vocabulary and language;
7. poetic and musical considerations.

The definition has been fully explored above. The second section on the received tradition emphasizes the use of the psalms in abbreviated or partial fashion in liturgical settings and the need to respect their integrity as poetry. The third section discusses the respect for ancient literary genres and the value of the dynamic equivalence approach to the present translation project. It also treats the importance of multivalent levels of meaning in words and the need for great care in rendering the Hebrew into English. Special note is made of the case of the divine name, YHWH. The fourth section deals with the critical and exegetical questions of handling the Masoretic text while balancing the later liturgical traditions that have grown up around Christian use, and at the same time respecting the nuances introduced by the Latin Vulgate translation into the Church's understanding of the psalms. The fifth section sets priorities concerning which psalms will be done first, and sketches future plans for the remainder. Section six treats questions such as the careful rendering of idioms, the power of liturgical language to create new insight, the value of repetition in Hebrew poetic style, and the value

---

[28] The twenty-three psalms that were the subject of the consultations in 1982 and 1984 were revised subsequently and published in *Psalms for All Seasons: From the ICEL Liturgical Psalter Project* (Washington, D.C.: NPM Publications, 1987).

[29] The latest published edition of the Brief is found in the *Consultation on a Liturgical Psalter* (Washington: ICEL, April 1984), 9-14.

in achieving gender-inclusive language. The final section emphasizes the need to pay close attention to the structures and literary forms of the poetic original when translating, and to musical considerations of strophe, refrains, and rhythm. Above all, the translation must be open to the settings and compositional patterns of contemporary musicians.

This Brief has been intended as a provisional statement that can be updated or amended, but also as truly *brief*. It does not argue the rationale for why the Masoretic Hebrew must be the original text source rather than the Greek Septuagint or Latin Vulgate which had formed the primary texts for Christians until modern times. It does not justify the historical-critical methods of modern biblical scholarship that place emphasis on identifying literary genres in the psalms. Nor does it try to answer all the objections that have been raised against the actual psalm translations the project has so far produced. It is a working guideline only.

It would be fair to characterize some of its emphases as more important than others to the actual process of producing a translation. I would like to treat four particular areas in more detail below. But first, three smaller points of significance can be noted. (1) The Brief has always guided the work in progress to guarantee that the basic principle of the fidelity of the translation is not lost. For example, at each stage in which further revision of wording is done, the working groups reconsult the base translation to prevent straying from the primary level of meaning and grammatical intent found in the Hebrew text. (2) A definite priority has also been given to the original Hebrew over any variations that are found in Greek or Latin versions or in traditional liturgical usage. (3) Finally, a careful balance is sought between too vulgar a translation and too high a level. This psalter must be clearly recognized as poetry that appeals to the spoken and heard language of our day.

TEXTUAL CONSIDERATIONS IN THE PSALTER PROJECT

Since the ICEL Psalter Project is intended to produce a faithful translation from the Hebrew original, special attention has been paid to the technical aspects involved in the process. Only scholars trained in biblical Hebrew and familiar with the problems of textual criticism have worked on the base translations. In each succeeding refinement of the English version, their judgments as to accuracy have guided the final decision on wording. The translator has taken the responsibility to establish what is the best or most probable text in the many cases where variant readings are available or where the text seems to be especially corrupt. The translator has also identified clearly the literary form of each psalm according to the best modern scholarship, and determined the poetic elements present: meter, stanza division, refrains, and identifications of different speakers within the text. As far as possible the translator also provides the working groups with current thinking on the age and setting of the psalm and its likely liturgical provenance in Israel. Finally the translator provides some textual and literary-critical notes on important or controversial words or images.

Since the translation has adopted a dynamic equivalence methodology, there is no attempt to duplicate either the rhythm of the Hebrew as such, or the exact parallelism that commonly occurs in the original. However, in general, the translation tries to keep as much of the flavor of the original as possible without sacrificing the freshness or concision of contemporary English poetry. Thus, the translation always respects the sense divisions of the original, such as the recurrence of refrains within a psalm, or major breaks in thought found in some psalms (for example, in Psalm 24:1-6, 7-10; or in Psalm 40:1-11, 12-18). It also respects changes in genre within a psalm (for example, Psalm 19:1-7, 8-15). The *selah* is always recognized as an interlude marker, even though its exact function has never been definitely established.[30] Even the Hebrew line divisions are respected wherever possible unless some factor of English poetic style suggests an alternative solution such as enjambment (see below under the heading, "Some Literary Considerations").

In metrical questions, Hebrew style usually follows a 3:3 beat for the two halves of a line in either psalms of praise or didactic poetry. In these cases, the standard English 3:3 meter serves well and has been employed the most often in ICEL's translations. But in lament psalms, a 3:2 meter is quite common in the Hebrew. It is usually called a "Qinah meter" from the Hebrew word for lament. ICEL has sought to reflect the limping or falling off effect of this type of beat by using English styles that create a similar effect. Staccato words or the use of hard dentals to close a line are two examples of this. Thus in Psalm 130, verses 1-2 read:

---

[30] N. H. Snaith, "Selah," *Vetus Testamentum* 2 (1952), 43-56.

From the depths I call to you,
Lord, hear my cry.
Catch the sound of my voice
raised up, pleading.

MUSICAL CONSIDERATIONS

Behind the decision to undertake the new psalter translation was the ultimate concern to broaden the musical possibilities for liturgical use of the psalms. Three factors already discussed were naturally of concern: (1) concision in language; (2) some regularity in line length; (3) division into strophes or stanzas. None of these is an absolute goal. Since meaning has the first priority, and is closely followed by the desire to retain the power and expressiveness of the key images found in the original, no attempt was made to construct completely regular lines or stanzas. In many cases, the Hebrew text itself indicates quite irregular stanzas, especially in those cases where the *selah* is inserted. Psalm 49, for example, has its first *selah* division after verse 13, but the second comes only two verses later (see also Psalms 9 and 30). Psalm 46, on the other hand, divides neatly into three nearly even stanzas by the placement of a *selah* after verses 3, 7, and 11.

The question of musical stanzas also plays a key role. On the practical level, there has been a real attempt to create regular stanzas as far as possible. By its nature, the Hebrew use of bicola and tricola in poetry often lends itself to stanza divisions of four or five lines. The ICEL translation has sought similar stanza divisions since the style of English hymn composition generally has stressed the use of stanzas which have a high degree of patterned consistency so that a single melodic unit can be repeated with each stanza. In this sense, the ICEL psalms are intended to invite hymn composers to try their hand at these psalms with as much flexibility as possible.

Finally, the concern for a translation open to musical setting requires that a number of practical factors be kept in mind:

1. the avoidance of many short vowels in a row so the meter does not weaken;

2. ending the line with a strong syllable, or no more than one weak syllable;

3. simple strong words which are easiest for musicians to employ;

4. frequent use of vowel sounds that can be stretched;

5. maintaining a sharp focus on the key concept or image to inspire the musical setting;

6. special effort to avoid uneven stanza lengths where possible;

7. keeping a rhythmic or lyrical quality to the pattern of syllables.

SOME LITERARY CONSIDERATIONS

The one factor in the Hebrew poetry of the psalms that has received the most attention is parallelism. Traditionally, parallelism has been understood to take three major forms: synonymous, in which two lines say the same thing in slightly different ways; antithetic, found largely in the Book of Proverbs, in which each line says the opposite in contrasting parallelism; and synthetic, in which there is no parallel as such between the two lines, but there is a connection of logic or consequence or additive quality.[31] Most analyses of psalm poetry since Bishop Lowth have also connected these three types to an accentual pattern in the poetic line, usually involving from two to four stresses.[32]

Since few psalms employ a significant amount of either synonymous or antithetical parallelism, the only true types, but rather are largely made up of various synthetic line pairs (or even occasionally single lines), other approaches to meter have received widespread attention in recent research. These involve either looking for rhythm based on the number of syllables per line,[33] or seeing parallelism itself as a type of balance between paired lines, often with the second half of the pair adding a new emphasis or more particular focus.[34] No consensus has emerged, and indeed one might well argue that the picture posed by Hebrew poetic studies is more confused now than it has ever been.

What is clear, however, is that parallel lines in Hebrew are not easily identified merely as two matching expressions of the same thought. The rhythm created by the use of balanced or paired lines

---

[31] See Robert Lowth, *De Sacra poësi Hebraeorium praelectiones academicae Oxonii habitae* (Oxford: University Press, 1753).

[32] See L. Alonso Schökel, *Estudios de Poética hebra* (Barcelona: J. Flors, 1963); Leopold Sabourin, *The Psalms: Their Origin and Meaning* (New York: Alba House, 1974), 25-28.

[33] See David Noel Freedman, "Acrostics and Metrics in Hebrew Poetry," *Harvard Theological Review* 65 (1972), 367-392.

[34] See James Kugel, *The Idea of Biblical Poetry: Parallelism and its History* (New Haven: Yale University Press, 1981).

had a pleasing quality that the Hebrews liked, was almost certainly felt to have a majestic and uplifting quality as religious language, and was treasured as a rich pattern for conveying nuanced variations in meaning. In short, the translator needs to recognize several possible levels of meaning in Hebrew couplets and not consider that a mechanical reproduction of paired lines always represents an adequate rendering of the text. The newer explorations of Hebrew poetry tend to strengthen the arguments of the dynamic equivalence scholars who want the emphasis in a translation to fall on the intended meaning. In the ICEL Liturgical Psalter project, for example, breaking through the limits imposed by a strictly parallel rendition is handled by a combination of means; one is the change in word structure from Hebrew to English, often by offering poetic alternatives to straight nominal patterns; a second is the use of enjambment. An example of the intentional change in word order is found in Psalm 51. Verse 3 reads in the literal version of the New American Bible (NAB):

> Have mercy on me, O God, in your goodness;
> in the greatness of your compassion wipe out my offense.

The chiastic pattern in this original (verb: adverbial clause / adverbial clause: verb, in which the sentence order is reversed) is not usual in English style.[35] The ICEL translators have dealt with this by retaining all four half-lines, but have striven for a fresher and more concise impression by accenting the power of the verbs over that of the nouns and adverbial structure:

> Have mercy, tender God,
> forget that I defied you.

The ICEL choice of "tender God" captures the combined sense of "goodness" and "greatness of compassion" in the NAB. The verb "forget" renders the NAB's "wipe out," which refers to blotting out a debt entry from an account book. Forgetting a debt conveys this same meaning. Finally, the verb "defied you" chooses a predicate form for the noun "offense." The idea of defying God comes much closer to the original Hebrew meaning of *pesha*ᶜ than does the NAB's weaker choice, "offense."

In Psalm 72:9, a literal version of the Hebrew would read:

> Before him shall bow down the *ṣiyyîm*,
> And his enemies the dust will lick.[36]

---

[35] In Hebrew, the text reads: *ḥannēnî 'ĕlōhîm kĕḥasdekâ / kĕrôb raḥămêkā mĕḥēh pĕšā'āy.*
[36] In Hebrew, the text reads: *lĕpānāyw yikre'û ṣiyyîm / wĕ'oyĕbāyw 'āpār yĕlaḥēkû.*

The New Jerusalem Bible (NJB) translates the difficult Hebrew word, *ṣiyyîm*, as "The Beast"; The New International Version (NIV) uses "The desert tribes"; and the Revised Standard Version (RSV) renders it "the foes." Even the Septuagint Greek, some two centuries before Christ, had difficulty and suggested "Ethiopians." Plainly the word is not known for certain in Hebrew although its root seems related to desert and to thirst. The ICEL translators eliminated the direct parallelism between *ṣiyyîm* in vs. 9a and "enemies" in 9b since the meaning cannot be established accurately or intelligibly at this time. Instead of duplicating the original Hebrew pattern of A:B:C: : A:B:C, ICEL used A:B:C::B:C, a very common alternate form in Hebrew parallelism, in order to preserve the sense without forcing it:

> Enemies will cower before him,
> they will lick the dust.

Since the *ṣiyyîm*, whoever or whatever they are, are the same as the enemies, the basic meaning is not lost but preserved.

The second means chosen for dealing with problems of parallelism is enjambment. Basically this involves a shift from what may be termed a synonymously parallel line to a synthetically parallel line. Instead of constructing two lines in parallel, it runs the thought of the two lines into a single sentence. Psalm 47:6, for instance, reads literally:

> God goes up to shouts of praise;
> The Lord to the sound of the trumpet.

ICEL renders this parallelism for the sake of poetic interest and concision in a combined phrase in which the cheers and trumpet blasts together welcome God:

> God ascends the mountain
> to cheers and trumpet blasts.

Beyond the simple enjambment, the word "mountain" is added, although not strictly present in the Hebrew, for the sake of clarity to a modern audience who might otherwise think God is ascending to the heavens, when the actual sense is clearly that of the divine procession up to the temple on Mt. Zion in Jerusalem.[37]

Psalm 51:7 also uses enjambment in the ICEL version for the sake of both accuracy and poetic concision. Literally, the text reads:

---

[37] For further elaboration of the theme of Zion traditions and the divine ascent of the mountain, see Richard Clifford, *The Cosmic Mountain in Canaan and the Old Testament*, vol. 4 of *Harvard Semitic Monographs*, gen. ed. F. M. Cross (Cambridge: Harvard University Press, 1972), 131-160.

> Behold in iniquity I was born,
> And in sin conceived me did my mother.[38]

The NIV chooses to translate this last difficult phrase as "Surely I have been a sinner since birth," understanding the reference to a person's own sins in life. A better sense of the original expression holds that the psalmist considers that God made him or her sinfully inclined in the very act of becoming human in birth. ICEL uses a two-line phrase that avoids the ambiguities in the NIV and makes the point clear:

> You see me for what I am,
> a sinner before my birth.

The dual expressions, "what I am" and "before my birth," retain an echo of the parallelism "born—conceived" in the original, and at the same time the "what I am" matches up with "sinner" to retain the echo of the parallelism of "iniquity—sin" in the Hebrew. Thus, the ICEL version allows "what I am" to do double-duty for both parallel expressions.

These are only two examples of how the ICEL translation attempts to remain faithful to the poetic insight of the original without losing the freshness of English poetic style which would be stifled by excessive parallelism. In all cases, the key word concepts and meaning are scrupulously maintained.

Concision is a major emphasis in modern English poetic work also, and generally the ICEL version seeks to express the Hebrew in a form as taut and concise as possible without sacrificing meaning or poetry.

Long consecrated religious words that are close to being abstractions are avoided as much as possible. Thus, instead of RSV's "I will bless the Lord at all times" in Psalm 34:2, ICEL has "I will never stop thanking God." In Psalm 27:1, RSV's "The Lord is my light and salvation" becomes "The Lord is my saving light." The principle is to render the Hebrew image as concretely as possible and as freshly as possible unless the loss of a favorite expression might seriously disturb the congregation or destroy the traditional use of a phrase in the liturgy.[39]

---

[38] The Hebrew reads: *hēn-be'awôn ḥôlāltî / ûbēḥēṭĕ' yeḥematnî 'immî.*

[39] One such example is Psalm 22, where ICEL has kept, "God, my God, why have you abandoned me?"—a rendition very similar to other standard translations.

Inclusive Language

From its beginning in 1978, the ICEL Liturgical Psalter project has been committed to the principle of achieving an English translation that employs inclusive language as far as possible. In particular this has meant that where the Hebrew uses a masculine singular pronoun to express a truth about all humans, male and female alike, a gender-neutral vocabulary has been employed in English. The same holds true for generic nouns in the Hebrew such as 'ādām, "mankind," 'îš, "man," ben 'ādām, "son of man," where these are intended to include all people. In a number of very concrete passages, an individual male is used as an example because he is male. Thus, in Psalm 128, the man described in verse 4 is clearly the ideal husband and father, with wife and children, and cannot be treated as an example of all human beings. In a further step, use of the masculine singular pronominal forms for God are also translated by gender-neutral alternatives.[40] However, some of the more common and important titles of God, such as Lord and King, are usually retained because they have significant historical and theological resonances that would be lost by developing a new terminology.

ICEL has considered this question carefully on many separate occasions because there has always been a small but consistent opposition to this usage among those who have reviewed and critiqued the completed psalm translations. The psalter subcommittee has been persuaded to take its present position, however, by numerous studies that point to the androcentric character of English usage as a reflection of the androcentric nature of a society in which women have been treated less than equally as a rule.[41]

Not only are such studies having a major impact in the United States, especially upon the women members of the Church community, but are more and more to the fore in Western Europe and in Australia and New Zealand as well. Indeed, the majority of respondents to the psalter consultation books of both 1982 and 1984 have applauded the efforts to use inclusive language.

The psalms themselves grew out of a liturgical assembly of Israel which was centered on the male. Faithful translation calls not

---

[40] See the discussion by Gail Ramshaw Schmidt, "De Divinis Nominibus: The Gender of God," *Worship* 56 (1982), 117-131.

[41] See Patricia Martin Doyle, "Women and Religion: Psychological and Cultural Implications," in *Religion and Sexism*, ed. Rosemary Radford Ruether (New York: Simon and Schuster, 1974), 15-40.

for suggesting a male-dominated community of faith, but a Christian covenant community that includes men and women. This is especially important since the ICEL translation is for use in the liturgical assembly, most often as a response psalm of the whole community to the reading of the word of God.

It can also be argued that concern for inclusive language has stimulated new ways to express the poetic power of lines, and to unlock images that had become fixed in stereotyped ways in the majority of existing translations. It creates a quite different effect from the familiar translations of the past in which strings of clauses each beginning or ending with a masculine pronoun referring to God were the most common feature. ICEL has tried new approaches, including more frequent use of the names or titles of God in sequence, more juxtaposed clauses without conjunctions, and shorter sentences in general. The translation has a sharper ring to it, sometimes criticized as harsh by listeners who cherish the older, more familiar translations. Most of all, there would hardly be a need for another translation of the psalms today that did not use inclusive language. Too many already are well-known. One of the ironies for those who criticize the ICEL version on these grounds is that the editorial committees of the older English translations (to which these critics point so proudly) are scrambling to develop inclusive language modifications of their own.[42]

CONCLUSION

This has been a brief survey of the major areas addressed by ICEL in undertaking a version of the Psalter that would be liturgically oriented and easily adaptable to musical settings on a broad scale. It was never intended that this translation would replace the standard translations available for study or proclamation in the liturgy. At this stage, the project has been in existence nearly ten years. About one-hundred psalms and canticles have been worked on and only about forty are actually completed. The pace will need to increase in the future, and ICEL is committed to finishing the Psalter as a whole by 1993. However, the measured step has not been with-

---

[42] Thus there have appeared revised versions with inclusive language of the New Testament portion of the New American Bible (New York: Catholic Book, 1986); of The New Jerusalem Bible (London: Darton, Longman & Todd, 1985; Garden City, N.Y.: Doubleday, 1985); and expected sometime soon a major revision of the Revised Standard Version.

out purpose. Just as important as the end result in total numbers of psalms completed is the careful development of the method used in arriving at these translations. And in its method the ICEL Liturgical Psalter project recognizes that poetic, musical, and liturgical expertise in collaboration can strengthen the work of Hebraists and other textual specialists and in the end lead to a stronger and more flexible translation for the liturgy.

No better ending could be suggested than a reading of two ICEL psalms as a sample of the results of this process.

PSALM 27

1 OF DAVID.
   The Lord is my saving light;
   what should I fear?
   God is my fortress;
   What should I dread?

2 When the violent come at me
   to eat me alive,
   a mob eager to kill—
   they waver, they collapse.

3 Should battalions lay siege,
   I will not fear;
   should war rage against me,
   even then I will trust.

4 One thing I ask the Lord,
   one thing I seek:
   to live in the house of God
   every day of my life;
   caught up in God's beauty,
   at prayer in the temple.

5 The Lord will hide me there,
   hide my life from attack:
   a sheltering tent above me,
   a firm rock below.

6 I am now beyond reach
   of those who besiege me.
   In the temple I will offer
   a joyful sacrifice;
   I will play and sing to God.

7 O God, listen to me;
   be gracious, answer me.
8 Deep in me a voice says,
   "Look for the face of God!"

   So I look for your face;
9 I beg you not to hide.
   Do not shut me out in anger,
   help me instead.

   Do not abandon or desert me,
   my Savior, my God.
10 If my parents rejected me,
   still God would take me in.

11 Teach me how to live;
   lead me on the right road,
   away from my enemies.
12 Do not leave me to their malice;
   liars swear against me,
   even breathing violence.

13 Yes, I shall see
   how good God is
   while I am still alive.
14 Trust in the Lord; be strong.
   Be brave. Trust in the Lord.

PSALM 95

1 Come, sing with joy to God,
   shout to our Savior, our Rock.
2 Enter God's presence with praise,
   enter with shouting and song.

3 God the Lord is great,
   over the gods like a king.
4 God cradles the depths of the earth,
   holds fast the mountain peaks.
5 God shaped the ocean and owns it,
   formed the earth by hand.

6 Come, bow down and worship,
   kneel to the Lord our maker.
7 This is our God, our shepherd;
   we are the flock led with care.

8 Listen today to God's voice:
   "Harden no heart as at Meribah,
   on that day in the desert at Massah.
9 There your people tried me,
   though they had seen my work.

10 "Forty years with that lot!
   I said: They are perverse,
   they do not accept my ways.
11 So I swore in my anger:
   They shall not enter my rest."

*INTERNATIONAL COMMISSION
ON ENGLISH IN THE LITURGY:
A QUARTER CENTURY OF SERVICE*

ICEL: THE FIRST YEARS

Frederick R. McManus

The International Commission on English in the Liturgy is defined as a joint commission of Catholic bishops' conferences. Now generally and widely known as ICEL, it was established in October 1963 at a meeting in Rome attended by bishops who themselves had been appointed for this purpose by ten conferences of bishops in countries where English is spoken.

ICEL's development and history can best be traced in the regular public reports of its program submitted to the bishops in their conferences and through them to the local Churches; in the lengthy enumeration of its translations, new texts, and other compositions and work; and in its impact on the celebration of the Roman liturgy in English. Little has been published, however, concerning its organizational beginnings and, more important, the plans and hopes of those who founded ICEL at the direction of the interested national episcopates.[1]

A reappraisal of these plans and hopes, after twenty-five years, reveals that ICEL has developed with remarkable consistency and quality of performance. Certainly it has gone beyond the vision of 1963, certainly it has had it weaknesses, but it has more than fulfilled the broad expectations of those days—and done so according to a pattern worked out as originally conceived, something unusual in Church undertakings. The defects in its work, moreover, have been slight compared to its success.

---

[1] This paper has been revised and much expanded from *ICEL: The First Years* (Washington: ICEL, 1981). In the preparation of the original article all available records of the first period of ICEL's work were examined, including correspondence, excerpts from diaries, and other materials provided by the participants in the establishment and early development of ICEL. The assistance of the living members of the first Episcopal and Advisory Committees, who read the original manuscript at that time, is gratefully acknowledged. The interpretations and judgments are of course the writer's.

FIRST STEPS

The first formal, organizational meeting of ICEL, then only the "English Liturgical Committee," took place during the second period of the Second Vatican Council—about two months before the promulgation of the Council's Constitution on the Liturgy *Sacrosanctum Concilium*. The meeting was attended by the appointed bishops and by the two English-speaking *periti* of the Conciliar Commission on the Liturgy. It took place as the revision of Chapters II-VII of the Constitution was being prepared, section by section, for submission to the conciliar Fathers. (The first chapter, as amended after debate, had been approved almost unanimously in a general congregation of the Council in 1962.)

At this point, mid-October of 1963, whatever skirmishes there might yet be over details of liturgical reform, the general principles were agreed upon. Most important for ICEL, the introduction and use of the vernacular in the Roman liturgy was to be at the discretion of the conferences of bishops, which bring together the local Churches of the respective country or region. Four of the dozen participants in the ICEL committee meetings of 1963 were themselves working day by day on the textual revision of the conciliar Constitution, and all were engaged in the daily meetings or general congregations of the Council. Thus the extent of the anticipated vernacular development motivated the discussions of the ICEL committee, but always within the context of the total reworking of the Roman rite and its future regional and cultural adaptation.

Some uncertainty remains, and must remain, about which of the founding bishops first conceived the plan for the International Commission on English in the Liturgy, a plan that had been less formally discussed at meetings in the fall of 1962, during the first period of the Council. A remote and rather indirect beginning can be traced to Archbishop Paul J. Hallinan of Atlanta, a nominee of the American bishops for election to the Conciliar Commission on the Liturgy in the first days of the Council. While the bishops of the world were gradually assembling in Rome, Archbishop Hallinan held a dinner meeting, small and informal, with a few bishops and others from English-speaking countries. At this time, however, Hallinan's concern was not so much with the use of English in liturgical celebrations—a cause to which he was already deeply committed—as with initial contacts for cooperation among English-speaking bishops in all liturgical matters.

Soon thereafter, Archbishop Hallinan and Archbishop Francis Grimshaw of Birmingham in England were brought into a friendly relationship as the English language members of the conciliar commission, together with the commission's only *peritus* from the English-speaking countries, Father Frederick McManus of The Catholic University of America, Washington. On the occasion of the many, almost daily, meetings of the conciliar commission during the 1962 period of the Council, the three naturally discussed means of collaboration among the English-speaking Churches in liturgical matters, especially the language of public worship.

The matter was brought forward by the rewriting of article 36 of the liturgical constitution during 1962. Situated in Chapter I, it reads rather restrictively—giving only instances of vernacular concessions—but is open-ended. It left the decision to the territorial bodies of bishops: whether to use, and how much to use, the respective languages, the decision subject to the confirmation or review of the Roman See. The later chapters of the Constitution completed in 1963 enlarged the instances of potential vernacular use and eliminated any language restriction at all in the case of the sacraments and services other than the eucharist.[2]

Despite subsequent, more cautionary developments, article 36 placed the responsibility for the actual translation of liturgical texts solely in the hands of the conferences of bishops. The Apostolic See, as the document plainly states and as the *acta* of the Council reveal, was to confirm the decrees of each conference concerning the extent of the use, if any, of the vernacular, but not to confirm or ratify the actual version.[3] Most important, as a matter of practical wisdom the Council suggested that the translations be approved by the conferences after they had taken counsel with the bishops of neighboring countries which employed the same language.

---

[2] Article 36 of *Sacrosanctum Concilium* was completed in 1962, while articles 54 (on the eucharist), 63 (on the other sacraments and sacramentals), 101 (on the divine office), and 113 (on music) were completed in 1963. In any case, even with regard to the eucharist, article 54 provided for unlimited extension of the vernacular, upon the proposal or request of a conference of bishops and the "consent" of the Apostolic See in accord with article 40 (on more profound liturgical adaptations). A policy of gradualism was followed, as in other aspects of the liturgical reform, and the Apostolic See gave general consent, for example, to the vernacular in the prefaces of the eucharistic prayer in April 1965 and in the entire eucharistic prayer in January 1967.

[3] See *Acta Synodalia Sacrosancti Concilii Oecumenici Vaticani II*, II (Rome: Vatican Polyglot Press, 1973), 5:526: the Conciliar Commission on the Liturgy responded negatively to the proposal (*modus*) that vernacular texts should require approval by the Apostolic See; II, 5: 45: the conciliar Fathers voted to accept this response, among others, from the commission.

This slight recommendation in the conciliar constitution is far removed from the later development of the international joint commissions, called *commissiones mixtae* in Latin, including ICEL. In 1962, when the text of article 36 was agreed upon, the Second Vatican Council could not anticipate the speed with which the conferences of bishops would embrace a full use of the mother tongues, nor, properly, did it wish to impose upon them any rigid uniformity in a given vernacular.

A COLLABORATIVE EFFORT

Toward the end of the first period of the Council in 1962, the desirability of formal liturgical collaboration among the English-speaking peoples and Churches was clearly evident to Archbishops Hallinan, Grimshaw, Guilford Clyde Young of Hobart, and Denis E. Hurley of Durban. The interest and informal discussions of these four archbishops were far from a plan of action, much less an official, representative committee of bishops, but the motivation and some expectations were already clear enough.

As Archbishop Hallinan later recounted, common liturgical texts were enthusiastically discussed by a small group of English and American bishops at a dinner meeting in December 1962. In addition to Archbishops Grimshaw and Hallinan, this included Archbishop (later Cardinal) Lawrence J. Shehan of Baltimore, Bishops Michael Hyle and Christopher Weldon from the United States, and Bishops George Beck and Edward Ellis from England. In the interim between the first two periods of the Council, in the spring of 1963, it was Archbishop Denis Hurley who took a practical initiative. Proposing a specific structure for an English language liturgical committee, he asked that Archbishops Grimshaw and Hallinan serve as conveners of the group when the conciliar Fathers would reassemble later that year. In a letter to Archbishop Grimshaw on 2 April 1963, he outlined the progress of discussions thus far and offered a specific proposal:

> Towards the end of the first session of the Council a few informal and unplanned meetings occurred in and about the coffee bars [in Saint Peter's Basilica] at which the topic of discussion was future English translations of liturgical texts. Your Grace and Archbishop Hallinan of Atlanta seemed to be the persons chiefly involved. . . .

Perhaps you have already carried your informational discussions a step or two further and evolved machinery for investigating the possibility of collaboration in the production of standardised or near standard translations. If not, may I intrude with a proposal for consideration?

1. That an English Language Liturgical Commission be set up in Rome during the next session of the Council consisting of representatives of all hierarchies of countries using English and of a select group of consultors (*periti*) with a view to investigating the possibility of making recommendations concerning the standardisation of English translations of liturgical texts, including scriptural passages used in the liturgy.

2. That the Commission consist of representatives of the following hierarchies:

Great Britain	1
Ireland	1
Canada	1
United States	6
India	2
Other Asian countries	1
Africa: East	1
West	1
Central	1
South	1
	16

(The U.S.A. has about six times as many dioceses as Great Britain or Ireland. The representation from Africa and Asia may be overloaded. Although English is used in those countries, it is by no means the predominant language of the faithful. A better representation may be 2 from Asia and 2 from Africa.)[4]

3. That 8 to 10 consultors (including Scripture men) be appointed as soon as possible.

4. That agreement be reached, if possible, on research that should be carried out before September [i.e. before the fall 1963 period of the council] and on important papers that should be prepared by members or consultors—such as—

---

[4] The proportions on the basis of Catholic population were later roughly determined in connection with the financial grants to ICEL made by ten conferences of bishops:

Australia	3.39%	Pakistan	.02%
Canada	4.46	Philippines	.51
England and Wales	6.39	Scotland	1.41
Ireland	5.11	South Africa	.52
New Zealand	.63	United States	77.36

(i) Requirements of a liturgical language (style, adaptability for public reading and for singing).

(ii) The style of singing best adapted to English.

(iii) English translations of Scripture in existence and in preparation:

    —merits and demerits;

    —copyright.

(iv) Translation procedure—committees, consultors, editors.

5. That if these proposals are in substance acceptable the representatives of British and American hierarchies (Your Grace and Archbishop Hallinan, I presume) act as a sort of unofficial convening committee and make the necessary preparation. . . .

As it happened, the preliminary steps recommended by Archbishop Hurley were not taken, and the organizational meeting which was called in the fall of 1963 included only one representative from each interested episcopate, except the United States, which sent two delegates.

In the discussions of 1962 and then in the regular meetings of 1963, the obstacles in the path of what came to be called ICEL were clearly recognized. The greatest obstacle, apart from the magnitude of the task, was thought to be the differing traditions of the several English-speaking peoples, above all the traditions on the two sides of the Atlantic. The older language and literary heritage of England and Wales, Scotland, and Ireland was and is different from that of North America, although these differences can be easily exaggerated. The vast majority, more than three-fourths of the English-speaking Catholic population, is in North America—in Canada, with its own distinct and distinguished literary tradition, and in the United States, with a literature and a cultural diversity now far removed from the English mother country. To bring these differences together in any kind of common literary expression appeared to be difficult. In the aftermath, it was ironic that some English critics of ICEL texts would deride or condemn them as Americanese, while some American critics felt that the same translations were too staid and British.

Given the conciliar mandate to reform all the Roman liturgical books—increasing greatly, as it turned out, the quantity of prayer texts to be translated—and to open up the changing Roman liturgy to cultural and regional variation, the magnitude of the undertaking was something that could not be exaggerated. And the weakness of any Roman Catholic precedents for liturgical language in English only increased the difficulties.

Archbishop Hurley had correctly adverted to the primary consideration in any style or styles of English liturgical language: "adaptability for public reading and for singing." This criterion was not at all verified, for example, in the existing hand missals with their English translations for individual use or study. The precedents for spoken and sung liturgical prayer in English, aside from hymns and a limited number of devotional texts, were not Catholic and were largely archaic in style.[5]

These questions were real, but they yielded to the common concern for a liturgical language in English of high quality and suitability for the celebration of Christian worship. Positive reasons for the project were far greater than the anticipated differences from country to country or the prospect of the extent of the work.

First of all, there was the likelihood of a much higher quality of translation from a collaborative effort that would draw upon the strengths of all the English-speaking peoples, certainly those on both sides of the Atlantic but also from Australia and New Zealand and even countries where English is only a secondary language. Next, the cultural traditions of the English-speaking peoples, in spite of all the divergencies, were sufficiently close—both in history and in contemporary relationships—to justify a concerted effort at common translation and, for that matter, common preparation of new texts and even non-verbal adaptations. Above all, English is a single language.

An appealing and, as it turned out, extremely important element was the service that the Churches in the larger nations could perform through ICEL for the smaller countries. None of these countries could be expected to mount a major enterprise of translation, and none of them—or the larger countries, for that matter—should be left at the mercy of publishing interests which up to that time had provided and owned unofficial liturgical translations. This aspect was a genuine expression of the communion of Churches and the collegiality of the episcopate.

Finally, the American participants in the initial discussions were well aware that liturgical reform was not widely supported or un-

---

[5] On English translations of the liturgy in the Catholic community after the Reformation, see J. D. Crichton, *Worship in a Hidden Church* (Dublin: Columba Press, 1988). The number of such translations prior to the twentieth century was much greater than is usually thought, although of course the texts were intended for those who would "follow" the liturgy or study it. Similarly, the many twentieth-century English versions of the missal, for example, were not translated for public speaking or singing; they varied from the elegant and the contemporary to the pedantic and slavish.

derstood in the United States—a stiuation common enough elsewhere as well. It would be important to have the balance or the influence of all the countries engaged in a cooperative effort.

BEGINNINGS OF THE EPISCOPAL COMMITTEE

As already mentioned, it was early in the second period of the
Council, in the second half of 1963, that the interested conferences
of bishops officially designated their representatives for the formal
organization of what Archbishop Hallinan called the "common market" of English liturgical translation. The initial meeting of the Episcopal Committee took place on Thursday, 17 October, at the
Venerable English College in Rome, according to a press release issued the following day. The episcopates of ten countries were interested in membership: Australia, Canada, England and Wales,
India, Ireland, New Zealand, Pakistan, Scotland, South Africa, and
the United States of America. (In 1967 the conference of bishops
of the Philippines was added as a member; other interested conferences are associate members, but with full consultation and involvement in the program.)

At the October 1963 meeting Archbishop Grimshaw was elected
chairman, with Archbishops Hallinan and Young as first and second vice chairmen. "Liturgy experts will meet regularly with the
group in Rome," it was announced, "and plans are being made to
include biblical scholars, musicologists, and stylists to ensure an English text true to the needs of public worship, as well as musical and
literary requirements. The goal is a text which will win acceptance
in those parts of the world where English is spoken." The primacy
of the "needs of public worship," even in this summary statement,
is worth noting: from the first the difference between language for
spoken and sung proclamation in the liturgical assembly and language for individual, silent reading was recognized.

Another public commentary on the projected program came a
few weeks later, when the American episcopal commission—then
called the Bishops' Commission on the Liturgical Apostolate and
chaired by Archbishop (later Cardinal) John F. Dearden of Detroit—
affirmed the commitment of the bishops of the United States to liturgical reform and, in particular, to "the concession of the vernacular
languages in the liturgy for the sake of the people's understanding,
piety, and participation." After explaining interim measures for as

extensive a use of English in the liturgy as was possible in the immediate aftermath of the conciliar constitution, this December 1963 statement offered a definition of what ICEL's role would be for the United States as well as for the Churches in other participating countries: ". . . the bishops of the United States authorized their representatives to work with an international committee; this committee will ultimately propose translations based upon the reformed rites for the consideration of the respective hierarchies of the English-speaking world."[6] Even at this point it was clear that ICEL would propose and that the conferences would dispose, each for the Churches in its own country.

Prior to the meeting on 17 October, four of the archbishops had taken the lead in making contact with the heads of other conferences or with individual bishops known to have liturgical expertise or special interest. In turn the latter had secured formal designation from the heads of their conferences. The actual decision to hold the organizational meeting was made on 2 October when the four most deeply involved members of the initial group met informally in the course of a general congregation in Saint Peter's Basilica. The four convening bishops were:

— Archbishop Hallinan, whose depth of pastoral, social, and ecumenical commitment was almost unmatched among the members of the American episcopate, although he reflected the views of only a progressive minority. He was prepared academically in the field of Church history and his religious enthusiasm, in the best sense of that term, had moved strongly in the direction of liturgical renewal soon after his ordination as bishop.[7] Along with Bishop Griffiths of New York, to be mentioned below, he was designated by the chairman of the Administrative Board of the American bishops.

— Archbishop Young of Australia was perhaps the best prepared in pastoral-liturgical matters, with a strong commitment dating back a quarter of a century and with the widest reading in the European

---

[6] The statement of the American commission was issued in Rome on 4 December 1963, the day on which the Constitution was enacted by the Council. For the full text of the statement, with a commentary, see Frederick R. McManus, ed., *Thirty Years of Liturgical Renewal: Statements of the Bishops' Committee on the Liturgy* (Washington: Office of Publishing and Promotion Services, United States Catholic Conference, 1987), 21-24.

At a meeting on 16 November 1963, the American bishops had agreed to employ the vernacular concessions in general (by vote of 130 to 5), to authorize the American commission to prepare interim translations (vote of 127 to 7), and to participate in ICEL (vote of 126 to 3). See *Thirty Years of Liturgical Renewal*, 11.

[7] Thomas J. Shelly, *Paul J. Hallinan, First Archbishop of Atlanta* (Wilmington, Del.: Michael Glazier, 1989); Paul J. Hallinan, *Days of Hope and Promise: The Writings and Speeches of Paul J. Hallinan, Archbishop of Atlanta*, edited by Vincent A. Yzermans (Collegeville, Minn.: The Liturgical Press, 1973).

literature on the liturgy and the liturgical movement as well as on ecclesiology and contemporary theology in general. A newly ordained priest at the beginning of World War II, he had gone as a liturgical pilgrim to Saint John's Abbey, Collegeville, Minnesota, the heart and head of such renewal in North America. His liturgical strengths can be traced to the summer spent there under the tutelage of Godfrey Diekmann, O.S.B.[8]

— Archbishop Hurley, like Hallinan a bishop of the greatest breadth of ecclesial and social concern and already well known outside South Africa, had taken a strong and supporting line when the Pontifical Central Preparatory Commission reviewed the draft of the liturgical constitution in the spring preceding the opening of the Council. At the time of ICEL's foundation, he was also playing an important role as a member of the Conciliar Commission on Seminaries, Studies, and Catholic Education.

— Archbishop Grimshaw had had direct experience as a translator and editor of a bilingual ritual for England and Wales prior to the Council. This valuable background sometimes made it difficult for him to accept the judgments of others concerning liturgical translation. On several occasions Grimshaw provided the generous hospitality of the Venerable English College for meetings of the Episcopal Committee and he served as its first chairman, as already noted.

In retrospect, it is possible to characterize the distinctive contributions of each of the four archbishops. Hallinan was the enthusiastic and effective activist, anxious to achieve unity and wide involvement in the common enterprise, which he envisioned as important in itself and as a sign of the communion of Churches in the post-conciliar period. Hurley had and has similar strengths and breadth of vision. Seeing the liturgy as the pre-eminent work of the Church but only as the center of its multifold mission in the world, he prepared for ICEL the concrete organizational recommendations already described and also, as a part of his constant involvement, the formal mandate to be quoted later. At a somewhat lower level of active involvement, Young combined lengthy pastoral experience as a bishop with personal knowledge of the length and breadth of the liturgical movement, its history and theology. And Grimshaw, whose service to ICEL was cut short by an early death, provided assurance of the support of the English-Welsh hierarchy and a certain

---

[8] W. T. Southerwood, *The Wisdom of Guilford Young* (George Town, Tasmania: 1989), includes hundreds of Young's addresses and homilies.

leadership in the liturgical collaboration of that conference of bishops with those of Ireland and Scotland.

During the formative period of ICEL in 1963 and 1964, two *periti* from the English-speaking world participated in the meetings of the Episcopal Committee. They were Father McManus and Father Godfrey Diekmann, O.S.B., of Saint John's Abbey, the distinguished editor of *Worship,* who had joined the Council's liturgical commission in the fall of 1963 as its second English-speaking *peritus.*[9] With academic backgrounds in sacramental theology and patristics on the one hand and in canon law on the other, the two provided pastoral and liturgical expertise from their own experience and from their intimate involvement in both the preparatory and conciliar liturgical commissions. Both had participated, moreover, in the international meetings of liturgical scholars in the 1950s which laid some of the groundwork for the Constitution on the Liturgy.

The other members of the Episcopal Committee, as initially constituted, were the following:

— Archbishop (later Cardinal) Gordon J. Gray of Saint Andrew's and Edinburgh, the head of the Scottish episcopate, who had an academic background in the field of English.

— Archbishop Joseph Walsh of Tuam, who had served as a consultor in the Pontifical Preparatory Commission on the Liturgy and was perhaps the member of the Irish episcopate most interested in liturgical renewal.

— Archbishop Michael O'Neill of Regina, who brought extensive pastoral experience and who headed the English language liturgical commission for the Canadian conference of bishops.

— Archbishop (later Cardinal) Joseph Cordeiro of Karachi, head of the small conference of bishops of Pakistan, who combined broad concern with all the major issues of the Council and complete openness to liturgical development.

— Bishop Leonard Raymond of Allahabad (later Archbishop of Nagpur), designated by the president of the Indian conference of bishops, Cardinal Valerian Gracias of Bombay, to represent the liturgical interests of the many English-speaking Catholics of India.

— Bishop Owen Snedden, auxiliary to the Archbishop of Wellington. Named to ICEL by Archbishop (later Cardinal) Peter McKeefrey

---

[9] A biography of Diekmann by H. Kathleen Hughes, R.S.C.J., will be published in 1990 by The Liturgical Press, Collegeville, Minn.

of Wellington on behalf of the small conference of bishops of New Zealand, he was a man with wide pastoral experience and total commitment to the purposes of the project.

— Bishop James H. Griffiths, auxiliary to the Archbishop of New York in the latter's capacity as military vicar. The active secretary of the American Bishops' Commission on the Liturgical Apostolate since 1958, he had played an important role in the publication of the American bilingual ritual and in the promotion of diocesan liturgical commissions in the United States, while also serving as liaison between the bishops and The Liturgical Conference of North America.[10]

Because this historical account is confined to the first years of ICEL, nothing will be said about the successors to the original members of the Episcopal Committee, except for the very first period.

Bishops Griffiths died in the early summer of 1964; he was replaced in the ICEL Episcopal Committee for a short period by Bishop William Connare of Greensburg and later by Bishop John Dougherty, auxiliary to the Archbishop of Newark. After Archbishop Hallinan's death in 1968, Bishop Dougherty continued as the single representative of the United States National Conference of Catholic Bishops. Although never a diocesan bishop, he had a breadth of ecclesial concerns similar to Hallinan's and was one of the American bishops known for deep involvement in the peace movement. A biblical scholar, writer, and broadcast preacher, he served also as president of Seton Hall University in New Jersey.

In March 1965 Archbishop Grimshaw died, and Archbishop Hallinan succeeded him as chairman until the resumption of meetings of the Episcopal Committee in Rome in the following fall. At that time Archbishop Gordon Gray was elected chairman, with Archbishop Young and Archbishop George P. Dwyer of Birmingham as first and second vice chairmen. Archbishop Dwyer had been named by the conference of bishops of England and Wales to succeed Archbishop Grimshaw.

PRELIMINARY ORGANIZATION

Some indication of the discussions, largely unrecorded, during the 1963 and 1964 meetings of the Episcopal Committee and *periti*

---

[10] For an account of the American commission and of Griffiths' role in it, see *Thirty Years of Liturgical Renewal*, 3-15.

may be seen in the following agenda for consideration in 1963. It is concerned with the charge to be given to the Advisory Committee of specialists about procedures and programs; it suggests some of the wisdom and foresight of the ICEL founders.

1. Structure of committee, specialists, translators, etc.
   a) secretary and secretariat (Archbishop Hallinan)
   b) committee of non-translator specialists for first judgment (liturgy, Scripture, English vernacular); suggestions
   c) body of translators; suggestions

2. Procedures for translation
   a) division:
      i) Scripture readings, etc.
      ii) psalmody and hymnody (music)
      iii) orations, collects, etc.
   b) sequence (dependent on order followed by post-conciliar committee [to be called the Consilium])
   c) single translators or group for section: committee of translators (methods of CBA—Catholic Biblical Association [of the United States], New English Bible, and Doubleday-Jerusalem Bible)

3. Practical questions
   a) permissions and royalties, esp. in interim period
   b) manner of publications (i.e. for official use in rites)
      i) *editio typica* published by hierarchy
      ii) choice of individual publishers
      iii) cooperative publication
   c) editorial and typographical control
   d) control by means of copyright or imprimatur
   e) protection of interests of publishers in interim
      i) publishers of liturgical books
      ii) publishers of popular missals

4. Directories or directives for instruction
   a) general plan: prepared by experts for examination by committee and subsequent submission to respective hierarchies for possible publication by them
   b) kinds
      i) (for the faithful directly) instruction in the meaning of liturgical texts and language, especially with a view to biblical orientation or appreciation of the spirit and peculiarities of Roman rite as revealed in language, etc.
      ii) (for the clergy, ministers, etc.) instruction in the reading and proclamation of the word of God, public praying in the vernacular, etc.

Several early preoccupations of the Episcopal Committee and their *periti* are worth noting, as seen in this listing of topics for consideration. One was the concern, already obvious enough, for public praying and hearing, for proclamation and song—with an evident recognition that the style of existing biblical translations was not suited to public proclamation in the assembly. Another interest was the integrity of future liturgical texts in English, balancing the legitimate rights of commercial publishers in the field of popular publications (or of the Latin liturgical books) with the radically different situation in the case of official English texts to be approved by the respective conferences of bishops. Finally, ancillary publications, directories, and instructions over and above the basic translation and provision of liturgical texts, were already on the table as part of the project.

Since organizational plans for the international committee had not developed as rapidly as expected (or as proposed by Archbishop Hurley in the letter quoted above), it was agreed that there would necessarily be a period during which provisional liturgical texts or existing translations would have to be used, awaiting the full plan for the joint project of translation and its execution. With the promulgation of the Constitution on the Liturgy on 4 December 1963, to be effective on 16 February 1964, each conference of bishops was obliged—if indeed it chose to permit the introduction of the vernacular at all—to approve particular texts.

Most of the participating conferences initially employed English texts taken from one or other of the popular missals or the versions of the ritual and divine office in English. The bishops of England and Wales, in addition, took the initiative in establishing common texts for the ordinary parts of the people in concert with the episcopates of Scotland and Ireland. Archbishop Grimshaw also set up a separate "Birmingham Committee" for the translation of the proper texts for Sundays; it was a project somewhat parallel to ICEL during the initial period.

Between the second and third periods of the Council, ICEL suffered a severe but temporary loss because of the grave illness of Archbishop Hallinan, who was unable to be in Rome in 1964. The meetings of the Episcopal Committee were resumed on 10 October of that year. It was possible to develop a mandate and constitution for the body and, above all, to appoint an Advisory Committee that would plan the ICEL program for translation and related aspects. Initially the two committees were distinctly and fully designated: the International Episcopal Committee on the Liturgy, the directing and governing body, and the International Advisory Committee on the Liturgy, the working and supervisory body.

THE MANDATE

The first major fruit of the extensive discussions of the Episcopal Committee in 1964 was the preparation of a formal mandate, which was then submitted for the approval of the sponsoring conferences of bishops represented by the individual members of the committee. The document was originally drafted by Archbishop Hurley with the assistance of the Irish pastoral expert and editor, Father James G. McGarry, who was later for a short time a member of the ICEL Advisory Committee.

The mandate was promptly adopted by the conferences—there was a slight delay in the case of one conference, which had to await its formal meeting—and constitutes the charter of ICEL. It is addressed to the advisory or steering body of specialists—the bishop-members already had their formal appointment to the Episcopal Committee—and reads as follows:

> The Hierarchies of England and Wales, Scotland, Ireland, the United States of America, Canada, Australia, New Zealand, India, Pakistan, and Southern Africa, having agreed to the establishment of an International Advisory Committee on English in the Liturgy with a view to achieving an English version of liturgical texts acceptable to English-speaking countries and bearing in mind the ecumenical aspects, entrust this Committee with the following Mandate:
>
> 1. To work out a plan for the translation of liturgical texts and the provision of original texts where required in language which would be correct, dignified, intelligible, and suitable for public recitation and singing;
>
> to propose the engagement of experts in various fields as translators, composers, and critics and to provide for the exchange of information with the sponsoring Hierarchies and with other interested Hierarchies; and
>
> to give special attention, within the scope of this plan, to the question of a single English version of the Bible for liturgical use or at least of common translations of biblical texts used in the liturgy.
>
> 2. To submit this plan to the interested Hierarchies with a view to obtaining their consent.
>
> 3. To implement the approved plan.

4. To submit final recommendations to the interested Hierarchies for their approval.

5. To use such funds as shall be made available for these purposes by the Hierarchies, under the general control of the Episcopal Secretary representing them for the time being, the Most Reverend Paul J. Hallinan, Archbishop of Atlanta.

Some points in this mandate deserve comment. It envisions, for example, the composition of original texts as well as translations from the Latin of the revised Roman liturgical books. Later it became even more evident that, while the primary task was the translation of Latin texts, liturgical development and adaptation would ultimately demand much more by way of creativity. At the end of the 1960s this became one of the normative principles of the Latin liturgical books themselves: they regularly left to the conference of bishops—and thus to their instrumentalities, the joint or international commissions like ICEL—the creation of new vernacular liturgical prayers wherever the Roman books offered alternatives. The point was summed up even more strongly by the Apostolic See in 1969:

> Texts translated from another language are clearly not sufficient for the celebration of a fully renewed liturgy. The creation of new texts will be necessary. But translation of texts transmitted through the tradition of the Church is the best school and discipline for the creation of new texts so "that any new forms adopted should in some way grow organically from forms already in existence (SC, art. 23)."[11]

The 1964 mandate does not speak directly to the kinds of commentaries, notes, and subsidiary aids which had already been considered and which soon came to be understood as the closely related responsibility of ICEL in serving the conferences of bishops and through them the local Churches of the countries where English is spoken. Again, the mandate does not explicitly direct the actual commissioning or composition of musical settings by ICEL, something which later proved both desirable and necessary, but it does include composers among those to be engaged in the program. More important, it does speak forcefully to the basic concept of provid-

---

[11] Consilium for the Implementation of the Constitution on the Liturgy [hereafter, Consilium], Instruction on the Translation of Liturgical Texts *Comme le prévoit*, 25 Jan. 1969, no. 43: *Notitiae* 5 (1969), 3-12. English text in ICEL, *Documents on the Liturgy 1963-1979: Conciliar, Papal, and Curial Texts* [hereafter, DOL] (Collegeville, Minn.: The Liturgical Press, 1982) 123, no. 880. The quotation concerning organic development of forms (applied, in the context of the Instruction, to liturgical texts) is from article 23 of *Sacrosanctum Concilium*.

ing texts that could be sung as well as spoken. (This goal is reflected in the choice of two of the eight members of the Advisory Committee, to be mentioned later.)

Finally, the original mandate is noteworthy for its ecumenical concern, thus recognizing the experience with the English vernacular which the other Churches and communities had had for several centuries. Nothing to match this experience could be found in the English-language Catholic tradition of the modern period, aside from a limited repertoire of hymns and despite the proliferation of popular missals in the twentieth century—even the best of which were translated with a view to silent reading and prayerful study rather than public proclamation.

The reference to "bearing in mind the ecumenical aspects" also embodies the significant impact of observers and delegates from other Churches and ecclesial communities during the Second Vatican Council. It is a recognition of the ecumenical contacts which showed how deeply the other Churches were committed to liturgical reform, including reform of liturgical language. This part of the mandate was later pursued by means of ICEL's participation in the (North American) Consultation on Common Texts, out of which developed the International Consultation on English Texts (ICET) and, much later, the English Language Liturgical Consultation (ELLC). In all of these ICEL became an important and supportive force.

THE CONSTITUTION

During the 1964 meetings of the Episcopal Committee a constitution was formally adopted for ICEL. (The civil incorporation did not take place until 1967, when it became necessary to protect the literary and liturgical integrity of ICEL texts by means of international copyright.)[12] In 1972 the original constitution was amended,

---

[12] ICEL was incorporated in Canada, in order to safeguard the international copyright of its texts, since the translators, authors, and the several committees which create or determine the final texts are from many countries, with no single individual ever identified or identifiable as "author." The corporate title is "International Committee on English in the Liturgy, Inc.," retaining the original name, "committee." In the early 1970s "committee" was changed to "commission," and an explanatory subtitle added: "a joint commission of Catholic bishops' conferences." Similarly, without changing internal relationships or responsibilities, the "Episcopal Committee" was renamed "Episcopal Board." The members of that (ecclesiastical) board are elected as members of the civil corporation upon their designation by the individual conferences of bishops—in whatever manner and for whatever term the respective conference determines—and are then also elected members of the Board of Directors of the corporation.

and the revision helps to demonstrate the development of ICEL in its first years.

While changing the nomenclature somewhat, the amended constitution remedied a defect in the original: the first document had been written largely in terms of the need to develop a plan and less in terms of the plan's execution, that is, ICEL's principal activity. The revision described, moreover, procedures for submitting texts to the participating and interested conferences of bishops according to the pattern that had been worked out after the experience of two or three years. The procedure expressed the responsibility of ICEL as the agent and instrument of the conferences, which direct ICEL through their episcopal representatives. It expressed in turn the responsibility of the conferences themselves to accept or reject the texts proposed by ICEL for their canonical approbation, each conference for the dioceses of its own territory.

The principal element in the ICEL constitution is of course the structured plan to relate the International Episcopal Committee on English in the Liturgy and the International Advisory Committee on English in the Liturgy as two parts of a single organization, both to be served by a secretariat and staff, and to seek the assistance of "translators, composers, and critics," as the mandate directed. The Advisory Committee was given the responsibility of planning the entire program and might perhaps have been better named the steering or coordinating committee. At one point the name of "critics' committee" was suggested, in the sense that the members would serve as the literary and liturgical critics or reviewers of texts.

The Advisory Committee, having been given the responsibility of planning the entire program and having created a plan, was then to execute the program if approved by the Episcopal Committee and, after widespread consultation, to submit its completed work— done under the administration of a secretariat—to the Episcopal Committee. The latter retained the ultimate responsibility of proposing liturgical texts to the parent conferences for definitive approval.

During this third period of the Council, in the fall of 1964, when the Episcopal Committee met several times, again with the participation of Fathers Diekmann and McManus, decisions were made concerning the initial membership of the Advisory Committee, establishment of a secretariat, and, of very great importance, funding of the project. On the basis of a tentative budget proposed by Father McManus, a proportionate assessment was suggested to the participating conferences of bishops—in proportion, that is, to the

English-speaking Catholic population of the individual countries as reported in official directories or as roughly estimated by members of the Episcopal Committee.

Nine of the conferences were able to provide grants in 1964 and 1965 for a total of $112,109. ICEL was later able, with income from royalties, to repay this entire amount and to make additional distributions of $272,272 to the conferences from funds not immediately needed for its program.

Also in the second half of 1964 the establishment of a secretariat, along with the temporary holding of funds, was entrusted to Archbishop Hallinan, who had now recovered sufficiently to carry on in these matters (and who was able to attend the fourth and final period of the Council), and to Father McManus. The Episcopal Committee discussed possible locations for such a secretariat. As in other matters, some effort was made to respect the proper balance between the traditions and interests on the two sides of the Atlantic, and a location in Canada or in Collegeville, Minnesota, was first considered rather than more logical locations in London or Washington, the centers of the conferences of bishops which reflected the two major traditions. The decision was made in favor of Washington, but with the expectation that a British priest or layperson would serve as executive secretary.

Beginnings of the Advisory Committee

Still, the choice of members of the Advisory Committee was the principal step taken by the Episcopal Committee in 1964. Unlike the Episcopal Committee, the Advisory Committee was conceived as representing not the participating conferences of bishops or the several countries but rather the diversity of specializations needed to plan and conduct a program of liturgical translations into English. The members were not themselves to be translators, although two or three of those appointed did have that competence and experience, but rather they were chosen as reviewers and revisers of the translated and other materials that would be commissioned. While respecting the right of each conference of bishops to veto the designation of a member of the Advisory Committee from its own country, the Episcopal Committee was anxious to retain the actual appointment to itself and did not wish to create a second body directly representative of the interests of the participating countries.

In addition to Fathers Diekmann and McManus, the original Advisory Committee chosen by the Episcopal Committee included the following:

— Father James G. McGarry, professor at Maynooth and editor of the Irish pastoral-liturgical journal, *The Furrow*. He was selected by the Episcopal Committee on the basis of recommendations, especially from the American participants and Archbishop Hurley, who were well aware of his deep liturgical interest and widespread pastoral influence both in Ireland and elsewhere.

Although he took part in the preliminary meeting of the Advisory Committee in early 1965, Father McGarry felt obliged to withdraw shortly afterward because of a misunderstanding on the part of others, who mistakenly felt that the appointment was of an Irish representative who should be a linguistic expert or a translator. After extensive consultation, the Episcopal Committee named a replacement:

— Father John Hackett, formerly a professor at Maynooth, a specialist in Greek and Latin, at the time a parochial curate. He brought to the project not only language and literary skills along with substantial patristic scholarship but also pastoral experience, breadth, and openness.

— Professor G. B. Harrison, English by birth and education, an eminent Shakespearean scholar who had emigrated to Canada and then to the United States. He was at the time a professor in the University of Michigan and had been recommended by Archbishop Dearden of Detroit.[13]

— Father (later Canon) Harold Winstone, parish priest of the Archdiocese of Westminster, who had extensive pastoral-liturgical experience and had been a teacher of classics for more than two decades. Well known as a writer in the liturgical field, he had also translated liturgical texts and papal documents, as well as German liturgical commentaries.[14]

— Professor H.P.R. Finberg, professor of local history in the University of Leicester, co-translator of the O'Connell-Finberg missal (often referred to as the Knox missal, because it employed the biblical translation of Ronald Knox). He had a strong background

---

[13] G. B. Harrison, *One Man in His Time: The Memoirs of G. B. Harrison 1894-1984* (Palmerston North, NZ: The Dunmore Press, 1985).

[14] A brief note on Harold Winstone may be found in the *New Catholic Encyclopedia* 18 (1989), 550-551.

in history, English style, and typographical design and had written in support of vernacular in the liturgy, although this included a commitment to archaic styles such as the "thou-form" of addressing God.

Both Winstone and Finberg were proposed by Archbishop Grimshaw, after other specialists had been considered, with the express purpose of providing between them a certain balance of expertise and ideology.

— Father Stephen Somerville, a diocesan priest from Canada, well known in North America. He was appointed by the Episcopal Committee in view of his musical expertise, especially in the field of liturgical composition.

— Father Percy Jones, of the Archdiocese of Melbourne, a graduate of the Pontifical Institute of Sacred Music, who was a reader in music in the faculty of the University of Melbourne and had long worked in Church and school music programs. He was chosen, largely upon the recommendation of Archbishop Young, because of his musical specialization, experience as a parish priest, and participation in the Pontifical Preparatory Commission on the Liturgy prior to the Council.[15]

PRINCIPLES AND PROCEDURES

With the initial funding in hand, the mandate and constitution approved, and the Advisory Committee appointed, it was possible to move directly to the planning of the ICEL program, which was the initial responsibility of the Advisory Committee. The first step was a preliminary meeting held in London in January 1965; for this the Episcopal Committee named Father Diekmann as convener and Father McManus as secretary pro-tem. The participants were Professor Finberg and Fathers McGarry, Winstone, and McManus, with McManus in the chair. At this meeting the new members of the Advisory Committee were made aware of developments thus far and the expectation that a secretariat would be set up in the next several months so that a full meeting of the Advisory Committee could be held in the second half of the year.

The principal work of the January 1965 meeting was the production of some "First Principles of Liturgical Translation Agreed by

---

[15] A biography, *Percy Jones: Priest, Musician, Teacher,* by Donald Cave (Melbourne: University of Melbourne Press, 1988), contains such extensive quotations from Father Jones as to make it in large part a personal memoir.

the Advisory Committee" to govern the program. Though put together a priori, before the enterprise actually began, a few of these
principles bear quotation even after twenty-five years:

> To be acceptable in substance, a translation must faithfully express
> the meaning, intention and character of the original, yet allow for
> adaptations required by pastoral needs. . . .
>
> To be acceptable in style, translation must take account of (a) the
> sacral character of the original texts; (b) the tradition of devotional
> writing in English; (c) contemporary linguistic usage; (d) eupho-
> ny; and (e) the practice of other Christian bodies. . . .
>
> Respect for the sacral character of the original texts and the demands
> of corporate public worship will prescribe a vocabulary and style
> not necessarily identical with those admissible in private and per-
> sonal prayer. . . .
>
> Respect for contemporary linguistic usage will dictate the avoidance
> of words and phrases not in living use today. . . .
>
> Respect for euphony will take into account that texts must be suita-
> ble for singing or speaking according to the liturgical context. . . .
>
> The word "acceptable" in the foregoing paragraphs is to be under-
> stood as requiring translators to work mainly with an eye to the mid-
> dle range of church-goers rather than to the least or the most
> intelligent and literate. . . .

Members of the group also visited with Cardinal John Carmel
Heenan, Archbishop of Westminster, and received his assurance,
on behalf of the episcopate of England and Wales, that no objection would be raised to the appointment of an American as executive secretary of ICEL, with offices in Washington. This agreement
was reached with the understanding "that the duties of the secretary would not include any translating or selections of translations,
or the formulation of any policies or principles of translation"—all
matters which were reserved to the corporate decision of the Advisory Committee. This agreement opened the way to a search by
Archbishop Hallinan and Father McManus for an executive secretary from the United States.

An initial effort was made to secure the services of the chancel-
lor of the Diocese of Fall River, Father John H. Hackett, a canonist
who had had considerable parish experience and had been involved
in liturgical promotional activities, having done extensive study of
the European liturgical literature as well. When Father Hackett was
unavailable, Archbishop Hallinan turned to Dr. Gerald A. Sigler,

then a priest of the Diocese of Erie, also a canonist, who had done a dissertation at the Gregorian University on the Roman Ritual. He possessed both pastoral-liturgical expertise and strong organizational and administrative abilities.

In August 1965 Father Sigler agreed to undertake the position of executive secretary and moved quickly to establish an office in Washington, in space provided by The Liturgical Conference, as well as to make preparations for the first full meeting of the Advisory Committee in Rome. The office of the secretariat was opened in September 1965, and the committee meeting was planned to overlap with the holding of an international congress on liturgical translation in Rome (9-13 November).

The congress, which was attended by members of both the Episcopal Committee and the Advisory Committee of ICEL, met under the auspices of the Consilium for the Implementation of the Constitution on the Liturgy, which had been established in January 1964 by Pope Paul VI, a few weeks after the promulgation of the liturgical constitution. There were 249 participants in the congress from sixty-nine nations, including representatives from other joint commissions for the major languages. Some seventeen reports were given on topics ranging from literary genre in the liturgy to the history of translation, from stylistic questions and difficulties to the publication and distribution of liturgical books.[16]

One of the papers given at the congress treated the organization of the work of liturgical translation in general, but was mostly the fruit of more than eighteen months of discussion in the English language group.[17] In fact the comments on structure, procedure, and policies were chiefly a description of ICEL up to that time. Some of the points made have already been mentioned: the task of the members of the Advisory Committee "to coordinate the entire work,

---

[16] Proceedings in *Le traduzioni dei libri liturgici, Atti del Congresso tenuto a Roma il 9-13 November 1965* (Città del Vaticano: Libreria Editrice Vaticana, 1966). An English translation of the address of Pope Paul VI to the congress on 10 November is found in DOL 113.

Soon after its establishment the Consilium had shown its interest in the matter of vernacular translations, in the letter *Le sarei grato* to papal representatives for communication to the conferences of bishops, 25 March 1964 (see DOL 79). Its policy was elaborated at greater length in the letter *Consilium ad exsequendum* of 16 October 1964 to the presidents of the conferences of bishops (see DOL 108); in this the president of the Consilium, Cardinal Giacomo Lercaro of Bologna, encouraged cooperative efforts among conferences and recognized what had already been accomplished by the existing joint commissions.

[17] Frederick R. McManus, "L'organizzazione del lavoro di traduzione," in *Le traduzione dei libri liturgici*, the proceedings cited in the preceding note. The quotations in the paragraphs summarizing the paper are from the Italian text; the paper was given in Latin, and no English version was published.

to critique and correct the translations, etc."; the crucial importance of texts that are not merely literary but "designed to be recited aloud or sung"—and at a middle level of intelligibility, neither for "the ignorant and inexpert" nor for the highly sophisticated.

The possible structures of translating bodies—in fact the new ICEL structures—were taken up in the paper with a definition of responsibilities, for example, spelling out not only the administrative responsibilities of a secretariat but also its task to inform the public, the Church community at large, about "the method and procedure of the work." This last represented the original concern of the founding bishops of ICEL, especially Archbishop Hallinan, that the translation project should have the broadest base of participation and public consultation as possible.

In reference to the qualities of translators—possibly working alone, possibly two by two—and again of consultants, competence in the English vernacular is judged to be even more important than the very necessary competence in the original language. Competence in Latin is seen as always providing a corrective function so as to include in the translation "all the spiritual and religious values contained in the original, but not to the exclusion of its literary style, suitably adapted." The importance of distinguishing "the nature of the literary forms (orations, prefaces, hymns, psalms, etc.)" is pointed out, along with the complex problems of biblical texts both in readings and as alluded to in prayer texts.

The paper expresses, more fully than the mandate quoted above, the ecumenical dimension of the ICEL enterprise—and thus recommends it to other translating bodies or commissions: "At least in some countries, for example those of the English language, the experts should consult with separated Christians, either as individuals or in their commissions on liturgical texts. It is very desirable to have common versions of some parts such as the *Gloria in excelsis, Sanctus, Pater noster,* psalms, and hymns."

Toward the end the paper, after describing ICEL procedures either in place or planned in mid-1965, deals with the matter of costs and policies affecting publication. First, it would be "the gravest error" not to offer adequate and just compensation to translators, "especially lay persons, both men and women," and to others who serve the program. Second, while the conferences of bishops should seek common editions published under their authority, the concept of "a monopoly of one or two publishers" is mentioned as unacceptable, especially in countries like the United States, and preference is stated for cooperative undertakings by commercial publishers. This is the first clear statement of ICEL's policy of granting publication rights on a non-exclusive basis to publishers of religious books, whether operating for profit or not, subject only to permissions from the respective conference of bishops.

The congress in November 1965 occupied only part of the time of the Episcopal Committee—which continued to meet occasionally during the fourth period of the Council and also held a joint meeting with the Advisory Committee while the latter was in Rome. It was the principal task of the Advisory Committee, however, to develop plans, in concert with the new executive secretary, for the actual prosecution of the ICEL program and to thrash out policies for the work to be done—especially matters of public consultation and the search for translators and consultants. Father Diekmann was chairman during the meetings from 8 to 17 November at the Collegio San Alberto near Vatican City and in the chambers of the Roman Rota in the Palazzo della Cancelleria, where the congress on translation was being held.

Much of the organizational and administrative detail was left to the executive secretary, Father Sigler, but the Advisory Committee worked up the plans for widely publicized surveys of opinion in the Church community concerning the translation of the *Ordo Missae*. The latter was then being revised and celebrated in Rome on a trial basis by the Consilium of implementation already mentioned. The Advisory Committee also undertook a basic explanation of the purposes and principles of the ICEL program and the selection of potential translators and consultants. Because the Advisory Committee itself did not then include biblical specialists, two American biblical scholars were invited to participate in one session. At another session three of the non-Catholic observers at the Council were present, initiating relationships which had been part of the 1964 mandate received by the Advisory Committee.

Some very particular questions were discussed at this first full meeting, such as the common or ordinary parts of the Mass, specimen translations of prayers in the collect-style, and the early issue—pressed by one of the members—of employing "thou" for "you" in the English liturgy. In this, as in other matters, pastoral considerations and contemporary needs prevailed, and it was quickly agreed that, whatever the differences of judgment, the translations should reflect the spoken language and be suited to public speaking and singing. In spite of the consultation with biblical specialists, it was obviously much too soon to reach any conclusions about preferred translations of the Bible for liturgical readings or the even more difficult question of suitable versions of the Psalter.

The first annual report of ICEL was issued to the participating conferences of bishops in November 1966, after the program of the Advisory Committee was well under way and the Washington secretariat had been in operation for a little more than a year. It included a report on the work discussed at the second Roman meeting of the Advisory Committee from 27 September to 4 October 1966. On 3 and 4 October the Advisory Committee met jointly with those members of the Episcopal Committee who were in Rome for the seventh plenary session of the Consilium of implementation.[18] From this point on the work of ICEL can be traced in its successive reports and other publications and especially in the list of liturgical texts and materials prepared and submitted to the conferences of bishops for their action.

CONCLUSION

As suggested at the beginning of this historical note, a remarkable feature of the ICEL development is the foresight of the bishop-founders and of the first members of the Advisory Committee. There was immediate agreement, as already noted, on the fundamental needs for English liturgical texts, both translated and original, which could be sung and spoken (and heard and understood) in the Christian assembly. A redefinition of fidelity of translation was sought, always respecting the meaning of the original but without slavish literalism—a position adopted fully in the 1969 Instruction of the Apostolic See on the subject.[19] In a sense ICEL had embraced, in

---

[18] Archbishops Dwyer, Gray, Grimshaw (until his death on 22 March 1965), Hallinan (until his death on 27 March 1968), Hurley, and Young were members of the Consilium; Fathers Diekmann, Jones, and McManus were consultors. In the course of his address to the plenary session of the Consilium on 13 October 1966, Paul VI referred to questions of liturgical language (see DOL 84).

[19] The 1969 Instruction (see above, note 11) is notable in that about two-thirds of its 43 sections are directed toward openness and freedom in translation. Its preparation benefited from the experience of the major joint commissions, including ICEL, whose executive secretary served on an ad hoc *coetus studiorum* of the Consilium for this purpose. ICEL was requested by the Consilium to prepare from the original text of the Instruction (in French, with some additions in Italian) the English text to be sent by the Consilium to the conferences of bishops; this involved the inclusion of textual examples in English, as was done in other languages.

For an account of the preparation of this Instruction, see Annibale Bugnini, *La riforma liturgica (1948-1975)*, Bibliotheca "Ephemerides Liturgicae," "Subsidia" 30 (Rome: CLV-Edizioni

matters of language, two goals and principles of the Constitution on the Liturgy: "to adapt more suitably to the needs of our own times those institutions [of the Church, including the liturgy] that are subject to change . . ." (art. 1), and to see that the rites of worship, including their words, "be marked by a noble simplicity; they should be short, clear, and unencumbered by useless repetitions; they should be within the people's power of comprehension and as a rule not require much explanation" (art. 34).

In other ways, the ICEL program mirrored and supported the new ecclesiological insights of the Second Vatican Council, from openness and collegiality throughout the whole Christian community to the special relationships among the Churches in Christian communion. The role of ICEL in relation to the conferences of bishops was clear as it moved into a program conducted on their behalf and as their instrument: all the final decisions about the acceptance and use of ICEL texts rested (and rests) with the territorial episcopates, the national or regional bodies in which resides traditional ecclesial conciliarity. From the first too, the independence of ICEL (and thus of Church authorities) from the ventures of commercial publishers was seen as necessary; all publishers were to be licensed on an equal basis, subject only to the approval of the respective conference of bishops. As mentioned already, collaborators in the work of ICEL, especially translators and critics or consultants (and, later, members of the small secretariat) were to be compensated justly. The greatest publicity was to be given to the program, and the public at large—the Christian community that is the Church—was to be invited to offer recommendations so as to elicit the most widespread criticism and involvement before decisions were taken.

Whatever the strengths or weaknesses of the original plans for ICEL in 1963-1965 or the later execution of these plans, it is possible a quarter-century later to appreciate an extraordinary accomplishment and contribution to the religious life of the Church in countries where English is spoken.

Liturgiche, 1983), 236-239. He draws attention (p. 239) to the significance of the final paragraph of the document, quoted above at note 11, on the need for newly created liturgical texts. The third part of the Instruction is concerned with commissions for translation, including joint international or mixed commissions. An English translation of La riforma liturgica is forthcoming from The Liturgical Press, Collegeville, Minn.

PERSONAL REMINISCENSES OF THE EARLY YEARS OF ICEL

The early history of ICEL is supplemented here by the personal reminiscences of two of the original members of ICEL's Advisory Committee, Dr. G. B. Harrison and Dr. Percy Jones. These accounts are given in the form of excerpts from *One Man in His Time: The Memoirs of G. B. Harrison 1894-1984* (Palmerston North: The Dunmore Press Ltd., 1985) and from the biography of Percy Jones by Donald Cave, *Percy Jones: Priest, Musician, Teacher* (Carlton: Melbourne University Press, 1988). This material is reprinted with the kind permission of the authors and publishers.

AN EXCERPT FROM CHAPTER SIX OF
ONE MAN IN HIS TIME: THE MEMOIRS OF G. B. HARRISON 1894-1984
(pp. 275-282)

In 1964 we celebrated our seventieth birthdays. This was the age when a professor of the University of Michigan reached the end of his career.

On 23 April 1964 Shakespeare's 400th birthday was celebrated all over the world. The annual bibliography of articles, books, theses, rose by more than 50%, to about 5000 items. I had my small share. The New York *Herald-Tribune* asked me to write an article on the foundation of a small private Shakespeare library, and then sent along a pile of books for review, at least four feet in height, and not one of any permanent value or interest. 'The time has come,' said my Guardian Angel, 'for you to turn to pastures new.'

Pope John XXIII had summoned the second Vatican Council to modernize the Church. Many new windows opened and much fresh air was let into dusty corners, as well as swarms of flies, gnats, and mosquitos. Among the first and most important matters, the Council determined to deal with the Liturgy which needed updating, especially for the lay folk. Hitherto Latin had been the language of the Church; now much was to be translated. Latin had been the religious language of Catholics everywhere, they worshipped, communicated, preached, lectured in one common language. While Latin was universally taught, even if only to the educated, that was sufficient, but it had almost disappeared. Meanwhile those who had broken away from the Roman Church had long since produced national versions for the Bible, for prayer, and for everything else. There were many of these versions but for the English everyone agreed that Cranmer's *Book of Common Prayer* of 1549 and the King James translation of the Bible in 1610 were the greatest glories of the English language. If English was to be used by Catholics, clearly these old translations were not appropriate. The translation must be in modern English; and it was most desirable that all who spoke English wherever they might live should use the same version everywhere. Where and how then should this new enterprise be organized?

America invited me to write an article on these problems, headed 'Words to Pray With.' The Canon of the Roman Mass, that is the prayer of consecration which is the most solemn moment in worship, was a set ritual, it went right back at least to the time of St. Gregory the Great who died in the year 604 and, as I discovered to my surprise, it had not been changed at all ever since. By this time although the rite was still performed in Latin it had been made easier for English worshippers because it had been translated into English so that they could follow the Latin as it was uttered. There was much debate, discussion and disagreement about the form a new translation should take. Most felt that the English version should be in good simple English; archaic, or worse, sentimental verbosity must be abandoned. Words such as 'vouchsafe', 'boundless', 'deem', 'deign', 'handmaid', were no longer in common use but where was the boundary between 'simple', and 'common'?

In one translation, instead of answering the priest's words 'The Lord be with you', with 'And also with you', the reply was 'Same to you Father', and for 'Hail Mary', some priests now said 'Hello Mary'. And what about the use of 'You' or 'Thou', when addressing God? Nowadays no one called an earthly father 'thou'.

The Lord's Prayer was the first test. There were several words that were no longer usual. 'Hallowed' is a lovely old word but archaic except in the United States of America in 'Hallow'een'—certainly not a hallowed or holy occasion. It could be used on sanctimonious occasions as when referring to the 'hallowed field' where some dreadful battle had taken place, or for a burial ground. So also the phrase which disturbs some small children 'asitisin'; and 'trespass' which has degenerated into 'keep off my grass'. As for 'lead us not into temptation' this is blasphemous. To lead young people into temptation means to introduce them to drink, drugs, sex, gambling and the like.

One great difficulty is that so many of the prayers in the *Book of Common Prayer* are in fact translations from the Latin which is by nature a polysyllabic language whereas the best modern English is monosyllabic—a fact seldom noticed.

The article was published in *America* in April and though short, produced quite a controversy. Two weeks later the editor printed a collection of comments, occupying two pages. One of the writers, who taught a class of 33 junior high school students, had at first questioned my objection to some of the common words of prayer, such as 'deign', 'handmaid', and 'vouchsafe'. He denied that there were difficulties; until he found, on inquiry, that only a third of his class knew that 'handmaid' meant servant, and that four spelt it 'handmade'. Some thought that 'oblation' meant 'obligation', few knew the meaning of 'vouchsafed', 'deign', or 'professor'. Most understood that 'trespass' meant fault, or sin, but only a few knew it had anything to do with property. One spelt 'hallowed' as 'harold', and only two realized that 'hail' was a greeting. Only a third were familiar with 'beseech' or 'bounden'.

The second Vatican Council came together in Rome in October, 1962, and one of its first accomplishments was to approve a Constitution on the Sacred Liturgy and its reforms. The purpose of the reforms was to encourage the people to take a more active part in the rites of the Church. To this end, the old rigid uniformity was relaxed. Each Episcopal Conference could adapt the liturgy to the special gifts of the people, provided that the substantial unity of the Roman rite was preserved. The vernacular language could be used, but no person, not even a priest, might add, remove or change anything in the liturgy on his own responsibility. Few in the Council had realized that when the gates are opened to a large and impatient crowd, they rush in and are no longer controllable. Once the vernacular was admitted, the demand for its full use was general and quite irresistible.

Both the Council and the new Pope, Paul VI, desired that when the same language was spoken by several countries, commissions should be established to make one text for all. As a result, the English-speaking bishops appointed an International Commission on English in the Liturgy, hereafter referred to as ICEL. This body consisted of two committees, the Episcopal Committee of representatives from different countries, a secretary and treasurer with offices in Washington, and other members of an Advisory Committee (at first of eight persons) to organize and oversee the translation. Archbishop Deardon of Detroit, enthusiastic about my article, was responsible for my being one of the two laymen on this committee.

From this meeting emerged our first publication – a pamphlet called *English for the Mass*. It set out different ways of translating such texts as the Gloria, the Credo and Agnus Dei. We asked for criticism and advice; *we got it!* Some 16,000 copies of the pamphlet were sent out; more than 4,000 replies came back, which revealed a great conflict of opinions, strongly held and often violently expressed. Some wished the committee to rewrite the Mass. Others demanded that we keep as close as could be to the language of Cranmer's *Book of Common Prayer* and all the ancient forms of liturgical language. Others again were as eager for the disappearance of the old familiar words, even 'almighty', 'everlasting', and 'amen'. A few urged us to follow the vocabulary of the Beatles as that of the generation to come.

A second pamphlet was issued a year later: *English for the Mass, Part 2*. This was a large collection of translations of the prayers, prefaces, and prayer endings. In the introduction, we pointed out that it was *not* our task to remake the liturgy but to translate what might be provided by Rome, and we replied to those who demanded that we use 'the contemporary idiom', that there was no such thing, for contemporary idiom changed from place to place, and year to year; the idiom that was modern and contemporary to a liturgiologist in Chicago was very different from the idiom natural to a taxi driver in London. The final translation, we claimed, could not be in any particular idiom–'it must aim at good straight, simple English which brings understanding to the unlearned and delight to the literate.' *English for the Mass, Part 2* produced very few answers and no offers from those with the gift of writing good, straight, simple English.

The original intention of the Council Fathers was that only certain parts of the Mass should be translated into the vernacular, and for some months the Mass was part English, part Latin. Pending official translations, different dioceses used what was available in existing missals for the Gloria, the Creed and other parts, but the offertory prayers and the Canon were still uttered inaudibly in Latin.

This hybrid was generally felt to be most unsatisfactory, and in the early Spring of 1967, the American bishops petitioned that the Canon might be said aloud in English. To their surprise, permission from Rome was given three weeks later; haste is not usual in such matters. The result was that ICEL was ordered to have the translation ready for use by the end of the year.

The Canon in English was published in October, 1967. It was greeted with startled screams by the conservatives. Long before it was ever heard in use, the London *Tablet* damned it in a harsh review and a harsher editorial, and for several weeks published letters from priests and laity. After a few Sundays the tone altered. And one of my former graduate students wrote to me that he thought the new translation was commonplace—until he heard it, and then to his surprise, it became a thing of simple moving dignity. These words were his, not mine.

The Advisory Committee developed a procedure for translating. For example, before the final version of the new Order of the Mass was published, it went through several stages. From the first we experimented with such texts as the Gloria. After the 4,000 comments had been received in 1966, an editor was appointed to study some 200 of the best and come up with a draft text for the Advisory Committee to scrutinize when it met in Rome in the Fall of 1967. At this meeting a text was evolved which was then sent around to a large body of consultors. They commented at length.

Meanwhile the Latin text had been so drastically revised that most of the comments had ceased to be relevant. So the latest Latin text and the comments were tossed back to the original editor to produce another text for the Advisory Committee to consider in 1968. In April, 1969, the authorized Latin text was officially published in Rome, and at last we could get down to a final translation. By early summer we had reached what in our jargon was called the Green Book stage. The Green Book was the committee's semifinal version, issued in a green cover and sent to our own Bishops' Committee, the various Ecclesiastical Conferences, the English-speaking bishops (all 750 of them) and to other interested parties. They responded with 300 pages of observations, some—but not all—helpful. Personally I found it embarrassing when a most respected archbishop made strong comments that were contradicted in equally strong comments by another highly respected archbishop. Either way we offended one if not both, but we grew hardened to that risk.

The next stage was the White Book. The Advisory Committee having considered all comments sat together in a common meeting with our Bishops' Committee.

ICEL was fortunate in that none of its members was a distinguished literary person. For some reason distinguished or well-known writers just cannot translate liturgical writing. We tried all we could find, and not one succeeded; they were our greatest disappointments. And when their work was criticized, they seldom revealed the virtue of humility. Nor for that matter did St. Jerome.

Apart from the problems of time and place, the greatest difficulty was the Latin text. The traditions of liturgical Latin were almost, but not quite, as old as Christianity. Educated men in the second and later centuries received an elaborate training in rhetoric; and in the Imperial Court at Rome or Byzantium they addressed the sovereign with obsequious phrases and gestures. Englishmen, also, in the sixteenth century and later, endured the same kind of education in rhetoric, and flattered the sovereign in the same way. Latin liturgical conventions were thus natural in Cranmer's *Book of Common Prayer*, and to those brought up on that book, its language seemed the only proper respectful way of addressing God.

This hyperbolical tradition was still strong in Vatican City. Even lay members of ICEL received letters addressed on the envelope 'To the Most Reverend, Most Learned, Professor'—to the irreverent amusement of their families. It sounds much better in Italian.

Modern masters of prayer have entirely rejected that mode: they no longer compose prayers in the style of a Loyal Address to the King of Kings by his abject slaves. Instead they prefer the direct speech of child to father, as Christ taught in the Lord's Prayer. The Gospels plainly show that in his prayers Christ used the simplest words. So too in his talk and his parables. 'Two men went up to the Temple to pray, one a Pharisee, the other a tax collector. . . . The tax collector stood some distance away, not daring even to raise his eyes to heaven; but he beat his breast and said: "God be merciful to me a sinner."' Seven words.

The tax collector's prayer was recast in one translation of the Collect for the fourth Sunday after Epiphany thus: 'God, who knowest that, set as we are amid such perils, our human weakness cannot stand fast, grant us health of mind and body, so that with thy help we may overcome the afflictions that our sins have brought upon us.' One sentence of 41 words.

Most of the severe critics of the ICEL translations failed to realize the facts of life. The texts were not for their own community or parish, but for every community. There are about 75,000,000 English-speaking Catholics throughout the world. Of these 82% live on the North American continent, 6% in England, and Wales. Most English-speaking Catholics, whatever their country, are simple people with small knowledge of the Bible, Church history or English literature. A translator should never forget he was providing words for public utterance to and by plain folk.

Hereupon the literate critic cried out in disgust: 'What! Basic English?' The answer was: 'Yes, basic English,' just as the Gospels were written in a kind of Basic Greek (the learned call it *koine*). They were intended not for educated Greek and Roman gentlemen, but for slaves, merchants, soldiers, shopkeepers, sailors and common people; and for that very reason, because the basic instincts of ordinary folk are more durable than the tastes of professional writers and critics, the Gospel narratives are still vivid and readable. Professional critics very seldom realize that simplicity is the supreme form of art—and the most difficult. Of the scores of translators who contributed to the work, I encountered only one to whom the gift of true simplicity had been given. Later he went to the seminary and was ordained a priest. He then translated into seminarese.

Our most vicious critics were the professional scholars . . . who abused our efforts, but very seldom told us how they would have translated a particular passage or prayer. The personal abuse some of us received was incredible. . . . As general editor I developed a skin as thick as a rhinoceros, and made a heroic attempt to cultivate that rare virtue known as 'holy indifference'. At times I retorted with ferocity. . . . It is perhaps forgivable if I add that in June 1981 Pope John Paul II included my name among those who were chosen as Knights of the Order of St. Gregory the Great.

✳ ✳ ✳

AN EXCERPT FROM CHAPTER FIVE OF
PERCY JONES: PRIEST, MUSICIAN, TEACHER
(pp. 8-88)

> *(The bulk of this book consists of memoirs collected in recording sessions held by the author, Donald Cave, with Percy Jones over a period of eighteen months)*

[Percy Jones] After the approval of the Constitution on the Liturgy the English-speaking bishops recognized that something definite had to be done as far as English language was concerned. During one of the last general sessions of the Council they met at the English College in Rome, to establish a committee for this purpose, consisting of bishops and priest consultors, under the chairmanship of Archbishop Hallinan. Dr. Young of Hobart and myself were elected to this Commission known as I.C.E.L., that is International Committee for English in the Liturgy. If it had been only a question of the readings from the Bible we would not have had to worry. I don't think anybody thought at the beginning of the Council that there would be such radical changes. In fact, I remember Cardinal Gilroy saying to me at the beginning of the Council that he thought that perhaps we would get the scripture readings and the prayers in the vernacular, but not much else. What happened was immensely more complicated than that. We were now confronted with the problem of translating the entire Liturgy into English. When one considers that this involved the formulae for the celebration of the Eucharist with variable parts for every single day of the year, the formulae for the celebration of the six other sacraments and the translation of the seven different prayer services, each with daily variations in readings, which make up the Divine Office, you have some idea of the task which confronted us. It meant that the English, Spanish, French, Germans, Italians, etc., all had to get down and do it. With the English groups, in no time at all, all manner of problems began to emerge. You can't imagine the trouble we ran into over the use of 'thou' and 'thee'. Fortunately there were some very inspiring bishops. The most inspiring as regards the translating into English was Archbishop Hallinan of Atlanta who unfortunately died shortly after the work began. He was highly thought of and respected. Archbishop Young of Hobart was one of the few bishops of the time who were out in front regarding the pastoral aspects of the Liturgy and he did tremendous work, as did Archbishop Hurley of Durban, South Africa.

[Donald Cave] At the conclusion of the Vatican Council in 1964 a committee with the name of the International Committee for Englishing of the Liturgy was set up (I.C.E.L.). Percy Jones and Father Steve Somerville from Canada were made members of the I.C.E.L. because of their 'musical expertise', so said the letter of invitation.

[Jones] There were one or two others who were good amateur musicians. Godfrey Diekmann, for example, was a good flautist and he could at least talk in terms of music, and several others were passable. On the other hand, there were three or four who were tone deaf and they were a blooming nuisance from the beginning. They simply could not understand arguments about assonance and the possibility of a text's being sung. I remember I had been told that when the Therry Society put on the pageant at the Melbourne Cricket Ground in 1939 they discovered that ten thousand people attempting to say the word 'penance' produced an extraordinary sound. It taught everyone a lesson. Great care has to go into the words proposed for group recital, but some of the committee were absolutely insensitive to this.

[Cave] In his work for I.C.E.L. and for the Australian bishops' commission of musicians, many strands of Percy's long professional career came together and he tackled the tasks in a particularly scholarly and practical way.

[Jones] I worked hard at this, the normal thing that you do if you are a scholar. That is to say you get to work and examine how musicians in the past have treated texts and, for what concerned us, to see how composers of the genius of Byrd and Tallis tackled English texts once the Anglican vernacular Liturgy was born. I studied the matter historically from the beginning until the present. I wrote about this in the book Geoffrey Chapman asked me to write. I was concerned to study cadence in the English language. People are finally beginning to discover that you can't just waffle on in English and expect to have cadence or a singable phrase.

[Cave] The amount of work, consultation and correction done in these early years was immense. An enormous number of persons throughout the English-speaking world were consulted regarding a translation of the Gloria, the Creed, the Sanctus and the Agnus Dei. A mountain of documentation was returned and Percy offered to put it in order. [This is a reference to preparation of the so-called ICET texts, thirteen liturgical texts used by a number of Christian Churches throughout the English-speaking world. They were prepared in an agreed upon ecumenical translation by the International

Consultation on English Texts, an ecumenical body in which ICEL provided the Roman Catholic representation. The ICET texts appeared under the title *Prayers We Have in Common* in three editions, 1970, 1972, 1975.]

[Jones] Whether it was stupidity or enthusiasm I don't know, but I offered to try to put some order in all these replies and brought them back to Australia with me. I was singularly fortunate in having with me for the summer two deacons who are now two of the top priests in the Archdiocese, Father Denis Hart who is the bishops' Australian secretary for the Liturgy, and Father Jerry Diamond who, after studies in Rome and Oxford, is Professor of Scripture at the diocesan seminary at Clayton. Being deacons they couldn't work in pubs as other students did, so I took them to work with me in Carlton. They did a tremendous job. We got through the whole thing in the summer holidays and I was able to take back to Rome the whole mass of documentation put in order: what variations there were; where they came from; the main tendencies; detailed reports of all the comments which had come in.

[Cave] From the cataloguing of this information a fact emerged which has been of significance in the planning of the I.C.E.L. group.

[Jones] One thing that we learnt from this task, and it was very important that we did learn it, was that nationality made little or no difference. The thing that made the difference was cultural background. The response to a suggested translation by a Methodist in England was almost always the same as that made by a Methodist in America. The same was true of Anglicans in England and Episcopalians in America. This went on all the time.

[Cave] This awareness of the international class, or cultural, preferences was immensely important for the Americans, for the I.C.E.L. group was constantly being accused by the English of producing American translations.

[Jones] It was an important lesson to learn and the American people at I.C.E.L. headquarters were immensely grateful. They were under attack from the English constantly. The office was in Washington, mainly because the American bishops had put up most of the money! The secretary was Father Gerry Sigler an excellent scholar. . . . One of the hardest things for those of us who had worked hard for I.C.E.L. is the charge or inference which comes up from time to time . . . that the I.C.E.L. translations are American. They are not. The people who did the translations and oversaw them were English. Professor Harrison was English, God knows; Professor Finberg couldn't have been more English; Harold Winstone who had translated everything except the Epistles and Gospels in what was known as the Knox Missal, was a superb translator and was English. Even Steve Somerville and I spoke some English. We weren't Esquimaux. The result was that I used to get furious and disheartened with the constant English harping that the I.C.E.L. translations were American.

[Cave] In defending the work of I.C.E.L., Percy shows the prudence of the true scholar. He is not pretending that the translations were perfect; they were not, but they were *English*. The task given to I.C.E.L. was enormous. Millions of English-speaking Catholics wanted an English-speaking Liturgy, and they wanted it now! After all they had waited centuries.

[Jones] What is true is that an attempt to follow what Pope Paul VI asked, namely that the language should be such that even the unskilled and minimally educated could understand, the balance often fell in favour of over-simplification. This is true and there is no point in denying it. But you've got to remember that people yelled and yapped for an English Liturgy and we had to get things done as quickly as possible. It was quite wrong that it happened that way, but it was a simple fact of life. Now, all that early work is being carefully revised and what is coming out is greatly superior to the early attempts.

[Cave] It would not be out of place to ask, even if one admired Percy's work with I.C.E.L. and considered it to be valuable, whether his commitments at the University were being fulfilled. He is most insistent that they were.

[Jones] Well, the task of I.C.E.L. was immense. Week after week new Missals, new texts of various sorts came out. Everybody wanted everything at once and quite frankly we were nearly driven mad. The work done at the Washington Secretariat was incredible and we all worked like slaves. Apart from the endless exchange of ideas by letter, we met twice a year for at least three years. I think I went at least twenty times around the world on I.C.E.L. business. I didn't resent it, but it was exhausting. The others held at least one meeting in what was their summer holidays, that is at a time when we were busy in Australia with the winter term. I was fortunate in having excellent colleagues like Don Thornton and Professor Loughlin who would (not in every case with enthusiasm) change their timetable for a couple of weeks to allow me to get away, and then I would double up on my return. I remember on one occasion I got off the plane at Essendon at 1 p.m. and began lecturing at 2 p.m. I've never been so close to being a horse asleep on its feet as I was that day. In the ten years on the committee I did not miss one lecture at the University and I am grateful that the University gave me so much help. [. . .]

✳ ✳ ✳

ICEL, 1966-1989:
WEAVING THE WORDS OF
OUR COMMON CHRISTIAN PRAYER

John R. Page

After its establishment in 1963 the early years of ICEL were largely given over to planning and preparation. The task of revising the liturgical books of the Roman Rite according to the mandate of the Second Vatican Council was under way in Rome, but it would be several years before the first results began to appear in finished form in the Latin *editiones typicae,* beginning with the ordination rites in 1968.

THE EARLY YEARS

In 1967 Pope Paul VI granted permission for the Canon of the Mass to be said in the vernacular. That same year ICEL issued its first text, a provisional translation of the Roman Canon. This was followed by a provisional text for the Order of Mass and a provisional text for the rite of baptism for children. It was necessary to issue a provisional text of the Order of Mass because the Consilium for the Implementation of the Constitution on the Liturgy had not yet finished its work. In the years immediately ahead ICEL frequently had to translate from provisional and draft texts while the Roman reform continued. For the most part these texts were for private study and comment, though in a few instances the texts were used as part of the Holy See's experimental use of the rites in process of revision. This was the case in the late 1960s with the *Rite of Funerals* and in the same period with early rites and texts of what would eventually be the *Rite of Christian Initiation of Adults.*

Two public consultations on the style of the English liturgical texts were carried out in 1966 and 1967. The consultation booklets, entitled *English for the Mass,* solicited comments on the English texts for the Order of Mass including collects and prefaces and on Scripture texts used in the Mass, psalms and readings. Several versions of each prayer, psalm, and reading were provided. The first consultation brought several thousand replies; the second only a small number.

The Roman Canon, issued as a text for consultation in 1967 and submitted to the conferences of bishops in final form in 1968, was the first example of the approach that ICEL took toward a vernacular liturgy. The text was clear, literate, and suited to public proclamation. The translation had pared down a number of the rhetorical elaborations of the original and provided a flow and coherence to the whole prayer not always evident in the original. The attempt to make the language of the prayer both reverent and contemporary was generally applauded. Some critics, however, said that the ancient prayer in its form and language had been mutilated, its reverence and sacrality sacrificed for reasons of popular intelligibility and a dubious liturgical renewal.

In 1968 the Holy See, acting on the request of many bishops, issued three additional eucharistic prayers for use in the revised Order of Mass. The ICEL translation of these prayers, the result of several drafts and the product of extensive consultation, was sent to the conferences in that same year. (Also at this time a slightly revised form of Eucharistic Prayer I was sent to the conferences of bishops.) In the same year sample provisional translations of the prefaces of *The Roman Missal* were sent to the bishops and a provisional translation of the *Ordination of a Bishop*.

By 1969-1970 ICEL was faced with a virtual avalanche of revised books coming from Rome. The Episcopal Board, the eleven bishops designated by their conferences, remained as the final voice in the approval of all texts and policies. The Advisory Committee, the body of specialists in various fields, oversaw the many stages needed to prepare the various books and to bring them to a finished form ready for submission to the board of bishops. The Advisory Committee reported all stages of its work to the Episcopal Board. It was also the Advisory Committee's responsibility to decide whether an English draft text (Green Book) was ready for the study of the bishops' conferences. All final English texts (White Books), the product of the consultation on the draft text, required the two-thirds majority vote of the Episcopal Board before being sent to the conferences of bishops. The Episcopal Board and Advisory Committee met at times apart and on other occasions in joint sessions. This arrangement has continued through the present, though the joint sessions are now fuller and longer than was the case in the early 1970s. From 1965 Archbishop Gordon Gray of Edinburgh served as chairman of the Episcopal Board. He was named a cardinal by Pope Paul VI in 1969, the first cardinal resident in Scotland since the sixteenth century. The Advisory Committee initially had a different chairman for each meeting, but in 1968 the members chose Father (later Canon) Harold Winstone, a priest of the Westminster Archdiocese, as continuing chairman. Father Winstone had a calm, easy manner and was able to bring consensus and resolution to debates within the Committee.

The Advisory Committee worked tirelessly in this period assisted by ICEL's able executive secretary, Father Gerald Sigler, to prepare the new texts as quickly as possible. The agenda by 1969-1970 included the following books: *The Roman Missal, The Liturgy of the Hours*, the *Lectionary for Mass*, the *Rite of Marriage*, the *Rite of Baptism for Children*, the *Rite of Confirmation*, and the *Rite of Ordination of Deacons, Priests, and Bishops*. ICEL was able to move quickly on the *Lectionary for Mass* (1969) since the task was somewhat limited, the readings being taken by decision of each bishops' conference from existing Scripture translations such as the Jerusalem Bible and the New American Bible. ICEL was also able to move fairly rapidly on the smaller ritual books, such as those for the rites of baptism, funerals, and marriage, all of which had been issued in final form in Latin by 1969 and in English translations by 1969-70.

The complete text of the *Missale Romanum* was not available until 1970. Up till that time ICEL, using drafts of the work in progress, was able to begin preparation for the considerable task of translating the Missal. One of the most difficult issues to be faced was how best to render the ancient collect form in English. Several consultations were held on this question from 1965 to 1970, and sample translations were solicited from experts proposed by a number of the conferences of bishops. By 1970 a clear answer had not been achieved. Experimentation and consultation continued even as the Latin text was issued. One school of opinion maintained that the succinct, classical form could not be reproduced in English, and, as a consequence, only paraphrases would be possible. Another body of opinion held that the collect form could be achieved in English only by an almost word-for-word adherence to the original and an almost exact reproduction of the Latin syntax in the English translation. A third group maintained that translations of the collect in order to be effective should be expansions on the Latin texts. In the end ICEL proposed and the conferences decided to provide both translations and original prayers for Sundays and solemnities. The original or alternative opening prayers were to be inspired by the Latin but fuller and freer. The task of overseeing the translation of the Latin texts, the work of various translators from different countries, and of coming up with a suitable English form was given over to a small team consisting of Father Harold Winstone, a classicist and expert in pastoral liturgy from England, Mr. Thomas Murphy, an Irish playwright, and Dr. Ralph Keifer, an American liturgist with an academic background. By 1971 samples of the draft translation of the collects were made available to the conferences for comment. The response was generally supportive. The final version of the 1324 collect-type prayers of the Missal was ready for inclusion in the White Book (final text) of *The Roman Missal* when it was issued in 1973. The style chosen for the collects was spare and direct both in vocabulary and syntax. Most of the prayers were rendered in two or three brief sentences. It was the opinion of the working group and of a majority of the Advisory Committee that the vernacular liturgy risked being too word-oriented and as a result the words of the liturgical texts should whenever possible be kept to a minimum. The reaction to this decision was in some quarters strongly negative. Perhaps no other texts in the ICEL corpus have caused such vigorous and continuing debate. The prefaces of *The Roman Missal* employed a somewhat fuller style in English translation than the collects. The more lyrical approach was in part dictated by the musical considerations integral to the prefaces. They were chiefly the work of a Scottish Jesuit, Father James Quinn, an expert in classics, and of Father John Rotelle, an American Augustinian with training in liturgical studies.

The work of ICEL and its approach to the provision of the English liturgical texts was greatly aided by the Holy See's 1969 Instruction on the Translation of Liturgical Texts. A brief word by way of background should be said about the genesis of the Instruction. Since 1965 the Consilium for the Implementation of the Constitution on the Liturgy had taken an interest in the work of the commissions involved in the preparation of the vernacular liturgical texts. ICEL members along with representatives of other major language groups were members of the *coetus* or working group of the Consilium that prepared the Instruction on the Translation of Liturgical Texts and the ICEL Advisory Committee provided the Holy See with the English language text of the Instruction with its examples of issues and questions of special concern for translators of the Latin liturgical texts into English. The Instruction, which was issued by the Holy See in a definitive English version as well as in other languages, served both to confirm in its major lines the approach that ICEL had taken up to that point and to guide ICEL's future work. The Instruction emphasized the need for texts that could be easily proclaimed by the celebrant and understood by the congregation. It also emphasized an approach to translation concerned with conveying the basic meaning of the original text rather than with a slavish adherence to the exact wording and syntax of the original. The Instruction also gave encouragement to the development of original or newly-composed liturgical texts.

After a number of years experience with the texts of the ICEL Missal—Order of Mass texts, collects, prefaces, and eucharistic prayers —it can be said that whatever their defects they showed that liturgical prayer in contemporary English was both possible and desirable. They advanced the question forward directly and concretely and broke the stranglehold of an approach to English liturgical prayer that often owed more to the nineteenth century than to the great treasures of the sixteenth. To some degree because of ICEL's pioneering work other English-speaking Christian Churches have looked anew at the question of English for the liturgy suited to the late twentieth century.

In the early 1970s the task of working to complete *The Roman Missal* and the four-volume Liturgy of the Hours was a severe strain on ICEL's resources, especially in the area of qualified experts. At the same time, of course, other smaller ritual books were in progress and the conferences of bishops were for understandable reasons intent on having all of the vernacular texts as soon as feasible. When various delays occurred in the preparation of the breviary translation, several of the sponsoring conferences, Australia, England and Wales, Ireland, and Scotland went ahead with their own breviary project. The result was *The Divine Office*, also known as the English Language Breviary, which was published in 1974-1975. ICEL's translation, *The Liturgy of the Hours*, was published in 1975-1976. In the twenty-five year history of ICEL the two breviary translations have proved to be the only significant exception to the acceptance by all the English-speaking conferences of bishops of the single text provided by ICEL.

ICEL's mandate from the founding conferences had emphasized the need for ecumenical cooperation whenever possible. This cooperation was set in motion when ICEL in 1966-1967 acted as one of the founders of the North American Consultation on Common Texts (CCT). In 1969 ICEL was also instrumental in the establishment of an international ecumenical body concerned with liturgical texts, the International Consultation on English Texts (ICET). The consultation included representatives from various Christian Churches, particularly in the British Isles and North America. This body produced in 1970 the first edition of *Prayers We Have in Common*, a booklet containing agreed upon English translations of various texts for the eucharist, for example, the *Gloria in Excelsis, Creed, Sanctus and Benedictus, Agnus Dei*, and texts used in the daily Office and other services such as the *Benedictus, Magnificat, Te Deum*, and *Nunc Dimittis*. Subsequent editions of *Prayers We Have in Common* were issued in 1972 and 1975. The texts were adopted by ICEL and proposed to the conferences of bishops. In time they were adopted by all the English-speaking conferences. ICEL also proposed the ICET version of the Lord's Prayer to the conferences, but this was then adopted by only three of the eleven member conferences in ICEL.

Several major changes took place in the leadership of ICEL in the early 1970s. Bishop G. Emmett Carter of London, Ontario, (later, Cardinal Archbishop of Toronto) Canada succeeded Cardinal Gordon Gray as chairman of the Episcopal Board in 1971. In 1975 Father Harold Winstone's term on the Advisory Committee came to an end. Father Winstone had served on the committee since 1965. Father (later Archbishop of Ottawa), Marcel Gervais, a biblicist and director of the Divine Word Institute in London, Ontario, was chosen by the Advisory Committee as its new chairman. And after five years of relentless work overseeing the day-to-day activities of ICEL, Father Sigler resigned in January 1970 to become director of the Woodstock Center in New York, a liturgical institute sponsored by two of the Jesuit provinces in the United States. Father John Shea, a Sulpician and formerly a professor of systematic theology at St. Mary's Seminary in Baltimore, succeeded Father Sigler. In 1972 Father Shea resigned and Dr. Ralph Keifer, at the time serving on the secretariat staff as general editor of *The Roman Missal*, took over temporary direction of ICEL. In May 1973 Father John Rotelle, O.S.A., then associate director and later director of the U. S. Bishops' Committee on the Liturgy, was appointed acting executive secretary of ICEL by the Episcopal Board meeting in Toronto.

The Middle Period

The middle period of ICEL's history, 1973-1981, saw the production of many of the liturgical books either in interim or final form. Father Rotelle moved decisively in early 1973 to bring *The Roman Missal* and other ritual texts to completion and he reorganized the translation project for the breviary. As a result *The Roman Missal* was issued in 1973 and all of the four volumes of *The Liturgy of the Hours* had been published by 1976. In 1976 a one-volume derivative of *The Liturgy of the Hours*, containing morning and evening prayer as well as the daytime hours and night prayer, was issued as *Christian Prayer*. The one-volume edition included in addition a limited number of musical settings provided by ICEL to encourage the singing of the Hours. Also issued in final form in the mid-1970s were the *Rite of Religious Profession*, the *Rite of Blessing of an Abbot or Abbess*, the *Rite of Consecration to a Life of Virginity*, the *Rite of Penance*, the *Rite of Reception of Baptized Christians into Full Communion with the Catholic Church*. Issued in interim form were the *Rite of Anointing and Pastoral Care of the Sick* (1973) and the *Rite of Christian Initiation of Adults* (1974). Two other texts issued in final form, the *Rite of Confirmation* and the *Ordination of Deacons, Priests, and Bishops* were delayed for a time owing to discussions between the Holy See and the conferences of bishops concerning the translation of the sacramental form for confirmation and the sacramental form for the ordination of a bishop. When these issues were resolved the *Rite of Confirmation* and the ordination rites were issued in final versions in 1975.

From the time that the three new eucharistic prayers were sanctioned by the Holy See, there were continuing requests from conferences of bishops for additional eucharistic prayers. In 1974 the Holy See issued for trial use three eucharistic prayers for Masses with children and two eucharistic prayers for Masses with the theme of reconciliation. English translations were issued by ICEL in 1975. In 1980 the Holy See removed the provisional status of these texts and granted them without the previous time limit to any conference that applied for their use according to the regular procedures governing additional eucharistic prayers.

Father Rotelle was instrumental in joining more formally to the work of ICEL fifteen associate-members conferences, the Antilles, Bangladesh, CEPAC (Fiji, Rarotonga, Samoa and Tokelau, Tonga), Gambia-Liberia-Sierra Leone, Ghana, Kenya, Malaysia-Singapore, Malawi, Nigeria, Papua New Guinea and the Solomons, Sri Lanka,

Tanzania, Uganda, Zambia, and Zimbabwe. In most of these conferences, English, though a secondary language, is used to some degree in liturgical celebrations. During the mid-1970s Father Rotelle visited many of the member and associate-member conferences to explain and report on the work of ICEL to the bishops and to solicit their views on the future work of ICEL. In his visits to the associate-member conferences Father Rotelle asked the bishops if there were ways in which ICEL could assist their liturgical work. As a consequence of his visits to the member and associate-member conferences, Father Rotelle proposed to the Episcopal Board the possibility of holding periodic meetings of the secretaries of the national liturgical commissions of the ICEL member and associate-member conferences. The first of these meetings was held in Singapore in 1975 with twelve secretaries taking part. Subsequent meetings took place in Rome in 1977 and 1982 and in Washington in 1988. By means of these meetings the secretaries were able to make recommendations and proposals for the ICEL program and its greater effectiveness, particularly its pastoral effectiveness.

In 1975 the Episcopal Board, meeting in London, elected Archbishop Denis Hurley of Durban, South Africa, as its chairman. Archbishop Hurley had been a leading participant in the founding of ICEL during the Second Vatican Council. And in 1978 Father (later Monsignor) Anthony Boylan of the Diocese of Leeds, England, succeeded Father Gervais as chairman of the Advisory Committee.

As a result of requests from the conferences of bishops and discussions of the secretaries of the national commissions, ICEL began in the latter half of the 1970s to explore ways of assisting the conferences beyond the preparation of the liturgical books in English. Efforts were undertaken to make information from ICEL and the conferences available to all the participating conferences and to encourage liturgical catechesis. Catechesis was considered important as a necessary step in deepening liturgical awareness and a richer and more pastoral understanding of the new liturgical books. Some planning along these lines had been done in the first years of ICEL, but the enormous amount of translation work prevented the Commission from going forward on projects such as a regular newsletter and a compilation of liturgical documents. In 1976 the ICEL newsletter began to appear on a regular basis and full reports of ICEL activities continued to be issued on an annual or biennial basis. Two booklets dealing with pressing pastoral liturgical topics were issued in 1977 and 1978, *Let Everyone Celebrate: guidelines and principles for liturgical celebrations particularly with the handicapped* and *Sunday Celebrations: guidelines to aid assemblies in preparing for celebrations held with a deacon or lay person presiding*. Both of these were translations from texts prepared by the national liturgical office of France. ICEL commentaries appeared on the *Dedication of a Church and an Altar* in 1977 and 1978, on *The Roman Pontifical* in 1978, and on the ordination rites in 1979 and 1980. The possibility of a journal containing translations of important articles on liturgical topics from various countries, especially pastoral-liturgical essays, was actively explored for several years at this time.

With major elements of the translation process finished or well in hand by the mid-1970s, ICEL established a standing subcommittee on music in 1974 in order to initiate several liturgical music projects. ICEL's earlier involvement with music had been limited to the ministerial chants of *The Roman Missal*. These new projects were undertaken with the hope that composers and publishers of liturgical music in various countries would be inspired to provide musical compositions for ritual texts in addition to those for the Mass. These texts had often been overlooked and little ritual music was available for the celebration of baptisms, funerals, and the other rites. In 1977 *Music for the Rite of Funerals and the Rite of Baptism for Children* was issued. And in 1978 *Music for the Rites: Baptism, Eucharist, and Ordinations* was made available. Efforts to foster the sung celebration of the Liturgy of the Hours were also begun with the provision of service music in *Christian Prayer* in 1976, followed in 1978 by an organ accompaniment book for this music. In 1979 a booklet was issued containing music for the celebration of evening prayer on Sundays and for the Liturgy of the Hours during the Easter Triduum.

In this period there were still liturgical texts to be prepared in interim or final form. The *Rite of Commissioning Special Ministers of Holy Communion* was issued in interim form in 1978, and that same year the interim text of the *Dedication of a Church and an Altar* was made available. The latter text marked something of a shift from earlier ICEL translations. The language used was somewhat fuller and richer than heretofore in keeping with the nature of these ceremonies, but it was also the result of continuing discussions on liturgical language within the Advisory Committee and the subcommittee on translations. One of the major efforts of these years was the preparation of *The Roman Pontifical*, published in 1978. The *Pontifical* made available in one book, according to the long-established tradition, the principal rites celebrated by a bishop such as ordination and confirmation.

Planning for the Future

ICEL's 1964 mandate from the conferences of bishops had included the preparation of a liturgical psalter and the translation of other biblical texts, particularly those used in the liturgy. The large amount of work in the early years had kept these projects from going much beyond discussion and a few sample texts. In the early 1970s there was some hope of an ecumenical liturgical psalter project but this was never brought beyond sixty texts. In 1978 ICEL convened a group of biblical and liturgical scholars to discuss the feasibility of providing a psalter prepared primarily for liturgical use. The scholars endorsed the undertaking and drew up a brief to guide the project. A special standing subcommittee was then established with the approval of the Episcopal Board and Advisory Committee to begin the work. A cognate project, which also came out of the 1978 meeting, was an exploration of the possibility of providing a lectionary for Mass translated with liturgical proclamation in view. Over the preceding decade a concern had been expressed in some countries that the English translations of Scripture approved for use in the liturgy, while admirably suited for study and private reading, often did not meet the special requirements needed for texts meant for public reading. A small task force was set up to prepare samples of selected biblical passages translated with proclamation in mind and to arrange for their experimental use.

From the first it had been foreseen that liturgical texts in the vernacular would need to be revised periodically. It had in fact been ICEL's original intention to issue *The Roman Missal* in 1973 in an interim version for a five-year period. After discussion the Episcopal Board decided, however, that *The Roman Missal* should be issued in a final form and without setting any recommendations to the conferences for restricting its use to a limited period. By the late 1970s ICEL was able to turn its attention to planning for the revision of the translation of the liturgical texts issued over the past decade. A number of full discussions on revisions took place within the Episcopal Board and Advisory Committee in the late 1970s. It was agreed that the process should be done slowly and methodically and that background study on the sources and vocabulary of the Latin texts should precede the actual work of revising them. This type of process had been planned for the first ICEL texts, but the pressure of pastoral needs made it necessary to produce the texts rapidly. It was also agreed that the revised books should include elements that were envisioned in the late 1960s and early 1970s but had been impossible to supply at that time owing to the sheer volume and urgency of the work. These included the provision of original prayers to supplement the texts translated from the Latin or to deal with pastoral situations not provided for in the Latin ritual books and common to the English-language Churches. Original texts had been encouraged by the 1969 Instruction on the Translation of Liturgical Texts and by the *praenotanda* of several of the revised Roman liturgical books. ICEL had provided original opening prayers for Sundays and solemnities in *The Roman Missal* as alternatives to the translated opening prayers. These had been welcomed by the conferences of bishops and readily approved. But these and a few brief texts in the Order of Mass had been the only instances of newly-composed prayers in ICEL's first decade and a half. With continuing discussion in the conferences on the desirability of additional eucharistic prayers, especially eucharistic prayers composed in English, ICEL committed itself to assisting the conferences' discussions of this question by providing examples of original eucharistic prayers for study and comment. As part of the discussion on eucharistic prayers, ICEL also undertook to provide translations of two ancient prayers, the Anaphora of Saint Hippolytus and the Anaphora of Saint Basil.

The Episcopal Board and Advisory Committee agreed that an important aspect of the revisions process should be careful attention to the layout and design of the liturgical books to ensure their promotion of good, pastoral celebration. ICEL had already provided a model for this important aspect of liturgical celebration with the publication of *The Roman Pontifical* in 1978. This book had been carefully designed and planned within ICEL, every page and element receiving the attention of experts in graphics as well as experts in pastoral liturgy. The resulting book, published by the Vatican Press in 1978, was regarded as an important achievement in the making of liturgical books.

Looking toward the preparation of this "second generation" of liturgical books, ICEL had begun to make major organizational changes in 1976. Up to that time the Advisory Committee had overseen the step-by-step preparation of each book. While many outside experts were consulted and a large number of translators from various countries were called on, a good deal of the preparation of each book was done by the Advisory Committee members themselves. Often major segments of the twice-yearly meetings were given over to one or more of the books then in preparation, especially in reviewing the translations. The members of the Committee would frequently meet in small groups, each group looking at some section or aspect of the text. The work from each group would then be brought back to the full Committee for discussion and possible decision. With the reorganization in the late 1970s three standing subcommittees, working under the direction of the Advisory Committee, were established. The membership of each subcommittee included two or three Advisory Committee members and several experts invited from outside the Advisory Committee. This had the beneficial effect of bringing a greater number of people directly into the work through membership on subcommittees and ad hoc groups, and in their selection an effort was made to have experts from as many countries as possible. The subcommittees met apart from the Advisory Committee, usually twice during each year. A subcommittee was established to deal with all matters related to translations and the revision of translations; a second group was set up to oversee the preparation of original or newly-composed texts; a third subcommittee was established to plan the presentation and layout of each book and, as needed, the preparation of pastoral notes and introductions to foster the pastoral celebration of the various rites. The subcommittee on music, which was already fully functioning, continued its work. The Advisory Committee was thus able to concentrate on steering and reviewing the various stages of each project before presenting it to the Episcopal Board.

In the late 1970s and early 1980s ICEL continued its service to the conferences of providing materials related to liturgical renewal and liturgical celebration. A major and monumental service of ICEL in this regard was the completion in 1982 of *Documents on the Liturgy, 1963-1979: Conciliar, Papal, and Curial Texts*. Work on this fifteen-hundred page collection had been done on and off through the 1970s but began to take definite shape in 1979 when Dr. Thomas C. O'Brien of the ICEL Secretariat was given direction of the project.

Other supplementary ICEL projects included further collections of liturgical music. In 1981 ICEL issued the *Resource Collection of Hymns and Service Music for the Liturgy* and in 1982 music for the Lectionary, *ICEL Lectionary Music: Psalms and Alleluia and Gospel Acclamations for the Liturgy of the Word*. A collection of traditional devotional prayers recast in more contemporary language was sent to the conferences in 1982 in a study booklet entitled *A Book of Prayers*. In 1981 ICEL initiated a series of occasional papers with Frederick McManus's "ICEL: The First Years." This was followed in 1984 by the "Language of the Liturgy" by H. Kathleen Hughes, R.S.C.J.

A major project of this period was the final version of the rite of anointing, entitled *Pastoral Care of the Sick: Rites of Anointing and Viaticum*. Although strictly speaking not a part of ICEL's revision program since it was a "first-generation" ICEL book going through the usual stages of Green Book (interim text) and White Book (final text), *Pastoral Care* came at a point when a number of the principles that were to govern the revision process had already been worked out and it was able to benefit from them. It is the first of the ritual books prepared by ICEL to be rearranged for greater pastoral effectiveness and to include extensive pastoral notes and reflections. It carefully distinguished in its rearrangement and parts anointing as the sacrament for the sick and viaticum as the sacrament of the dying. *Pastoral Care* contained in addition a number of newly-composed prayers, the first ICEL text to do so since *The Roman Missal* in 1973. There were protracted discussions with the Congregation for Divine Worship before *Pastoral Care* was sent to the conferences of bishops in 1982. Much of the discussion centered on the translation of the word *periculose* with reference to the qualified subject of anointing. The ICEL translation of the *praenotanda* used the word "seriously" ill in this context. Eventually this translation was accepted by the Roman authorities with the addition of a footnote which read: "The word *periculose* has been carefully studied and rendered as 'seriously,' rather than as 'gravely,' 'dangerously,' or 'perilously.' Such a rendering will serve to avoid restrictions upon the celebration of the sacrament. On the one hand the sacrament may and should be given to anyone whose health is seriously impaired; on the other hand, it may not be given indiscriminately or to any person whose health is not seriously impaired."

From 1975 the question of inclusive language in the liturgical texts was given study and attention by ICEL. An ad hoc subcommittee on discriminatory language was formed in 1976. Meetings dealing with the question were held at intervals over a six-year period, and from 1975 a careful effort was made to avoid discriminatory language, particularly with reference to women, in the liturgical texts. In 1980 the Green Book, *Eucharistic Prayers*, containing several proposed interim revisions in the eucharistic prayers, mainly for purposes of inclusive language, was sent to the conferences of bishops. This Green Book contained in addition a major statement from ICEL's Advisory Committee on the question of inclusive language and a foreword endorsing the Advisory Committee's statement from Archbishop Denis Hurley.

In the early 1980s several projects in progress or under study had to be suspended or set aside owing to the press of work or other considerations. The lectionary translated for proclamation had been tested in 1981 before it was decided that the project was simply too large and costly to undertake. Also set aside were plans for the journal, *ICEL International*. For several years a project to provide two additional cycles of non-biblical readings for the Office of Readings in *The Liturgy of the Hours* had been under way. Work on the project was suspended in 1980.

The Second Generation

In 1980 Father John Fitzsimmons, a priest of the diocese of Paisley in Scotland, was elected chairman of the Advisory Committee. Father Fitzsimmons, for a number of years a professor of Scripture at St. Peter's Major Seminary in Glasgow, was later rector of the Scots' College in Rome. Also in 1980 Father Rotelle, after directing the day-to-day work of ICEL for seven years, resigned as executive secretary to accept a position in the provincial curia of the U.S. Eastern province of the Augustinians. The Episcopal Board, meeting in Rome, appointed Mr. John Page to succeed him. Mr. Page had been associate executive secretary since 1974. Archbishop Denis Hurley has continued to serve as the chairman of the Episcopal Board throughout the 1980s.

The long-planned process of revisions began in earnest with the issuance in 1981 of a special consultation book on the revision of the *Rite of Funerals*, a text first issued by ICEL in 1970. The consultation book invited comments on all the translated texts of the funeral rite and also on the possible need for original prayers to supplement the texts offered in the Latin or to deal with special pastoral situations not addressed in the *Ordo exsequiarum*. The consultation, involving all the member and associate-member conferences of ICEL, ran for eight months until August 1981. The results were tabulated and studied in the ICEL Secretariat and then reviewed by the three subcommittees charged with the three major areas of revision: translations, original texts, and presentation of the text. The revised ritual book, the *Order of Christian Funerals*, was presented to the conferences of bishops in 1985 and approved by the conferences in 1985 and early 1986. Difficulties followed over the Roman *confirmatio* and the revised funeral rite was not able to be implemented by the conferences until late in 1989 and early in 1990.

While the funeral rite was being revised, the preliminary steps toward the revision of *The Roman Missal* were taken. A consultation book on the revision of the presidential prayers of *The Roman Missal* was issued in 1982. It contained a special introduction, which invited comments on the Missal prayers and carefully set out the major reactions, critical as well as laudatory, that had been made about the Missal prayers since their appearance nearly a decade before. Work on revising the 1324 presidential prayers was started in 1985. To guide the work the Advisory Committee drew up a set of principles, which it approved in 1982. Among other things these principles allowed for the possibility of texts that were somewhat fuller and richer in vocabulary and syntax than the 1973 texts. The translations and revisions subcommittee followed this new approach in their work but kept always as its principal guide the 1969 Instruction on the Translation of Liturgical Texts with its emphasis on the need for proclamation and intelligibility and avoidance of a slavish literalism. The Episcopal Board and Advisory Committee endorsed the approach being taken by the translations and revisions subcommittee. A special report on the progress of the work of revising the presidential prayers was issued by ICEL to the conferences of bishops in 1988. In addition to giving examples of the revised texts, the report explained the steps being followed in the revision of the texts and gave examples of the critical background research that ICEL had done on *The Roman Missal* texts in preparation for their revision. A second consultation on the revision of *The Roman Missal*, focusing on the Order of Mass and the prefaces and eucharistic prayers, took place in 1986. Revision of these texts began in 1989.

In the early 1980s three eucharistic prayer texts were prepared by ICEL for the study and comment of the bishops' conferences. The *Eucharistic Prayer of Saint Hippolytus* was issued in 1983 in a new translation along with the Latin texts, French translation, and notes found in Dom Bernard Botte's *La Tradition Apostolique de Saint Hippolyte*. The ICEL translation of Hippolytus brought important responses from Roman Catholic experts as well as scholars from other Christian Churches. In 1985 a translation and slight adaptation of the *Eucharistic Prayer of Saint Basil* was offered to the conferences for their study. The first original eucharistic prayer prepared by ICEL was issued in 1984. After a period of consultation lasting one year, revisions were made in the text, and following on the approval of ICEL's Episcopal Board the text was sent to the conferences of bishops early in 1986 as *Eucharistic Prayer A*. Eight conferences voted to approve the text for liturgical use. The Roman authorities did not, however, confirm the conferences' decisions.

In 1985 a decision was made by the Episcopal Board to go ahead with the full liturgical psalter project, including, in addition to the 150 psalms, fifty-five Old and New Testament canticles used in the liturgical books. The guiding brief for the project, first drawn up in 1978, was revised subsequently in light of the public consultations on the liturgical psalter project in 1982 and 1984.

ICEL's commitment to ecumenical initiatives continued in the 1980s through its participation in the North American Consultation on Common Texts (CCT) and the successor to ICET, known as the English Language Liturgical Consultation (ELLC). In 1983 the CCT produced a Sunday eucharistic lectionary for trial use. Entitled the *Common Lectionary*, this is an ecumenical lectionary based in large part on the Roman *Ordo lectionum Missae* of 1969, a development encouraged by the substantial agreement since the early 1970s on the use of the Roman Lectionary among a number of Christian Churches in North America. The CCT also issued *Ecumenical Services of Prayer* (1983), *A Christian Celebration of Marriage: An Ecumenical Liturgy* (1987), and *A Celebration of Baptism: An Ecumenical Liturgy* (1989). When it became apparent in the early 1980s that there was considerable interest among the English-speaking Christian Churches in establishing a successor to ICET, ICEL and the CCT invited representatives of the Churches to explore the possibility of establishing a new international ecumenical body to deal with liturgical matters. As a result of these exploratory discussions the English Language Liturgical Consultation (ELLC) was established in 1985. The ELLC is made up of ICEL and five national and regional ecumenical liturgical associations, having a total of thirty-five participating Churches. One of the first results of this new collaboration was the revision of *Prayers We Have in Common*. The revised texts and notes were made available to the participating Churches in 1987, and issued publicly in 1990 as *Praying Together*. The ELLC has expressed its interest in the development of an international ecumenical lectionary and has endorsed the *Common Lectionary* as the most promising basis on which to begin study of such a lectionary. The ICEL secretariat has from the first served as the coordinating secretariat for the Consultation on Common Texts as well as for the International Consultation on English Texts and its successor body, the English Language Liturgical Consultation.

On 17 October 1988 as ICEL completed twenty-five years of service to the Churches in the English-speaking conferences of bishops, the revision of the Missal was the principal project on its agenda. In addition to the revision of the translated texts, ICEL was preparing some three hundred original prayers, including opening prayers for Sundays related to the Scripture readings, for inclusion in the revised Missal. ICEL also continued to prepare translations of further books of the Roman reform. In 1987 the interim text of the *Book of Blessings* was issued, and in 1989 ICEL completed the translation of the *Ceremonial of Bishops*. In addition, an interim edition of the *Collection of Masses of the Blessed Virgin Mary* was issued in 1989. Work was also under way on a second volume of *Documents on the Liturgy*, covering the years 1979 to 1989.

On 22 June 1989 the Center for Pastoral Liturgy at the University of Notre Dame conferred its Michael Mathis Award on ICEL. The text of the citation read out on that occasion seems a fitting conclusion to this overview of ICEL's first quarter century:

> The Notre Dame Center for Pastoral Liturgy presents the 1989 Michael Mathis Award to the International Commission on English in the Liturgy in recognition of its steadfast commitment to the pastoral implementation of liturgical reform by providing words for our prayer, music for the words, and presenting them in a fashion that is worthy of the dignity they possess and the function they serve in the public prayer of the Church. In the twenty-five years since it was established, ICEL has dedicated itself to the faithful translation of the official Latin texts, the creative composition of original English texts, the careful preparation of ritual commentary, and the pastorally effective arrangement of the liturgical books. ICEL has been a model of collegiality, collaboration, and consultation for the universal Church. Searching out the many gifts which the Spirit gives, ICEL has engaged women and men of every English-speaking nation in the challenging and awesome task of weaving the words of our common Christian prayer.

CONTRIBUTORS

— Horace T. Allen, Jr. is Assistant Professor of Worship in the School of Theology at Boston University. An ordained minister of the Presbyterian Church (U.S.A.), Dr. Allen is the author of *A Handbook for the Lectionary* (Philadelphia: The Geneva Press, 1980).

— Frederick Amoore is the former Bishop of the Anglican diocese of Bloemfontein, South Africa. Bishop Amoore retired in 1987 after serving a term as the Provincial Executive Officer of the Church of the Province of Southern Africa.

— Lawrence Boadt, C.S.P., is a Paulist priest and Associate Professor of Biblical Studies at the Washington Theological Union. He has been a member of the Advisory Committee of ICEL since 1985 and of ICEL's subcommittee on the liturgical psalter since 1978. An editor for Paulist Press, Dr. Boadt is the author of *Reading The Old Testament: An Introduction* (Mahwah, N.J.: Paulist Press, 1985).

— Andrew Borello, a priest of the diocese of Johannesburg, South Africa, works at present in the archdiocese of Cape Town. In addition to various pastoral assignments, he has served as lecturer in liturgy at the major seminary and has initiated a pastoral training center in the Johannesburg diocese.

— Patrick Byrne, a priest of the diocese of Peterborough, Canada, is pastor of St. Michael's Parish in Coburg, Ontario. From 1971 to 1987 Msgr. Byrne was Assistant Director and Editor for the National Liturgical Office in Canada, during which time he was also editor of the *National Bulletin on Liturgy*.

— G. B. Harrison became a member of ICEL's Advisory Committee in 1964 and, in 1975, was made a lifetime member of the Committee in recognition of his many contributions to the work of ICEL. An expert on Shakespeare and Elizabethan England, he had a distinguished teaching career at King's College, London, Queen's University, Kingston, Canada, and the University of Michigan at Ann Arbor. Dr. Harrison retired from teaching in 1964 and lives now in Palmerston North, New Zealand.

— J. Frank Henderson is Professor in the Department of Biochemistry of the University of Alberta and a lecturer in liturgy in the Newman Theological College, Edmonton, Canada. He served on ICEL's Advisory Committee from 1978 to 1985 and on two of ICEL's subcommittees: the ad hoc subcommittee on discriminatory language and the subcommittee on translations and revisions (which he chaired for several years and of which he is still a member). Dr. Henderson is a former chairperson of the National Council for Liturgy in Canada and is the editor of the *National Bulletin on Liturgy*.

— Michael Hodgetts is a school teacher by profession and was for thirteen years head of the religious education department at St. Thomas More School in Walsall, near Birmingham, England. He has been a member of ICEL's subcommittee on translations and revisions since 1976. From 1969 to 1985 he was editor of *Recusant History* and is now general editor of the Catholic Record Society. His book *Secret Hiding Places* was published in 1989 by Veritas Publications, Dublin.

— H. Kathleen Hughes, R.S.C.J., a Religious of the Sacred Heart of the United States Province, is Associate Professor of Liturgy at the Catholic Theological Union in Chicago. She served on ICEL's Advisory Committee from 1980 to 1987, the last five years of which she chaired ICEL's subcommittee on original texts. Dr. Hughes is the author of a forthcoming biography of Godfrey Diekmann, O.S.B., to be published by The Liturgical Press, Collegeville, Minnesota.

— Percy Jones, a priest of the archdiocese of Melbourne, Australia, became a member of the Advisory Committee in 1964 and was named an emeritus member of the Committee in 1975. Dr. Jones served as a consultant to the Second Vatican Council's preparatory commission on the liturgy (1960-1962) and is an expert in the area of liturgical music. For many years he was on the faculty of the Conservatory of Music at the University of Melbourne and he now lives in retirement in Newtown, Australia.

— Thomas A. Krosnicki, S.V.D., a Divine Word Missionary, is Assistant Professor of Liturgy at the Washington Theological Union. He served in the secretariat of the United States Bishops' Committee on the Liturgy, as Associate Director beginning in 1973 and as Executive Director from 1978 to 1981. Dr. Krosnicki is the author of *Ancient Patterns in Modern Prayer* (Washington, D.C.: The Catholic University of America Press, 1973).

— Frederick R. McManus, a priest of the archdiocese of Boston, is Professor of Canon Law at The Catholic University of America, Washington, D.C. He was one of the founders of ICEL and has served as a member of the

Advisory Committee since 1964. He was one of two English-speaking *periti* to the Second Vatican Council's commission on the liturgy (1962-1965), and he served also as a consultant to the Second Vatican Council's preparatory commission on the liturgy (1960-1962) and to the post-conciliar Consilium for the Implementation of the Constitution on the Liturgy (1964-1970). Msgr. McManus edited and provided the commentary in *Thirty Years of Liturgical Renewal: Statements of the Bishops' Committee on the Liturgy* (Washington, D.C.: Office of Publishing and Promotion Services, United States Catholic Conference, 1987).

— Gilbert W. Ostdiek, O.F.M., a Franciscan priest, is Professor of Liturgy at the Catholic Theological Union in Chicago, where he also has served as dean of the faculty. He is the author of *Catechesis for Liturgy*, published in 1986 by The Pastoral Press, Washington, D.C.

— John R. Page is the Executive Secretary of ICEL.

— Mary Alice Piil, C.S.J., is a member of the Congregation of St. Joseph of Brentwood, New York. Dr. Piil is Professor of Liturgy at Immaculate Conception Seminary in Huntington, New York.

— Paul Puthanangady, S.D.B., a member of the Salesian Congregation, is Director of the National Biblical, Catechetical, and Liturgical Centre (NBCLC) of the Catholic Bishops' Conference of India. He is the editor of *Word and Worship*, a review published by the Centre, and the author of *Initiation to Christian Worship* (Bangalore: Theological Publications in India, 1979).

— Eileen M. Schuller, O.S.U., is a member of the Ursuline Sisters of Chatham. Dr. Schuller is Lecturer in Old Testament and Hebrew at the Atlantic School of Theology in Halifax.

— Mark Searle, a native of Bristol, England, is Associate Professor of Theology in the Graduate Program in Liturgical Studies at the University of Notre Dame. He was Associate Director of the Notre Dame Center for Pastoral Liturgy from 1977 to 1983. Dr. Searle is the editor of (and has an essay in) volume 2 of *Alternative Futures for Worship: Baptism and Confirmation* (Collegeville, Minn.: The Liturgical Press, 1987).

— Rembert G. Weakland, O.S.B., is Archbishop of Milwaukee. From 1967 to 1977 he was Abbot Primate of the confederated congregations of the Order of St. Benedict. Archbishop Weakland chaired the committee that prepared the United States Catholic bishops' letter on the economy, *Economic Justice for All: A Pastoral Letter on Catholic Social Teaching and the United States Economy* (Washington, D.C.: United States Catholic Conference, 1986).